D1215489

# Slavery, Capitalism, and Politics in the Antebellum Republic

The second and concluding volume of Professor Ashworth's study of American antebellum politics, this book offers an exciting new interpretation of the origins of the Civil War. The volume deals with the politics of the 1850s and with the plunge into civil war.

Professor Ashworth offers a new way of understanding the conflict between North and South and shows how northern free labor increasingly came into conflict with southern slavery as a result of both changes in the northern economy and the structural weaknesses of slavery.

John Ashworth was born in Lancashire, England, and studied at the Universities of Lancaster and Oxford. He is currently Professor of American History in the School of American and Canadian Studies at the University of Nottingham.

Professor Ashworth is the author of *'Agrarians' and 'Aristocrats': Party Political Ideology in the United States, 1837–1846*, and *Slavery, Capitalism, and Politics in the Antebellum Republic: Volume 1: Commerce and Compromise, 1820–1850* (both published by Cambridge University Press), and of numerous articles and reviews in learned journals.

# Slavery, Capitalism, and Politics in the Antebellum Republic

Volume 2: The Coming of the Civil War, 1850–1861

JOHN ASHWORTH

*University of Nottingham*

CAMBRIDGE
UNIVERSITY PRESS

CAMBRIDGE UNIVERSITY PRESS
Cambridge, New York, Melbourne, Madrid, Cape Town, Singapore, São Paulo, Delhi

Cambridge University Press
32 Avenue of the Americas, New York, NY 10013-2473, USA

www.cambridge.org
Information on this title: www.cambridge.org/9780521885928

First published 2007

Printed in the United States of America

A catalog record for this publication is available from the British Library.

Library of Congress Cataloging in Publication Data

Ashworth, John.
Slavery, capitalism, and politics in the antebellum Republic / John Ashworth.
    p. cm.
Contents: v. 1. Commerce and compromise, 1820–1850
1. Slavery – Economic aspects – United States – History – 19th century.
2. Capitalism – United States – History – 19th century.   3. United States –
Politics and government – 1815–1861.   4. Working class – United States –
History – 19th century.   5. United States – Economic conditions – To 1865.
E441.A86   1996
331.11'734'0973 – dc20        95009957

ISBN   978-0-521-88592-8 hardback
ISBN   978-0-521-71369-6 paperback

*To my parents, Eric and Freda Ashworth*

# Contents

# Acknowledgments

It is a pleasure to acknowledge the help I have received over the many years I have been engaged upon this volume (and its predecessor). I should like to express my gratitude to the Arts and Humanities Research Council for a grant which enabled me to take a much-needed study leave. As far as fellow academics are concerned, Eric Foner has been a constant source of engagement and of constructive criticism and special thanks are due to him. Bruce Levine provided me with an excellent critique of an earlier version of the entire manuscript and the book is far better for his criticisms. Thanks also to James Oakes for many helpful points, to William W. Freehling, with whom I have exchanged many e-mails on the subjects addressed in this volume, and to two other anonymous critics, employed by Cambridge University Press, who offered not only criticism but also encouragement that was most welcome. On this side of the Atlantic, my colleague Richard King at Nottingham made some extremely helpful observations about my treatment of southern militants before the Civil War and Owen Butler, a former graduate student, gave the section on the Whig party a very thorough critical reading. Michael Heale, my teacher many years ago, and a friend now for many decades, read the whole manuscript and his comments and support were of incalculable value. Profound thanks also to my father, Eric Ashworth, who also read the manuscript in its entirety – a time-consuming task – and made many very helpful observations. I should also like to express my gratitude to my children Jackie and Mcash. Mary Paden and her team at Aptara Inc. saw this volume through from manuscript to its final form and I am very grateful to her. Last, but certainly not least, I must thank my editor Frank Smith at Cambridge University Press in New York for the immense amount of support, help, and encouragement he has provided over three books and more than twenty years.

# Introduction: Explaining the Civil War (1)

The slaveholders of the South thought they knew their slaves. They were certain that they understood the capabilities and the limitations of their "negroes." They believed that, in the main, enslavement suited African Americans and accorded well with their natural endowments, or the lack of them. Historians used to believe the same. Ulrich B. Phillips, for example, referred to the slaves' "courteous acceptance of subordination" and their "readiness for loyalty of a feudal sort." American slaves were well-suited to their condition.[1]

Yet, Phillips and the slaveholders of the Old South erred grievously. Historians now know what contemporaries and most scholars of previous generations did not: in most cases, slaves did not want to be slaves and instead yearned for freedom. Although this insight has emerged from the social history of African Americans before the Civil War, it has only recently made an appearance in the historiography of the Civil War itself. In fact, the opposition of the slaves to their own enslavement is the fundamental, irreplaceable cause of the War.[2]

This is not to say, of course, that the slaves were able actively to plan or to seek, or to bring about a civil war between North and South. A war could only come about as a result of a whole series of actions taken within the political arena by those who were legally able to take them. Slaves were not, in this sense, political actors at all. Nor were they able to mount a revolutionary challenge to their masters; slave rebellions in the Old South were rare and comparatively unsuccessful. To this extent, the masters were able to contain their slaves.

1. Ulrich B. Phillips, *American Negro Slavery* (Baton Rouge, 1918), p. 291.
2. African-American resistance to slavery was emphasised in the first volume of this study. Since then, it has emerged in some recent writings on the politics of the era – see, for example, William A. Link, *Roots of Secession: Slavery and Politics in Antebellum Virginia* (Chapel Hill, 2003), p. 1.

Nevertheless, to appreciate the importance of slave resistance, one need only imagine how different the history of these years would have been had the slaves conformed to Phillips's stereotype. In such circumstances the great controversies of the prewar decades would have been drained of most of their significance. If slaves had accepted rather than resisted enslavement, they would not have wished to flee from their masters. Hence, there would have been no controversy over fugitive slaves. If slaves had willingly accepted enslavement, there would have been little reason for southerners to fear abolitionist propaganda, whether from hostile northerners, such as William Lloyd Garrison and William Seward, or from southern "traitors" like Hinton Helper. If slaves had willingly accepted enslavement, would there even have been an abolitionist crusade? It seems unlikely.[3] Moreover, the free-soil movement, which in southern eyes brought with it the threat of abolition at some future date, would not have been so menacing. If slaves had willingly accepted enslavement, there would have been no danger of servile rebellions, the fear of which struck terror into the hearts of so many of their masters.

Moreover, if the slaves had willingly accepted enslavement, there would have been little reason for the South to engage in the series of actions which were taken in the 1850s and earlier and which did so much to fuel northern fears of a Slave Power. Similarly, it can be argued that southern economic development was severely constrained by the problems of controlling a potentially recalcitrant labor force in cities and in industry. The resulting feature of the southern economy, its limited development, was another huge source of conflict with the North. If the slaves had willingly accepted enslavement, this constraint would probably have been removed.

Historians have been slow to recognize the political significance of this black resistance to slavery. Their analyses have focused on, for example, the struggles over the Fugitive Slave Law, or the series of crises that erupted in Kansas. These struggles and these crises are indeed of importance and the Civil War cannot be explained without full reference to them. But one has only to imagine a series of counterfactuals to appreciate that they cannot compete in importance with black resistance to slavery. One can imagine a civil war taking place without the Fugitive Slave Act of 1850 and even without the attempt to organise the territory of Kansas in the mid- and late-1850s. But one can scarcely imagine a civil war if the slaves had acted in the way that their masters and previous generations

---

3. Not only would the abolitionist project, demanding enough as it was, have become immensely more difficult but some of the behaviour of the masters, which called forth the antislavery onslaught, would have been far less in evidence. Thus, whippings would presumably have been far less frequent and separation of families or the threat of it would not have been used so often as a punishment.

of historians believed. From this, one must conclude that black resistance to slavery is a more fundamental and thus a more important cause of the Civil War.

It is a central proposition of this work that such resistance is endemic in slavery. It is also a central proposition of this work that such resistance constitutes class conflict, whether or not the individuals concerned possess class consciousness and regardless of whether they act collectively or individually.[4] Yet, the class conflict that existed between slave and master, though enormously important, was not of itself enough to unravel the southern social fabric. It would be quite wrong to assume that the South in 1860 was on the verge of a servile rebellion or that the resistance of the slaves, without outside pressure from the North, was sufficient to destroy slavery in the region.

For this, something else was needed, and it is here that we must give attention to the structure of northern society. Once again, there was no question of revolutionary upheaval: the North in 1860 was no more on the verge of a social cataclysm than the South. But the North was, in the decades prior to the Civil War, making a series of adjustments to the unprecedented growth of wage labor. Without wage labor, it is virtually certain that the northern economy could not have developed to the extent that it did and in such sharp contrast to the economy of the South. Northerners were struck by the differences between their region, where urbanisation and industrialisation were advancing with great strides (especially in the northeast), and the South, where these processes were either retarded or entirely absent. Equally important were the ideological adjustments that northern society was making. Wage workers had, traditionally in European society, been held an extremely low esteem. In the same way, the American democratic tradition, the tradition of Thomas Jefferson, Andrew Jackson and John Taylor of Caroline, looked upon them with suspicion. Wage workers were thought servile, lacking the independence that was the hallmark of republican freedom. In the final antebellum years, these attitudes, though never entirely absent, became far less widespread. Instead, many northerners now took pains to emphasise the advantages that the free, northern wage worker enjoyed. He was free to follow his conscience, he was free to enjoy the benefits of a family "not marketable," he was free to rise in society. Moreover, his freedom was guaranteed by a set of civil and political rights and underwritten by the esteem in which his labor was held. It is scarcely surprising that these ideological shifts took place: they were occasioned by, and in turn helped facilitate, the development of wage labor in the North. But each of them made slavery seem increasingly unacceptable. Did the slave not

4. These issues are discussed throughout the first volume of this study.

lack the ability to follow his conscience? Was his family not subject to the whim of another: a master who had the right to take his wife and child to market and sell them? What social mobility could there be under slavery for either the slave or, since the plantation employed so few whites, the nonslaveholders of the South? Did slaveholders not scorn the civil and political rights not merely of their slaves but also of their nonslavehold- ing whites, and set them aside whenever the need arose? And did not the fact that so much labor was performed by a degraded class of slaves result in labor itself being discredited in the South, as some southerners acknowledged? The Republican party, as we shall see, reached the conclu- sion that slavery disorganised a community politically, economically and, many added, morally. This conclusion reflected not merely the southern social order but also the priorities and perceptions of a northern society that was itself undergoing fundamental changes.

The interpretation in these volumes does not suggest that there is any simple relationship between classes and political parties. Where there was a tendency for certain groups to favour certain parties at certain times, I have pointed this out. Thus, as everyone knows, slaveholders increas- ingly favored the Democratic party in the final years of the antebellum Republic, while upwardly mobile Protestants in the expanding rural areas of the North, it is equally widely recognised, were much more likely to vote Republican. Thus, party affiliation was, in many instances, linked to socioeconomic position. But there were many exceptions and in no sense can the parties or the party conflict be reduced to simple expressions of class interest or of class conflict.

Instead, we need a more subtle notion of class, one which focuses upon relationships at the point of production. This work identifies a clash between northern and southern labor systems at the heart of the sec- tional conflict and traces their impact upon the political system. Slavery produced a distinctive set of relations of production, of class relations; wage-labor capitalism produced a different set. The values generated by each labor system, by each set of relations of production, proved increas- ingly difficult and finally impossible to reconcile. Southerners were able to contain the resistance, actual and potential, from their slaves just as northerners were able to forestall the resistance, actual and potential, from a previously despised class of wage workers. But the elite in each section could manage this accommodation only at the cost of a widening rift with the other section.

The ideology of the political parties and the competition between them are the central concerns of this volume and they reflect, albeit in a highly mediated form, this complex process of struggle, containment, and con- flict that was occurring deep within the American social order. The story I relate tells of the rise to dominance of the northern labor system, with wage labor an indispensable part of it. The challenges to that dominance resulted in more than a decade of mounting strife and, finally, in a Civil War. But northern victory in that war would be both cause and consequence of the superiority of the northern social system, or, conversely, of the inferiority of the slave mode of production. The Civil War would thus confirm that the northern way would become the American way. It would be the United States' bourgeois revolution.

## II

It is scarcely surprising that the Civil War, the largest, most dramatic event in the history of the United States, has generated a huge historical literature. Here, it is only necessary to examine what are perhaps the three major schools of thought, to assess their current viability, and to begin to situate the conclusions of the present work in reference to them.

Some two years before the outbreak of war, New York's Republican Senator William Henry Seward described the clash between the sections as an "irrepressible conflict" and, ever since, historians have been debating the proposition. Many have endorsed Seward's view, at least in its barest essentials. Even here, however, there has been no consensus. In accepting that conflict was inevitable, some scholars have insisted that moral issues were uppermost. For them, slavery was at the heart of the sectional controversy and slavery was itself primarily a moral question. This was very much the attitude of James Ford Rhodes, who wrote a highly celebrated multivolume history of the Civil War at the turn of the twentieth century and who believed that the slavery controversy had involved irreducibly moral issues and had indeed generated an "irrepressible conflict."[5]

A second school of thought also found intractable issues at the heart of the conflict but found them in the competition of economic interests rather than the clash of moral values. In its most extreme version, this interpretation dismissed the question of slavery entirely and insisted that the struggle was instead one between rival economic interests, with the North representing the forces of industrial or protoindustrial capitalism and the South embodying the values of agriculture and agrarianism. This tradition owes something to the writings of Karl Marx, who contributed a number of articles on, and in his letters made many references to, the Civil War, it owes more to the vulgar Marxism that was displayed by some of his followers writing in the early twentieth century, and it owes most of

5. James Ford Rhodes, *History of the United States from the Compromise of 1850*. 7 vols. (New York, 1893–1906). Ford was not the first to advocate this view. Indeed, it was held by many of the abolitionists and radical Republicans at the time of the war itself.

all to the work of Charles and Mary Beard, who were themselves almost certainly heavily influenced by these vulgar Marxists. The Beards argued that the Civil War marked no less than a "Second American Revolution," a crucial dividing line between the agricultural and industrial eras, a time when the grasping industrialists of the North expelled from power the southern planters and their agrarian allies. For the Beards, as for the early Marxists who wrote upon the subject, the Civil War was both cause and consequence of the development of industrial capitalism in the United States.[6]

Despite the fundamentally different viewpoints of Rhodes and the Beards, they agreed on the intractability of the sectional conflict. The third great school of Civil War historians instead argued that the war could have been averted had not a "blundering generation" failed to find the compromises that could have brought peace to the nation. This interpretative schema, dubbed "Civil War revisionism," flourished in the 1930s and 1940s. Emphasising the errors of the "blundering generation," scholars such as Avery Craven and James Randall denied that the differences between North and South were sufficient to justify war. Instead, they found, in the historical record, mistakes and misperceptions, emotionalism, and irrationality, rather than uncompromisable moral values or irreconcilable economic interests. For the revisionists, Seward's references to an "irrepressible conflict" demonstrated not an admirable awareness of the moral or economic dimensions of the struggles between North and South but rather a lamentable failure to engage in the constructive statesmanship that might have brought an end to them.[7]

## III

Few scholars today are prepared unreservedly to endorse any of these three historiographical positions; modern scholarship has recorded many advances upon the writings of Rhodes, the Beards, Craven, Randall, and their disciples. In this work, I have employed the insights of a veritable army of scholars who have refined, revised, and supplemented the work of these pioneers. Following modern scholarship I argue that the relationship between ideas and interests, for example, was far more subtle and complex than Charles and Mary Beard realised. In common with the vast majority of historians, I accord a central place to slavery in the

---

6. See Algie M. Simons, *Social Forces in American History* (New York, 1911); Charles A. and Mary R. Beard, *The Rise of American Civilization.* 2 vols. (New York, 1927). II, pp. 2–54. This view too was advanced by contemporaries in the 1850s and 1860s, normally southerners, almost invariably Democrats.
7. Avery Craven, *The Repressible Conflict 1830–1861* (Baton Rouge, 1939), J. G. Randall, *Lincoln the President: Springfield to Gettysburg.* 2 vols. (New York, 1945).

sectional conflict and argue that the conflict cannot be reduced to a clash between agriculture and industry. Like most historians, I recognise that slavery generated considerable moral outrage but that the political and economic criticisms of the institution were more frequently heard than the moral indictment. I follow other historians in disputing the claim that the War years occupy a privileged place in the transition from agrarianism to industrialism. I echo other scholars, too, when I reject the notion that the sectional conflict erupted into war because of the failings of a "blundering generation." In these, and in other respects, the present work reaffirms conclusions that other scholars have offered.

Some arguments, however, will be less familiar to readers.[8] In these volumes, I place a heavy emphasis upon the weaknesses of slavery in comparison with wage labor. I argue that these weaknesses were a result of the conflicts, actual and potential, between slave and master that were endemic to the regime. I suggest that, in the 1850s and at the time of secession, southerners, although they scarcely realised it, were responding to these weaknesses and searching for a means of overcoming them. Secession was the ultimate, drastic remedy. But secession failed for the very reason that it became necessary. The South lost the Civil War essentially because of slavery.[9]

My quarrel with Civil War revisionism is also relevant in this connection. Unlike many contemporary historians, I fully accept the revisionist claim that statesmen on both sides of the Mason-Dixon Line made fundamental errors and misperceived much of what was happening around them.[10] I also accept that these errors and misperceptions were of considerable importance in bringing about the Civil War. On the other hand, I suggest that they should not be seen as the products of a "blundering generation" but should be viewed instead as having been structurally generated. These errors and misperceptions were the product of underlying ideas and assumptions which should be understood in terms of the entire ideology of which they were a part. These ideologies were inscribed with, and structured by, certain economic and class interests which they in turn furthered. In other words, there is an intimate connection

---

8. Although my general approach is heavily derived from Marxist categories and Marxist analysis, I should perhaps point out that neither Marx, nor any scholar working within the Marxist tradition has (to my knowledge) presented an argument along the lines offered here.

9. One historian who has stressed the role of slavery in bringing about Confederate defeat is William W. Freehling. See Freehling, *The South vs. The South: How Anti-Confederate Southerners Shaped the Course of the Civil War* (New York, 2001). See also John Ashworth, "William W. Freehling and the Politics of the Old South," *American Nineteenth Century History* V (2004), pp. 1–29.

10. Most scholars, it is fair to say, note these errors almost in passing, without acknowledging the support they afford to the revisionist position.

between misperceptions and economic interests. The dichotomy between errors and economic interests implied by revisionism must therefore be dissolved.

Similarly, when I look briefly at the impact of the war, I also attempt to embrace a wider view of economic interests. Thus, although I claim that the war constituted a bourgeois revolution, I do not argue, as some Marxists have done (and as Beard came close to doing), that the war was needed to remove impediments to the continued development of northern capitalism. Instead, I suggest that one must again transcend the division between interests and values by emphasising that the triumph of free labor and the demise of slavery made capitalist ideology itself triumphant. Although no economic historian has even attempted to place a value upon this ideological shift, there can be no doubt that especially over the long haul it was in financial terms immensely advantageous to the employers of labor and their allies. Its value indeed was, in both senses of the term, incalculable.

## IV

This volume is essentially a history of American politics between 1850 and 1861. Although it locates the ultimate cause of the sectional conflict in the different relationships entailed by wage labor and slave labor economies, its focus is not upon this underlying social history or upon the underlying labor systems but rather upon their political repercussions. Thus, the reader who believes (despite the mountain of historical scholarship to the contrary) that African Americans were quite content to be slaves will find very little evidence marshalled here to challenge his preconceptions. More important, those who are curious to know how the traditional suspicion of wage labor shaped the history of the American labor movement in the North will also find little in these pages that addresses this important question. On the other hand, the reader who wonders how that suspicion fed into the sectional conflict or the reader who understands that African Americans were far from content to be slaves but wonders how this contributed to the outbreak of the Civil War will, it is to be hoped, find a great deal more. In other words, this volume, like its predecessor, builds upon the work of social historians, especially those who have studied the slaves of the South, and traces the political effects of their findings. Some readers have observed that the dramatis personae of my account, the white politicians whose views fill most of the pages of this volume, and its predecessor, are not those to whom, in explaining the Civil War, causal primacy is accorded. This is an accurate observation. But, if this is an unusual approach, it is, I hope, neither contradictory nor perverse.

Most histories of the 1850s and of the secession crisis adopt a narrative and chronological approach to their subject, the advantages of which are perhaps too obvious to be spelled out. Such an approach does, however, entail certain disadvantages too. I believe that to a very considerable extent, the events of the 1850s and early 1860s are to be understood by reference to the ideologies of the principal protagonists, and I have, therefore, striven to present those ideologies as systematically as possible. This work is thus divided primarily by reference to sectional, political, or ideological affiliation and stance and only secondarily according to chronology. I present the events of the period from four different perspectives, those of southern militants, of Republicans, of (primarily northern) Democrats, and of what I term "Whigs and neo-Whigs," and I seek to achieve an empathic understanding of the events from each of those perspectives. As a result, some of the key events or processes of the period recur in each chapter. Secession, for example, features in each chapter, although with a different focus in each. Similarly, I consider the Kansas-Nebraska Act in each chapter, in two of them (those dealing with southern militants and northern Democrats) concentrating upon the origins of the Act; in the others assessing its impact (upon Republicans, Whigs and the party system, in general). The attitudes of the various groups towards the economic changes of these years mean that the banking and tariff questions are treated on more than one occasion, although again with a different focus each time. Readers will decide for themselves whether this arrangement of materials is, or is not, an appropriate one. In any event, I should perhaps state that I have found much that is ironic in the history of these years and, as I have already noted, not a few misperceptions and errors on the part of its leading statesmen. I have also, however, found little that, once placed within its ideological context, was irrational, foolish, or unintelligible.[11]

---

11. Some repetition is inevitable, but I have tried to keep this to a minimum. It is, of course, the case that some topics could as easily have been treated in one chapter as in another.

# PART I

*Slavery versus Antislavery*

# 1

# Combating the weaknesses of slavery: Southern militants, 1850–1861

### Introduction: The weaknesses of slavery

On March 4, 1850 John C. Calhoun of South Carolina entered the Senate to present his last great speech. He had been for almost twenty years the leading, though not always the most extreme, exponent of the view that the South must awaken to the dangers of abolition, must unite to demand her rights under the Constitution, and must, if those rights were not granted, be prepared to secede from the Union. As soon as it was known that the South Carolinian was to speak, queues formed on Capitol Hill. In fact Calhoun had less than a month to live and his speech had to be read by James Mason of Virginia. Nevertheless, it was listened to, one onlooker reported, "with the deepest attention."[1]

By 1850 Calhoun's warnings had acquired fresh urgency in the minds of many southerners. The huge accession of territory (covering California, Nevada, Utah, most of New Mexico and Arizona, and parts of Oklahoma, Wyoming, Colorado, and Texas) that followed the nation's triumph in the recent war with Mexico had reintroduced the question of slavery in the territories. Large numbers of northerners had in the late 1840s rallied behind the proviso which bore the name of David Wilmot and which sought to exclude slavery from these newly acquired lands. Most southerners regarded the Wilmot Proviso as an outrageous violation of their equal rights within the Union and for Calhoun it was confirmation, if any were by now needed, that antislavery sentiment in the North had attained fearsome proportions. In his final speech Calhoun reiterated that this hostility to slavery, if unchecked, spelled utter ruin for the South. The South was the minority section and, if the Union were to be preserved, it was up to the North to make concessions and to cease the agitation of

---

1. Allan Nevins, *Ordeal of the Union: Fruits of Manifest Destiny 1847–1852* (New York, 1947), p. 281.

the slavery issue. Otherwise a break-up of the Union would be inevitable. It was concession or secession.[2]

Calhoun repeatedly referred to the South as the "weaker" section. By this he meant that it was in a minority in the Union. On this score he was right. Here was an elemental fact, one which gave the sectional controversy immense significance. Out of a population of more than twenty-three million in 1850, the slaveholding states had fewer than ten million. As Calhoun knew, this population imbalance left the South vulnerable, or at least potentially vulnerable, to what he regarded as the tyranny of the "numerical majority." As Calhoun also knew, the minority status of the South was even more pronounced than these figures suggested. Some three million of her population were slaves, who counted, for purposes of representation, as only three-fifths of a person. As Calhoun did not know however, those slaves would prove, in an armed conflict with the North, not an asset but a severe liability. As he also did not know (though he might have suspected), the loyalty to the South of some of those slave states, the ones which bordered the North, could also not be relied upon in an armed conflict. Events would show that the majority of the two million people in the four states of Kentucky, Delaware, Virginia, and Maryland, when compelled to choose, would throw in their lot with the North.

Calhoun was also well aware that, even if the four border states were classed as southern, the South could expect in the future to control only a minority of states in the Union. In 1850 the Union comprised thirty states, fifteen slave and fifteen free. But Calhoun foresaw the creation in the next decade of an additional five free states but not a single new slave state. This opened up the possibility that the North might, at a later date but still in the not-too-distant future, control three fourths of the States, and thus be able to alter the Constitution, and abolish slavery. In states controlled, as in population, therefore, the South was indeed the weaker section.

Calhoun reminded his listeners that the South's minority status was of comparatively recent origin. There had been equality between North and South when the Union had been created. How had the imbalance arisen? Calhoun attributed it entirely to the operations of the federal government, which had favoured the North at the expense of the South by levying taxes upon the South that were then used to fund expenditures in the North, and by outlawing slavery in many of the lands acquired since 1776. Thus for Calhoun the weakness of the South was in no sense attributable to slavery.

---

2.  The speech can be found in *Congressional Globe*, 31st Cong., 1st Session, pp. 451–455 (hereafter cited in the form *CG*, 31/1, pp. 451–455).

Here he was wrong.[3] The South was indeed, in ways that Calhoun did not himself understand, the "weaker" section. But his understanding, and his misunderstanding, of the sectional controversy in 1850 were both highly typical of southerners in the final antebellum decades. As the conflict between North and South deepened, protagonists on both sides of the divide were driven to offer elaborate defences of their own section. Not surprisingly, those who most enthusiastically defended the South were, like Calhoun, also those who were most convinced of the viability, even the superiority, of slavery there. These militants did not hesitate to proclaim their commitment to their system of unfree labour, and they followed Calhoun once again in insisting that if forced to choose between slavery and the Union, the South should unhesitatingly opt for the former. The southern militant thus exhibited an enormous confidence in the strength of slavery, a confidence which finally, and most dramatically, propelled him in 1860–1861 to recommend the dismemberment of the nation and the creation of a separate southern confederacy.[4]

Ironically, however, the same southerner was in fact responding in 1860–1861, as Calhoun had in 1850, and many southerners before him, to the weaknesses of slavery. These he could not admit; in most cases he, like Calhoun, could not even recognise them. To be blind to a problem, however, is not to be immune to its effects, and militant southerners in their attitudes and actions in the 1850s (as previously) in fact quietly illustrated the weaknesses and vulnerabilities of chattel slavery even as they loudly proclaimed its superiority and its strengths.

From one standpoint, however, southerners were correct to proclaim the strength of their peculiar institution. In comparison with other systems of unfree labour, located elsewhere in the world, southern slavery was indeed extremely powerful. In 1850, slavery still existed in Ecuador, Peru, Brazil, Venezuela, Cuba, and Puerto Rico; and there were more than twenty million serfs in Russia. But nowhere else in the nineteenth century did a class of slaveholders exercise the power wielded by the planters of the South. This power was in part political in that the South enjoyed a

---

3.  Calhoun's logic and facts were extremely shaky here – see Volume I of this study, pp. 455–456.
4.  The best analysis of southern politics in the final antebellum years is, in my view, to be found in the work of Willliam W. Freehling. I have learned more about the South from Freehling than from any other historian, though I fundamentally disagree with many, perhaps most, of his conclusions. See Freehling, *The Road to Disunion: Secessionists at Bay, 1776–1854* (New York, 1990) and *Road to Disunion: Secessionists Triumphant, 1854–1861* (New York, 2007). For an extended discussion of the first of these volumes and other works by the same author see John Ashworth, "William W. Freehling and the Politics of the Old South," *American Nineteenth Century History* V (2004), pp. 1–29. For an assessment of the second volume see my review in *Reviews in American History* (forthcoming) entitled "Democracy and Despotism: Roads (and Railroads) to Disunion."

huge and disproportionate influence over the destinies of the American Republic. It was also economic in that by comparison with many other nations in the world, the southern economy was highly developed and highly advanced. This economic strength would even allow the South to fight a bitter civil war for four long years. Nevertheless, as the outcome of the War would confirm, it was in comparison with the North that the southern social system, rooted in human slavery, would be found wanting. And when southerners boasted of the strength of their labour system, it was the comparison with the North that they usually had in mind. As the outcome of the War would also confirm, this was indeed the relevant comparison.

The weaknesses of slavery took many forms and left the South vulnerable to criticisms from the North that were moral, economic, and political in nature. They also left the South vulnerable to the majority of its own population who were neither slaves nor slaveholders. But underlying these threats from the North and from the nonslaveholders of the South lay a still closer and more potent threat, one that came from the slaves themselves. At the core of the sectional controversy was a problem which no spokesman for the South was able to recognise, let alone remove: the slaves did not wish to be slaves. It was this which probably constrained the economic development of the South by impeding the progress of industrialisation and urbanisation there and by ensuring that in the race to colonise the West, the South would be the loser. It was this which also constrained southern democracy, by curtailing the rights of free speech and free discussion where slavery was concerned. And it was this which made the relationship between slaveholders and the nonslaveowning population of the South so delicate and so difficult. Underlying all these dangers was the threat of abolition itself, a horrific prospect but one which, in reality, derived its potency from the slaves' desire to throw off their chains.

None of this was understood either by Calhoun in 1850 or those who led the South in the decade after his death. Yet these southerners were all responding to the effects of slavery's weakness. Like Calhoun they were all too aware that their section was lagging far behind the North in terms of states controlled and in terms of population. And like Calhoun they realised that the settlement of 1850, the great compromise between the sections, could not alter the fact that the South was indeed the minority section. Calhoun did not live to see the details of the Compromise of 1850 confirmed. Had he done so, he would, like most southern militants, have opposed it,

As he, and those who followed him, recognised, the minority status of the South in the Union had been a defining feature of the sectional controversy; it would continue to be so in the decade that preceded its final climax. Northern power in Washington meant that the militant southerner, who by definition was unwilling simply to trust northerners to act properly towards him, had two choices. One was to leave the Union, a course of action which some recommended in 1850 (and earlier), which would be frequently threatened in the 1850s, and which would finally triumph in 1860–1861. The alternative was to seek to make the Union safe for the South and its peculiar institution. How could this be achieved? There were in turn three ways. One was to seek to re-educate the North. Although few southern militants believed that northern antislavery zealots could be cured of their fanaticism, many more came to believe that if proper views of the Constitution (and especially of the constitutional power of Congress over slavery), could be established among sufficient numbers of northerners, then the Union might yet be made safe. This might mean persuasion, but it might also mean threats. Northerners might be induced to abandon their crusade against slavery if they were forced to confront its possible consequences. The ultimate threat was of course that of secession itself, and it was accordingly made with great frequency, usually with conditions attached, in the 1850s. A second way of making the Union safe for the South was to reduce or even eliminate the northern advantage in political power by acquiring more slave states. Southern militants in the 1850s would devote a huge amount of time and attention to this possibility. The third possibility was to address the vulnerabilities of the slave system in the South either in locations where it was, or seemed, weakest or among groups whose conduct gave most cause for unease.

Between 1850 and 1861 militant southerners would try each of these strategies. Yet none of them could touch the weaknesses of slavery, the most fundamental of which was the slaves' desire for freedom. Accordingly, each would fail, and fail quite spectacularly.

## The Compromise of 1850 and its legacy

### I

For many southerners the crisis of midcentury was a defining moment in the history of the American Republic. By the end of 1851, the Compromise measures of 1850 had been accepted and all but a few of the most militant southerners hoped that the settlement would prove permanent. Outside South Carolina there had been few outright secessionists in 1850 but there had been far more who had asserted the right of secession. On their reading of the hallowed document, the Federal Constitution was a compact between sovereign states which preexisted the Union, which had voluntarily joined it, and which thus retained the right to leave it whenever they so wished.[5] In the main these southerners feared that by the terms of the Compromise the South had surrendered too much and the North had given too little. They had thus acquiesced in, rather than embraced, the settlement, in many cases simply because it had become apparent that, once again outside South Carolina, public opinion was unwilling to countenance further resistance.[6]

Who were these southern militants? After the death of Calhoun, there was no single leader around whom they could rally, although Jefferson Davis of Mississippi probably came closest to fulfilling this role.[7] Moreover between the time of the Compromise and the late 1850s they had relatively few complaints to make of the federal government and of the men who headed it. Indeed the administrations of Pierce and Buchanan were viewed in these years with some warmth even by southerners who had been highly critical of the Compromise. There was thus in the middle years of the decade no issue upon which they needed to take a distinctive, oppositional stand and they therefore had no need of separate institutional support.

Southern militants thus formed neither a party, nor even an organised pressure group. There was no newspaper circulating throughout the 1850s in large numbers across the entire South that spoke for them and they did not even meet regularly as a congressional group. Moreover their numbers were unstable, some individuals moved in and out of their ranks, and they were by no means unanimous in their views. Hershel Johnson of Georgia and Pierre Soulé of Louisiana, for example, adopted more extreme positions on sectional questions in the early 1850s than they would assume later in the decade. A figure as important as Robert Toombs of Georgia pursued an erratic course in the 1850s: on some occasions threatening secession in unmeasured terms, on others counselling caution and moderation. Some militants, as we have seen,[8] favoured the reopening of the African slave trade, others might insist upon the right to reopen but declare it presently inexpedient, while still others were strongly opposed both in principle and in practice. Even on a question as fundamental as secession, and the conditions in which it would be justified, they did not take a single, consistent line.

Nevertheless southern militants shared certain traits. They were far more likely to be Democrats than Whigs. When the Compromise was

5. Other southerners derived the right of secession from the right of revolution, to which almost all Americans were, of course, committed.
6. Allan Nevins, *Fruits of Manifest Destiny*, pp. 346–379; David Potter, *The Impending Crisis, 1848–1861* (New York, 1976), pp. 122–130; Holman Hamilton, *Prologue to Conflict: The Crisis and Compromise of 1850* (New York, 1964)
7. Even Calhoun, it should be noted, had had his critics within their ranks.
8. See volume I of this study.

under consideration a majority of southern Democrats had initially been ranged against it and, as we shall see, although that opposition would disappear after the Compromise had been ratified, the underlying attitudes and principles would persist. Indeed the choice for these militants would usually be either to support the Democratic party or to support no party at all. Even more strikingly, they were more likely to be from the Deep South rather than the Middle South and least likely to be from the border states.[9] The typical southern militant was thus a Democrat from the Deep South. He might be in a position of great influence and power, he might occupy a seat in the United States Senate or a governor's mansion, indeed, as the examples of Jefferson Davis of Mississippi and John Slidell of Louisiana suggest, he might be the most powerful man in his state. Especially in the Deep South he and his fellow militants might well be a major and sometimes a controlling force in a Democratic party which itself might well be a major or controlling influence in the state.

Southern militants were also almost invariably slaveholders but in this they did not differ from almost every other southern leader, especially in Washington. Their distinguishing features were not slave ownership *per se*, but rather the depth of their commitment to slavery, their doubts about the trustworthiness of the North, and their common sense of grievance.

It is important to understand the precise nature of these grievances. Like northerners, and indeed virtually all Americans, the militant southerner now examined the past and projected recent developments into the future. Unlike northerners, however, he ended up with a vision of a South in which slavery had been abolished, three million slaves emancipated and left to run riot, and his civilisation and prosperity permanently destroyed. It was this vision which provoked southern anxieties before the Compromise measures were enacted and which continued to nourish those anxieties afterwards.

In 1849 in one of his periodic attempts to unite the South across party lines, Calhoun had written the *Address of the Southern Delegates in Congress to their Constituents*. In it he had provided a vivid account of the northern encroachments upon southern rights that had already taken place and warned that these alone might "perhaps," if not checked, "end in emancipation, and that at no distant day." But he insisted that the further aggressions now contemplated would assuredly have that effect. The Address was signed by forty-eight southerners, almost all of them

---

9.  The border states were Kentucky, Missouri, Delaware, Maryland, and, technically, given that what is now West Virginia borders Ohio and Pennsylvania, Virginia. In other respects, however, Virginia belonged to the Middle South, along with Tennessee and North Carolina. Similarly Arkansas is usually characterised as part of the Middle South, but sometimes classified with South Carolina, Georgia, Florida, Alabama, Mississippi, Louisiana, and Texas as the Deep South or the Lower South.

Democrats. This neatly anticipated the alignment of 1850 in which southern Democrats formed (along with northern Whigs, who were hostile for opposite reasons) the most solid force mobilised against the Compromise. It anticipated the alignment of that year too in demonstrating that such militancy, while visible far beyond the boundaries of the state of South Carolina, and perhaps able to command the support of a majority of southern Democrats, could not yet command the support of a majority of all southerners.[10]

By 1850 southern militants had become accustomed to reviewing the progress of abolitionism and antislavery (which to them were virtually one and the same) in the North since the early 1830s. Such reviews had been for some time a part of the repertoire of John C. Calhoun and his disciples,[11] and southern militants continued in this vein until the moment at which they tried to leave the Union in 1860–1861. In 1851 Robert W. Johnson of Arkansas in an *Address to His Constituents* reminded them that "twenty years ago, (which is a short time), there was not an abolition newspaper in the entire North." Yet now with "exceptions barely enough to establish the rule, they are all such, by the principles of Free-soil." "Indeed," he noted, "we now have more abolition prints now published and patronized within our Southern limits than were to be found in the entire North." Johnson then sounded the necessary warning: "the Constitution will not protect us in ten years." The Vermont legislature had already claimed that slavery could be legislated on except in the original five slave states. "Time," Johnson felt, "will sanctify this idea." And while the notion might seem monstrous, he pointed out that abolition in the District of Columbia or the territories had been similarly viewed only a few years earlier. Johnson's specific fear, of a distinction being made between the original slave states and the newer ones, proved unfounded but his general point about the growth in antislavery sentiment would be vindicated time and time again in the following decade. As Jacob Thompson of Mississippi declared, also in 1851, "this anti-slavery feeling will be onward till the whole power of the Government shall be wielded for the overthrow of slavery."[12]

The midcentury crisis had revealed three specific southern fears or concerns. One of these was over the return of fugitive slaves.[13] Another

---

10.  *Address of the Southern Delegates in Congress to their Constituents* (n.p., n.d.), p. 11. At the time of the *Address*, there were about 120 southerners in Congress.
11.  See Volume I of this study, pp. 133–139.
12.  "Address of Congressman Robert W. Johnson to his Constituents Jan. 29, 1850" in Helena (Arkansas) *Southern Shield*, July 12, 1851; *Address of the Hon. Jacob Thompson of Mississippi to His Constituents* (Washington, D.C., 1851), pp. 10–11. See also *To the Hon. W. J. Grayson by One of the People* (n.p., n.d.), p. 9.
13.  For a discussion of this issue, see, pp. 35–43.

concerned the proposed action by Congress on the subject of both slavery in the District of Columbia and the interstate slave trade. At one time it had seemed as if outright abolition in the District and of the interstate slave trade were both on the northern agenda but in the event it was merely the slave trade in the District that was outlawed.[14] The third item was the imposition of the Wilmot Proviso which attempted to prohibit slaveholders from taking their slaves to the territories newly acquired from Mexico. All three issues were important and each caused resentment in its own right but it is important to note that these, and virtually all other measures proposed at this juncture, were viewed by many southerners as part of an unfolding pattern of northern antislavery militancy and aggression. The fear was that each northern demand or piece of agitation would, if unchecked, encourage another even more dangerous act. And the culmination of the process would be the abolition of slavery in the states where it existed.

This was very much the message offered by those who attended, and endorsed the address of, the first of the Southern Conventions which met at Nashville in 1850 The address was written by Robert Barnwell Rhett, as ardent a secessionist as anyone in the South, but it was considerably toned down to suit the moderate temper of the Convention and it limped to the conclusion that the Missouri Compromise line at 36° 30′ should be extended to the Pacific. But Rhett's analysis of the current crisis was far more compelling than his specific demands. The Address, which was directed at all the citizens of the slave states, posed a question:

> If you were to yield everything the North now request, and abolish slavery in the District of Columbia, submit to be legislated pirates for conveying slaves from one State to another, let trial by jury and the writ of *habeas corpus* wrest from you in the North every fugitive slave, give up all your territories to swell northern arrogance and predominance, would things stop there?

The answer was, of course an emphatic negative: "surrendering one of these means you will but inflame the power by which another will be exacted." All were simply "means, aiming at one great end – the abolition of slavery in the States."[15]

The same approach, which sought to extrapolate a pattern from recent events, and then use it to predict the future, was perhaps universally adopted by southern militants from the late 1840s (and by a small minority even earlier). No one advanced the argument with greater force or

14. And even this turned out to be less than was once feared since only the most flagrant (and antipatriarchal) examples of slavetrading were banned.
15. "Address of the Southern Convention to the People of Delaware, Maryland, Virginia . . ." in Mobile *Advertiser*, June 29, 1850.

clarity than Albert Gallatin Brown, Representative and then United States Senator for Mississippi and, with the possible exception of the South Carolinians, as militant on the slavery question as anyone in the Senate. Except for a short period when the sectional controversy seemed to be in abeyance Brown continued throughout the 1850s not so much to threaten northerners as to make explicit the circumstances in which he thought their actions would lead to, and justify, the break up of the nation. He claimed that his position was that of nineteen-twentieths of southerners and whilst this was a considerable exaggeration he certainly spoke for a significant strand of southern opinion. Thus in 1850 he acknowledged that neither the exclusion of slaveholders from the territories nor abolition of the interstate slave trade, the slave trade in the District, or even slavery itself there would justify secession. Yet he nevertheless warned that "at the first moment after you consummate your first act of aggression upon slave property, I would declare the Union dissolved." There was no contradiction here because "such an act perpetrated after the warning we have given you would evince a settled purpose to interpose your authority in the management of our domestic affairs."[16]

It was thus the growth in antislavery sentiment which most alarmed Brown and those who thought like him. He could derive no consolation from the denials, repeatedly offered by antislavery northerners, that they wished to abolish slavery in the states where it existed. Even if these northerners spoke the truth, their promises were worthless since they would soon be replaced by more extreme men. In 1858 Brown boasted that he had been more hostile to the Compromise measures of 1850 than any man in Congress and he clearly believed that his course had since been vindicated. But yet again he made it clear that it was the future progress of antislavery that was so alarming. He now invited any northerner to "point out any spot short of absolute ruin to ourselves, and desolation to our section of the country, and give us the guarantee that when you have gone to that point, these aggressive and perplexing measures, legislative and others, shall certainly cease." In such an eventuality "we will say to you at once, go to that point." But Brown's conclusion was again that of 1850: "defend the outposts" and "yield not an inch of ground." The danger once again was that "the whole northern free soil phalanx will be turned loose in one mighty assault upon slavery in the States." Brown had "taught my people, as I would teach them to-day, to prepare for this assault" on the grounds that "it is better to die defending the door-sill than admit the enemy and then see the hearth-stone bathed in blood."[17]

16. M. W. Cluskey (ed.), *Speeches, Messages, and Other Writings of the Hon. Albert Gallatin Brown, A Senator in Congress from the State of Mississippi* (Philadelphia, 1859), pp. 477, 169
17. *Speeches, Messages, ... of ... Albert Gallatin Brown*, pp. 170, 538–539, 477,.

These were common sentiments in 1850 (and after). The Milledgeville *Federal Union* offered in that year to give up all claims to the territories in question, "humiliating" though such a concession would be, if only peace on the slavery question could be established and agitation ended. But "no sane man," the newspaper continued, "in view of the history of the past, can anticipate such a result." Once again the danger was cumulative: "if the South submit now to the exactions demanded of her, she will soon be called to submit to other and still more exorbitant demands."[18]

Southern militants were acutely aware that abolition could be achieved within the Constitution, as soon as the North had sufficient political power. Since the early years of the Republic, northerners and southerners alike had been concerned with the balance of sectional power. The policy of paired admissions of new states, one slave and one free, had been established in the time of Jefferson, confirmed in 1820 with the admission of Missouri (coupled with Maine) and retained until 1850. Thereafter the creation of additional free states was doubly threatening to the South. It not only conferred additional power on the North in the Senate, which could then be mobilised on everyday legislative matters, it also greatly increased the chances of constitutional revision. To change the constitution, of course, required not only a two-thirds majority in each chamber but also ratification by three-fourths of the states. In this context, an increase in the ratio of free to slave states was ominous indeed.

These fears had been voiced as early as 1820 and they re-emerged at midcentury. In 1849 Calhoun and the forty-eight signatories of his *Address of the Southern Delegates* had predicted that "at no distant day" the North's policy of monopolising the territories would provide her with the necessary votes to amend the Constitution and then "emancipate our slaves." In that and the preceding year, Jefferson Davis of Mississippi repeatedly drew attention to the same danger. Similarly the Southern Convention that met in Nashville in 1850 predicted that there would be twenty new nonslaveholding states within fifty years. Hence abolitionists would no longer need to scorn the Constitution, as was the practice of William Lloyd Garrison. They would instead be able to amend it and annul its safeguards. It was with this process in mind that the delegates at Nashville warned the people of the South that "your condition is progressive." In 1851 *De Bow's Review* predicted on the basis of the experience of the last three years that the North would soon obtain fifteen or twenty new states while the South would obtain at most three or four (to be carved out of Texas). These fears too would be frequently voiced in the following decade.[19]

---

18. "Milledgeville Federal Union" in *Raleigh Standard*, June 26, 1850.
19. *Address of the Southern Delegates*, pp. 11–12; Lynda Lasswell Crist *et al.* (eds.), *The Papers of Jefferson Davis*. 11 vols. (Baton Rouge, 1971), III, p. 354, IV, pp. 19–20,

This was the context in which the creation of the new state of California was viewed. The admission of California as the thirty-first state and a sixteenth free state would immediately end the sectional parity in the Senate. It was viewed by many southerners, therefore, as a critical stage in the process by which northerners were establishing their supremacy. By virtue of its faster growing population, the North had already acquired a majority of seats in the House of Representatives. Accordingly, when the bill for the admission of California was passed, Jefferson Davis, destined to play a leading role in the South's attempt to resist the northern majority, warned that Congress was now "about permanently to destroy the balance of power between the sections of the Union, by securing a majority to one, in both Houses of Congress." "Let us sleep now for a few years," one South Carolinian warned, "and we will then be roused to find the slaveholding States struggling with a government in which they will be a weak and helpless minority."[20]

## II

If the measures of 1850 were as symbols unacceptable to militant southerners, most of them were in addition highly objectionable in themselves. Ironically perhaps the measure that attracted least attention was based upon a principle which, when applied four years later, would provoke more controversy than any other. The territories of New Mexico and Utah were in 1850 to be organised in accordance with the principle of congressional nonintervention. Since this area seemed far less attractive to most southerners (and northerners too for that matter) than California, and since there was a hope that one or both of these territories would establish slavery, this measure gave rise to relatively little discussion. It should be noted, however, that the principle of congressional nonintervention was shrouded in ambiguity. Congress should refuse to establish a policy regarding slavery in a given territory but in the absence of such a policy, at what point were the settlers in the territory to make the crucial decision? Would it be in the territorial stage, as Stephen A. Douglas of Illinois and others believed, or would it be, as most southerners argued, only at the very end of the territorial stage, when the territory was about to join the Union as a fully fledged state? This was an important question, since

32–46, 49; "Address of Southern Convention"; *De Bow's Review*, XI (1851), p. 319; Nevins, *Fruits of Manifest Destiny*, pp. 224–225. *Address of the Committee of the Mississippi Convention to the Southern States* (n.p., n.d.), p. 2.

20. CG, 31/1, App., p. 1533; *To the Hon. W. J. Grayson by Another of the People* (n.p., n.d.), p. 14. See also *To the Hon. W. J. Grayson by One of the People*, p. 9; Anthony Gene Carey, *Parties, Slavery and the Union in Antebellum Georgia* (Athens, GA, 1997), p. 163.

it would determine whether slaveholders would be present at the moment of statehood and thus able to influence the final outcome. This ambiguity would assume momentous proportions later in the decade but it received relatively little attention in 1850, partly because the territories in question were eclipsed by California and partly because there was an additional uncertainty concerning the status of Mexican law during the territorial phase. It is safe to say that if the organisation of these two territories had been the sole issue in 1850, few southerners would have either warned of impending doom or threatened disunion.[21]

Very different was the southern reaction to the proposal to admit California as a free state, bypassing the territorial stage entirely. This unprecedented act seemed to many southerners nothing less than an outrage. They charged the North with having rejected the proposal to extend the Missouri compromise line in the late 1840s and then also rejecting, for California, the policy of popular sovereignty. Once again, they acknowledged, as almost all southern militants were to do both in 1850 and 1861, that the people of a territory could indeed exclude slavery at the time of their entry into the Union but insisted that they must be a people, must be citizens of the United States, and must have allowed slaveholders, prior to admission into the Union, equal opportunities to enter the territory. None of these conditions applied, it was argued, in the case of California. According to Pierre Soulé of Louisiana, the constitution proposed for California had been drawn up by "a handful of adventurers, most of whom had not a three months residence in the territories." Southerners would recall this later in the decade when the question of the admission of Kansas as a slave state, again under highly irregular conditions, arose. But in 1850 they complained bitterly that so far as California was concerned, there had been, in effect, a prohibition of slaveholders every bit as oppressive and unconstitutional as that contained in the Wilmot Proviso.[22]

Was there ever any real prospect of planting slavery in California? Here the evidence is mixed. Jefferson Davis for one insisted that there was no reason slavery could not flourish in California and other southerners noted that slaves could easily and profitably have been employed in mining in that area.[23] On the other hand, for Robert Toombs of Georgia the issue was instead one of honour. California, he believed, could never become a true slave state but it was essential that the moral slur cast upon slavery

21. One South Carolinian, however, argued that the continuance of Mexican laws at the territorial stage meant the exclusion of slavery and was thus equivalent to the Wilmot Proviso – *To the Hon. W. J. Grayson by One of the People*, p. 6.
22. *To the Hon. W. J. Grayson by One of the People*, pp. 5–7; *Mr Soulé's Speech at Opelousas, La. Delivered 6 Sept. 1851* (New Orleans, 1851), p. 6.
23. *CG*, 31/1, App., pp. 149–157; Crist *et al.* (eds.), *Papers of Davis*, IV, pp. 28–30, 66; *Speeches, Messages, . . . of . . . Albert Gallatin Brown*, p. 181.

and slaveholders by the Wilmot Proviso be removed. Similarly the Raleigh *Standard*, the leading Democratic newspaper in North Carolina, took the editor of its Whig counterpart, the *Register*, severely to task for arguing that Congressional action in regard to California was not important since "the laws of nature bar slavery from there." The *Standard* did not disagree about the prognosis for slavery in California but nevertheless underlined the importance of the principle involved and the need to resist the North, for northerners desired an exclusion of slavery from the territory as one of their *"entering wedges to complete an universal emancipation."*[24]

It is impossible for the historian to determine who was correct or even which view was predominant. The difference of opinion never came into sharp focus since advocates of each view were agreed on the policies to be pursued. Moreover, as future developments were to indicate, in determining the prospects of slavery in a region far more was involved than the questions of climatic suitability or the availability of raw materials. Of equal importance was the political and legal infrastructure. Would there be any protection offered to the slaveholder in the territorial stage? Would he be conceded the right to lynch anyone he suspected of anti-slavery proclivities? This was perhaps a brutal question but if this right or privilege were not allowed, then the chances of creating a slave state would, as southerners themselves would later concede (at least implicitly), diminish sharply.[25]

Similar issues of principle governed the southern militant's response to the other concession offered to the North in 1850, the abolition of the slave trade in the District of Columbia. A similar degree of resentment was also created. In this case, however, there was little discussion of the practicalities of the question since the ban had little direct effect on slavery itself even in the District, let alone in the rest of the South. But the principles were, nonetheless, important for many southerners. The measure, it was claimed, was deliberately intended to demonstrate the power of Congress to abolish slavery itself in the District. Its "first great purpose" was "to condemn and stigmatize, by a national vote, the transfer of slaves from one owner to another upon slave soil" while, even more alarmingly "its second great end was to establish a precedent for emancipation." To the Raleigh *Standard* it was another of the North's "entering wedges" designed to facilitate abolition.[26]

---

24. Robert Toombs to John J. Crittenden, Jan. 22, 1849, in Ulrich B. Phillips (ed.), *The Correspondence of Robert Toombs, Alexander H. Stephens, and Howell Cobb*, American Historical Association *Annual Report 1911*, II (Washington D.C., 1913), p. 141; Raleigh *Standard*, June 20, 1849.
25. Historians have not always appreciated this aspect of the issue and have assumed that the viability of slavery in California (and elsewhere) was a simple "either/or" formulation.
26. *Reply of Hon. John J. McRae to the Speech of Senator Foote* (New Orleans, 1851), p. 17; *Address of Thompson*, p. 8; *Raleigh Standard*, June 20, 1849.

The measures of 1850 were, of course, a package,[27] and those responsible for them believed that much had been offered to each section. But what, southern militants asked, had the South, in return for all her sacrifices, received? Very little, was the answer, other than the Fugitive Slave Law, about which they in any case, as we shall see, entertained strong reservations.[28] Thus the conclusion seemed inescapable: after a crisis provoked essentially by the Mexican war, southern men, who had served with great distinction in that war and made disproportionate sacrifices to win it, had been robbed of their rightful share in the fruits of victory. Instead they had had to make major concessions, some of which involved direct practical losses, others of which created dangerous precedents for the future, and all of which merely invited further aggressions from an increasingly belligerent and tyrannical North.[29]

### III

It is generally agreed that one of the effects and indeed one of the purposes of the federal system in the United States has been to allow regional differences to flourish. These have been, at different times, economic, cultural, political, and ethical. In so decentralised a polity, it has sometimes been difficult to gauge public opinion, within the nation as a whole or even within a region. In the middle of the nineteenth century, it was difficult even for politicians to know precisely where their own constituents stood on even the most critical of questions, let alone the constituents of politicians in other counties, states, or regions. The crisis of midcentury had many effects, but one of them was to begin to lay bare the state of opinion within the South on slavery, the Union, and the relationship between the two.

It soon became apparent that there was a spectrum of opinion on slavery and the Union with the great majority of southern politicians clustered at various identifiable points along it. The most extreme are the most easily identifiable positions of all. At one extreme was an unconditional unionism.[30] Thus Governor Neil S. Brown of Tennessee declared that he was "for the Union at every hazard and to the last extremity." In reporting this comment, the *Mississippian*, which took a very different view of the Union and of the sectional controversy, demonstrated why the Tennessee Governor's view was both highly unusual and, to many, highly dangerous. In terming the declaration "the most unfortunate sentiment ever expressed by a prominent and influential Southern man,"

---

27. They were recognised as such even though they were passed separately.
28. The other measure relevant here was the reduction in the area of Texas. See *To the Hon. W. J. Grayson by One of the People*, p. 6
29. *Reply of McRae*, p. 17; *Soulé's Speech at Opelousas*, p. 4.
30. For the views of southern moderates and Unionists see Chapter 4.

one contributor to the *Mississippian* clearly appreciated that Brown's words left the South ultimately defenceless if a northern majority launched an assault upon slavery in the states. Of course, Brown himself and those who thought like him were confident that such an assault would never take place and this reminds us that attitudes towards the Union were inextricably bound up with perceptions of the motives and actions of the North and the nature of antislavery sentiment there. In a like vein Henry Clay, also of course a Whig from the Upper South, observed that if Kentucky left the Union he would himself move against her. In other words, his loyalties were to the Union rather than to his state. Indeed he indicated that he would not even be swayed (as others from the Upper South would be in 1861) by majority opinion in favour of Kentucky and against the Union.[31]

These utterances were rare at midcentury, if only because southern Unionists did not feel that they would have to make such a choice. Far more common was a somewhat less extreme but still enthusiastic unionism which, while not offering guarantees of loyalty under all circumstances, simply assumed that reasonable behaviour on the part of southerners would stimulate a corresponding moderation in the North so that sectional harmony could prevail. This was probably the predominant attitude among southern Whigs, most of whom were, until well into the 1850s at any rate, almost as likely to blame southern extremists as northerners for the sectional rift. Although the unionism of these southerners might be in a literal sense conditional, they deliberately did not spell out the conditions (since they believed such a pronouncement would itself be confrontational) and were generally and accurately viewed as staunch supporters of the Union.[32]

At the opposite pole lay those whose can be classed as disunionists. Again there were two subgroups. The more extreme elements advocated immediate secession, and by a single state if necessary. Such a bold move was, of course, intended to preserve slavery and to signal a formal renunciation of a Union which seemed irredeemably polluted by antislavery fanaticism. Those who advocated immediate secession by a single state were concentrated in South Carolina. They had only a handful of coadjutors in other states. Men such as Edmund Ruffin of Virginia or John A. Quitman of Mississippi or George Gayle of Alabama were as enthusiastic as anyone in South Carolina for secession. How much influence did they wield? Quitman was unusually influential in that he was Governor of his state (though his extreme views had not really helped him obtain

31. Nashville *Republican Banner*, Oct. 6, 1849; *Mississippian*, May 10, 1850; CG, 31/1, App., pp. 1486–1488. John J. Crittenden made similar statements.
32. These Unionists, mainly Whigs, are dealt with in Chapter 4 in this volume.

the position). Ruffin was more typical in that he had comparatively little influence even in his own state.[33]

Events demonstrated that the more extreme elements did not even control the state of South Carolina, for in 1851 a unique confrontation took place there. It pitted not the advocates of the Compromise against its enemies, which was the alignment in some other states, but rather advocates of immediate secession by South Carolina alone against those who would have liked a dissolution of the Union but only in concert with other southern states. (These "moderate" secessionists were joined by the small number of more orthodox Unionists in the State.) The result was a resounding defeat for the separate-state secessionists. But elsewhere in the South these groups were too weak even to stage such a confrontation.[34]

Those who advocated immediate secession but only if it could be achieved in concert with other states were dominant in South Carolina though nowhere else. Even in other Deep South states they were in a small minority. At the second of the Nashville Conventions of 1850, Langdon Cheves of South Carolina urged secession, partly on the grounds that the principle of Free Soil, which had triumphed in relation to California, would almost certainly presage abolition. He added that even if it did not, it would diminish both the security and profitability of slave property. Meanwhile the abolition of the slave trade in the District of Columbia was a precedent for the abolition of the interstate slave trade. Accordingly "secession" was "the only practicable remedy." Yet Cheves acknowledged that secession by a single state would not work. South Carolina needed at least three others. But this position was far too advanced for most of the delegates at Nashville who, having made little impact on the South as a whole, adjourned once again, this time *sine die*.[35]

This leaves the large body of southerners who can accurately be termed "conditional Unionists." Some might as easily be termed "conditional secessionists." Thus Pierre Soulé of Louisiana announced in September 1851 that he was "not for breaking this Confederacy," and "not for advising this State to join in any social movement which may be made by other States." Speaking at a time when it looked as if South Carolina might secede, he admitted that the Palmetto State might be too rash and precipitate and that he could not urge his own state to follow her. But he

---

33. J. Mills Thornton, III, *Politics and Power in a Slave Society: Alabama 1800–1860* (Baton Rouge, 1978), pp. 203, 244–245.
34. As the Charleston *Mercury* observed a decade later, much of South Carolina had, for ten years, favoured a dissolution of the Union, the difference of opinion in 1851 being over the means rather than the ends – *Charleston Mercury*, March 10, 1860.
35. *Speech of Hon. Langdon Cheves, in the Southern Convention at Nashville, Tenn., Nov. 14, 1850* (n.p., 1850), pp. 10–20. For instances of southerners threatening secession, see Hamilton, *Prologue to Conflict*, p. 63.

insisted that South Carolina had the right to secede and that he could not "but respect, and love, and admire her noble daring and her heroism." Soulé did not advocate secession and if he had done so he would surely have been repudiated by the voters of Louisiana, but he left his audience in no doubt of his fears. His task, he announced, was to sound the alarm.[36]

An assessment of the nature and strength of Unionist sentiment across the South as a whole is made more difficult because the events of 1849–1851 produced not merely a crystallisation of opinion but also a constantly changing environment in which the views of many politicians underwent significant shifts. Thus as important a figure as Robert Toombs of Georgia at one point threatened secession (under certain specific but, as he then feared, all too imminent conditions) only to re-emerge a little later as a key defender of the Compromise. As the crisis of midcentury unfolded, the spirit of compromise proved contagious in that concessions on the part of one side not unnaturally strengthened the hand of moderates on the other. For southerners, no event was more important than the North's abandonment of, or at least retreat from, the Wilmot Proviso. Although this, as we have seen, by no means satisfied all southerners, it did suggest to many that the North was not so bent on aggrandizement or gripped by abolitionist frenzy as had been feared. The passage of the Fugitive Slave Law had a similar effect, despite the doubts expressed by many southerners as to its efficacy.[37]

After South Carolina the three states in which proslavery militancy was strongest were Mississippi, Alabama, and Georgia. In all three the mainly Democratic opponents of the Compromise, now calling themselves the Southern Rights party, were faced by a coalition of Whigs and pro-Compromise Democrats, now styling itself a Union party. And in each state the pro-Compromise Union forces triumphed. The anti-Compromise forces, however, had stopped far short of demanding secession. A typical attitude was that of the *Mississippian*, which denounced the Compromise bitterly on the grounds that it gave the North everything and the South nothing.[38] But the militancy of southerners who took this view produced a demand not for secession but instead for resistance to the Compromise, perhaps by economic nonintercourse with the North or perhaps by the summoning of yet another southern convention which would then engage in yet further discussions and planning. Similarly, the vast majority of pro-Compromise forces in these states (and in others of the Deep South) were

36. *Soulé's Speech at Opelousas*, pp. 14–15.
37. CG, 31/1, pp. 18–28. "Address of . . . Robert W. Johnson."
38. *Mississippian*, May 24, 1850. For an example of a Floridian who favoured southern rights but not secession, see *Address of E. C. Cabell of Florida to his Constituents* (n.p., n.d.), pp. 1–4.

in no sense unconditional Unionists of the Henry Clay stripe or even the strong (if not quite unconditional) Unionists who dominated Upper-South Whiggery. Instead they achieved victory in a sense by undercutting the Southern Rights parties and laying down stringent conditions for their continued commitment to the Union. These conditions were most clearly spelled out in the so-called Georgia Platform. This platform was drawn up after a Convention summoned in Georgia specifically to consider the Compromise that assembled in December 1850. Unlike the gatherings at Nashville the same year, their deliberations produced results of great significance. The delegates agreed that whilst the state of Georgia could not "wholly approve" of the Compromise, she would nevertheless "abide by it as a permanent adjustment of the sectional controversy." They then put forward a series of resolutions, of which the fourth was by far the most important:

> *Resolved*, That the State of Georgia, in the judgment of this Convention, will and ought to resist, even (as a last resort) to the disruption of every tie which binds her to the Union, any future act of Congress abolishing slavery in the District of Columbia, without the consent and petition of the slaveholders thereof; or any act abolishing slavery in places within the slaveholding States, purchased by the United States for the erection of forts, magazines, arsenals, dock-yards, navy-yards, and other like purposes; or any act suppressing the slave trade between slaveholding States; or any refusal to admit as a State any Territory applying, because of the existence of slavery therein; or any act prohibiting the introduction of slaves into the territories of Utah and New Mexico, or any act repealing or materially modifying the laws now in force for the recovery of fugitive slaves.

Thus although unionism triumphed in these three key states of the Deep South, it was a highly conditional unionism.[39]

The Georgia Platform, after the defeat of the anti-Compromise forces, became a point of reference or rallying cry for militant southerners as well as for Unionists throughout the next decade. Not all viewed it in the same way, however, or rather it would be more accurate to say that different groups offered different estimates of its chances of success. These, in turn, were based upon widely contrasting attitudes towards the North, towards northern politicians and towards northern public opinion. In South Carolina most statesmen were entirely confident about the Compromise – confident that it would fail. In 1850 and 1852 the State's Governors announced that it was merely a question of time before further aggressions, including those of which the Georgia Platform had warned, would occur. These would then, it was hoped, propel the South out of the

---

39.  Helena (Arkansas) *Southern Shield*, Jan. 4, 1851.

Union. Only a little more hopeful about the possibility of a lasting settlement with the North was Felix Huston of Louisiana. Huston told the
delegates at Nashville that he was "extremely doubtful" about the Compromise but added that it must be tried. On the other hand, the triumvirate
that formed in Georgia in defence of the Union, consisting of Democrat
Howell Cobb and Whigs Robert Toombs and Alexander H. Stephens, displayed far more optimism about the settlement of 1850. The three were
far more likely to trust northern politicians and the northern public.[40]

IV

Most southern militants, whether they proclaimed a desire for secession in
1850, declared their resentment of the Compromise, or even announced
a highly qualified and perhaps reluctant acceptance of it, were expressing
attitudes that were closely correlated with, and partly driven by, their perceptions of the North. Ironically, the weaker they believed the North inherently to be, the greater the danger they apprehended from that quarter. The
reason was that a society, such as that in the North, which lacked stability and which could only prosper by exploiting another was necessarily, if
only for the sake of self-preservation, a predatory one. Those southerners
who developed, especially from the 1830s onwards, an overtly proslavery argument rang the changes upon these themes: the North with its
free labour system was inherently unstable, subject to violent paroxysms,
economic dislocation, and ruinous internal competition; the South was in
all essential respects and because of her slave labour base, its antithesis.
Some southerners argued that the predatory nature of northern society
derived ultimately from the Puritan heritage of New England and there
were even in the 1850s sporadic speculations that a new Union might be
formed composed of the southern states and those of the lower North. In
other words, the fanatics of New England and of New England descent
would be somehow excluded or expelled. Somewhat more common was
the claim (which would later be taken up by historian Charles Beard and
form the centrepiece of his interpretation of the sectional conflict) that
northern aggression derived not so much from the Puritan heritage but
rather from the inherent hostility of "the commercial and manufacturing
interests of the North" to the South, the region where Jeffersonianism
naturally flourished. Here, after all, "was found the great agricultural

40. *Journal of the Senate of the State of South Carolina, Being the Annual Session Commencing November 25, 1850* (Columbus, 1850), pp. 28–29; *Journal of the Senate
of South Carolina, Being the Extra and Annual Sessions of 1852* (Columbus, 1852),
p. 30; *Address of Gen. Felix Huston, To the Members of the Southern Convention,
To be Held at Nashville, 3 June 1850* (Natchez, n.d.), p. 1.

interest that refused to favour class legislation, conferring bounties upon one pursuit, and burdens upon another."[41]

Although these arguments were deeply problematic from even a southern militant's perspective, they undoubtedly pointed to a cardinal tenet of that southerner's faith. Since the Puritan legacy would not simply disappear and since the manufacturing and commercial interests of the North could not be expected to wither away and might even, at least in the short term, expand in power and influence, the future of the South within the Union was highly uncertain. Southern militants even in 1850 looked closely at the state of northern opinion and they did not like what they saw. Jacob Thompson of Mississippi reported that northern sentiment was almost unanimous in the belief that slavery was an evil and should therefore be abolished. According to the *Mississippian*, which was also hostile to the Compromise, it would be both dangerous and foolish of southerners to believe that antislavery in the North would prove transitory or that it had sprung from anything but the deepest sources. Instead northern sentiment posed an ever-growing menace:

> The agitation now going on, far from being – as some affirm it – merely to subserve a present partisan end, and be lost in the vortex of demagogue expediency forever – proceeds from a fixed and unalterable principle in the religious, the moral, and social creeds of the millions at the North, and is gathering strength every day – that *slavery is an evil in the sight of God – a dark spot upon our character as a nation*, and ought by every means consistent with prudence and the dictates of wisdom, to be abolished. The agitation will go on – it will never cease.

This implied a fatalistic attitude towards both the Compromise and, more fundamentally, the Union itself.[42]

An alternative stance, however, was adopted by those who claimed that resistance on the part of the South, whilst obviously beneficial in itself, would also serve to check northern aggressions. Here was a slightly different perception of the North, one which viewed northerners not so much as blind, desperate fanatics, driven to exploit southern wealth and influence because they had no option but rather as more cunningly and subtly parasitical, taking only what they were allowed to take and retreating when the host environment became insufficiently benign. Thus the Raleigh *Standard* argued (quite plausibly) that Daniel Webster's famous pro-Compromise speech of March 7, 1850 had been prompted only by threats of southern resistance. The conclusion was that resistance on the part of the South would help the cause of sectional harmony by compelling

41. *De Bow's Review*, XXVIII (1860), pp. 7–16; *Address of Thompson*, pp. 11–13.
42. *Address of Thompson*, p. 11; *Mississippian*, Nov. 8, 1851.

northerners to act with a greater sense of justice and fairness. It was a paradoxical conclusion. David S. Reid, campaigning to be Governor of North Carolina took this approach only a little further when, having argued that "the best and surest means . . . to preserve and perpetuate the Union," was "for the State to take a firm and decided stand in favor of her rights, against the encroachments of the North," he ended with a ringing endorsement of the Union. "I yield," he proclaimed, "to no man in devotion to this glorious Union." This posture, perhaps more frequently adopted in the Upper than in the Lower South, allowed Reid to combine unionism with a strong defence of southern rights.[43]

In all these analyses, the South was, of course, the innocent and aggrieved party. These southerners disagreed merely over the precise nature and source of northern aggressions. The disagreement never came into sharp focus. A slightly different approach was taken, or at least a slightly different emphasis was given, by those who pointed out how easy and painless it would be for the North to bring about sectional peace and harmony. Clearly this view, by implication at least, denied that the North was driven by some irresistible cultural or economic imperative to war upon the South and some southern militants went so far as to suggest that northerners, in order to treat the South justly, need not suffer any financial losses at all. Thus John J. McRae, faithfully following the strategy of fellow Mississippian Jefferson Davis, having denied that he or Davis favoured secession, was one of many southerners who maintained that the fate of the Union, after the Compromise, rested squarely with the North. The platform on which he stood (which resembled the Georgia Platform) required of northerners, he claimed, "no sacrifice of their honor, their interests, or their rights." This implied that previous northern exploitation of the South, however momentous in consequences, was motivated by a desire for gain that was, in the sense that it could be shrugged off at will, after all quite superficial.[44]

In any event, and whatever the ultimate source of the northern desire for domination and aggrandizement, it was, the southern militant concluded, up to the South to stand firm. This meant, above all, unity and resolution in the South. Those who opposed the Compromise feared that it had been created by, and would further strengthen, the tendency to weakness and capitulation in the South. The task of those who engineered the settlement of 1850 was to ensure that each side should retreat from some of its more uncompromising utterances and in this they succeeded. In making

---

43. Raleigh *Standard*, March 20, 1850; David S. Reid, "Address to the People of North Carolina" in Wilmington (NC), *Journal*, July 12, 1850. See also "Address of . . . Robert W. Johnson," *Mississippian*, June 28, Oct. 25, 1850.

44. *Reply of McRae*, p. 20. See also *Speeches, Messages, . . . of . . . Albert Gallatin Brown*, p. 164; *Mississippian*, May 10, 1850.

concessions, however, southern moderates necessarily antagonised those militants who believed that the North would respond only to firmness and resistance and that concessions would merely lead to a demand for even greater and more damaging sacrifices of political principle and economic interest. Thus it was noted that the Virginia legislature, for example, had in 1849 urged the citizens of the state to view the abolition of the slave trade in the District of Columbia as "a direct attack upon the institutions of the Southern States, to be resisted at every hazard." Yet within a few short months, the usurpation had been perpetrated and the state of Virginia had tamely submitted.[45]

How had such surrenders occurred? As we shall see, many in the Deep South had grievous doubts about the reliability of those in the Upper South on the slavery question. But it was also felt that the blandishments of power had corrupted many southerners. It was noted that most of the separate acts that comprised the settlement of 1850 could not have been passed if significant numbers of Congressmen had not carefully absented themselves when the crucial votes were taken. Indeed the disaggregation of the various measures proved indispensable to the success of the entire settlement: congressmen would be present when they needed to vote "aye" and "absent" when they might have voted "nay." Whilst this was scarcely an unprecedented legislative tactic, it nevertheless aroused great suspicion and provoked accusations of betrayal, especially when the individual under suspicion had previously been identified with opposition to the Compromise. Such was the fate of Henry Foote of Mississippi, for example, who was denounced for having succumbed in precisely this way.[46]

## V

In accordance with the terms of the Compromise, California quickly gained admittance into the Union as a free state, the slave trade in the District of Columbia was suppressed (if only in part) and the territories of New Mexico and Utah were organised on the basis of popular sovereignty (however ambiguous the doctrine). The first two quickly became *faits accomplis*, the third attracted relatively little attention. The fugitive slave question, however, was very different. Although the Fugitive Slave Act might itself soon become a *fait accompli*, this in no way guaranteed that any slaves would actually be recovered from the North under its provisions, for many northerners were implacably opposed to the Act and fiercely determined to thwart it. Southerners knew this but the more

45. *Soulé's Speech at Opelousas*, pp. 6–12; Staunton *Vindicator*, Feb. 10, 1860.
46. *Reply of McRae*, pp. 21–22.

militant among them offered no concessions. On the contrary, they insisted upon its enforcement. According to the *Southern Literary Messenger*, "the continued existence of the United States, as one nation, depends upon the full and faithful execution of the Fugitive Slave Bill."[47] This implied secession if either the citizens or the states of the North failed to carry out the measure. Far more common, however, were threats that would be carried out in the event of a congressional repeal of the Act. According to the *Mississippian* even those in favour of the Compromise would in that eventuality desire to dissolve the Union. Similarly Governor John S. Roane of Arkansas, while avowing himself "no disunionist" announced that he would favour secession in those circumstances. Meanwhile, in Virginia, Governors Floyd and Johnson in 1850 and 1852 respectively pointed out that the South had made great sacrifices in the interests of peace and harmony, sacrifices which would be proved worthwhile if the Compromise provided a final settlement of the slavery issue. Floyd, however, observed that if "this reasonable expectation prove fallacious and the abolition agitation be still contained in the halls of Congress," then "it will furnish proof, convincing and conclusive, of that fixed and settled hostility to slavery on the part of the North, which should and will satisfy every reasonable man, that peace between us is impossible." The Fugitive Slave Act would thus present the litmus test. "Virginia," the Governor concluded, "and I think all the slaveholding States can, and ought, calmly but explicitly to declare, that the repeal of the fugitive slave law, or any essential modification of it, is a virtual repeal of the Union." Floyd then explained that such a stance would in fact strengthen moderate northerners. But even if this were true, it was a strategy that would entail the highest possible risk to the survival of the nation.[48]

In fact many southerners, from the start, had little faith in the new law. If the Governors of Virginia believed the survival of the nation ought to depend upon its retention, one of her Senators, and he the one who actually drew up the legislation, believed from the start that there was little prospect of its being enforced. According to James M. Mason, "the disease is seated too deeply to be reached by ordinary legislation," and he predicted that "it will be found that even this law will be of little worth in securing the rights of those for whose benefit it is intended." Nor was he the only prominent southerner to take this view; at least three

---

47. *Southern Literary Messenger*, XVI (1850), p. 597.
48. *Mississippian*, Dec. 13, 1850; "Message of Governor John S. Roane of Arkansas, Nov. 5, 1851" in Washington (Arkansas) *Telegraph*, Nov. 21, 1851; *Journal of the Senate of the Commonwealth of Virginia ... 2 Dec., 1850* (Richmond, 1850), pp. 32, 34; *Journal of the Senate of the Commonwealth of Virginia ... 12 Jan., 1852* (Richmond, 1852), p. 27.

other Senators said much the same. In other words, a measure that was believed essential to the maintenance of the Union was thought by its main proponents to be of little practical use.[49]

There was further irony. One might have thought that the law had been intended symbolically, to allow northern states and northern officials to demonstrate a willingness to comply even if a minority of their own citizens made full compliance impossible in all cases. In such circumstances, the measure might have demonstrated the good faith of the North overall, if not of every northerner. But such was not the intention. Instead the law had been framed very rigidly and could scarcely have been more stringent if the goal had in fact been to make full and universal compliance impossible. By its terms federal officials were created and made responsible for its execution. Slaveholders were empowered to seize a slave, or rather a suspected slave, themselves and bring him or her before a commissioner or federal judge. There would then be a hearing and if the case were made the commissioner or judge would issue a certificate. At the hearing testimony from the prisoner was not to be permitted. The commissioner or judge then received $5 if he found for the captive but, ostensibly because the paper work involved would be greater, $10 if he issued a certificate for rendition. Moreover, all northern citizens were required to lend aid when appropriate and financial penalties or even jail sentences were to be imposed on those seeking to thwart the law.[50]

Although this act was an integral part of the Compromise settlement, it was itself no compromise. On the contrary, it was intended to be a wholly prosouthern measure that would, it was hoped, offset wholly pronorthern measures such as the abolition of the slave trade in the District. One historian, calling it "utterly one-sided," has pointed out that, had it not been part of a package, it would have been judged far too severe and probably could not have been passed. It was therefore certain to provoke intense controversy in the North. Thus whether the law had been intended for its symbolic or its practical value, it seemed as likely to aid the secessionists as the Unionists.[51]

There were many objections to the Act, some of them inherent in any effective measure for the return of fugitive slaves, some of them specific to the Act of 1850. Undoubtedly the Constitution required a fugitive slave to be "delivered up on claim of the party to whom...[his] service or labour may be due." But it was not clear who should do the delivering. Nor was it clear how the rights of free blacks (who might be mistakenly

49. *CG*, 31/1, pp. 233, 1588, App., pp. 79, 1622.
50. Stanley W. Campbell, *The Slave Catchers: Enforcement of the Fugitive Slave Law, 1850–1860* (Chapel Hill, NC, 1968).
51. Don E. Fehrenbacher, *The Slaveholder's Republic: An Account of the United States Government's Relations to Slavery* (New York, 2001) p. 227.

or wilfully misidentified as slaves) were to be secured. The absence of due legal process was the norm in the case of a slave but not in the case of a free black and this problem became acute when the purpose of the trial was precisely to determine whether the prisoner was a slave or a free black. The requirement on all citizens to aid in the recovery of fugitives was, in one sense, understandable since there was no federal bureaucracy that could take on these potentially expansive duties but it conflicted hopelessly with the sensibilities of many northerners. The many northerners who believed that the conscience should be the infallible guide to action were utterly repelled by the Act of 1850 and they viewed the system of differential payments as the most sordid and disgraceful bribery. Northern militants unhesitatingly advised resistance to the law and out of their resentments would come Harriet Beecher Stowe's masterpiece of antislavery propaganda, *Uncle Tom's Cabin*.

Those who defended the new Act merely ignored these objections, which they in any case believed hypocritical, and also ignored the dangers now faced by free blacks, whose rights they in any case believed inconsequential. At the heart of the problem was the simple but inescapable fact that, in the words of one historian, "effective recovery of fugitive slaves was incompatible with effective protection of free blacks against wrongful seizure." The result was that northern state authorities took their own action to protect free blacks. Such actions had taken place before 1850 and had done much to bring about the Act of that year. They continued after 1850, but now, of course, in a far more highly charged atmosphere.[52]

The controversy over fugitive slaves was both cause and consequence of the growing controversy over slavery itself. The first Fugitive Slave Act of 1793 had been, especially in the 1840s, circumvented by northeastern states, some of which had forbidden their officials from arresting free blacks or accepting jurisdiction in fugitive slave cases. Some cases, such as *Prigg v. Pennsylvania* (1842), achieved national prominence and although the United States Supreme Court in effect found for the slaveholder the outcome was of little practical value to southerners. In the Van Zandt case (1847), a group of Kentuckians seeking to recapture some alleged fugitives were forced to leave Michigan under threat of violence and were even fined for trespass. Pressure accordingly mounted for a new Fugitive Slave Act.

Northerners had at first responded to the question of fugitive slaves on a piecemeal basis or simply to safeguard the rights of their free blacks. But by the 1840s resistance to the law was becoming, as it would remain after 1850, part of a coordinated antislavery strategy. It was increasingly

---

52. Fehrenbacher, *Slaveholder's Republic*, p. 213.

claimed that violations of northern rights were inherent in legislation for the return of fugitive slaves and indeed inherent in slavery itself. On the northern side, therefore, the fugitive slave question both reflected and created antislavery sentiment.

Consequently the passage of the Act of 1850 intensified northern resentment. Although it enabled many southerners successfully to reclaim their slaves, a number of cases achieved great notoriety. In February 1851 a coffee-house waiter in Boston named Shadrach was rescued from jail by a number of free blacks and helped to flee to Canada. The President ordered that all who aided him should be prosecuted. Another case in Boston involved an alleged fugitive named Thomas Sims, who was successfully recovered but only at a cost of $20,000. In September 1851, in Christiana, Pennsylvania a slaveholder was killed while attempting to recapture two fugitives and in Syracuse another incident resulted in a mob freeing a fugitive from jail. As a result of the Shadrach, Christiana and Syracuse incidents a total of seventy-five northerners were indicted but only one conviction was obtained.[53]

By now the Fugitive Slave issue was deeply implicated in the sectional controversy in a way that it simply had not been even ten or fifteen years earlier. The inclusion of the new Act in the Compromise package of 1850 and its identification as an overtly prosouthern measure reinforced the link. By the mid-1850s a clear tendency had emerged: rather than compliance with the Act generating sectional harmony, sectional conflict brought about by issues largely unrelated to fugitives, instead produced violations of the Act. Hence when the South scored a remarkable triumph in 1854 with the passage of the Kansas-Nebraska Act, a string of northern states responded by passing Personal Liberty Laws, which were ostensibly intended purely to safeguard the rights of free blacks against kidnapping but which were, in addition, calculated to strike a retaliatory blow against slavery and slaveholders. In 1854 Joshua Glover was taken into federal custody at Racine, Wisconsin but was then rescued by a mob and his pursuer arrested for kidnapping. A couple of months later a slaveholder attempted to recapture Anthony Burns from Boston. The attempt was successful but there was a riot in the courthouse and some Bostonians tried to free him. Massachusetts and Wisconsin (along with Michigan and the other New England states) then passed their Personal Liberty Laws which in effect nullified the Fugitive Slave law within their borders. Burns became the last fugitive to be extradited from anywhere in New England and the state of Wisconsin, which alone had formally repudiated

---

53. Potter, *Impending Crisis*, pp. 130–140; Allan Nevins, *Ordeal of the Union: A House Dividing 1852–1857* (New York, 1947), pp. 150–154, *Fruits of Manifest Destiny*, pp. 380–390.

the Fugitive Slave Act as unconstitutional, remained in conflict with the federal judiciary right up to the outbreak of the Civil War.[54]

## VI

Why did southerners attach so much importance to the Fugitive Slave Act both prior to and after the passage of the Act of 1850? The question becomes the more pressing when we recall that in demanding northern compliance with the provisions of the new law, southerners were essentially laying aside their own commitment to state's rights and local autonomy, principles which they invoked again and again in the years of the sectional conflict and in defence of which they would ultimately break up the nation itself.

In effect there was a coalition forged between the states of the Upper and those of the Lower South, each of which gave the matter intense scrutiny but for somewhat different reasons. The border states were of course most directly exposed to the danger of runaway slaves. One newspaper in Kentucky in 1860 claimed the state lost between 1,500 and 2,000 slaves per year and warned that if Personal Liberty Laws spread to the Lower North the result would be that all border counties would have no slaves at all.[55] The slaves in those areas would then have little value as property and, even if they did not manage to flee, their owners would be impelled to sell them further south. In this eventuality, it was noted, the territory occupied, and thus the political influence wielded, by slavery would significantly shrink. But this was not the only danger to be apprehended from fugitive slaves. According to the Governor of Missouri in 1860, his state could claim the distinction of having suffered more than any other from runaway slaves. But he reminded his audience that, having fled from their masters, these slaves posed additional problems. Theft, murder and arson had, he claimed, left several counties in the state severely depopulated[56]

Yet the impact of the problem was still greater. According to Charles Faulkner, a Congressman from Virginia, it was the effects upon the entire

54.  Richard J. Carwardine notes that many northern evangelicals said that the repeal of the Missouri Compromise absolved them of the need to observe the Fugitive Slave law – Carwardine, *Evangelicals and Politics in Antebellum America* (New Haven, 1993), pp. 238–239.
55.  Modern assessments of the numbers of fugitive slaves range from about a thousand per year in the 1850s to five thousand.
56.  Louisville *Daily Courier*, Feb. 22, 1860 quoted in Dwight L. Dumond (ed.), *Southern Editorials on Secession* (New York, 1931), pp. 359–360; *Journal of the Senate of the State of South Carolina, At the Extra Session, Nov. 6, 1848, and Regular Session, Nov. 27, 1848* (Columbus, 1848), pp. 26–27; *Speech of Mr Amistead Burt of South Carolina in Favor of Adopting a Resolution to Exclude Abolitionist Petitions* (n.p., n.d.), p. 6; Buel Leopard and Floyd C. Sheomaker (eds.), *The Messages and Proclamations of the Governors of the State of Missouri* (Columbia, MO, 1922), III, p. 143.

slave population in the border areas that were most to be feared. Thus it was "not the mere money value of the slaves who escape into the free States which has aroused the united action of the South on this question." Instead it was "the fact, well known to us, that if such a provision did not exist in the constitution, and was not faithfully enforced, a spirit of insubordination would very probably be infused into our slave population that would lead to the most fearful and tragic consequences." From this premise Faulkner was able to conclude that "upon the faithful execution of this plain and express guarantee of the constitution depend her [the South's] domestic tranquillity and peace."[57]

The priorities of those in the Deep South were somewhat different. Jeremiah Clemens of Alabama acknowledged that his state lost (to the North) one fugitive slave approximately every five years. But he also declared that if the law of 1850 could not be enforced then the Union should end. This juxtaposition was neither uncommon nor irrational. Not only was there a natural fraternity with the slaveholders of the Upper South whose property was under more direct threat, there was also the concern, already noted, that the consequent sale of slaves from that region, acceptable enough in itself, would nevertheless weaken slavery within the nation as a whole. As we shall see, militant Democrats from the Deep South harboured suspicions of their Upper South brethren and they most emphatically did not wish to see the region's commitment to slavery further attenuated.[58]

Yet the main reason for their intransigence on the question was the one we have already encountered. Fugitive slaves tested the depth of antislavery fervour (or "fanaticism") in the North as a whole. What future could there be for slaveholders in a Union in which nonslaveholders would not come to their aid and help them recover their rightful property? Southerners believed, and most northerners did little to dispel the belief, that the requirement to return fugitive slaves was one of the "sacred compromises" of the Constitution, without which it would never have been signed. As a historical fact this was highly questionable but there is no doubt that southerners were convinced of its accuracy. In this way, northern willingness to enforce the law was a measure of northern willingness to respect the Constitution itself. And the Constitution was the ultimate, perhaps the only, barrier within the Union to the abolition of slavery.[59]

The controversy over fugitive slaves represented in microcosm the sectional conflict in a fundamental way. In one of the more curious utterances

57. *Speech of Hon Charles James Faulkner of Virginia, At Reading, Pennsylvania Sept 7, 1852* (Washington, D.C., n.d.), p. 9. See also *CG*, 31/2, App., p. 299.
58. *CG*, 31/2, App., p. 304, 32/1, p. 1951.
59. Fehrenbacher, *Slaveholder's Republic*, p. 251

on the subject Thornton Stringfellow claimed that fugitive slaves were "constantly returning to their masters again, after tasting the blessings, or rather the awful curse to them, of freedom in nonslaveholding States."[60] If this process were indeed "constantly" occurring then his readers might have wondered why southerners had become so exercised about the problem in the first place while if, (as is infinitely more likely) such occurrences were extraordinarily rare then they might have wondered why Stringfellow had made the point at all. In fact his remark unwittingly pointed towards the weaknesses at the very heart of the slave regime. Why did the slave want to escape at all, if, as the southern militant claimed, slavery so fitted his needs? When they considered this and other equally graphic illustrations of slave discontent, southerners normally, as we shall see, blamed it entirely upon external groups who, they insisted, poisoned the otherwise healthy and wholesome relationship between master and slave: northern "emissaries," treacherous southern whites, free blacks. Stringfellow's comment, by its very absurdity, serves to remind the historian that flight was in fact an indication of slave discontent and that Fugitive Slave laws were needed precisely because it was impossible to reconcile significant numbers of slaves to their condition. The fugitive slave was the product of conflict between master and slave.

This in itself might have been posed no threat at all to the antebellum republic if northerners had been willing to cooperate fully. But the problem was – and here we encounter the issue at the very heart of the sectional controversy – that such cooperation conflicted utterly with the process by which, for many in the North, northern society was itself legitimated. Southerners were wont to dismiss northern concern for slaves, whether fleeing or not, as pure hypocrisy or fanaticism but this obscured the deep social roots of antislavery in the North. Many of the northern abolitionists and antislavery militants who led the opposition to the Fugitive Slave law (and who indeed frequently participated in the highly dramatic attempts to obstruct it) believed that the finest feature of northern society was that it allowed its members the freedom to follow the dictates of their own consciences. This belief played a key role in the legitimation of a social order in which increasing numbers of northerners lacked the ownership of productive property, traditionally the badge of republican citizenship, and in which wage labour was becoming increasingly widespread.[61] But if the injunction to hear and heed the voice of the conscience helped legitimate the northern social order, it could only do so by simultaneously rendering odious all attempts to compel northerners to ignore that voice and aid in such nefarious enterprises as the recovery of the fugitive slave.

60. Thornton Stringfellow, *Scriptural and Statistical Views in Favor of Slavery* (Richmond, 1856), p. 139.
61. See Volume I of this study, pp. 168–173.

How important was the fugitive slave issue in bringing about sectional conflict? Undoubtedly it was a significant cause of discord. But as we have seen it was also a symptom of that strife and there is little doubt that alone it could not have disrupted the Union. It derived much of its force from its inclusion in the Compromise of 1850 as an overtly prosouthern measure. Thus when southerners found it failed to meet their demands they were left, especially as northern gains in California and the District of Columbia were irreversible, with the feeling that they had been cheated. In much the same way, the southern gains secured after the passage of the Kansas-Nebraska Act left many northerners determined to retaliate by repudiating or circumventing the Fugitive Slave law, and this in turn further antagonised southerners. This reciprocating process of action, reaction, and counteraction again represented in microcosm the wider process by which the nation would be torn apart. As we shall see, it culminated in the winter of 1860–1861 with the states of the Deep South, as they explained the decision for secession, giving great prominence to the failure of northerners to enforce the Fugitive Slave Law. This they viewed as tantamount to a failure to honour and uphold the Federal Constitution. With few exceptions secessionists believed that by then the Fugitive Slave Act was of little or no use to the South.[62]

Immediately after the passage of the Act, however, the hopes of some southerners had been considerably higher. And despite the various *causes celebres* of the following years the Act at first worked with some success. By the end of 1853 about seventy fugitives had been returned under its provisions with only fourteen or so released or rescued from custody. At the end of 1851 President Millard Fillmore claimed that the problem was being gradually resolved and both major parties endorsed the Fugitive Slave Act in their platforms for the presidential election of 1852. Notwithstanding the occasional dramatic incident, public interest in the issue almost certainly diminished in 1852 and 1853 (despite the numbers who were enthralled by *Uncle Tom's Cabin*) and this, coupled with the apparent resolution of the other issues of 1850, meant that the sectional controversy itself now seemed to have been resolved, precisely as the champions of compromise had hoped and believed.[63]

In January 1854 the Charleston *Mercury* was still complaining that the Compromise was merely "a hollow truce" but this was now an aberrant view within the South. The Governor of Virginia reported in a message delivered at the end of 1853 that the abolitionists in the North had been rebuked in the last two years, whilst the Governor of Missouri at the

62. William D. Porter, *State Sovereignty and the Doctrine of Coercion: 1860 Association Tract no 2* (n.p., n.d.), p. 36; *Speech of Louis T. Wigfall on the Pending Political Issues, Delivered at Tyler, Smith County, Texas, Sept. 3, 1860* (Washington, D.C., 1860), p. 25.
63. Fehrenbacher, *Slaveholder's Republic*, p. 235

same time declared, with evident pleasure and satisfaction, that sectionalism had almost been banished from national politics. Future Confederate
leader Jefferson Davis acquiesced in the nomination of Franklin Pierce
as Democratic candidate in 1852 and all the southern states, including
even South Carolina, did likewise. In the South the final, lingering gasp of
opposition to the Compromise took the form of a new Southern Rights
party which received in the election a paltry four thousand votes. (Pierce
received more than one and a half million.) In the United States Senate
Albert Gallatin Brown, who in 1850 had believed that it might be necessary to take slaves into California and defend them with arms, and that the
North would betray the South at the first opportunity, now felt impelled
to repudiate the charge that he was or ever had been a disunionist. In
1860 he would again remark that he had believed for twenty years that
slavery and the Union were incompatible but in late 1851 he denounced as
"FALSE AND SLANDEROUS" "the charge laid against me that I was,
or ever have been, for *disunion*, or *secession*." A few months later he
announced that the southern rights movement, which he had supported
in 1850–1851, was dead. And his verdict on the movement, he announced,
was – "let it die." Thus the Compromise of 1850 appeared to have been
as successful as might have been hoped and the compromisers of 1850
seemed to have ample reason to be proud of their efforts.[64]


## VII

It is important to remind ourselves of the role of slave resistance in the
crisis of 1850. The slaves were not, of course, active participants in the
drama that unfolded in Washington, when the Compromise was being
hammered out, or in the various state capitals, when it was in effect being
ratified. Nevertheless their role was a crucial one.

This was most obviously the case with those who had attempted, successfully or unsuccessfully, to flee from their masters. The Fugitive Slave
law was a direct response to their actions. But the role of slave resistance
went far beyond the few thousand fugitives who went north each year.
The minority status of the South, which so preoccupied southern militants
at this time, cannot be understood except in terms of the weaknesses of

64. Charleston *Mercury*, Jan. 26, 1854; *Journal of the Senate of the Commonwealth
of Virginia...5 Dec., 1853* (Richmond, 1853), p. 26; *Messages and Proclamations
of Governors of Missouri*, II, p. 328; *Speeches, Messages,...of...Albert Gallatin
Brown*, pp. 176, 190, 243, 264, 597; Nevins, *House Dividing*, p. 38. See also
*Richmond Enquirer*, July 6, 1853; Ronald P. Formisano, *The Birth of Mass Parties:
Michigan 1827–1861* (Princeton, 1971), p. 215; Harold S. Schultz, *Nationalism and
Sectionalism in South Carolina, 1852–1860: A Study of the Movement for Southern
Independence* new edition (New York, 1969), p. 52.

slavery. The inability of the South to keep pace with the North in terms of population was attributable in large part to her inability to attract immigrants. As her leaders often acknowledged, the South did not want immigrants, lest they bring opposition to slavery with them. Slavery was so vulnerable to the opposition of nonslaveholding whites that the southern militant preferred to risk minority status within the Union rather than see an increase in their numbers.

Far more important than the actions of a small minority of fugitives, and investing the potential disaffection of the immigrant with its significance, was the longing for freedom of the great mass of slaves. It was this which energised the antislavery movement, the fear of which so gripped militant southerners at this time and indeed throughout the era of the sectional conflict. The abolitionist project, daunting enough as it was, would have been unimaginable had the slaves embraced their chains. Every time the southern militant reacted to the prospect of abolition, he was confirming the role of black resistance to slavery.[65] Had the slaves been content in their enslavement, abolitionism would have been made almost entirely innocuous. The simple fact that slaves did not wish to be slaves gave abolitionism its bite. It was thus a necessary condition of the crisis of 1850.

## Triumph of the southern Democrats: The Kansas-Nebraska Act, 1854

### I

The Compromise had succeeded because it had detached the more moderate elements North and South from their more militant colleagues. While the Fugitive Slave issue had been, in the short term, highly contentious, the controversy surrounding it had, by the end of 1853, in good part abated. The territories of New Mexico and Utah, however ambiguous the principles on which they were organised, largely disappeared from public consciousness.[66] Texas's boundaries ceased to be of great concern outside Texas and the abolition of the slave trade in the District of Columbia was of equally little concern even within the District. Moreover, since there was now no territory for which federal policy had not been determined, it seemed as though there was little prospect of a renewal of sectional animosities. Small wonder therefore that the years 1852 and 1853 marked a time of relative peace and harmony between North and South.

---

65. To repeat an argument made throughout these volumes: this point is in no way weakened by the fact that southerners were convinced that their slaves were content in their enslavement.
66. This was true at least so far as the sectional controversy was concerned; the Mormons in Utah continued to attract attention for other reasons.

Unfortunately, however, the work of the politicians could not touch the deeper processes operating within the nation. Nothing that had been achieved in 1850 could alter the basic fact that there was an ever-increasing imbalance between North and South, and nothing could alter the even more basic fact that the friction between master and slave could only be controlled by measures that would inevitably, and for equally profound reasons, alienate the North. These processes would soon shatter the calm of 1852–1853 and they would burst forth in the crisis that engulfed the nation after 1854 as it sought to determine the fate of Kansas.

The territories of Kansas and Nebraska lay within the area purchased by Thomas Jefferson in 1803. They were therefore subject to the provisions of the Missouri Compromise, which had decreed that slavery should not exist in areas north of 36° 30′. In short, they were to be free. Since the nation had after 1850 acquired an important new state, California, on the Pacific, it was imperative that the territories of Kansas and Nebraska, which lay between the Pacific and the older states, be organised. For this reason among others, Stephen A. Douglas of Illinois introduced his famous Nebraska bill, later to become a Kansas-Nebraska bill, in early 1854.[67] Originally Douglas had not wished to amend the Missouri Compromise at all but southerners pressured him not merely to amend but to repeal it entirely. It was apparent by 1854 if not earlier that, primarily by virtue of their power within the Senate, southerners had an effective veto on the opening up of Kansas and Nebraska. Douglas's motives, both for introducing the Act and for succumbing to southern pressure will be examined elsewhere in this study; here it is necessary to understand why southerners placed this pressure upon him.

There were four principal reasons. One was the fear of additional free states and its corollary, the desire for more slave states. If Kansas and Nebraska were organised in accordance with the Missouri Compromise, they would of course enter as free states. The fear of ever-expanding free territory had been awakened (or reawakened) by the Wilmot Proviso in 1846 and as we have seen, it had been one of the factors that impelled many southerners to voice the strongest objections to the admission of California. By now any southern writer or statesman who expressed concern about new free states scarcely needed to add that the ultimate danger was of an amendment to the Constitution which would then allow a direct assault upon slavery in the states. This fear was ever-present in the 1850s and, as we shall see, it would play an important part in the drive for secession in 1860–1861.[68]

---

67. The original bill envisaged a single territory, Nebraska; later versions divided it into two.
68. *De Bow's Review*. XXII (1857), pp. 585–587; Robert E. May, *The Southern Dream of a Caribbean Empire* (Gainesville, 2002), pp. 10–11.

The result was that most southerners could see little reason to support Douglas's bill in its original form (that is, with the Missouri restriction intact). It offered nothing but the prospect of additional free states, nothing therefore but the loss of additional political ground. Why should southerners, as Albert Gallatin Brown later asked in a somewhat different context, "help to swell that hostile power at the North which has already given us so much trouble?"[69] On the other hand, a repeal of the Missouri Compromise would change all. It would open up the possibility of additional states for the South, attainable by one of two routes. First and most obviously, Kansas herself might enter the Union as a slave state. But in addition there was the prospect that other states, perhaps far removed from Kansas, might enter on the basis of the policy of Congressional nonintervention, if that became the federal government's settled and agreed policy for the territories.

Southerners were divided as to whether slavery was actually viable in Kansas. Some Missouri Congressmen, who were closest to the area in question, were sure that it was, as were some of their colleagues from Tennessee and Virginia. On the other hand, some Arkansans said the opposite, as did the Richmond *Enquirer*. Other southerners expressed uncertainty or voiced no opinion on the question or were inconsistent in their assessments. R.M.T. Hunter of Virginia, for example, began by believing that Kansas would be fertile soil for slavery, then changed his mind. On the other hand, a large number of southerners, who initially had been pessimistic about Kansas, went in the opposite direction and after a few months or years began to demand that slavery be formally recognised there. Jefferson Davis, meanwhile, argued that slavery might gain a foothold in Kansas but doubted whether it would be permanently established there. Thus a wide range of opinions found expression. A representative attitude was perhaps struck by the *Mississippian*, which in welcoming the measure, acknowledged that whether Kansas could become a slave state "remains to be seen."[70]

Even those who had doubts about Kansas herself, however, entertained hopes for slave states elsewhere, whose creation would be facilitated by the Kansas-Nebraska Act. For if the policy of congressional nonintervention, inaugurated in 1850, were reintroduced in 1854 in the Kansas-Nebraska Act, would it not then be firmly established as federal policy, to be

69. *Speeches, Messages, . . . of . . . Albert Gallatin Brown*, pp. 593–594.
70. CG, 31/1, pp, 140, 206–207, 221, 232, 408–414, 437, 530, 559–560, 844, 1303; Manisha Sinha, *The Counterrevolution of Slavery: Politics and Ideology in Antebellum South Carolina* (Chapel Hill, NC, 2000) p. 189; Nevins, *House Dividing*, p. 117; *Mississippian*, 2 June 1854; James A. Rawley, *Race and Politics: 'Bleeding Kansas' and the Coming of the Civil War* (Lincoln, NE, 1969), p. 80; James M. Woods, *Rebellion and Realignment: Arkansas's Road to Secession* (Fayetteville, AR, 1987), pp. 66–67; Schultz, *Nationalism and Sectionalism in South Carolina*, pp. 53–65; Freehling, *Road to Disunion: Secessionists at Bay*, pp. 549, 626.

automatically applied when organising future territories yet to be acquired? Some southerners explicitly stated that they valued the repeal of the Missouri Compromise primarily because it would facilitate expansion into the tropics. This was a powerful political motive for repeal.[71]

Alongside the political imperative for additional slave states, however, lay an economic imperative. Here was a second factor that induced southerners to put pressure on Douglas in 1854. Yet it is important to note that there had been prior to 1854 no sustained call for the repeal of the Missouri Compromise, if only because southerners thought such a goal unattainable. There had therefore been, prior to 1854, no sustained demand for the spread of slavery into Kansas. Nevertheless the socioeconomic argument for the expansion of slavery had been advanced with increasing frequency since the 1840s and it helped make some southerners profoundly receptive to the possibility of expansion into Kansas, if only once again to create a precedent or to clear the way for expansion elsewhere. In other words the economic case for the spread of slavery was critical to the arguments that developed over future and existing territories. And it was the Kansas question that both relaunched the controversy over the territories and dominated the ensuing discussion for the remainder of the decade.

## II

In the 1850s many Americans, both North and South, favoured territorial expansion, and for a wide variety of reasons. Much interest focussed on the Caribbean and especially on Cuba, but Mexico and Central America also attracted considerable attention. Northerners and southerners alike emphasised the commercial gains that might be available if some of all of this territory were acquired. In the case of Cuba southerners also stressed the danger of abolition there, should Spain, the colonial power, encourage or at least fail to prevent it, and in the case of Mexico, they focussed upon the opportunities for escape across the border that were offered to slaves in Texas, for example. Nevertheless, in the 1850s as in the 1840s, territorial expansion had a genuine appeal in the North too and for this reason it received a ringing endorsement from the Democratic party throughout the decade.[72]

Southerners indeed had a variety of reasons for desiring additional territory. As we have seen, the political need for additional slave states was

---

71. Thus the New Orleans *Picayune* declared that the Kansas-Nebraska Act had established the principle "upon which alone, if Cuba is ever acquired, it can be received safely to the Southern States" – *Picayune*, June 9, 1854 quoted in May, *Southern Dream of a Caribbean Empire*, pp. 37–38.
72. For this reason too, it is treated in this volume in Chapter 3.

ever present and had been confirmed by the loss of parity in the Senate.[73] But there was also a socioeconomic case for additional slave territory. At its heart lay a fear that the slave population was increasing at a rate which, in some parts of the South at any rate, was highly alarming. At a meeting in support of the Nashville Convention in 1850 C.R. Clifton of Mississippi estimated that there would be within a generation eight million slaves in the South and sixteen million by 1900, his fellow Mississippian Albert Gallatin Brown suggested seven or eight million by 1880 and other southerners made similar predictions.[74] These estimates were based upon details obtained from the federal census, which again confirmed that the United States (alone among new-world slave regimes) was able to increase its slave population through natural reproduction. But some southerners viewed this demographic trend with great dismay. They had serious doubts whether the anticipated numbers of slaves, if confined to the present boundaries of the South, could be profitably used by their masters. The Governor of Virginia in 1846 believed it "unquestionably true, that if our slaves were to be restricted to their present limits, they would greatly diminish in value, and thus seriously impair the fortunes of their owners," while the *Mississippian* in 1850 raged that the northern policy of free soil would leave southerners "pent up until the value of the labor of our slaves will not equal their food and clothes, or until it will be cheaper to employ white labor than buy black." Thus the South would suffer a catastrophic economic decline and southern capital would flow north. The newspaper added that this was already happening and in a similar way other southerners drew attention to this, the problem of an "overgrown" slave population.[75]

The consequences of this surplus of slaves were not, however, merely financial. Governor Smith of Virginia warned that it would lead whites to emigrate so that "finally, the slave will become the owner of the present slaveholding States." In other words these states would then be controlled by a population of free blacks which, according to one Missourian, was "the worst of all classes with which they could be afflicted." As if this possibility were not bad enough, others foresaw an even more frightening prospect. "One of two things," according to C. R. Clifton, was "inevitable": "the white population will exterminate the slaves, in order

73. May, *Southern Dream of a Caribbean Empire*, p. 261.
74. "Speech of C. R. Clifton 8 April, 1850" in *Mississippian*, May 10, 1850; *Speeches, Messages, . . . of . . . Albert Gallatin Brown*, p. 324, William L. Barney, *The Secessionist Impulse: Alabama and Mississippi in 1860* (Princeton, 1974), p. 17.
75. Message of Governor William Smith in *Journal of the Senate of the Commonwealth of Virginia . . . 6 Dec. 1847* (Richmond, 1846), p. 28; *Mississippian*, Oct. 4, 1850. See also *De Bow's Review*, XII (1852), p. 182; Robert F. Durden, "J. D. B. De Bow: Convolutions of a Slave Expansionist," *Journal of Southern History*, XVII (1951), pp. 441–461.

to avoid being exterminated, or they will be compelled to abandon the country to the slaves." In other words, a race war was in prospect for the South. Clifton added that this was precisely the goal of free-soil northerners.[76]

In much the same way, Albert Gallatin Brown noted, as many southerners did, and had done for many years, that slaves were being drained from more northerly to more southerly regions. Just as the New England states had seen their slaves sold south, so Virginia and Maryland were experiencing the same process. But Brown demanded that the slaveholders of Mississippi too should in the future be offered the same option. For "when the slaves have become profitless or troublesome, we, too, want a South to which we can send them." According to Brown, southerners "want it, we cannot do without it, and we mean to have it." The alternative, in the absence of an "outlet" would be "that sort of disaster which you would have if you damned up the mouth of the Mississippi river." What Brown obliquely referred to was the spectre other southerners explicitly invoked when they predicted nothing less than a repetition of the bloodshed and violence that had taken place early in the century in Santo Domingo. As they had for many decades, the slaveholders of the South saw this as the ultimate calamity.[77]

Those southern militants who predicted economic ruin and social cataclysm for a South that was unable to expand did not always explain the process by which these calamities would occur. Ironically, those who did gave what amounted to, though was scarcely intended to be, an indictment of the economic performance of slavery in the South that rivalled anything produced by the most unrestrained northern critic. As we have seen, the authors of more formal proslavery tracts were bedevilled by this problem and it resurfaced when southerners presented the economic case for territorial expansion.[78]

The state of Mississippi was one of the wealthiest in the South and its successes illustrate what has been termed the allocative efficiency of slavery: the ability of the slave regime to shift resources into geographical

76. *Journal of the Senate of the Commonwealth of Virginia....6 Dec, 1847* (Richmond, 1847), p. 29; *Journal of the Senate of the Commonwealth of Virginia....3 Dec. 1849* (Richmond, 1849), p. 22; "Speech of Clifton," in *Mississippian*, May 10, 1850; *Letter of James S. Green of Missouri* (n.p., n.d.), pp. 11–12.
77. *Speeches, Messages,...of...Albert Gallatin Brown*, p. 324; Louisville *Daily Courier*, Jan. 10, 1861, in Dumond (ed.), *Southern Editorials on Secession*, p. 392; Benjamin M. Palmer, *A Thanksgiving Sermon, Delivered at the First Presbyterian Church, New Orleans, November 29, 1860* (New York, 1861), p. 19. See also *Southern Slavery Considered on General Principles; Or, a Grapple with Abstractionists by a North Carolinian* (New York, 1861), p. 20. Calhoun had raised the spectre of a repetition of the events of Santo Domingo in the Senate in April 1848 – see *CG*, 30/1, App., p. 505.
78. See Volume I of this study, pp. 246–262.

regions where they could be most productively employed. But even Mississippi's economy gave considerable cause for concern to some observers. The *Mississippian* in 1860 sounded the alarm:

> We have reached that period in our history where something must be done for progress, or our declension in resources of strength will be rapid and evident. We need not ask what will be the fate of those vast tracts of worn-out lands, now lying everywhere as useless as the bills of spurious and broken banks; but what will become of those on which we rely now, not merely for the articles of our export – cotton, etc., but for bread, the staff of life? They are rapidly falling into the condition of the former... An improvident agriculture has already ruined millions of the best acres of our soil, and if persisted in, will ultimately turn the whole country into a wide, ruinous waste.

Similarly George Sawyer of Virginia declared that "in some of the old Slave States," "the soil, from long cultivation, is fast becoming exhausted." He pointed out that in North Carolina, South Carolina and "even Alabama and parts of Mississippi" there were "large tracts of country" which "must be annually abandoned, and the inhabitants... compelled to seek new and fresh lands to reward their labors." Hence the desire to move West. Sawyer argued that "millions and millions of acres of the richest and most productive lands upon the face of the globe, that have for years, and will for hundreds of years to come, lay unoccupied in the West, invite them, by the most tempting rewards, to seek new homes in these vast realms of the pubic domain." Then he delivered the sombre conclusion. Whoever had witnessed this exodus could "feel most sensibly the weight of the death-blow that would be inflicted upon the industry, wealth, and enterprise of these States, were their citizens denied this privilege." Thus for Sawyer the problem of soil erosion made territorial expansion an absolute necessity for the South.[79]

On the basis of similar reasoning Jefferson Davis argued that slavery should be "diffused." This was partly because slaves were, he claimed, better treated in such circumstances but more fundamentally it was, as he did not claim or even clearly understand, because of the economic weaknesses of slavery. In a phrase that would have been applauded by any Republican or abolitionist Davis termed "slave labour" "wasteful labour." Hence "it requires a still more extensive territory than would the same pursuits if they would be prosecuted by the more economic labor of

---

79. *Mississippian*, Aug. 10, 1860; George S. Sawyer, *Southern Institutes or, An Inquiry into the Origin and Early Prevalence of Slavery and the Slave Trade* (Philadelphia, 1858), p. 354.

white men." "We at the South, he concluded, "are an agricultural people, and we require an extended territory."[80]

If this was a problem even in a state like Mississippi it was all the more acute in the states of the South East. Those who advocated the reopening of the African slave trade sometimes pointed to the faltering economy of South Carolina and some of those who demanded additional territory for slavery similarly warned that without it soil erosion and other evils would bring disaster. Edward Shepard, in the North Carolina State Senate in 1850 painted a vivid picture of the condition to which his state would sink if measures like the Wilmot Proviso were implemented. Shepard claimed that while excellent for opening up new lands, the labour of the slave nevertheless "impoverishes" the soil. "Even now," he continued, "unless upon the best cotton, rice, and sugar plantations, his labor is not remunerative." Shepard then asked "what ... must it be, when the number is enormously increased, and that increase restricted to worn and impoverished soils?" Since North Carolina had "but little territory peculiarly adapted to the profitable occupation of slave labor," she would suffer more than any other state. Already "much of her soil is ... worn down by constant cultivation and needs the resuscitation of rest and economical and skillful husbandry, which can never take place when burdened by a superabundant population of slaves." And by 1890 there would indeed be a "superabundance." Shepard predicted 860,000 blacks in the state, "nearly all of them agricultural laborers drawing a scanty support from a worn out and impoverished soil." The nonslaveholders would be compelled to emigrate, the few slaveholders would engross the land "until the State becomes one vast plantation, barely providing enough to sustain in the cheapest and scantiest manner, her teeming black population." Hence expansion into the West (or elsewhere) was imperative for the purpose of North Carolina "relieving herself partially of this population."[81]

For these reasons, therefore, and with these dystopian visions before them, many southerners pressed the case for territorial expansion. Some argued that even if the need was not yet urgent, action should still be taken quickly; it was the task of the statesman to anticipate and thus forestall future crises. Nor should expansion be limited to areas suitable for the cultivation of cotton. Many southerners considered that slaves might be profitably employed in mining and some even speculated on the possibilities in the grainbelt of the Northwest. Albert Gallatin Brown, as ardent a southern expansionist as anyone in Congress, urged the occupation of parts of Central America – but only if slaveholding could be established in them.

80. "Speech of Jefferson Davis, February 13 and 14, 1850" in *Mississippian*, May 3, 17, 1850.
81. "Speech of Mr Shepard in the North Carolina Senate ... Nov. 27" in Raleigh *Standard*, Dec. 14, 1850

Brown acknowledged, quite openly, that he wanted Cuba, Nicaragua and parts of Mexico for the spread of slavery. He wanted, he reiterated in January 1853, "an outlet for slavery." Both Democratic presidents of the 1850s, Franklin Pierce and James Buchanan, though northerners, would prove highly sympathetic to these southern demands.[82]

Hence despite the levels of prosperity enjoyed in the South (as well as the North) in the 1850s these demands did not disappear and, as we shall see, were still heard when secession was under consideration in 1860–1861. Nevertheless it is important to note that the economic case for territorial expansion by no means united all southerners. Those who from the mid-1850s campaigned to reopen the African slave trade, for example, generally argued that there were in fact too few slaves in the South, even in the areas already held, and that those slaves commanded prices that were in fact too high. The goal of these radicals was to reduce the price of slaves, not least in order to increase their numbers in the states of the Upper or Middle South (such as Shepard's North Carolina) where, they believed, slavery was highly vulnerable. In part, but only in part, the two contradictory strategies were responses to different economic conditions, with the slave trade enthusiasts addressing problems of prosperity and consequent high prices and the territorial expansionists responding to economic decline and consequent low prices. This distinction is blurred, however, by the persistence of the territorial argument into the prosperous years of the 1850s and the claim, made by some slave trade enthusiasts, that more Africans were needed to reinvigorate the southern economy.

Similarly many southerners, without explicitly confronting the question of slavery's need for additional territory, simply opposed, and for a variety of reasons, all schemes for expansion into Latin America or the Caribbean. Thus some argued that Mexico was unsuitable, on climatic grounds, for slavery and that Mexicans were in any case unsuitable, on racial grounds, for citizenship (or slavery!) in the American Republic. Other southerners found in the racial deficiencies of the Cubans a fatal objection to the annexation of their island. Finally the process by which expansion might occur caused great disquiet in some quarters; many condemned unreservedly the filibustering efforts that were repeatedly made in the 1850s. And it is important to note that among the enemies of expansion were some of the most militant southerners of all. Thus Edmund Ruffin of Virginia questioned the value of Cuba, while almost all the South Carolinians (with the possible exception of James Orr and his coterie), remained very hostile to all imperialist enterprises.[83]

82. Eugene D. Genovese, *The Political Economy of Slavery: Studies in the Economy and Society of the Slave South* (New York, 1967), pp. 254–260; *Speeches, Messages, . . . of . . . Albert Gallatin Brown*, pp. 324, 212, 593–595.
83. May, *Southern Dream of a Caribbean Empire*, pp. 15, 201–203; Sinha, *Counterrevolution of Slavery*, p. 65; Lacy Ford, Jr., *The Origins of Southern Radicalism: The*

Nevertheless there were many southerners who advocated territorial acquisitions in the 1850s, many of them on explicitly proslavery grounds, and many on the basis of slavery's chronic and more-or-less urgent economic need for more land. The policies they favoured became embroiled in the struggle over the Kansas-Nebraska Act. Thus the economic case for territorial expansion, though unable in the 1850s to command universal acceptance even among southern militants, was nevertheless present as a second motive impelling southerners to seek repeal of the Missouri Compromise.

## III

As we have seen, the political case for new slave states had an unmistakable appeal to most southerners who wished to retain slavery in the South. The economic case for additional territory, as we have also seen, appealed to some, though by no means all, of the staunchest defenders of the system. But almost every southerner by 1854 found the opportunity to erase the Missouri Compromise from the statute book difficult, on constitutional grounds alone, to resist. Here was a third reason for supporting the Kansas-Nebraska Act and indeed for pressuring northern Democrats to include repeal within its provisions.

As we have seen, there was no prior movement in the South for the repeal of the Missouri restriction. Indeed in the late 1840s there had been a widespread desire among southerners to extend it to the Pacific. But northerners had voted this down. In so doing, they created, though it was scarcely understood at the time, a large southern constituency in favour of congressional nonintervention or, as it was often called, popular sovereignty, at that time an entirely untried and untested policy. For otherwise, how were any new slave states to be created? Northern objections that had applied to an extension of the line to the Pacific would presumably apply with equal force to any other policy that required the federal government to authorise slavery in any latitude at all, including territories that might be subsequently acquired in Central America or the Caribbean. Thus a complete repudiation of congressional control over the territories seemed the only way by which the South might expand.[84]

---

*South Carolina Upcountry, 1800–1860* (New York, 1988), pp. 182–185; Schultz, *Nationalism and Sectionalism in South Carolina*, pp. 68, 121, 179–180; William W. Freehling, *The Reintegration of American History* (New York, 1994), pp. 168–172; May, *Southern Dream of a Caribbean Empire*, p. 249.
84. In fact there was another alternative: a slave code for the territories. Calhoun had advocated something like this, as had William Lowndes Yancey in February 1848 but in the early 1850s it had relatively few supporters, not least because it seemed such an extreme proposal.

Moreover, the success of the Compromise measures in general (at least when viewed from the vantage point of late 1853) and of the territorial policy respecting New Mexico and Utah in particular widened the appeal of nonintervention still further. Thus the only policy that might produce territorial expansion in the South seemed to have been successful. By 1854 there were therefore three effects that southerners might expect or hope for from a repeal of the Missouri restriction. First, it would allow for the possibility of the spread of slavery into Kansas itself. Second, even if slavery did not in fact go into Kansas, repeal of the Missouri Compromise would nevertheless confirm a federal policy for the territories which alone seemed to offer the prospect of more slave states, wherever they might be located. We have seen that some southerners believed this indispensable to the health of the institution on economic as well as political grounds. And third, even if no expansion took place anywhere at all, repeal would roll back the power of the federal government and help confirm that it lacked the constitutional power to infringe the rights of slaveholders.

Even before the Kansas-Nebraska Act was introduced, some southerners expressed deep regret that the South had acceded to the Missouri restriction in 1820. Albert Gallatin Brown as early as 1848 lamented the fact that the South, in so doing, had admitted the power of Congress to exclude slavery. This was "the first, greatest, and most fatal error in our legislation on the subject of slavery," since "it violated at once the rights of one half the Union, and flagrantly outraged the Federal Constitution." Missouri, according to Brown, had had a perfect right to enter the Union in 1820 as a slave state and there was therefore no reason for the North to have extracted a price in the form of an exclusion of slavery in other territory. So for Brown the correct view of the constitution had prevailed until that date. "Give us the Constitution as it was administered from the day of its formation to 1819 and," he promised, "we are satisfied." Similarly in 1849 the *Address of the Southern Delegates in Congress* confirmed that prior to 1819 there had been no problem with regard to federal policy on the territories.[85]

Both Brown and Calhoun (who wrote the Address) had nonetheless been willing, on grounds of expediency and as a gesture of goodwill, to extend the Missouri line to the Pacific. But some southerners noted that all the constitutional arguments directed against the Wilmot Proviso applied equally to the Missouri restriction. In this way northerners who demanded free soil in the late 1840s and beyond unwittingly strengthened

---

85. *Speeches, Messages, ... of ... Albert Gallatin Brown*, pp. 133, 207, 331; *Address of the Southern Delegates*, pp. 1–2. Southerners who took this view noted that the Northwest Ordinance predated the signing of the Federal Constitution and thus did not form an exception to the pattern described.

the possibility that, if offered the opportunity to abrogate the Missouri Compromise, the South would take it, even though the effect might be to antagonise the North and thus strengthen the northern demand for free soil still further. In this curious way, as the North became increasingly attached to the Missouri Compromise, though unwilling to extend it, southerners viewed it with ever greater hostility, though they were prepared to see its scope expanded to cover many thousands of square miles of additional territory.[86]

Some years after the passage of the Kansas-Nebraska Act Senator James Mason of Virginia observed that he had never met a southern statesman who had not regretted the surrender of southern rights made in 1820. This was perhaps an exaggeration but it does serve to confirm the fact that southerners had ample reason to support the principle contained in Douglas's bill, even before the bill itself had seen the light of day. As a result when it did pass, most southerners were delighted. And, in general, the deeper the attachment to slavery, the greater the delight. The Milledgeville *Federal Union*, the leading Democratic paper in Georgia, noted that "for more than thirty years" the South had "borne the unjust and unconstitutional restrictions embraced in the Missouri Compromise for the sake of peace." Yet "submission did not bring peace, it only encouraged the enemies of the South to greater demands." By the late 1840s the free soilers, "having grown bold and insolent by their former success," would not abide by the Missouri Compromise, "which would have given them half of the new territories, but instead demanded the whole territory." Similarly the *Mississippian* avowed itself "gratified" by the Act, "because it erases from the statute-book, as unconstitutional and a most odious enactment to the South, degrading her institutions, and asserting her inferiority in the Union." Passage of the Act meant that "the power thus unwisely yielded thirty-four years ago, to Congress, to prohibit slavery in the territories, is revoked." Even more fundamentally, "the dangerous precedent is done away with" so that now "the standard of Equality between the States, is raised aloft; and the doctrine of the Constitution once more reigns supreme."[87]

As their polemical remarks indicated, southerners were convinced that the withdrawal of Congressional power over the territories would not

---

86. Phillips (ed.), *Correspondence of Toombs, Stephens, and Cobb*, p. 93; Charles M. Wiltse, *John C. Calhoun, Sectionalist, 1840–1850* (New York, 1951), p. 304; J. G. De Roulhac Hamilton, *Party Politics in North Carolina, 1835–1860* (Durham, NC, 1916), p. 129; Sinha, *Counterrevolution of Slavery*, p. 68.

87. CG, 35/1, App. p. 76; Milledgeville *Federal Union*, Feb. 14, 1854; *Mississippian*, June 2, 1854. The Missouri restriction was to some southerners all the more galling since it seemed to prevent even *states* and not merely *territories* north of 36°30′ from establishing slavery – hence its danger as a precedent.

merely serve to establish proper constitutional principles but would also administer a severe blow to those northerners who wished to agitate the slavery question. This indeed was Douglas's expectation. He had some time previously reached the conclusion that the discussion of slavery in Congress gave northern agitators scope for mischief they would otherwise not possess. It allowed them to manufacture controversy where none need exist. Historians know with hindsight, of course, that the Kansas-Nebraska Act had precisely the opposite effect in that it produced a disastrous intensification of sectional hostilities but it is important to realise that if Douglas himself, perhaps the most popular statesman in any party in the North, made these predictions about the effect of his measure on northern opinion, it was scarcely surprising that many southerners shared them.

Thus a proper view of the constitutional limitations on Congressional power would be promoted by the Act and this is turn would have a salutary and regenerative effect on northern opinion. It was not surprising, therefore, that the *Mississippian* upon the passage of the bill looked forward to "the banishment of the slavery question from the National councils." The process by which northerners had been led to demand one concession after another, each greater and more threatening than the last, would now be put into reverse. For southern militants this was an outcome most fervently to be desired.[88]

## IV

Even the prospect of these gains, substantial as they appeared to be, did not exhaust the attractions of the Kansas-Nebraska Act for southern militants. Not only was there a political incentive for new states, an economic incentive for territorial expansion, and a constitutional incentive to deny Congress power over slavery, there was also a fourth factor. This comprised a set of more localised concerns which played a key part in the genesis of the Act, in its operation and in making the measure truly irresistible in the South. They concerned the state of Missouri. Indeed it is scarcely too much to say that affairs in the state of Missouri made the territory of Kansas the powder keg that it quickly proved to be.

Like other border states Missouri contained relatively few slaves.[89] In 1850 the total was about 90.000 (approximately the same as in Maryland). They farmed hemp and tobacco primarily in the western counties.

---

88. *Mississippian*, March 31, 1854. See also Phillips (ed.), *Correspondence of Toombs, Stephens, and Cobb*, p. 344.
89. Virginia was the exception that proved the rule. The border areas (now West Virginia) had few slaves, even though the tidewater areas, far away from the border, had a great many, giving Virginia in absolute numbers more slaves than any other state.

But the politics of slavery in Missouri were unique. The state had been admitted into the Union, of course, more than thirty years earlier in the sharpest sectional controversy the nation had yet experienced. From that time onwards the slavery question had lain largely dormant in the politics of the state until the late 1840s when controversy erupted once again. For many Missourians choosing between North and South proved then, as it would until the end of the Civil War, an extremely difficult and painful process.

In the 1850s the range of opinion on slavery within Missouri's political mainstream was extraordinarily wide, wider in fact than in any state in the Union. Men like U.S. Senator David Rice Atchison were utterly southern in their loyalties; Atchison was a close friend and messmate of some leading southern Senators and utterly determined to protect the interests of slavery and slaveholders in Missouri. On the other hand, leaders like Thomas Hart Benton looked instead to the North and in Benton's case openly acknowledged that, although a slaveholder, he wished there were no slaves in the state. Later in the 1850s an abolition party would emerge in Missouri and the Republicans would in 1860 carry the city of St Louis, the focus of antislavery sentiment in the state. The position was complicated by the fact that Missouri, unlike Maryland for example, was still a frontier state desperate to recruit new settlers and later in the decade many would conclude that slavery was retarding her growth and ensuring that in a competition with Illinois, for example, she would lose. On the other hand, Atchison and his followers feared that an influx of free-state settlers might further weaken slavery in the state. Yet by the early 1850s it was becoming increasingly difficult for them to resist the mounting pressure placed upon them by constituents who demanded the opening up of neighbouring Kansas.[90]

Atchison, like many other southerners, believed that the prohibition of slavery above the line of 36° 30′ had been one of the most catastrophic errors in the history of the Republic. Until at least 1853 however, he, again like many other southerners, saw no hope of its repeal. But by that year he had realised that the pressure from his constituents to open up Kansas could no longer be resisted. He now faced a dilemma. Preventing the organisation of Kansas would alienate his nonslaveholding supporters (always a large majority in Missouri); allowing the territory to be organised in accordance with the Missouri Compromise would damage the interests of the slaveholders. This problem was particularly acute since

90. P. Orman Ray, *The Repeal of the Missouri Compromise* (Cleveland, 1909); Freehling, *Road to Disunion: Secessionists at Bay*; Roy F. Nichols, "The Kansas-Nebraska Act: A Century of Historiography," *Mississippi Valley Historical Review*, XLIII (1956), pp. 187–212.

Benton, defeated in his campaign for re-election to the Senate two years earlier, was thirsting for revenge and exploiting Atchison's dilemma to the full. But there was, for Atchison, a way out: open up Kansas but with the odious restriction on slavery repealed.[91]

At first Atchison did not press for this. But what tipped the scales was his concern for the fate of slavery not merely in Kansas but also in Missouri. In fact it was the weakness or potential weakness of slavery in both areas that produced the pressure for the alteration in Douglas's bill that would see the Missouri Compromise repealed. One of his supporters wrote Atchison that silence on the question of slavery in Missouri (essentially Benton's policy) would prove ruinous to the slaveholders there, partly because more nonslaveholding immigrants would further dilute the political strength of the slaveholders. Atchison must therefore agitate the question of slavery in Kansas in order to bring to public attention the "thousands" of "covert" abolitionists in Missouri, "who now from policy hide their hellish designs." Similarly Claiborne Fox Jackson, a prominent Missouri Democrat and future Governor, wrote to him that if Kansas were to become "'free nigger' territory, Missouri must become so too, for we can hardly keep our negroes here now." Jackson was referring to the alleged "kidnapping" of slaves that would then occur from a free Kansas, to the impact that free settlers in Kansas would have if they moved into Missouri, and even to the "insidious sabotage from Missourians who were ostensibly in favor of silence" on the slavery question.[92]

The problem was greatly aggravated by the geographical location of the state which left Missouri, alone among border states, vulnerable to virtual encirclement by free states. For, as the St Louis *Republican* warned, if Kansas "be made a free territory then will Missouri be surrounded on three sides by free territory, where there will always be men and means to assist in the escape of our slaves." The newspaper concluded that "with the emissaries of abolitionists around us, and the facilities of escape so enlarged, this species of property would become insecure, if not valueless in Missouri." These opinions were almost certainly widely shared within the slaveholding community in Missouri. A little later, in the summer of 1855, a proslavery convention in Lexington explained that, facing the prospect of the organisation of Kansas with the slavery prohibition intact, Missouri's position had been "truly unenviable":

> With two states on her northern and eastern border, in many portions of which the Constitution of the United States, and the Fugitive Slave

91. The best brief account of the impact of Missouri politics is Freehling, *Road to Disunion: Secessionists at Bay*, pp. 536–565.
92. E. A. Hannegan to Atchison, Sept. 1, 1853, C. F. Jackson to Atchison, Jan. 18, 1854, quoted in Freehling, *Road to Disunion: Secessionists at Bay*, p. 549.

Law, passed in pursuance thereof, were known to be as inefficacious
for the protection of our rights, as they would have been in London
or Canada, it was left to the will of Congress, by enforcing the restriction of 1820, to cut Missouri off almost entirely from all territorial
connexion with States having institutions congenial to her own, and
with populations ready and willing to protect and defend them. No
alternative was left to that body but to repeal the restriction, and
thus leave to the Constitution and the laws of nature, the settlement
of our territories, or, by retaining the restriction, indirectly to abolish
slavery in Missouri.

Thus "the enforcement of the restriction in the settlement of Kansas was
virtually the abolition of slavery in Missouri."[93]

Atchison himself took very much to heart the suggestion that he should
agitate the slavery question. He too noted that "the State of Missouri is
now bounded on two sides by free States." Thus if Kansas were organised "as free territory then we are bounded on three sides by free States or
Territories." Public meetings now denounced the Missouri Compromise
and highly inflammatory rhetoric was employed. "If the Territory shall be
opened to settlement," one proslavery group declared, "we pledge ourselves to each other to extend the institutions of Missouri over the Territory at whatever sacrifice of blood or treasure." Atchison himself avowed
that he would "rather see the whole of Nebraska [including Kansas] in
the bottom of hell, than see it a Free State." Such was the militancy of the
proslavery forces in Missouri. And this militancy fed directly into the
demand for a repeal of the Missouri Compromise.[94]

Southerners like Atchison claimed that events in Kansas would have
an impact on Missouri directly and also indirectly on other parts of the
South. As we have seen, the sectional controversy had generated anxiety
in the minds of many southerners about the future of slavery in the border
states. A widespread fear in the 1850s was of a domino effect, whereby
pressure on Missouri, for example, would weaken states further South.
Atchison himself cited Arkansas and Texas as well as the other territories
not yet settled as being vulnerable to this process. "We are playing," he
informed Virginia Senator R. M. T. Hunter for a mightly [sic] stake." It
is certain that other southerners were aware of this.[95]

Nevertheless, it would be a mistake to assume that the entire South rallied to the Kansas-Nebraska Act out of concern for Missouri. Although it

93. St Louis *Republican* quoted in Nevins, *House Dividing*, p. 92; *Address to the People
of the United States, Together with the Proceedings and Resolutions of the Pro-Slavery
Convention of Missouri, Held at Lexington, July 1855* (St. Louis, 1855), p. 5.
94. Rawley, *Race and Politics*, p. 81; Nevins, *House Dividing*, p. 93; Freehling, *Road to
Disunion: Secessionists at Bay*, p. 551.
95. David Rice Atchison to R. M. T. Hunter, quoted in Rawley, *Race and Politics*, p. 81.

received an occasional mention, most newspapers outside the immediate area did not give this aspect of the issue great prominence. For many, the constitutional issue was more weighty. Moreover, as we have seen, many southerners doubted whether Kansas was in any case suitable for slavery, in which case repeal of the Missouri Compromise would have, from this point of view, no beneficial effect whatever upon affairs in Missouri herself. It is true that the vulnerability of the border states was an extremely delicate issue and at least one historian has suggested that those who denied slavery could be established in Kansas were being disingenuous and merely seeking to lull northerners. But this ignores the fact that if a crisis of the border states were genuinely imminent, publicity within the South was precisely what was needed. Moreover it ignores the fact that if slavery were indeed to go to Kansas, then slaveholders from other parts of the Union would have to migrate there; in such circumstances, public utterances about the unsuitability of the territory would prove utterly counterproductive.[96]

## V

The combination of factors that led southerners to desire the repeal of the Missouri Compromise meant that the great majority of southerners were delighted when the Kansas-Nebraska Act was passed. Some years later, one southern newspaper referred to it as "the most universally popular act in the South ever considered by Congress on the subject of slavery." It was so popular indeed that southern Whigs, as we shall see later, with few exceptions felt compelled to support it, even though it resulted in the virtual disbanding of their party. It became in the South a measure almost impossible to resist.[97]

As a result, even the most militant southerners now found that the Democratic party might, after all, safeguard their rights within the Union. Northern Democrats in general and Douglas himself, in particular, now became heroes in the South, even to many of those militants who had been highly sceptical of the product of their labours on behalf of the Compromise in 1850. The Milledgeville *Federal Union* honoured the northern Democrats as men on whom the South could "rely for justice in the hour of need." The Act had proved extremely difficult to pass, as a result of the most determined opposition from northern Whigs (and some northern

96. Charleston *Mercury*, Feb. 3, 1856; Robert Russel, "The Issues in the Congressional Struggle over the Kansas-Nebraska Bill, 1854," *Journal of Southern History*, XXIX (1963), pp. 187–210.
97. Staunton *Vindicator*, Oct. 5, 1860; Freehling, *Road to Disunion: Secessionists at Bay*, p. 536. Southern Whig reactions to the Kansas-Nebraska Act are treated in Chapter 4 of this volume.

Democrats). But as in 1850 and indeed for the previous half-century northern Democrats had rallied to support the South. The *Federal Union* noted that these men had withstood attacks from press and pulpit alike in the North and the help they had given "should never be forgotten." "Whilst we have such men in our national councils," the paper concluded, "we need not despair of the Republic." Even more fulsome praise came from the *Mississippian* which referred to them as "a glorious band, whose names will live, when their traducers will have been forgotten, or be remembered only to be despised."[98]

This gratitude to the Democrats of the North was destined to be short-lived, a casualty of the clash that would subsequently occur between northern and southern interpretations of congressional nonintervention. Southerners with few exceptions continued to believe that popular sovereignty should mean that only at the time of admission into the Union could a territory-state exclude slavery, whereas the great majority of northerners believed with Douglas himself that the decision could be taken much earlier by the territorial legislature. This division of opinion was visible from the start; indeed it had existed in 1850. In 1854 the Charleston *Mercury*, as always representing the most extreme opinion in the South, denounced the northern interpretation (frequently and opprobriously referred to as "squatter sovereignty") in unmeasured terms. But the standard southern Democratic approach was the same as that taken by Douglas himself. The *Federal Union* announced that it could "see no use in raising the issue at this time." For "it can do no good, while it may occasion much evil to the Democratic party." A pragmatic view should be taken: "if the bill is a good one and suits all parties, why should we quarrel about a provision which is both admitted and denied – why peril the bill by an unnecessary dispute as to some *supposed* admission or denial of a doctrine?" Hence the editor announced that "we deprecate all discussion at present, as useless and provocative of controversies that can only end in hurt." In fact he went a little further and offered to open the columns of the newspaper to those arguing on either side of this question. Clearly the gains offered by the Act seemed in 1854 more than enough to compensate for any ambiguity that might inhere in it as to its application.[99]

Indeed the Kansas-Nebraska Act seemed to offer the South an extraordinary political harvest. Some southerners hoped it would strengthen slavery in Missouri; some believed the creation of a new slave state would at least reduce the impact of new free states; others found in it reason to believe that it would facilitate territorial expansion elsewhere if not in Kansas; almost everyone thought it would overturn an odious restriction

98.  Milledgeville *Federal Union*, May 30, 1854; *Mississippian*, March 31, 1854.
99.  Charleston *Mercury*, Feb. 14, 1854; Milledgeville *Federal Union*, April 18, 1854.

that set a dangerous constitutional precedent. Moreover these aspirations were not contradictory. None ruled out the others. The more general effects could be expected to ensue even if the more specific ones did not.

It was therefore not surprising that it produced a sharp sectional division in Congress. Apart from those northern Democrats who rallied to the bill (and many did not), it pitted, with only a trivial number of exceptions, northerners against southerners. The bill got through the Senate relatively easily. In the House northern Democrats were subjected to almost unprecedented pressure to support it and on May 22, 1854 it was passed. The South, it seemed, had won a remarkable victory.

What few people realised, however, was that this Act, which seemed to promise so much for slaveholders, and which had assumed its final, highly controversial form as a result of the power they wielded, was in fact a testimony to the underlying weaknesses, as much as the strengths, of slavery. All the reasons that converged to make it possible have this in common. They can perhaps be best illustrated by a comparison with northern society which suffered from no analogous weaknesses. Thus the need for additional slave states was a consequence of the failure to match the North in the race to develop the West and colonise new territory. The fear of an "overgrown" slave population had no counterpart in a North where the demand for additional labour (in the form of immigration, for example) was in most years quite insatiable. The need to propagate a strict construction of the Federal Constitution in order to protect slavery from a hostile majority had no parallel in the North, whose employing class had no fears that the federal government would threaten its relationship with its wage workers. And no northern state's labour system needed to be shored up in the way that slavery in Missouri needed support. Although they did not (and could not) see it in these terms, the Kansas-Nebraska Act was an attempt on the part of southerners to overcome the constraints imposed upon them by the slave mode of production, at the heart of which lay the conflict, actual or potential between master and slave. Since it was beyond the power of any act of Congress to overcome those constraints or to resolve that conflict, it is not surprising that the Kansas-Nebraska Act would prove to be an abject failure.

## Crisis in Kansas, 1854–1858

### I

The problems that quickly afflicted the territories of Kansas had several causes. For one thing there were some 10,000 Native Americans there for whom Congress had made little or no provision. Nor was there a coherent land policy for the territory. But the major difficulty lay elsewhere and it concerned the fate of slavery in Kansas. In April 1854 Eli Thayer of Massachusetts obtained a charter for the Massachusetts Emigrant Aid Society (later renamed the New England Emigrant Aid Company). This was both a money-making operation and an attempt to ensure that Kansas became free territory. Thayer had a talent for self-publicisation and he announced he would raise millions of dollars and send 20,000 free-state settlers into Kansas. In the event, he raised far less and helped send perhaps 2,000 settlers.[100]

In neighbouring Missouri, however, this project was viewed with the greatest consternation. Seeing a threat to the prospects of slavery in Kansas and to the continued safety of slavery in Missouri herself, Missourians led by, among others, David Rice Atchison, determined to take action. Not once but repeatedly over the next few years they would cross into Kansas, intimidate free-state settlers and vote illegally in the elections that would either directly or indirectly determine the fate of slavery in the territory. Not surprisingly the free-soil settlers also engaged in violent and illegal activities.

The consequence was that when elections took place the results were clearly the product of frauds on a large scale. Nevertheless a proslavery territorial legislature was established at Shawnee (it later moved to Lecompton) which then enacted draconian measures in support of slavery. Those who denied slavery was legal in Kansas, for example, could be imprisoned and only proslavery men could hold office. In response the free-soil settlers established their own assembly at Topeka, which then sought to prohibit slavery in the territory after July 1857. This was submitted to a popular vote and overwhelmingly endorsed but the election was boycotted by the proslavery elements whose leaders denounced the Topeka movement as treason. President Pierce meanwhile was unwilling to intervene with any vigor, partly because, as a good state's-rights Democrat, he doubted whether the federal government had the authority. But he too viewed the Topeka government as revolutionary. By the end of 1855 the disorder in Kansas had already resulted in the dismissal of one governor and there were now rival governments, each with its own armed supporters, and each heaping abuse upon the other.

The following year was still more eventful. Atchison was now appealing to other southern states for aid, in the form of additional manpower, in order to make Kansas a slave state and to defend slavery in Missouri. Northerners were by now also calling for weapons, the famous Sharps rifles, to be sent into the territory to defend free-state settlers against the so-called Missouri ruffians. There was even bloodshed, though on a small

---

100. Good accounts of events in Kansas can be found in Nevins, *House Dividing*, Potter, *Impending Crisis*, and Rawley, *Race and Politics*. The best of all, however, is in Freehling, *Road to Disunion: Secessionists Triumphant*.

scale. Then in May 1856 came one of the most celebrated events of the entire Kansas saga: the "sack of Lawrence." Again there was little bloodshed though much destruction of property. By now violence was occurring on both sides, there were widespread guerrilla activities as well as burning and pillaging and, as a direct result of the sack of Lawrence, John Brown, the militant abolitionist, brutally murdered five men at Pottowatomie in Kansas. One historian estimates that between November 1855 and December 1856 perhaps two hundred lives were lost and perhaps two million dollars worth of property destroyed.[101]

Congress became increasingly absorbed by events in Kansas. The newly formed Republican party, which had sprung into existence in the wake of the passage of the Kansas-Nebraska Act to resist the spread of slavery, received a great boost from the chronic unrest in the territory. When, in response to the actions perpetrated by the proslavery forces in Kansas, Charles Sumner of Massachusetts, denounced slavery in general and South Carolina and one of her Senators, Andrew Butler, in particular, Preston Brooks, a relative of Butler, retaliated with a physical assault upon Sumner which kept him out of the Senate and unable to resume his duties for several years. The result was a further polarisation of opinion with southerners sending Brooks canes to replace the one broken in the affray, and northerners denouncing the assault as fresh evidence of southern barbarism. The election of 1856 was thus played out against the background of "Bleeding Kansas" and "Bleeding Sumner." These were the direct or indirect effects of events in Kansas and they redounded to the benefit of the nascent Republican party.[102]

By the start of 1857 it was evident that the free-soil settlers, who had probably outnumbered bona fide proslavery settlers (as opposed to Missouri insurgents) from the very first, were now in a large majority. But the Lecompton legislature, not at all prepared to surrender its cause, drew up plans for the admission of Kansas into the Union as a slave state. It was now on a collision course with the third governor of the territory. John W. Geary opposed these plans, had his vetoes overridden and finally, after an unsuccessful appeal to President Pierce for federal troops, resigned.

When James Buchanan took office he chose a fourth Governor, Robert J. Walker. Walker urged the free-soil settlers to participate in the upcoming elections to the Constitutional Convention. He expressed his opinion that Kansas was unsuited to slavery by virtue of her climate. This, however, deeply antagonised not merely the proslavery groups in Kansas but also many southerners in Congress, who still believed that Kansas could and should be admitted as a slave state. Meanwhile the Constitutional

101. Rawley, *Race and Politics*, p. 160.
102. Newspaper reaction to the Sumner beating can most conveniently be found at http://history.furman.edu/editorials/see.py – an excellent collection of material.

Convention at Lecompton did its utmost to guarantee slaveholders' rights. The right to hold slaves already in the territory was reaffirmed and the voters were to be allowed to determine whether in the future more slaves could be introduced. To some observers this seemed like a choice between two proslavery options, since the voters could not reject the constitution in its entirety. In fact even this limited form of popular participation was a concession. For the very good reason that they feared defeat, the proslavery forces had contemplated not submitting the constitution to the people at all (as had happened in the case of some territories previously) despite a prior promise to do so.[103]

The result of the referendum on the Lecompton constitution was a ringing endorsement of the proslavery position. Those in favour of "the constitution with slavery" numbered 6,266, while those in favour of "the constitution without slavery" (which in fact guaranteed the possession of slaves already in the territory) totalled 567. But the free-soil settlers had boycotted the referendum entirely and a subsequent investigation found that no less than 2,700 votes had been fraudulent. This now struck Walker, Stephen A. Douglas, and the great majority of northern Democrats as absurd and they refused to accept the Lecompton constitution. But many southerners insisted that it be accepted and that Kansas enter the Union as a slave state. President Buchanan succumbed to this pressure and endorsed Lecompton. Walker resigned and Douglas now broke with the Democratic administration. No event in the entire history of the Kansas affair was more fateful for it presaged the catastrophic split in the party of 1860, the split which helped the Republicans to their momentous victory.

In February 1858 Buchanan sent a message to Congress in which he urged the immediate admission of Kansas under the Lecompton Constitution and denounced the Topeka government as treasonous and revolutionary (as Pierce had). He even claimed that Kansas was now as much a slave state as Georgia or South Carolina. Some in the Deep South went so far as to threaten secession if Kansas did not enter the Union as a slave state. After an extraordinary legislative battle, when the administration used all means including bribery to promote the Lecompton constitution, it was finally submitted to the voters of Kansas. In what was, by the standards of 1850s Kansas, a remarkably fraud-free election, the voters rejected the Lecompton constitution in August 1858 by 11,200 to 1,788. This doomed the hopes of the proslavery forces, either in Kansas or Washington, DC and two and a half years later Kansas entered the Union – as a free state.[104]

103. On this and related points see especially Potter, *Impending Crisis*, pp. 296–327.
104. James D. Richardson (ed.), *A Compilation of the Messages and Papers of the Presidents 1789–1897* (Washington, D.C., 1899), V, p. 479; Mark Summers, *The Plundering Generation Corruption and the Crisis of the Union, 1849–1861* (New York, 1987), pp. 249–255.

## II

From the standpoint of the southern militant, the extent of the disaster can scarcely be exaggerated. As we have seen, many southerners had doubted whether slavery could take root in Kansas at all. But the process by which this prediction had been verified had proved utterly ruinous. The creation of a seventeenth free state was in fact the least damaging of the effects. In Missouri the cause of antislavery was strengthened and plans for the ending of slavery were actually submitted. In 1860 the Republicans ran strongly in some parts of Missouri and this confirmed fears (or hopes) that the state would soon become free. Even this, important as it was, was not the main effect of the Kansas imbroglio.[105]

Instead the major consequence was the impact on northern opinion. Kansas gave a huge boost to antislavery sentiment in the North as a whole since it seemed to validate so many of the criticisms of slavery made by abolitionists and free soilers. The passage of the Kansas-Nebraska Act itself had seemed bad enough, but the events that then transpired in the territory of Kansas apparently confirmed what had been said by antislavery militants for many years: slavery was an inherently disruptive and fatally disorganising force.

As a result, the other gains that had been expected from the repeal of the Missouri Compromise now evaporated. Indeed they were transformed into catastrophic losses. Northerners now redoubled their efforts to prevent the spread of slavery; this was the very *raison d'etre* of the Republican party which, by the time of the Lecompton crisis, controlled most of the states of the North. It was now impossible for southerners to hope for an extension of slave territory whether to Kansas or anywhere else – so long as they remained in the Union.

So with the constitutional argument for the Kansas-Nebraska Act. The principle of congressional nonintervention contained in the Act was not formally repudiated by the Democratic party or either of its two presidents in the 1850s. On the contrary it became a fixed party principle. And the southern construction of the doctrine received a ringing reaffirmation both from President Buchanan and in the Supreme Court's Dred Scott decision of 1857. But this was no victory for the South, or at least not for those within the South who wished to remain within the Union. Once again the effect on northern opinion was crucial. Rather than settle the slavery controversy by denying antislavery agitators scope for their

105. On Missouri see B. Gratz Brown, *Extracts from a Speech of B. Gratz Brown of St. Louis, Delivered in the Missouri House of Representatives, Feb. 12, 1857* (Philadelphia, n.d.); Richard H. Sewell, *Ballots for Freedom* (New York, 1976), pp. 318–320; Barbara L. Green, "The Slavery Debate in Missouri, 1831–1855" (Unpublished Doctoral Dissertation, University of Missouri-Columbia, 1980); Robert W. Duffner, "Slavery in Missouri River Counties, 1820–1865 (Unpublished Doctoral Dissertation, University of Missouri, 1974), pp. 154–163; Missouri *Democrat*, May 24, 1857.

actions, the Kansas-Nebraska Act, both when under discussion and when in operation, offered them unprecedented opportunities. The debates of 1854 and the legislative manoeuvrings accompanying them generated an extraordinary degree of controversy but once again these were as nothing compared with the heat generated and regenerated whenever news of a fresh crisis in Kansas reached Washington.

In this way the Kansas-Nebraska Act brought the very opposite of what had been hoped for and expected. At first it had seemed to commit the Democrats to a view of the constitution that satisfied almost all southern militants. Then, largely as a result of the subsequent events in Kansas, the ambiguity in the doctrine of congressional nonintervention could no longer be tolerated and it transpired that the views of most northern Democrats were, after all, not acceptable to the South. Finally, it became apparent that northern opinion, again largely as a result of the events in Kansas, would not tolerate the southern militant's view of the constitution and any Democrat who espoused it would face almost certain electoral defeat.

Such were the strange fruits of the Kansas-Nebraska Act. Designed to facilitate southern expansion, it instead made that expansion virtually impossible. Offering the hope that slavery might be strengthened in Missouri, it ended by leaving Missouri slaveholders more exposed than ever before. Promising to quell antislavery agitation, it instead raised that agitation to levels which made southern participation in the Union increasingly doubtful.

What had gone wrong? Why were the outcomes so dramatically at odds with the expectations? It is tempting to assign responsibility to those who, in drawing up, or supporting the Act, made predictions that were wholly mistaken. To do so would be, of course, to join those historians who, in assigning responsibility for the Civil War to a "blundering generation" of statesman, formed the so-called "revisionist" school. But this approach is highly unsatisfactory. As we have seen, the case for the Kansas-Nebraska Act looked extremely compelling. Moreover, how else were southerners to arrest the processes by which the South was being outvoted, slavery confined to regions in some of which its prospects were uncertain, slaveholders in Missouri threatened with encirclement and a dangerously latitudinarian view of the constitution propagated? Southerners realised that the Kansas-Nebraska Act would be extremely controversial but they believed the advantages were worth the risk. Here they were mistaken but their strategy was anything but a foolish one.

This does not, however, explain the gulf between expectations and outcomes. The key effect was on northern opinion. It was this which frustrated one by one all southern hopes and wrecked all the southern projects. Northerners of an even moderately antislavery persuasion and some who had never previously been antislavery at all, found southern attitudes throughout the protracted crisis over Kansas quite outrageous. They therefore warrant a brief examination.

Many of these attitudes were prominent when the Lecompton constitution was under consideration. It might be thought that Lecompton was simply indefensible, since it was the product, to a considerable degree, of fraudulent voting, coercion and a process of electoral consultation that was an affront to standard contemporary American practice. After all, even including the fraudulent votes only 6,000 were cast by an electorate estimated to number 20,000. Yet southerners did defend it. Some of them made a comparison with California's admission into the Union in 1850. Thus Lucius Lamar of Mississippi reminded the House that on that occasion "without any previous assent of Congress, without even the authority of a Territorial Legislature; without any census, a band of roaming adventurers was lugged into the Union over all law and precedent, as the coequal of the oldest State in this Union, because it happened to be a free State." Why then should such a fuss be made over Kansas? The answer was that northerners were operating a double standard:

> when a State applies for admission with a constitution excluding slavery, no irregularity can be too enormous, no violation of precedent too marked, no disregard of constitutional procedure too palpable, no outrage can be too enormous for its admission as a State into the Union; but when a State applies for admission with slavery in its constitution, no excuse can be too trivial, no pretense too paltry and ignoble, to keep her out.

Other southerners accepted that there had been frauds in Kansas but insisted that they had been "equally great on both sides." Moreover, these were the responsibility of the state of Kansas, not of Congress. Indeed the very principle upon which the Kansas-Nebraska Act had been based was that of congressional noninterference. If a majority were truly opposed to slavery in Kansas, then there would be ample opportunity to revise the Constitution in the future. Many southerners argued that the opposition to the Lecompton constitution was simply the product of a covert antislavery: the constitution was unacceptable because it established slavery in Kansas.[106]

Yet these defences did not move northerners. For them the crucial events in the territory were the repeated incursions by the "Missouri ruffians" and the fraudulent votes which they repeatedly cast. While not necessarily defending these illegal votes, southerners insisted that the Missourians

---

106. *CG*, 35/1, App., pp. 51, 69, 77; Lucius Q. C. Lamar to Howell Cobb. July 17, 1857, in Phillips (ed.), *Correspondence of Toombs, Stephens, and Cobb*, p. 417.

had been acting under extreme provocation and acquitted them of ultimate responsibility for the disastrous course of events that had ensued in the territory. Here was the real sticking point. If the Missourians were guilty as charged, Lecompton was utterly unacceptable; if not there might be grounds for ignoring the electoral irregularities and letting Kansans determine their own fate as citizens of a recognised and respected slave state within the Union.

It is at this point that the weaknesses of slavery play a decisive role. Ironically they were reflected in the very arguments employed in defence of the Missourians and in defence of slavery in both Kansas and Missouri. To a man militant southerners denounced the Emigrant Aid societies as abolitionist in inspiration and then argued that, faced with such a threat, Missourians had had little choice. In so doing, those who defended the Missourians unwittingly demonstrated that a slave regime could only survive by taking the most draconian, antidemocratic and even lawless actions against those expressing antislavery sentiments. They thus unwittingly highlighted the weaknesses of slavery.

It is therefore important to examine the defences offered. In 1855 at a Pro-Slavery Convention held at Lexington, Missouri, the various speakers vied with each other to heap abuse on the Emigrant Aid societies. They were denounced as "*hirelings* – an army of hirelings – recruited and shipped indirectly by a sovereign State of this Union, to make war upon an institution *now* existing in the Territory to which they are transplanted, and thence to inflict a fatal blow upon the resources, the prosperity and the peace of a neighboring State." Thus they were "*military* colonies, planted by a State government." The Convention affirmed that such men would use rifles and would, with no compunction, stir up servile insurrections. "That such a population [in Kansas] would be fatal to the peace and security of the neighboring State of Missouri," the report concluded, "is too clear to admit of argument." Indeed "a horde of our western savages, with avowed purposes of destruction of the white race, would be less formidable neighbors." At the same Convention another speaker, Judge William B. Napton, announced that the slaveholders of Missouri "do not hold it necessary or expedient to wait until the torch is applied to our dwellings, or the knife to our throats, before we take measures for our security and the security of our firesides." Within Missouri, he continued, twenty-five million dollars worth of property would soon become valueless with such a population "of hired fanatics, recruited, transported, armed and paid for the special and sole purpose of abolitionizing Kansas and Missouri."[107]

---

107. *Address to the People of the United States, Together with the Proceedings and Resolutions of the Pro-Slavery Convention of Missouri, Held at Lexington, July 1855* (St. Louis, 1855), pp. 7, 23.

What actions should be taken? At the same convention another speaker, James Shannon, explained that "the practical abolitionist, who labors to impair a vested right of property in slaves, is a *negro-thief*." And a negro thief, he continued, "should be regarded and treated as a horse-thief, a burglar or any other sort of thief." Moreover, "those who give them aid and comfort should be regarded and treated as their accomplices in guilt." It followed that "an organized band of such persons, and for such ends, should be treated as an organized band of conspirators against the lives and property of the citizens, enemies alike to God and man." Hence "slaveholding communities have just the same rights to take all *necessary measures of defence, whether legal or extra-legal, judicial or extra-judicial* [emphasis added], against a negro-thief, or an organized band of negro thieves, as they have a right to take, and are universally acknowledged to have a right to take, against horse-thieves, or house thieves." The Convention then passed resolutions which promised all possible aid to the slaveholders of Missouri (who were concentrated on the state's western border):

> Resolved, That the fanatical and persevering efforts of Abolitionists and Abolition societies to render our slave property insecure, and to excite the evil passions of those slaves to insubordination, has a direct tendency to incite them to servile war, with all its attendant horrors; and is such an invasion of our rights, that we feel justified in pledging our lives, our fortunes, and our sacred honor, to each other, to the State, and to our sister slave States that we WILL ABATE IT, to the utmost extent of our ability, peaceably if we can, forcibly if we must.

> Resolved, That the whole State is identified in interest and sympathy with the citizens on our western border; and we will cooperate with them in all proper measures to prevent the foul demon of Abolitionism from planting a colony of negro-thieves on our frontier to harass our citizens and steal their property. It matters not whether that colony be imported from European poor-houses and prisons, or from pestilential hot-beds of New England fanaticism.

Missouri's slaveholders thus invoked the right of self-defence to justify their actions.[108]

Moreover Shannon stressed that it was not only those who were overtly antislavery who should be targeted. For "it is not to be expected that any man in a slave State will acknowledge himself an abolitionist, or an emissary of abolitionists... such an acknowledgement, if it did not endanger their persons, would at least in a great measure destroy their capacity for mischief." How then were these public enemies to be identified? The speaker offered some valuable practical advice:

---

108. [James Shannon], *An Address Delivered Before the Pro-Slavery Convention of the State of Missouri...July 13, 1855, on Domestic Slavery* (St Louis, 1855), p. 28.

> By their fruits ye shall know them.... They must be judged by their
> acts. If they labor to weaken the South by keeping alive the foul demon
> of party spirit; if they are ready to palliate the aggressions of the
> negro-thieves, and the States and parties by which they are sustained;
> if they are prompt to exaggerate and denounce the measures of neces-
> sary self-defence that an injured and exasperated community may be
> compelled to take in providing new guards for their future security;
> and, especially, if they denounce by opprobrious epithet those whose
> only alleged offense is too great devotion to the constitutional rights
> of the South, – you neither need, nor can get, better evidence of their
> complicity with our enemies.

Thus anyone who found the proposed actions to be taken against the
"abolitionists" of Kansas excessive should himself fall under suspicion.[109]

One of the slaveholding counties of Missouri was Platte county, home
of David Rice Atchison himself. A pamphlet entitled *Negro Slavery, No
Evil*, which was a report written for the benefit of the revealingly named
Platte County Self-Defensive Association, painted a still more vivid picture
of the plight of Missouri slaveholders. Again the fear was of Kansas being
"abolitionised" and again the danger was that this would stimulate the
enemies of slavery within Missouri to greater and bolder acts. "Situated on
the border of Kansas," the Report explained, "we were the first to receive
the attack." As a consequence "those among us, who had hitherto been
restrained by fear, emboldened by the prospect of such efficient aid, begun
[sic] openly to avow their sentiments; the timid became free soilers; the
bold, abolitionists." Who were these traitors? The Report cited "among
our traders and merchants... those who at heart were against us" and
"others who loved money so much more than their country" that "they
would, for the gain from the abolition trade, encourage them to come
among us." In addition there was "a large number of free negroes, most
of them, as usual, of bad character; their houses, the natural places of
resort for abolitionists; at which to meet and tamper with slaves, corrupt
them, entice them to run away, and furnish them facilities for escape."[110]

The most obvious danger, according to the Report, was of slaves escap-
ing. Since the laws of Missouri were not sufficient to prevent this, it followed that all good citizens had to be active and vigilant. But the Report
also explained that much more was involved than the loss of property:

> The security of our slave property was not alone involved; our very
> lives were endangered. The negro-thief, the abolitionist, who induces
> a slave to run away, is a criminal of a far more dangerous character

109. [Shannon], *Address Delivered Before Pro-Slavery Convention*, p. 27.
110. *Negro Slavery, No Evil: or the North and the South: A Report Made to the Platte
County Self-Defensive Association* (St Louis, 1854), pp. 4–7.

than the house-breaker, or the highway-robber, – his crime of a far higher grade than that of the incendiary, – it ranks, at least, with that of the midnight assassin. To induce a slave to escape, involves not merely to the master the loss of that slave, of that amount of property; but it brings in its train far more serious consequences. Other slaves are thereby induced to make like attempts; a hatred for their masters, whom they begin to regard as their oppressors, is thus begotten; and this, too, often is followed by arson and murder.

Hence the need for action: "to guard as far as possible against such fearful evils, was the immediate cause of our organization."[111]

The Report then insisted that such niceties as due process and the rule of law could and should be disregarded in these circumstances. The problem was that no suitable laws existed to prevent the dangerous talk of which the Association complained. "In a slaveholding community," it was said, "the expression of such sentiments is a positive act more criminal, more dangerous, than kindling the torch of the incendiary, mixing the poison of the assassin." Once again the right of self-defence was invoked and a comparison made with bloodthirsty Indians. The New Englanders sent by the Emigrant Aid societies were "to us as would be a band of Blackfeet or Camanches who should encamp upon our borders for the avowed purpose of stealing our cattle and horses, of plundering our farms and villages." The analogy was clearly intended to justify acts of violence against the free-soilers: for "we would be justified in marching to their camp and driving them back to their dens, without waiting for the attack." Indeed "we are not bound to wait until they have 'stolen our negroes,' 'burned our slaveholding towns'." The basic and inescapable fact was that "robbers and murderers have no right to call upon the law for protection"

The Report avowed that the ultimate goal should be to expel from Kansas and Missouri all free blacks and all antislavery whites. The stakes were indeed high because if Missouri were lost then she would herself be wheeled into line to attack the states south of her. Thus "Missouri vanquished, Arkansas and Tennessee are looked upon as easy victims." Finally with little territory available for the millions of slaves in the nation, the events of Santo Domingo would be re-enacted.

Such were the dangers feared by Missourians. In these circumstances, it seemed extraordinary that their actions, motivated entirely by self-defense, should elicit criticism from northerners. One writer expressed a genuine astonishment:

> And in view of these facts, anti-slavery people . . . expect the people
> of Missouri in particular, and slave States in general, to sit quietly

---

111. Material in this and the following paragraphs is from *Negro Slavery, No Evil*, pp. 4–8.

and permit such things to be done – aye, affect to think Missourians unnecessarily sensitive, and opprobriously denounce them as
mobocrats and lawless savages, because they oppose force to force
in a case involving not simply their peace but their safety, their social
existence indeed.

From this perspective the actions of the Missourians in Kansas were
entirely appropriate.[112]

It is important to note that these perceptions were not, as might be
assumed, merely those of a fringe group of wild frontiersmen. The actual
leader of the "border ruffians" was, as we have seen, former U.S. Senator
David Rice Atchison;[113] equally prominent in the movement were Benjamin F, Stringfellow, a former attorney general of Missouri, and William
B. Napton who was a Justice of the Missouri Supreme Court. Moreover,
defences were also made in Congress of the actions of the Missourians.
Thus Virginia Senator James Mason also placed the responsibility for all
the outrages that had taken place in Kansas firmly on the shoulders of the
Emigrant Aid societies and blamed the Republicans for having encouraged these "abolitionists" to enter the territory in the first place. Similarly Albert Gallatin Brown of Mississippi attributed the problems of the
territory to the character of the northerners who had moved there. These
were men who had gone "not with the artisan's tools or the implements of
husbandry in their hands, but with rifles, bowie knives, and other deadly
weapons" and their purpose had been "to fan the flames of discord."
Hence "they went for mischief, and they got it; they sowed the whirl-
wind and reaped the storm." Brown also argued that the Republicans
in the Senate and in the northern states bore the ultimate responsibility
since they had organised, or at least promoted, the Emigrant Aid societies.
Thus the so-called Border Ruffianism was merely a response by Missourians to a fear of Kansas and then Missouri becoming "abolitionised." On
these grounds, Brown argued that the Proslavery party were not the true
culprits in Kansas: "on the broad principle . . . that he who commits the
first fraud cannot afterwards be allowed, in a court of equity, to complain
that his adversary has committed frauds," Brown concluded, "I claim a
judgment in this case."[114]

Unprecedented though the sequence of events in Kansas was, it should
be noted that the treatment recommended by the Missourians for those

---

112. Peter G. Camden, *A Common-Sense, Matter-of-Fact Examination and Discussion of
     Negro Slavery in the United States* (St Louis, 1855), p. 14.
113. Atchison himself argued that a horse thief should merit a fair trial but an abolitionist
     should not – Atchison to Jefferson Davis, Sept. 24, 1854, in Crist *et al.* (eds.), *Papers
     of Davis*, V, p. 84.
114. *CG*, 35/1, App., p. 78; *Speeches, Messages, . . . of . . . Albert Gallatin Brown*, pp. 497–
     498, 545.

avowing antislavery sentiments, or even for those suspected of holding them, was entirely in accordance with practice in other slaveholding states. The slaveholders of South Carolina, for example, prided themselves on their cultivation and refinement, fostered within a community radically different from anything that could be found on the frontier. But their attitude towards abolitionists, or suspected abolitionists, was very similar. As we shall see, throughout the South extralegal actions were recommended to combat the abolitionist threat and they were seen as entirely legitimate, fully justified by reference to the fundamental and unchallengeable right of self-defence.[115]

In this way therefore, slavery's weakness had resulted in recourse to extralegal activities, the abandonment of due process and the repudiation of civil liberties. The northern response to these departures from standard American, or at any rate northern, practice did much to ruin the expectations that southerners had had of the Kansas-Nebraska Act. But there was a second process by which the weaknesses of slavery fatally undermined southern aspirations for Kansas. Why had the proslavery forces needed the "Border Ruffians" at all? The reason was, of course, that slaveholders had shown insufficient interest in migrating to Kansas. At the height of the unrest it was estimated that there were no more than two hundred slaves in the entire territory. Why did slaveholders shun Kansas? To understand this it is only necessary to compare Kansas with Texas or Arkansas, both of which had considerable amounts of land still uncultivated in the mid-1850s. Ironically the very reasons men like Atchison wanted a slave state out of Kansas explain why he failed to get it. Even if slavery could operate profitably in Kansas, why should anyone expect it to be any more secure than in Missouri? The domino effect, much feared by the Missourians, might have led them to a different conclusion. Might slavery not be even weaker in Kansas than in Missouri and thus become the first domino with Missouri the second? If so the result would be greater not less insecurity for Missouri slaveholders. Moreover the unrest itself in the state put slaveholders off. Again the comparison with Texas or Arkansas is instructive. Not only did experience suggest that these states were far more suitable for slavery than Kansas; there was far less political opposition to slavery there. Not surprisingly therefore, the slaveholders of the South stayed away from Kansas.[116]

A comparison with the free-labour forces in Kansas is instructive. Whether they expected to work independently or for wages they faced no threat comparable to the loss of their slaves, whether by flight or insurrection, feared by the slaveholders. Such difficulties simply did not

115. See pp. 93–96.
116. Freehling, *Road to Disunion: Secessionists Triumphant*, pp. 124–128.

exist in the northern free labour economy of the 1850s. And climate did not constrain the northern settlers as it did the slaveholders. For this reason it was always probable that in the race to settle the plains of Kansas, they would be the winners.

## III

The Kansas saga is replete with ironies. If the Kansas-Nebraska Act had been ultimately a response to the weaknesses of slavery, the failure of the hopes it stimulated was attributable to the same cause. Kansas proved a disaster for all southern militants who hoped to make the Union safe for slavery. The contrasting (but not contradictory) hopes that had made different southerners support the Kansas-Nebraska Act in 1854 were wrecked beyond repair. Another free state was created, Missouri became still more exposed, prospects for the expansion of slavery were utterly blighted and were now dimmer than at any time in the history of the Republic and a new party had emerged to control the North with views on the Constitution that posed the direst threat to slavery in the South. Although they did not (and could not) perceive it in these terms, southerners had sought an escape from the weaknesses of slavery but were beginning to learn that there was indeed, within the Union at least, no escape. In this remarkable and ironic way, the weaknesses of the slave regime, with slave resistance at their core, thus destroyed the very hopes and aspirations to which they had given birth.

## The weaknesses of slavery (1): Free blacks

### I

In 1850 there were in the South as a whole fewer than a quarter of a million free blacks. They were not spread evenly within the region. No fewer than a third of them were in the single state of Maryland, which actually had more free blacks than all the states of the Deep South combined. Moreover, the free black population of Maryland, estimated in 1850 at 74,000 was not far short of the state's slave population (90,000); over the next ten years the gap would almost disappear. Across the South as a whole the problems posed by free blacks were always recognised and they did much to spur interest in the decades-old project of colonisation (by which free blacks would be sent to Africa or, as was later mooted, Latin America) but only in Maryland, and to a lesser degree Virginia, (which had 54,000) did they present a political issue of the first magnitude.[117]

117.  There is an excellent discussion of free blacks in Maryland in Barbara J. Fields, *Slavery and Freedom on the Middle Ground: Maryland During the Nineteenth Century* (New

Throughout the South free blacks consorted with slaves, often worked side by side with them and, not infrequently, intermarried with them. They tended to live in cities; a third of Maryland's free blacks, for example, were in the city of Baltimore where they carried out a variety of tasks. Some were barbers, skilled mechanics and petty tradesmen but most were poorly paid domestic servants or unskilled labourers. And in Maryland their labour filled a gap. Indeed many thousands of them had been freed not simply out of humanitarian sentiment (sometimes by masters who were in fact their fathers!) but precisely because there was a need for the labour they could supply as free men and women. In the northern part of the state, where slavery had reached an advanced stage of disintegration and decay they worked as agricultural labourers engaged in the production of wheat. Wheat needed much labour at harvest time, relatively little in other seasons. For this reason and others it was unsuited to slave labour. The result was to make free blacks in this sense a highly desirable class – of permanent exploitees.[118]

In Maryland the relative decline of slavery owed much to the decline of tobacco production in the state. From a dominant position in the colonial economy tobacco accounted for a mere fourteen percent of total agricultural production by the time of the Civil War. As free blacks increased in number and as the sectional controversy in the nation as a whole intensified, they provoked ever-deeper suspicion and resentment. In 1856 and 1857, there were fears of slave insurrections in Maryland as elsewhere but in Maryland as in no other state the status of free blacks became the pre-eminent political question of the day.

Slaveholders throughout the South had long resented free blacks. In 1846 Governor William Smith of Virginia denounced the free black man as "essentially and hopelessly degraded," a man who "corrupts the slave with whom he habitually associates, and becomes the ready instrument of the unprincipled white man, and too frequently his shield." Here the Governor hinted at the two objections habitually levelled against free blacks. The first was that they set an example of idleness. Their freedom, according to Edmund Ruffin of Virginia, "serves to cause discontent to

Haven, 1985), pp. 63–89, and the analysis presented here is greatly indebted to it. See also Freehling, *Reintegration*, p. 19 and especially Freehling, *Road to Disunion: Secessionists Triumphant*, pp. 185–201 which offers conclusions very similar to those advanced here. In the tiny state of Delaware, it should be noted, the proportion of free blacks was by 1860 so high that the state was only nominally slave. In fact the proportion was so high, and the number of slaves so low that re-enslavement or expulsion of free blacks, in order to safeguard slavery, would probably have been an absurdity.

118. For an alternative view of the relationship between slavery and wheat farming, see Gavin Wright, *Slavery and American Economic Development* (Baton Rouge, 2006) pp. 71–90, 116. On free blacks, see Ira Berlin, *Slaves Without Master: The Free Negro in the Antebellum South* (New York, 1974); Leon Litwack, *North of Slavery: The Negro in the Free States* (Chicago, 1961).

the slaves." As a good proslavery ideologue Ruffin insisted that although free blacks were actually worse off than slaves, the slaves did not always appreciate this fact since "it is the general characteristic of the negro race to prefer idleness to labor." The free black was thus a threat to slave productivity.[119]

Far more important than this, however, was the encouragement free blacks gave, or were thought to give, to the forces of abolition. Conditions faced by free blacks in the South had almost certainly deteriorated from the early 1830s onwards partly on account of Nat Turner's rebellion and this confirms that, in the minds of many southerners, free blacks and slave insurrections were closely linked. In the words of the New Orleans *Picayune*, free blacks were "a plague and pest in the community" because they brought "the elements of mischief to the slave population." Accordingly, as the sectional conflict intensified, southern militants urged that action be taken. In 1849 Governor Whitemarsh Seabrook of South Carolina recommended that all free blacks who did not own real estate should be removed on the grounds that they were "spies in our camp" who "disseminate through the entire body of our slave population the poison of insubordination, prepared in the great laboratory of northern fanaticism." Ruffin in his pamphlet outlining the *Two Great Evils of Virginia* went still further. The two evils, he held, were free blacks and abolitionists but he claimed it was possible to be rid of both simultaneously. Expelling free blacks would automatically eliminate the threat from abolitionists. The reason was that "the negro slave, if not seeing other Negroes free, would scarcely think of his servitude as a hardship." But "with this example of exemption from labour always before his eyes, he is taught to desire also to be free, and to be discontented and unhappy because he is a slave." In the same way "Python," author of a series of highly influential articles in *De Bow's Review* on the eve of the Civil War, referred to the free blacks of the border states as "as a fruitful source of future insurrectionary trouble." A resolution passed by a proslavery group in Maryland put it even more succinctly: "free negroism and slavery are incompatible."[120]

Southerners were thus able to discern a link between free blacks and abolition. As usual, however, they misperceived it. Although the presence of free blacks may well have deepened the discontent of slaves (by confirming the African American's fitness for freedom), it was in no sense

119. *Journal of the Senate of the Commonwealth of Virginia . . . 6 Dec., 1847* (Richmond, 1846), p. 17; Edmund Ruffin, *Two Great Evils of Virginia, and Their One Common Remedy* (n.p., n.d.), p. 7.
120. New Orleans *Picayune*, March 8, 1856; *Journal of the Senate of the State of South Carolina At Its Annual Session Commencing Nov. 26, 1849* (Columbus, 1849), p. 24; Ruffin, *Two Great Evils*, p. 7; *De Bow's Review*, XXVIII (1860), p. 255; Clement Eaton, *The Growth of Southern Civilization* (New York, 1961), pp. 93–94; Fields, *Slavery and Freedom*, p. 69.

the cause; slaves did not need the spectacle of free blacks to resent enslavement. But to this the slaveholders were blind and the free black man thus took his place alongside the abolitionist as a scapegoat for the weaknesses of the regime.

By the southern militants' logic the obvious solution was to remove free blacks and their pernicious influence from the states of the South. Accordingly in the 1850s many states considered laws that were designed to accomplish precisely this. The legislatures of Louisiana, Alabama, Mississippi, Georgia, and Tennessee each at various points in the decade debated measures that sought to impose the most stringent penalties upon free blacks, including re-enslavement and removal from the state. Most of these proposals either foundered on the opposition of one of the legislative branches, or succumbed to an executive veto; in some cases they raised a storm of protest, for reasons we shall presently consider. In 1859, however, Arkansas succeeded in passing a law which ordered the expulsion of all her free blacks. Here, perhaps, was a cue for other states to act.[121]

Many of them indeed gave this policy serious consideration. But it was one thing for Arkansas to contemplate the removal of a free black population numbering well under a thousand, quite another to implement the same policy in Maryland or Virginia. The attempt was nevertheless made. In Maryland as in other southern states the Brown raid of 1859 led to renewed fears of slave rebellions and renewed hostility to free blacks. In the state legislature Curtis W. Jacobs, a militantly proslavery Democrat, led the movement to expel the free blacks. He had long believed that they should be either expelled or re-enslaved and the panic that followed the Brown raid saw him precipitated into a position of considerable influence. His Committee on Colored Population now proposed to eliminate the free blacks as a class by requiring them, under threat of re-enslavement, to leave the state or to be required to work under contract and under white supervision for periods of ten years or more (with their children to be re-enslaved). These proposals were too much even for the state legislators, who toned them down, and far too much for the voters of Maryland, who summarily rejected them.[122]

Why did they fail? In most of the southern states the movement to expel free blacks encountered insuperable obstacles. In Maryland their labour was simply too valuable to be dispensed with; it was even required by slaveholders in the middle and southern parts of the state. "Who, it was asked, "is to supply the places of the free colored women who are hired

---

121. Sinha, *Counterrevolution of Slavery*, pp. 214–215; Paul D. Escott, *Many Excellent People: Power and Privilege in North Carolina 1850–1900* (Chapel Hill, 1985), p. 11. Allan Nevins, *The Emergence of Lincoln: Prologue to Civil War, 1859–1861* (New York, 1950), pp. 152–156; Eugene D. Genovese, *Roll, Jordan, Roll: The World the Slaves Made* (New York, 1972), pp. 398–413.
122. Fields, *Slavery and Freedom*, pp. 63–89.

by the week, month, or year as cooks or house servants, in thousands of families throughout the state?" Other Marylanders objected on humanitarian grounds. But it was the problems of agriculture in the northern part of the state that were most intractable. If free blacks were not available to work on the wheat crop, who would take their place? There were not enough slaves in the state and even if there had been, experience had shown that slave labour was not well suited to wheat. This left only one possible alternative: a white agricultural workforce. But this prospect, even if it could be realised, was even more alarming than the employment of free blacks. As one journal noted, the danger would then arise of "a class of free white labor that would be hostile to slavery, would be entitled to vote, and might finally dictate terms to slavery itself." How important was this fear of a white agricultural proletariat? According to one historian it was "the most widely stated grounds for opposition to Jacobs's proposals."[123]

In Virginia the Arkansas enactment was also subjected to careful scrutiny. As we have seen, Edmund Ruffin found much to applaud in it. But even he felt compelled to admit that "free negroes, with all their defects, are useful in the towns as labourers and servants – or more so than their substitutes whether hireling country slaves, or white foreigners." In Staunton Virginia the *Vindicator*, a Democratic newspaper, published in February 1860 an article entitled "What Should be the Policy of the South towards Free Negroes?" Here humanitarian sentiment surfaced, but in a muted form. Moreover, the writer found it difficult to reconcile his defence of local free blacks with his own racist assumptions. But he denounced the proposed law as "hostile to every feeling of kindness and philanthropy" on the grounds that it condemned the "industrious and law-abiding" as much as the "indolent and vicious."[124]

The writer nevertheless felt impelled to reaffirm his racist credentials. He reassured his readers that he had "no more sympathy than any other philanthropist for that unfortunate class of beings, whom God in his Providence has made black, and whom man in his improvidence has made free." Yet "if the majority of them are degenerated, degraded creatures, without the least knowledge of virtue or the least awakening of morality," there were nonetheless "some who deserve the approbation and encouragement of every friend of civilization." Indeed some of these free blacks, he claimed, were "far better in their personal character and mode of life than the majority of the lower white class." At this point his readers might have wondered how such persons, despite being "degenerate in color and in mind," had "by their industry and morality, rendered themselves worthy of the society in which they moved." How had they "by their

123. Fields, *Slavery and Freedom*, p. 88.
124. Ruffin, *Two Great Evils*, p. 16; Staunton *Vindicator*, Feb. 3, 1860.

industrious and upright life...amassed considerable money, and...
gained the applause of every good and honest man"? The answer was
a curious one: the very fact that they had not been in competition with
whites had been their means of salvation. Thus "to make such persons
exiles from their native State, would be like driving them into a city of the
plague or a den of robbers." In such circumstances "they would be morally
as well as pecuniarily ruined." For "the state of inferiority in which they
are held by our better citizens, and the honorable and honest manner in
which they are dealt with, is the secret of their success amongst us." If
instead they were to be sent "to a free State," they would then "have no
such bulwark to protect them." In other words racial discrimination in
the South was very much in the interests of her free blacks. It had allowed
some of them to thrive and those free blacks should not be penalised for
their success. Here was a most unexpected and ironic conclusion.[125]

## II

The growing numbers of free blacks in a state like Maryland was in part
a testimony to the humanitarian sentiment of those who had freed them
(or their ancestors). To a greater degree, however, it reflected the fact that
a slave labour system could not accommodate the agricultural realities of
northern Maryland, the most advanced rural area of the state, any more
than it could encompass the commercial realities of Baltimore, its leading
urban centre. The weaknesses of the labour system thus generated the
initial problem.[126]

Free blacks gave the slaveholders a dilemma. Since it was a cardinal
tenet of the proslavery ideology that blacks fared better in slavery than
in freedom, and indeed that blacks were congenitally incapable of coping
with the burdens of liberty, a large number of free blacks, hardly any of
whom ever sought re-enslavement, furnished a living challenge to the slave

---

125. The writer then advocated a more humane approach: "One of the best remedies seems
to be this: Let a law be passed to the effect, viz.: That every free negro must depart
the State before a certain time, or bring to the County Court of the county, in which
he or she resides, a certificate signed by at least six responsible men, of his or her
neighbourhood, certifying to his or her good moral character and industrious habits.
Let this certificate be placed upon record and renewed regularly within a certain given
time; and, if this does not remove an evil of which many complain – if this does not
purge our society of the dross of this species, while the purer metal remains, then I
say take the severer remedy used by our sister State." In a final flourish, and to drive
home the point about the worthiness of the free blacks, he pointed to the admirable
conduct of those among them who had, in the wake of the Brown raid, offered to help
the authorities either as soldiers and then, when this offer was declined, as servants
of soldiers – Staunton *Vindicator*, Feb. 3, 1860.
126. William W. Freehling points out that some opponents of the repressive legislation also
argued that it was only the prospects of freedom that made some border slaves work
at all – Freehling, *Road to Disunion: Secessionists at Bay*, pp. 79–82, *Secessionists
Triumphant*, pp. 98, 193.

regime. Because of their association with both slaves and nonslaveholding whites of dubious character, they were thought to embody a real threat even to the survival of the regime – hence the draconian proposals to remove or re-enslave them.

The need to resort to such extreme measures was a second indication of the weaknesses of the regime. In effect, the battle to expel free blacks pitted those for whom the political threat they posed, especially to slaveholders, outweighed the commercial benefit their labour conferred, even upon slaveholders. Whichever side had won, it would have illustrated the weaknesses of slavery in Maryland. Ultimately the commercial incentives proved the stronger and free blacks were allowed to remain in the state – though subject to increasingly stringent restrictions. Hence they continued to pose a set of problems to which the slaveholders had no real solution. The reason for this failure was simple: in Maryland, Virginia, and indeed wherever free blacks existed and worked in significant numbers, there was, in the 1850s, no solution.

### The weaknesses of slavery (2): Nonslaveholding whites

#### I

In all but two or three of the states of the South free blacks were too few in number to pose a major problem for the slaveholding elite. Very different, however, was the position of the nonslaveholding whites. In 1850 only one southern family in three owned slaves; ten years later it was one in four. While the number of those with an indirect stake in the institution was obviously much higher, the potential danger was nonetheless clear for all to see. And not only did nonslaveholding whites hugely outnumber free blacks, the great majority of the adult males had the vote.

Historians have often wondered why the nonslaveholders of the South acquiesced in a social system which conferred such huge benefits upon those who owned slaves but which was less obviously beneficial to those who did not. Although attempts have been made to demonstrate that slaveholders adopted a paternalistic stance towards their nonslaveholding white neighbours, it is doubtful whether this can provide anything like a full explanation.[127] Instead we need to remind ourselves of the ideological context in which American democracy functioned. By the final decades of

---

127. Equally unpersuasive is the much heralded attempt to argue that gender issues were vital here. The claim that white males united in order to defend their gender-based privileges founders on the fact that there was little or no threat to those privileges, and southerners rarely suggested otherwise – see Stephanie McCurry, *Masters of Small Worlds: Yeoman Households, Gender Relations and the Political Culture of the Antebellum Lowcountry* (New York, 1995).

the antebellum years, the era in which slavery entered its most dramatic period of expansion and enjoyed its greatest successes, there were two political traditions to which southerners, like northerners, were heir. Neither was significantly antislavery, indeed each implied an accommodation with slaveholding and an acquiescence in the rule of slaveholders.

This was obviously true of the Federalist-Whig tradition, in which the property of the slaveholder was essentially placed alongside that of the farmer, the merchant, and the manufacturer, the interdependence between them stressed and the legitimacy of the southern elite thus confirmed. Classic Whiggery, as expounded by Henry Clay and Daniel Webster, did not invite assaults upon propertied interests and southern Whiggery did not, therefore, invite assaults upon the property of the slaveholder.[128]

The situation of the Democratic party was more complex. The Democratic tradition, the tradition of Thomas Jefferson, John Taylor of Caroline and Andrew Jackson, did indeed allow for an attack upon the nation's social elites and one might have thought that the slaveholders of the South would have presented an obvious target. Yet it is a primary contention of this work that Democratic ideology tended to undercut antislavery at every point. Thus its insistence that moral issues (such as antislavery) should not be introduced into politics, its attachment to limited government and state's rights, and its racism – all of this tended to blind Democrats to the evils of slavery. Indeed one may push this analysis further and argue that it was precisely because Democratic egalitarianism was not directed against slaveholders that the Democratic party was able to command such strength in the South and thus in the nation as a whole. American democracy was born with an umbilical link to southern slavery.[129]

The economics of the slave system reinforced these tendencies. Slavery was irreducibly commercial, in that slaveholders produced for distant, indeed transatlantic, markets. But it left large parts of the South, particularly the upcountry areas where the nonslaveholders predominated, with only limited participation in the market economy. This could be a strength in that it allowed slaveholders to leave these regions of the South alone; fully occupied exploiting black labour, they scarcely needed to concern themselves with that of the whites. And by the tenets of the Democratic faith, the nonslaveholding whites in these regions, left to enjoy the fruits of their labour, were indeed both "free" and "equal."[130]

Yet this did not guarantee that the slaveholders would remain in control forever. From a different perspective, the very lack of economic

128. See Volume I of this study, pp. 350–358.
129. This is one of the main themes of the first volume of this work. See also Chapter 3 of this volume.
130. Steven Hahn, *The Roots of Southern Populism: Yeoman Farmers and the Transformation of the Georgia Upcountry, 1850–1890* (New York, 1983), p. 84.

development in some parts of the South, if slavery and slaveholders could be blamed for it, could itself be construed as a form of exploitation or at any rate of oppression when contrasted with the progress of the rural North, for example. The danger was that northerners – or indeed southerners – might launch an appeal to the nonslaveholders of the South on precisely these grounds.

## II

Notwithstanding this danger or perhaps because of it, many southerners vigorously denied that the nonslaveholders, apart from a handful of individuals, were in any way disloyal to slavery. Thus Albert Gallatin Brown in a public letter that attracted great attention when it appeared in 1860 acknowledged that "a few" nonslaveholders might be disloyal but nevertheless insisted that the great mass of whites, whether they owned slaves or not, had ample reason for preserving the institution. He claimed, quite plausibly, that the general level of prosperity in the southern states depended upon the financial value attached to slaves and also contended that if abolition were attempted or carried out, the rich would be insulated from its effects to a far greater degree than the poor, who would then be reduced to an equality with the newly freed blacks. Brown thus played the race card and, like many proslavery ideologues, suggested that slavery united all whites by preserving an equality of esteem which would be the first casualty of a successful antislavery movement.[131]

Defenders of slavery frequently asserted that all southerners had a stake in the institution. Emancipation, it was claimed, would create millions of men (and women) who were entirely unsuited for inclusion in American democracy and in American society. On some occasions it was, of course, their potential for violence, the possibility that the scenes of Santo Domingo would be re-enacted in the South, that was stressed. Beyond this, however, blacks were assumed to be congenitally lazy. As Ruffin put it, "it is the general characteristic of the negro race to prefer idleness to labor." Southern whites were thus invited to close ranks in order to ensure that the southern economy should not be blighted by the presence of several million freed men and women, all determined to exert themselves as little as possible. It is a measure of the success of this stratagem that even those southerners who wished to rid their region of slaves almost invariably wished to rid it of freed ex-slaves too.[132]

131. Albert Gallatin Brown, *Letter of Hon. Albert Gallatin Brown, On the Interest of Non-Slaveholders in the South in the Perpetuation of African Slavery* (n.p., 1860).

132. Ruffin, *Two Great Evils*, pp. 2–7. For other examples of southerners castigating blacks for idleness, see Albert T. Bledsoe, *An Essay on Liberty and Slavery* (Philadelphia, 1856), p. 266 and John Townsend, *The Death of Slavery in the Union: Its Safety Out of It* (Charleston, SC, n.d.), pp. 19–22.

In stressing the common interest of all whites in resisting emancipation, this strategy clearly operated to diminish the class antagonisms within the white community, especially in the more heavily enslaved lowcountry areas of the South. Racism in this sense weakened class consciousness. However, it is important to note that these racist sentiments themselves were the product of class conflict, in this case that between master and slave. Historians now know that slaves had a powerful incentive to appear unmotivated and "lazy," in order to diminish the expectations, and thus the demands, of their masters. Although the image of the lazy slave may well have operated to unite the white community, it was itself the product of a deeper social antagonism.[133]

Oblivious to all of this, southern militants continued to stress that the nonslaveholders had an identity of interest with the slaveholder. Felix Huston told the Nashville Convention of 1850 that those who owned no slaves were fully aware that abolition would degrade them to the same level as the blacks, and ten years later prominent southern writers, politicians and propagandists were saying the same.[134] In some of the intervening years *De Bow's Review* had been calling for the encouragement of greater levels of immigration into the South and, since some southerners had traditionally questioned the loyalty of immigrants, this was in effect another display of confidence in the white nonslaveholder.[135]

De Bow himself in 1860 wrote an extremely interesting pamphlet entitled *The Interest in Slavery of the Non-Slaveholder.* Here he argued that the number of southerners who were directly or indirectly interested in slavery numbered at least two million and concluded that "of no other property can it be said, with equal truthfulness, that it is an interest of the whole community." He also argued that wages were high in the South, that most southerners who did not yet own slaves had enviable opportunities to acquire them in the future and that they, rather than the slaveholders, would suffer most from abolition. De Bow dwelt too on the alleged equality that bound the white race together and ending by apologising for even having stooped to rebut the northern claim that the nonslaveholders might be disloyal.[136]

Even here, however, De Bow acknowledged that in some counties of Maryland, Missouri and Kentucky there were pockets of antislavery

---

133. This should remind us, once again, that class should not be reduced to class consciousness and that one cannot simply assess its importance, relative to race, by determining whether southern whites were more aware of race than class.

134. *Address of Huston,* pp. 7–8; Kentucky *Statesman,* Oct. 5, 1860, in Dumond (ed.), *Southern Editorials on Secession,* p. 175. See also A. O. P. Nicholson of Tennessee in the U.S. Senate – CG, 36/1, p. 624; Lawrence Shore, *Southern Capitalists: The Ideological Leadership of an Elite* (Chapel Hill, 1986), pp. 69–70.

135. *De Bow's Review,* XI (1851), p. 319, XVII (1854), p. 182, XX (1856), pp. 56–57.

136. [J. G. B. De Bow], *The Interest in Slavery of the Non-Slaveholder* (Charleson, 1860), pp. 4, 6–12.

sentiment. But what makes his pamphlet unusually significant is the fact that he almost certainly concealed some of his private thoughts on this subject, for by now De Bow had become an enthusiastic advocate of the African slave trade. As we have seen, the main concern of the slave trade devotees was to lower the price of slaves in order to make it easier for the nonslaveholder to purchase them. Reopening was intended, above all, to allow a higher proportion of southern whites to become slaveholders. It was intended, therefore, to address the disloyalty, either actual or potential, of the nonslaveholders.[137]

Yet the fear of the nonslaveholder extended far beyond the ranks of the slave trade campaigners. Thus Robert Harper of Georgia, in a tract which explicitly opposed reopening, sounded a familiar warning against the use of slaves in other than agricultural activities. The result of this practice, he warned, was to convert many of the whites forced to compete with slaves into enemies of slavery itself. Harper in fact claimed that this competition had "hitherto" been no less than "the secret spring by which abolition movements have been originated and propelled." Here were animosities "at once the most easily brought into action and the most difficult to allay." According to Harper competition between whites and slaves was disastrous: "it is this sensitive chord which has been touched by impious and designing hands, in such slave states as Delaware and Maryland, Kentucky, and Missouri, and the result has been, to force upon society there that unholy strife which should have been kept forever between the distant sections." "Upon this train of thought," he concluded, "much might be said – but there are some points on which it is perhaps wiser to reflect than to write."[138]

By the mid 1850s De Bow in his *Review* had reversed a previous opinion and was arguing strongly that the South should discourage immigrant white labour. Again the danger was that such immigrants might bring with them a European hostility to slavery. In a letter to William Yancey, De Bow in 1859 asserted that the South did not want immigrant labour. (He added, quite correctly, that even if this were not true, immigrant white labour did not want the South.) Similarly his *Review* printed the records of the Southern Commercial Conventions, now increasingly absorbed by the controversy over the African slave trade. One delegate to the Savannah Convention fretted about the Upper South's loss of slaves. The danger, he warned, was that these slaves would be replaced by immigrant free labour and that free soilism would then triumph.[139]

---

137. Shore, *Southern Capitalists*, pp. 75–76; Ashworth, *Slavery, Capitalism and Politics*, I, pp. 267–279.

138. Robert G. Harper, *An Argument Against the Policy of Re-Opening the African Slave Trade* (Atlanta, GA, 1858), pp. 71–72.

139. *De Bow's Review*, XXVII (1859), pp. 232–233, XXII (1857), pp. 216–224, esp. pp. 216–218. See also XXIX (1860), pp. 70–72.

Nor were these the only fears voiced. The southern city remained an object of suspicion. "Every city," one militant warned, "is destined to be the seat of free-soilism." Similarly Edmund Ruffin of Virginia in 1857 singled out the cities of the South as the areas where antislavery sentiment was already most developed and most to be feared, for here were to be found "traders, mechanics and laborers, or sailors." The cities were suspect partly because they received a steady influx of European immigrants but also because of the numbers of northerners to be found there. In 1850 the *Mississippian* drew attention to the pernicious influence of Yankee merchants in New Orleans and referred to the "free-soilism in that city" and ten years later *De Bow's Review* agreed that "the settlement of Northerners among us is fraught with danger."[140]

By the early 1850s many southerners believed that significant numbers of spies were in their midst. Iveson Brookes of North Carolina declared that "the abolitionists of Texas and the North have their spies and agents engaged in personal presence and in secret action in our midst." "Is it not time," he asked, "for the South, everywhere to have her faithful sentinels in post, and to watch with jealous suspicion the movements of Northerners and foreigners amongst us, whose feelings, interests and prejudices being dissimilar to ours unfit them to approve the genius of our institutions?"[141] In 1857 Edmund Ruffin warned that there were many abolitionists secretly working in the South, while Charleston, South Carolina was by now one of many cities where vigilance associations routinely interrogated all northerners to ensure that they were sound on the slavery question.[142]

It was now widely held that there were abolition "emissaries" in the South who were "scattered abroad throughout the length and breadth of our land, who permeate the whole of Southern Society, who occupy our places of trust and emolument." These fears had been present since at least the 1830s but in the final years of the antebellum South they reached a crescendo. By 1856 to claim that Congress had power over slavery in the territories was to court condemnation as an "incendiary." Vigilance committees, which had been established in many communities in the wake of Nat Turner's rebellion and the almost simultaneous emergence of the demand for immediate abolition, became active as never before. Hotels and taverns were routinely inspected, baggage was checked, and itinerants who were found merely talking with slaves risked being lynched.

---

140. *Southern Quarterly Review*, X (1854), p. 453; Ruffin in *De Bow's Review*, XXIII (1857), p. 547. *Mississippian*, June 14, 1850; *De Bow's Review*, XXVIII (1860), p. 1.
141. [Iveson L. Brooks], *A Defence of Southern Slavery against the Attacks of Henry Clay and Alexander Campbell . . . By a Southern Clergyman* (Harrisburg, SC, 1851), p. 28.
142. *De Bow's Review*, XXIII (1857), p. 546; Steven A. Channing, *Crisis of Fear: Secession in South Carolina* (New York, 1974), p. 34.

Many southerners by now identified the Republican party with abolition and, after 1859, abolition with the Brown raid. The presidential elections of 1856 and 1860 were thus thought to provide direct encouragement to the forces of abolition within the South and they consequently took place against a background of mounting fear in many of the southern states. Insurrections, it was felt, were being planned. Fears were rampant of an abolitionist conspiracy to burn down towns and to provide slaves with supplies of poison. The shock waves reverberated throughout the South. Such events seemed to confirm the presence of the abolition "emissaries."[143]

Although it was politically more expedient to blame either outsiders (from Europe or the North), or marginal groups (such as itinerants or propertyless urban workers), they were not the only targets. Often, as when the case for reopening the African slave trade was being made, generalisations were offered about the dangers to be apprehended from the nonslaveholding community of the South *en masse*. In the late 1850s discussions of the African slave trade were the occasion for the expression of renewed fears concerning the loyalty of the border states. According to William Lowndes Yancey there was "no denying that there is a large emancipatory interest in Virginia, and Kentucky, and Maryland and Missouri, the fruits of which we see in Henry Winter Davis, Cassius M. Clay, and Thomas H. Benton."[144]

Once again, however, the fears went beyond the ranks of the slave trade enthusiasts. In 1860 *De Bow's Review* published more articles written by "Python," who now sounded the alarm about abolitionism in the South. "Python" (son of former President John Tyler) informed his readers that he had recently toured the South and his findings must have alarmed them profoundly. Where were the exposed areas? "Python" reported that they comprised Delaware and Maryland, many of the northern and western counties of Virginia, the east and north of Kentucky, western North Carolina and east and middle Tennessee. As if this were not enough, the merchants of the cities of the Gulf Coast were unsound on the slavery question as were managers and employees of southern railroads, steamboats and hotels and many involved in journalism. Many of these, "Python" acknowledged, as yet held only "suppressed" abolitionist sentiments but they would, he had no doubt, speak out when the appropriate time came.[145]

In the same way some southerners made some highly revealing remarks in private letters. Writing to Benjamin Yancey in 1859, one clergyman

---

143.  Russell B. Nye, *Fettered Freedom: Civil Liberties and the Slavery Controversy 1830–60* (Urbana, 1972); Barney, *Secessionist Impulse*, pp. 168–170, 166;. *De Bow's Review*, XXIX (1860), p. 70.
144.  *De Bow's Review*, XXIV (1858), p. 587.
145.  *De Bow's Review*, XXVIII (1860), pp. 254–255.

worried about the "opposition [to slavery] among the working classes in the towns & up country." This, he felt, "must soon show itself and then who shall say where the end will be?" Similarly, in early 1860 Daniel Hamilton, a federal marshal in Charleston, South Carolina, posed a dramatic question to William Porcher Miles, the city's secessionist Congressman. "Think you," he asked, "that 360,000 Slaveholders will dictate terms for 3,000,000 of non-slaveholders at the South?" He gave his answer: "I fear not. I mistrust our own people more than I fear all of the efforts of the Abolitionists." By the end of the 1850s it was relatively common for southern spokesmen, especially those in the South Atlantic states, to voice fears of the nonslaveholding white majority in many of the states of the South.[146]

Thus behind the confidence frequently expressed about the nonslaveholders lay, in the minds of many southerners, deep forebodings. Europeans were suspect, northerners could not be trusted, cities might become centres of antislavery insurgency and border states residents were flirting with abolition. By 1860 if not before, to the southerner who was determined to protect slavery, the future looked uncertain indeed.

## III

Against this background came, in 1857, the most direct and dramatic appeal to the nonslaveholders of the South to rise up and put an end to the slave oligarchy. Hinton Helper's *Impending Crisis of the South* was a lengthy indictment of the slaveholders of the South. Helper was then an unknown North Carolinian, previously a Whig, now a Republican, who was living safely in exile from his native state. His critique of slavery in the South made the odd reference to the slaves, whom he conceded had been unjustly treated, but its primary concern was with the nonslaveholding whites whom, he believed, the slaveholders had continuously exploited and impoverished. Helper devoted many pages to a demonstration of the poor performance of the southern economy by comparison with that of the North, and his conclusion was that southern nonslaveholding whites should cease to vote for slaveholders or conduct business with them. Helper aimed at nothing less than the liquidation of the slaveholding class and to bring this about he proposed a punitive level of taxation to be levied upon every slave in the South.[147]

---

146. Reverend B. E. Habersham to Benjamin C. Yancey, June 14, 1859, Daniel Hamilton to W. P. Miles, Feb. 9 1860 quoted in Channing, *Crisis of Fear*, pp. 255–256.
147. Hinton R. Helper, *The Impending Crisis of the South: How to Meet It* (New York, 1857). The best work on Helper is probably David Christopher Brown, "The Logical Outcome of the Non-Slaveholder's Philosophy? Hinton Rowan Helper on Race and Class in the Antebellum South" (Unpublished Doctoral Dissertation, University of Hull, 2000).

Sometimes Helper hinted that violence might be necessary in the South; more often he assumed that peaceful change would be possible. At no point, however, did he address his remarks to the slaves, for whose welfare he had little concern. It was therefore apparent from his text that if there were to be violence, it was to be carried out by the nonslaveholding whites and perhaps their northern allies.

The reaction in the South was equally explosive. Both book and author were denounced. Helper, it was discovered, had been convicted of pilfering much earlier in his life and southerners made much of this. They also attacked the statistics he had compiled to demonstrate the alleged poor performance of the southern economy. But their outrage was primarily provoked by the virulence of his attacks upon them. Many Republicans, it transpired, had endorsed his book, many of them, it further transpired, without having read it. Among the latter group was John Sherman, a moderate within the party and a candidate for the Speakership when the thirty-sixth Congress convened in December 1859. But the Helper endorsement ruined his chances. The book was widely denounced as "incendiary" on the grounds that it sought to incite the nonslaveholders of the South and Sherman was accordingly adjudged unfit to be Speaker of the House. Some southerners even declared that the South should leave the Union if he were elected.

A significant feature of many of the attacks on Helper was that those who made them misunderstood his message and his purpose. Shelton F. Leake of Virginia asked whether the House was to "elect a man who, while I am here in the discharge of my public duties, is stimulating my negroes at home to apply the torch to my dwelling and the knife to the throats of my wife and my helpless children." Here Leake made two significant assumptions. The first was that Sherman endorsed the Helper strategy. This was not in fact the case, though it was quite understandable that southerners should have thought so. The second was that Helper had exhorted the slaves to use violence. For this there was, or seemed to be, no justification whatever. This was a mistake, or at least an apparent mistake, made by many southerners. Thus R. M. T. Hunter of Virginia referred to Helper's book as one which called for a servile war. For this reason, by the late 1850s, mere ownership of the book constituted treason in most states of the South. In North Carolina, for example, the Reverend Daniel Worth was arrested and tried for distributing it.[148]

148. *CG*, 36/1, p. 21; *Speech of Hon. R. M. T. Hunter, of Virginia, on Invasions of States ... delivered in the Senate of the United States, Jan 30, 1860* (Washington D.C., 1860), pp. 5–6.; Nye, *Fettered Freedom*, p. 160; Martin Crawford, *Ashe Country's Civil War: Community and Society in the Appalachian South* (Charlottesville, VA, 2001), pp. 64–65.

IV

The slaveholders' fears of those whites who did not own slaves were real and important. They derived not only from the highly publicised examples of those who overtly criticised their power, such as Helper, but also from the movements that were afoot within some of the southern states, during the late 1840s and especially the 1850s, to diminish the power of the slaveholding elite. In these years there were three major initiatives. One of these concerned "free suffrage," the demand that property qualifications for the suffrage (and in some cases for office holding) be swept away. Another was the demand that legislative seats be apportioned not on the "mixed" or federal basis, which counted slaves as three fifths of a person (and thus augmented the power of the slaveholders), but instead upon the "white basis" (by which all votes cast by whites had equal weight). The third initiative was the proposal to increase taxes on slaveholders, by taxing property in slaves according to the *ad valorem* principle rather than at a low *per capita* rate. These movements were concentrated in the states of the Atlantic seaboard.[149]

They caused considerable controversy. None of them was an attack upon slavery; indeed their proponents were often slaveholders and did not hesitate to claim that the effect of the planned reform would be to make slavery more secure, essentially by increasing the stake of nonslaveholders in the *status quo*. But slaveholders sometimes viewed them in a very different light. Thus Kenneth Rayner of North Carolina in 1860 complained bitterly that the *ad valorem* advocates had "infused among the ignorant people, the idea that there is an antagonism between poor people and Slave-owners;" they had in effect "insidiously preached" nothing less than Seward's "'irrepressible conflict.'"[150]

It is important to ask, however, how these fears related to the sectional controversy. It has been argued that they did much to produce an "internal crisis of the South" which in turn "necessitated secession." According to

149. On these movements see, for example, Paul H. Bergeron, *Antebellum Politics in Tennessee* (Lexington, 1982), p. 24; Charles Bolton, *Poor Whites of the Antebellum South: Tenants and Laborers in Central North Carolina and Northeast Mississippi* (Durham, NC, 1994), pp. 114–115, 132–134; Carey, *Parties, Slavery and the Union*, pp. 123, 133; Daniel Crofts, *Reluctant Confederates: Upper South Unionists in the Secession Crisis* (Chapel Hill, 1989), pp. 156, 193–194; Escott, *Many Excellent People*, pp. 15, 27–30; Fields, *Slavery and Freedom*, p. 21; Hahn, *Roots of Southern Populism*, p. 8; Clarence C. Norton, *The Democratic Party in Ante-Bellum North Carolina, 1833–1861* (Chapel Hill, 1930), pp. 131–135, 172–173, 199–206; Schultz, *Nationalism and Sectionalism in South Carolina*, p. 99; Chilton Williamson, *American Suffrage from Property to Democracy, 1760–1860* (Princeton, 1960), pp. 223–241.
150. Kenneth Rayner to Thomas Ruffin, Dec. 25, 1860 quoted in Norton, *Democratic Party in North Carolina*, pp. 204–205.

this view, secession was in part an attempt on the part of political elites to reverse, in the name of a "patriarchal republic," the democratic reforms that had swept the nation in the nineteenth century and the states of the South Atlantic most recently.[151]

There is some truth in this analysis. Without doubt some secessionists harboured deep contempt for the masses. They tended to be located in the states of the southeast, in Virginia, Georgia and especially South Carolina, where such antidemocratic sentiment had long flourished. Many of these secessionists favoured constitutional arrangements and legislative enactments that were deeply antidemocratic and strikingly at odds with mainstream American practice. Finally, the sectional conflict itself, which pitted a minority South against a majority North not unnaturally produced, among many southerners, a weakening of confidence in majority rule *per se* and thus in one of the cardinal tenets of the American democratic faith. It produced a parallel weakening of confidence in political parties, which had since the time of Andrew Jackson been viewed as essential channels through which popular sentiment should be conveyed.[152]

Yet in the South as a whole there is no correlation between secessionist sentiment and hostility to democratic forms. The states of the Lower Southwest, where egalitarian sentiment was strongest, were, taken as a whole, every bit as keen on secession as those of the South Atlantic, where it was weakest: if South Carolina was the state where secessionist ardour was most intense, Mississippi and Alabama were probably ranked second and third, significantly ahead of Georgia and far ahead of Virginia. At the individual level, some of those who were lukewarm towards secession, such as Alexander Stephens, retained a Whiggish fear of the people just as Kenneth Rayner of North Carolina, whose objections to *ad valorem* taxes we have already noted, was a moderate on sectional issues throughout his career. Meanwhile Albert Gallatin Brown of Mississippi, for example, was a committed secessionist but an equally committed populist. Secession was not, therefore, an attempt to overcome a pre-existing political crisis within the states of the South.[153]

As we shall see, however, it was an attempt to ensure that the nonslaveholding white majority in the South should not be "corrupted" by an incoming Republican administration. In this sense, it was an attempt to forestall a future political crisis, one brought about not by the existence of

---

151. Michael P. Johnson, *Toward a Patriarchal Republic: The Secession of Georgia* (Baton Rouge, 1977), pp. 53–54, 65–70, 87–94, 101, 130–131, 159, 167.

152. Just as the same process produced a strengthening of majoritarian sentiment in the North.

153. See Bruce Collins, *The Origins of America's Civil War*, pp. 141–142; Carey, *Parties, Slavery and the Union*, pp. 323–324.

democratic practices in themselves, but by the opportunities those demo-cratic practices offered to nefarious and unscrupulous outsiders.

Slaveholders faced a dilemma. They could not turn their backs upon the nonslaveholders. The potential danger the nonslaveholders posed made it more rather than less important that they acquiesce in the regime. Deny-ing them voting rights, particularly rights that they currently enjoyed, risked provoking precisely the conflict that Hinton Helper so desired and that slaveholders so dreaded. On the other hand, it was essential to ensure that these nonslaveholders should not use their freedoms to agitate against slavery. Prior to 1860 such agitation had occurred on only a limited scale and its impact was, as yet, still more limited. But could the same be guaran-teed in the future? Many southerners doubted it and these doubts helped push them to seek an independent nation, one in which they could be sure that the nonslaveholders could enjoy their democratic rights but in a way that would not prevent the southern elite from continuing to enjoy the fruits of the labour of several million enslaved blacks.

## V

Southern reactions to the threats from nonslaveholders in general and from disaffected nonslaveholders like Helper in particular are highly revealing. Helper could not after 1857 have risked a return to his native state; anyone suspected of abolitionist activities was subject to vigilante action which might take the form of tarring and feathering, expulsion from the locality or state, even lynching. As we have seen, these were the actions taken by Missourians during the prolonged crisis over Kansas. But they were also the actions recommended by other southerners. From the 1830s Committees of Vigilance had been set up in the Deep South and they did not hesitate to recommend extralegal action when necessary. As one such Committee in South Carolina observed: "where the laws of the land are insufficient to meet the emergency, the laws of natural jus-tice and self-preservation shall supply the deficiency." The justification, if any were needed, was that "we are deliberately and advisedly deter-mined that the guilty shall not escape!"[154] It is even possible that South Carolina, despite the aristocratic pretensions of many of her slavehold-ers, was the state in which, by virtue of her high concentration of slaves, such extralegal action was most widely recommended. Thus James Henry Hammond, a former Governor of South Carolina and a future Senator, boasted in 1845 that the only time a "mob" could be seen in the South was when an abolitionist was being dealt with. Yet in reality "this is no more of a mob, than a rally of shepherds to chase a wolf out of their

154. Nye, *Fettered Freedom*, p. 179.

pastures would be one." Sixteen years later in a private letter he boasted that when abolitionists came into his state, "we hang all of them we can catch." In the same way John Townsend, also of South Carolina, in 1860 asked what treatment an abolitionist could expect if found in a slaveholding state: "whilst leaving his own home, and intruding himself, with such fiendish purposes, upon the peaceful homes of other men, what does the insane and malignant wretch deserve but to be shot down like any wolf, or wild cat, which is found prowling around the quiet sheep fold?" As one South Carolinian observed in 1859, "defence at home is a matter that takes precedence of every other consideration, and is antecedent in men's minds to the formality and technicality of the law."[155]

Yet these were southern and not merely South Carolinian responses. In 1848 Henry Foote of Mississippi (and Tennessee) was given the sobriquet of "Hangman Foote" by announcing to the Senate that if John P. Hale, New Hampshire's antislavery Senator, should enter his state, then "if the arm of the law happened to be too short or the spirit of the law too slumberous" it would be the "duty" of the people to "inflict summary punishment." By this he meant "death upon the scaffold." Jefferson Davis, also of Mississippi, endorsed Foote's recommendation Two years later the editor of the Montgomery *Advertiser*, perhaps the leading newspaper in Alabama, announced that while "we have great veneration for the laws of the land as a general thing," nevertheless "when we see a man putting a torch to our dwelling and enacting means for the butchery of our wives and children, it is criminal to wait for the slow, uncertain process of the law." Similarly Iveson Brooks, referring to Cassius Clay's antislavery activities in Kentucky, exclaimed that "if any work of the devil would justify the infliction of summary punishment by the protectors of female virtue and sacred homes, it is the establishment of an abolition press in the midst of the firesides of any slaveholding community."[156]

The problem with the established processes of law was, of course, that they might not achieve the desired effect of extinguishing antislavery sentiment or antislavery activities. It is important to ask, however, why the attitudes of southern nonslaveholders were deemed to be of such enormous importance. Why could slaveholders not tolerate a legitimate difference of opinion within the white community on the desirability of slavery?

155. *Governor Hammond's Letters on Southern Slavery: Addressed to Thomas Clarkson* (n.p., n.d.), p. 7; Channing, *Crisis of Fear*, pp. 38–42, 31; [John Townsend], *The South Alone, Should Govern the South* (Charleston, 1860), p. 43. Atchison to Jefferson Davis, Sept. 24, 1854 in Crist *et al.* (eds.) *Papers of Davis*, V, p. 84.
156. CG, 30/1, App., pp. 504–505; Montgomery *Advertiser*, Aug. 28, 1850; [Brooks], *Defence of Southern Slavery*, p. 20; Barney, *Secessionist Impulse*, pp. 170–177; Nevins, *Prologue to Civil War*, p. 159.

In part the slaveholders were simply rallying to the defence of their property. By the late 1850s the rising price of slaves meant that their total value in the United States was somewhere between three and four billion dollars. Here was a strong reason for defending it. Yet it cannot alone explain the extralegal actions southerners took or their refusal to allow normal democratic practices to operate whenever slavery was under threat. The United States in the final antebellum years saw few concerted attacks on property rights (other than those in slaves) and when such attacks were mounted they did not result in such draconian countermeasures. After all the banking interest had been of major concern in the 1830s and 1840s but its defenders had never had to abandon due process. Equally, those who defended the manufacturing interest never resorted to lynchings. What was different about slavery?

The difference was, of course, that slaves were people and not merely property. As such they could do what no bank or factory could do: they could resist their owners either by fleeing or by rising up and murdering them. Southerners sometimes recognised this. In the aftermath of John Brown's raid *De Bow's Review*, reminding its readers of the dangers posed by northern settlers in the South, conceded that "not one in twenty of such settlers might tamper with our slaves and incite them to insurrection," yet one in twenty might be enough, for "one man can fire a magazine, and no one can foresee where the match will be applied." Here was an interesting metaphor, almost certainly more interesting than the writer who employed it himself realised since it served to highlight in the most dramatic way the vulnerability of a slaveholding community. Other southerners employed the metaphor. According to William C. Preston of South Carolina, "we are a magazine round which crackers are exploding." Although such was not the writer's purpose, no image more graphically illustrated a slave society's susceptibility to the forms of resistance which it characteristically engendered among its slave population and the dangers to be apprehended, as a result, from its nonslaveholding whites. Thus no image more graphically conveyed the weaknesses of the slave mode of production.[157]

There was therefore ample reason to prevent the spread of antislavery propaganda. As *De Bow's Review* observed a few months before the appearance of Hinton Helper's *Impending Crisis*, "the public sentiment of the South will not tolerate a hostile discussion of slavery, for the very obvious reason that such discussion, if unrestricted, would lead to servile

---

157. *De Bow's Review*, XXVIII (1860), p. 1; William C. Preston to David Campbell, Aug. 22, 1857 quoted in Channing, *Crisis of Fear*, p. 77. It is perhaps unnecessary to add that the weaknesses of slavery illustrated here resulted from the slaves' unwillingness to be slaves and their potential for resistance.

insurrection." The writer then made a crucial comparison with the North, though almost certainly without appreciating the full import of what he had said: "there is no such danger in the North and the largest freedom of speech can be safely allowed."[158]

Here too was the reason for the apparent misreading of the Helper volume. Although Helper never addressed his often inflammatory remarks to the slaves, many southerners responded as if he had. Their assumption was that, as soon as the nonslaveholding whites had been corrupted by Helperism, they would at best cease to cooperate with the slaveholders in maintaining order or at worst would themselves incite the slaves to insurrection or arson. Little wonder, therefore, that possession of the book was regarded as treason.

At the most fundamental level, ownership of slaves differed from ownership of banks or factories because there could be no class conflict between a bank and its owner. Such conflict, however, suffused the slave system. Southerners, as we shall see, were never able to recognise this fact. But they attended to its consequences. One of these consequences was that the position of free blacks in one or two states of the South became, as we have seen, a matter of considerable significance. A more important consequence was that the attitude of nonslaveholding whites became a matter of desperate concern. And to ensure that the attitude of those whites remained "correct," southerners were driven to equally desperate measures, regardless of their devastating and ultimately fatal impact on northern opinion.

## The weaknesses of slavery (3): Slaves

### I

As we have seen, fears for the security of the master–slave relationship and thus for slavery itself underlay southern responses to the problems posed by free blacks and nonslaveholding whites. The renewal of sectional hostilities following the introduction of the Kansas-Nebraska Act produced a steady escalation of these fears. The presidential election of 1856, the first contested by the nascent Republican party, was fought in much of the South in a climate of intense fear. In early fall rumors of an insurrection caused a panic which began in Kentucky and Tennessee, from where it spread to Missouri and Arkansas before reaching the Gulf States, Virginia and Maryland by the end of the year. According to one southern proslavery writer "plans of insurrections in various localities in the Slave States were secretly laid by the slaves, in anticipation of the

158. *De Bow's Review*, XX (1856), p. 667.

Black Republicans in November, 1856." The result was that "great consternation prevailed among the inhabitants, and night patrols were kept, and every precaution used to detect these conspirators."[159]

The late 1850s saw a further intensification of these fears. The Brown raid helped produce, as we have seen, a backlash against free blacks in several states and an attempt to crack down upon the hiring out of slaves. South Carolina was now gripped by what has been aptly described as a "crisis of fear"; "the flood tide of vigilance activity broke in the final months of 1859 and did not recede again." Fears of slave murders and arson were widespread; indeed in Charleston such fears were almost a part of daily life.[160]

The election of 1860 witnessed even greater alarm than that which had accompanied the contest of 1856. In Dalton, Georgia thirty-six blacks were arrested and accused of plotting to burn the town and kill its inhabitants. A lynching took place in Talladega Alabama, there were rumors of insurrections in Louisiana and Mississippi, and Texas was gripped by hysteria following a wave of suspected arson in the northern part of the state. Southerners were convinced that the election was responsible for "disturbances among the slaves." One Alabama newspaper struck a note that was being sounded throughout much of the South when it urged its readers not to "slumber whilst the enemy is prowling about our very doors, and the torch of the incendiary lights up the whole Northern horizon in the onward march of the enemy."[161]

As this editorial indicates, southerners did not always explain who was ultimately responsible for these cases of arson or the attempts at insurrection. Consequently it was not always apparent who "the enemy" was. Was it northern "emissaries," disloyal nonslaveholding southern whites, free blacks, slaves or some combination of these groups? Many southern expressions of fear and even panic were extremely vague in this respect.

Yet it is clear that overall southerners were confident that such activities were rarely if ever carried out by slaves alone and on the few occasions that they were it was under the insidious influence of others, even if they were located far away in the antislavery North. Here was a cardinal tenet, indeed the fundamental article, of the proslavery faith: slaves were inherently contented with their enslavement.

From at least the time of the rebirth of antislavery in the early 1830s southern defenders of slavery had insisted, time and again, that blacks were contented under slavery. As early as 1835, when the North Carolina

---

159. Sawyer, *Southern Institutes*, p. 385; Barney, *Secessionist Impulse*, p. 165.
160. Channing, *Crisis of Fear*, pp. 22, 26, 43, 47, 48, 256. See also *CG*, 36/1, p. 454.
161. Nevins, *Prologue to Civil War*, pp. 306–307; Montgomery *Advertiser*, quoted in Barney, *Secessionist Impulse*, p. 167.

legislature responded to the emergence of a militant abolitionism in the North, this was the message promulgated to the people of the state. "Left to themselves," the slaves would be "a laboring class as little dangerous to society as any in the world." But the problem was, of course, that the slaves were not being left alone. The report continued by insisting that "others shall not teach them evil, of which they think not themselves" and that they should not be "stimulated by the base and violent of other lands, to deeds of bloodshed." In other words, however contented the slaves might be, they were easily converted into murderous savages who would then pose a dire threat to their masters and to themselves alike.[162]

For the next thirty years southerners continued, with remarkable unanimity and consistency, to present this argument. In 1842 one South Carolina Congressman declared that "our slaves are as light-hearted a race of beings as there is to be found on the face of the earth." They were "generally pretty well contented with their condition, and will probably remain so until taught differently by the officious intermeddling of those who, whether ignorantly or hypocritically, would most cruelly convert into a galling yoke that servitude which they have hitherto borne with cheerfulness." The reasons for the slaves' contentment were not difficult to find: "in general" they "appear to entertain for their masters and their families not only respect and esteem, but sincere friendship." Then came the inevitable warning: "they, however, exist among us, a separate race, and are capable of being converted into our deadliest enemies."[163]

Such opinions were widespread among slaveholders. In 1848 Jefferson Davis informed the United States Senate that he had "no more dread of our slaves than I have of our cattle," for they were "happy and contented" and "are rendered miserable only by the unwarranted interference of those who know nothing about that with which they meddle." By 1850 therefore, despite or perhaps even as a result of almost two decades of antislavery agitation and pressure, southerners' faith in the inherent loyalty of their slaves was undiminished. One South Carolinian confirmed the conclusion his state had reached at the time of nullification: the only

162. *Remarks to the People of North Carolina, In Connection with the Report of the Joint Select Committee of the Legislature of 1835 on the Subject of Abolition* (n.p., n.d.), p. 6.
163. *Speech of John Campbell of South Carolina in the House of Representatives, April 15, 1842* (n.p., n.d.), p. 16. See also Herbert Fielder, *The Disunionist: A Brief Treatise Upon the Evils of the Union Between the North and the South* (n.p., n.d.), pp. 42–46; *Speech of R. M. Saunders, of North Carolina, Against Receiving, Referring, or Reporting On Abolitionist Petitions* (Washington, D.C., 1844), pp. 9–10. A somewhat less common view was to the effect that blacks were so docile that even abolitionists could not move them. See Mathew Estes, *A Defence of Negro Slavery As It Exists in the United States* (Montgomery, Alabama, 1846) p. 225 for the argument that "those who fear the result of abolition excitement among the Negroes, know but little of their character."

power that could destroy slavery was the federal government. At the time of the Compromise, when secession looked possible and war not impossible, some southerners took care to emphasise that the slaves would, in such circumstances, be a source of strength. Blacks, it was held, "despise poor white men who will put themselves on an equality with them." Some writers and publicists continued to acknowledge that in parts of the South there were problems. Thus when Felix Huston reviewed the history of the abolition movement over the last generation, he claimed that the record demonstrated both that slavery was not an evil and that except in one or two towns and along the border states, "the slaves are perfectly repugnant to any white interference." "At no time," he maintained, "has more security been felt throughout the whole south than at the present moment." Indeed "we feel as little danger from our negroes as we do from our horses and mules." Consequently "nothing can alienate our slaves from us if we are true to ourselves and to them."[164]

The mounting attacks on the South that accompanied the midcentury crisis and especially the controversy created by *Uncle Tom's Cabin* placed additional demands upon the defenders of slavery. With increasing vociferousness northerners demanded to know why most slaves were not taught to read and write. The answer was that "the laws against reading were the only barrier we could devise against the flood of incendiary publications that threatened our safety." Hence "the responsibility" for slave illiteracy "must rest upon other shoulders than ours." As another proslavery theorist explained, if the slaves would read only the Bible there would be no problem. But the danger came from those who would urge him to read instead the Declaration of Independence:

> The temptor is not asleep. His eye is still, as ever of old, fixed on the forbidden tree; and thither he will point his hapless victims. Like certain Senators and demagogues, and doctors of divinity, he will preach from the Declaration of Independence, rather than from the Bible. He will teach, not that subordination, but that *resistance*, is a duty. To every evil passion his inflammatory and murder-instigating appeals will be made.

Ironically the writer then attributed the fact that slaves might respond to the Declaration to their racial inferiority. For "stung by these appeals and maddened, the poor African, it is to be feared, would have no better notions of equality and freedom, and no better notions of duty to God or

---

164. Crist *et al.* (eds.), *Papers of Davis*, III, p. 315; *To the Hon. W. J. Grayson by another of the People*, p. 8; *Address of Huston*, pp. 5–6, 18.

man, that his teachers themselves have." Thus to teach him to read was "to prepare the slave for his own utter undoing."[165]

These assertions continued to be made throughout the 1850s. *De Bow's Review*, semiofficial spokesman for the slave South, played a prominent role in disseminating them. Having been "born in servitude," the slaves "have never known any other condition, and but few ever desire to change it." Negroes were naturally subservient and "no sense of wrong pervades the race." The reason was that the slave "has no conception" of liberty and "unless the emotions were industriously cultivated, we believe that there are no people on earth that have less occasion, or are less inclined, to disturb the existing state of society around them."[166]

On the other hand, some southerners did acknowledge that abolitionist doctrines could have a damaging effect upon the slaves, even if no attempt at insurrection were made. *De Bow's Review* declared that in the South generally "the continual efforts to excite mutiny and insurrection, even if failing to produce any open or violent act, cause discontent and unhappiness, and a spirit of insubordination in the slaves, and much injury to their owners and to the commonwealth." Without this interference, the slaves would be able to inhabit a veritable paradise of unfreedom:

> If all such emissaries and agents were shut out from intercourse with our slaves, and deprived of their present facilities for deluding them, it would be very rare for any slave, without influence from abroad, to attempt, or to desire, to escape permanently from his home and his condition of slavery. And the spirit of discontent which Northern abolitionists have produced by false representations, and the consequent spirit of insubordination thus rendered necessary – all being the direct results of abolitionist action – are the only serious disadvantages, and sources of suffering to the slaves, and the only thing to prevent them being the most comfortable, contented, and happy laboring class in the world.

The problem was that the abolitionists, in the words of Robert Toombs of Georgia, induced the slaves, who otherwise would present a spectacle of "happiness, cheerfulness, and contentment" to "take counsel rather of their passions than their reason."[167]

The southerners' understanding of their slaves was enormously important throughout the sectional crisis. It became still more important in

165. [E. J. Pringle], *Slavery in the Southern States, By a Carolinian* (Cambridge, MA, 1852), p. 25; Bledsoe, *Essay on Liberty and Slavery*, p. 125.

166. *De Bow's Review*, VII (1849), p. 489, XXI (1856), p. 547, see also XIV (1853), p. 274; XXV (1858), pp. 47, 292.

167. *De Bow's Review*, XXIII (1857), pp. 547–549; Robert Toombs, *A Lecture Delivered in the Tremont Temple, Boston, Massachusetts on 24 Jan. 1856* (Washington, D.C., 1856), p. 14.

1860 as secession loomed. The unrest that had accompanied the contests of 1856 and 1860 did not result in any change of opinion within the South. Instead it was easily fitted into the ideological framework that had been in existence for some decades. Indeed the John Brown raid, which resulted in no uprising of slaves (at least in the way that Brown had hoped), if anything confirmed the southern stereotype: the slave was inherently safe and dependable.

Some southerners complained that the Republican campaign of 1860, like that of 1856, had infected some slaves with the spirit of liberty. There were reports that some of them believed that Lincoln's victory meant emancipation (as indeed it ultimately did). But this did nothing to dampen southern confidence in the inherent loyalty of the slave and the inherent stability of the slave system. John Townsend of South Carolina in a best-selling secessionist tract made the rather doubtful claim that the abolitionists appealed to the slaves as an oppressed people and exhorted them to rise up violently against their masters. But this strategy foundered on the inherent qualities of the slave. In a curious and ironic inversion of standard logic, Townsend insisted that the abolitionists had too low an opinion of the slaves:

> the slaves are not the brutes and savages which the Abolitionists suppose them to be. God has placed conscience in their bosoms; they have the common feelings of humanity in their hearts; many of them are governed by the holy precepts of Christianity, and understand the duties of "obedience" which God has enjoined that the slaves show to their master. Many of them, again, have been brought up in the families of their masters; have been the companions of their childhood and youth, and have acquired a sincere friendship and attachment for them; whilst there is scarcely one of them who cannot recall to mind many faults forgiven, and numerous favors conferred.

One result was that if they heard about insurrections, slaves informed their masters. Townsend concluded that "if let alone they would live with us all the days of their life in harmony, and with the kindliest good offices." He had "not a distrust of them if left to themselves." Similarly when the state of Alabama engaged in a formal debate over secession in early 1861, the same confidence in the uncorrupted slave was in evidence. "In nine cases out of ten," it was said, "in positive contentment, the Alabama slave is happier than his master." The reason was that "his cottage is built for him, his food provided, his meals prepared; his hearth to spread with substantial comforts, and his long nights are for those blissful dreams that are undisturbed by the knowledge of coming necessities." Nevertheless, the convention at which these words were uttered was also the one which took Alabama out of the Union, not least because of the fear of the actions of which this same slave might be capable.[168]

The dangers of slave insurrections, stirred up by northerners, and encouraged by traitorous nonslaveholding whites or free blacks, were appreciated throughout the South. As we have seen, Missourians were alarmed by the possibility that their slaves might be tempted into rebellious acts if Kansas were "abolitionised." Yet insurrections or acts of individual violence were, not surprisingly, most acutely feared in the black belt regions of the South, those areas with the heaviest concentration of slaves. Here the problems of maintaining control were most obvious. The areas most at risk were primarily in the Deep South in the states of Georgia, Alabama, Mississippi, Louisiana and of course South Carolina.

This danger in a way complemented the threat posed by nonslaveholding whites and together they illustrate the vulnerability of the slave system. As we have seen, there was widespread concern about the nonslaveholding whites throughout the South, but the areas thought to be most at risk were those in which slaveholding was less common and slaveholdings smaller. In these border areas the nonslaveholders could more easily mount an attack upon the institution. Cassius Clay in Kentucky, Benjamin Gratz Brown in Missouri, the Blairs in Maryland and Missouri – these had no counterparts in the Deep South. But where the slave population was densest the fear of the subversive nonslaveholders receded – only to be replaced by the still more terrifying prospect of the rebellious slave. What then was the ideal concentration of slaves? Neither contemporaries, nor historians have ever been able to answer this question.

## II

It is highly ironic that the final antebellum years witnessed not only mounting alarm and a sense of deepening crisis but also extravagant claims about the loyalty of the very slave whose resistance to his enslavement was ultimately responsible for the alarm and the sense of crisis. Southerners of course saw matters very differently. As far as they were concerned, the crisis was attributable to northern antislavery activities. The drive for secession was, in their eyes, a wholly logical attempt to counter those activities. As William H. Trescot of South Carolina put it, a southern confederacy "would suppress that of which alone we complain, *legislative agitation*." If political action in the North were indeed the cause of slave unrest then the ending of that action would necessarily end the unrest.[169]

---

168. Channing, *Crisis of Fear*, p. 271; Townsend, *Death of Slavery*, pp. 24–25; William R. Smith (ed.), *The History and the Debates of the Convention of the People of Alabama, Begun and Held in the City of Montgomery, on the Seventh Day of January, 1861* (Montgomery; 1861), p. 201.
169. William H. Trescot, *The Position and Course of the South* (Charleston, n.d.), p. 18.

Yet however logical this argument might be, it was utterly flawed. Historians now know that the slaves were not reconciled to their enslavement in the way that southerners believed. Resistance was in fact endemic in the relationship between master and slave, simply because the exploitation suffered by the slave was so naked and obvious. Slaveholders were surrounded with the evidence of this. Many of the slaves who sought to flee from the South, many of those who malingered or deliberately worked poorly, all of those who plotted rebellion or who secretly followed and applauded the progress of the antislavery parties of the North – these slaves were confirming the existence of the conflict that lay at the heart of the master/slave relationship. But southerners simply could not see it.

This was partly because there was indeed some evidence to suggest that their slaves were affected by antislavery activity in the North. Unfortunately these are matters on which it is very difficult for historians to pronounce. Yet there is evidence to suggest that the three major slave insurrections planned in the nineteenth-century South, those of Gabriel Prosser, Denmark Vesey and Nat Turner, were triggered in part by events outside their immediate localities: respectively the conflict with France, the debates over slavery in Missouri, the debates over slavery in Virginia. During the 1850s many southerners reported that there was growing insubordination among their slaves and they of course unhesitatingly connected it with national political events. They also claimed that northern defiance of the Fugitive Slave law encouraged some slaves to run away and, as we have already noted, the elections of 1856 and 1860 gave rise to similar concerns. There was almost certainly some truth in these claims; slaves often did hear about what was happening in the North and in the federal capital and they knew far more about the debates over slavery than their owners wanted them to know.[170]

Yet the causal pattern was very different from that which the masters discerned. It was the conflict within the master–slave relationship which played the key role, external influences afforded opportunities or encouragement but they were not necessary conditions for slave resistance and would have been worthless if the slaves had been the happy, contented, child-like figures the masters believed them to be.

Once again, however, it would be quite wrong to view this as one of the blunders made by an allegedly "blundering generation." An accurate identification of the problems entailed by slaveholding was simply not compatible with continued resistance on the part of the slaveholding class to the forces of antislavery. If southern militants had recognised that

170. Genovese, *From Rebellion to Revolution: Afro-American Slave Revolts in the Making of the New World* (New York, 1979), pp. 26, 45; Rodney D. Green, "Urban Industry, Black Resistance, and Racial Restriction in the Antebellum South: A General Model and a Case Study in Urban Virginia," (Ph.D. dissertation, American University, 1980), pp. 547–548; CG, 30/2, pp. 317, 31/1, p. 136, 31/2, p. 579.

slaves could not be reconciled to their enslavement, their defence of the institution could not have reached beyond the level of expediency. They would then been have been forced to recognise themselves as an exploitative class and, having done so, could then scarcely have called upon each other or upon the nonslaveholders of the South, or upon their remaining northern allies, to make the sacrifices that would be necessary to preserve the institution. Least of all would they have been able to contemplate breaking up the nation in order to maintain it.[171]

Consequently they utterly misunderstood the nature of the threats around them. Indeed they had an inverted image of reality. They were confronted by three threats either real or potential, ranged in effect in concentric circles around them. Closest to them was the threat from their own slaves. Next came the threat from the nonslaveholding whites and the free blacks of the South. Finally came the threat from the North. As we have seen, the nonslaveholding whites and the dangers presented by free blacks assumed such large proportions only because of the conflict, actual or potential, between slave and master. Southerners however reversed the formulation and believed that it was these groups who were, in good part, responsible for the conflict between master and slave. Finally, southerners reacted so vehemently to the threat from the North because they believed it responsible for the problems posed by both slaves and nonslaveholding whites. In reality, however, that threat was activated by the prior existence of those problems.

These misunderstandings were profound and yet necessary. As we shall see, they continued to distort southern perceptions of reality up to and including the time when southern militants made the most desperate gamble of all and attempted to set up shop for themselves. The shop would be the Confederate States of America.

## The southern economy

The 1850s were a decade of advancing, indeed unparalleled, prosperity for the South, as for the nation as a whole. After the economic dislocations of the late 1830s and early 1840s, recovery really began in the South in 1845 when cotton prices, previously at alarmingly low levels, began to revive. After 1848 the recovery accelerated and the 1850s were characterised by rising slave prices and, for most of the larger producers of cotton, and other plantation-based crops, unprecedented profitability. Unlike

---

171. On one occasion Eugene Govenese dismisses these sentiments as "cant" – see Genovese, *From Rebellion to Revolution*, p. 116. However, there is no evidence for this. Moreover, as Genovese himself was among the first to recognise, the slaveholders needed to believe that slavery was good for the slave. From this the notion of a "contented slave" followed inexorably, however inaccurate it might have been.

in previous decades, however, no major speculative bubble formed and so when the Panic of 1857 struck, the South was able to surmount the difficulties with relative ease.[172]

In the 1850s, to a greater extent than ever before, slaves brought great wealth to their owners. If northern and southern levels of per capita non-slave wealth are compared then the North is far ahead. But when wealth in the form of slaves is included the picture alters and it is the South which appears the wealthy section. The result was that although the South in the 1850s was far behind in population, in land values and in manufacturing, her slaveholders were enjoying unexampled prosperity. The former trend does much to explain northern criticisms of the southern economy, with slavery at its base and the latter does even more to explain the reluctance of most southern leaders, slaveholders virtually to a man, to accept those criticisms.[173]

Yet the weaknesses of southern slavery transcend considerations of per capita wealth, however measured. For one thing, the lack of economic development and diversification in the South meant that the wealth of the region was highly dependent on the price its slave labour force could command, which in turn was heavily dependent upon the overseas demand for its staple crops, in particular cotton. The northern economy, by contrast, was much more broadly based. Moreover in terms of per capita income, as opposed to wealth, the North was again far ahead.[174] But even the successes of the southern labor system, as measured by the wealth generated by slaves, brought problems in their wake. Slavery offered the greatest rewards in the states of the Deep South and especially the Southwest and the result was a continued draining of slaves out of the border regions. Both Maryland and Delaware, for example, lost slaves in the 1850s over-all while in the other border states (Kentucky, Missouri and Virginia) the proportion of slaves in the total population fell. In each of these states the result was, from the slaveholders' perspective, a dangerous loss of polit-ical as well as economic power, one which neatly anticipated the refusal in the following decade of each of these states, or in the case of Virginia, a portion of the state, to join the Confederacy. Thus even when slavery was economically successful it brought political problems which simply had no counterpart in the North.

These were years in which more and more southerners (like northerners) were sucked into the market economy, even though a "safety first" strategy

172. Douglass C. North, *The Economic Growth of the United States, 1790–1860* (New York, 1966), pp. 206, 208.
173. Wright, *Slavery and American Economic Development*, pp. 58–61.
174. The margin was in 1860 about forty percent – see Robert W. Fogel and Stanley L. Engerman, *Time on the Cross: The Economics of American Negro Slavery* (London, 1974), p. 248.

(by means of which southerners would cater to their subsistence needs first and only then produce a "marketable surplus") continued to characterise large swathes of southern agriculture. The 1850s witnessed a railroad boom in many parts of the South (though on a lesser scale than in the North) and the result was to enhance opportunities for some producers, even as others found themselves unable effectively to compete. Rising slave prices might mean dazzling wealth for many but the result was almost certainly increasing social stratification as the price of a prime field hand soared well beyond the means of hundreds of thousands of small farmers. For thousands in the South even land ownership was becoming an impossibility and tenancy and even agricultural wage labour became increasingly common in some localities.[175]

The pattern of economic growth in the South was geographically uneven too. States like Arkansas and Texas moved more fully into the southern orbit. In Arkansas cotton boomed as total production soared from six million pounds in 1840 to almost a hundred and fifty million two decades later. The state was drawing more and more of its population from the Deep South and apart from its northwestern counties was coming to resemble the plantation areas of the Lower South. An identical process was converting east Texas from a frontier area with more in common with the northwest into another region whose economy was beginning to resemble the plantation society of the Deep South. Even in these states, however, regional variations were marked. The Ozark counties of north central and northwest Arkansas contained few slaves (some counties having less than one percent of their populations enslaved) while north Texas continued to resemble the Upper South (from where most of its inhabitants had in fact originated).[176]

In other parts of the South, similar regional variations remained prominent. The eastern counties of Virginia, for example, became increasingly black in population, whereas the northwestern part of the state continued to strengthen its links with the neighbouring free states and the free-labour economies of Ohio and Pennsylvania. Despite the demise of cotton production in Virginia and despite the widespread practice of selling slaves

---

175. Bolton, *Poor Whites of the Antebellum South*, p. 88; Bill Cecil-Fronsman, *Common Whites: Class and Culture in Antebellum North Carolina* (Lexington, 1992), pp. 124–132; Escott, *Many Excellent People*, p. 8; Hahn, *Roots of Southern Populism*, pp. 22, 47; Ford, *Origins of Southern Radicalism*, p. 253; Carey, *Parties, Slavery and the Union*, pp. 16, 137, 214; Joseph P. Reidy, *From Slavery to Agrarian Capitalism in the Cotton Plantation South: Central Georgia, 1800–1880* (Chapel Hill, 1992), pp. 81–101.
176. Woods, *Rebellion and Realignment*, pp. 8, 17, 21, 25, 30, 90, 124, 170; Randolph B. Campbell, *An Empire for Slavery: The Peculiar Institution in Texas, 1821–1865* (Baton Rouge, 1989); Walter L. Buenger, *Secession and the Union in Texas* (Austin, Texas, 1984), pp. 10, 16, 34, 64, 68, 167.

into the markets of the Deep South there, slavery continued to maintain a strong presence in most of the state as it did in North Carolina and Tennessee. In much of the Deep South and even some parts of the Middle South, cotton spread into new areas, though landholding and slaveholding became more concentrated, especially in the South Atlantic states.[177]

Still more striking and varied were the conditions in the largest cities of the South. Baltimore, St Louis, and New Orleans dwarfed all other southern cities. All three were in economic terms success stories, though in different ways and in different degrees. Baltimore, third largest city in the nation, saw its population double between 1840 and 1860. It alone had more industrial workers than were to be found in eleven of the fifteen slave states. But from a southern, sectional perspective the problem was that slavery was increasingly marginal to its economy. On the eve of the Civil War a mere two percent of its population was enslaved. As in New Orleans, immigrants were present in large numbers and although their labour was a vital source of urban growth and development, they lived and worked beyond the supervision and control of the slaveholders who aspired to lead and direct southern society. St Louis was, from a southern sectionalist's viewpoint, even worse. Not only was slavery precariously poised in Missouri, it was increasingly irrelevant to the growth of her largest city whose black population, free and slave, had collapsed from twenty-five percent in 1830 to two percent in 1860 and even more alarmingly, was widely viewed as an impediment to St Louis's bid for leadership of the northwest and a liability in her rivalry with Chicago. These large cities were, of course, to prove highly problematic within the Old South; two of the three states in which they were located would remain loyal to the Union after 1861 and the third would harbor large numbers of Union sympathisers throughout the war years.[178]

The crucial question, however, concerns the relationship between the economic changes of the final antebellum decade and the movement for southern independence. Some historians have claimed that secession was triggered not merely by northern antislavery pressure but also by the commercial development taking place within the South itself. In other words, it has been suggested that in some states at least, secession was

177. William G. Shade, *Democratizing the Old Dominion: Virginia and the Second Party System, 1824–1861* (Charlottesville, 1996), p. 20; William A. Link, *Roots of Secession: Slavery and Politics in Antebellum Virginia* (Chapel Hill, 2003), pp. 29–33. Bruce Levine, *Half Slave and Half Free: The Roots of Civil War* (New York, 1992), p. 38; Hahn, *Roots of Southern Populism*, p. 41; Cecil-Fronsman, *Common Whites*, pp. 124–132; Carey, *Parties, Slavery and the Union*, p. 16.
178. Frank Towers, *The Urban South and the Coming of the Civil War* (Charlottesville, 2004), pp. 1, 3–4, 7, 22, 31–32, 46, 203–204.

a reaction against the economic changes of the era. Southerners, it is argued, were wedded to Jacksonian notions of liberty and equality and were unwilling to accept the restrictions upon individual freedom entailed by increasing involvement in a market economy. Secession was thus an attempt to escape these restrictions. More specifically the insistence upon the right to plant southern social practices and to establish southern social norms in the new territories was an attempt to ensure that an escape route from social stratification remained open to large numbers of southern agriculturists.[179]

There is no doubt that from time to time southerners sounded the alarm about the dangers to be apprehended from the processes of commercialisation. In the same way, they sounded the alarm about the dangers to the individual of excessive dependence and warned that those who lacked the ownership of productive and especially landed property all too often lacked the independence that was necessary for republican citizenship. Thus Louisa McCord, the daughter of Langdon Cheves of South Carolina, declared that "he who has not the right to dispose of his own labour becomes consequently and necessarily, to a greater or lesser extent... the serf or bondsman of the individual or government, thus shackling or limiting his exchanges." Another South Carolinian similarly warned that a victorious Republican party would make the yeomen of the South "serfs of the manufacturers like the coolies of India or the Peons of Mexico." This was the traditional fear of wage labour, the belief that the proletarian or wage worker could not be a fit citizen of a Republic.[180]

Even more important than these comments, however, were the suspicions voiced by many southerners about the cities and especially the biggest cities of the South. Proslavery apologists like J. G. B. De Bow and Edmund Ruffin feared that the Republicans would soon control Baltimore, precisely as they had controlled St Louis. In Louisiana John Slidell, the state's leading Democratic chieftain, informed President James Buchanan that the large numbers of Irish and Germans of New Orleans were "at heart abolitionists." The large cities of the South, and to a lesser extent, the smaller towns too, posed a challenge to the hegemony of the planters simply because the web of impersonal relations that characterised urban life, and the transient population of immigrants (together with free blacks) who resided there made it difficult to maintain the network of personal controls upon which slavery depended.[181]

179. Thornton, *Politics and Power*, pp. xix, xx, 206–216. 268–276; Ford, *Origins of Southern Radicalism*, pp. 84, 244.
180. Ford, *Origins of Southern Radicalism*, pp. 355, 361.
181. Towers, *Urban South and Coming of the Civil War*, pp. 31–32; Roger W. Schugg, *The Origins of Class Struggle in Louisiana* revised edition (Baton Rouge, 1967), pp. 145–146.

Along with this antiurbanism went, in some southern states in the 1850s, a traditional agrarian hostility to banks and banking. Nowhere was this more pronounced than in Georgia where Governor Joseph Brown exploited the banking issue as no statesman had done in any state for more than a decade. In the aftermath of the Panic of 1857, the voters of north Georgia in particular roared their approval of Brown's neo-Jacksonianism. Even more common in the states of the South in the 1850s were profound controversies over railroads, which in a state like Alabama shook the political system to its core. Between 1854 and 1858 the issue proved hugely controversial and deeply divisive and there is no doubt that once again neo-Jacksonians voiced their protests against the network of commercial relations that was forming in their midst.[182]

Yet it is incorrect to assume that these protests played a major role in precipitating the South towards secession. Across the South as a whole there is simply no correlation between commercialisation and secessionist sentiment. The Upper South was, in general, the area where commercial development and market relations developed most rapidly; it was also the area of the South where secession was weakest. Within this region Arkansas, as a trans-Mississippi state, was less commercially advanced than any other, in 1861 she had not a single bank to her name but was probably keener on secession than any other state in the Middle South. Moreover, even in Alabama the banking system remained on the eve of the Civil War modest in scale. (The state had only eight banks in 1860; Ohio, by comparison, had fifty-four.) This was even more the case in neighbouring Mississippi, where the state government was far less active in promoting commercialised agriculture. In 1860 Mississippi could boast the sum total of two banks. Moreover, those who advocated southern rights, such as Jefferson Davis, far from reacting against these developments, repeatedly in the 1850s urged his fellow Mississippians to diversify their economy, to construct more railroads and even to build more factories. In the same way, the Natchez *Free Trader*, which repeatedly urged the creation of a southern confederacy, at the same time repeatedly called for "the building of railroads, trunks and branches, uniting all the cities, towns and villages of the South by one common and indissoluble bond" as well as "the encouragement of Southern colleges and schools" and "the building up and the sustaining of Southern factories, foundries, and manufactories." Even in Georgia, where twenty-seven new banks had been chartered between 1850 and 1857, Joseph Brown's crusade against the

182.  Hahn, *Roots of Southern Populism*, p. 89; Carey, *Parties, Slavery and the Union*, p. 214; Bruce Collins, "Southern Secession in 1850–1," in Susan-Mary Grant and Brian Holden Reid (eds.), *The American Civil War: Explorations and Reconsiderations* (Harlow, 2000), pp. 39–67. (Collins, it should be noted, makes some extremely telling points in relation to the modernisation thesis.)

banks subsided rapidly after the Panic of 1857 and both he and his supporters in northern Georgia actually championed the process of railroad construction that was underway in these years.[183]

Thus it is not possible to view secession as the product of a revolt or reaction against modernisation or commercialisation. The error of those historians who have claimed otherwise lies in their assumption that changes in the southern social structure in the 1850s were responsible for the break up of the Union. In fact by 1850, as we have seen, large numbers of southerners had made it clear under what circumstances they would leave the Union and when the Republicans were victorious in 1860 those conditions had been met. As we shall see, the predominant view in the Deep South was that, unless the Republicans were willing to retreat from, indeed abandon, their programme, the nation did not deserve to continue in its present form.

In some respects, however, the economic changes of the 1850s did play a part in secession. If the decade had been one of economic reverses for the South, confidence in slavery and in slave society might have been eroded.[184] Although it is safe to assume that many southerners would, even in these circumstances, have kept faith with slavery (and would no doubt have blamed northerners for their economic adversities), others might have had their confidence dampened. They might have been less certain that cotton was king, or that a southern confederacy would be able to withstand an armed struggle with the North, should one have ensued. These are matters which historians can ponder but about which they can never reach a firm conclusion.

In another sense too the economic changes of the 1850s did play a role, or perhaps it would be truer to say that the absence of change played a role. Despite the prosperity and commercial growth of the 1850s, the South remained woefully retarded in industry. And the deeper the commitment to slavery, the more conspicuous the failure in this regard. Moreover, the same was true of towns and cities, where the contrast with the North was equally sharp. And even where the South did experience change, in the construction of railroad lines, for example, she remained, as we have noted, far behind the North.

There were two momentous consequences. First, this lack of diversification and development, as we shall see, fuelled the economic critique of slavery that was an integral part of the Republican critique of slavery and

---

183. Crist *et al.* (eds.), *Papers of Davis*, IV, pp. 41, 277, VI pp. 124, 138–139, 160, 211; Percy L. Rainwater, *Mississippi, Storm Center of Secession, 1856–1861* (Baton Rouge, 1938), pp. 70–72; Hahn, *Roots of Southern Populism*, p. 102.
184. It may be worth noting, however, that the patrician elite of the South Carolina low-country experienced economic adversity but this in no way diminished the commitment to slavery.

the South. Republicans, in common with virtually all other antislavery crusaders in the antebellum Republic, were utterly convinced that slavery retarded the growth of the southern economy and this was one of their principal reasons for opposing it. Second, these same economic weaknesses would return to haunt the Confederacy, once it had been established. Even with the accession of the four states of the Middle South, the Confederacy would prove to be hopelessly deficient in industrial might. As we shall see, this would prove a fatal handicap in war.

Thus southern economic performance had contradictory effects. It was strong enough to promote an overweening confidence in southern slave-based society and in the South's military capacity. It would even prove strong enough to allow the South to wage war for four years. On the other hand, as events would show, it was not strong enough to forestall criticisms of slavery's economic performance before the war, criticisms that would play a key role in generating the opposition of northern antislavery militants. Nor was the southern economy strong enough to prevent defeat in the war that followed, a defeat which confirmed that the opposition of those militants would ultimately prove fatal not only to the Confederacy but also to slavery itself.

## Crisis in the Democratic party and in the nation, 1857–1860

### I

When Democratic president James Buchanan was inaugurated in March 1857 his party had been in control of the White House for all but four years since 1845 and for all but eight years since 1829. Although the Republicans had run very strongly in the North, the new President believed that this was entirely because of a series of artificial crises, needlessly stirred up by those, primarily northerners, who took extreme views of the slavery question. He was confident that he would be able soon to settle the sectional controversy. He hoped to pacify Kansas and he hoped too that the Supreme Court would play a major role in establishing harmony. Then peace would return to the Kansas prairies, harmony would be restored in Washington and the Democratic party would recover its former strength in the North.

For their part, militant southerners had few fears about the federal government under its new Chief Magistrate. Although they viewed the Republican party with abhorrence and its evident popularity in the North with anger and dismay, their confidence in the Democratic party and its new leader was high. At this stage they had hopes that Kansas would become a slave state and many hoped too that slavery and the South might after all be safe within the Union.

Instead by the time of Buchanan's departure from office, although Kansas had ceased to be a subject of much controversy, this was because the proslavery forces in the territory had been utterly routed. More important, the general question of slavery in the territories had escalated to the point where it had broken up the Democratic party, helped the Republicans win the presidency for the first time and plunged the nation into the deepest crisis in its history. Southern militants now despaired of the Democratic party as a national force since it was reduced to a powerless minority throughout most of the North. Out of a total of 183 electoral votes available from the eighteen northern states in 1860, the Democrats won only three (of New Jersey's seven). A party which had carried every northern state but two in 1852 had eight years later failed to carry even a single one in its entirety.

The loss of strength in the North dated, of course, from the time of the Kansas-Nebraska Act; Buchanan had hoped to reverse a trend which his presidency actually succeeded only in accelerating. Southerners controlled his administration to a very considerable degree and, on the whole, prior to the secession crisis they had few complaints to make of it. Yet these were the years in which the party's northern wing suffered further catastrophic losses. At first glance, it appears that these southerners can be heavily censured for their actions in these years, for they certainly made life extremely difficult, perhaps impossible, for their northern allies. When the Democratic party split in 1860 it was a portentous event and many historians have blamed the rift on the alleged "irrationality" of southern militants. The reality, however, is rather different.[185]

## II

On the very day of his inauguration Buchanan knew that Chief Justice Roger Taney, who was administering the oath of office, was about to hand down what turned out to be one of the most famous or notorious Supreme Court decisions in American history. The decision was duly announced two days after he had been sworn in. In the Dred Scott case the court made two momentous judgments. One was that African Americans could not be citizens of the United States. This had major implications for their status even in the North but in importance it was the lesser of the judgments. The other was that neither Congress nor a territorial legislature had the power to exclude slavery from a territory. In other words the Court found for the version of popular sovereignty for which most southerners had contended all along. This meant not only that the Republican policy of congressional

---

185. David Potter, for example, argues that most explanations offered are "too rational" – Potter, *Impending Crisis*, p. 414.

exclusion was unconstitutional but that so too was the Douglas version of popular sovereignty, dubbed "squatter sovereignty," which allowed the territorial legislature but not Congress to rule upon slavery during the territorial phase.[186]

Here, it seemed, was a major southern victory. The Richmond *Enquirer* was jubilant. "The *nation*," it stressed "has achieved a triumph, *sectionalism* has been rebuked, and abolitionism has been staggered and stunned." Like other southerners the writer assumed that the decision would be respected. If so it seemed as though the territorial controversy was well on the way to resolution. Hence "another supporting pillar has been added to our institutions; the assailants of the South and enemies of the Union have been driven from their *point d'appui*; a patriotic principle has been pronounced; a great, national, conservative, union saving sentiment has been proclaimed." Similarly the Milledgeville *Federal Union* thought that the decision would strengthen the forces of moderation (as southerners defined it) within the nation as a whole. Noting that the Republicans wished to reject the decision, the newspaper argued that while the immediate effect might be another burst of antislavery agitation, the final result would be to quell the unrest. Even New Englanders, it was thought, as fanatical as they were, would "hesitate to enter the ranks of a political party, organised for the express purpose of overturning a decision of the Supreme Court of the United States." In this sense "the fury of the storm has passed" and the "treasonable conduct of the leaders of the Black Republican party" would soon "be rebuked at their very doors." The *Federal Union* predicted that "the true-hearted, Constitutional, law-abiding men of the North, and thousands who followed Frémont and 'bleeding Kansas,'" would soon find themselves "allied with the Union men of the country, in sustaining the determination of the Supreme Court in the Dred Scott case." In other words, the sanctity of the Supreme Court would undermine the antislavery cause.[187]

Overlooked in this prognosis was the possibility that the antislavery cause was now so powerful that it might instead undermine the sanctity of the Supreme Court. This process, however, took a little time. Initially, when the decision was delivered, Douglas was in considerable difficulties. His solution was to seek to salvage his own interpretation of popular sovereignty by amending or perhaps amplifying it. The so-called Freeport

---

186. On the Dred Scott decision Don E. Fehrenbacher, *The Dred Scott Case: Its Significance in American Law and Politics* (New York, 1978) is invaluable. See, however, Freehling, *Road to Disunion: Secessionists Triumphant* for a challenge to the view that the decision was a genuinely proslavery, rather than pro-Union one. It is of course the case that there was some controversy as to whether the Court's opinion on the territorial issue was *obiter dictum*.

187. Richmond *Enquirer*, March 10, 1857; Milledgeville *Federal Union*, March 31, 1857.

Doctrine, formally enunciated in 1858 but anticipated in some of Douglas's (and some other Democrats') prior utterances, asserted that while a territorial legislature might not be able to prohibit slavery directly, it could nevertheless achieve the same result indirectly by refusing to pass the policing regulations necessary in any slaveholding community. Thus Douglas sought both to accept the Dred Scott decision but also to retain the appeal of popular sovereignty in the North. Northerners were reassured that, despite the decision, they could easily achieve a prohibition on slavery in the territorial stage. In effect, therefore, Douglas offered the South the form, the North the substance.[188]

Initially southerners did not greatly resent Douglas's strategy. But in 1858 the issue became entangled with events in Kansas. With the possibility of winning both the form and the substance in Kansas, southerners now began to think the worst of those northerners who wished to deny them either. As we have seen, Lecompton became, in southern eyes, a test of northern attitudes towards slavery and most northerners – most northern Democrats and all Republicans – failed the test. This gave a new significance to the Dred Scott decision and to the Freeport Doctrine.

The result was the southern demand for a congressional slave code for the territories. If adopted this would have committed Congress to intervene to protect slavery there and, if necessary, ensure that the required policing regulations were in place.[189] Utterly unacceptable to Douglas, not least because it would ensure the annihilation of the Democratic party in the North, it was for the same reason judged unwise by some southerners, including some whose devotion to the cause of slavery was unimpeachable. Thus both of South Carolina's Senators, James Chesnut and James Henry Hammond, together with James L. Orr, also of South Carolina and Robert Toombs of Georgia thought it inexpedient to press the demand at that time, however justifiable the underlying principle might be. Nevertheless this was precisely the demand made when the Democratic party national convention met in 1860 first at Charleston and then at Baltimore. The rupture of the party and the nomination of two different tickets were the predictable results.[190]

The conduct of southern Democrats is therefore of great importance and it is essential to understand their increasing alienation from the majority of their erstwhile northern allies, whose most popular leader was, by a wide margin, Stephen A. Douglas of Illinois. The key question is why

---

188. Robert W. Johannsen, *Stephen A. Douglas* (New York, 1973), pp. 669–671.
189. See Freehling, *Road to Disunion: Secessionists Triumphant*, pp. 276–339 for the claim that, in the view of Jefferson Davis, John Breckinridge and many others, the slave code was to be invoked only in the event that the territorial legislature failed to pass the necessary legislation.
190. See Fehrenbacher, *Dred Scott*, p. 512.

they pressed for a platform upon which, as they had been repeatedly told, those northern allies simply could not stand. There were several reasons. A small minority of southerners actually wanted secession and wanted to bring it about directly. These out-and-out disunionists, as they might be termed, were still not, except in South Carolina, in a position of power. Edmund Ruffin of Virginia might be numbered among them but even a southerner as militant as William Lowndes Yancey of Alabama, who more than any other individual was responsible for pressing the demand for a slave code on the party convention, was not prepared to turn his back on the possibility of continued coexistence with the North, even if he believed the ultimate prospects bleak. Some contemporaries claimed that the southern goal was to throw the presidential election into the House of Representatives and by that route secure the defeat of the Republican candidate. Yet this was a consequence rather than a cause of the schism within the party for if Douglas had been acceptable to southern militants in 1860 he could have been nominated in the normal way and there need have been no recourse to a putative House election.[191]

The actions of the southerners were in fact far more principled and far more rational than some historians have allowed. For one thing, as Louis Wigfall of Texas observed, for southerners to support Douglas would have been to damage their "true friends" in the North, that relatively small number who were prepared to accept without reservation the southern interpretation of popular sovereignty. Those northerners would then have been exposed to the charge that they were prepared to do more for the South than southerners themselves. Yet this point too depended on the prior existence of a split within the Democracy and was thus more a consequence than a cause of the schism.[192]

To some degree the dispute between the southerners and Douglas turned on constitutional questions. Douglas sometimes argued that, in excluding slavery, a territorial legislature derived its power from Congress even though, as he acknowledged, the Dred Scott decision had ruled that Congress itself did not possess the power. Thus Congress could authorise a territorial assembly to do what it could not itself do. Most southerners viewed this as an absurdity. Since Congress itself set up a territorial government, Douglas's doctrine seemed a clear case of the creature being vested with greater powers than the creator.

---

191.  Potter observes that there was another motive: some southerners hoped to pressure Douglas into concessions but found out that this was impossible. They could then not back down – hence the claim of "irrationality." There is some truth in this but it is highly misleading. Southerners could indeed not easily back down, but their paramount objective was to make the Union safe for slavery, and there was nothing irrational in that.
192.  *Speech of Wigfall*, p. 29.

Alternatively Douglas and his supporters sometimes derived the power to exclude slavery from the inherent right of self-government. This was much the same right as Democrats had invoked in the early 1840s in the famous "Dorr war." At that time, southern Democrats, apart from the small band who followed John C. Calhoun, had endorsed this right but by the late 1850s their attitudes had altered sharply. They now found it quite unacceptable. As Albert Gallatin Brown observed, if Douglas were right in 1858 then Dorr had been right in 1842. Brown added that he had thought Dorr wrong.[193]

In addition to the dispute over the constitutional questions involved, southerners took exception to the unqualified unionism which Douglas, on some occasions at least, affirmed. This struck many of them as quite extraordinary and highly injurious, indeed fatal, to the South. On the one hand, Douglas sometimes denounced Republicans and abolitionists as vehemently as any southerner and shared the southern view of the catastrophic consequences implied by the policy of emancipation. But, on the other hand, in 1860 he toured the South threatening to hang every practising disunionist as a traitor. Thus William Porter of South Carolina in an avowedly disunionist tract reminded his readers that Douglas had condemned Abraham Lincoln for advocating a war of extermination but now was proposing to "put the South to fire and sword, because it would retire peacefully from the field, rather than become a party to this fratricidal strife of sections, or a meek and submissive victim to this relentless war of extermination." When Douglas made these threats at Norfolk Virginia, a group of forty eminent southerners from Virginia, Louisiana, North Carolina, South Carolina, Florida and Texas made a public protest. They could, they maintained, "conceive of no doctrine more dangerous to the South." Douglas had confused resistance to the law on the part of individuals, which should certainly be punished, with "the peaceable Secession of States from a compact no longer consistent with the interest or existence of its constituents." Moreover – and here the document touched upon a vital difference between northern and southern Democrats – Douglas had misunderstood the nature of the Union. He seemed to view it "as a perpetual bond, exacting unconditional submission, forever, from a weaker to a stronger section." The southerners then spelled out the dangers of his approach:

> It strips the States of the chief attribute of Sovereignty, to wit: the right to determine when their existence is put to hazard as to the means necessary to their preservation, and affirms that, while it is legitimate

193. *Speeches, Messages, . . . of . . . Albert Gallatin Brown*, pp. 564–565. For a short discussion of the Dorr war, see John Ashworth, *'Agrarians' and 'Aristocrats': Party Political Ideology in the United States, 1837 – 1846* (London, 1983), pp. 225–231.

in the people of the North having control of the General Government, through it, to inflict upon the States of the South whatever wrongs it may be consistent with their interest or feelings to impose, it would be treason in the people of the South to obey the orders of their States in opposition of Federal authority.

As the Richmond *Enquirer* concluded, even Republicans like Abraham Lincoln and William Seward were no worse than Douglas in their assaults upon the rights of the southerner for while "the former would rob him, regardless of the Constitution, of his means of subsistence," "the latter would shoot him if he had the courage to resist."[194]

Thus by 1860 the two wings of the party though in agreement on the abstract question of "state's rights" were in profound disagreement as to the precise nature of those rights. In a sense Douglas was true to the unqualified unionism of Andrew Jackson, the southerners were the heirs of Calhoun.

Even this, however, does not take us to the heart of the differences between Douglas and the southern militants for the most dramatic statements of his unionism came *after* the Democratic convention and thus after the schism in the party. They were made as he became increasing aware of the likelihood of a Republican triumph. Prior to that he had sometimes implied that a Republican victory would indeed be grounds for secession.[195]

Instead the southern case against Douglas turned upon the allegation that he had betrayed the principle of equal rights upon which the Kansas-Nebraska Act had been based, and thus had betrayed the South herself. Many southerners argued that the Douglas policy of squatter sovereignty was, in practice, an exclusion of the South from all the common territories and was thus every bit as injurious to their interests as the Wilmot Proviso had been a decade earlier. Thus the Staunton *Vindicator* referred to squatter sovereignty as one of the "expedients of abolition ingenuity" and indeed argued that, of all of them, it "aims the truest and deadliest blow at the institution of slavery." According to the Richmond *Enquirer*, the doctrine should meet with "unqualified abhorrence" from all true Democrats. In its practical application it was no better than the policy of congressional exclusion advocated by the Republicans. "Of what advantage," asked "Python" in *De Bow's Review*, "is it to the South to be destroyed by Mr Douglas through territorial sovereignty to the exclusion of Southern

---

194. Porter, *State Sovereignty*, p. 24; Richmond *Enquirer*, Sept. 28, 1860. The protest was reprinted in, for example, Richmond *Enquirer*, Sept. 11, 1860.
195. This was surely a legitimate inference given that he had placed the blame for the Brown raid, for example, squarely upon the Republicans. Could Southerners reasonably be expected to submit to the rule of such a party?

institutions, rather than by Mr Seward through Congressional sovereignty to the same end?" Similarly an electioneering address of 1860 claimed that Douglas differed from the Republicans only "in making insidious, instead of open, war upon the South," while Louis Wigfall, Democratic Senator from Texas, denounced Douglas as "a Democrat in name" but "a Red Republican in practice." At the Democratic Convention in Charleston, many Douglas supporters were told to go and join their kindred spirits – at the Republican convention.[196]

Douglas himself could, with some justification, have argued that he had not in fact changed his principles at all, that he had always favoured squatter sovereignty and that its avowal in 1854 had not prevented him from becoming a hero throughout the South. What had happened in the meantime? The most obvious event had been, of course, the Dred Scott decision. Douglas had always promised to acquiesce in the decision of the Court concerning the true meaning of popular sovereignty. His subsequent attempt to extricate himself from the consequences of that commitment produced both rage and scorn in the South. John C. Breckinridge, campaigning in Kentucky shortly before the voters went to the polls in 1860, reviewed the history of this controversy. The Dred Scott decision, he argued, had seemed to offer tranquillity. Since "the equality of rights of persons and property of all the States in the common Territory" had now been "stamped by the seal of judicial authority," it followed that "all good citizens might now acquiesce." Southern militants had then hoped that the sectional controversy might now be laid to rest. "The time seemed to be at hand," Breckinridge recalled, "when the agitation would be confined to a little handful of political Abolitionists, which the conservative sentiment of the country would soon put down." "Least of all," the candidate continued, "was any renewal of agitation to be expected from any portion of those who had agreed by the Kansas bill to refer the Constitutional question to the Court." The Dred Scott decision seemed to auger "the end of the struggle"; "the spectre of slavery agitation seemed to be laid forever."[197]

Here was the allegation that was at the heart of the case against Douglas. Some of his enemies in the North echoed the southern criticisms. Thus Daniel Dickinson, who had advocated popular (and squatter) sovereignty even earlier than Douglas himself, agreed that it must be qualified "in

196.  Staunton *Vindicator*, Jan. 20, 1860; Richmond *Enquirer*, Sept. 7, 1860; *De Bow's Review*, XXVIII (1860), p. 382; *Address to the Democracy and the People of the United States By the National Democracy Executive Committee* (Washington, DC, 1860), p. 2; *Speech of Wigfall*, p. 28; Milton, *The Eve of Conflict: Stephen A. Douglas and the Needless War* (Boston, 1934), p. 429.

197.  *Speech of Hon. J. C. Breckinridge, Delivered at Ashland, Kentucky, Sept. 5, 1860* (n.p., n.d.) p. 9.

harmony with the constitution." This meant that the Supreme Court must determine the issue. Once the Court had spoken, the entire controversy was, or should have been, laid to rest. For "if all had acquiesced in this decision, like good citizens, and had yielded willing and cheerful obedience to it as an authentic construction of the fundamental law, by the highest tribunal, the question of slavery in the Territories would have been at rest, and the democratic party would have been on its way rejoicing."[198]

Yet according to Breckinridge this had not happened because a year later, in his celebrated debates with Lincoln, Douglas had advanced the view (the Freeport doctrine) that "there was a mode by which subordinate authorities may over-rule the opinion of the highest tribunal in the Union." This had occurred "for the first time in the history of American politics." As another Democratic broadside put it in 1860, the so-called Freeport doctrine had invested the territorial legislature with the power to annul a decision of the United States Supreme Court. No southerner emphasised the enormity of this more than William L. Yancey, one of the prime movers in the demand for a slave code in the territories. A slave code was needed because the Freeport doctrine authorised the people of a territory to "take away the constitutional rights of the slaveholder there."[199]

In other words, the failure of Douglas to abide by the Court's decision seemed to southerners to demonstrate his faithlessness to the constitution. Breckinridge noted that Douglas himself termed it an "abstract question" but according to Breckinridge it was "one involving the equality of the States of the Union and the vital rights of nearly half of the Confederacy." Douglas's conduct seemed to demonstrate that even northern Democrats, let alone Republicans or abolitionists, could no longer be trusted to defend the rights of the South.[200]

For some southerners this abstract right to take slaves into the territories was all-important. Yet in 1860 there were no territories in which the right could be effectively exercised. Slavery had no existence in Colorado, Dakota, Washington, Nevada or Nebraska, while Utah and New Mexico contained at that time fewer than a hundred slaves between them. The point was, however, that the Constitution was the only safeguard for the South against an increasingly aggressive and exploitative North. According to Yancey, who did not himself think that territorial expansion was necessary for the South, it was "a vital issue, a constitutional principle . . . which could not be compromised without yielding our

198. From the *New York Herald of July 19, 1860 Breckinridge and Lane Campaign Documents*, No. 5 (Washington, D.C., 1860), pp. 11–12.
199. *Speech of Breckinridge*, 9; *Speech of the Hon. William L. Yancey, of Alabama, Delivered at Memphis, Tenn, Aug. 14, 1860* (Frankfort, KY, 1860), p. 14.
200. *Speech of Breckinridge*, pp. 9–11.

constitutional position of equality in the Union, and to that degree taking from our breast the Constitution, which is our only shield and protection against Northern majorities." The point for Yancey and those who thought like him was that if the provisions of the Constitution were to be set aside or circumvented by even northern Democrats then the South had to look elsewhere for self-preservation. And that could mean only the establishment of a southern confederacy.[201]

For others, however, the right to take slaves into territories was, as we have seen, a matter of direct practical concern and therefore of vital importance in itself. Southerners had not previously been unaware of the importance of protective legislation for slavery in the territorial stage. Thus as early as 1850 the *Mississippian* had been concerned that in establishing popular sovereignty in New Mexico and Utah, the architects of compromise had left slavery unprotected in those territories. There were "no laws creating a police over slavery." Here was a sharp contrast with the law in Mississippi, for example. Then the newspaper described the manner in which the law operated:

> where a runaway secrets himself in the fastnesses of a swamp or wood, any justice of the peace of a county where the slave us supposed to lurk, may direct the leader of a patrol detachment to take such power with him *as he shall think fit and necessary* for the effectual apprehension of the slave; and the State agrees to pay one fourth of a reward of thirty dollars for each slave recovered. We in Mississippi know the value of regulations of this kind. They are essential to the peaceable possession of our property.

In Mississippi if the slave were then to resist the law, the slave patrol "may...maim or kill him." In a territory like Utah, by contrast, the patrolmen would risk a murder charge. The effect on the institution of slavery would be akin to that of the Wilmot Proviso. Indeed "a slave in a territory would in fact be so voluntarily."[202]

Nevertheless, this issue had not been in focus during the debates over the Kansas-Nebraska Act. At that time southerners were so pleased to receive from Douglas in particular and the North in general what seemed a windfall that concerns over policing regulations in the territorial stage seemed insignificant in comparison. Now, however, in the light of the Freeport doctrine, they came sharply into focus. Although it was clearly too late for a slave code to apply to Kansas, and no other territory was an obvious candidate, some southerners seemed to look forward to the creation of future slave states for the settlement of which a slave code would

201. Fehrenbacher, *Slaveholder's Republic*, p. 275; Nevins, *Prologue to Civil War*, pp. 178, 403; *Speech of Yancey*, p. 4.
202. *Mississippian*, June 7, 1850.

be needed. This was perhaps implicit in the remarks of the Staunton *Vindicator* which in January 1860 stressed the importance of a slave code. The newspaper in fact referred to "protection for our slave property in the Territories" as a "jewel," which, if retained, would make "the institution of slavery . . . as firm and immovable as the everlasting hills." But if "this sacred constitutional right" were taken away then "slavery in the Union is a condemned and doomed institution." Here it is probable, but by no means certain, that the right was to be exercised in practice rather than defended merely as a matter of principle. Somewhat more explicitly the Richmond *Enquirer* complained that Douglas's policy would "utterly preclude the admission into the Union of another slave State." In explaining the operation of squatter sovereignty, the newspaper showed the impact that events in Kansas had had on southern attitudes. For under the operation of "squatter sovereignty," "New England Aid Societies . . . would speedily and effectually secure the control of any new territorial government which may hereafter be established, even where the element was not unfriendly to the prosperous existence of the institution of the South." The *Enquirer* stated that "such territory there is, already in the embraces of the Union, which, at a day not remote, may ask for admission as a sovereign State or States." Where was this territory? Unfortunately the *Enquirer* did not say, but the writer probably had in mind some parts of the Louisiana Purchase. For he then argued that squatter sovereignty was not merely as bad as "that disgraceful proposition," the Wilmot Proviso, but actually "worse" since "it affects territory which was acquired as *slave* territory, nearly a half a century before the annexation of Texas."[203]

There were therefore two reasons for southerners to denounce Douglas's Freeport doctrine. It could be condemned either as a barrier to the creation of any new slave states or it might be denounced as a betrayal of constitutional pledges and commitments, themselves essential to the preservation of slavery within the Union. But these were not the only criticisms of Douglas. His course over the Lecompton constitution produced even more resentment than the Freeport doctrine. According to Louis Wigfall, Douglas had always intended that Kansas should enter the Union as a free state. When the legitimate territorial government established slavery, however, Douglas, "the great non-interventionist," had then intervened in order to deny the proslavery forces their victory. In other words Douglas had, from the first, been out to deceive and betray the South and Wigfall went so far as to denounce him as "a demagogue" who had now deliberately disrupted the Democratic party in order to elect a Republican and dissolve the Union. Then Douglas might become president of a northwestern confederacy. William Yancey offered a similar set of

203. Staunton *Vindicator*, Jan. 20, 1860; Richmond *Enquirer*, Sept. 7. 1860.

accusations. He too believed that Douglas had had "designs upon the
unity of the Democratic party ever since the Northern people failed to
obtain, under the operation of the Kansas-Nebraska Act, the dominancy
in the Territory of Kansas." Then, "when it became apparent that the
Southern men had obtained advantages under that act, and that Kansas,
under these advantages, if fairly dealt by, would be admitted into the
Union as a slave state," Douglas had "determined to war against the true
principle of the Kansas-Nebraska bill" in order "to keep Kansas out of
the Union as a slave State." He was also prepared "if necessary, to dis-
member the Democratic party, and to rely for support in that controversy
upon the antislavery sentiment of the Northern States."[204]

While it was true that Douglas had allied with the Republicans against
the Lecompton constitution, little else in this indictment was accurate.
Although Douglas insisted time and again that it was not the proslavery
features of the Lecompton constitution to which he objected but rather
the undemocratic mode of its creation and adoption, militant southerners
gave little credence to the claim. Hence it was that Douglas was widely
regarded, especially in the Cotton States, as a traitor to the South by
1860. So it had been with Martin Van Buren a dozen years earlier. Van
Buren, it was pointed out, had previously served the Democratic party
with great distinction but by 1848 had to be "loathed by every disciple
of the Jeffersonian school." This, it was urged, should be Douglas's fate
in 1860.[205]

## III

In this intraparty dispute who was right? Historians have often criticised
southerners for their intransigence, their refusal to accept a platform and
a candidate who alone might have brought success to the party in the
North. But this is to misunderstand the objectives of the southerners who
bolted from the Charleston convention and ultimately nominated John
C. Breckinridge. Their goal was not primarily to win the election but
rather to ensure the permanent safety of the South. It was not enough
for them to defeat the Republicans; rather the task was to fortify the
South by preventing the Democratic party in the North from becoming a
vehicle for antislavery. The choice for them was not between a Democratic
and a Republican victory but rather between secession and a Democratic
victory won in such a way as to make secession unnecessary.[206] Hence the

204. *Speech of Wigfall*, p. 27; *Speech of Yancey*, pp. 3–4.
205. Richmond *Enquirer*, Sept. 7, 1860.
206. This view in turn rested on the assumption that, *whether the South took action or
not*, antislavery sentiment in the North would spread and deepen. Hence action was
required even if it meant that that same antislavery sentiment would spread and deepen
even more. It is a principal contention of this work that, although these southerners

emphasis upon constitutional guarantees. Nor should the abstract nature of the debate over a slave code be adduced as evidence of their irrationality. After all, the argument that no concrete interests were involved cut both ways: it should by the same token have been all the easier for northerners to acquiesce.[207]

Yet it was clear that Douglas could not have accepted a slave code. To do so, as Lincoln realised in 1858, would have ruined him in his home state and throughout the North. In this sense there was simply no room for a compromise between the two sides. When Douglas wrote a public letter to the effect that he would only accept the nomination on the basis of the Freeport doctrine, the effect of this, as his critics observed, was to put out of the party its president, all but two of its Senators and all but some half dozen of its Congressmen. Thus the schism in the Democratic party had already occurred before the Convention actually met.[208]

There was great irony in the conflict. Each side believed that it was demanding equality for all, northerners and southerners alike, in the territories. This was obviously true of Douglas, who proposed to treat slave property like any other and refused to give it special protection. His doctrine allowed the settlers to choose freely between slavery and free soil without any interference from Congress. But it was also true of the southerners who believed that without congressional protection slave property would not in fact be on an equal footing with any other. In other words, congressional intervention would establish and underwrite, rather than subvert, equality. This point was made with great force by Yancey who vehemently rejected the idea that a slave code would in any way force slavery upon a territory. "Because a Southern man goes to Kansas with his slave and demands that it shall not be taken away from him," he asked rhetorically, "is that forcing slavery on the people? Does it interfere at all with the principle of self-government if you shall leave your neighbor alone?" Yancey demanded to know "how it interferes with the people of Kansas governing themselves to require them to leave their neighbours alone with their slaves." Far from being a violation of equal rights, a slave code for the territories instead "indorses the doctrine," laid down in the Dred Scott decision, "that one man is on a level with his brethren."[209]

This was a valid argument in that slaveholders would not take their slaves into a territory if they thought the surrounding community hostile. But there was a profound paradox: a benign environment for slavery, the

---

did not understand the mechanisms or processes at work, they were right: antislavery in the North had deep social and economic roots.

207. See Roy F. Nichols, *The Disruption of the American Democracy* (New York, 1948); Daniel Crofts, "And the War Came," in Lacy K. Ford (ed.), *A Companion to the Civil War and Reconstruction* (Malden, MA, 2005), p. 185.

208. *Address to the Democracy*, p. 3.

209. *Speech of Yancey*, pp. 11–14. See also Crist *et al.* (eds.), *Papers of Davis*, VI, p. 140.

essential precondition for southern equality, seemed to result, as the experience of Kansas amply demonstrated, only in a denial of the equal rights of nonslaveholders whose freedom of (antislavery) expression and (antislavery) opinion had to be severely and, if necessary, violently curtailed. Thus both sides demanded equality; each approach necessarily violated it.

Here we encounter a further irony. Both sides also believed that slave property was akin to any other. Douglas constantly made this point and was wont to claim that just as Congress did not intervene to protect the property of the rum seller, for example, in a territory, so it should refrain from protecting that of the slaveholder. Southerners too asserted that slave property resembled any other. As Breckinridge put it, "between slave property and other property no distinction exists." They sought to assimilate slavery to other forms of property in order to broaden the basis of its support and rally to their cause the defenders of property rights of all kinds.[210]

Yet slavery was unlike other forms of property. If the rum seller did not convince his fellow citizens of the desirability of liquor he might fear that they would vote to exclude his business. There was little danger that they would steal his liquor and none at all that they could induce his liquor to flee of its own accord or to rise up against him. Hence with liquor the stakes were far lower; the need for extralegal action greatly diminished. Property in slaves was simply different from property in inanimate objects or livestock.

Once again therefore the resistance, actual or potential, between master and slave had a decisive effect on the politics of the final antebellum years. The Democratic schism, the split that pitted Douglas Democrats against southern militants saw both sides claiming that slavery was simply a form of property that should be placed on an equal footing with other forms of property. But in reality because of the conflict between master and slave, slaves were a profoundly different of property and no equality was actually possible.

## IV

As if the controversies within his party were not enough, the Buchanan years witnessed perhaps the most dramatic single event in the history of the sectional controversy to date. In October 1859 such calm as remained was shattered by the news of John Brown's abortive raid into Harpers Ferry, Virginia. Brown had hoped that the slaves would be inspired by his capture of the federal arsenal at Harpers Ferry and demand their freedom.

210. *Speech of Breckinridge*, p. 9.

When the expected uprising failed to materialise and he was captured and convicted, he played the role of martyr with consummate skill, winning the grudging respect even of the Virginia authorities. Brown was executed on December 2, 1859.

Southern reaction to the entire episode was mixed. All, of course, condemned it outright but not all drew the same conclusions. On the one hand, it seemed to confirm the loyalty of the slaves. According to one South Carolina newspaper, "the tone and temper of the slave have been exhibited in a striking light – assuring us of that faithfulness, that happy and contented disposition which the South has always claimed for him." Ironically neither Brown nor the southerners understood the slaves' response. Brown failed to appreciate that their chances of achieving emancipation were negligible, given the enormous naked power at the disposal of the Virginia authorities. The southerners did not appreciate that it was this, in conjunction with problems of logistics and communication, rather than any deep loyalty to their masters or any innate, racially determined subservience that prevented an insurrection. In this instance therefore, they concluded, even the interference of northerners had not been enough to corrupt their slaves.[211]

But far more important than this was what the raid revealed to them about the North. Brown had been backed by a number of influential northern abolitionists including Gerrit Smith, Theodore Parker and Thomas Wentworth Higginson. How many of the details of the raid they knew, or wanted to know, is difficult to determine but for southerners their complicity in it was confirmation, if confirmation was needed, of abolitionism's diabolical intent. According to the Governor of South Carolina Harpers Ferry was merely "the truthful illustration of the first act in the drama to be performed in a southern theatre." Similarly the Charleston *Mercury*, although believing the raid in one sense "a small affair" saw it as a portent of the future. It was "a pregnant sign of the times" and "a prelude to what must and will recur again and again, as the progress of sectional hate and Black Republican success advances to their consummation." The threat was particularly acute in the border states where slave property was coming to be seen as a "dangerous and troublesome nuisance" and slaves could "neither be kept nor managed." Unless resistance were offered "the Cotton States, which are vitally interested in the institution, are actually allowing slavery to be carried out of the border states" and encouraging the formation of an abolition party within the South. For the *Mercury* the raid, like almost every event in the sectional controversy, confirmed the need for an independent South; northerners

211. Yorkville, South Carolina, *Enquirer*, Oct. 27, 1859.

would no more seek to foment slave rebellions in a southern confederacy than in Cuba or Brazil.[212]

Many Democrats, north and south, quickly attributed the raid to the teachings of the Republicans and abolitionists. According to one election pamphlet Brown and his band had been "incited to the wildest extremes by the dangerous teachings of a false philanthropy." Stephen A. Douglas made the same claim in the United States Senate. In the South the Milledgeville *Federal Union* declared that they had "received indirect encouragement from William H. Seward, Joshua Giddings, Horace Greeley and other Republican leaders, who, by their speeches and writings, have encouraged fanatics to such deeds as this." In the same way a Tennessee newspaper refused to allow northern Republicans to dissociate themselves from the raid. Instead "the Republican party of the North is responsible for it"; "the fanatics engaged there would never have dared the attempt at insurrection but for the inflammatory speeches and writings of Seward, Greeley, and the other Republican leaders." Even Robert M. T. Hunter of Virginia, who acknowledged that the Republicans did not support Brown, noted that the raid was the final fruits of sectional hatred and pointed out that in no state had the party proposed any legislation to punish or forestall such attacks in the future.[213]

More specifically it was noted that a few months prior to the raid William Seward had made his "irrepressible conflict" speech in which he had offered a vision of the future of slavery, or rather of its lack of a future, within the Union. Southerners linked the Brown raid with Seward's speech, not because the New York senator was thought to have been directly implicated but because it was thought that violent abolition was the direct outcome of the doctrines he and his party preached. Seward had declared "war to extermination . . . against the institutions of slavery in the southern States" and the raid was "the legitimate result of Sewardism," "the commencement of what Seward spoke of as the "irrepressible conflict." Moreover, after the speech and the raid the northern electorate had an opportunity to rebuke the Republicans at the polls and the Richmond *Enquirer*, for example, called upon them to do so. "Let them send from the polls," it was urged, "greetings of overthrow that shall, if possible, restore confidence, and cement the broken fragments of attachment for the Union." But southerners who hoped for such an

---

212. *Journal of the House of Representatives of the State of South Carolina: Being the Session of 1859* (Columbus, SC, 1859), p. 22; Charleston *Mercury*, Nov. 14, Oct. 19, Nov. 1, 1860.
213. *Address of the National Democratic Volunteers* (New York, 1860), pp. 3–4; CG, 36/1, p. 553; Milledgeville, *Federal Union*, Nov. 1, 1859; Nashville, *Union and American*, Oct. 21, 1859; Charleston *Mercury*, Nov. 24, 1860; Richmond *Enquirer*, Oct. 25, 1859; *Speech of Hunter*, p. 5.

outcome were grievously disappointed. No rebuke was offered and instead the Republicans carried both branches of the New York legislature, and by increased majorities, the effect of which was to ensure Seward's re-election to the Senate.[214]

At the same time, southerners watched as northerners increasingly demonstrated their sympathy for Brown in the days up to and including his execution. On the final day, December 2, 1859 bells tolled, guns were fired, prayer meetings were held. It seemed as though there was an outpouring of grief, a day of mourning throughout the northern part of the nation.

As we have seen, southerners drew much consolation from what they took to be the loyalty displayed by their slaves. Similarly, those who had long been counting the value of the Union were gratified to see a hardening of attitudes in the South, and especially in the Upper South. The Charleston *Mercury* hoped and believed that the raid would operate on Virginia as a "slap in the face" to awaken her to an awareness of the dangers around and to stiffen her resolve. The Richmond *Enquirer* claimed that the raid had "advanced the cause of Disunion, more than any other event that has happened since the formation of the Government." It had "rallied to that standard men who formerly looked upon it with horror" and it had "revived, with ten fold strength the desire of a Southern Confederacy." In some of the states of the Upper South an Opposition movement had been developing which might have resulted in an alliance or at least an *entente* between anti-Democrats in those states and northern Republicans. The raid damaged this movement and southern militants derived some grim satisfaction from the fact.[215]

## V

Prior to the election of 1860 the four main events or processes of the Buchanan years were the Dred Scott decision, the battle over the Lecompton constitution, the Democratic schism, and the John Brown raid. They were clearly very different in character, ranging from legal wrangles to partisan disputes to purportedly extralegal, indeed revolutionary, action. Yet they perhaps had at least one common feature: all were, in all likelihood, the product of events in Kansas. This was obviously true of the debate over Lecompton but it was scarcely less true of the Dred Scott decision and the Democratic schism. What made *Dred Scott* so very controversial and so alarming to northerners was that it seemed to confirm their fears

214.  Charleston *Mercury*, Nov. 24, 1859; Nashville *Union and American*, Oct. 21, 1859; Richmond *Enquirer*, Oct. 25, 1859.
215.  Charleston *Mercury*, Nov. 28, 1860; Richmond *Enquirer*, Oct. 25, 1859.

about an advancing Slave Power whose most repressive, authoritarian and outrageous acts had been committed in Kansas. What made it so important to southerners was its apparent guarantee that slavery would not be threatened in future territories as it had been in Kansas. And what made the Democratic split so deep was the legacy of events in Kansas, which had illustrated (though few had seen it in this light) the difficulty, indeed the impossibility, of placing slavery on an equal footing with other forms of property in an environment where it was strongly resented by one group but resolutely defended by another. The John Brown raid, utterly unpredictable though it had been, may also have been an effect of the crisis in Kansas. Certainly many in both North and South thought so and it may well be that the violence in Kansas had done much to push Brown towards his insurrectionary action. In this sense, therefore, the nation's route to Civil War was indeed via the plains of Kansas.[216]

## Secession and war, 1860–1861

### I

In the South the election of 1860 was fought in an atmosphere of fear and crisis. Memories of the Brown raid were fresh in the minds of all, the progress of the Republican party was viewed with the deepest misgivings and rumours of insurrectionary plots were rife. As it became clear who the candidates were to be and increasingly possible that the Republicans would amass enough electoral votes to carry the day, southerners had to decide what action they would take. Essentially there were four possible responses. One was to do nothing and simply acquiesce in the election as if it were akin to any other. No southerner who had displayed any militancy in the preceding decade was willing to do this. The second was to wait for an overtly threatening act from the Republicans; this course of action recommended itself to many in the Upper South and to the most conservative elements, the most cautious spirits, in the Deep South. A third possibility was to demand that the Republicans recede from some or all of their programme in a last ditch attempt to maintain the Union. Among southern militants, this was perhaps the most widely favoured option. The final possibility was to move immediately towards secession itself, perhaps with each slave state acting alone, perhaps with some or many

216. The Charleston *Mercury*, for example, commented as follows: "successful in Kansas, is it surprising that the emissaries of abolition should turn to the frontier States to carry out within their limits the policy of insurrection and freesoil domination? The one was the natural consequence of the other" – Charleston *Mercury*, Nov. 8, 1860. As far as the North is concerned, Nevins claims that "a hundred journals" attributed Brown's raid to his experiences in Kansas – Nevins, *Prologue to Civil War*, p. 86.

of them acting in concert. Militant southerners adopted one of these last two strategies, advocating either immediate secession or a final, desperate effort, in effect an ultimatum to the North, in order to save the Union.

By 1860 they well understood, or at least thought they understood, the dangers facing them. In effect, threats surrounded them in three concentric circles. First was the "turbulence and discontent," as John Townsend of South Carolina put it, among the slaves, though this Townsend, as a good southerner, attributed almost entirely to "meddlesome intrusion" from abroad. Second, there was the threat, only a little more remote, posed by the nonslaveholders of the South. Several months before the presidential election of 1860 "Python," having warned in *De Bow's Review* of the "feeling of deep-rooted jealousy and prejudice, if not hostility, to the institution of negro slavery" that existed in Delaware and Maryland and in parts of Virginia, North Carolina, and Tennessee, concluded that it threatened "the most serious consequences, the moment Black-republicanism becomes triumphant in the Union." And here of course was the third threat, posed by the Republicans, geographically the most distant but politically the most urgent, the one which, southerner believed, largely mistakenly, activated the other two. By the start of 1860 if not much earlier, it was clear that the Republican party had a real chance of winning the presidency.[217]

Historians have often wondered whether the decision to secede was a rational one or whether highly emotional stereotyping had replaced dispassionate analysis in the minds of secessionists. Clearly much depends on the legitimacy of southern fears in 1860–1861 and upon the accuracy of southern perceptions of the Republican party, its history, its character and its intentions. What was the nature of the Republican threat to the South? Southerners were not slow to spell this out. Many announced in advance that they believed the election of Lincoln or Seward (when it seemed as though he would receive the party's nomination) would itself be sufficient grounds for secession. This belief was itself often the product of a lengthy and detailed review of the party's record. One such review was provided by William D. Porter of South Carolina in a tract written for the election of 1860:

> How can we judge of this Republican party otherwise or more fairly than by their own acts and declarations? What they have done is but an earnest of what they will do. The persistent agitation of the slavery question in the most offensive and insidious forms; the exclusion of the South from the whole of California – a territory for which the

217. [Townsend], *The South Alone . . .*, pp. 16; *De Bow's Review*, XXVIII (1860), p. 255. See J. William Harris, *Plain Folk and Gentry in a Slave Society: White Liberty and Black Slavery in Augusta's Hinterlands* (Middletown, CT, 1985), pp. 137–138,

South had expended more of blood and treasure than any other section of the Union; the dismemberment of Texas, with the bayonet in one hand and a bribe in the other; the rejection of Kansas because the Constitution of Lecompton protected slavery; the raid into Virginia, the burnings and poisonings in Texas, and the movements, incendiary and insurrectionary, of Northern emissaries even now lurking in other parts of the Southern country; the sympathy with John Brown, at first largely disguised, but now open and unmasked – a sympathy which is calculated if not expressly designed, to incite other deluded fanatics to an imitation of his treason and a coveting of his traitorous doom; the endorsement of the atrocious Helper book by some sixty members of their party in the present Congress, and the broadcast circulation of it as one of their campaign documents in the current canvass – and these things, and more, many more, which it sickens me to rehearse, demonstrate, beyond all doubt or cavil, a hostility of purpose, an antagonism of spirit and feeling, a deep and settled hate which, so far from being consistent with the duties and relations of brethren and fellow countrymen, would be a shame and a disgrace to natural and hereditary foes!

Several features of this indictment require comment. Much of it was quite accurate, however intemperate its tone. But there were significant inaccuracies and some highly questionable assertions. These fall into two categories. First, there was the conflation of all forms of antislavery in the North and the ascription to Republicans of events for which other northerners were responsible. Thus the actions of free-soilers and Whigs in 1850 and the activities of abolitionists like John Brown were conflated with Republicanism to create a misleading impression of a monolithic threat from the North. Second, there was the tendency to attribute to Republicans responsibility for events from which no northerner was responsible. Thus there was no evidence for the charge that the wave of "burnings and poisonings in Texas" was the work of Republicans or any other northerners. These were significant errors. As we shall see, however, this does not mean that the fears they generated were groundless, or that the demand for secession was in any way irrational.[218]

In 1860–1861 Southerners had two sets of fears, related but distinct. Few believed that slavery would cease to exist, or be abolished, the moment a Republican president took office. Rather they feared that a Republican Chief Magistrate would be able to inflict some dangerous blows upon the institution which would weaken it in the short, medium or long term, almost certainly fatally. They also believed that a Republican victory would confirm the ever-deepening antislavery convictions of the North. It would confirm that antislavery was on the march in the North and within the nation as a whole. And it would demonstrate that in

218. Porter, *State Sovereignty*, pp. 22–23.

the future still more extreme antislavery measures could be expected. The election of a Republican would thus in itself expose the South to some dangerous, perhaps deadly, attacks and would, at the same time, confirm and accelerate the progress of antislavery in the North, the result of which would be further assaults, even more numerous and still deadlier in nature.

## II

When the seven states of the Deep South took the decision to secede from the Union their leaders announced their reasons to the world, either by official messages and proclamations or in individual speeches and addresses. These documents are important to the historian although in themselves they do not offer a full exposition of secessionist thinking. One of the questions that received much, indeed perhaps disproportionate, attention was the fugitive slave issue. By 1860 the law passed ten years earlier had become unenforceable in many of the northern states and southerners dwelt upon the injustice of the Personal Liberty Laws that obstructed it. Thus South Carolina's official document of secession referred to the constitutional provision for the return of fugitives as one without which the Union would not have been established and then recounted the history of the Fugitive Slave laws:

> The States of Maine, New Hampshire, Vermont, Massachusetts, Connecticut, Rhode Island, New York, Pennsylvania, Illinois, Indiana, Michigan, Wisconsin and Iowa, have enacted laws which either nullify the Acts of Congress or render useless any attempt to execute them. In many of these States the fugitive is discharged from service or labor claimed, and in none of them has the State Government complied with the stipulation made in the Constitution. The State of New Jersey, at an early day, passed a law in conformity with her constitutional obligation; but the current of anti-slavery feeling has led her more recently to enact laws which render inoperative the remedies provided by her own law and by the laws of Congress. In the State of New York even the right of transit for a slave has been denied by her tribunals; and the States of Ohio and Iowa have refused to surrender to justice fugitives charged with murder, and with inciting servile insurrection in the State of Virginia.

It is noteworthy that South Carolina in this document gave more attention to the fugitive slave question than to the territorial issue.[219]

---

219. *Declaration of the Immediate Causes Which Induce and Justify the Secession of South Carolina from the Federal Union.* See also *First Message of Governor Isham Harris to the Tennessee Assembly, Jan 7 1861; Mississippi Resolutions on Secession; Alabama's Letter to the State of North Carolina, Resolutions on Secession from Floyd County, Georgia* – all these documents are available at

Yet this emphasis is misleading. As we have seen the fugitive slave prob-
lem affected the Upper South states far more than those of the Deep South.
Yet it was the Deep South which seceded in the winter of 1860–1861.
Only after war had broken out did the Upper South states follow. And
the states most vulnerable of all to the danger of slaves fleeing, Kentucky,
Missouri, Delaware, and Maryland, did not secede at all. Moreover the
election of Lincoln did little to alter the situation regarding fugitives. The
Personal Liberty laws were state measures and Lincoln himself would,
he announced, have been "glad" to see them repealed. Although some
Republicans took a very different view, the party as a whole was prepared to compromise on the question in 1860–1861. But concessions on
this issue were not enough to prevent secession. Even the more directly
affected states like Virginia announced that the issue was in itself a relatively minor one. Although the Richmond *Enquirer* in October 1860
argued that the violation of the law of 1850 constituted a breach of the
contract between North and South, as a result of which the Union no
longer truly existed, a month later the same newspaper denounced those in
the South who were satisfied with "the poor boon of apprehended fugitive
slaves." Such a strategy "abandons the other and more important issues
of the slavery question," and "should not influence the Legislature in this
severest trial of our people." After all "the escape of slaves is a grievance
peculiar to the border states" and Virginia "must not expect the Southern
States to become satisfied with the repeal of Northern laws nullifying the
fugitive slave law." Such repeal "would be indeed an encouraging sign"
but "it is neither all, nor yet the greater part of Southern grievances." As
Henry Benning put it in Georgia's formal debates over secession, although
the South certainly needed new measures regarding fugitive slaves, "that
question bears no higher relation to that great one, the intention to abolish
slavery, than a cent does to a dollar. It is a mere trifle compared with the
question whether or not slavery shall be abolished at the South." In the
words of Georgia Senator Alfred Iverson, those who, like him, advocated
disunion "look infinitely beyond this petty loss of a few Negroes."[220]

http://members.aol.com/jfepperson/causes.html. See also *CG*, 36/2, p. 356; Smith
(ed.) *History and Debates*, pp. 374–377.
220. David Potter, *Lincoln and his Party in the Secession Crisis* (Baton Rouge, 1995),
p. 100; Kenneth M. Stampp, *And The War Came: The North and the Secession
Crisis, 1860–61* (Chicago, 1950), p. 185; Richmond *Enquirer*, Oct. 23, Nov. 27,
1860, see also Dec. 21, 1860; "Henry L. Benning's Secessionist Speech" in William
W. Freehling and Craig M. Simpson (eds.), *Secession Debated: Georgia's Showdown
in 1860* (New York, 1992), p. 121; *CG*, 36/2, p. 49. For another example of southern
resentment concerning fugitive slaves, see "Robert Toombs' Secessionist Speech,"
in *Secession Debated*, pp. 41–43. It should, however, be noted in this connection
that some borderites were by 1860 claiming that slavery was unsustainable in their
regions because of the problem of slave flight, brought about, as they believed, by "the
influence of abolitionism" – see George H. Reese (ed.), *Proceedings of the Virginia*

Why then did southerners give so much attention to this question in their official or semiofficial declarations? There are two reasons. First, they felt that their case was unanswerable. The laws of the land, the provisions of the Constitution, had been set at naught. Second, the failure of northerners to enforce the law demonstrated their faithlessness to the Constitution. The Personal Liberty Laws thus illustrated northern hostility to the rights of the South, a hostility that threatened far more serious consequences in other areas whether in the immediate or more distant future.

## III

Flight was, of course, a classic form of resistance to slavery and it highlighted one of the weaknesses endemic in the system. And aiding fugitives was a charge of which some northerners could be convicted. An even more dramatic form of resistance, indeed the most dramatic of all, was violence against slaveholders, whether undertaken collectively in the form of insurrection or individually in the form of attacks by single slaves (or perhaps small groups of slaves) on the person or the property of their master. The Brown raid of 1859 had demonstrated that a small number of northerners at least were prepared to encourage this mode of resistance. Moreover, Brown's death and martyrdom seemed to have shown that Republicans and many northerners seemed to regret that it had not been more successful.

Southerners did not correctly perceive the nature of northern involvement in the raid. On the one hand they ascribed it, as we have seen, to the teachings of Republicans and abolitionists even though neither group had collectively set out to stir up slave rebellions. On the other hand, the involvement of the few who had known of Brown's plans, the so-called Secret Six, all of whom were militant abolitionists, was even deeper than southerners yet knew. One of them, Gerrit Smith, was a former Congressman who had contributed $500 to the Frémont campaign. In these circumstances some southerners not unnaturally identified the Republican party with the cause of slave insurrection.[221]

Those who did so were consequently driven to urge secession as soon as a Republican victory was achieved. Thus John Townsend of South Carolina struck the classic note, a mixture of confidence and trepidation, when he announced that he had no fear of insurrection unless it

*State Convention of 1861*. 4 vols. (Richmond, VA, 1965), I, p. 134, II, p. 69, III, p. 106.

221. Foner, *Free Soil, Free Labor, Free Men: The Ideology of the Republican Party Before the Civil War* (New York, 1970), p. 303.

were encouraged by outside forces. His "apprehensions," he announced, "spring from the operation of laws, and the alteration of the constitution" which a Republican victory portended. Thomas Clingman of North Carolina predicted that a hundred Brown raids might occur in a single year with a Republican in the White House. And "though the negroes left to themselves" were "harmless," yet "when assisted and led on by Europeans in St. Domingo, they destroyed the white inhabitants." Clement Clay of Alabama, defending in early 1861 his state's decision to leave the Union, condemned the Republican platform of the previous year for being "as strong an incitement and invocation to servile insurrection, to murder, arson, and other crimes, as any to be found in abolition literature."[222]

Similarly South Carolina's Senator James Henry Hammond in a letter drafted for the state legislature announced that the "irrepressible conflict" of which Republicans like Seward spoke, was "no mere political or ethical conflict." Instead it was "a social conflict in which there is to be a war of races to be waged at midnight with the torch, the knife and poison." At what has aptly been termed Georgia's "showdown," the occasion when in the aftermath of Lincoln's election her leading statesmen in a number of set speeches and public letters debated secession, Robert Toombs publicly expressed fears of insurrection at home, while Thomas Cobb described the climate of fear in which the state's slaveholders currently lived. Cobb reminded his listeners that the Union had been formed to promote "domestic tranquillity" and then invited them to contrast this with their own domestic environment:

> Recur with me to the parting moment when you left your firesides, to attend upon your public duties at the Capitol. Remember the trembling hand of a loved wife, as she whispered her fears from the incendiary and the assassin. Recall the look of indefinable dread with which the little daughter inquired when your returning footsteps should be heard. And if there be manhood in you, tell me if this is the domestic tranquility which this "glorious Union" has achieved. Notice the anxious look when the traveling peddler lingers too long in conversation at the door with the servant who turns the bolt – the watchful gaze when the slave tarries long with the wandering artist who professes merely to furnish him with a picture – the suspicion aroused by a Northern man conversing in private with the most faithful of your Negroes, and tell me if peace and tranquility are the heritage which this Union has brought to your firesides. Take up your daily papers and see reports of insurrections in every direction. Hear the telegram read which announces another John Brown raid. Travel on your Railroads and hear, as I did this day, that within seven miles of this Capitol, a gang of slaves have revolted from their labor, declaring

---

222. Townsend, *Death of Slavery*, pp. 25–27; CG, 36/1, p. 455, 36/2, p. 486.

themselves free by virtue of Lincoln's election, and say if such fruits as these grow on the good tree of domestic tranquility.

Like most southerners Cobb was confident of the innate loyalty of his slaves – so long as they were not incited by others. They were, left to themselves, "the most happy and contented, best fed and best clothed and best paid labouring population in the world" and thus "the *most faithful* and least feared." But the problem was that "a discontented few here and there" when "instigated by the unscrupulous emissaries of Northern abolitionists," would "become the incendiary or the poisoner." Then he underlined the need for immediate action: "what has given impulse to these fears, and aid and comfort to those outbreaks now, but the success of the Black Republicans – the election of Abraham Lincoln."[223]

These were extreme fears conveyed in highly alarmist rhetoric. Yet there is no reason to dismiss them as mere hyperbole or hypocrisy; historians have found no evidence that private belief belied public utterance. The fear of slave insurrection was widespread in the South, it united the border states with the Deep South. Yet not all southerners were convinced that a Republican administration would, of itself, result in slave revolts, Brown raids or waves of arson. Most of those who predicted such consequences probably had other grounds, sufficiently strong in themselves, for favouring secession while the dominant opinion in a state like Virginia, which had after all played host to Brown, was that secession was not yet justified. If all southerners who feared slave insurrections and other forms of violent resistance had believed that a Republican victory would itself bring them about, then eleven or perhaps even fifteen states would presumably have left the Union immediately. The sheer horror with which almost all southerners viewed slave insurrections suggests that outside the ranks of already-committed secessionists, most of them did not believe the election of a Republican president in itself made them significantly more likely to occur.

## IV

Abraham Lincoln's election in November 1860 had both practical and symbolic consequences. Some of the practical consequences flowed directly from the assumption by a Republican of the powers of the executive. Robert Toombs, in advocating secession, referred to the "executive

223. Hammond: *draft of letter to the Legislature of South Carolina Nov. 1860* quoted in Channing, *Crisis of Fear*, p. 286; "Toombs' Secessionist Speech," in Freehling and Simpson (eds.), *Secession Debated*, p. 49, "Thomas R. R. Cobb's Secessionist Speech," in Freehling and Simpson (eds.), *Secession Debated*, pp. 11–12. See also Porter, *State Sovereignty*, p. 32.

power" as "the last bulwark of the Constitution," and argued that it had "been swept away," with the result that "we now stand without a shield." This, however, was open to question, since the Republicans in 1860 did not control either chamber in Congress, nor did Republican opinions hold sway in the Supreme Court, which had, after all, only recently handed down the (in the South) much acclaimed Dred Scott decision.[224]

Nevertheless, the loss of the executive was an immense blow to southerners. What could an antislavery president do? Apart from the huge symbolic value of the victory, and the enormous boost it would give to the antislavery cause throughout the nation, Lincoln as president would now be able to wield certain well-defined powers. Among these was the power of the patronage and the prospect of this power being exercised by a Republican caused intense consternation among southern militants.[225] These fears had been prominent since the inception of the new party in the mid-1850s. Prior to that date, southern militants had frequently denounced southern Whigs for being insufficiently loyal to the South, for surrendering too much to the North and for being prepared to collaborate with northern antislavery partisans like William H. Seward. They had rarely, however, argued that a Whig president would actually use the powers of the patronage to build up an overtly antislavery party throughout the South. Before the mid-1850s when fears of presidential power being mobilised against the South had been aired, they were usually in the context of vague speculations about events that might occur in the more distant future involving political organisations that had not yet seen the light of day.[226]

The birth of the Republican party transformed the situation. In the wake of the election of 1856, when the new party had performed remarkably well, southerners began to raise the alarm about the potential use or abuse of the patronage. Writing in *De Bow's Review*, Edmund Ruffin in 1857 referred to the "open, unassailable, and powerful influence" that would then be brought to bear. In such circumstances, "the zealous and active exertions of these many thousands of Government officials and employees, down to the lowest labourers on any Government work, would be counted on and secured, to operate against the institution of slavery and the interests of slaveholders." In early 1860 Robert Toombs of Georgia registered a similar fear of the Republicans in a letter to Alexander H. Stephens when he noted that the recent election of a Republican speaker

---

224. "Toombs' Secessionist Speech," in Freehling and Simpson (eds.), *Secession Debated*, p. 45.

225. See Freehling, *Road to Disunion: Secessionists Triumphant*, pp. 104, 253, 264, 289, 336–337, 367–371, 397, 455, 512 for an excellent treatment of this issue.

226. See, for example, Montgomery *Advertiser*, June 1, 1850 quoted in Thornton, *Politics and Power*, p. 217.

had given a great impetus to the antislavery cause in the locality of the federal capital and warned of the dangers of Republican control over the other branches of government. The effect would be to "abolitionize Maryland in a year, raise a powerful abolition party in Va., Kentucky and Missouri in two years, and foster and rear up a free labour party in [the] whole South in four years." At that point "the strife will be transferred from the North to our own friends" and at that point too "security and peace in our borders is gone forever."[227]

As the election of 1860 loomed, these concerns came increasingly to the fore. The Washington *Constitutionalist*, newspaper of the Buchanan administration, warned that a Lincoln administration would put anti-slavery officeholders into every community and flatly declared that the South could not be expected to submit to this outrage. The election also witnessed a high degree of activity on the part of vigilance committees, sometimes dubbed "Minute Men" organisations throughout the Deep South. Some of them were explicitly told to be alert to the danger of Republican sympathisers receiving federal offices in the event of a Lincoln victory. In Mississippi, for example, one newspaper announced that it would be the duty of such organisations not to permit "a corrupt and mercenary band of officeholders to be installed in their midst by a Black Republican President." Although "the enemies of the South" might seek to "demoralize her people and to divide her . . . ranks," it was possible for countermeasures to be taken "with a view to block this avenue to power in our midst"[228]

By polling day southern militants were aware that a Republican triumph was imminent. Some Breckinridge supporters in the South warned that many of their opponents, who now claimed to be merely Unionists, would soon metamorphose into Republicans or even abolitionists. The New Orleans *Delta*, a leading Democratic newspaper in Louisiana, similarly warned that there were in the South "very many, as there must be very many in every community, who would yield to the pressure of a majority, to the allurements of office, to the seductions of power." Such men would "in a short time, after Lincoln's election, should the South submit to his Administration . . . fill the Federal offices, would wield all the influence of the Federal Government within the Southern States, and with their followers and friends would compose the Administration party." Thus they "would be the basis of a Black Republican organization, having

227. *De Bow's Review*, XXII (1857), p. 588; Robert Toombs to Alexander H. Stephens. Feb. 10, 1860, in Phillips (ed.), *Correspondence of Toombs, Stephens, and Cobb*, p. 462.
228. Washington *Constitutionalist*, Sept. 21, 1860, quoted in Nevins, *Prologue to Civil War*, p. 290; *Vicksburg Weekly Citizen* quoted in Bolton, *Poor Whites of the Antebellum South*, pp. 165–166.

more or less strength in every Southern State." Consequently it was a delusion to believe that "when this Black Republican party is formed in every Southern State, it will be without followers and sympathizers"[229]

The power to nominate or appoint officeholders, from postmasters and port collectors to Supreme Court justices, now received full consideration from many southerners. One after another, as the election approached, they predicted the dire consequences that would inevitably follow when this power was exercised. The most obvious, but still catastrophic, effect would be the creation of a Republican party in every state of the South. In 1860 Lincoln was not even on the voting ticket in most of the states of the South and some southerners fretted that even the Douglas Democrats within the region, if not led by slaveholders, would pose a threat. Little wonder then that the prospect of a Republican party was so alarming. The Richmond *Enquirer*, the leading newspaper in Virginia and perhaps in the entire South, decreed in October 1860 that "no patriot, south of Mason and Dixon's line, must hold an office under the administration of Lincoln, any more than he would hold an office under a foreign potentate who was [in?] open hostility to our cherished institutions" And any states that furnished officeholders were "so fallen that it matters not at what time they unresistingly lay their heads upon the executioner's block." Yet there was a real danger that "Mr. Botts [of Viriginia], or Mr. Rives [of Virginia], or Mr. Etheridge [of Tennessee], or Mr. Anybody-else" would be offered and would accept a major role in a Lincoln administration. What would be the effect? The *Enquirer* conceded that on Lincoln's accession to power it "would apprehend no direct act of violence against negro property." Yet "by the use of federal office, contracts, power and patronage," there would occur "the building up in every Southern State of a Black Republican party, the ally and stipendiary of Northern fanaticism, to become in a few short years the open advocate of abolition, the confiscation of negro property by emancipation sudden or gradual, and eventually the ruin of every Southern State by the destruction of negro labor." The *Enquirer* also conceded that "no act of violence may ever be committed, no servile war waged" and yet "the ruin and degradation of Virginia" would be "as fully and fatally accomplished as though bloodshed and rapine ravaged the land."[230]

Similarly, and almost simultaneously, in the Deep South the Charleston *Mercury*, long the acknowledged voice of secession and disunion, expressed deep concern about the loyalty of some elements within the

229. Crofts, *Reluctant Confederates*, p. 92; Barney, *Secessionist Impulse*, p. 123; New Orleans *Delta*, Nov. 1, 1860, in Dumond (ed.), *Southern Editorials on Secession*, pp. 202–203.
230. Barney, *Secessionist Impulse*, p. 123; Richmond *Enquirer*, Oct. 23, July 10, 1860.

South. "With the control of the Government of the United States, and an organized and triumphant North to sustain them," the newspaper warned, "the Abolitionists will renew their operations upon the South with increased courage." At that point traitors would be found. For "the thousands in every county, who look up to power, and make gain out of the future, will come out in support of the Abolition Government." More specifically "the BROWNLOWS and BOTTS in the South" would "multiply"; they would "organize; and from being a Union Party, to support an Abolition Government, they will become, like the Government they support, Abolitionists." The result would be "an Abolition Party in the South, of Southern men" and from that point onwards "the contest for slavery will no longer be one between the North and the South" but instead "will be in the South, between the people of the South."[231]

These fears reached a crescendo when news of Lincoln's victory, and in the North by such a large margin, finally broke. Those who were already advocating secession immediately redoubled their efforts; some of those who had previously been devoted to the Union quickly changed tack. In Georgia Howell Cobb wrote a public letter to the people of his state advocating secession. In so doing he explicitly confronted the point, now being made by many Unionists, that there was still a majority in Congress against Lincoln, a majority upon which the South could rely. Cobb posed a series of questions:

> Can that majority in Congress control the power and patronage of President Lincoln? Can it stay his arm when he wields the offices and patronage of the Government to cement and strengthen the anti-slavery sentiment which brought his party into existence and which alone can preserve it from early and certain dissolution? Can it prevent the use of that patronage for the purpose of organizing in the South a band of apologists – the material around which Black Republicanism hopes during his four years to gather an organization in Southern States to be the allies of this party in its insidious warfare upon our family firesides and altars?

His conclusion was that "true but over-anxious friends of the Union at the North, faithful but over-confiding men of the South, may catch at this congressional majority straw, but it will only be to grasp and sink with it."[232]

231. Charleston *Mercury*, Oct. 11, 1860, in Dumond (ed.), *Southern Editorials on Secession*, p. 179. An almost identical point was made in private by Lawrence Keitt of South Carolina – see Keitt to Porcher Miles, Oct. 3 1860 in Barney, *Secessionist Impulse*, p. 123.
232. "Howell Cobb to the People of Georgia," in Phillips (ed.), *Correspondence of Toombs, Stephens, and Cobb*, p. 514.

In the weeks and months following Lincoln's victory and as the debate over secession raged, so one southerner after another drew attention to the dangers to be apprehended from a Republican president. Thus John J. Allen of Virginia, president of the state's Supreme Court, addressing a mass meeting in Botetourt County in December 1860 called for concerted action on the part of the southern states and warned of the dangers now facing the South. The new president would be "clothed with the patronage and power incident to the office" and this included "the authority to appoint all the postmasters and other officers charged with the execution of the laws of the United States." Here, Allen declared, was "a standing menace to the South – a direct assault upon her institutions, an incentive to robbery and insurrection, requiring from our own immediate local government... prompt action to obtain additional guarantees for equality and security in the Union; or to take measures for protection and security without it." A few months later, when Virginia held her own convention to debate secession, another slaveholder warned that the new president would create a Republican party in the South leaving "Black Republicans upon every stump, and organizing in every county." "That," he concluded, "is the peace we shall have from this 'glorious Union'."[233] Similarly Stephen F. Hale of Alabama, sent as a commissioner to the state of Kentucky, addressed some questions to her Governor:

> Shall we wait until our enemies shall possess themselves of all the powers of the Government? Until Abolition Judges are on the Supreme Court bench, Abolition Collectors at every port, and Abolition Postmasters in every town, secret mail agents traversing the whole land, and a subsidized Press established in our midst to demoralize the people? Will we be stronger then, or better prepared to meet the struggle, if a struggle must come?

He then offered a succinct answer to his own questions: "No, verily!"[234]
    Although these southerners were all convinced of the dangers posed by a Republican in the White House, they did not all advance the same prognosis. The power of the patronage involved above all, perhaps, the right to appoint postmasters in every locality. This in turn had two consequences. First, the mere availability of these offices was itself an allurement, an incentive to southerners to endorse Republican policies and betray the South. Second, and equally important, postmasters were in a position to

---

233.  Reese (ed.), *Proceedings of Virginia State Convention*, I, p. 257.
234.  *The Botetourt Resolutions of Judge John J. Allen... Offered in a large mass meeting of the people of Botetourt County, December 10th, 1860, by the Hon. John J. Allen, President of the Supreme Court of Virginia* available at http://www.geocities.com/bobscivilwar/docs1861/doc61g.html; "Letter of S. F. Hale, Commissioner of Alabama to the State of Kentucky, to Gov. Magoffin of Kentucky, Dec. 27, 1860," in Smith (ed.), *History and Debates*, pp. 382–383.

influence, if not to control, access to antislavery material in the mails. Since the controversy over the mails in the mid-1830s such material had been sent into the South but retained at local post offices. Antislavery postmasters, however, could reverse this policy and thus generate a new debate over the peculiar institution within the South.[235]

This prospect brought panic to southern militants. Sometimes they drew attention to the possibility that the slaves themselves would be directly affected. Thus David Clopton, Alabama's Commissioner to Delaware, in a letter to Delaware's Governor, warned in January 1861 that Lincoln would "exert all his powers, influence, and patronage" in order to place slavery on the path to ultimate extinction. This process would be facilitated "by the possession of the channels through which to circulate insurrectionary documents and disseminate insurrectionary sentiments among a hitherto contented servile population." Similarly the Montgomery *Mail* in August 1860 predicted that "if Lincoln . . . shall be elected, every postmaster will be a tamperer with slaves, every marshal and other Federal functionary a promoter of rebellion." Thus the fear of servile rebellion re-emerged and indeed reached new heights, stimulated by both the Brown raid of 1859 and the prospect of a Republican in the White House. The Charleston *Mercury* specifically linked the Brown raid with the growth of a Republican party in the South and predicted social convulsions for the slaveholders in a Union dominated by the Republicans. "If, in our present position of power and unitedness," the *Mercury* argued, "we have the raid of JOHN BROWN – and twenty towns burned down in Texas in one year, by abolitionists," then "what will be the measures of insurrection and incendiarism which must follow our notorious and abject prostration to Abolition rule at Washington, with all the patronage of the Federal Government, and a Union organization in the South to support it?"[236]

On other occasions secessionists emphasised the threat that might now be posed by the nonslaveholding whites, newly contaminated by Republican propaganda. According to the Wilmington, NC *Journal*, "federal patronage within our limits will become the nest to hatch black republican eggs, and a nucleus around which will gather a black republican squad." The dissemination of Republican ideas would thus stir "jealousies between the slaveholder and the non-slaveholder" and the "minds of the uneducated" would be "systematically demoralized upon the subject." Another possibility, equally terrifying, was of an alliance forged

235. Fehrenbacher, *Slaveholder's Republic*, p. 302.
236. *"Hon David Clopton to the Governor of Delaware,"* Jan. 1st, 1861, in Smith (ed.), *History and Debates*, p. 440; Montgomery *Mail*, Aug. 16, 1860 quoted in Avery Craven, *The Coming of the Civil War* (Chicago, 1957), p. 424; Charleston *Mercury*, Oct. 11, 1860, in Dumond (ed.), *Southern Editorials on Secession*, pp. 179–180.

by a Republican president, between slaves and nonslaveholding whites. Thomas Clingman of North Carolina predicted that a Republican president would "fill the southern States with postmasters, and other officials, whose efforts would be directed," in general, "to dividing, as much as possible, the people of the South," and, in particular "to forming connections with the Negroes." This policy, or some variant of it, would "doubtless...be adopted before any direct blow was struck at slavery anywhere." Some southerners did not distinguish between these possibilities, or rather they claimed that a combination of some or all was entirely possible, indeed probable. Thus Governor Joseph Brown of Georgia predicted that "as soon as the Government shall have passed into Black Republican hands, a portion of our citizens must, if possible, be bribed into treachery to their own section, by the allurements of office." Alternatively, Brown warned, "a hungry swarm of abolition emissaries, must be imported among us as office-holders, to eat out our substance, insult us with their arrogance, corrupt our slaves, and engender discontent among them; while they flood the country with inflammatory abolition documents; and do all in their power to create in the South, a state of things which must ultimately terminate in a war of extermination between the white and the black races." Brown was here more prescient than he knew since the groups he described would indeed subsequently emerge – as Scalawags and Carpetbaggers respectively during Reconstruction.[237]

Whatever the process, southerners were convinced that an army of officeholders, owing loyalty to a Republican president, would soon be marshalled against the South. How seriously did they take this threat? Missouri Senator Trusten Polk described in detail the scene that awaited the South when a Republican president exploited the power of the patronage:

> Cohorts of Federal office-holders, Abolitionists, may be sent into her midst to exert the patronage, influence and power of their offices, and to plot and conspire against her property, her peace. Postmasters – more than thirteen thousand – with all their employees, controlling the mails and loading them down with incendiary documents. Add to these, land officers, surveyors of land, surveyors of ports, collectors of customs, assistant treasurers, judges and marshals, each of these, with all his employees, intent upon one aim.

Polk clearly believed that no danger facing the South was of comparable importance; "against almost everything else but this, the South might

237. Wilmington (NC) *Journal*, Jan. 3, 1861 quoted in Crofts, *Reluctant Confederates*, p. 93; *CG*, 36/1, p. 455; *Journal of the Senate of the State of Georgia at the Annual Session of the General Assembly...1860* (Columbus, 1860), p. 47.

protect herself." But "what institution," he asked, "could withstand such an invasion, such sapping and mining?"[238]

Sometimes southerners singled out the potential effects on the border states. Senator Alfred Iverson of Georgia also displayed more prescience than he knew when predicting that northern power would soon be augmented by the resources of the border states. Iverson posed a question. "Let the post office and the mails be put into the hands of the Republican party, disseminating their seditious tracts through every hole and corner of the southern States, encouraging incendiarism, John Brown raids, murderings, poisonings, and revolts, and what," he asked, "will be the condition of the border states?" He then gave an answer: slavery would become a "burden" to them and those slaves that did not manage to escape would be "sent down to the cotton States to be sold, and Maryland and Virginia and Kentucky and Missouri will, in a few years, add to the power and arrogance of the free States of this Confederacy." Iverson's predictions were, in part, borne out. Although the process would not be the one he had anticipated, within a few months three of those four states (along with Delaware, on which he had presumably already given up) would indeed be ranged against the other slaveholding states of the South.[239]

Among the slaveholders in the border states themselves, these fears were also prominent. In a letter to the Nashville *Patriot* one correspondent predicted that a Republican president would use "soft language," "kind words," "money without measure" in order to "poison the fountains of public sentiment." By the time of the presidential election of 1864 a "Black Republican ticket" would be "openly run in Tennessee" and the whole process would culminate in the state's slaveholders selling their slaves to the Lower South. For "does not every man know that all the Negroes among us will, as a matter of self-preservation, have to be carried South?" Thus the Republicans would be able to put an end to slavery in the border states not by dint of violent revolution, or even as a result of a political struggle, but by stimulating ordinary and routine commercial processes.[240]

Other southerners, also focussing upon the border region, warned of a domino effect, whereby a newly installed Republican president would undermine slavery in the border states, which would in turn facilitate emancipation in the Deep South. According to the Richmond *Enquirer*, "by gradual and insidious approach, under the fostering hand of federal

---

238. *CG*, 36/2, p. 357.
239. *CG*, 36/2, p. 49. See also Carey, *Parties, Slavery and the Union*, pp. 240–241.
240. Letter to editor of Nashville Weekly *Patriot* quoted in Crofts, *Reluctant Confederates*, pp. 93–94. The point about selling slaves southward is of great importance and has received heavy emphasis in Freehling's writings. See Freehling, *Reintegration*, p. 156.

power, abolition will grow up in every border Southern State, converting them into free States, then into 'cities of refuge' for runaway negroes from the gulf States."[241]

Yet patronage was not the only weapon available to a Republican president. Some southerners drew attention to his role as Commander-in-Chief. "The very inauguration of your candidate," Thomas Clingman of North Carolina told the Republicans, "makes him commander of the Army and Navy" and "one of his first acts would be, doubtless, to station them advantageously, while, at the same time, he could carefully remove from the South all the public arms, lest the people should take them for defense." The lack of a Republican majority in Congress would not, southerners noted, diminish this power. Similarly John Townsend of South Carolina asked whether southerners should "*wait*, until, as Commander-in-Chief of the Army and Navy of the United States, he takes possession of those engines of power to compel obedience; and of the Treasury of the Government . . . to bribe traitors amongst ourselves, the more securely to establish his power?" That this was purely a rhetorical question was clear from the very title of Townsend's pamphlet: *The South Alone, Should Govern the South*.[242]

For a variety of reasons, therefore, southerners deeply feared Republican occupancy of the White House, even if it were not reinforced by Republican control of Congress. As we have seen, some southerners predicted that the appointment of Republicans to federal offices within the South would give a direct impetus to slave rebellion and revolt. Some, however, believed that the opposite would occur in that extralegal action would be rendered unnecessary. Thus Robert Toombs of Georgia advocated secession on the grounds that Republicans would now be able to use the power of the federal government and would consequently not need to resort to extralegal action:

> Hitherto they have carried on this warfare by State action, by individual action, by appropriation, by the incendiary's torch and the poisoned bowl. They were compelled to adopt this method because the Federal executive and the Federal judiciary were against them. They will have possession of the Federal executive with its vast power, patronage, prestige of legality, its army, its navy and its revenue on the fourth of March next. Hitherto it has been on the side of the Constitution and the right; after the fourth of March it will be in the hands of your enemy.

Consequently Toombs was unable to derive any consolation from the anticipated switch in Republican strategy following the party's electoral

---

241. Richmond *Enquirer*, July 10, 1860.
242. "Cobb's Secessionist Speech," in Freehling and Simpson (eds.), *Secession Debated*, p. 25; *CG*, 36/1, p. 455; [Townsend], *The South Alone . . .*, pp. 14–15.

triumph. Rather than let a Republican president assume the powers of the executive, Toombs counselled resistance: "strike while it is yet today."[243]

It was therefore highly rational for southerners to fear the consequences of Republican victory in 1860. Although Lincoln himself promised not to appoint "obnoxious strangers" to office in the southern states, many of those whom secessionists feared, however obnoxious they might be, were anything but strangers in the localities in which they operated. It should be noted that some Republicans themselves had virtually identical expectations of the growth of their party within the South and before war broke out Lincoln and others were already receiving applications for office from below the Mason-Dixon Line. Nor was the potential disloyalty of southern nonslaveholders (who would be the targets of Lincoln's patronage policy) a concern that surfaced only in 1860. As we have seen, the dangers, real or potential, posed by the white nonslaveholders had precipitated the furore over the Helper volume, they had been the major concern of those seeking to reopen the African slave trade; and they had done much to feed the antiurbanism which had long been a feature of the Old South. Thus the prospect of a Republican in the White House activated some long-standing fears and was one from which southerners had indeed good reason to recoil.[244]

## V

As far as formal policies were concerned, however, the Republicans' main commitment was to stop the further spread of slavery. In the secession winter of 1860–1861, numerous attempts at compromise were offered but all foundered, essentially on the territorial question. Lincoln avowed himself "inflexible" on the issue and the southerners who were by now in control of the states of the Deep South were scarcely less so. More than any single area of controversy it was the extension of slavery which created an unbridgeable gulf between the sections.

Yet however tightly southern militants might unite in opposition to the policy of free soil, they did not always advance the same reasons for

---

243. "Toombs' Secessionist Speech," in Freehling and Simpson, (eds.), *Secession Debated*, p. 47. There was, at least in theory, the possibility that southerners might block the appointment of any southerners whose loyalty to slavery was in doubt. But as Thomas Cobb of Georgia put it, the result might be to prevent the formation of a cabinet or an administration. "What is this," he asked, "but revolution and anarchy?" – "Cobb's Secessionist Speech," in Freehling and Simpson, (eds.), p. 24.

244. Roy F. Basler (ed.), *The Collected Works of Abraham Lincoln*. 9 vols. (New Brunswick, 1953–1955), IV, p. 49. It should perhaps be noted that the fear of a Republican party being created in the South received little attention in the official Ordinances of Secession since the priority there was to demonstrate unity rather than announce the potential for internal strife or dissent. These documents resembled declarations of war not because war was anticipated or generally desired but because unity and strength of resolve were clearly at a premium.

that opposition. It was not always clear which aspect of the case against exclusion in the territories was uppermost. As we have seen, the widespread enthusiasm in the South for the Kansas-Nebraska Act had masked contrasting, though not contradictory, priorities. Some had wanted and expected Kansas to become a slave state, others had hoped for more territory elsewhere but probably not in Kansas, still others had been motivated by the need to purge the legislative record of an unconstitutional prohibition. Those who had demanded additional territory had in turn advanced different arguments, sometimes stressing political factors, on other occasions emphasising economic considerations. These different priorities had coexisted throughout the 1850s; they were still present during the secession crisis.

Some southerners continued to insist that the economic needs of the slave system were such that additional territory for the South was essential. For these southerners territorial expansion required a southern Confederacy, given Republican policies, and a southern Confederacy would in turn require territorial expansion. They drew attention to the longstanding fear of an excess of slaves in the South. Although this concern had perhaps been most marked in times of economic hardship, it was still apparent in the final, prosperous antebellum years. The problem was one we have already encountered: the rate of increase of the slave population. Thus Thomas Cobb warned his fellow Georgians at the Milledgeville debates on secession that "ere long you will be imprisoned by walls of free States all around you" and "your increasing slaves will drive out the only race than can move – the whites." The result, Cobb continued, employing a simile that was widely used in the secession crisis, would be that "the masters who still cling to their fathers' graves, will, like the scorpion in a ring of fire, but sting themselves to die." "This," he concluded, "is your destiny in the Union."[245]

Others voiced similar fears. At the same gathering Robert Toombs calculated that if the historic growth rate of the slave population were maintained, there would be eleven million slaves by 1900. What was to be done? Toombs insisted that "we must expand or perish": "we are constrained by an inexorable necessity to accept expansion or extermination." From these calculations and from a review of the history of the expansion of slavery into new territories since the Revolution, he concluded that the issue was no mere abstraction. Indeed "those who tell you that the territorial question is an abstraction...are both deaf and blind to the history of the last sixty years." According to Toombs, "all just reasoning, all past history condemn the folly." And northerners themselves,

---

245. "Cobb's Secessionist Speech," in Freehling and Simpson (eds.), *Secession Debated*, p. 29.

he warned, were well aware of this. Hence their policy had been for twenty years to surround slavery "with a border of free States, and like the scorpion surrounded by fire, they will make it sting itself to death."[246]

Secessionist sentiment was, of course, much weaker in the Upper South than in a state like Georgia. Nevertheless, Judge John J. Allen of the Virginia Supreme Court declared publicly that the Republicans' hatred for the South was displayed "in their openly avowed determination to circumscribe the institution of slavery within the territory of the States now recognizing." For the "inevitable effect" of this "would be to fill the present slaveholding States with an ever increasing negro population, resulting in the banishment of our own nonslaveholding population in the first instance, and the eventual surrender of our country to a barbarous race, or, what seems to be desired, an amalgamation with the African." Here was the old fear, clearly expressed during the Missouri crisis by Virginians forty years earlier, highlighted at midcentury, and displayed again at the time of the Kansas-Nebraska debates, of slavery being "penned up" in the states where it already existed. Former President John Tyler, although a prominent advocate of compromise in the secession winter, voiced the opinion that Virginia would "never consent to have blacks cribbed and confined within prescribed and specified limits and thus be involved in all the consequences of a war of the races in twenty or thirty years."[247]

In the states of the southwest, themselves the product of the relatively recent expansion or "diffusion" of slavery, these concerns were perhaps still more in evidence. Sometimes there was a specific territory or foreign country targeted. For example, O. R. Singleton of Mississippi told the House of Representatives that there was "but one mode" by which slavery could be "perpetuated to any considerable number of years." This was "by expansion." "And that expansion," he added, "must be in the direction of Mexico." Similarly, when the delegates to Alabama's secession convention assembled, some of them referred to the need to spread slavery and thus expand the infant southern confederacy not only into Arizona but also into Mexico, Cuba, and other parts of Central America.[248]

More often, however, the territory into which slavery should spread was left unspecified. When Alabama's Commissioners to North Carolina sent an official letter to their hosts, they predicted that the Republican policy

246. "Toombs' Secessionist Speech," in Freehling and Simpson (eds.), *Secession Debated*, p. 39. Toombs added that it was entirely mistaken to believe that expansion required a reopening of the African slave trade.
247. Botetourt Resolutions of... Allen; "*John Tyler to – ,*" *Nov.* 16, 1860, in Channing, *Crisis of Fear*, p. 213; Ashworth, *Slavery, Capitalism and Politics*, I. pp. 62–63.
248. CG, 36/1, p. 53; Smith (ed.), *History and Debates*, pp. 236–237, 208–209. See also Thornton, *Politics and Power*, pp. 206–213.

of preventing the creation of any more slave states "must, of itself, at no distant day, result in the utter ruin and degradation of most, if not all of the Gulf States." The reason was that "Alabama has at least eight slaves to every square mile of her tillable soil" and her slave population could be expected to double "in less than thirty years." Hence "the children are now born who will be compelled to flee from the land of their birth, and from the slaves their parents have toiled to acquire as an inheritance for them, or to submit to the degradation of being reduced to an equality with them, and all its attendant horrors." Consequently there was an indisputable need for territorial expansion: "our people and institutions must be secured the right of expansion, and they can never submit to a denial of that which is essential to their very existence."[249]

These views did not, however, command universal acceptance, even among those advocating secession. For one thing, there were in fact vast supplies of land available in the South in 1860. As we have seen, many southerners had for more than a decade questioned the economic rationale for additional territory and this scepticism persisted. Thus at the same secession convention in Alabama other delegates rejected the call for additional territory. One of them noted that in seceding from the Union the state had lost all claim to the existing territories. This left, he claimed, Mexico as "the only outlet." Yet Mexico was utterly undesirable; both the white man and the slave would "degenerate" there. Clearly for this delegate secession did not require territorial expansion after all. Similarly William Lowndes Yancey, at the same convention, also believing that Mexico was "our only outlet for expansion" registered a comparable disdain for her population. According to Yancey, it was "at least, doubtful whether we should wish an expansion in that direction, that would bring with it the recognition of such a mass of ignorant and superstitious and demoralized population, as Mexican States, if annexed, would necessarily bring." On this reasoning the South did not need, and should not seek, more territory, given the racial inferiority of those occupying it.[250]

These differing priorities precluded a consistent set of policy recommendations for the new Southern Confederacy. Alongside the doubts some southerners expressed about Mexico's suitability for slavery, there continued to be divisions over Cuba. Thus Jefferson Davis, the Confederate President, was in favour of its acquisition, whereas Robert Toombs, his Secretary of State, was not. Owing to the outbreak of war, this and other issues were never resolved and it is extremely difficult for historians

249. "Alabama's Letter to the State of North Carolina," in Smith (ed.), *History and Debates*, pp. 432–436.
250. Gavin Wright, *The Political Economy of the Cotton South: Households, Markets and Wealth in the Nineteenth Century* (New York, 1978), pp. 132–133; Smith (ed.), *History and Debates*, pp. 203, 251. See also pp. 236–237.

to know where the balance of opinion among secessionists actually lay. Moreover, one cannot assume that even those who shared Davis's view were motivated by the fear of a superabundant slave population, since the acquisition of Cuba, which had a slave density comparable to that of Alabama, would do nothing to reduce the ratio of slaves to territory. One can only conclude that when southerners took their states out of the Union and founded their new Confederacy there was no consensus among them on the need for additional territory, still less a consensus that the growth in the slave population actually mandated it.[251]

These vagaries notwithstanding, southern militants were united in their opposition to the Republican demand for free soil. The idea that no more slave states could be created was anathema to all secessionists, whether or not they perceived an economic imperative for additional slave territory. There were two additional sets of reasons, each of which had been advanced for many years and each of which we have already encountered. The first set was political: the fear that the Republicans intended to create additional free states, at the same time as they prevented the creation of additional slave states. Thus in time they would control three quarters of the states and would then be able to amend the constitution and abolish slavery. These fears had been expressed many times throughout the 1850s. They had caused many southerners to view the admission of California as a sixteenth free state (with no new slave state to accompany her into the Union) as a disaster and to look to Kansas, to Central America and to the Caribbean for additional territory and additional slave states. With the rise of the Republican party and the strife over Kansas, these fears became increasingly intense. In 1856, for example, a campaign tract directed at the South on behalf of Buchanan had alerted southerners once again to the need for additional slave states. Otherwise, additional free states would be created which would then be mobilised in the war against slavery. Here was "the way by which your ruin may be effected 'lawfully under the Constitution,' unless you secure the right for the admission of new slave States."[252]

Four years later a crescendo was reached. Prior to the election Lucius Lamar of Mississippi challenged Republican congressmen to acknowledge that by excluding slavery from the territories they would have "taken the initial and most decisive step towards the destruction of slavery in the States," while John Townsend of South Carolina in an election pamphlet predicted that the North would be able to abolish slavery constitutionally within ten years. When the election was over and the result known,

---

251. Crist *et al.* (eds.), *Papers of Davis*, VII, pp. 44, 65.
252. *The Agitation of Slavery Who Commenced! And Who Can End It!! Buchanan and Fillmore Compared* (n.p., n.d.), p. 7.

Governor Andrew B. Moore of Alabama declared that slavery would now be excluded from the territories and free states admitted into the Union "in hot haste" until northerners had the power to alter the Constitution. Meanwhile, his state's envoy to Kentucky, Stephen F. Hale, prophesied that eight new nonslaveholding states would be admitted into the Union within as few as four years.[253]

Parallel fears were expressed in other states. Henry Benning told his Georgia audience to expect eighteen new free states within the foreseeable future and one of Mississippi's formal resolutions, passed when the state officially seceded from the Union, levelled at the Republicans the following charge:

> That they . . . seek by an increase of Abolition states "to acquire two-thirds of both houses," for the purpose of preparing an amendment to the Constitution of the United States abolishing slavery in the states, and so continue the agitation that the proposed amendment shall be ratified by the legislatures of three-fourths of the states;

Some southerners linked this fear with the other dangers to be apprehended from a Republican administration. The refusal to allow slavery to expand, it was noted, was entirely consistent with the use of the patronage to build up Republican power within the southern states and especially the border states. Both policies worked to diminish the number of slaveholding states prior to a reform of the Federal Constitution. No fear played a greater role in pushing southerners towards secession in 1860–1861.[254]

Even this, however, did not exhaust southerners' objections to Republican policy for the territories. Alongside the political arguments about the number of free and slave states lay a second set of more general constitutional concerns: a party which was prepared to trample upon the Constitution by preventing the creation of new slave states could be expected to violate it again and again, whenever the need arose. Thus when South Carolinians spelled out their reasons for secession, in their official *Address to the Slaveholding States*, they referred to the recent Dred Scott decision which the Republicans planned to set aside, and then posed a telling question. "If it is right to preclude or abolish Slavery in a territory," then "why should it be allowed to remain in the States?" For "according to the decisions of the Supreme Court of the United States," "the one is not at all more unconstitutional than the other." A party that was prepared to

---

253. *CG*, 36/1, p. 45; Townsend, *Death of Slavery*, p. 14; "Letter from Governor Moore," "Letter of S. F. Hale," in Smith (ed.), *History and Debates*, pp. 15–16, 381.
254. "Benning's Secessionist Speech," in Freehling and Simpson (eds.), p. 118; "Python" in *De Bow's Review*, XXVIII (1860), pp. 252–256. "Python" thought the North would have the votes for a constitutional amendment "within a single lifetime."

attack slavery in the territories, in flagrant violation of the constitution, would not shrink from a direct assault on slavery in the states.[255]

As we have seen, the economic argument in favour of new territory for slaves did not unite all those who advocated secession upon Lincoln's election. No secessionist dissented, however, from the political and constitutional arguments; no one who sought a Southern Confederacy in late 1860 or early 1861 doubted that the Republican policy for the territories was profoundly and alarmingly unconstitutional, or that the Republicans would shrink from mobilising, for the most nefarious of purposes, a three-fourths majority of the states. Hence it did not matter that there were no territories in the nation whose fate was not yet decided; all future territories and finally all existing states, would become free; nor did it matter, from this perspective, that in leaving the Union, the South might jeopardise her claim to the existing territories. In effect, therefore, though the territorial question might propel the South out of the Union, it might then lose much of its urgency. With the constitutional and political motives for expansion removed, a southern Confederacy might not then need to acquire additional territory. Some southerners explicitly acknowledged this. Thus R. M. T. Hunter of Virginia observed that the newly created Southern Confederacy no longer needed to acquire Cuba, since there was no longer a need for political parity with the North. In so doing he confirmed that the political and constitutional objections to the Republican policy for the territories appealed to a wider audience than that which focussed upon the economic need for additional slave territory.[256]

Whatever the relative importance of the arguments enlisted against the Republican territorial policy, there can be no doubt of their cumulative impact. Secessionists united in believing that the Republican policy of free soil revealed that the party's ultimate goal was abolition in the states, however it might be achieved. Thus even those who denied that the territorial question was in itself of much importance were able to derive no consolation from the fact. The Richmond *Enquirer*, for example, now committed to secession, declared, when discussing the Republican attitude to slavery, that "the war upon its extension is but one development of the deep seated hostility to its existence, and it is in this view that the present issues assume an importance to which intrinsically they may not be entitled." Here the claim was that although the extension of slavery, at least in 1860, was not itself an urgent issue, Republican policy disclosed the party's ultimate abolitionist goal. This was a fundamental article in

255. *South Carolina's Address to the Slaveholding States*, written by Robert Barnwell Rhett, can be found at http://americancivilwar.com/documents/south_carolina_address.html.

256. May, *Southern Dream of a Caribbean Empire*, p. 253.

the secessionist creed: Republicans, as revealed by their territorial policy, were in essence abolitionists. Indeed Republicans and abolitionists shared the same goals for while "the latter would expel slavery, wherever it be found, by compulsory laws, or by fire and sword if necessary," "the former would merely confine it where it is, exclude it from all territories, in whatever latitude...and thus slowly but surely accomplish its destruction." Thus "both aim at the same end." According to one delegate at the Alabama convention called to debate secession, the Republican platform of 1860 called for "exclusion from the Territories of the United States, with the ultimate extinction of slavery as the consequence of such exclusion." At the same convention another delegate posed a question: "And why not submit to this exclusion from the Territories, the common property of all the States?" He then answered it: "because the South believes this Northern policy of restricting slavery to its present limits, would ultimately destroy the institution." From this perspective, the Republicans' emphasis upon freedom for the territories, together with Lincoln's refusal to compromise on the issue constituted an unmistakable confirmation of their abolitionist intent.[257]

## VI

Although Lincoln's intransigence on the territorial question doomed attempts to achieve a compromise during the secession crisis, the new president was, within his own party, a moderate on the slavery question. The radical Republicans wanted to go much further. Their programme called for the separation of the federal government from slavery and this meant abolition in the District of Columbia, in federal forts and dockyards as well as the abolition of the interstate slave trade. These measures were intended to ensure the abolition of slavery, not immediately but over a period of time, and without an unconstitutional assault upon slavery within the states. Some southerners gave this programme, or aspects of it, careful scrutiny. Thus both Louis Wigfall of Texas and John Townsend of South Carolina declared that abolition in the forts and dockyards was intended not simply to free the small number of slaves working there but rather to make such places, in Townsend's words, "the

257. Richmond *Enquirer*, Oct. 2, 1860. See also CG, 36/1, p. 624. Barney, *Secessionist Impulse*, p. 313; John F. H. Claiborne, *Life and Correspondence of John A. Quitman.* 2 vols., II, p. 265. Smith (ed.), *History and Debates*, pp. 27, 208. See also Barney, *Secessionist Impulse*, pp. 24, 101. For more examples of the secessionist belief that Republican victory meant abolition, see Charles B. Dew *Apostles of Disunion: Southern Secession Commissioners and the Causes of the Civil War* (Charlottesville, 2001), pp. 23, 27, 29, 33, 48, 50–52, 57–58, 61–62, 77.

asylums and harbors of refuge to every disaffected slave who may retreat to them." It would then be as difficult for southerners to recover slaves who had escaped to these safe havens as to recapture those who had fled to Massachusetts or Vermont. But the evil effects would not end there, for, as Townsend pointed out, there would be a catastrophic effect upon the wider slave population. "What subordination," he asked, could be preserved, "among the slaves within the cities of Norfolk, Wilmington, Charleston, Savannah, Mobile, New Orleans, or upon the plantations for a hundred miles around...if the slave" were able "for any fancied grievance" to "leave his master and find security, and release from his service, within the walls of a fort?" The result would be that "any sudden petulance occasioned by some mild, but well-deserved rebuke or punishment, would be resented upon the master; and a walk of twenty minutes to some contiguous dockyard, or a voyage of a few miles in a paddling canoe, to some fort within sight, would take him to *free soil*, where the master would be powerless in retaking him."[258]

The radical programme was thus profoundly menacing to the South. Southerners did not always distinguish carefully between the policies that were specific to the radicals and those to which the party as a whole was committed. Thus Trusten Polk of Missouri looked ahead in early 1860 to the prospect of a Republican victory and asked what it would mean. "What," he asked, "could the slaveholding States expect...but that all the patronage and all the power of the Federal Government, in all its departments, would be brought to bear upon the institution of slavery in the South, in order to compass its destruction?" "How long," he wondered, could the South "retain the institution of slavery after the whole power of the Federal Government shall have been brought to bear upon her for its destruction?" Polk invited his audience to "think what could be effected by the Federal legislation." There would be "abolition of slavery in the District of Columbia; abolition in the arsenals, dockyards and forts; outlawry of it on the high seas, and wherever the flag of the Union floats; exclusion of it from the common Territories belonging equally to all the States; circumscribing it as with a wall of fire within the States." No institution could withstand such an assault.[259]

Just as they did not usually distinguish between radical and moderate Republican objectives, so southern militants did not always spell out the

---

258. Townsend, *Death of Slavery*, pp. 15–16; *Speech of Wigfall*, p. 28. This fear too had been anticipated by Calhoun in the late 1840s – see *Address of the Southern Delegates*, p. 11.
259. *CG*, 36/2, p. 357. See also "Letter from Governor Moore," [of Alabama], Nov 14, 1860, in Smith (ed.), *History and Debates*, p. 15.

specific effects of a single Republican action or policy. Very frequently they lumped together several possible Republican acts and then offered a prediction of their cumulative impact. Thus Congressman William Boyce of South Carolina in a public letter cited both the danger of the patronage being used against the South and also the Republican threat to reform the Supreme Court. In common with many others, he stressed the special vulnerability of the border states. The Governor of one of those states, John Letcher of Virginia, similarly referred to the prospect of a Republican exercising control over both the federal patronage and the army and navy as one that "cannot be entertained by the South for a moment." William W. Avery of North Carolina likewise listed the prohibition on new slave states, the reform of the Supreme Court, abolition in the District of Columbia, and the fugitive slave issue in an attempt to alert the South to the impending catastrophe. William Porter of South Carolina drew attention to fugitive slaves, the patronage, the restructuring of the Supreme Court and also made a rare reference to the three-fifths clause, which he judged vulnerable to Republican assault. Robert Toombs of Georgia cited the exclusion of slavery from the territories, the refusal to return fugitive slaves and the attempt, by agitation of the slavery issue, to incite rebellion in the South and concluded that "the open and avowed object of Mr. Lincoln and the great majority of the active men of his party," and one which "he himself expressly avows," was "ultimately to abolish slavery in the States." One of the more vivid and more detailed descriptions of the future that awaited the South was offered by Georgia's governor, Joseph Brown, in a public letter advocating secession. Brown predicted that if Lincoln "places among us "his Judges, District Attorneys, Marshals, Post Masters, Custom House officers," then "by the end of his administration, with the control of these men, and the distribution of public patronage, he will have succeeded in dividing us to an extent that will destroy all our moral powers, and prepare us to tolerate the running of a Republican ticket, in most of the States of the South, in 1864." Brown noted that if the Republicans managed only a few thousand votes in each southern state they might still hold the balance of power and thus be able to control elections. Thereupon a series of measures would be enacted: abolition in the District of Columbia, abolition in the forts, arsenals and dockyards, and abolition of the interstate slave trade. "These steps," he warned, "would be taken one at a time, cautiously, and our people would submit." Then "finally, when we were sufficiently humiliated, and sufficiently in their power, they would abolish slavery in the States." Brown also noted that "it will not be many years before enough of free States may be formed out of the present territories of the United States, and admitted into the Union, to give them sufficient strength to change the Constitution, and remove all Constitutional barriers which now deny to Congress this power." Here was a succinct summary of the case for secession following Lincoln's election.[260]

Those who advocated secession at this time were thus quite certain that the Republican party would sooner or later abolish slavery in the states, and not merely prevent its extension into the territories. They were fully aware that Lincoln had declared that "a house divided" could not stand and that it was his duty to place slavery where the public mind could "rest in the belief that it is in the course of ultimate extinction."[261] It was for this reason that southern secessionists so often conflated Republicanism with abolition and associated Abraham Lincoln with William Lloyd Garrison. Moreover, they noted that even some abolitionists who had shunned the major parties desired a Republican victory. John Townsend of South Carolina looked carefully at the relationship between Republicans and Garrisonians. He acknowledged that many Republicans "looking to party success, and the spoils of office" were prepared to "disavow ... these sentiments of the Garrisonian wing of the Anti-Slavery party, as *extreme* and going further than they intend." Yet southerners should not be misled for "when analysed, the difference between the Garrisonians, and the Black Republican wings of the Great Anti-Slavery Party, is just that, between the advanced guard of an army which goes ahead as *pioneers*, to remove obstructions and prepare the way (or as Garrison expresses it, to 'regenerate public opinion') and the main body of the army which soon moves forward and occupies the ground, which has thus been prepared for them." "The ultimate design of both," he warned, "is the same; only the main body advances more *cautiously* so as to ensure success."[262]

Similarly A. O. P Nicholson was one of many who argued that the Republicans did insidiously what the abolitionists advocated openly, while Robert Toombs and Henry Benning told the Georgians gathered at Milledgeville to debate secession that the Republicans' primary goal was the abolition of slavery in the states. In the words of Benning "the meaning of Mr Lincoln's election to the Presidency is the abolition of slavery as soon as the Republican party shall have acquired the strength to

260. Channing, *Crisis of Fear*, pp. 235–236; Nevins, *Prologue to Civil War*, p. 176; *Speech of William T. Avery in the House of Representatives, April 23, 1860* (n.p., n.d.), p. 7; Porter, *State Sovereignty*, p. 36; "Robert Toombs to E. B. Pullin and Others, Dec. 13 1860," in Phillips (ed.), *Correspondence of Toombs, Stephens, and Cobb*, pp. 520–221; "Joseph E. Brown's Secessionist Public Letter," in Freehling and Simpson (eds.), *Secession Debated*, p. 148. See also *Mississippian*, Sept. 27, 1850; James P. Holcombe, *The Election of a Republican President an Overt Act of Aggression on the Right of Property in Slaves: A Speech Delivered before the People of Albemerle, 2 January 1860* (Richmond, 1860), pp. 12–13.
261. Republican attitudes to slavery and abolition will be considered in detail in Chapter 2 of this volume.
262. [Townsend], *The South Alone ...*, p. 28.

abolish it." In his capacity as official envoy of the state of Georgia, Benning took this message to Virginia's Secession convention where he informed his audience that his state has seceded out of "a deep conviction" that "separation from the North" alone "could prevent the abolition of her slavery."[263]

Probably every southerner who favoured secession in 1860 or early 1861 believed that large numbers of northerners were gripped by "fanaticism" and as Thomas Cobb of Georgia observed in a secessionist speech in the aftermath of Lincoln's victory "fanaticism is madness, is insanity." Would it ever stop? "All history," according to Cobb," speaks one voice" and he challenged his listeners to tell him "when and where the craving spirit of fanaticism was ever gorged with victims; when and where its bloody hands were ever stayed by the consciousness of satiety; when and where its deaf ears ever listened to reason, or argument, or persuasion, or selfishness; when and where it ever died from fatigue, or yielded except in blood." Cobb concluded that it would count for little if Lincoln should "prove to be a conservative" for "would not these bloodhounds only seek in Seward, or Sumner, or Hale, a less scrupulous and more faithful servant?"[264]

Southerners of this persuasion were therefore convinced that compromise was futile. They had been saying for many years that any concession to antislavery opinion would "but inflame the power by which another will be exacted" and events seemed to have vindicated these predictions. Could the Republicans in any case be trusted to honour an agreement, even if one could be reached? "What faith" asked Benjamin Palmer of Louisiana, "can be placed in the protestations of men who openly avow that their consciences are too sublimated to be restrained by the obligation of covenants or by the sanctity of oaths?" The Republicans, he was certain, would never give up until "the dreadful banquet of slaughter and ruin shall glut the appetite." Thus it did not matter that Lincoln had promised to administer the nation in a conservative manner. Even if this were true, other more radical figures would soon follow. Thomas Clingman in 1860, before the election, set out the case for immediate action. Again the possibility was considered, and discounted, that a Republican president might prove more conservative than was now expected. Such an outcome would be "only a reprieve to us" for "the very fact of his election" together with "our submission" would both "destroy our friends

263. *CG*, 36/1, p. 628; "Toombs' Secessionist Speech," in Freehling and Simpson (eds.), *Secession Debated*, p. 46; "Benning's Secessionist Speech," in Freehling and Simpson (eds.), *Secession Debated*, p. 118; Reese (ed.), *Proceedings of Virginia State Convention*, I, pp. 62–66.
264. "Cobb's Secessionist Speech," in Freehling and Simpson (eds.), *Secession Debated*, pp. 20–24.

in the North" and "demoralize and degrade our own people and render them incapable of resistance." The result would be that "our enemies, flushed with success," would "elect more ultra agents." Unlike the majority of southern leaders in the Middle South, Clingman refused to wait for an "overt act" of hostility on the part of a Republican president for "no other 'overt act' can so imperatively demand resistance on our part, as the simple election of their candidate."[265]

Southerners who advocated secession were convinced that at the heart of the problem lay northern public opinion. Many of them recognised what historians have often missed: even if the South did nothing, antislavery sentiment in the North would almost certainly grow ever deeper and the threat to the South would become ever greater.[266] As they had done since 1850 (and even earlier), southerners reviewed the progress of antislavery in the North and in the nation and projected a similar rate of increase in the future. It seemed that nothing could be done to arrest its growth. Noting that hatred of slavery was "ineradicable" in the North, Henry Benning also observed that many southerners had warned what the effect would be of electing a Republican president. But northerners had been undeterred. The only solution was thus for the South to assume entire responsibility for the defence of slavery, leave the Union, and determine her own destiny.[267]

## VII

When news of Lincoln's election reached the South on November 7, 1860, southern militants possessed a formidable battery of arguments which they could deploy in favour of secession. But how was it to be achieved? The previous month Governor William Gist of South Carolina had sent confidential letters to the governors of six other southern states asking them to predict their states' reaction to a Republican victory in November. The answers were mixed. The Governor of Florida said his state would not take the lead in seceding but would follow any other state, while the

---

265. "Address of Southern Convention"; Palmer, *Thanksgiving Sermon*, p. 15; CG, 36/1, p. 455.
266. Fielder, *Disunionist*, p. 20; Palmer, *Thanksgiving Sermon*, p. 12; [Townsend], *The South Alone...*, p. 13. This is not to say, of course, that southerners had correctly identified the mechanism by which antislavery sentiment was becoming increasingly widespread in the North. As we shall see in Chapter 2, the legitimation of northern society and the emerging northern labour system had powerful antislavery implications.
267. Benning's Secessionist Speech," in Freehling and Simpson (eds.), *Secession Debated*, pp. 121–124. It is worth noting that some other arguments for secession were occasionally advanced. Thus a few southerners made reference to the tariff. Overall, however, this was a minor issue in 1860–1861.

Governors of Alabama and Mississippi said their states would perhaps follow one or two others out of the Union. The Governors of Georgia, Louisiana and North Carolina meanwhile were more discouraging: their states would need an "overt act" of aggression from the President before they would secede. Several of the Governors spoke favourably of a southern convention, to which all the slaveholding states might be invited.[268]

Thus there were important tactical issues for secessionists to consider. First, should there be a southern convention? Such a convention might unite the South, but was it not equally possible that it would quickly bog down in debate and irresolution, just as previous conventions, and especially those at Nashville a decade earlier, had done? Second, if there were to be no southern convention, and secession should occur on a state-by-state basis, which state should lead? South Carolina was the obvious candidate but she was, by virtue of her very extremism, the object of considerable suspicion even in the South. But if not South Carolina, then which other state?[269]

In the event, South Carolinians did, of course, take the lead. On receiving news of Lincoln's election the state had initially decided to delay a formal decision on secession until a convention had met in January. The hope was that in the interim another state would start the ball rolling. But, impressed by secessionist sentiment specifically among a party of visiting Georgians and, more generally, elsewhere in the Deep South, the South Carolina legislature brought the convention forward to December. Thereafter the other states of the Deep South, with the exception of Texas, followed suit and by the end of November Georgia, Alabama, Mississippi and Florida had called state conventions, while Louisiana had convened a special session of the legislature in order to achieve the same result. On December 20 the South Carolina convention unanimously adopted an ordinance of secession and in the next three weeks elections were held in six other states to choose delegates to the conventions.

In these elections traditional party labels disappeared and most delegates were elected either as "secessionists" who favoured immediate secession on a separate-state basis, or "cooperationists" who favoured concerted action across the South or at least the Deep South, probably to be achieved by means of a southern convention. The cooperationists,

---

268.  John G. Nicolay and John Hay, *Abraham Lincoln: A History*. 10 vols. (New York, 1890), II, pp. 306–314.

269.  On secession see, amongst other works, Barney, *Secessionist Impulse*; Buenger, *Secession and the Union in Texas*; Carey, *Parties, Slavery and the Union*; Channing, *Crisis of Fear*; Freehling, *Road to Disunion: Secessionists Triumphant*; Potter, *Impending Crisis*, Rainwater, *Mississippi, Storm Center of Secession*; Schultz, *Nationalism and Sectionalism in South Carolina*; Sinha, *Counterrevolution of Slavery*; Thornton, *Politics and Power*; Schugg, *Origins of Class Struggle in Louisiana*.

however, were themselves divided over the merits of secession, once cooperation with other states had been achieved. Some then favoured secession without further ado, others a final ultimatum to the Republicans,
still others had a stronger attachment to the Union. The elections were
complicated by the fact that some local leaders were chosen on the understanding that they would hear the arguments on both sides and then make
up their minds. The elections were further complicated by the progress of
events in Washington, where efforts at compromise were being put forward but were meeting, on the whole, little enthusiasm from the victorious
Republicans.[270]

In each state the elections were won by secessionists but these results
probably underestimate the support for secession in principle, since in no
state were the cooperationists, or even a significant proportion of them,
unqualified supporters of the Union. When the conventions met, secession
was adopted by wide margins, with many cooperationists acquiescing in
the majority view in order to present a united front to the North and to the
world. Only in Texas was secession submitted to a popular referendum for
ratification and here it was endorsed by a huge majority. By February 1,
seven states had left the Union and were ready to form the Confederate
States of America.

Some of the secessionist leaders declared, sometimes in private, sometimes in public, that it was their duty not to wait for popular approval,
but rather to shape and guide it. Some of them, especially the South
Carolinians, expressed little confidence in the people. Throughout the
Deep South, those opposed to secession were subjected to intimidation
and the threat, sometimes the reality, of violence. Moreover, it is clear
that some secessionists had planned a domino effect whereby secession
in South Carolina, where sentiment was most favourable to their cause,
would change the nature of the entire debate, and impel other states to
follow. Noting these facts, some historians have argued that secession was
contrary to the views of the majority in the Deep South and was in effect
a proslavery *coup d'etat* or *putsch*.[271]

Yet this is a mistaken view. Secession had been threatened again and
again prior to the election. Thus every one of South Carolina's Senators
and Representatives, except for James Hammond, was on record as
favouring immediate secession in the event of Lincoln's election. Elsewhere men who were universally recognised as leaders and opinion

---

270. These compromise attempts will be discussed in later chapters.
271. The leading advocate of this view is William Freehling. See Freehling, *Reintegration*,
     pp. 215–216 and Freehling, *Road to Disunion: Secessionists Triumphant*, pp. 343–
     534. I have offered criticism of it in my review in *Reviews in American History*
     (forthcoming). Other scholars, notably David Potter, have doubted whether secession
     had mass support in the South – see Potter, *Impending Crisis*, pp. 495–513.

formers in the Deep South advocated secession in the same circumstances: Alfred Iverson and Robert Toombs of Georgia, Albert Gallatin Brown, John J. Pettus of Mississippi, John Slidell and Governor Thomas Moore of Louisiana, David Yulee and Governor Madison S. Perry of Florida, John Reagan and Louis Wigfall in Texas and Andrew B. Moore and Clement Clay of Alabama. Major newspapers like the Montgomery *Advertiser* and the Jackson *Mississippian*, took the same approach. Even men like Howell Cobb and James Orr who had been advocates of the Democratic party were now strongly in favour of secession. The example of Texas is a revealing one. Governor Sam Houston opposed secession (until it had been achieved). But the exception proved the rule because Houston's stance led to his being deposed.[272]

Across the Deep South there was scarcely an unconditional Unionist of any note. In Mississippi Jefferson Davis, future President of the Confederacy, was somewhat more guarded than many of his colleagues but he was essentially a secessionist and did not believe that the South should wait for an overt act of aggression from Washington. In Georgia Alexander Stephens, soon to become his vice president, was by some margin the leading advocate of compromise and further negotiation but even he demanded concessions from the Republicans that could not be obtained. The result was that across the entire Deep South those who opposed secession lacked leaders of stature.[273]

One should not assume that secession was unpopular with the masses. In 1859 as many as fifteen Democratic country conventions in Mississippi, for example, passed resolutions affirming the need for secession if the government fell into Republican hands.[274] Although intimidation was certainly used throughout the South, there is no reason to believe that it was decisive. Unionism was by now so unpopular that its advocates had to assume the guise of cooperationists in order to retain any influence at all.[275] Historians should not be surprised at the popularity of secession, or perhaps it would be better to say the unpopularity of any alternative. To have remained in the Union, the citizens of the Deep South would have had to repudiate virtually all their leaders, and to reject all the arguments those leaders had been advancing for many years, in order to insist upon being governed by a party which had no existence in the Deep South, whose candidate for the presidency had not even been on the ticket in the

272. Barney, *Secessionist Impulse*, pp. 191–192 Bolton, *Poor Whites of the Antebellum South*, p. 183; Buenger, *Secession and the Union in Texas*, pp. 120, 143, 156; Carey, *Parties, Slavery and the Union*, p. 227; Schultz, *Nationalism and Sectionalism in South Carolina*, pp. 166, 187; Sinha, *Counterrevolution of Slavery*, p. 231; Schugg, *Origins of Class Struggle in Louisiana*, p. 422.
273. For Davis's view see *CG*, 36/1, pp. 1937–1941. For Stephens's see pp. 609–610.
274. Rainwater, *Mississippi, Storm Center of Secession*, p. 95.
275. This point, extremely damaging to his claim that secession lacked mass appeal, is made by Potter – *Impending Crisis*, p. 495.

November election and which was thought to be at war with their fundamental institutions and interests. There is therefore no mystery about the refusal of the Deep South to continue in a Union headed by a man who openly expressed the desire to put slavery on the path to ultimate extinction. Long before 1860 slaveholders in the Deep South had successfully identified slavery with the South. This was the ultimate illustration of their hegemony in the region. Although force and intimidation were certainly employed in 1860 and 1861 the probability is that the slaveholders did not need them: they already ruled the Deep South politically, economically and ideologically.[276]

## VIII

In the minds of those who favoured secession in 1860–1861 no contrast could have been sharper than that between the fate of the South within the Union and her future outside it. In 1850 the relatively few southerners who had discussed the question had concluded that there was then little danger of a civil war since the North would not fight and that even if this prediction were proved wrong, the South was in any case invincible. The prosperity of the 1850s, even though it had benefited northerners and southerners alike, further strengthened southern confidence in the prospects of the independent nation they now sought to create.[277]

Some southerners even thought that war might in some respects be desirable since it was "a truth of history, untouched by an exception, that no nation has ever yet matured its political growth without the stern and scarring experience of civil war." But even this writer believed that, as long as the South were united, "the apprehension of civil war is the idlest of fears." The overwhelming majority of secessionists shared his opinion. When secession was being debated no secessionist recommended that the South should deliberately initiate a war so of course it followed that only northern aggression could bring it about. Yet this seemed inconceivable. There would have to be "madness in the head and worse than folly in the heart, before the North could seriously entertain the thought of possible aggression." The problem for the North was that so many of her citizens were so dependent on the South that they would neither fight themselves

---

276. A number of points made by Mills Thornton are highly pertinent here: Thornton observes that "an analysis of secession which argues that the fire-eaters manipulated the event, or that South Carolina's decision forced the issue, leaves unexamined the most important element – the support, ranging from acquiescence to enthusiasm, of nearly the entire electorate of the Lower South." Thornton also observes that (in Alabama and elsewhere) "at any time during these years, the voters could have halted the movement towards secession" and he concludes that "the decision was taken because the voters wanted it taken." – Thornton, *Politics and Power*, p. 457.

277. *Address of Thompson*, p. 14; *Address of Huston*, pp. 1–5; *Mississippian*, Dec. 6, 20, 1850.

nor allow others to fight. Northerners simply could not afford to wage war on the South.[278]

Why was the South so strong? One Georgia secessionist declared that "we have more financial power and resources than the North has" and this view was perhaps universally held by secessionists. Yet by "financial power" this Georgian and those who shared his view did not refer to the banking and commercial infrastructure of the South, which all agreed was less extensive than that of the North, but rather to the economic power that accrued as a result of the South's main export, its cotton crop. Here was a key to southern strength, the trump card which southerners could play in the event of war or whose very existence would preclude any aggressive act on the part of the North and thus maintain peace.[279]

Southerners here took their cue from James Henry Hammond, whose famous "Cotton is King" speech of 1858 reflected southerners' confidence in their economic well-being and potential. Hammond had in effect challenged the North by declaring that northerners did not "dare" to make war upon cotton and this confidence was undoubtedly strengthened by the South's relative immunity to the financial difficulties that had afflicted the North as a result of the Panic of 1857. But the confidence had existed prior to, and did not diminish after, the Panic. Hammond himself a decade earlier had declared that "no calamity could befall the world at all comparable to the sudden loss of two millions of bales of cotton annually" and had predicted that such an event would precipitate the collapse of both the northern and the British economies. Even some of those who would in 1860 be lukewarm towards secession, like Alexander H. Stephens of Georgia, subscribed to this view of cotton. "There is not a flourishing village or hamlet in the North, to say nothing of their towns and cities," Stephens told his constituents in 1857, "that does not owe its prosperity to Southern cotton." Moreover, "England, with her millions of people and billions upon billions of pounds sterling, could not survive six months without it." Hence southerners were in an enviable situation: "we emphatically hold the lever that wields the destiny of modern civilization in its widest scope and comprehension; and all we have to do is to realize the consciousness of our power and be resolved to maintain it."[280]

Some three years later, when secession was imminent, fellow Georgian Joseph Brown, now Governor of the state, sought to demonstrate the

278. Trescot, *Position and Course of South*, p. 16; Holcombe, *Election of a Republican President an Overt Act of Aggression*, p. 13; *Journal of the Senate of the State of Georgia at the Annual Session of the General Assembly...1860* (Columbus, 1860), pp. 49–51; "Benning's Secessionist Speech," in Freehling and Simpson (eds.), *Secession Debated*, pp. 131–132; Buenger, *Secession and the Union in Texas*, p. 128.
279. "Benning's Secessionist Speech," in Freehling and Simpson (eds.), p. 131.
280. *Selections from the Letters and Speeches of the Hon. James H. Hammond of South Carolina* (New York, 1866), pp. 311–322.; *Hammond's Letters on Southern Slavery*, p. 28; Phillips (ed.), *Correspondence of Toombs, Stephens, and Cobb*, p. 415.

impossibility of a northern invasion of the South since such an act "would cut off a single crop of Cotton," and thus "would shake the pillars of the English throne." The resulting "cry of 'bread or blood' would at once control the actions of the Government, the Army and the Navy of Great Britain." William L. Yancey of Alabama similarly believed that "great as is the prosperity of the North, of England, and of France, and of Germany, that prosperity would wither like a weed pulled up by the roots in mid-summer, were they deprived of their trade in our cotton bales." In the same vein, another Georgia secessionist argued that cotton would be not only "an unfailing supply of money to us" but also a source of immense political strength since without it four million Britons would starve. Thus Great Britain would be compelled, in the event of war, to intervene against the North. Even this did not exhaust the expectations of southern militants. Confirmed secessionists like William Trescot and John Townsend of South Carolina were convinced that the South's economic power would allow her to establish close alliances with manufacturing nations, especially Britain, so that "the South would be, in the maturity of her strength, the guardian of the world's commerce." Alternatively, the South might develop her own manufacturing interests to a far greater extent than hitherto.[281]

This confidence was widespread in the South by 1860 and it entailed a matching and equally widespread contempt for the northern economy. Those who favoured the reopening of the African slave trade, for example, were wont to insist that, however morally repugnant the trade might be to them, northerners would simply not be able to resist a concerted southern demand for reopening, such was the vulnerability of their own economy. But this perception of northern weakness went far beyond the ranks of the slave trade devotees. Many southerners offered apocalyptic warnings to the North in which it was predicted, for example, that without the southern states, the North would divide, with the New England states perhaps ranged against the rest. While an independent South could face the future with boundless confidence, for the northerners the outlook was bleak indeed.[282]

---

281. *Journal of Senate of Georgia . . . 1860* (Columbus, 1860), p. 49; Smith (ed.), *History and Debates*, p. 250; "Benning's Secessionist Speech," in Freehling and Simpson (eds.), *Secession Debated*, p. 131; Trescot, *Position and Course of South*, p. 13; [Townsend], *The South Alone . . .*, pp. 19–20; *Speech of Hunter*, p. 7; Palmer, *Thanksgiving Sermon*, p. 11. See also Eric H. Walther, *The Fire-Eaters* (Baton Rouge, 1992), pp. 185, 255, 262; *Vicksburg Sun*, Nov. 12, 1860 quoted in Rainwater, *Mississippi, Storm Center of Secession*, p. 164; Nevins, *Prologue to Civil War*, p. 38; Nevins, *The Emergence of Lincoln: The Improvised War 1861–1862* (New York, 1959), pp. 19, 94–99.
282. William Miller, *Address on Re-Opening the Slave Trade at Wylde-Moore August 29, 1857* (Columbia, SC, 1857), p. 10; Leonidas W. Spratt, *The Foreign Slave Trade the Source of Political Power and of Material Progress, of Social Integrity, and of Social Emancipation to the South* (Charleston, 1858), p. 9; [Townsend], *The South Alone . . .*, p. 19.

Why was the North so weak? It was not simply that she lacked cotton, important though that was. Rather it was her labour system that made her vulnerable. Since at least the 1830s, southerners had been predicting revolution in the North, a social cataclysm which would pit labour against capital in a ruinous conflict. At that time southerners had claimed that their influence and economic power were doing much to prevent such an occurrence. Now, in 1860, some southerners prophesied that the day of reckoning was imminent if the southern states left the Union. The war of labour against capital would erupt and the principal casualty might even be representative government and democratic institutions in the North. In such circumstances, the North would cease to be a democratic republic and would instead become an aristocracy.[283]

If northern vulnerability were the product of her free labour economy, the strength of the South was instead a product of slavery. Even more than cotton, slavery was the key to southern prosperity. Proslavery writers had for a generation argued that slavery alone allowed an advanced economy to avoid the conflict of labour with capital and as the demand for secession grew louder in the final antebellum years and months, this confidence became still more pronounced and still more important. Little that was new, however, had to be added in 1860. On the other hand southerners did need to confront, more squarely than in previous decades, the possibility that slavery might be a source of weakness in war. This had been a concern following the war of 1812 and had at that time even been a source of antislavery sentiment. By 1860, however, southerners were confident that far from being a weakness in war, slavery would instead be a source of immense strength. Again Hammond in 1845 struck a note which many others would later sound. He cited the examples of Ancient Greece and Imperial Rome to refute the idea that slavery necessarily entailed military weakness and then, with a moralistic fervour that Jefferson Davis would later evince when reacting to the Emancipation Proclamation, referred to the possibility that some "foreign nation" might be "so lost to every sentiment of civilized humanity, as to attempt to erect among us the standard of revolt, or to invade us with Black Troops, for the base and barbarous purpose of stirring up servile war." In such circumstances, however, "their efforts would be signally rebuked." The reason was that "the present generation of slaves" would never contemplate revolt "unless instigated to it by others."[284]

By this reasoning there was no danger of the slaves rising up against their masters. This alone demonstrated the superiority of the southern social system and its greater military potential. But secessionists' confidence in

283. [Townsend], *The South Alone...*, p. 19; Fielder, *Disunionist*, pp. 68–69.
284. *Hammond's Letters on Southern Slavery*, p. 6.

the loyalty of their slaves did not end there. Thomas Clingman of North Carolina, who believed that there was "in fact, about as much reason to apprehend a general insurrection of the horses as of the slaves of the South when left to themselves" argued that the slaves would in war be "a positive element of strength, because they add to the production of the country, while the white race can furnish soldiers enough." In other words, the slaves could be left to their labours, and this would release the South's white manpower for her armies. The consequence was that the South would be simply invincible in war.[285]

Southerners thus concluded that war was highly unlikely, perhaps not entirely undesirable, and in any case certain to result in triumph. Most believed the South would gain a speedy victory. For those southerners who embraced secession, the possibility of war was not a powerful deterrent. But their fondest hope was, of course, for a peaceful resolution to the conflict, in which northerners accepted the secession of the southern states and the two nations coexisted harmoniously. In such circumstances, it was anticipated, all the problems the South had experienced for a generation would vanish. Northerners would then take no more interest in southern slaves than in those of Cuba or Brazil and their racism would induce them to expel any fugitives who escaped from the South. They would no longer seek, or be able, to stir up discontent among either the slaves or the nonslaveholders of the South and in the absence of such efforts peace and harmony would reign. Even the threat of abolition in the border states would disappear for border slaveholders would no longer fear the escape of their slaves to the North. The process by which the Upper South was being drained of its slaves would either cease of itself or, if necessary, additional measures could be taken to arrest it. Even if such measures failed, there would now be no danger of those states being "abolitionised" by northerners and then used to secure the necessary votes for constitutional change. Whether it brought peace or war, secession seemed to guarantee a glorious future for a new southern confederacy.[286]

The southern militant's world view, with slavery as its foundation, attained a new maturity at the moment secession was accomplished. This was true not in the sense that he had achieved a fuller understanding of the world around him; on the contrary, his belief in southern superiority

---

285. *CG*, 36/1, p. 454. See also [Augustus Baldwin Longstreet], *A Voice from the South* (Baltimore, 1847), pp. 25–26; "Cobb's Secessionist Speech," in Freehling and Simpson (eds.), *Secession Debated*, p. 29; *Speech of Hunter*, p. 7; *The Democratic Demonstration at Poughkeepsie: Speech of Hon. R. M. T. Hunter, of Virginia* (n.p., n.d.), p. 12.

286. "Benning's Secessionist Speech," in Freehling and Simpson (eds.), *Secession Debated*, p. 128 – to maintain slavery in the Border areas, Benning proposed a tax on slave imports into the Deep South.

and in an inevitable southern victory should an armed conflict ensue was to prove hopelessly and catastrophically wrong. But the maturation of his worldview occurred when his evaluation of slavery and of free labour escaped all empirical controls and became part of what was simply taken for granted. It was not merely southern strengths and northern weaknesses that were now adduced as evidence of the superiority of slavery. In addition, any significant weaknesses the southern social system displayed were blamed squarely upon the North; any real strength the northern social system exhibited was attributed unhesitatingly to its parasitic attachment to the South. In this way, the dedication to slavery was complete and a closure had been achieved. It illustrated more clearly than ever before the slaveholders' hegemony within the seven states that had now seceded.

On this wave of pride, confidence, and self-assertiveness, the Confederate States of America were launched. The leaders of the Deep South believed in all sincerity that they were honouring the legacy of the constitution makers of 1787 and following in the footsteps of the men of 1776. It was they who were true to the values of the Revolution and the Federal Constitution, values that northerners had betrayed. Although forging a new nation, the Confederates were convinced that they were creating a purified version of the old.[287]

By the time of Lincoln's inaugural in March 1861, the new nation, or would-be nation, was in existence. By this time, too, all eyes were focussed upon Fort Sumter in Charleston Harbor. When Lincoln decided to reprovision it, the Confederates were faced with a momentous decision. But although one or two voices urged caution, the predominant and entirely understandable view was that it was intolerable to allow the fort to remain in the hands of what was now after all a foreign power. Many Confederates hoped that armed conflict would induce some (or all) of the remaining slave states to secede from the Union and join them; in this they were not disappointed. A nationalist fervor gripped the new nation and hubris, generated by confidence in the Confederate economy and social system, ruled the hour. Most believed the war would be short and glorious. Senator James Chesnut of South Carolina had already offered to drink all the blood that would be spilt as a result of secession; others now predicted that it could all be wiped up by a pocket handkerchief or else contained in a lady's thimble. One or two demurred, including Confederate President Jefferson Davis. But none foresaw the slaughter that lay ahead.[288]

---

287. This theme is developed very effectively in Michael A. Morrison, *Slavery and the American West: The Eclipse of Manifest Destiny and the Coming of the Civil War* (Chapel Hill, 1997).
288. Nevins, *Improvised War*, pp. 49, 68–69; Potter, *Impending Crisis*, p. 490.

## Conclusion

The creation of the Confederate States of America was the occasion for much rejoicing among those who had spent the previous decade reiterating the warning that Calhoun had delivered in 1850 (and earlier) to the effect that the South must choose between slavery and the Union. In a sense the events of 1860–1861 saw the efforts of the southern militant, who was by now the southern secessionist, crowned with success. Only later would he learn that his course was to end in abject ruin.

Yet for most of even these southerners, the renunciation of the Union was tinged with regret, as indeed it assuredly would have been for Calhoun, had he lived to see it. With few exceptions they would have been happy to remain in a Union that gave them what they believed to be their constitutional guarantees and entitlements. It is true that many had shared, for at least part of the time, doubts about the strategies they had pursued in the 1850s in order to make the Union safe for slavery in that they had been at least partially prepared for them to fail. Nevertheless, one must seek to explain this failure. Why had it proved impossible to make the Union safe for slavery?

To answer this question it is necessary to remind ourselves of the nature of the danger slaveholders faced within the Union. It proceeded from first, the growing opposition of northerners to southern slavery, second, the power that those northerners especially by virtue of their superior numbers and the ever-growing number of free states could wield, and third, the susceptibility of slavery in the South to that power when wielded by that northern antislavery majority. In the 1850s each of these factors elicited a reaction from those southerners who sought to make the Union safe. In response to the growing opposition of northerners to southern slavery militant southerners sought to re-educate the North, partly by issuing threats but also by seeking to inculcate "correct" constitutional principles. In response to the growing power of the North, they sought to augment southern power by acquiring new slave states. And in response to the vulnerabilities of their own system, they sought to shore it up in geographical locations where it was weakest and among groups whose loyalty was most questionable. Ironically, however, the very strategies by which southerners tried to make the Union safe for slavery ended by intensifying antislavery sentiment in the North, confirming northern power and leaving the slave system as vulnerable as ever, indeed more vulnerable than ever. Thus the experience of the 1850s in effect confirmed that the dangers facing slavery within the Union were in reality beyond the control of even the most powerful and determined slaveholding class in the modern world.

As we shall see, northern opposition to slavery was partly political in motivation, a reaction against southern political activities and initiatives, but also partly a socially generated phenomenon. In fact its social roots were deep and spreading: they would have continued to spread and bear fruit even if southerners had reacted in an entirely passive manner. But passivity was precisely what the southern militant could not countenance. He wanted action. Yet ironically the course he pursued ended by producing an intensification of antislavery sentiment, of which he was fully aware, and by confirming the superiority of the northern social system, of which he was totally unaware, indeed upon the denial of which he based his entire political strategy.

The campaign to re-educate the North consisted in part of threats. Southerners made it clear that they would not support northerners who espoused the "wrong" doctrines. Any overtly antislavery statesman immediately fell under this ban but even Democrats like Stephen A. Douglas, who were in no meaningful sense antislavery, could also feel its force. By 1860 northerners were being told that if they were not prepared to endorse a slave code for the territories they could not win the highest offices in the nation, not, at any rate, with southern support. And if those offices were instead won without southern support, then an even more drastic threat would be invoked: the break-up of the nation itself.

As the case of the slave code indicates, these threats were accompanied by the promulgation of "correct" constitutional principles, to which northerners were now expected to subscribe. Earlier in the decade, as we have seen, southern militants had pursued the same strategy when trying to promote the doctrine of congressional nonintervention in the territories. Northerners were then expected, once again helped along their way by a number of threats, to repudiate the Missouri Compromise and to renounce, perhaps in theory only, perhaps in practice too, the benefits that it had offered in the more northerly latitudes of the Louisiana Purchase.

Yet both the constitutional principles enunciated and the threats applied served merely to strengthen antislavery sentiment in the North. The constitutional principles, even when enunciated by the Chief Justice of the United States Supreme Court, seemed to many northerners merely a cloak for the ambitions of a minority class in a minority section. Similarly the threats seemed an even more blatant attempt to promote the interests of that minority by the simple expedient of intimidating the majority. The attempt to re-educate the North thus foundered upon one of the problems it was designed to combat: the minority status of the South in the Union.

This brings us to that very issue. Southerners understood all too clearly that they were vulnerable politically to the growing population imbalance between the sections, combined with the increasing disparity in the number of free and slave states. One solution to this problem was to create more slave states. In the 1850s these efforts centred upon the settlement of Kansas and its entry into the Union as a slave state. Once again however, the results were precisely the opposite of those intended and once again the problems that were being combated resurfaced to doom the strategy that had been designed to overcome them. Slave labour had proved unable to compete with free labour across almost the entire northwest; even without any congressional prohibitions it was unviable across most of these northern latitudes. Kansas was a little more promising but only a little. Even if it were as suitable for slavery as Missouri (and this was questionable), slavery in Missouri was itself extremely vulnerable. In part (but only in part) for reasons of climate and soil, the experience of slavery and slaveholding in Kansas would mirror that of slavery and slaveholding in the northwest as a whole with the result that in any competition to settle new territories; free labour would generally win. In this sense the settlement of Kansas, though intended to counter the inequality between slave and free labour, instead merely reproduced it. By the time Kansas was ready to enter the Union as a free state, southerners were left in an even more decidedly minority status.

The third prong of the southern strategy was to shore up slavery at its weak points. As we have seen, this meant that certain groups in southern society, and certain regions within the South, should be targeted. Free blacks were one of these groups, since they were held to be a danger to the stability of southern slavery because of both the pernicious example they offered, and the temptations they presented, to their enslaved compatriots. Yet here again the southern reformer was unable to make headway: once again, in Maryland as in Kansas, slave labour had proved unable to compete with free labour, not only in an urban location such as Baltimore, but also in the northern counties, the most agriculturally advanced region of the state. Free blacks were simply too important to Maryland's economy to be removed from the state. This relative failure of the slave system had been in large part responsible for the creation of the free black problem in Maryland; the same failure doomed the efforts that were made to solve it.

An even greater source of at least potential vulnerability within the South was her nonslaveholding white population. The fear of this group gave rise to many specific concerns and resulted in a whole series of warnings or initiatives. The demand for the reopening of the African slave trade, for example, had its genesis in the belief that too few whites were now able to purchase slaves and that, as a result, too few were sufficiently committed to the maintenance of the slave system. In the same way, many southerners stressed that if slaves were employed in other than agricultural activities, the nonslaveholding whites with whose labour they competed would be converted into enemies of the regime. In addition, immigrants, foreigners, and northerners living or working in the South all fell under suspicion. Cities were widely thought to be points of vulnerability as were all other parts of the South where the proportion of nonslaveholding whites to slaves was comparatively high. The list of southerners of whom suspicions were entertained thus added up to an indictment of a large slice of southern white society.

But once again there was no easy way of addressing these problems. The African slave trade was rejected because reopening it would create at least as many problems as it solved. Hostility towards immigration, industrialisation and urbanisation was not easily translated into specific policies though it was almost certainly a cause as well as a consequence of the South's relatively poor performance in these areas. Yet if this under-performance met certain needs, it too created many problems. It left the South highly vulnerable to the appeal of a Hinton Helper whose message was precisely that the South should be regenerated economically and her society and labour system brought into line with those of the North. Only then would the interests of nonslaveholding white southerners be properly advanced. Nor was Hinton Helper the only, or even the most important, exponent of this approach. Similar, even identical, criticisms of the southern economy lay at the heart of the Republican critique of slavery in the South. And these Republicans would, in time, administer the *coup de grace* to southern slavery.

Much closer to home than the Republicans or even the nonslaveholding whites of the South were the slaves themselves. Here the slaveholders exhibited enormous confidence: their slaves were inherently faithful, loyal, contented. Modern historians know better than to accept the myth of the contented slave. But for the masters ignorance was anything but bliss. They were compelled to respond again and again to the resistance, actual or potential, of their slaves even as, with perfect sincerity, they denied its existence. As we have seen, the threats posed by free blacks, by nonslaveholding whites, and by northern antislavery groups, in fact derived much of their force from the slaves' discontent, their desire not to be slaves, their awareness that their masters were filching from them the fruits of their labour. Contented slaves would have been impervious to antislavery propaganda and antislavery pressure. Contented slaves could not have been roused to acts of resistance by free blacks or nonslaveholding whites. Contented slaves would not have fled to the North in significant numbers and, in so doing, have created a need for Fugitive Slave Laws, which in turn generated enormous opposition in the North and finally a conviction in the South that northerners could not be trusted to abide by constitutional guarantees. In Missouri contented slaves would not have been susceptible to propaganda from antislavery elements and would not have wished to flee to neighbouring Kansas. In Kansas, or any other territory, contented slaves would not have needed special laws to police them, introduced in order to give slavery an equal chance with free labour.

The reality, however, of discontented slaves showed that southerners could not even understand the true nature of the dangers facing them, let alone remove them, with the result that the attempts to shore up their system ended in failure. They could not reconcile their slaves to their enslavement, they could not tackle the problem of free blacks, they could not compete with free labour in most of the land which comprised the United States of America and they could not remove the threats posed by slaves, by nonslaveholding whites or by antislavery northerners. The highest priority of these southerners was to protect slavery, a need which owed much to the system's weaknesses. The same weaknesses would make it impossible to find the protection they sought.

Secession was in essence a recognition that such protection could not be had within the Union. Throughout the decade militant southerners had agreed that slavery in the South faced a growing danger from the North; they had not been able, and often had not tried, to rank the specific threats to which they were exposed. In 1860 some believed, as they had done earlier in the decade, that territorial expansion was an economic necessity. Others were more concerned with the political power that additional states had brought, and would continue to bring, to the North. Some believed that the South needed more slaves; others feared that in the future she would have too many. Some concentrated upon the dangers posed by nonslaveholding whites, others proclaimed that those whites were entirely reliable and focussed instead upon the North, or upon free blacks.

In 1860 few believed that the inauguration of a Republican president would result in the instant destruction of southern slavery. But the essence of the secessionist case was that antislavery had been growing in the North for a generation and that its triumph in 1860 marked a turning point in the nation's history in both symbolic and practical terms. A Republican in the White House would be able to strike a series of extremely damaging practical blows against the South and his very presence would confer further legitimacy upon free labour and antislavery throughout the nation. On the premise that slavery could and should be perpetuated, secession was a highly rational action; it proceeded from the entirely rational conviction that slavery would no longer be safe within the Union.

The further irony of course was that once again actions taken to defend slavery merely increased the attacks upon it. For their own reasons, northerners would not allow southerners to leave the Union and the resulting War would make all previous attacks upon slavery seem mild by comparison. But irony did not even end here. Once again the slaveholders' attempts to defend their labour system would fail. And, as we shall see,[289] once again the failure would be attributable to the weaknesses that had called forth the defence. In 1850 Calhoun had described the South as the "weaker" section and Calhoun was regarded, by southern militants, as by far the most profound statesman in the land. But this proved a far more profound remark than either he or they realised. Slavery was indeed weaker than free labour. Slavery and its weaknesses had brought about the War; slavery and its weaknesses would doom the southern attempt at independence. Slavery gave birth to the Confederacy and slavery would ultimately destroy it.

289. See Conclusion and Appendix to this volume.

# 2

# *The antislavery challenge: The Republicans, 1854–1861*

## Introduction: The Republican party[1]

### I

In December 1859, in response to a request for some autobiographical information, Abraham Lincoln recorded that in the early 1850s he had been "losing interest in politics." But then in 1854 came an event which, he recalled, "aroused me again." The event was "the repeal of the Missouri Compromise," brought about, of course, by the passage of the Kansas-Nebraska Act. It was this which renewed Lincoln's interest in politics, and which propelled him on a course that would lead to the White House within a mere seven years.[2]

Lincoln was not alone in reacting so decisively to the repeal of the Missouri Compromise. Indeed others had been far more virulent in their opposition. One of the most dramatic and effective of all the attempts to combat it was launched by a manifesto signed by six antislavery Senators and Representatives but written primarily by Salmon P. Chase of Ohio which appeared as early as January 1854. The *Appeal of the Independent*

---

1. The classic work on the antebellum Republicans is, of course, Eric Foner, *Free Soil, Free Labor, Free Men: The Ideology of the Republican Party before the Civil War* (New York, 1970). All scholars are greatly indebted to this work. The approach taken here, however, differs in three principal respects. First, I attempt a fuller discussion than Foner needed to undertake of the relationship between Republican ideology and those of the Democratic and Whig parties in previous decades. Second, and far more important, I offer a different view of Republican attitudes towards wage labour. Third, I suggest that the Republicans' social philosophy had a vitally important legitimating function in the North. See also Eric Foner, "Free Labor and Nineteenth Century Political Ideology," in Melvyn Stokes and Stephen Conway (eds.), *The Market Revolution in America: Social, Political, and Religious Expressions, 1800–1880* (Charlottesville and London, 1996), pp. 99–127, *Slavery and Freedom in Nineteenth-Century America* (Oxford, 1994).
2. Roy F. Basler (ed.), *The Collected Works of Abraham Lincoln*. 9 vols. (New Brunswick, 1953–1955), III, p. 512.

*Democrats* went further than Lincoln would ever go in denouncing the measure. "We arraign this bill," Chase wrote, "as a gross violation of a sacred pledge; as a criminal betrayal of precious rights; as part and parcel of an atrocious plot to exclude from a vast unoccupied region, immigrants from the Old World and free labourers from our own States, and convert it into a dreary region of despotism, inhabited by masters and slaves." According to Chase, Stephen A. Douglas, its instigator, was perpetrating "a bold scheme against American liberty, worthy of an accomplished architect of ruin."[3]

Lincoln had been, prior to 1854, a Whig and his reaction to the Kansas-Nebraska Act had typified that of northern Whigs. The signatories of the *Appeal* were antislavery radicals, men who placed the antislavery cause ahead of any political party. The third group to be galvanised by the Act were northern Democrats, men who had in many cases fought for years against what they believed to be the increasingly southern orientation of their party and who now were prepared to abandon it rather than submit to further dictation. Thus Kinsley Bingham of Michigan regarded the repeal of the Missouri Compromise as "but a part of a stupendous scheme into which certain northern statesmen have been drawn, for securing to the slaveholding interests, a permanent preponderance in the measures and actions of the Federal government." Despite their differences, these three groups, former Whigs, former Democrats, and radicals, would unite and form the Republican party which within a decade would preside over the destruction of slavery in the southern states.[4]

In opposing the Kansas-Nebraska Act, its enemies sounded the themes that would reverberate again and again over the remaining years of the antebellum Republic. All the groups composing the Republican party agreed that the extension of slavery would blight the prospects of free labour and of free men in the territories affected. All agreed too that the repeal of the Missouri Compromise confirmed that the Slave Power, a profound threat to the democratic values and practices of the nation, was on the march. Many (though not all) agreed, moreover, that slavery was a moral blot upon the nation and that they had a duty, as Chase put it, "to behold in every man a brother, and to labor for the advancement and regeneration of the human race." The groups that made up the Republican party, despite the significant differences between them, thus developed a multifaceted critique of slavery and of southern slaveholders, and an ideological framework within which would they could explain the momentous events of their times.[5]

---

3. Salmon P. Chase *et al.*, *An Appeal of the Independent Democrats* (Washington, DC, 1854), pp. 1, 6–7. Foner, *Free Soil*, p. 94.
4. Message of Kinsley S. Bingham (1855) in George N. Fuller (ed.), *Messages of the Governors of Michigan*. 4 vols. (Lansing, 1926), II, p. 297.
5. Chase *et al.*, *An Appeal of the Independent Democrats*, p. 7.

## II

As we shall see, at the heart of the Republican ideology was a basic satisfaction with northern society, either as it was or as it could readily become. No Republican doubted that a free-labour economy and society were inherently superior to any that might be based upon slavery. As we shall also see, some of the claims Republicans made about their own society and some of the accusations they levelled against southerners were in fact far wide of the mark. Nevertheless these Republicans were more successful than southern militants in defending their social system. As we have already noted in Chapter 1, southerners could not in their thinking or in their everyday lives escape the problems of slavery, at the heart of which was the brute fact that slaves did not wish to be slaves. Although Republicans almost certainly exaggerated the attractions of wage labour in the North and almost certainly overestimated the enthusiasm with which wage workers contemplated their condition, the conflict within the northern labour system was radically different from, and less significant than, that which suffused slavery in the South. As a result, the northern social system was simply less vulnerable to conflict from below, as it were, than its southern counterpart.

As we shall see, Republican ideology reflected the fact that the 1850s witnessed what has been termed "the emergence of the wage earner." In the antebellum North there were often extremely wide disparities in wealth and in economic, social and political power, between employers and employees. Here, as southerners never tired of pointing out, was a potential source of deep conflict, especially since the United States was heir to a European intellectual tradition in which wage workers were thought not to possess the propertied independence that was the badge of full republican citizenship. Yet northern antebellum society was able to accommodate this potential conflict and adjust to these changes with relative ease and this process too was reflected in the outlook of the Republican party, by 1860 the North's dominant political force.

It is important to ask how this adjustment was made. In fact there were many features of the wage-labour relationship which could be, and were, emphasised in order to demonstrate that it was a just and harmonious one and that the wage earner was in no sense exploited by the employer. Chief among these was the voluntary nature of the contract between them. The labourer had "freely" consented to sell his labour power to the employer. In drawing up their bargain both had been free to enter into the contract or to decline it, in this sense there was therefore equality between them. Since the wage worker had entered into the relationship freely, under normal circumstances he had no incentive to flee and no reason to take the actions so feared by slaveholders: arson, poisoning, sabotage. There was therefore no need for the employer to concern himself with the private life of the employee, who could be left to enjoy the right to a family and a home. The employee, just like the employer, could also act according to the dictates of his conscience. Even if he lacked ownership of land or other means of production, he had interests as a consumer. His labour could be esteemed by the wider society. He could hope for, and in some cases achieve, a marked improvement in his or his children's economic fortunes and perhaps even cease to be a wage labourer. All these advantages could be, and were, pointed out and genuinely celebrated by Republicans when they defended the northern social order.

At the heart of this adjustment to the spread of wage labour lay the greater degree of consent given, sometimes reluctantly, sometimes enthusiastically, by the wage worker. Consent was obtained because of the formal equality which we have just noted between wage worker and employer. Here was a stark contrast with the relationship between slave and slaveholder. No one has grasped this better than Karl Marx. "On the basis of the wages system," Marx wrote, "even the unpaid labor [i.e., the surplus value derived by the employer] seems to be paid labor." But "with the slave... even that part of his labor which is paid [i.e., the amount required to feed and clothe him] appears to be unpaid."[6] The equality and freedom contained in the wage relationship was real and important; wage labour was as a result infinitely more attractive to the wage earner than slavery could ever be to the slave. But this same equality operated both to mask and to legitimate huge inequalities of wealth and power and the same freedom masked and legitimated the severely curtailed choices of the wage worker in comparison to those of his employer. Here is the key to the relative stability and the resilience of the capitalist system, both in the 1850s and since.[7]

The problem for the antebellum Republic, however, was that all the features of the wage relationship that were celebrated by northerners and which eased the transition to wage-labour capitalism were either much less in evidence or totally absent in southern slavery As northern society made its adjustment to the growth of wage labour, so it generated a deadly opposition to slavery. Civil war would be the result.

## Democratic antecedents

### I

Although most Republicans were former Whigs, a significant number came instead from the Democratic party. These Democratic-Republicans,

6. Karl Marx and Friedrich Engels, *Selected Works*. 3 vols. (Moscow, 1969–1970), II, pp. 59–60.
7. It is perhaps unnecessary to emphasise that this stability is relative and not absolute.

as they may be termed, reached their new home by a different ideological route from that taken by former Whigs. Both groups discarded some opinions or beliefs, and modified or retained others but of course the inherited political cultures and ideologies were in some respects sharply at odds. Moreover, although former Democrats were able to coalesce with their erstwhile enemies within the same party, they remained in conflict over certain issues and at all times were conscious and protective of their distinctive political heritage. In other words the Democratic-Republicans not only emerged from a separate political culture, but also ended up at a somewhat different ideological resting-place.[8]

A main theme of American politics in the 1850s was the growing disillusionment of northerners with the Democratic party. The cause was the apparently increasing southern orientation, and even domination, of the party. Not all northern Democrats, of course, were so deeply concerned at this development. As we shall see, the party maintained a measure of support, especially in the lower North throughout the decade and even during the Civil War Democrats formed what one historian has termed "a respectable minority" within the North. But by 1860 some of these were displaying considerable animosity towards the southern wing of their party. Indeed in the free states by 1860 the Douglas Democrats, although not intending to defect, were bitter in their denunciations of the South (as well as being, in many cases, resolute defenders of the Union in the aftermath of secession). Other Democrats had displayed this resentment rather earlier and it had carried them by the mid-1850s into a new party. They were the Democratic-Republicans.[9]

There are perhaps three important sets of questions to be asked of the Democratic-Republicans. First, which Democrats left the party and why? Second, which views did they change or abandon and which did they retain? Third, and perhaps most important, what economic, social or political factors explain these ideological shifts? All these questions are critical to an understanding of the antebellum Republican party.

---

8. Foner's, *Free Soil* contains an excellent chapter on the Democratic-Republicans, see pp. 148–185. See also Richard H. Sewell, *Ballots for Freedom, Antislavery Politics in the United States, 1837–1860* (New York, 1976); Roy F. Nichols, *The Democratic Machine 1850–1854* (New York, 1923). I attempted a preliminary analysis of this subject in "The Democratic-Republicans before the Civil War: Political Ideology and Economic Change," *Journal of American Studies*, 20 (1986), pp. 375–390. See also John Ashworth, "Free Labor, Wage Labor and the Slave Power: Republicanism and the Republican Party in the 1850s," in Melvyn Stokes and Stephen Conway (eds.), *The Market Revolution in America: Social, Political, and Religious Expressions, 1800–1860* (Charlottesville, 1996), pp. 128–146.

9. Robert W. Johannsen, "The Douglas Democracy and the Crisis of Disunion," *Civil War History*, 9 (September 1963), pp. 229–247, *Stephen A. Douglas* (New York, 1973), pp. 788–789; Joel H. Silbey, *A Respectable Minority: The Democratic Party in the Civil War Era, 1860–1868* (New York, 1977).

## II

To answer each of these questions, however, it is important to understand the history of the Democratic-Republicans and, in addition, to recount their own version of that history. Like all northern Democrats they venerated the name of Jefferson, not merely the Jefferson who warred in the 1790s against Hamilton's financial system but also the antislavery Jefferson of the Northwest Ordinance. As James Doolittle of Wisconsin put it in 1859, "there is not a plank in our platform today which does not conform to the principles of Jefferson." This was of course, to say the least, a somewhat simplified view of the Jeffersonian legacy, a legacy whose effect was, as I have argued throughout these volumes, to give support to the slaveholders of the South rather more than to stimulate opposition to them, but it does illustrate the Democratic-Republicans veneration for the Sage of Monticello.[10]

Although Jefferson was a hallowed figure in the antebellum Democratic party, the Democratic-Republicans gave as much praise and attention to Andrew Jackson. Again Jackson had waged war upon the dominant financial interests of his day (as represented especially by the Bank of the United States) and although he had not pursued any overtly antislavery policies he had played a vital role in combating southern aggression in the form of nullification. The Democratic-Republicans viewed the Jacksonian era in Manichean terms with absolute good represented by Old Hickory, the heir of Jefferson, and absolute evil by his archenemy John C. Calhoun, the plotter of treason and would-be architect of national ruin. As Joseph Stringham of New York put it in 1856, "if Jefferson was the Angel of Light of the party, Calhoun was its Prince of Darkness."[11]

According to the Democratic-Republicans, Calhoun's goal since the early 1830s had been either to place himself in the White House, or, failing that, to set up a southern confederacy, with himself of course at its head. In 1856 Francis P. Blair, Andrew Jackson's close adviser and confidant, wrote a public letter in which he reviewed the history of the Democratic party. Calhoun's career received close scrutiny. The South Carolinian had begun in public life by espousing the tariff. When this failed to win the White House he had then performed a spectacular *volte-face* and become a bitter opponent of all protective duties. It was, Blair acknowledged, "true that agriculture was indeed oppressed by an excessive tariff" but

10.  *Congressional Globe*, 35th Congress, 2nd Session, p. 1267 (hereafter cited in the form *CG*, 35/2, p. 1267); *Celebration of Jefferson's Birthday in Washington, April 13, 1859* (Washington DC, 1859), pp. 4–5, 11. See the brilliant treatment of Jefferson's reputation in the 1850s in Merrill D. Peterson, *The Jefferson Image in the American Mind* (New York, 1962), pp. 189–209.
11.  Foner, *Free Soil*, p. 151; Joseph Stringham, *An Address to the Republican Club of Buffalo* (n.p., n.d.), p. 4.

Calhoun had had ulterior motives. He had "insisted that the whole burden fell on the South, although the North paid double the duties drawn from the South." The real motive had been to form a southern confederacy.[12]

With this goal in mind Calhoun had next manufactured a crisis over slavery. Citing "speculative enthusiasts" like Garrison and the Tappans, he had then sought to "impress the feeling" that their associations "portended the invasion of the rights of Southern slave-owners by the power of the Northern States." Yet "there was not the slightest pretext for the apprehension," since "the great majority in all the free States condemned interference with the domestic institutions of the South." But "Mr. Calhoun was not content with this demonstration of public feeling in the free States" and began to demand restrictions on free speech in the North, a demand which only served to increase the abolitionists' appeal. Indeed he now strove to persuade the entire South to threaten disunion unless he were made President. Yet fortunately the South in the 1830s had recognised that "all the abolitionist pamphlets were but waste paper" and Calhoun's ambitions had been thwarted.[13]

In that decade Calhoun had been vanquished by Andrew Jackson, the great Democratic-Republican hero. The wild heresies of nullification had been rejected and the Union triumphantly vindicated. Jackson had not hesitated to threaten force against the South Carolinians who had then, of course, backed down. For the Democratic-Republicans the moral was clear: nullification and disunion were treason; both should be resisted to the last.

In the 1840s, however, Calhoun had had much more success. As Secretary of State under Tyler he had made the "shameless boast to the world" that the nation's purpose was to spread slavery. Southerners now gave him greater support. The nation had had a legitimate claim on Texas, but no one, Blair contended, had realised that Calhoun planned to take additional provinces from Mexico and introduce slavery into them. Before long he was demanding the whole of New Mexico for slavery, and threatening disunion if the demand were not met.[14]

The key event of the 1840s, however, had been, according to Blair and virtually every other Democratic-Republican, the Democratic national convention of 1844 held at Baltimore. Here the Democratic party had

---

12. *A Voice from the Grave of Jackson! Letter from Francis P. Blair, Esq to a Public Meeting in New York, Held April 29, 1856* (n.p., n.d.), p. 1. See also "Blair to Jackson, July 7, 1844," in John S. Bassett (ed.), *The Correspondence of Andrew Jackson.* 7 vols. (Washington DC, 1926–1935), pp. 299–300; *Speech Delivered by Hon. Thomas Hart Benton at Jefferson ... Mo. ... 26 May 1849* (n.p., n.d.), pp. 16–17. Ashworth, *Slavery Capitalism, Politics,* I, pp. 423–424, 449–450.
13. *Voice from Grave of Jackson,* pp. 1–2.
14. *Voice from Grave of Jackson,* pp. 2–3.

adopted the rule which required the nominee to receive not a simple majority but instead two thirds of the votes cast. As a result Martin Van Buren, who had opposed the immediate annexation of Texas, had been overthrown and James K. Polk nominated in his place. Few events bulked larger in Democratic-Republican thinking. The two-thirds rule, according to Joseph Stringham, was "the radical evil in the present Democratic organization." It had been adopted "at the instance of the Tyler-Calhoun party" and had had calamitous effects ever since. Calhoun, "beaten and disgraced by Jackson," had, after the Old Hero's retirement, "compromised with Van Buren and ruled Tyler." Although most delegates had been pledged to Van Buren, yet "the genius of Calhoun was not balked." The nominating convention "opened to his enterprising mind a field too inviting to be overlooked." Hence the two-thirds rule, by which he had managed to seize control of the party. "From the day it was adopted," Stringham concluded, "the faction which Jackson crushed with his heel, and which Van Buren thought to humor into duty," had "usurped the control of the democratic organization and... dictated its policy."[15]

From 1844 the party's descent had been rapid. That year had been the last in which the Jackson–Van Buren issues had been dominant. Van Buren was sacrificed to the demand for additional slave territory and Francis P. Blair himself, as editor of the *Globe*, had been sacrificed (by Polk) in order to end all criticism of Jackson's old enemies, the nullifiers. Indeed from 1844 the nullifiers had been increasingly in control of the party and northerners had been required to submit to southern dominance. "From that year," according to Timothy Day of Ohio, "we date doughfaceism; from that year the decadence of the principles of democracy."[16]

Thus it was the Van Burenites who had first mobilised against southern domination of the Democratic party in the mid-1840s. In New York, Van Buren's home state, his supporters, universally referred to as Barnburners, formed the radical wing of the party. This would prove to be a common pattern throughout the North in the 1840s and 1850s: antislavery Democrats would come disproportionately from the ranks of radical Democrats. In New York, the Barnburners were engaged in a more-or-less permanent battle for control of the party with their enemies, the Hunkers, who represented the conservative wing.[17]

15. Stringham, *Address to Republican Club of Buffalo*, pp. 4, 5, 8; Charles G. Sellers, Jr, *James K. Polk, Continentalist, 1843–1846* (Princeton, 1966), pp. 36–162; James C. N. Paul, *Rift in the Democracy* (Philadelphia, 1951), pp. 144–168. In effect, Van Buren was defeated by a combination of conservative Democrats and Southern expansionists.
16. Stringham, *Address to Republican Club of Buffalo*, pp. 9–10; CG, 34/1, App. p. 415.
17. Herbert D. A. Donovan, *The Barnburners* (New York, 1925); Foner, *Free Soil*, p. 169.

It is important to note that in Jackson's era the radicals had been distinguished less by their opposition to slavery and the South (which was not then a dominant political issue) than by their stance on the economic and financial questions of the day. Both at state level and in Washington they were enthusiastic champions of Democratic antibank policies. In New York they were also strongly opposed to the canal building policy favoured by both Whigs and Hunkers. Indeed the intraparty dispute in New York, though echoed in most other states, was of exceptional bitterness and severity.[18]

This split now contributed to the Barnburners' growing disenchantment with Polk, of whom they had initially had quite high hopes. Polk indeed had had reasons to support them but he had also had equally compelling reasons to support the Hunkers. Although the Barnburners were far more enamoured of Polk's financial programme than the Hunkers, it was the Hunkers who were able to applaud his territorial acquisitions with little concern about the possible spread of slavery into them. As a result they received a significant portion of the federal patronage going to New York state, much to the disgust of the Barnburners, who regarded them as false to Democratic doctrines on the tariff and bank questions and utterly subservient to the South on sectional matters. The Hunkers, equally resentful of the Barnburners, in 1846 gave only lukewarm support to Silas Wright, since Van Buren's retirement the leader of the Barnburners, in his unsuccessful campaign for re-election as state governor. That year too David Wilmot, himself a radical Democrat from Pennsylvania and a future Democratic-Republican, had introduced his famous Proviso banning slavery from any territory that might be acquired from Mexico. Conservative Democrats, in New York as elsewhere, despite originally supporting the Proviso, soon retreated from it when they saw the degree of opposition it provoked in the South.[19]

At this point state and federal issues decisively converged. When the next Democratic national convention met in 1848, again at Baltimore, two rival delegations from New York arrived, each claiming to represent the state. They were, of course, the Hunkers and the Barnburners. The convention then devised a compromise by which each delegation was to

18. It should be added, however, that this radical–conservative dispute existed in almost every state without being quite so protracted. See John Ashworth, *"Agrarians" and "Aristocrats": Party Political Ideology in the United States, 1837–1846* (London, 1983), pp. 87–174.

19. John Mayfield, *Rehearsal for Republicanism, Free Soil and the Politics of Anti-slavery* (New York, 1980); Chaplain W. Morrison, *Democratic Politics and Sectionalism, The Wilmot Proviso Controversy* (Chapel Hill, 1967); Joseph G. Rayback, "Martin Van Buren's Break with James K. Polk: the Record," *New York History*, 36 (January 1955), pp. 51–62; Sellers, Polk, Continentalist, pp. 162–213; *Sewell, Ballots for Freedom*.

deliver half the votes of the state. But as always the Barnburners were disinclined to accept a compromise:

> If the Convention recognize as the representatives of the Democracy of New York men among whom may be found those who opposed the Independent Treasury, who were hostile to the debt paying of our state in 1842; who lobbied against the tariff of 1846 ... who treacherously defeated Silas Wright, the regular candidate for Governor in 1846 ... who, living in a State which owes its greatness to the dignity and influence with which its liberal institutions have clothed the arm of free labor, unblushingly advocate the extension of slavery into territory now free, and upon that ground claim to be entitled to seats in this Convention as Representatives of the New York Democracy – we have no hesitation in saying that if we should consent to divide with them our seats and our votes, we should betray the principles and forfeit the confidence of the pure and fearless party whose commission we bear. We therefore respectfully decline to take our seats upon the terms proposed by the Convention.

The Barnburners then walked out of the Convention. And the Convention proceeded to nominate for President another of their arch-enemies, Lewis Cass of Michigan.[20]

Democratic-Republicans viewed Cass, as they would later view Stephen A. Douglas, as the epitome of the northern "doughface," a politician who, in order to gratify his ambitions, would sacrifice true principle in order to secure southern support. Cass had not only repudiated the Wilmot Proviso, but had denied that the constitution gave Congress power over slavery in the territories. Accordingly the Barnburners and their allies in other states, joined with other antislavery groups to form the Free Soil party of 1848. In part their purpose was, as Benjamin Butler put it, "to teach the South a lesson" and "thus render a great and lasting service to the country and the world." But in part too the goal was to teach the North a lesson, to let "the ambitious and the aspiring" know, as David Wilmot later put it, "that they cannot reach the Presidency by a base bowing down to the power of slavery."[21]

The wholesale retreat by large numbers of northern Democrats from the Wilmot Proviso fuelled radical Democratic fears of the South and of southern political power. Yet in the North in 1848 regular Democrats were able to defuse the Free Soil appeal by claiming that Cass's doctrine

20. John Bigelow (ed.), *The Writings and Speeches of Samuel J. Tilden.* 2 vols. (New York, 1885), I, pp. 244–245; Frederick J. Blue, *The Free Soilers, Third Party Politics, 1848–1854* (Urbana, 1973).
21. Butler quoted in Patricia M. McGee, "Issues and Factions: New York State Politics from the Panic of 1837 to the Election of 1848," (Unpublished Doctoral Dissertation, St John's University, 1969), p. 183; CG, 31/1, App., p. 941.

of congressional nonintervention in the territories would in fact result in free states throughout the area of the Mexican cession. As a result Martin Van Buren, who headed the Free Soil ticket, carried not a single state. Nevertheless, those who had defected from the Democratic party at least had the satisfaction of seeing Cass fail in his efforts to procure the ultimate political prize.[22]

When the Compromise measures of 1850 were devised, northern Democrats as a whole, along with southern Whigs were their strongest supporters. The Democrats who had defected to the Free Soil party tended to be far less enthusiastic. But they acquiesced in the agreement as a final settlement of the territorial question and returned to the fold to support Franklin Pierce in 1852. So Pierce, when elected, immediately faced a dilemma. Should he deny the former Free Soilers any share of the federal patronage and force them out of the party or should he, in the spirit of harmony, seek to unite all elements regardless of their past activities? He opted for the second course, much to the disgust of groups like the New York Hunkers who understandably believed that, having defended the national party throughout the preceding four years, they should receive all its patronage plums. As a result, despite the supposed "finality" of the Compromise of 1850, intraparty disputes in New York and elsewhere were far from resolved.[23]

But the key event of the 1850s, exceeding in importance even the Baltimore convention of 1844, was the introduction of the Kansas-Nebraska Act. Once the repeal of the Missouri Compromise had been proposed, southern Democrats (together with President Pierce) insisted on making it a test of party loyalty, partly because the presence of northern Free Soilers in the northern Democracy gave southern Whigs valuable ammunition. If the objective was to drive them away from the party, the strategy was highly successful. Although older Democrats like Martin Van Buren and Thomas Hart Benton could not bring themselves to leave the party, many of the prominent Democratic Free Soilers, together with others who had stayed loyal in 1848, defected and over the following months and years joined the newly formed Republican party.

Indeed no action could have been better calculated to spread alarm among antislavery Democrats than the repeal of the Missouri Compromise. At a stroke it confirmed their deepest fears over southern influence

22. "The Election of 1848," in Arthur M. Schlesinger, Jr and Fred L. Israel (eds.), *A History of American Presidential Elections, 1789–1968*. 4 vols. (New York, 1971), II, pp. 865–896.
23. Nichols, *Democratic Machine*. In New York the more conciliatory Hunkers merged with the Barnburners to become the "Softshell" faction or "Softs"; the more intransigent Hunkers became the "Hardshell" faction or "Hards." The old bitterness in no way diminished in the 1850s. See CG, 33/1, App., p. 156.

in the party, fears they had harbored for many years, and it revealed what they now took to be the ultimate objective of southern Democrats. According to Kinsley Bingham of Michigan, a radical Democrat and Democratic-Republican, this was "to nationalize slavery and its interests, and to sectionalize freedom." In the words of Nathaniel Banks of Massachusetts, "the repeal of the Missouri Compromise was the most stupendous public wrong ever committed in this country, or that men will ever live to commit."[24]

The circumstances of its passage seemed to many Democratic-Republicans proof that a conspiracy existed. According to Galusha Grow of Pennsylvania, the splitting of the original Nebraska territory into two had been intended to make it more difficult for free labour to take possession of the entire territory. Others noted that the Washington *Union* in 1854 at first condemned the attempt to repeal the Missouri Compromise explicitly but then suddenly reversed itself and made the repeal a test of party orthodoxy. Surely this was proof that improper influences had been brought to bear. What was their source? Why had a measure that had stood on the statute book for a third of a century suddenly been swept aside? Inevitably perhaps, John C. Calhoun was heavily implicated, despite having been dead for four years. In the election campaign of 1856 Joseph Stringham noted that Presidents Pierce and Fillmore bore some responsibility for the disasters of recent years. But as a good Democratic-Republican, Stringham located the ultimate responsibility elsewhere:

> I look behind *them* to the *influence* behind the throne greater than the throne, which imposed measures upon them so offensive to all liberty loving, kind hearted, and generous men, and I find it to be precisely the same as that which thwarted the will of the majority of the democratic party in 1844, which assassinated Silas Wright (politically) in 1846, and which now proposes to elect James Buchanan president in 1856. It is the disunion party founded by Calhoun and Tyler.

According to James Doolittle of Wisconsin, 1854 was the year in which the Democratic party ceased to be worthy of its name.[25]

In the following years the Democratic-Republicans continued to assert that the South had taken over the Democratic party. According to Frank Blair, Jr, "Mr. Buchanan was nominated to carry out the policy of his predecessor, which was to fix slavery upon Kansas by force or fraud." He added that "in my opinion, not only Kansas, but the whole continent

---

24. Message of Kinsley S. Bingham (1855) in Fuller (ed.), *Messages of Governors of Michigan*, II, pp. 297–299; *Address of His Excellency Nathaniel P. Banks, to the Two Branches of the Legislature of Massachusetts, Jan. 6, 1860* (Boston, 1858), p. 31.
25. Stringham, *Address to Republican Club of Buffalo*, p. 9; CG, 34/1, App., p. 147, 35/2, p. 1267.

is embraced in this conspiracy." Other former Democrats in the Republican ranks carefully examined the policies and personnel of their old party. They did not like what they saw. The party used to be "radical," Timothy Day noted, and had been opposed to the "'law and order' of conservatism." But now it was "a receptacle of all that is selfish, all that is conservative." "Instead of being the party of the people," it was "the party of privileged power." Its twin principles, according to another Democratic-Republican were "slavery and office." Lyman Trumbull of Illinois declared that "to call the party that now calls itself Democratic, the successor of the old Democratic party, is a misnomer. It is no more the successor of that party than the Republican party." Another former Democrat went still further and claimed that the Democratic party had been disbanded in 1854 and was now called the Republican party.[26]

According to the Democratic-Republicans the ultimate goals of the Democratic party were either to spread slavery throughout the nation or to bring about disunion.[27] Francis P. Blair Junior and Lyman Trumbull in the aftermath of the Dred Scott decision shared the view of prominent Whig-Republicans (including Lincoln) that the next step would be for the Supreme Court to legalise slavery in every state of the Union. Little wonder, then, that prominent among the leading men of the Democratic party were those who had been Jackson's enemies. Francis P. Blair examined its personnel and found everywhere Calhoun's disciples (Butler of South Carolina, Hunter and Wise of Virginia, Yulee of Florida, Atchison of Missouri), former Whigs (Toombs and Stephens of Georgia) or out-and-out secessionists (Soulé of Louisiana). True Democrats like Thomas Hart Benton had been pushed aside and in their place were the nullifiers who, he concluded, had controlled the party since the election of Polk. As a result, "the Jefferson-Jackson Democracy is utterly scouted." It had been "sold out to Mr. Calhoun's nullifying party." Calhoun had posthumously triumphed.[28]

## III

Historians are agreed that the Democratic-Republicans tended to come disproportionately from the radical wing of the party. Those who were

---

26. *CG*, 35/1, p. 1282, 34/1, App., p. 414, 36/1, p. 39, 34/1, App., p. 1269.
27. For a discussion of this issue see pp. 250–264.
28. *Speech of Senator Trumbull at Chicago* (n.p., n.d.), p. 5; *CG*, 35/1, p. 1282; *Voice from Grave of Jackson*, pp. 8–10; One former Democrat noted that Buchanan, who had favoured the Whig tariff of 1842 over the (Democratic) Walker tariff of 1846, had recently tried to read Robert J. Walker out of the party! – see *CG*, 35/1, p. 1043. The Democratic-Republican newspaper, *The Republic* generally referred to secessionists as nullifiers. See also George Weston, *The Federal Union – It Must Be Preserved* (July 1856), p. 15.

radical on economic questions like banking and currency were likely to be sympathetic to the free soil cause. In 1844 they supported Martin Van Buren. Lewis Cass meanwhile was the accredited conservative candidate. This correspondence between economic radicalism and antislavery sentiment obtained again in 1848 when the Free Soil party was launched, and yet again when the even more important wave of Democratic defections occurred in the mid-1850s as a result of the Kansas-Nebraska Act. Why was this so?[29]

It is tempting to find an explanation in the simple motive of revenge. After all the Van Buren Democrats were denied the nomination in 1844 by southerners determined, it appeared, to spread slavery into the West. They were indeed bitterly anti-Southern and there can be little doubt that the motive of revenge was prominent in the minds of many Democratic-Republicans. Yet this is an inadequate explanation. The Barnburners and other Van Burenite groups were from the outset alarmed at the prospect of slavery spreading; their free-soil sympathies were the cause rather than the consequence of their defeat in 1844. If Van Buren had been willing to embrace the immediate annexation of Texas that year, he would undoubtedly have been nominated. Moreover by the early 1850s, as we have seen, there had been a rapprochement between the former Free Soilers and the Democratic regulars. The cause of the new breach was the introduction of the Kansas-Nebraska Act for which the Democratic-Republicans had been in no way responsible. Finally, feelings of revenge are quite compatible with a hostility based upon principle. Indeed, the two are frequently mutually reinforcing rather than mutually exclusive. Explanations of behaviour in terms of emotion are not necessarily in competition with explanations which emphasise ideas. They simply occupy a different conceptual space. To understand why the radical Democrats in disproportionate numbers joined the Republican party it is necessary to examine their ideas and principles.

What then were the fundamental principles of the Democratic-Republicans? Here it is necessary to recur briefly to the founding fathers of the Democratic party. The Democratic-Republicans were the heirs not merely of Jefferson and Jackson but of the radical wing of Jeffersonian Democracy, whose ideas were most forcefully expressed by John Taylor

29. Donovan, *Barnburners*; Foner, *Free Soil*, p. 169; Floyd B. Streeter, *Political Parties in Michigan 1837–1860* (Lansing, 1918), pp. 45, 142, 183. In a speech in Cincinnati in 1848 John Van Buren asserted that four-fifths of the Democrats in the Free Soil Party in New York state were from the radical wing. The speech was quoted in the New York *Evening Post*, Nov. 2, 1848. Note that although Foner observes the correlation between radicalism and antislavery within the Democratic party he does not seek to explain it.

of Caroline, and of the radical Jacksonians, who adopted most of these ideas wholeheartedly. Radical Democrats took from Taylor an unqualified faith in majoritarian government. This was based on the belief that, as Taylor put it, "however splendidly a minority may live upon the labors of a majority...a majority cannot subsist upon those of a minority." Taylor's conclusion was that "it would be as unnatural for majorities to fatten upon minor interests, as for pastures to eat the herds grazing on them."[30]

The simile was, for Taylor's purposes, an apt one. For just as herds would eat the pasture so the minority would inevitably seek to fatten itself off the labour of the majority. In his famous *Inquiry into the Principles and Policy of the Government of the United States* Taylor devoted hundreds of pages to an analysis of this process which he showed to have been ever-present in other countries and which, he believed, threatened to re-emerge in the United States and to subvert its democratic experiment. The danger to which he was seeking to alert his fellow countrymen was that of aristocracy. In Taylor's words, "a transfer of property by law is aristocracy and aristocracy is a transfer of property by law."[31]

These ideas were central to Taylor's thought. They provided an explanation for the injustices which human history had witnessed over the centuries as well as an urgent political lesson for his newly independent nation. The immediate target for criticism was the Hamiltonian financial programme and Taylor launched a powerful assault on the tariff and the banking and funding systems. In the Jacksonian era those Democrats who waged the bank war most vigorously (the radicals) simply repeated the substance of Taylor's criticisms. They shared the same suspicion of the minority and placed their confidence in the majority. Once again the source of inequality was political. Once again the threat was from the privileged minority. Once again the only way it could be combated was by mobilising the majority. The radical Democrats believed that history exhibited a long continuous struggle on the part of the masses – the many – to restrain the holders of power – the few. "All past history," it was argued, presented the same dismal spectacle: "governments taking some of the rights of the Many and giving them to the Few." There was "an eternal struggle" in society: "a portion of mankind" constantly sought to "pervert the laws and institutions of society to their own temporary aggrandisement and to the permanent oppression of the mass of their fellow creatures." How did the radical Democrats propose to counter this

30. John Taylor, *Arator* (reprint, Indianapolis, 1977), pp. 94–95.
31. John Taylor, *An Inquiry into the Principles and Policy of the Government of the United States* (reprint, London, 1950), pp. 86, 255, 352.

threat? By mobilising the self-interest and the power of the majority, on the grounds that "a majority cannot subsist upon a minority."[32]

We are now in a position to understand how the radical Democrats in the North could so easily become free soilers and then Republicans. For if the leaders of the southern Democracy had wanted to antagonise them they could hardly have performed the task better. To begin with, the slaveholding interest that they represented was indisputably a minority interest in the nation and even, it could be argued, within the South itself. Yet it was seeking to control the Democratic party and thus the destinies of the nation. Through this ideological lens the key events of the Jacksonian era instantly came into focus. The nullification crisis revealed, radical Democrats believed, the true colours of their archenemy, John C. Calhoun. Calhoun had made no secret of his scorn for majority rule and his entire theory of nullification was explicitly intended to protect the (slaveholding) minority against the aggression of a (northern) majority. Similarly in the Baltimore Convention of 1844 the Democratic party had abandoned Van Buren, to whom a majority of the delegates had been pledged, and had symbolically confirmed its repudiation of the majoritarian principle by adopting the two-thirds rule. By thus conferring privileges upon a mere minority the party had acted, as John M. Niles of Connecticut put it, "in violation of the fundamental principle of our political system." By empowering the minority, the two-thirds rule operated, in the words of Joseph Stringham, "contrary to the principle of the rule of the majority."[33]

Throughout the sectional crisis of the 1850s and the early 1860s the Democratic-Republicans emphasised that southern demands were those of a mere minority and thus should not be conceded. "Is it seriously proposed," asked George Weston during the election of 1856, "that seventeen States shall yield to fourteen States; that thirteen millions of people shall yield to six millions?" Again and again Democratic-Republicans insisted that the majority must rule. In 1860 Governor Samuel Kirkwood of Iowa, contemplating the threats of secession, justified his majoritarian stance in terms which bore a remarkable similarity to those used many decades before by John Taylor of Caroline:

> In a government like ours, without privileged classes, and where the laws affect all alike, we need not fear that a majority of our people will deliberately pursue a policy intended to operate injuriously upon

32.  Samuel Young, *Oration at New York, 1840* (New York, 1841), pp. 5, 9; *The Crisis Met* (n.p., n.d.), p. 2; *CG*, 25/2, App. p. 423; Washington *Globe*, Sept. 16, 1842, Jan. 13, 1842; *Democratic Review*, 1 (October 1837), p. 4. See Ashworth, *"Agrarians" and "Aristocrats,"* pp. 87–111.

33.  "Letter of Senator John M. Niles to the Free Soil State Convention of Connecticut" in *The Barnburner*, Aug. 12, 1848; Stringham, *Address to Republican Club of Buffalo*, p. 8.

the public welfare, because by so doing they would be acting contrary
to their own best interest.

Here was the ultimate security for the South. The majority, acting in its
collective self-interest, was the guardian of freedom, of equality, and of
democracy.[34]
From the moment they joined the Republican party, the former
Democrats were insistent majoritarians, adamantly opposed to compromise with the southern minority. But their confidence in the majority and
their fears of the minority were not merely politically based: they had an
important social and economic rationale. The minority which threatened
the nation was a minority of the rich and powerful. Once again the ideological inheritance from Jefferson, Jackson and John Taylor of Caroline
was enormously important.[35]
This time, however, it was not the nullification crisis but rather the
Jacksonian struggle with the Bank of the United States and, to a lesser
extent, with the protective tariff, which bulked large in the minds of the
Democratic-Republicans. In each case an aristocratic minority had sought
to use the powers of government to enhance its own wealth and power
at the expense of the rest of the community. Here was the ideological
prism through which the Democratic-Republicans viewed the events of
the sectional conflict. What they observed in their struggle with the South
in the 1840s and 1850s slotted comfortably into, and reinforced, the
pattern of beliefs and assumptions inherited from previous generations.
Thus according to Governor Kinsley Bingham of Michigan, experience
suggested that the struggle then (in 1857) taking place in Kansas would
continue. "The contest between free labor and slave labor, between free
society and slave society," he announced "will not probably terminate
with the struggle in Kansas, whatever may be the result there." For, he
continued in language that might have been employed twenty years earlier
in the struggle against the banks, "history teaches us that privilege never
restrains its ambition to rule, nor abates a whit of its pretensions, and so
long as in our country, it can surround itself with flatterers and parasites,
it will continue to struggle for enlargement and preponderance." David

34.  Weston, *Who Are Sectional* (Washington DC, 1856), p. 3; Kirkwood in Benjamin
    F. Shambaugh (ed.), *The Messages and Proclamations of the Governors of Iowa.* 7
    vols. (Iowa City, 1903–1905), II, p. 230. There is no doubt that the Democratic-
    Republicans were sincerely convinced that the federal government was being "pros-
    tituted to slavery." See George T. Palmer (ed.), *Letters from Lyman Trumbull to John
    M. Palmer, 1854–1858* (Springfield, 1924), p. 5. For an identical public utterance,
    see *Speech of Senator Trumbull at Chicago* (n.p., n.d.), pp. 4–5.
35.  For other examples of Democratic-Republican majoritarianism, see George M.
    Weston, *The Federal Union – It Must Be Preserved.* Tract no. 1. (July 1856), p. 5;
    *Speech of Trumbull at Chicago*, p. 5; Shambaugh (ed.), *Messages of Governors of
    Iowa*, II, pp. 237, 253; New York *Evening Post*, Oct. 28, 1846.

Wilmot of Pennsylvania was still more explicit in linking the sectional controversy with the financial battles of the Jacksonian era. "The instincts of money," he announced in Congress, "are the same the world over. – the same here as in the most grinding despotism of Europe." "Money," he warned, "is cold, selfish, heartless" and had "no pulse of humanity, no feelings of pity or of love." He then made the link explicit: "interest, gain, accumulation are the sole instincts of its nature; and it is the same whether invested in manufacturing stock, bank stock, or the black stock of the South. Intent upon its own interest, it is utterly regardless of the rights of humanity." Wilmot referred to the slave interest as "a heartless money aristocracy" comprising sixteen hundred million dollars and before which the nation was being asked to "bow down." He then illustrated the affinity between Democratic radicalism and antislavery by boasting that his district in Pennsylvania was "the most radical, thorough, inflexible Democratic district in the State ... opposed to a high protective tariff, to a national bank, to extravagant schemes of internal improvements by the General Government" but "in favour of the independent treasury and ... of every other measure with which the Republican [i.e. Democratic] party has been identified for the last twenty years." As a true radical Jacksonian Wilmot announced that he was "deadly hostile to the control of capital in this Government." For that reason he had been a Free Soiler in 1848 and would be a Democratic-Republican in the 1850s.[36]

Other Democratic-Republicans voiced similar sentiments. Galusha Grow, also of Pennsylvania, noted at the time of the Kansas disturbances in 1856 that "a moneyed interest in any country always struggles to seize upon its Government, and to wield it for its own advantages." Again language that might have been directed against the advocates of a national bank was here used to refer to the slaveholding interests of the South. Again the comparison was made explicit. Grow, now a Republican, argued that "the Democracy of the country, in the days of its glory and triumph, resisted the attempt of the moneyed interest of the country, invested in banking, to seize upon this Government, to use it for its own purposes." "They also," he noted, "resisted the attempt of the moneyed interest engaged in manufacturing to use the Government for its purposes." "And yet," he declared, "here is a united, concentrated moneyed interest – compared to which either of those was but a drop in the bucket to the ocean – endeavoring to use this Government for the promotion of its interests and the advancement of its ends." James Doolittle of Wisconsin likewise referred to the slave power as exercising a "similar despotism" to that wielded by the Bank of the United States, though the latter was "a mere

---

36. "Message of Kinsley S. Bingham (1857)," in Fuller (ed.), *Messages of Governors of Michigan*, II, p. 319; CG, 31/1, App., pp. 941–942.

pigmy" in comparison with the former. Finally Frank Blair, representing St Louis, Missouri, reminded Congress that the Democratic party had destroyed the Bank of the United States and dismantled the protective system. It had been the defender of the rights of man rather than the rights of property and the enemy of "monopolizing institutions." Now a similar struggle was taking place against "a colossal aggregation of wealth." Blair then concluded that the struggle over slavery was ultimately not a sectional one at all and, in so doing, testified to the remarkable persistence of radical Democratic thought:

> This is no question of North and South. It is a struggle between those who contend for caste and privilege and those who neither have nor desire to have privileges beyond their fellows. It is the old question that has always, in all free countries, subsisted – the question of the wealthy and crafty few endeavoring to steal from the masses of the people all the political power of the government.

The radical Democratic reading of the past provided a ready explanation for the struggle over slavery.[37]

Thus it was the radical Democrats who were quickest to conclude that slaveholders constituted an "aristocracy." Their commitment to equality (as displayed in the bank war) and their natural inclination to fear the political and social power of an elite minority were, quite simply, greater than those of conservative Democrats, who had been for much of the Jacksonian era in dread of the politics of conflict pursued by the radicals. The conservatives had a different view of history and of political power. They were not so disposed to look for instances of the minority oppressing the majority.[38]

Hence those Democrats who had been conservatives and who remained in the party throughout the 1850s were slower to perceive a threat from

37. *CG*, 34/1, App., p. 148, 35/2, p. 1267, 35/1, pp. 964, 1284. Not surprisingly, similar sentiments underlay the defection of 1848. William Cullen Bryant, editor of the New York *Evening Post* (and later to be a Democratic-Republican), in 1848 surveyed the recent past and compared the slave power with the advocates of paper money and a high tariff. Those in favour of protection, he noted, had tried everything to retain their privileges – "but in vain." for "like the paper money interest" the tariff interest "was in conflict with equal political rights and it could not be sustained." Now for a third time the struggle was being waged: "The slave interest at the South now seems to be acting this part. It claims to be the whole South, instead of a mere interest that extensively prevails there. It looks up to the constitution of the United States as its shield and as pledged to be the instrument of its diffusion across the continent. It threatens terrible things. It will not allow us to have a President unless of its own selection, so talked the paper money interest. But Andrew Jackson came into office for a second term, like a mighty conqueror. It is no new thing for a sectional interest to set itself up for the sole interest...of the whole country." – New York *Evening Post*, May 4, 1848. See also April 27, 1848.
38. Ashworth, *"Agrarians" and "Aristocrats,"* pp. 132–146.

the South. It was not that they liked slavery, or that they wished to see it expand into the territories. It was rather that their ideology did not lead them to expect a "despotic, monopolizing interest," as William Cullen Bryant put it, to undermine the wellbeing of the individual citizen or the health of the nation. Fundamental ideological continuities explain the tendency of radical, rather than conservative, Democrats to defect to the Republicans party.[39]

## IV

Their long established and recurrent fear of a social and political elite was by no means the only ideological asset that the former Democrats brought to the Republicans. Throughout the prewar decade they reacted to southern threats of secession precisely as Jackson had reacted to the nullification crisis. Many attached as little credence to the claim that slavery was under threat in 1860 as Jackson had at the time of nullification. Thus Frank Blair Jr declared that the alarm caused by the Brown raid was once again entirely bogus. Slave prices, he noted, were rising throughout the South and southerners surely knew that Republicans would immediately quell any slave rebellion. For Blair, as for other Democratic-Republicans, the secession crisis was merely nullification revisited. Hence in the crucial days prior to the outbreak of hostilities they rallied to the defence of the Union and were extremely reluctant to entertain proposals for compromise. Secession, they argued, was rebellion and rebellion was treason. Both were merely the culmination of the pernicious doctrines that had been taught for the previous thirty years and which had originated with John C. Calhoun of South Carolina. Secession meant a resort to force. As one Democratic-Republican Governor put it, it would "strike a blow, which, if not arrested, will crumble the fabric of our Government into ruins." Other Democratic-Republicans claimed that it meant not merely the break-up the Union but also "the destruction of the democratic principle of government, and the substitution of an aristocracy in its stead." Above all secession was an affront to the democratic principle and to the rights of the majority.[40]

Yet as good Jacksonians the Democratic-Republicans combined a veneration for the Union with a scrupulous regard for the rights of the states. While southern militants in the 1850s often associated state's rights with secession, this was by no means a necessary correspondence. In fact more than any other group Democratic-Republicans adhered to the Jacksonian rationale for state's rights. As we shall see, northern Democrats, led

---

39.  New York *Evening Post*, Dec. 15, 1858.
40.  *Journal of the Indiana State Senate ... Special Session ... Commencing April 24, 1861* (Indianapolis, 1861), p. 24.

by Stephen A. Douglas, were finding new justifications for maintaining the rights of the states, emphasising the "variety" and the diversity of interests of the different states rather than the need to maintain strict control, in the name of the majority, over those in power in Washington.[41] Southern Democrats, by contrast, were increasingly linking state's rights, as Calhoun had done, with the defence of slavery and the rights of minorities. But Democratic-Republicans took a different view. According to Francis P. Blair, "State's rights will sustain no man in resisting the installation of a legally elected President." Instead "the honest champion of the rights of the States will be equally tenacious of the powers granted to the Federal government." As true Jacksonians, the Democratic-Republicans were enthusiastic Unionists, committed majoritarians and defenders of the rights of the states.[42]

Consequently they denounced the southern claim that the federal government should intervene to protect slavery in the territories (by means of a slave code) as a departure from state's rights principles. According to the New York *Evening Post* the modern democratic party was "a centralizing, sectional party, comprising democrats, whigs and nullifiers, who have adopted a new territorial policy with a view to nationalize and extend slavery, by the unwarranted assumption of power on the part of the federal government." Equally, one of their reasons for repudiating the alleged plot to legalise slavery in the North was that it rode roughshod over the rights of the states and threatened to convert the nation into "a consolidated despotism." Thus as in Jackson's era the Democratic-Republicans felt they were witnessing an attempt to "confer exclusive advantages on a particular portion of them [the states] by an unwarranted exercise of federal power."[43]

This emphasis upon state's rights was also allied, as it had been in Jackson's day, to a belief in limited government, at state as well as federal level. The Democratic-Republicans continued to embrace the Jacksonian and Jeffersonian ideal of a limited, inactive government. The newspaper established in Washington to expound their views, *The Republic*, warned its readers about the recent high level of government spending "which, if not checked in some way, could have had no other termination than the extinction of all public integrity." This, the editor asserted, would have been "followed inevitably by the overthrow of Republican institutions." Similarly Democratic-Republican Governors throughout the North continued to deliver warnings about the dangers inherent in "over

41. See pp 381–383.
42. *Celebration of Jefferson's Birthday*, p. 13. In this context, it should be noted, Jackson's Force Bill was not, as his opponents charged, a violation of state's rights principles.
43. New York *Evening Post*, Dec. 15, 1858; CG, 35/1, p. 1043.

legislation." "One of the evils under which we suffer," according to Hannibal Hamlin of Maine, was "excessive and useless legislation." In the words of William Bissell of Illinois, "too much legislation, a tendency which is greatly increasing with us, is a serious evil." Although the question of legislative power within the states was of minor importance compared to the slavery controversy, the Democratic-Republicans were here faithful to their Jacksonian heritage.[44]

These views on government and federal power helped differentiate the Democratic-Republicans from the former Whigs in the party. Yet this aversion to Whiggish views on government was only one of the distinctive features of the Democratic-Republicans. In general they were more tainted by racism than the bulk of the former Whigs within the party. It can be argued that this too is only comprehensible in the light of the Democratic world view. Ironically Democratic egalitarianism militated against justice for the racial minorities in the United States. Democrats sought a large measure of equality and came to argue in effect that the franchise guaranteed not merely the right to vote but also the right to social and economic equality. In the New York Constitutional Convention of 1846 Bishop Perkins, a Barnburner, warned that "you could not admit the blacks to a participation in the government of the country unless you put them on terms of social equality with us." Unable to accept African Americans (or Native Americans) as social equals, many former Democrats agreed with Lyman Trumbull of Illinois that "we, the Republican party, are the white man's party." Trumbull acknowledged that he wanted "to have nothing to do either with the free negro, or the slave negro." Similarly in 1856 an Indiana Republican who had recently left the Democratic party asserted that "the mass of the people of the free States prefer not to have the African race among them." For it was not only slavery to which they were opposed: "both the race and the institution are distasteful to them." Hence when many Democratic-Republicans looked forward to the termination of slavery in the nation, they also desired the colonisation of the freedmen.[45]

44. *The Republic*, Dec. 17, 1858; Message of Hannibal Hamlin in *Journal of the Senate of Maine for...1857* (Augusta, 1857), p. 22; Message of Lott Morrill in *Journal of the Senate of Maine for...1858* (Augusta, 1858), p. 20; Message of William Bissell in *Journal of the Senate of the Twenty-First General Assembly of the State of Illinois...* (Springfield, 1859), p. 19; Message of Governor Ralph Metcalf in *Journal of the Honorable Senate of the State of New Hampshire...1855* (Concord, 1855), p. 21.
45. Foner, *Free Soil*, p. 267; Perkins quoted in Ernest P. Muller, "Preston King, A Political Biography," (Unpublished Doctoral Dissertation, Columbia, 1957), pp. 379–380; *Speech of Trumbull at Chicago*, p. 9; *An Enquiry into the Equal Rights of the States, as to the Non-Extension of Slavery into the Territories, By an Indianian* (Indianapolis, 1856), p. 8; Ashworth, *"Agrarians" and "Aristocrats,"* pp. 221–223 and also "The Jacksonian as Leveller," *Journal of American Studies*, 14 (December 1980),

These racist sentiments were almost certainly strongest in the western states. Yet they were also expressed by easterners. David Wilmot of Pennsylvania, at the time he introduced his Proviso, explained that his hostility to slavery was based entirely upon his estimate of its effects upon the white race. He acknowledged that he cared nothing for its impact upon the blacks. Wilmot's was to be the typical Democratic-Republican stance. George M. Weston of Maine, editor of *The Republic*, in a tract entitled *The Poor Whites of the South*, went so far as to claim that even if Southerners were right and slavery were indeed a blessing to the blacks yet "the price paid for it is too costly." Weston argued that "an equal number of people of the Caucasian stock" (here he was referring to the eponymous poor whites) had been forced to pay this price, "thus reversing the natural order of Providence, and sacrificing the superior to the inferior race." And even a Republican like John P. Hale of New Hampshire, who had left the Democratic party in the 1840s, and who took pride in his efforts on behalf of African Americans, on occasion made it clear that the wellbeing of his "own kith and kin...the white Saxon" was paramount.[46]

Partly as a consequence of this intense racism, most Democratic-Republicans gave relatively little attention to the moral indictment of slavery. Their critique was of its economic and political power, rather than of its effect upon the slave or upon the conscience of the slaveholder. Of course economics and morality are often related and former Democrats did stress that one of the effects of slavery was to make labour dishonourable, to the moral as well as the economic detriment of the entire community.[47] Nevertheless, the characteristic concern of radical Republicans (and abolitionists) with the moral impact of enslavement upon the slave, or of slaveholding upon the conscience of the master, or of slavery upon the families of both, received very little attention from the former Democrats. Indeed David Wilmot actually went so far as to concede that he was not as alive to the sufferings of the slave as he wished. It should be remembered that the Democratic-Republicans were from a tradition that frowned upon the intrusion of moral questions (understood as those which involved an appeal to personal morality and the individual conscience) into politics. Hence although they became staunch enemies of

pp. 407–421. It might be worth noting that, despite these utterances, Trumbull spent a good deal of time as a lawyer defending the rights of Illinois blacks. It is also the case that many former Whigs were equally attracted to the colonisation scheme.
46. *CG*, 29/2, App., pp. 217–218; George M. Weston, *The Poor Whites of the South* (Washington, DC, 1856), p. 7; *CG*, 33/2, App. p. 1520. In the words of the New York *Evening Post*: "that the black man is somewhat below the normal standard of manhood, we presume will not be disputed." – New York *Evening Post*, Aug. 11, 1853. See also Morrison, *Democratic Politics and Sectionalism*, pp. 69–74.
47. This theme was all but universal among the enemies of slavery.

slavery, their hostility was not primarily based upon moral considerations.[48]

## V

As we have seen, the Democratic-Republicans carried into their new party the commitment to majoritarian democracy which they had earlier displayed. This presented few major problems within the Republican party, not least because, as we shall see, their colleagues who had formerly been Whigs had themselves abandoned the fear of the majority which many prominent Whigs had displayed in the 1830s and 1840s. In other words, a consensus was here emerging (precisely at a time when minoritarian sentiment was on the increase in the South). Yet this in no way meant that all the political differences between former Democrats and erstwhile Whigs in the new party had been erased, for the Democratic-Republicans adhered to other principles and policies which led them to view their new allies, the former Whigs, with a certain suspicion. It is a mistake to assume that the party system which was created in the 1850s obliterated the differences which had long divided Whig and Democrat. Rather interparty struggles became in the North intraparty tensions.

Although differences existed on the race question, these did not neatly accord with the alignment of the second party system since some former Whigs had as little concern for the African American as the former Democrats. Nor did Democratic-Republican concern for the rights of immigrants, also a traditional Democratic characteristic, differentiate them from Whigs of the Seward stripe, even though some more conservative Whigs had traditionally displayed strong nativist tendencies. But the concern for limited government and state's rights did produce one major disagreement. Former Whigs came from a political tradition which, especially in the North, emphasised the need to protect American industry by means of a tariff. As we have seen, Democrats, by contrast, had traditionally viewed the tariff as yet another device by which the few sought to employ government for their own benefit and at the expense of the rest of the community. After the Panic of 1857 there were renewed calls for protection in the North, especially from Pennsylvania, a state which, it was recognised, would be a crucial battleground in 1860. Some ex-Democrats became alarmed at the pressure exerted by former Whigs to commit the party to a higher tariff. Thus the New York *Evening Post* in March 1860 detected "a deeply-laid conspiracy...to pervert the Republican party to the purposes of the owners of coal and iron mines, by forcing the Chicago convention to nominate for the presidency an old Clay Whig, whose merits

48. *CG*, 31/1, App., p. 942.

consist in his advocacy of tariffs and rivers and harbors improvements." William Cullen Bryant, editor of the *Evening Post*, was here being faithful to his Jacksonian roots.[49]

In addition to their opposition to the tariff many Democrats took with them into the Republican party their Jacksonian distrust of banks and paper money, another attitude that had sharply differentiated them from the Whigs. According to Governor Morrill of Maine "the multiplicity of banks in the state" was "an evil," while further west in Michigan Governor Kinsley Bingham both drew the legislature's attention to the dangers to be feared from small notes and referred to "the suffering and distress" which some of the state's banks had occasioned. The desired reform, an outlawing of small notes, was widely sought by Democratic-Republican statesmen in the 1850s.[50] This hostility to banks peaked in the aftermath of the Panic of 1857, at which time Democratic-Republicans renewed the criticisms of the commercial order that had been heard in the late 1830s and 1840s. Thus Morrill in Maine warned that the pecuniary embarrassments had come about "because we have not accumulated by frugality." Another echo of the anti-entrepreneurialism of the Jacksonian era was heard in 1858 when Governor Alexander Randall of Wisconsin complained that in the last few years "business had been overdone." The problem was that "the great majority of businessmen were rejoicing in an imaginary, and not real, prosperity" with "people forgetting that a dollar acquired without labor is taken from someone else." Randall concluded, in classic Jacksonian fashion, that "too many are endeavoring to live without labor, and to get money without earning it."[51]

In view of these priorities, it is scarcely surprising that the former Democrats to some degree retained a separate identity within the Republican party. They insisted upon, and generally obtained, a share of the major offices and were keen to have a balance struck between former Democrats and Whigs when Republican tickets were drawn up. Above all they strove to ensure that the doctrines of Whiggery should not become party orthodoxy. The depth of their concern is suggested by an entry in

49. New York *Evening Post*, March 1, 1860.
50. Message of Lott Morrill, p. 19; Message of Bingham in Fuller (ed.), *Messages of Governors of Michigan*, II, pp. 288–292, 315. For additional instances of Democratic-Republican hostility to banks and paper money see Governor Kirkwood in Shambaugh (ed.), *Messages of Governors of Iowa*, II, pp. 361–363; *Address of His Excellency Nathaniel P. Banks, to the Two Branches of the Legislature of Massachusetts, Jan. 7, 1858* (Boston, 1858), pp. 13–14; "Message of the Governor of Ohio, to the Fifty Third General Assembly at the Regular Session, Commencing Jan. 4, 1858," in *Message and Report Made to the General Assembly and Governor of the State of Ohio for the year 1857. Part 1* (Columbus, OH, 1858), pp. 356–358.
51. *Annual Message of Alexander W. Randall, Governor of the State of Wisconsin, delivered Jan. 15, 1858* (Madison, 1858), pp. 42–43.

Gideon Welles' diary during the Civil War. Despite the feelings of solidarity engendered by over a decade of sectional strife and by three years of warfare against a common enemy, Lincoln's Secretary of the Navy expressed his contempt for the former Whigs:

> The Whig element is venal and corrupt, to a great extent. I speak of the leaders of that party. They seem to have very little political principle, they have no belief in public virtue or popular intelligence; they have no self-reliance, no confidence in the strength of a righteous cause, and little regard for constitutional restraints and limitations.

These were the very charges which Democrats had been leveling against the Whigs in the mid-1830s.[52]

## VI

Yet for a variety of reasons questions of banking and the tariff did not prove as divisive as might have been feared. Democratic hostility to banking had grown out of the fear that a process of commercialisation that was artificially promoted by banks would bring demoralisation and, most importantly, inequality in its wake. The banking failures and suspensions of the late 1830s and early 1840s had, of course, fuelled these fears so that in the West, which was hardest hit, the Democrats had often gone so far as to demand the destruction of all banks. The Democratic-Republicans, as we have also seen, carried their suspicion of banks into the Republican party but by this time banking was no longer so significant an issue. In part this was because the Democrats had successfully reformed the banks but more fundamentally it was the economic recovery which blunted antibank radicalism. With the discovery of gold in California and renewed foreign investment, the nation's specie reserves expanded rapidly and banks were able to conduct their operations with more safety that had been possible a decade earlier.[53] When the Panic of 1857 struck and the Democratic-Republicans voiced some of the old criticisms of banking, by now the goal of an entirely specie currency was seen by most of them to be impractical. Governor Ralph Metcalf of New Hampshire supplied the reason:

> The banking system of the country has become so interwoven with its industrial interests and monetary affairs, that the abandonment of a paper, and the adoption of an exclusively specie, currency is now

52. Howard K. Beale (ed.), *The Diary of Gideon Welles*. 3 vols. (New York, 1960), II, p. 122; Foner, *Free Soil*, pp. 167–168.
53. Thomas D. Willett, "International Specie Flows and American Monetary Stability, 1834–1860," *Journal of Economic History*, XXVIII (March 1968), pp. 28–50; Jeffrey G. Wilkinson, *American Growth and the Balance of Payments, 1820–1913* (Chapel Hill, 1964), p. 111

as much an "obsolete idea" as that the establishment of an United States bank is necessary to regulate exchanges.

Democratic-Republican Governors in the 1850s combined their criticism of the banks with an admission that they were more stable than in previous eras and would continue to exist for the foreseeable future. Thus William Bissell conceded in 1859 that "our present system of banking is, in the main, satisfactory." Others acknowledged that the banks within their states were, on the whole, safe and recognised that they were still needed to supply credit. Thus even in the wake of the Panic most Democratic-Republicans probably agreed with Preston King of New York that prosperity and progress would soon return. For most of the North, this optimism was well-founded.[54]

If the Panic had had a greater and more lasting impact upon the northern economy, it is possible that the old Jacksonian issues would have climbed much higher up the political agenda. But the recovery (in most of the North) meant that the compromise of the early 1850s was maintained: those who looked unfavourably upon banks would tolerate them provided they behaved in a responsible manner. Meanwhile, as we shall see, former Whigs had reached a similar conclusion: criticism of banks was acceptable and a national bank would not be re-established, provided that the goal of an exclusively specie currency was abandoned. Thus, once again, a compromise with the former Whigs had emerged.[55]

More fundamentally, however, the Democratic-Republicans had here come to terms with the realities of an expanding commercial economy. And they in fact sought to accelerate its development by sponsoring transportation improvements, the most spectacular of which would be the creation of a railroad to the Pacific. More significant even than this, however, was their new enthusiasm for manufacturing. This was perhaps the principal factor which prevented the tariff issue from inflicting irreparable damage upon the newly formed party.[56]

For a variety of reasons the tariff did not prove as divisive an issue as might have been feared. To begin with, the Panic of 1857 did not have such severe effects as that which had struck twenty years earlier and so outside states like Pennsylvania the pressure for change was limited. And even in Pennsylvania the Republicans were no more unfavourably placed

54. Message of Governor Ralph Metcalf in *Journal of the Honorable Senate of the State of New Hampshire, June Session 1856* (Concord, 1856), pp. 20–21; Message of Bissell, p. 23. *Journal of the Senate of Maine, 1857*, p. 28. For other examples of Democratic-Republican tolerance of banking, see: *Message of Hamlin*, p. 28; Sharp, *Jacksonians versus Banks*, pp. 121–122, 206–207, 319, 328–329.
55. See Chapter 4.
56. Shambaugh (ed.), *Messages of Governors of Iowa*, II, p. 243; *Annual Message of Randall, 1858*, pp. 32–33.

than the Democrats, who of course had a much stronger commitment to low tariffs. Moreover, the traditional formula, by which the revenue principle would govern the setting of duties but with "incidental" protection provided to American manufacturing, was itself a compromise acceptable to most within the Republican party. These were some of the factors which allowed the new party to avoid a damaging split over the tariff.

The principal cause, however, probably lay elsewhere. It reveals a fundamental discontinuity between the Jacksonian era and the 1850s. Although Democratic-Republicans brought their traditional dislike of the tariff into the new party, a subtle change had occurred. Classic Democratic theory had denounced the tariff not merely as an aid to manufacturers but as an aid to manufacturing, which they had traditionally disliked. The tradition inspired by Jefferson and John Taylor of Caroline had frowned upon all forms of manufacturing (except the household variety) chiefly because wage labour was perceived as a threat to the society of autonomous equals which a republic required. Thus tariffs were denounced as an artificial means of promoting American manufactures and of creating a dependent class of wage labourers. The desire for free trade had, therefore, generally been accompanied by a dislike of manufacturing. Gradually, however – and this shift occurred at different times with different individuals in different regions – antitariff sentiment in the North came to denote a hostility not to manufacturing *per se* but instead to manufacturers who grasped at what were deemed to be excessive profits. These were precisely the grounds upon which William Cullen Bryant of the New York *Evening Post* now opposed protection. Bryant indeed defended the lower duties of the Walker Tariff of 1846 by claiming that they had actually accelerated the growth of manufacturing in the nation. Lower duties, he argued in 1846, would result in lower prices and lower unit profits for manufacturers, as a result of which more units would be produced. Six years later he claimed that manufacturing functioned best when not protected, when lower prices allowed cheap iron, for example, to replace wood. Few former Democrats were more hostile to the tariff than Bryant but his hostility did not convey the traditional fear of manufacturing as anti-republican.[57]

This did not mean that Democratic-Republicans ceased to pronounce eulogies upon the farmer. Thus Alexander Randall, Governor of Wisconsin, in 1858 declared that "tilling the soil is an ancient occupation; in itself the most honorable of any engaged in by civilized men." He added that "the highest good to all mankind, depends more than in [sic] any other one avocation, upon the wise and successful prosecution of agricultural pursuits." Other Democratic-Republican Governors in the states of Michigan, New Hampshire and Maine made similar utterances, each

---

57.  New York *Evening Post*, Oct. 30, 1846: May 13, 1852.

affirming that agricultural interests were the most important in his own state. Indeed they went further. Ralph Metcalf of New Hampshire implied that this was, or should be, true of all states, while Lott Morrill of Maine and Kinsley Bingham of Michigan each assumed that the primacy of agriculture would continue forever.[58]

At the same time, however, the Democratic-Republicans were far more enthusiastic than the radical Democrats of the Jacksonian era had been towards manufacturing. Thus while for Metcalf "the products of the earth" might indeed be "the basis of all wealth," it remained true that manufacturing was "a branch of industry giving employment to thousands" and "a source of great wealth to the state." Although New Hampshire was, of course, far less advanced industrially than some of her New England neighbors, Metcalf insisted that "our natural advantages for pursuing the business are not surpassed by those of any other State." Here he had in mind waterpower, to be derived from the state's "never-failing water-falls," which he believed "sufficient, if improved to their utmost capabilities, to furnish motive power for machinery enough to manufacture for half the globe." In the same way Salmon P. Chase, when Governor of Ohio, claimed that his state's abundance of raw materials like iron and coal demonstrated "the vast capacity of Ohio for mineral production and for manufactures." Similarly Alexander Randall in 1861 announced that "an increased development of manufacturing interests in Wisconsin" was "a great necessity ... to the welfare of our people, present and prospective." Even more strikingly, he displayed what an earlier generation would have seen as impeccable Whig credentials when he observed that "our people follow too exclusively a single pursuit." Randall then suggested that the state should offer tax concessions to manufacturers for the next five or ten years. And George Weston, editor of the *Republic*, in surveying the prospects for the future development of the nation, insisted that the area between the Alleghanies and the Rockies should not always be devoted to agriculture. "It is itself," he predicted, "to be the seat of manufactures, to which many circumstances invite." Thus while ex-Democrats and former Whigs still disagreed upon the policy of tariff protection they were now in much closer agreement on the far more important question of the desirability of manufacturing itself. It was now a conflict over means rather than ends.[59]

58. *Message of Randall*, 1858, p. 14; Message of Bingham (1855), in Fuller (ed.), *Messages of Governors of Michigan*, II, p. 283; Message of Metcalf in *Journal of the Hon Senate of the State of New Hampshire 1855*, pp. 21–22; *Journal of the Senate of Maine for the Year 1858*, p. 20.

59. *Message of Metcalf* (1855), pp. 21–22; "Message of the Governor of Ohio," p. 351; *Annual Message of Alexander W. Randall, Governor of the State of Wisconsin ... 1861* (Madison, 1861), pp. 17–18; *The Republic*, Aug. 28, 1858. For

How then did the Democratic-Republicans view northern society? Despite their residual doubts about the behavior of certain banks or the greed of certain factory owners, there can be no doubt that they were satisfied with their society and pleased to contemplate the changes it was now undergoing. Thus Salmon P. Chase, when Governor of Ohio, boasted that since entering the Union Ohio's "social progress has been a sublime triumph." Similarly Governor William Bissell of Illinois, a state which was developing with extraordinary rapidity prior to the Civil War, in 1859 invited his fellow Illinoisans to congratulate themselves upon their recent progress:

> Our physical, intellectual and moral condition is advancing with a rapidity probably never equaled at any age nor among any people on the globe. Our almost limitless prairies are being converted, as if by magic, into fertile and teeming fields, the produce of which, finding cheap and speedy transit over our magnificent rivers and railroads, to the best markets in the world, is enriching our farmers, and creating and sustaining a healthful business, in all the useful departments of life.

It was significant that Bissell claimed that economic progress was accompanied by moral improvement. For ex-Democrats, like Republicans generally, believed that theirs was an age of progress, one in which "the dominating idea among the civilized nations of the earth" was "freedom." Where radical Democrats had during the Jacksonian era viewed contemporary social changes in the North with great unease, by the 1850s this unease had given way to a sense of gratification and confidence.[60]

Yet the very social and economic forces which muted the Democratic-Republicans' criticism of northern society simultaneously deepened their reservations about the South. Here Democratic-Republican criticisms of the South were indistinguishable from those offered by former Whigs. If the age were indeed one of enhanced freedom for the "civilized nations" of the earth, where did this leave the South? "Serfdom, vassalage and slavery," it was argued, were retreating "everywhere" before "freedom" – everywhere, that is, except in the South, whose leaders had since the 1820s and 1830s become increasingly committed to slavery. To the Democratic-Republicans it seemed that the slaveholding minority or "aristocracy" was seeking to reverse the tide of history. Thus in Kansas in 1857 it had inspired "laws repugnant to humanity and to the age in which we live." At

additional examples of Democratic-Republican support for manufactures, see Shambaugh (ed.), *Messages of Governors of Iowa*, II, pp. 288–289; New York *Evening Post*, Nov. 11, 1846.

60.  "Message of the Governor of Ohio...1858" in *Message and Reports Made to the General Assembly and Governor of the State of Ohio for the Year 1858*. Part II (Columbus, 1859), p. 79; Message of Bissell, p. 17; Shambaugh (ed.), *Messages of Governors of Iowa*, II, pp. 281, 315.

the time of the Mexican war, it had promulgated "the idea of marching, in the nineteenth century, with the immense power of this Republic . . . and forcing upon . . . [the Mexicans] the institution of slavery." The South, it seemed, was backward both morally and materially. The explanation was simple: slavery retarded both economic and moral improvement.[61]

Democratic-Republicans were as eager as former Whigs to make comparisons between free and slave states. Moreover, they reached an identical conclusion: the southern states had suffered grievously because of slavery. As we shall see, former Democrats joined with erstwhile Whigs in their insistence that slavery degraded labour in the South, reduced wages and opportunities for upward mobility and thus doomed an economy to virtual stagnation. In a striking reversal of traditional Democratic theory George Weston complained that "the wages of labour are always low in countries exclusively agricultural." The reason was that "industry begins to be fairly rewarded, when it is united with skill, when employments are properly divided, and when the general average of education and intelligence is raised by the facilities afforded by density of population." Weston concluded that "agricultural countries are comparatively poor, and manufacturing and commercial countries are comparatively rich; because rude labor, even upon rich soils, is less productive than skilled labor, aided by machinery and accumulated capital."[62]

The result was that the nonslaveholders could not better themselves; they could only sink into barbarism. Hence the South lagged behind the North not merely in the creation of wealth but also in the provision of schools and libraries, in charitable institutions and in moral reform movements. While northern society was progressive in every sense, the South was languishing with a stagnant economy and a retrograde social structure. When Southerners denounced northern wage workers as slaves, Democrats and Whigs alike rallied to the defence and their responses were indistinguishable. A consensus was emerging on the desirability of wage labour in particular and on the northern social structure in general to match that which united former Whigs and Democrats in defence of the rights of the majority and in support of the Union.[63]

## VII

As we shall see, the Democratic-Republican vision of northern society did not by any means fully correspond with reality. Republicans of all persuasions generally exaggerated the opportunities for mobility open to the

61. "Message of Lott Morrill," in *Journal of the Senate of Maine for . . . 1860* (Augusta, 1860), p. 39; Message of Hamlin, 17; Muller, "Preston King," p. 422.
62. Weston, *Poor Whites of the South*, pp. 2–5; CG, 35/1, pp. 815, 1005, 1044.
63. New York *Evening Post*, Nov. 11, 1846, Foner, *Free Soil*, pp. 40–72.

free and the wage labourer. As we shall also see, Democratic-Republicans were again at one with former Whigs in grossly exaggerating Unionist sentiment in the South.[64] But their most distinctive error, the one to which former Democrats within the party were especially prone, derived from their understanding of the Democratic party itself. Although they invoked Jefferson as an ardent enemy of slavery and in effect a proto-Free-Soiler, they ignored the Jefferson who had ridden to power on the basis of a disproportionate degree of southern and slaveholder support, who as President had extended the area open to slaveholders by purchasing Louisiana, and who at the time of the Missouri crisis had come down firmly on the side of the South. The Jeffersonian legacy was far more ambiguous and unclear than they allowed.

More fundamentally, however, what these erstwhile Jacksonians failed to perceive was that Democratic, and before that Jeffersonian, ideology had been inherently and functionally pro-southern from the start. The traditions of *laissez-faire* and states rights, the tendency to mistrust and misperceive northern antislavery sentiment, the distaste for the intrusion of moral and humanitarian issues into politics, and the deep conviction of white racial superiority – all this meant that the Democratic party was especially suited to the defence of southern interests. Thus the Democratic-Republicans, although correctly identifying the southern orientation of their party, exaggerated the extent to which it was attributable to the machinations of certain southern politicians, and especially John C. Calhoun, aided by northern dupes. They often saw a conspiracy when in truth none had been needed. This is not to say, of course, that Democratic ideology did not itself alter in these years. On the contrary, as a result of the increasing pressures to which southern slavery was now exposed, major shifts occurred. In effect, what had been covert protection offered to slaveholders, now became increasingly overt and the leading personnel in the party changed correspondingly. The Democratic-Republicans perceived these changes in personnel and ideology and reacted vigorously to them, but they nevertheless failed to understand the underlying ideological and material factors facilitating them.

The fact that they refused to tolerate these accretions of southern power within their party is explicable primarily in terms of their egalitarian principles. As former radical Democrats, they were predisposed to search for, and to find, evidence of an elite minority seeking to take possession of the government and enhance its own wealth and power at the expense of the rest of the community. The actions of the southern elite were easily fitted into their pre-existing categories of thought. Thus it is reasonable to conclude that they were indeed profoundly anti-southern, provided that we

64. These misperceptions are discussed on pp. 260–264.

remember that their hostility was directed against the slaveholding minority of the South and its dupes and not against southerners in general.[65] But
it is not quite accurate to conclude that they were more anti-southern than
antislavery. Their hostility to the southern elite derived entirely from its
political and economic power, which in turn derived entirely from slavery.
It would be more appropriate to conclude that their opposition to slavery
came from a conviction that it was economically and politically disruptive or disorganising. As we have seen, where many Republicans expressed
their moral opposition to slavery, this concern was far less apparent among
former Democrats. They held that slavery was an economic and political
blight upon both the South and the nation and that for these reasons it
must be resisted – and with all the firmness and vigor that the followers
of Andrew Jackson could muster.

## Whig antecedents

### I

Important though the former Democrats were to the Republicans, by
far the largest accession of strength to the new party at its birth in the
mid-1850s came from the ranks of the northern Whigs. Some historians indeed have argued that the Republicans were little more than the
Whig party in another guise.[66] Although this view is mistaken, there are
without doubt important similarities between the two groups and the
comparison between Whigs and conservative Republicans, in particular,
is a telling one. But even here there were important dissimilarities and if
the scope of the analysis is widened to embrace the moderate Republicans,
to say nothing of the former Whigs within radical Republican ranks, then
the differences between Whiggery and Republicanism become even more
marked. These continuities and divergences are also worthy of the closest attention, for they illustrate some of the pressures operating upon the
antebellum polity in its final years and therefore help make intelligible the
cataclysm that would follow the election of the first Republican president.

### II

In the era of the second party system, northern Whigs had generally been
more hostile to slavery than northern Democrats. This pattern had been

65. Indeed they believed that they were acting in the very best interests of the nonslaveholders of the South.
66. William B. Heseltine, *Lincoln and the War Governors* (New York, 1948), p. 18.
Charles and Mary Beard, *The Rise of American Civilization*. 2 vols. (New York,
1933), II, pp. 3–54.

visible both within the states, when the relevant issues arose, and, more commonly, in Washington, DC. In the federal capital slavery-related issues arose in every Congress from the inception of the second party system in the 1830s to its collapse in the 1850s and the partisan alignment was discernible whenever the parties voted on these issues. In these years Congress had to deal with a variety of questions which included resolutions relating to the extension of slavery, the rights of free blacks, the reception of antislavery petitions, the fugitive slave question and the three-fifths clause. On every issue from the mid-1830s to the 1850s northern Whigs showed themselves to be either more hostile to slavery and the South or more sympathetic to free blacks than northern Democrats. This process culminated in 1850 when the Compromise measures were passed, with the support of a large contingent of northern Democrats but over the opposition of a large majority of northern Whigs.[67]

At the time of its birth in 1834 the Whig party had been concerned primarily with the financial issues of the Jackson presidency and, more generally, with the populistic forces which Jackson had sought to unleash. Even in the mid-1830s, however, slavery issues had never been absent. The abolitionist inspired campaigns which sought to flood the South with antislavery propaganda and to flood Congress with petitions calling for the ending of slavery (primarily in the District of Columbia) produced sharp responses from the South. The mails were intercepted so that abolitionist literature could not get through and a gag law was passed, according to which antislavery petitions were immediately to be tabled with all discussion forbidden.

These reactions on the part of the defenders of slavery were only made possible by the acquiescence of a sufficient number of northerners. But it was overwhelmingly northern Democrats who acquiesced. Thus one typical vote saw the northern Democrats divide fifty-nine to fifteen in favour of the gag, while out of forty-seven Whigs all but one were opposed. Similarly a resolution defending slavery in the District of Columbia received the support of sixty-eight out of seventy-five northern Democrats but only four out of forty-two northern Whigs.[68]

The northern Whigs who were critical of slavery were motivated by a number of considerations. Very few were sympathetic to the Garrisonian project of immediate abolition. Nevertheless there was at this time, as there had been for many decades, considerable resentment of southern

67. Thomas B. Alexander, *Sectional Stress and Party Strength: A Study of Roll-Call Voting Patterns in the United States House of Representatives, 1836–1860* (Nashville, TN, 1967), pp. 12, 27, 33, 39, 53, 59, 65, 67, 72, 81, 87.
68. Leonard L. Richards, "The Jacksonians and Slavery," in Lewis Perry and Michael Fellman (eds.), *Antislavery Reconsidered: New Perspectives on the Abolitionists* (Baton Rouge, 1979), pp. 99–118.

political power within the nation, together with a scorn for the South's economic performance and a sympathy for the nation's black population which, though by no means enough to erase racial prejudice entirely, was far greater than that felt by most Democrats. All these concerns would persist into the 1850s and would carry most Whigs into the Republican party.[69]

In the early 1840s northern Whigs had continued to voice these concerns, until in 1844 the gag rule was finally repealed. In that year southerners surrendered on the gag issue, however, in part because they then grasped for a greater prize: Texas. To this northern Whigs were unanimously opposed. The reasons were varied. Some simply emphasised the need to prevent the extension of slavery. Others stressed their opposition to any territorial acquisitions, in part because of the impact on the sectional balance of power. Still others objected to the aggressive and bellicose foreign policy pursued by the Democrats. When this opposition proved futile and the Polk administration went to war with Mexico, northern Whigs sought again to prevent the extension of slavery. Despite its author's Democratic affiliation, the Wilmot Proviso received much greater support from northern Whigs than northern Democrats. A vote taken in February 1847, for example, revealed the northern Whigs unanimously in favour of the Proviso, while more than thirty percent of northern Democrats were against it.[70]

In the late 1840s, as northerners began to appreciate the depth of southern opposition to the Proviso, some from each party retreated from it. But again it was the Democrats who were more willing to compromise. Although the support of northern Whigs like Daniel Webster was extremely important, what proved crucial in facilitating the passage of the Compromise measures, were the votes of northern Democrats who in effect abandoned the Proviso. In the case of the Fugitive Slave Act, for example, a key vote in 1850 enlisted the support of sixty-two percent of northern Democrats but only six percent of northern Whigs. Most northern Whigs remained strongly opposed both to the Fugitive Slave Law and to the Compromise measures as a whole.[71]

---

69. I have discussed the spectrum of Whig opinion on slavery in the first volume of this work, pp. 350–361.
70. Richards, "Jacksonians and Slavery," p. 113. Of course the percentages varied slightly from roll-call to roll-call. Thus a vote taken two weeks earlier saw one Whig out of fifty-five vote against the Proviso and sixteen out of fifty-eight Democrats. But the broad pattern is unmistakable. For an exhaustive history of the Whig party in the late 1840s and 1850s, see Michael F. Holt, *The Rise and Fall of the American Whig Party: Jacksonian Politics and the Onset of the Civil War* (New York, 1999), pp. 330–985.
71. I have calculated these percentages from Alexander, *Sectional Stress and Party Strength*, p. 211. (roll-call 58).

No sooner had those measures been passed than their defenders began to demand pledges from presidential candidates that they were committed to the Compromise as a "final adjustment" of the sectional controversy. After 1850 the territorial issues were, it seemed, now resolved but hostility to the Fugitive Slave law mounted as southerners in a number of highly publicised cases sought to recover their slaves in the North.[72] Partly for this reason many antislavery Whigs refused to pledge allegiance to the compromise measures as a "finality." Winfield Scott, the Whig presidential candidate in 1852 gave "finality" only lukewarm support. The price he paid was electoral humiliation in the Deep South and a ringing defeat in the nation as a whole.[73]

Within the states the Whig party was also experiencing considerable difficulties, partly as a result of the emergence of temperance and nativism as major issues.[74] Nevertheless a devastating blow to the party's survival as a national institution came when Stephen A. Douglas introduced his Kansas-Nebraska Act. The opening of Kansas and Nebraska to slavery and the repeal of the Missouri compromise outraged northern Whigs. With complete unanimity they denounced the measure. This might not have doomed their party, however, had the southern wing, with a few exceptions, not felt obliged to support the Act. Even then, it is possible that the party might have survived, if the Kansas issue had been speedily resolved in favour of the free-state settlers. But the continued disturbances in Kansas shattered the Whig party and between 1854 and 1856 propelled the great majority of northern Whigs into the newly formed Republican party either directly or indirectly after a short period within the ranks of the Know Nothing party.

It is important to note that northern Whiggery had never been free from factionalism and intraparty strife. Conditions varied from state to state, of course, but the key division was between conservatives like Daniel Webster of Massachusetts and liberals such as William Seward of New York. In Massachusetts, Webster was faced in the late 1840s by antislavery or "conscience" Whigs, who were more hostile to slavery and the South than Webster and his "cotton" Whig allies. Similarly in New York, Seward was engaged throughout the life of the second party system in a vicious battle with the so-called Silver Gray faction of the party, who were also relatively sympathetic to the South and who, like the cotton Whigs of Massachusetts, embraced the Compromise measures of 1850.[75]

---

72. See Chapter 1.
73. Holt, *Whig Party*, pp. 673–764; Allan Nevins, *Ordeal of the Union: A House Dividing 1852–1857* (New York, 1947), pp. 3–42; David M. Potter, *The Impending Crisis, 1848–1861* (New York, 1976), pp. 121–144.
74. See Chapter 4.
75. Kinley J. Brauer, *Cotton versus Conscience: Massachusetts Whig Politics and Southwestern Expansion, 1843–1848* (Lexington, KY, 1967); Leo H. Warner, "The Silver

The introduction of the Kansas-Nebraska Act and the continued strife in Kansas sent virtually all the more liberal Whigs together with some conservatives into the Republican party. But other conservatives held aloof. After trying unsuccessfully to maintain the Whig party, many of them in 1856 supported the Know Nothings whose presidential candidate, former president Millard Fillmore, was himself a Silver Gray.[76] Fillmore's poor showing in the election however, convinced many of these conservative Whigs that they must find another way of resolving the sectional controversy. At the same time many Republicans concluded that to carry the next presidential election, they would need to recruit more heavily from the ranks of the conservative or "Old Line" Whigs as they were now known. The result of these twin pressures was that the Republicans made more conservative Whig converts in the late 1850s and in 1860. These new recruits joined and strengthened the ranks of the conservative Republicans.

### III

Although the intraparty division within the Whig party arose in part from different attitudes towards slavery and the South, there were other issues that were, until at least the mid-1840s, more important. Crucial policy differences were involved, particularly over a national bank, which conservatives were keen to recreate but which liberals feared would prove a severe electoral liability. But behind this difference lay an even more significant divergence of opinion concerning democracy itself. While liberal Whigs like Seward had made their peace with the populistic forces unleashed by Jackson, the conservatives were far more cautious. Some openly lamented the passing of the Federalist party and freely invoked the memory of Alexander Hamilton. Although these attitudes were fading in the North, they had by no means disappeared even in the 1850s and conservative Republicans, heirs of the conservative Whigs, continued to express many of them, if sometimes a little forlornly. In so doing they helped replay within the Republican party, the intraparty struggles that had been so prominent within Whig ranks.[77]

A key issue concerned the quality of statesmanship within the Republic. Those critical of democracy had always worried that it would enthrone the demagogue or the spoilsman and from its earliest years the Whig party had denounced Andrew Jackson for his alleged debasement of political life.

Grays: New York State's Conservative Whigs, 1846–1856" (Unpublished Doctoral Dissertation, University of Wisconsin, 1971).

76. Others supported Buchanan in 1856. See Rufus Choate, *The Duty of Conservative Whigs in the Present Crisis* (Boston, 1856).

77. Ashworth, *"Agrarians" and "Aristocrats,"* pp. 87–174. Evidence for my statements about Whig beliefs in the 1830s and 1840s can be found in this volume.

The claim had been that Jackson, inspired and controlled in good part by Martin Van Buren, had appointed politicians rather than statesmen to the highest offices in the land. The political party had thus acquired a ruinous hold upon the political system; mere partisans had replaced statesmen of enlightened vision and superior talents. More than twenty years later this was very much the line of reasoning adopted by Illinois Republican Orville H. Browning. Reporting in his diary in July 1856 a meeting with fellow conservative John McLean, he observed that "a new system of dispensing patronage and managing the government" had been introduced during "the administration of Genl. Jackson" with the result that "high official station had been cheapening, and coming more and more within the reach of inferior and corrupt men." Browning concluded that "the present deplorable state of things" could be blamed above all upon Martin Van Buren, who had manipulated Jackson and "made him debase the offices of the Government by bestowing them upon demagogues in reward of mere partisan services."[78]

A jeremiad such as this, however, which had been standard Whig fare in the 1830s, was rarely heard in the 1850s. More common now was the claim that slavery debased political life. Thus William M. Evarts complained that a *"degradation of politics"* had occurred. Since the slavery question had risen to the top of the political agenda, good men did not enter politics. The conclusion was simple: stop asking whether men were for slavery as a national institution "and you will have your politics purified."[79]

Complaints such as these fuelled a Republican assault upon the Buchanan administration, which was probably more vulnerable to charges of corruption than any in the antebellum Republic. Yet Evarts's contention was that northern politics had been polluted by the slavery question and this tacit admission of sectional weakness (whatever the ultimate source of the pollution) did not suit the political temper of the late 1850s. While it was possible to claim instead that it was southern statesmanship that was impaired by the slavery question, this charge ran counter to the criticism more often leveled against the South: her leading men, as a result of slavery, it was said, were both enabled and compelled to concentrate upon politics to the exclusion of all other worthwhile activities and had as a result obtained a disproportionate share of federal offices. Thus though by no means oblivious to the Whiggish concern with the quality of statesmanship in the Republic, even Whig-Republicans did

78.  Theodore C. Pease (ed.), "The Diary of Orville Hickman Browning," *Collections of the Illinois State Historical Library* XX, vol 1, 1850–1864 (Springfield, 1925), pp. 244–245.
79.  Sherman Evarts (ed.), *Arguments and Speeches of William Maxwell Evarts*. 3 vols.(New York, 1919), II, p. 450

not give this as much emphasis as they might have done a generation earlier.

For some of the more conservative Whig-Republicans this was probably a matter of some regret. Some of them would surely have liked to stress the exceptional gifts and capacities of Republican candidates for the highest offices in the nation, if only they could have identified them. Presidential elections were particularly awkward in this respect. Frémont, the Republican candidate in 1856, had had little of the political experience that Whigs who venerated the memory of Henry Clay or Daniel Webster deemed invaluable. Worse still, he had been a Democrat. Four years later, Abraham Lincoln was a little better, but only a little. As historians must constantly remind themselves, Lincoln was then a comparatively unknown Illinois Republican who had served only a single term in Congress and who had participated in a losing (if still highly creditable) campaign for the United States Senate. The difficulties were compounded in that year by the presence of John Bell and Edward Everett, standard-bearers of the Constitutional Union Party, which was recognised by friend and foe alike as the Whig party reincarnated. Bell and Everett indeed could far more plausibly claim the pedigree of disinterested statesmanship that some Republicans sought in presidential and vice-presidential candidates.[80]

For those conservatives who attached great importance to these matters the solution, insofar as there was one, was to maintain that Lincoln and his fellow Republicans, however lacking in the experience of the great Whig leaders, were nevertheless inspired by the greatest Whig leader of all, Henry Clay. Thus Browning claimed that in 1860 the Republican party on the slavery question did "but follow the teachings of the immortal Clay, the great apostle of Republicanism," while John Sherman, a moderate Republican, in tracing the "history and policy" of the Republican party in the same year also laid claim to the mantle of Henry Clay, "the standard of all that is manly or noble." Indeed Clay's stature, in the decade following his death, was so great among some former Whigs that spokesmen for the Republican party who had only recently enlisted in its ranks, having previously been Know Nothings, took great pains to claim that Lincoln was the Clay candidate.[81]

These claims, however, were by no means straightforward in 1860. Not only were Bell and Everett in the field that year, with apparently

80. *Speech of the Hon. Thomas Ewing, at Chillicothe, Ohio Before a Republican Mass Meeting, Sept. 29, 1860* (Cincinnati, 1860), p. 13.
81. *Speech of Hon. O. H. Browning Delivered at the Republican Mass Meeting, Springfield Ill, Aug. 8, 1860* (Quincy, 1860), p. 5; John Sherman, *The Republican Party – Its History and Policy* (n.p., n.d.), p. 5. For the views of former Know-Nothings in the Republican party see Chapter 4.

superior Clay credentials on display, but even Stephen A. Douglas was able to appeal to the great man's memory. Douglas claimed, with some justice, that in 1850 he and his followers had set aside traditional party animosities and cooperated fully with Clay and the Whigs to create and implement the Compromise measures of that year. Perhaps aware of the potency of this claim, some conservative Republicans went out of their way to rebut it and condemn Douglas instead as the archenemy of Clay. For Clay was identified with the Missouri Compromise line, the erasure of which in 1854 many conservative former Whigs held responsible for all the sectional turmoil of the mid- and late-1850s. In this sense, therefore, Douglas and his followers were not the political descendants but rather "the political butchers of Mr Clay."[82]

Lincoln himself assisted in the process by which he became Henry Clay *redivivus* by asserting that "during my whole political life, I have loved and revered [Clay] as a teacher and leader." Nevertheless, these claims were of limited significance and carried limited conviction. Despite his love of Clay, Lincoln had refused to support him in 1848. Moreover, though Clay had certainly had (mild) antislavery convictions, they had never been his primary concern. With the Republicans, however, these priorities were reversed and slavery was far higher on their agenda than Clay's American System or any of its components. Moreover, Democratic-Republicans had little love of the man who had been their primary antagonist for more than twenty years and many radical Republicans who had deserted the Whig party for the Free Soil movement felt that Whigs of the Clay and Webster stripe had betrayed antislavery throughout their careers and were especially critical of their conduct in 1850. Thus the presence within the Republican ranks of these groups inhibited the tendency of former Whigs to claim that the Republicans were the party of Clay. But even those who had remained Whigs until the creation of the Republican party could not always agree where Clay was concerned. Although conservative Whigs venerated his memory, the Seward wing of the party was far cooler and properly so given the record of its leaders (Seward and Weed, his alter ego) in their quadrennial efforts to frustrate Clay's presidential ambitions. Thus although the Clay mantle was important to some within the Republican party, the Clay devotees tended to be conservatives who needed reassurance or who needed, as late as 1860, to be won over to the party.[83]

Indeed despite the occasional criticism of the processes introduced into American politics by Andrew Jackson, Republicans in practice often

82. *The Duty of Americans: Speech of Gen. G. A. Scroggs, and of Hon. Geo. B. Babcock, also of Hon. James A. Putnam*s (n.p., n.d.), p. 15.
83. Daniel Walker Howe, *The Political Culture of the American Whigs* (Chicago, 1979), p. 272; Basler (ed.), *Works of Lincoln*, IV, p. 49.

demonstrated the extent to which they had succumbed to them. In its choice of presidential candidates the early Republican party opted not for their most illustrious or experienced statesmen, probably William Seward or Salmon P. Chase, but instead for John C. Frémont and Abraham Lincoln, neither of whom had held high executive office or served in the United States Senate. Like most or indeed all major parties since the election of Jackson, they employed the patronage so as to cement party loyalty in a way that Martin Van Buren would have applauded and Daniel Webster (in theory at least) would have condemned. And in their electioneering, the Republicans continued the unabashed populism that the Jacksonians had displayed in the 1820s and 1830s.[84]

Whiggish doubts about those populistic tendencies had, in the 1830s and early 1840s, been greatly intensified by the financial turbulence of that era and the political protest that had accompanied it. Perhaps if the 1850s had witnessed a similar degree of economic instability these concerns would have been equally prominent. This possibility is strengthened by the reaction of some Republicans, and especially former Whigs within the party, to the one episode that evoked the fiscal uncertainties of the 1830s and early 1840s: the Panic of 1857. Thus James Watson Webb of the New York *Courier and Enquirer* complained about the response of Democratic Mayor Fernando Wood to the economic crisis of that year. Wood warned that the sufferings of the poor might impel them to resort to violence. "Could plainer language be used," Webb asked, "short of an appeal in terms to the laboring classes to sack the houses and rob the safes of their present or their late employers?" Here was the standard Whig fear of demagogues inciting the masses. Yet even in 1857 these fears were not widespread within the Republican party and the rapid economic revival that most northern states experienced helped quell them. Even Webb himself, the most irascible of newspaper editors, was far calmer in the 1850s than he had been twenty years earlier.[85]

Nevertheless, vestigial traces of Whig elitism and disdain for popular democracy did occasionally surface within Republican ranks. They rarely took the form of outright hostility to the populace, however. Instead marginal groups were singled out and criticised as unfit for the political rights or privileges conferred upon them. Immigrants were one such group,[86] westerners newly arrived in the territories another. Here Douglas's policy of popular sovereignty, which conferred vitally important rights upon settlers in the territorial phase, was an object of some

84. William E. Gienapp, *The Formation of the Republican Party, 1852–1856* (New York, 1987), pp. 375–411.
85. New York *Courier and Enquirer*, Oct. 26, 1857. James L. Crouthamel, *James Watson Webb: A Biography* (Middletown, CT, 1969).
86. See Chapter 4.

criticism on precisely these grounds. The policy was square in the logic of Democratic theories of sovereignty, which empowered an electorate regardless of its past experience or the extent to which it was bound together by commonality of sentiment or shared values. But for the same reason it drew fire from some Whig-Republicans. In February 1858 the *Atlantic Monthly* in an article entitled "The Kansas Usurpation" traced all the calamities that had befallen that territory to the hopelessly misguided policy of "popular sovereignty:"

> They [the Territories] were declared fully formed and fledged before they were out of the shell. A mere conglomeration of emigrants, Indian traders, and half-breeds was invested with all the functions of a mature and ripened civilization. Long ere there were people enough in any territory to furnish the officers of a regular government, – before they possessed any of the apparatus of court-houses, jails, legislative chambers, etc., essential to a regular government, – before they lived near enough to each other, in fact, to constitute a respectable town-meeting, – before they could pay the expenses or gather the means of their own defense from the Indians, these wonderful entities were held to be endowed with the right of entering into the most complicated relations and of forming the most important institutions for themselves, – and not only for themselves, but for their posterity.

Though the elitism of this passage is unmistakable, its disdain for the migrants who had entered Kansas did not equate to a denial of democratic rights for the West as a whole. Eastern states were, by implication, superior, but western states properly constituted had their place too. Many Whigs had shared these beliefs.[87]

Douglas's policy had been intended to defuse the slavery question by removing it from Congress and empowering local communities to determine their own destinies. Orthodox Whig doctrine instead decreed the opposite: that the federal government should preside over the process. Since the time of the *Federalist*, conservatives had believed that the federal government would attract the nation's elite and would therefore exhibit a higher standard of statesmanship than the state governments, to say nothing of territorial administrations. As they denounced Douglas in 1860, some Republicans demonstrated that these assumptions were still very much intact. "Will you now reward him [Douglas]," George Babcock asked, for "a policy which makes this quarrel [over slavery] eternal, takes it out of the hands and power of Congress, and refers it to the fierce passions of a frontier people, without law or authority to guide them, and compels them to resort to civil war as the only practical arbitrament?"

87. *Atlantic Monthly* I (Feb. 1858), p. 494.

Evidently the "fierce passions" of frontiersmen, like those of many immigrants, made them unsuitable candidates for citizenship in a republican polity.[88]

For Babcock it was not the federal government in general but Congress in particular that should provide inspiration and leadership. This too was orthodox Whig belief. Lincoln himself, ironically perhaps in view of the expansion in executive power over which he would himself later preside, in his single congressional term had promised that Zachary Taylor, if elected, would, unlike Democratic incumbents, defer to Congress. For while the president did indeed represent the people, Lincoln doubted whether he could, "in the nature [of] things, know the wants of the people, as well as three hundred other men, coming from all the various localities of the nation." Otherwise, Lincoln asked, "where is the propriety of having a Congress?"[89]

This veneration of Congress undoubtedly owed something to the uses to which Andrew Jackson and his Democratic successors had put presidential power. But it had deeper roots. As James Madison had argued, the superior talents of an elite in Congress should be used to benefit the nation as a whole. The superiority of Congressmen would lie especially in their ability to take an enlarged view of the national interest. This meant that they must be representatives and not delegates. They should not merely echo the views, nor even confine themselves to furthering the interests, of their constituents. A high-minded elite, after appropriate discussion and deliberation, should instead promote the general interest. It was this reasoning which prompted Thomas Corwin, a conservative Republican, to insist in the House of Representatives that "every man on this floor is the Representative of every man, woman and child in the Republic." This attitude had led most Whigs in the 1830s to refuse to give pledges to the voters, and to reject the idea that United States Senators could be instructed by state legislatures. In the 1850s even radical Republicans like Charles Sumner continued to express similar views. Thus, refusing to make pledges, Sumner insisted that, when elected to the United States, he must be "in all respects an independent man, bound to no party, and to no human being, but only, according to my best judgment, to act for the good of all." These were sentiments quite alien to northern Democrats.[90]

Yet however much they might in theory exalt the role of the congressman, Republicans could not easily draw confidence from the conduct of

---

88. *The Duty of Americans*, p. 8. As Daniel Howe observes, the Kansas-Nebraska Act outraged the Whig sense of history as progress – Howe, *Political Culture of American Whigs*, pp. 275–279.
89. Basler (ed.), *Works of Lincoln*, I, p. 504.
90. Josiah Morrow (ed.), *Life and Speeches of Thomas Corwin* (Cincinnati, 1896), p. 445; *The Works of Charles Sumner*. 15 vols. (Boston, 1870–1883), III, p. 99.

Congress itself in the 1850s. The acrimony, vituperation, and sheer violence exhibited there meant that many Republicans sought not merely to replace territorial with congressional rule but also to purify the nation's primary deliberative and representative body. This fed into the concern to resolve the slavery issue as a first step towards restoring the polity as a whole. Indeed for some conservative Whig Republicans, the primary task was to elect a Republican in order not to attack slavery but instead quickly and quietly to remove the slavery question from the nation's councils so that other, more important issues, traditional Whig or neo-Whig ones, could then be tackled. This meant a revival of the Whig role of government. Thus Thomas Ewing applauded the Republican platform of 1860 on the grounds that it "advances *sound* old Whig doctrine as to the fostering care which Government owes to the industry of its people."[91]

Once again, however, these Whiggish preoccupations did not easily translate into Republican priorities. Once again the Democratic-Republicans inhibited the process, for they were, as we have seen, jealous guardians of the Democratic traditions of limited government and state's rights. Radical Republicans, moreover, resented any dilution of antislavery by the reintroduction of Whiggish economic policies, to most of which they were at best quite indifferent, and their principal governmental concern was separation of the federal government from slavery in its entirety, a policy which owed nothing to Whig traditions. As a result, the attempt to use the federal government in the way that Henry Clay might have applauded never quite in the antebellum years became Republican orthodoxy.[92]

On the other hand, many Republicans did claim for government a moral and educative role. Thus Lincoln constantly complained that Douglas's policy of nonintervention poisoned public opinion by promoting indifference to slavery among the electorate. This was much closer to Whig than to Democratic traditions in that it implied a critically important leadership role for those in government, who were clearly something more than, as Democrats often claimed, delegates, and whose aspirations and ambitions should not, as Democrats were wont to argue, be viewed with fear and suspicion. Yet, as we shall see, even here the Republicans departed from Whig orthodoxy when they spelled out the precise message which they believed should emanate from the federal government.[93]

In its heyday the Whig party had not only proclaimed its hostility to the Democratic political creed but had also, notwithstanding the antislavery

---

91.  *Speech of Ewing at Chillicothe*, p. 13.
92.  Edward L. Pierce (ed.), *Memoir and Letters of Charles Sumner*. 4 vols. (Boston, 1877–1893), III, p. 254. The exigencies of the Civil War, of course, would later produce very different effects.
93.  Basler (ed.), *Works of Lincoln*, II, p. 255, III, pp. 89–90.

convictions of many of its northern spokesmen, sought to distance itself from extremists on the slavery question. In the 1850s some Whigs continued to display similar concerns. They emphasised the absurdity of the abolitionist doctrine, espoused also by some radicals in their own party, that the conscience was the surest, if not the only, guide to political action. William Evarts, a Websterite, argued in 1850 that to claim for one's *"private conscience* the right of *veto* on the public legislation" was to deny "the rightful existence of *society."* Evarts would later join the Republican party. Nine years after this utterance Thomas Corwin, also now a Republican sympathiser, employed an argument that would have warmed Daniel Webster's heart when he insisted that "there can be no government possible, if any and every individual may determine, for himself what law he will obey and what he will not obey." On both occasions the immediate focus of interest was the clause in the Fugitive Stave Act of 1850 which compelled northerners to assist in the return of fugitives and which later in the decade would be in effect nullified by the passage in some northern states of Personal Liberty laws.[94]

Yet the larger question was the relationship of the individual to government and to society. Orthodox Whigs repudiated the abolitionist view and insisted that governments should impose restraints upon all citizens, and require all to consult the general interest. On the many occasions when it proved necessary, citizens should graciously accept the need for compromise, even on deeply held moral issues. Thus Ewing was one of those who denounced the notion that "the individual will, dominant in the minds of excited men" should be supreme. He and many other conservative former Whigs within the Republican party insisted that the Fugitive Slave Law should be enforced, a view which was shared by moderate Republicans like Lincoln. In this regard constitutional stipulations assumed great importance and, for conservative Republicans, overrode abstract notions of right. Thus Corwin dismissed the idea that the slave had an "inherent right...to run away from his master" since such a "right" clearly "ceases, if the constitution has said his master may follow and reclaim him." Here it was the constitution which effected or facilitated the compromises upon which government and society for these Republicans necessarily depended.[95]

As a result, they did not hesitate to declare their opposition not merely to Garrisonian abolitionists but also to the radicals in their own party. Thus John Sherman, writing to his brother William, acknowledged that there

---

94. Evarts (ed.), *Arguments and Speeches of Evarts,* II, p. 432; Morrow (ed.), *Life and Speeches of Corwin,* p. 382.
95. *Speech of Ewing, at Chillicothe,* p. 12; Morrow (ed.), *Life and Speeches of Corwin,* p. 382. See also *Speech of Browning at...Springfield,* p. 7; Evarts (ed.), *Arguments and Speeches of Evarts,* II, p. 451; New York Times, May 28, 1854.

were many things done and said by Republican leaders that he detested and it was the moral absolutism preached and practised by the radicals that he had in mind.[96]

Yet as good Whigs, the Clay supporters or Websterites in the party did not seek to overlook or set aside the moral question entirely when discussing slavery. Indeed like most other Republicans they resented Douglas's moral neutrality on the slavery question. Orville Browning expressed the view of the conservatives with great clarity when he reiterated that "we believe slavery to be morally wrong" and reminded his audience that "the moral aspects of the question" "ought not wholly to be overlooked" in the way that Douglas overlooked them. What these conservatives wanted was thus an approach that would seek to balance, in a statesmanlike manner, interest and morality, principle and expediency.[97]

For conservative Republicans, therefore, it was imperative to maintain contact with the animating but also controlling traditions of the American republic. The problem was that the Democracy, increasingly dominated by the slaveholders of the South, was abandoning these traditions. As Corwin explained, it was the duty of the Republican party to return to them:

> You have abandoned the great highways of the past – the good macadamized roads made for you – every milestone of which was red with revolutionary blood; you have strayed away from them, and wandered after wills-o'-the-wisp into swamps and by-paths. All that the Republican party wish to do is, to stand up and call you back as a mother calls to her lost child, and put you on the safe old road again.

For these conservatives the Republican party was thus to be a restorative agency, returning the Republic to the hallowed ways of old.[98]

## IV

This emphasis upon restoration was particularly evident in the speeches and writings of the more conservative Republicans. Their political ideal was a return to the Clay and Webster era, though perhaps with rather more frequent electoral triumphs for their followers than the two sages had themselves enjoyed. Although the conservative Republicans had been forced to place slavery at the top of their political agenda, this was an adjustment forced upon them; they would have preferred to retain, and

96. Rachel S. Thorndike (ed.), *The Sherman Letters* (New York, 1969), p. 87.
97. *Speech of Browning at . . . Springfield*, p. 15.
98. Morrow (ed.), *Life and Speeches of Corwin*, p. 454.

indeed hoped to revive, the older Whig agenda. But these were probably the views only of a minority, even within the Whig-Republican ranks.

Other Whig-Republicans had other priorities. At first glance it appears that the restorative impulse was universal within the party. Radicals, moderates and former Democrats all announced, time and again, that they sought to return the nation to its founding principles.[99] There is no reason to doubt their sincerity. Yet the emphasis upon restoration requires careful inspection. The appeal to the past obscured the real changes in the political system and the political process that Republicans had introduced, welcomed, or at least tolerated,

In part these changes were forced upon them by circumstances over which they had no control. In the course of the 1850s many Republicans were compelled to revise their opinions of the judiciary, and especially of the federal Supreme Court. Classic Whig and Federalist doctrine had encouraged an exaltation of the judiciary, in part as a bulwark against the power of the majority unleashed by a democratic system. That these associations were still made in the 1850s is apparent from a speech given by Richard Henry Dana at the Massachusetts Constitutional Convention held in 1853, just prior to the emergence of the Republican Party. Dana, who would soon become a Republican himself, denounced the proposal to make the judiciary elective. He acknowledged that it was theoretically possible to elect judges every month but exhorted his fellow members of the convention instead to retain the appointive principle. "Let us," he urged, "put upon us this SELF-RESTRAINT" since "there is no greater virtue in a free people than the willingness to exercise self-restraint." This association of republicanism with self-restraint had its roots in Antiquity and was at the core of classical republicanism. Dana then spelled out his reasoning: "the minority needs protection against the majority." "How," he asked, rhetorically, "can that be had, unless you establish a tribunal above the mere will of the majority?" For "if you constitute the Supreme Court as that tribunal, how can it accomplish that purpose unless you make it independent, not only of the executive, but of the legislature and of the temporary will of the majority of the people?" Dana reminded his fellow delegates that "the history of democratic governments shows that they may be as arbitrary as any absolute monarchy."[100]

For Democrats in the Jacksonian era the role of the judiciary had been primarily to check the tendency towards partial legislation that benefited a minority and oppressed the majority. The alternative view, expressed

99. See, for example, *Speech of Hon. J. Z. Goodrich of Massachusetts, Delivered in the Peace Convention in Washington, Feb. 1861* (Boston, 1864), pp. 3–4; Bancroft (ed.), *Speeches, Correspondence etc of Schurz*, I, p. 146.
100. Richard Henry Dana, Jr, *Speeches in Stirring Times* (Boston, 1856), pp. 88, 90–91, 191.

by Dana, that its role was to defend the minority, continued to be echoed in the 1850s and even as late as 1860. In that year William Evarts, on the same wing of the Republican party, declared that "a free people must maintain their judiciary or they have no defence for their liberties." He then referred to "the Supreme Court of the United States, that venerable tribunal, against which neither by tone, by gesture, nor by implication will I ever raise my voice." This would have been orthodox Whig doctrine two decades earlier. But its reiteration in 1860 may have been a response to the very different attitudes expressed by other Republicans at that time. For the southern orientation of the Supreme Court in the 1850s meant that Republicans were driven to voice a most un-Whiggish hostility. Thus Charles Sumner acknowledged that whilst he respected judges, and especially Supreme Court judges, he viewed them without "superstitious reverence," for "judges are but men, and in all ages have shown a full share of human frailty." Indeed, according to Sumner, "the worst crimes of history have been perpetrated under their sanction" with the result that "the blood of martyrs and of patriots, crying from the ground, summons them to judgment."[101]

Like many other radicals, Sumner had here left the Whig tradition far behind. But such opinions were not confined to the radical wing of the party. Abraham Lincoln, for example, in his celebrated debates with Douglas in the Illinois Senatorial election of 1858, repeatedly mocked his adversary's reverence for the Court and its pronouncements. Lincoln charged that for Douglas its every utterance was a "thus saith the Lord." Lincoln was a moderate within the party. Even more remarkable was the criticism of conservative Orville Browning who, after acknowledging that the Court was "entitled to our profoundest respect" and that he was one of those who "habitually bow, respectfully and deferentially, to the decisions of all judicial tribunals," nevertheless reminded his listeners that it was no more infallible than a Pope. He also criticised the Dred Scott ruling on the grounds that it went beyond the Court's remit. In the same vein the Indiana Republican platform of 1858 contained a resolution reaffirming "the doctrine, that Congress has the constitutional power to exclude slavery from the national territories, notwithstanding the extra judicial opinion of the Supreme Court of the United States to the contrary." It is perhaps significant that Indiana was probably the northern state in which radical Republicanism was weakest; even conservatives and moderates were prepared to challenge the Court.[102]

---

101. Evarts (ed.), *Arguments and Speeches of Evarts,* II, p. 523; *Works of Sumner,* III, p. 468.
102. Basler (ed.), *Works of Lincoln,* III, pp. 27–28; *Speech of Browning at . . . Springfield,* pp. 11–12; William E. Henry (ed.), *State Platforms of the Two Dominant Political*

The parties had in this respect switched roles, with the Republicans adopting Jackson's attitude towards the Court and the Democrats taking a line that Whigs and even Federalists might have followed. A similar reversal took place in relation to the age-old (and closely linked) question about majority and minority rights. Once again mainstream Republicans espoused what had been orthodox Democratic views, while the Democratic party in the South inclined increasingly to a minoritarian position and in the North had great difficulties in maintaining any consistent approach at all.[103]

Of course Republican majoritarianism owed much to the party's recognition that it represented the North, where a large majority of the population resided. But other factors were present too. The Republicans were majoritarians within the states as well as at the federal capital and their beliefs here reflected a larger shift that occurred between the eras of the Whig and Republican parties. Whereas the Whigs had fretted about the power of the majority, particularly when exploited by unscrupulous demagogues, Republicans in the mainstream of the party displayed little or no anxiety on this score, and indeed rarely discussed the problem. Typical of that mainstream, in this as in so many respects, was Lincoln himself, who spent little time worrying about minority rights but instead strove to further the interests of the majority. In his first inaugural he briefly discussed the question and roundly condemned secession as a violation of majority rights. Indeed he declared that "the central idea of secession, is the essence of anarchy." Lincoln predicated this observation with the word "plainly," characteristically presenting his own favoured solution as the only one that a rational mind could possibly countenance. "The only true sovereign of a free people," he announced, is "a majority, held in restraint by constitutional checks, and limitations, and always changing easily, with deliberate changes of popular opinions and sentiments." Here the possibilities that the majority might exercise a tyranny over the minority or, conversely, that the "changes of popular opinions and sentiments" might be so frequent and sweeping as to create chronic political instability, were entirely ignored, despite their long pedigree within American political discourse. In effect the danger of anarchy or tyranny was dismissed – until the alternative, anti-majoritarian position, was discussed. At that point the threats resurfaced. Lincoln announced that "whoever rejects" majority rule "does, of necessity, fly to anarchy or to despotism." In a single sentence he set out his reasoning: "unanimity is impossible; the rule of a minority, as a permanent arrangement, is wholly inadmissible;

*Parties in Indiana, 1850–1900* (Indianapolis, 1902), pp. 13–20. Here, of course, the claim was that the Court's ruling on the Missouri Compromise had been *obiter dicta*.
103. See Chapter 3.

so that, rejecting the majority principle, anarchy, or despotism in some form, is all that is left." Clearly for Republicans like Lincoln the Union had come to symbolise an unproblematic commitment to majority rule. Here as elsewhere their attitudes were closer to those of the Jacksonian Democrats than to those of the Whigs.[104]

In the Federalist and Jacksonian eras the abstract fear of majority tyranny and demagogic politicians had drawn upon the highly concrete experience of Revolutionary and Napoleonic France. Federalists had recoiled in horror from the French Revolution and most Whigs had exhibited similar fear and trepidation. Republicans, however, took a different view. A radical like Charles Sumner was fulsome in his praise, referring to "that great outbreak for enfranchisement" but even a conservative like Henry J. Raymond, editor of the *New York Times*, found much to admire in revolutionary France. Equally striking was the Republicans' attempt to clothe themselves in the Jeffersonian mantle. Jefferson had, of course, been anathema to the Federalists. In the Jacksonian era, the Whigs had been more ambivalent, with conservatives denouncing him and more liberal Whigs either maintaining a discreet silence or offering for the most part qualified praise. With few if any exceptions Whigs had preferred Madison. Republicans, however, took a different line. Even those who had been Whigs fondly invoked his memory.[105] Partly it was because an antislavery Jefferson, the Jefferson who had excoriated slaveholders as tyrants and who had been responsible for the Northwest Ordinance of 1787, had an obvious and immediate political value in the 1850s. But more strikingly, even Whig-Republicans directed attention towards the Jefferson who had written the Declaration of Independence. The Declaration indeed now assumed a role for Republicans that it had previously had for Democrats, whilst at the same time the Democrats themselves were, in the face of the Dred Scott ruling, restricting its scope and explicitly confining its application to the white race. Once again the parties had apparently changed places.[106]

---

104.  Basler (ed.), *Works of Lincoln*, IV, p. 268.
105.  *Works of Sumner*, II, p. 334; *New York Times*, Dec. 6, 1854. The majority view of Jefferson was probably expressed by Charles Francis Adams who claimed that the Republicans were the party of Jefferson, "the great apostle of modern democracy" – Adams, *What Makes Slavery a Matter of National Concern* (Boston, 1855), p. 19. A minority within the party, however, argued that Jefferson the president had merely furthered the interests of slavery – see [John G. Palfrey], *Five Years Progress of the Slave Power* (Boston, 1852), p. 11. But there were few if any objections to Jefferson for his democratic leanings.
106.  Henry Wilson, *How Ought Workingmen to Vote in the Coming Election? Speech of Hon Henry Wilson, at East Boston, Oct. 15, 1860* (n.p., n.d.), pp. 1, 8; Charles Francis Adams, *An Address Delivered before the Members of the School and the Citizens of Quincy, July 4, 1856* (Boston, 1856), p. 29; Howe, *Political Culture of American Whigs*, pp. 280–296.

The Jeffersonian tradition had emphasised natural rights and many Whigs had viewed such appeals as pure demagoguery. In particular they had tended to present the suffrage as a privilege rather than a right. William H. Seward, however, repudiated this approach entirely when in 1854 in the Senate he declared that "the right of suffrage is not a mere conventional right, but an inherent natural right, of which no government can rightly deprive any adult man who is subject to its authority, and obligated to its support." This statement was not merely at odds with conventional Whig opinion; it also implied a repudiation of the universal Whig view of the Dorr rebellion which had erupted in Rhode Island in 1841, a view which had been conspicuously shared by the then Governor of New York, one William H. Seward.[107]

Criticising the Supreme Court, asserting the rights of the majority, cherishing the memory of Jefferson, celebrating the French Revolution, drawing inspiration from the Declaration of Independence – these Republicans had clearly left far behind them the Whiggish fears of an excessively populistic political system. Some indeed went out of their way to heap the most fulsome praise upon American democratic institutions. Henry Wilson told an audience in 1860 that it was their and his "privilege" to be "citizens of this Democratic Republic of North America, with its achieved free institutions based upon the recognition of the rights of human nature, with millions trained in self-government, and in complete possession of the citadel of consummated power – the ballot box." What conservatives had traditionally objected to in appeals of this sort was the implication that American democracy had overturned the established wisdom of the ages. After all if their system of government were so superior, why should Americans attend to the experience, or heed the warnings, of the past? Those who shared these concerns were particularly incensed by many of William Seward's pronouncements. According to Seward, "the world has never before seen a state assume a perfect organisation in its very beginning, and extend itself over a large portion of a great continent, without conquests, without colonies, and without undergoing any change of constitution." On another occasion he claimed that "under the republican system established here, the people have governed themselves safely and wisely, and have enjoyed a greater amount of prosperity and happiness than under any form of constitution, that was ever before or elsewhere vouchsafed to any portion of mankind."[108]

Even these appeals and claims, however, did not exhaust Republican populism. The traditional conservative fear, expressed by Federalists and

107. George E. Baker (ed.), *The Works of William H. Seward.* 5 vols. (New York., 1853–1884), III, p. 460.
108. Wilson, *How Ought Workingmen to Vote?*, p. 1; Baker (ed.), *Works of Seward* I, p. 156, IV, p. 139. See also Carl Schurz, *Speeches of Carl Schurz* (Phil, 1865), p. 237.

Whigs, was that the demagogic politician would exploit the vulnerability of a republic by making impassioned appeals to the electorate, who would then engage in reckless assaults upon the social elite. In other words, the demagogue ultimately threatened to bring not merely political unrest and turmoil but also social upheaval. If all his utterances were to be condemned, then the most wicked of all were those which set the masses against the elites.[109]

Such inflammatory rhetoric had been the hallmark of the Jacksonian Democrats, and in particular of the more extreme Democrats who had drawn their inspiration from Jackson's destruction of the Bank of the United States and taken their cue from his warnings about the dangers posed by the rich and powerful. It is scarcely too much to say that the Whig party had come into existence primarily to combat the prospect of social upheaval which many had believed imminent in the 1830s. In the 1850s, however, even former Whigs within the Republican ranks engaged not infrequently in precisely this kind of rhetoric. Radical Republicans were particularly attracted to it, partly because their more extreme antislavery had not found favour with the social elites of the North. As a result, they did not hesitate to open fire upon the members of that elite. The precedent was perhaps set by Charles Sumner, who in 1848 had memorably denounced the nomination of Zachary Taylor as the consequence of a "conspiracy" brought about "between the politicians of Louisiana and Mississippi and the cotton-spinners and traffickers of New England, – between the lords of the lash and the lords of the loom." Somewhat later Sumner conceded that the eminent in the North were not imbued with antislavery sentiment. "Alas," he exclaimed, "it is only according to the example of history that it should be so." For history showed that "it is not the eminent in Church and State, the rich and powerful, the favourites of fortune and of place, who most promptly welcome Truth, when she heralds change in the existing order of things." Instead "it is others in poorer condition who open hospitable hearts to the unattended stranger." For Sumner this was "a sad story, beginning with the Saviour, whose disciples were fishermen, and ending only in our own day." In the same way Zachariah Chandler of Michigan, himself a merchant, denounced the mercantile community for its truckling to the South. "From the days of Carthage to those of James Buchanan," he complained, "the great mercantile centers have been peaceable – ever ready to hire defenders not to furnish them, ever ready to buy immunity but not to fight for it." And as we shall see, other radicals went out of their way to expose the social

---

109. This fear, more than any other factor, generated the opposition to democracy that existed throughout Europe prior to the nineteenth century (and even after it).

evils of the North and to denounce those responsible for them, whatever their social rank.[110]

Such criticisms of northern elites, however, were not characteristic of Republicans in the mainstream of their party. More common were attacks upon the southern elite. Thus Lincoln, once again claiming Jefferson as the party's patron saint, condemned the Democrats of the 1850s for believing that "the *liberty* of one man" was "absolutely nothing, when in conflict with another man's right of *property*." This contrasted sharply with the Republicans who "on the contrary," were "for both the *man* and the *dollar*, but in cases of conflict, the man *before* the dollar." Even more pointedly, in September 1859, he insisted upon the right of the labourer to eat the bread that he had earned. In so doing, he employed an argument that the great majority of Whigs would in the 1830s have found demagogic and thus abhorrent:

> I hold that if the Almighty had ever made a set of men that should do all the eating and none of the work, he would have made them with mouths only and no hands, and if he had ever made another class that he had intended should do all the work and none of the eating, he would have made them without mouths and with all hands.

Lincoln of course was directing attention to the evils of slavery, and it was African Americans in the South rather than northern labourers whom he believed were under threat. Nevertheless, it was striking that he was prepared to employ this rhetoric regardless of the possibility (of which Whigs earlier would have been acutely aware) that it might encourage similar assaults upon the northern elite.[111]

Other Republicans made similar remarks. Thus William Seward observed that "property...has always a bias toward oppression, and it derives power to oppress from its own nature, the watchfulness of its possessions, and the ease with which they all can combine." For Seward history revealed that "whenever a property class is invited by society to oppress, it will continue to oppress." In a slightly different vein, Henry Waldron in Congress described the two major parties in terms that the Jacksonians would have used a generation earlier. The party system, he announced, pitted the party "of the pampered capitalist" against "the

110. *Works of Sumner*, II, p. 81, IV, p. 38. Philip S. Foner, *Business and Slavery: The New York Merchants and the Irrepressible Conflict* (Chapel Hill, 1941), pp. 251–252. See Henry Wilson, *How Ought Workingmen to Vote*, p. 2 for the suggestion that the poor labourer had more at stake in the pending election than the rich.
111. Basler (ed.), *Works of Lincoln*, III, p. 375; Roy F. Basler (ed.), *Collected Works of Lincoln Supplementary Volume* (Westport, CT, 1974), p. 44. See also Basler (ed.), *Works of Lincoln*, I, p. 412.

hardy son of toil." But once again the parties had reversed themselves for now it was the Democrats who were said to represent capital and their opponents, now the Republicans, labour.[112]

More generally, when Republicans claimed that a "Slave Power" had gradually taken control over the nation, they were deliberately stirring up the hostility of the North to a social elite, albeit one in the South.[113] In a sense this was a dramatic rejection of the offer that John C. Calhoun had made to the North in the 1830s and 1840s. Calhoun's strategy (or rather one of his strategies) had then been to unite northern and southern conservatives in an alliance of propertied classes to resist both abolition-ism and radical Democracy. And many Whigs had then found this an attractive prospect. But in the 1850s even conservative ex-Whigs in the Republican party endorsed the Slave Power concept and thus demon-strated their willingness to encourage attacks upon one elite, regardless of the possibility, to which Calhoun had sternly drawn their attention, that it might stimulate assaults upon another. It is easy for historians to underestimate the importance of this process since the stability of democratic systems of government in the developed world is now largely taken for granted. But the Whig view, that democracy endangered an elite, however meritorious it might be, had a long history. By Whig stan-dards Republican attacks on the southern elite were setting a dangerous precedent.

Republican confidence in the majority and in the nation's populistic political system thus allowed even former Whigs to borrow rhetorical devices and modes of argument that most Whigs would once have found quite unacceptable. Much of this borrowing was done from the Democrats and, less immediately, from the antislavery tradition of Thomas Jefferson. Nevertheless Whig-Republicans even borrowed from abolitionism. Not only had the abolitionists first publicised the Slave Power concept but they had also insisted that hostility to slavery should, if necessary, override constitutional obligations. Garrison's ceremonial burning of the Consti-tution was the most potent symbol of this attitude and it was one that no Republican endorsed. But in their criticisms and even mockery of the Supreme Court, some Republicans went much further than the Whigs would have gone. Even the willingness to join a political party in which radicals on the slavery question were highly conspicuous and held senior positions marked a step beyond orthodox Whiggery. Moreover, when Seward asserted that there was "a higher law than the Constitution," he

---

112.  Baker (ed.), *Works of Seward*, IV, pp. 254, 272; *CG*, 36/1, pp. 1871, 1873. See also Benjamin W. Arnett (ed.), *Hon. J. M. Ashley Souvenir* (Phil, 1894), p. 28 for the claim that a truly democratic government would protect the poor and defenceless against the rich and powerful.

113.  On the Slave Power, see pp. 244–264.

was, however ambivalently, advancing an opinion that was anathema to
Whigs of the Webster school.[114]

It is true that Seward's views were unusual within the Republican party
(with the result that historians have found it difficult to place him along
the radical/conservative spectrum). It is also true that Seward in his Whig
years had sometimes made utterances that revealed a similar confidence
in American democracy and a similar willingness to criticise established
elites. In other words he had traveled a shorter ideological distance than
most of his colleagues. But if Seward was exceptional, his example proves
the rule about the Republican party, for in the 1830s and 1840s he had
been something of a maverick figure within Whig ranks, far more liberal
on a host of issues than most of his colleagues and accordingly viewed
with considerable suspicion and mistrust. He had never been a serious
candidate for the presidency. In the 1850s he was the leading Republican
statesman and until the last moment was favourite to become its standard
bearer in 1860.[115]

Thus most Whig-Republicans in their views on government had moved
some considerable way from the opinions and attitudes that had held sway
within the Whig party. A minority of conservative Republicans remained
unrepentant members of the Clay and Webster school of politics and
wished to see that school recapture its former glories. Even these Republicans, however, were less alarmed about the dangers posed by democracy
and demagogues than a generation earlier.

At the opposite extreme were the radicals Republicans, many of whom
had formerly been Whigs but who had abandoned most, though not quite
all, of these Whiggish attitudes. The radicals strove to keep the moral
question of slavery uppermost and they set out to agitate the question in
order to ensure that the electorate remained sensitive to it. In this sense,
therefore, they were committed populists. Yet the vestiges of Whiggery
were still in evidence, for if the populism of the radicals was as intense
as that of the Jacksonian Democrats in the 1830s, it nonetheless took a
different form. The Jacksonians had sought to enlist the populace in order
to offset the power of the elite and to prevent the passage of legislation
which would further the interests of that elite. Jacksonian man was motivated by self-interest and this was particularly true of men in government,
who were held to pose a constant threat to liberty and equality. The solution was to ensure that they were allowed only to express the opinions
and further the interests of the majority. But the populism of the radical
Republicans required those in government – and here the radicals had
themselves in mind – to lead public opinion and inspire a moral crusade.

114. Baker (ed.), *Works of Seward*, I, p. 74
115. Ashworth, *"Agrarians" and "Aristocrats,"* pp. 160–168.

This was a highly moralistic populism; it was in effect a synthesis of traditional Democratic populism with the old Whig emphasis on moral betterment, led by a governing elite.

Between these two extremes in Republican ranks lay the moderates. Like the radicals, men like Abraham Lincoln had gone well beyond conservative Whiggery and displayed a far greater degree of satisfaction with American democracy. Like the radicals too, although they spoke of restoring the legacy of the Founding Fathers, they had in their views on government embraced, sometimes enthusiastically, many of the changes that had been controversially introduced by Jefferson and Jackson in the heat of partisan conflict. As late as the 1840s the Whigs had set their faces against the Democrats' "Manifest Destiny" crusade, not only because they were sceptical about the need for additional territory in the West, but also because they were suspicious of the vainglorious boasting about American democracy that infused it. But, as we shall see, mainstream Republicans viewed the West quite differently and, as we have already seen, their spokesmen in the 1850s could now vie with the Democrats in heaping praise upon the nation's democratic institutions and in proclaiming its redeeming influence in the world. Once again Lincoln, the archetypal moderate Republican, expressed a whole host of Republican attitudes in a few sentences when, in a speech at Peoria in 1854, he explained why he hated the indifference to slavery that seemed widespread in the North:

> I hate it because of the monstrous injustice of slavery itself. I hate it because it deprives our republican example of its just influence in the world – enables the enemies of free institutions, with plausibility, to taunt us as hypocrits – causes the real friends of freedom to doubt our sincerity, and especially because it forces so many really good men amongst ourselves into an open war with the very fundamental principles of civil liberty – criticising the Declaration of Independence, and insisting that there is no right principle of action but *self-interest.*

Here Lincoln combined Democratic and Whig beliefs in what was an original Republican synthesis. From the Whigs he had taken the emphasis upon morality as the transcendence or renunciation of self-interest as well as the principle of antislavery itself, always more prominent within the northern Whig party than among northern Democrats. But from the Democrats he had taken the emphasis upon the Declaration of Independence and the image of American democracy as a beacon in the world. In the following decade this Republican synthesis would receive still more memorable expression when the first Republican president would have the task of presenting the Civil War to the North and to the rest of the world.[116]

Thus it is important to note the vital differences that existed within the Republican party on political questions, even among those who had formerly been Whigs. To a considerable degree the differences between radicals, moderates, and conservatives on the slavery question reinforced and were reinforced by, their divergent views on government. The radicals were prepared to countenance, indeed actively set out to promote, a politics of conflict in the belief that they must enlist the northern masses in a crusade against the enormity of slavery. For them the scale of the problem meant that compromises were futile and even counterproductive; the solution was to create a radicalised electorate which would then demand the implementation of a constitutional programme of abolition. At the opposite extreme, the conservatives held that a conflict could easily be averted, so long as leaders of the appropriate caliber, with full electoral backing, firmly but courteously asserted northern rights. Although slavery was indeed an evil, it did not necessitate an "irrepressible conflict" between North and South and agitation of sectional issues, especially if it inflamed the electorate, would merely diminish the room for maneuver available to disinterested statesmen and thus jeopardise the Union. For these Republicans, the election of Lincoln would itself be enough to bring an end to the agitation of the slavery question.[117]

## V

The differences within the Republican party over political issues were mirrored by contrasting attitudes towards social and economic questions. Once again it is essential to keep in mind the distinction between radicals, moderates, and conservatives, while simultaneously delineating the area of agreement between them. Once again it is important to trace the continuities and the discontinuities between Whiggery and Republicanism in order to understand the significance of the Republican victory of 1860, the victory which heralded the collapse of the antebellum Republic.

---

116. Basler (ed.), *Works of Lincoln*, II, p. 255.
117. This was put very well by Thomas Ewing: "And our rights asserted firmly, with dignified courtesy, will be much more readily conceded than if we mingled with their assertion, contumely, and reproach. Thus disposed of – and I think we shall dispose of it amicably – the irrepressible conflict will be repressed, for there will be nothing remaining for which a conflict can be maintained." – see *Speech of Ewing, at Chillicothe*, p. 20. Or as one Republican merchant expressed it: "Let Mr. Lincoln be elected tomorrow, and the irrepressible conflict about which we have heard so much will instantly subside" – see Foner, *Business and Slavery*, p. 203.

That the North was superior to the South was an article of faith for Republicans. It was a fundamental principle, from which no party member dissented, however conservative, moderate or radical he might be. As we shall see, Republican spokesmen again and again announced that the southern economy lagged far behind that of the North. Although former Democrats endorsed this conclusion as wholeheartedly as those who had previously been Whigs, it had distinctively Whiggish connotations. In the first place, some conservative Whigs, always fearful of provoking political conflict, hoped that the economic argument against slavery might facilitate an appeal to the pocketbook of the slaveholder, and thus obviate the need for the moral denunciations which were the trademark of radical Republicans. Thus William Sherman in 1856 was convinced that Kansas would become a free state (and that emancipation must soon follow in Missouri and Kentucky). But this was to be achieved not by agitation but simply by letting "things go on as now, showing the eminent prosperity of the free States, whilst the slave States get along slowly." "Self-interest" was "the great motor." Sherman presumably had in mind not the self-interest of the slaves, nor that of the nonslaveholding whites, but instead that of the masters. Such was also the view of the *New York Times* which, in 1854 announced itself "perfectly satisfied" that "all appeals and arguments, rhetorical or logical, which treat the question as exclusively one of conscience and religion, are worse than useless – they do hurt, rather than good, so far as the removal of Slavery is concerned." Instead "with the South the question is mainly one of *Social and Industrial Economy*, – to be canvassed as involving the material interests of the slaveholding classes themselves, and to be decided, when a decision is reached at all, on that basis." According to the *New York Times*, "the economical aspects of the question" should be afforded "a large if not a preponderating influence." Apparently the superiority of the North was so marked that it might even persuade southerners of the error of their ways and thus remove the need for an emphasis, distasteful to many conservative Whigs, upon the immorality of the slaveholder.[118]

There was, however, an even more important link between Whiggery and the economic indictment of slavery. As they criticised southern society for its lack of growth and development, Whig-Republicans displayed their Whiggish heritage. From its inception the party of Clay and Webster had welcomed, indeed rejoiced in, the processes of social and economic development which the Republicans applauded in the 1850s. Moreover even in the 1830s it had been evident that these processes were more advanced in the North than in the South. One consequence had been the Whigs' greater electoral strength north of the Mason-Dixon Line. It was

118. Thorndike (ed.), *Sherman Letters*, p. 55; *New York Times*, April 7, 1855.

no coincidence that the party had been strong in the most industrially advanced states of Massachusetts and Rhode Island, weakest in the least advanced, the Deep South. More important, however, had been the desire of southern Whiggery, especially in its Upper South heartland, to emulate the economic successes of the North, though without sacrificing its interest in slavery. In essence the Whig party had had an electoral and an ideological orientation towards the North.[119]

This Whiggish heritage was both confirmed and modified by the Republicans. Whiggery's northern orientation had been only implicit in the party's first decade or so. Orthodox northern Whigs had deprecated overt criticism of the South and its economy and had instead striven to bind the two sections together. They had thus underwritten, for the present, the existence of slavery in the South even while entertaining, for the future, vague hopes of its ultimate disappearance. In the 1850s the former Whigs who had joined the Republican party had a different perspective. Now the comparison between North and South was not only explicit rather than implicit but had become no less than the fundamental principle of their political creed. So with slavery itself. The hope that it would ultimately disappear was now more fervent than ever even though the process by which it was to occur was still very nebulous. But gone was the respect for, and easy tolerance of, its current function in the South and in the nation as a whole.

The frequent comparisons of North and South, however, despite confirming the inferiority of the South, did not, of course, imply that northern society was incapable of further improvement. Indeed one of the advantages adduced in favour of free society over slavery was that it facilitated progress, both moral and material. There could thus be no room for complacency about the North, however marked its superiority to the South. Yet most Republicans, as we shall see, believed that northern society should be celebrated for the freedoms, the social justice and the equality which it promoted. This was very much the attitude of Abraham Lincoln, who, as we shall also see, constantly emphasised the extent of social mobility within the North. This perception of the northern social order was, once again, squarely within the Whig tradition. Yet, as always there were several differences of emphasis.

First, Lincoln and other Republicans frequently cited the West as an important source of economic revitalisation. Lincoln saw the West as a safety valve regulating eastern wages and underwriting opportunities for northern labourers. Whigs, on the other hand, had more often viewed it as a threat to the labour supply and thus the process of industrialisation in the East and had wondered whether democratic institutions could be

119. I have discussed this at some length in the first volume of this study.

extended over the enormous area which by the late 1840s the nation covered. But these were not Republican sentiments. For the Republicans the West had become a support for American freedom, rather than a threat to it.

Second, and perhaps more important, for the Whigs, equality of opportunity, social mobility and classlessness had had a defensive role. Their function had in part been to secure order and to maintain and legitimate inequalities in the face of an insurgent Democratic radicalism. In a sense they were defences against the democratic onslaught. In the 1850s, however, they had lost this defensive quality. In effect the same ideals had become not defences against, but instead supports for, the democratic order and the typical Republican enthused equally about democracy and classlessness in a way that had been possible for only an unrepresentative minority of Whigs. And there was a further sense in which this defensive orientation had disappeared. For Republicans now cited these features of the northern social order not to defend the status quo but rather to draw attention to the failures of the South. As they analysed or criticised, damned or derided southern society, the Republicans used old ideals to generate a new belligerence.[120]

Finally it should be noted that some Republicans, as we shall see, advanced some significant criticisms of northern society. Although these were by no means consensual within the party, and although some Whigs had also been similarly critical, it is fair to say that some Republicans, and especially radical Republicans, were more critical of northern society than the typical Whig had been. Yet if their criticisms of the North were contrary to mainstream Whig traditions, the ideal against which the North was being measured, an economically vibrant, morally improving society based firmly upon free labour, had been implicit in the northern variant of Whiggery from the first. Thus while this critique of the North was far removed from mainstream Whiggery, the social aspirations upon which it rested were not.

## VI

This expanding and expansive confidence in the superiority of northern society was thus, in a broad sense, a reaffirmation of northern Whig values. Despite important differences of tone, Republicans and Whigs shared a similar enthusiasm for economic and commercial development. The greater confidence and optimism of the Republicans in large part reflected the increased stability and maturity of the northern economy in

---

120. Ashworth, *"Agrarians"* and *"Aristocrats,"* pp. 66–73; Sean Wilentz, *The Rise of American Democracy: Jefferson to Lincoln* (New York, 2005), pp. 482–518.

the 1850s but as far as specific policies were concerned, the effect was profoundly paradoxical: the more fully Whig hopes for the northern economy seemed to be vindicated, the less need there seemed to be for the policies themselves.

This meant that despite the veneration of Henry Clay, his holy trinity of economic policies, the protective tariff, national internal improvements, a national bank, were now in headlong retreat. The American System had, of course, received a pounding from the Democrats and in effect the former Whigs conceded that they had lost the battle for specific policies even though they were winning the war for the economic development those policies were intended to promote. In part their retreat was forced upon them by the need to retain the support of the former Democrats, most of whom, as we have seen, still viewed the Whig economic policy agenda with suspicion or even contempt. Thus, as we have noted, many Democratic-Republicans remained resolutely and vigilantly opposed to any attempt to revive the American System or any of its components. As late as 1860, as we have seen, former Democrats like William Cullen Bryant were vehemently resisting the attempt to have a former Clay Whig nominated, lest the result be an increase in the tariff and the passage of a whole raft of federal legislation for internal improvements projects. In that the nomination went to Lincoln, a self-avowed Clay Whig, Bryant might have been disappointed. But if so, he would have drawn considerable comfort from Lincoln's insistence that, despite his continued reverence for Clay's tariff policy, the question should not even be discussed at the Chicago convention. The simple but inescapable reality was that, as John Sherman put it, the party was "composed ... of whigs and democrats, ... holding somewhat opposite creeds on the question of the tariff."[121]

There was, however, far more than *realpolitik* in the Republican retreat from the tariff. A radical like Charles Sumner, despite being from Massachusetts, since the 1820s one of the most protectionist states in the Union, avowed himself "absolutely uncommitted on the tariff." Yet few Republicans were more enthusiastic about commercial development than Sumner. Another inescapable reality, and a more profound one, was that, as Samuel Foot put it, the tariff by the mid-1850s was a "hopeless" cause "in part because many of our manufacturing interests have become so well established as not to require protection."[122]

Similarly northern economic development had obviated the need for a national bank and, at the same time though for different reasons, removed

---

121. Basler (ed.), *Works of Lincoln*, IV, p. 49; Sherman, *Republican Party*, p. 12.
122. Pierce (ed.), *Memoir and Letters of Charles Sumner*, III, p. 254; Samuel A. Foot, *Reasons for Joining the Republican Party* (n.p., n.d), pp. 1–3; *Works of Sumner*, III, p. 228.

the need for the advocates of commercial development to defend even state banks. For a working compromise had been effected by which a national bank was viewed as unattainable and unnecessary, while state banks were viewed as indispensable and therefore permanent. In 1857 the New York *Tribune* voiced its desire for a national bank but at the same time acknowledged that this was an impossibility. At the same time the *Courier and Enquirer*, closely identified with the commercial interests and the commercial elite of New York City, announced that both a national bank, traditionally the centrepiece of the Whig economic programme, and an exclusively metallic currency, formerly dear to the hearts of most radical Democrats, were equally obsolete ideas. By now even Whigs were prepared to criticise the conduct of banks in the knowledge that this criticism would not fuel a more far-reaching assault on the nation's commercial infrastructure. In a sense the northern economy had outgrown the banking controversy: banks now could be criticised even if banking *per se* was sacrosanct.[123]

The greater success and stability of the northern economy thus deeply coloured the Republican worldview. There was simply less need for a paternalist government than in the Whig era. Whereas the Whigs had championed the mixed corporation, part privately financed, part government financed, by the 1850s a much larger pool of private capital was now available. Thus the Republicans were ironically both the inheritors and the repudiators of the Whig creed. They inherited its concern with enterprise, its enthusiasm for development, its emphasis on social mobility, and its denial of class divisions. But at the same time they repudiated its fears for the survival of these aspirations in the face of the democratic challenge. They repudiated also the spirit of paternalism which had hung over much of northern Whiggery. In this sense, and to a greater degree than Whiggery, Republicanism reflected the hopes of northern capitalism, the confidence of northern capitalists in the northern social system and the conviction that the populace in the North would, if invited, enthusiastically rally to its defence. The outbreak of the Civil War would demonstrate that these beliefs were indeed well-founded.

## Slavery and morality

### I

The critique of slavery that developed in the United States in the final decades of the antebellum Republic contained three related but distinct strands. One was a political argument, centring upon the claim that

123. New York, *Tribune*, Nov. 5, 1857; New York *Courier and Enquirer*, Oct. 21, 1857.

the slaveholding elite constituted an undemocratic and tyrannical "Slave Power" that was intent on controlling the destinies of the nation. Another was a set of socioeconomic criticisms of the peculiar institution which together amounted to the claim that slavery was irremediably inferior to free labour in productive capacity and developmental potential. The third was a moral critique which emphasised the immorality of holding one's fellow man in a state of servitude.

All three sets of arguments were advanced by Republicans and abolitionists alike. For the abolitionists, as we have seen, the moral critique was uppermost.[124] What of the Republicans? Here the question is more complex because as a mass political party the Republicans contained within their ranks a far greater diversity of opinion that could be found among those who advocated immediate abolition (despite the latter's penchant for in-fighting and schism). The most conservative Republicans merely wanted to place in power northern neo-Whigs (and perhaps their southern sympathisers), who would spend little time on the slavery question and who would instead revive Whiggish economic policies designed to benefit the entire nation, southern slaveholders included. Although these Republicans sincerely disliked slavery, they were at the same time deeply suspicious of those within their party who wished to embark upon uncompromising moral crusades, particularly crusades designed to benefit the nation's African-American population. Similarly, those Republicans who had formerly been Democrats came from a tradition that had shown scant concern for the African American. But the other constituents of the Republican coalition had different priorities. The moderates in the party insisted that a place be found for the moral indictment of slavery while for the radicals this critique was of paramount importance.[125]

Who were the radical Republicans and how had their careers been shaped prior to the creation of the Republican party? Although some individuals, such as William Seward and Horace Greeley, are not easily situated along a radical-conservative continuum, most of the radicals can be easily identified. They were the most militant antislavery element within the Republican ranks and they had come from both major political parties and from neither. A small number, such as John P. Hale of New Hampshire or Salmon P. Chase of Ohio had once been Democrats. More commonly, radicals had formerly been conscience Whigs. William Seward and Horace Greeley (assuming that they qualify as radicals) in New York, Charles Sumner and Charles Francis Adams in Massachusetts, Benjamin Wade and Joshua Giddings in Ohio, George Julian in Indiana, and many others

---

124. I have discussed abolitionism in the first volume of this study, pp. 125–191.
125. Foner, *Free Soil*, is an invaluable source on the divisions and the different groups within the Republican party, and I have borrowed his typology.

had all previously been Whigs, and highly prominent Whigs at that. Some of these individuals (Chase, Hale) had defected relatively early in their careers to the Liberty party; an even greater proportion of the radicals, though by no means all, had supported the Free Soil party in 1848. In the 1840s they had been outraged by the attempts to spread slavery into the Southwest and by the indifference of both the major parties to the antislavery crusade. After 1848 many of them remained either partially or entirely alienated from the two major parties. To a man they opposed the compromise measures of the 1850s; to a man they displayed the bitterest hostility to the Kansas-Nebraska Act.[126]

The radical Republicans were, in many respects, ideologically midway between moderate Republicans and abolitionists. Like William Lloyd Garrison, they aimed at the abolition of slavery in the states where it existed. Unlike Garrison, however, they sought to use federal power or at least federal policy, to achieve the result. "Give me the power to cut up slavery, root and branch, wherever the federal authority legitimately extends," George Julian proclaimed, "and I will open veins enough to bleed the monster to death." Here in essence was the radical programme. It scarcely differed from that of the Liberty party in the 1840s as devised by Salmon P. Chase, himself a leading radical Republican in the 1850s. According to the radicals the federal government gave slavery and slave-holders enormous support and sustenance without which the peculiar institution would wither and die. Hence Julian concluded, Republicans must insist that abolition was their "ultimate purpose."[127]

Radicals conceded, sometimes regretfully, that the federal government did not have the power to attack slavery directly in the states of the South. Hence abolition would be a gradual process. How would it unfold? The key was the divorce of the federal government from slavery. This would have important direct and indirect effects. The most obvious direct effect would be to restrict slavery to the states where it already existed. Most Republicans (along with many southerners) believed that slavery had to expand or die and it is in this context that the Republican refusal to allow the spread of slavery into the territories should be seen. According to Henry Wilson of Massachusetts, the Republican party, "recognising the rights of the States," did not "claim power to abolish slavery in the States by Congressional legislation." Instead "it claims the power to exclude slavery from the Territories, and by the blessing of God it will use every legal power and make every honorable effort to expel slavery from every rood of the Territory of the Republic." But for Wilson, as for many other

---

126. On the radicals, see Hans L.Trefousse, *The Radical Republicans: Lincoln's Vanguard for Racial Justice* (New York, 1969).
127. George Julian, *Speeches on Political Questions* (New York, 1872), pp. 146, 149. See also Salmon P. Chase, *An Argument for the Defendant...in the Case of* Wharton Jones v. John Van Zandt (Cincinnati, 1847), pp. 82, 100.

Republicans, non-extension meant ultimate abolition. Hence he did not contradict himself when, in the same speech, he announced that the party "is opposed to slavery everywhere." To restrict Slavery within its present limits," according to the New York *Tribune*, "is to secure its speedy decline and ultimate extinction."[128]

A federal prohibition on the spread of slavery was not, however, the only plank in the radical platform. Direct action against slavery in the District of Columbia, the repeal or at least the negation of Fugitive Slave laws, and, even more dramatically, the prohibition of the interstate slave trade, were intended to exert direct pressure on the peculiar institution. "With these principles established," Chase announced, "and an administration based upon them, Slavery would come to a speedy end."[129]

A reorientation of federal policy towards slavery would have indirect as well as direct effects. Of primary importance was the impetus it would give to the antislavery movement within the South itself. "Who," asked Chase, "does not see that the divorce of the General Government from slavery. . . . would exert a great moral influence for Freedom in those States?" Chase then explained the process. "The People of those States, encouraged by the example of the General Government, and stimulated by its legitimate influence," he predicted, "would themselves take up the work of enfranchisement; and slavery would disappear speedily, certainly, peacefully, from the whole land."[130] Here ironically was a description of the impact of a radical Republican administration that in almost all essentials duplicated that envisaged by the most determined defenders of slavery.[131] The federal government was to become the agent not of slavery and the Slave Power but instead of freedom and democracy. Thus by indirect and direct means, and gradually rather than immediately, abolition would be secured.

As we shall see, the concern with the Slave Power united virtually all Republicans. To remove the control slaveholders exerted over the federal government was a priority for all Republicans, whether radical or conservative. For the conservatives this need not result in the abolition of slavery; for the radicals it must. As Charles Sumner frequently asserted, to destroy the Slave Power would be to destroy slavery itself. Carl Schurz similarly connected abolition with attacks upon the Slave Power by warning that either slavery would have to be gradually abolished, or freedom itself would gradually die.[132]

---

128. Wilson, *How Ought Workingmen to Vote?*, p. 8; New York *Tribune*, Oct. 15, 1856.
129. Chase to Editor of American Citizen, April 2, 1845 quoted in Foner, *Free Soil*, p. 117.
130. *Politics in Ohio: Senator Chase's Letter to Hon. A. P. Edgerton* (n.p., n.d.), p. 15.
131. The only difference was, of course, that the southerners expected the process to be anything but peaceful.
132. *Works of Sumner*, IV, p. 228; Frederic Bancroft (ed.), *Speeches, Correspondence and Political Papers of Carl Schurz*. 6 vols. (New York, 1913), I, p. 146.

II

Radical Republicans and abolitionists.shared more than a common ultimate goal. Not only did both groups aim at abolition, they also advanced
similar criticisms of southern slavery. Many of these criticisms focussed
upon the sufferings of the slaves themselves. Both groups viewed slavery
as a monstrosity, an abomination in the eyes of God and they described
its evil effects with great gusto. Foremost among these effects, perhaps,
was the impact of slavery upon the slave family. Why was this given such
prominence? The reason is to be found in the extraordinarily high expectations which so many antebellum northerners had of the family. Henry
Ward Beecher, for example, perhaps the most popular of all Republican
clergymen, proclaimed that in the North nothing could be more sacred
that a man's family and his children. The family was "by far the strongest
as it is the most sacred of all institutions." Similarly, George Julian, in
defending the Homestead law, claimed that it "throws the broad shield of
the government over that greatest and most beneficent or all institutions –
the family." "Home," he declared, was "the great school of virtue, the
centre of the heart's best affections, 'the birthplace of every good impulse,
of every sacred thought.'" Owen Lovejoy told members of Congress to
"take away what there is of earthly happiness growing out of the endear-
ments of home," and then asked "how much of human felicity have you
left?" The link with abolition was of course that under slavery the family,
abolitionists and radical Republicans alike believed, was set at naught.
Slavery, as Beecher put it, left the family "like a bale of goods, to be
unpacked, and parcelled out, and sold in pieces." "What rights," asked
Horace Mann, "are more sacred or more dear to us than the conjugal
and the parental?" Mann noted that savage nations and even animals
respected them; it was "only in the land of slaves that they are blotted out
and annihilated." When Charles Sumner in summary form listed the five
main objections to slavery, no fewer than two concerned its impact upon
the family.[133]

In the same way, radical Republicans followed the abolitionists in their
emphasis upon the individual conscience. One of the main criticisms of
slavery was that in subjecting the slave to the will of another it necessarily prevented him from following the dictates of his own conscience.
Hence "slavery," in the words of Horace Mann, "is an unspeakable wrong
to the conscience." But the impact of slavery upon the conscience went

---

133. *Great Speech Delivered in New York City by Henry Ward Beecher on the Conflict
between Northern and Southern Theories of Man and Society, January 14, 1855*,
(Rochester, 1855), pp. 8, 9, 14; Julian, Speeches, p. 58; Owen Lovejoy, *Human Beings
Not Property* (n.p., n.d.), p. 5; CG, 30/1, App., p. 841; *Works of Sumner*, IV, pp. 207–
208. See also CG, 35/1, p. 1358.

even beyond this. Both radical Republicans and Garrisonians were bitterly opposed to the stringent Fugitive Slave Law of 1850 partly on the grounds that it required all citizens to aid in the recapture and return of fugitives, contrary to the promptings of their individual consciences. In this sense it was, according to Charles Sumner, a "detestable, Heaven-defying Bill." (Sumner refused to dignify it with the title of "Act.") Yet once again the radical Republicans distanced themselves from the Garrisonian abolitionists when they assessed the constitutionality of the measure. Garrisonians tended to see the Fugitive Slave law as a confirmation of their view of the constitution as a slaveholder's charter and the Union as an obstacle to emancipation. Radical Republicans, on the other hand, tried to argue that the measure was unconstitutional since it denied the right of trial by jury to those African Americans who were apprehended under its provisions.[134]

In a more general sense radical Republicans, like abolitionists, were convinced that they were part of a moral crusade to end slavery in the Americas, and perhaps in the entire world Both groups were quick to invoke transcendent moral forces against which majorities, legislative enactments and political maneuverings would ultimately prove futile. Thus George Julian believed it impossible to control "those moral forces by which American slavery shall perish," while in the (for antislavery militants) bleak aftermath of the Compromise of 1850 when many were proclaiming that the slavery question had been resolved, Charles Sumner insisted that it was in reality far from settled. "Nothing," he declared, "can be settled which is not right. Nothing can be settled which is against Freedom. Nothing can be settled which is contrary to the Divine Law."[135]

These arguments differed sharply from those which mainstream Whigs had made in the 1840s and which conservative Republicans were continuing to offer in the 1850s. In 1850 William Seward claimed that the law of God, as revealed to the individual conscience, was a "higher law" than the constitution. With its enthronement of the individual conscience this claim was one which abolitionists could certainly applaud but it was also one from which conservative northerners, like southerners, could only recoil.[136]

This moral absolutism assuredly made many of the radicals implacable enemies of slavery but at the same time it made them unreliable participants in the normal give-and-take of political life. They were likely to put

134. *CG*, 30/1, App., p. 841; *Works of Sumner* II, p. 404.
135. Julian, *Speeches*, p. 48; *Works of Sumner* II, p. 413.
136. It has been suggested that Seward merely intended to say that the "higher law" was operative only when the Constitution was silent. But Seward did little to ensure that his listeners and readers so construed his words – Willaim R. Brock, *Conflict and Transformation The United States 1844–1877* (Harmondsworth, 1973), p. 111.

the antislavery crusade above all other considerations, sometimes above even the nation itself. Here too they went some way in the direction of the abolitionists. Though dissenting entirely from Garrison's disunionism, some of them, on some occasions at least, made it clear that they attached greater importance to antislavery than to the Union. Thus George Julian declared that he would "rather see the breaking up of the Union than the extension of slavery into our Territories either by the action or permission of the government." Some radicals, especially in their gloomier moments, were prepared to contemplate a division of the nation, although in practice these musings amounted to relatively little. More significant, perhaps, was a resemblance between the Garrisonian and the radical view of political parties and of the political process itself. Garrison held that involvement in political activities would inevitably corrupt the antislavery crusader and the antislavery movement itself. Radicals, as fully fledged members of a major party, could not of course go so far. But they did make it clear that for them the party was a means rather than an end; more importantly they made it clear that if the Republican party diluted its antislavery principles too much they would bolt and form a new one.[137]

Even more alarming to conservative opinion, north and south, than the invocation of a "higher law," was the violence of language employed by some radicals. Here again the resemblance with the Garrisonians was unmistakable. Thus Joshua Giddings referred to emancipation as "a work which, if not accomplished by the voice of truth and justice, will be perfected in blood." Even more pointedly Giddings referred with open disgust to the plan to reimburse, from the federal coffers, those slave masters whose slaves had managed to escape to the North. He then announced that he "would sooner see every slave-holder of the nation hanged, than to witness the subjugation of northern freemen to such a humiliating condition." These too were sentiments from which conservatives could only recoil.[138]

Giddings was only one of many radicals who could claim to be motivated by a sincere desire to improve the lot of the African-American. Thus Salmon P. Chase in a private letter congratulated Charles Sumner on his "earnest desire to inaugurate the deliverence [sic] of millions from oppression." And as they denounced slavery in the abstract, radical Republicans necessarily emphasised the humanity of the slave. Thus in describing slavery in the South, Henry Wilson of Massachusetts referred to the "auction blocks" of the South as places "where man, made in the image of God, is sold like the beasts that perish." In the final years of the antebellum Republic racism was intense and there was an increasing tendency to

137. Julian, *Speeches*, p. 26.
138. Joshua R. Giddings, *Speeches in Congress* (Boston, 1853), pp. 485, 498.

seek compromise between the sections by stressing the inferiority of the African American, whether slave or free, and by pointing to the dangers that freedmen and women would pose if emancipation took place. Moreover, there were few votes to be gained in the North by stressing the injustices suffered by slaves or free blacks. It is in this context that the radical Republican (and abolitionist) concern for the African-American population should be seen.[139]

Many radicals in fact had a distinguished record of support for not only the abolition of slavery in the South, but also for attempts to improve the lot of the free blacks in the North. Outside New England most states did not allow free blacks to vote and some states of the Northwest would not even allow blacks to enter, whether slave or free. Many radicals fought against these and other forms of discrimination in the North and advocated not only legal but also full political rights for African Americans as well as giving assistance to fugitive slaves, sometimes via the underground railroad, sometimes by donating their legal services. Some radicals even wanted full social equality for the races, a rare demand in the antebellum Republic. The range of opinion within the party on the race question meant that there could never be a single policy regarding the rights of free blacks, but radicals in particular were far in advance of mainstream northern opinion and, of course, even further in advance of the traditionally and yet now increasingly racist northern Democrats.[140]

Some final considerations on the relationship between radical Republicans and Garrisonian abolitionists may be in order. Although radicals made it clear that they repudiated abolitionist denunciations of the Constitution and of the Union, this did not prevent them from praising the Garrisonians on occasion. George Julian, for example, declared that among the immediatists were "some of the purest and most gifted men in the nation." On occasion too, abolitionists praised the speeches and the actions of the radicals. Perhaps their most astute but also their most fair-minded critic was Wendell Phillips, whose judgement upon them merits a brief review. Phillips praised the radicals and he fully accepted that if their policy for the federal government were implemented, slavery would indeed be deeply damaged in the South and in the nation at large. But he also argued strongly that more was needed and in so doing emphasised the protection that the Constitution gave to the slaveholder. Thus Phillips noted that the radicals demanded on behalf of all blacks who were seized in the North as alleged fugitive slaves a jury trial and the right of

139. Chase to Sumner, July 16, 1858 in "Diary and Correspondence of Salmon P. Chase," *Annual Report of the American Historical Association 1902*, vol. II (Washington, DC, 1903), p. 278; Wilson, *How Ought Workingmen to Vote?*, p. 8.
140. Foner, *Free Soil*, pp. 281–295.

*habeas corpus.* This, however, for Phillips, was not enough since "if the slave catcher can get past these, he can have the slave." More generally Phillips challenged the radical programme by questioning the view of the past upon which it was based. Referring specifically to Charles Sumner (though the observation held good for the radicals as a whole), he noted that Sumner wanted to bring the federal government back to where (according to the radicals) it had been at its inception in 1789. Such, according to Sumner and the radicals, would be the position it should occupy if the constitution were correctly construed. But, asked Phillips, "has the voyage been so very honest and prosperous a one, in his opinion, that his only wish is to start again with the same ship, and the same sailing-orders?" As a loyal Garrisonian, Phillips was convinced that the Constitution necessarily functioned as a bulwark of slavery. He was also convinced that even if the radical programme were implemented it would not be sufficient to seal the doom of slavery. Its implementation would indeed be "a momentous gain, a vast stride." But, he warned, "let us not mistake the half-way house for the end of the journey."[141]

Who was right? Would slavery have survived the onslaught the radicals had in mind? It is impossible for the historian to know but the very fact that the issue was never put to the test reminds us once again of yet another assumption, this time quite fallacious, that the two groups shared. There was never the slightest chance of the South submitting to the radical programme yet ironically both Garrisonians and radicals did not doubt that, given the inherent weaknesses of slavery, southerners needed the Union so much that they would have no choice but to acquiesce in its implementation. Neither group took southern threats of secession seriously. Each group, along with other factions within the Republican party would learn better as the secession crisis unfolded.

### III

For the radicals within the Republican party the moral critique of slavery was enormously important. For the conservatives it was far less significant, though not entirely negligible. What of the moderates, those at what might be termed the party's ideological centre of gravity? Not surprisingly, they shared some of the radicals' views, while dissenting from others. Abraham Lincoln was the quintessential moderate. Indeed he owed his nomination and election in 1860 to his position at the centre of the party. And on some important issues, he departed from the radicals. Thus he believed that the Fugitive Slave law should be honestly enforced in the

141. Julian, *Speeches*, pp. 5, 10. Wendell Phillips, *Speeches, Lectures and Letters* 1st Series (Boston, 1863), pp. 121, 138–139, 142–145, 148.

North. At the same time he did not engage in the denunciations of southerners which some of the radicals practised. Nor did he employ the violent language in which Joshua Giddings, for example, specialised. Moreover Lincoln made it clear that he did not believe that African Americans were the equal of whites and he was a strong advocate of colonisation, the policy to which many Whigs had traditionally been committed. Nevertheless, in some crucial respects Lincoln agreed with the radicals. His goal, like theirs, was not merely the confinement of slavery to the states where it now existed, but rather, as he said in his "House Divided" speech of 1858, to place it where "the public mind shall rest in the belief that it is in course of ultimate extinction." Although he was extremely vague on the details and the timing of this process, Lincoln wanted and expected slavery to die in the states of the South and was committed to policies which, he believed, would bring about that result.[142]

Equally important, Lincoln believed that African Americans had rights that should be respected. Moreover he insisted that the moral case against slavery must be made. "If slavery be not wrong," he observed, "nothing is wrong" and in his debates with Stephen A. Douglas he repeatedly chided his adversary for ignoring this moral dimension of the struggle, for teaching other northerners to do the same and thus for polluting public opinion in the North. Although they did not necessarily take precedence in his mind over the other criticisms of slavery (based upon political and economic factors), these moral considerations were of considerable importance to Lincoln. Indeed they formed part of his entire outlook upon the world in which he lived. As we have seen Lincoln made it clear that slavery was for moral as well as for economic and political reasons at war with the fundamental principles of the Republic.[143]

## IV

The moral case against slavery was important for many reasons. The desire for the abolition of slavery, at however distant a day, and by whatever means it might be accomplished, sprang in part from the belief that it was a moral blot upon the nation. Militant southerners in the secession winter were quite certain that the Republicans intended to launch a war upon slavery not merely in the territories but also in the states where it existed. Lincoln was able to say quite truthfully that he had no such project in mind. But he did believe that the confinement of slavery to the states

142. Basler (ed.), *Works of Lincoln*, II, p. 515. He used the same phrase in a speech at Chicago also in 1858 – see p. 492.
143. Basler (ed.), *Works of Lincoln*, II, p. 255; Don E. Fehrenbcher: *Prelude To Greatness: Lincoln in the 1850s* (Stanford, 1962).

in which it already existed would seal its doom throughout the nation. He never spelled out the process he envisaged but he probably believed that if the federal government set an example and prevented the spread of slavery into the territories, southerners themselves would sooner or later take action to be rid of it.

Lincoln's insistence that he intended no attack upon slavery in the states thus gave no comfort to militant southerners, even to those who did not question his veracity. And beyond Lincoln, of course, stood the radicals, who proclaimed in the most unambiguous terms, their desire to bring about abolition. As we have seen, it was the fear of abolition that above all prompted secession and the attitudes of the Republican party, and especially those which grew out of its moral condemnation of slavery, confirms that that fear was eminently well founded and entirely rational.

## Republicans and the Slave Power

### I

The moral indictment of slavery, though of great importance, did not unite all Republicans, given the indifference of many conservatives and former Democrats in the party to the welfare of the slave. The political indictment, however, was different. Virtually all Republicans believed that slavery posed a real political threat to the nation. These fears crystallised in the concept of the "Slave Power."

Although the phrase had been employed time and again by Republican spokesmen in the 1850s, and by abolitionists since the 1830s, Jefferson Davis as late as 1860 asked in the United States Senate what it meant since, in his view, the South was acting not aggressively but merely in defence of her vital and constitutionally guaranteed interests. Henry Wilson of Massachusetts then spelled out what he understood by the Slave Power and in so doing gave a clear definition of the term. "When I speak of the slave power of this Government," Wilson explained, "I mean the political influence of slavery in the Government of this country." He then reminded the Senate that when the Constitution was drawn up there had been only six hundred thousand slaves in the nation, worth on average less than $100 each. At that time "slavery, as an element of political power," had been "utterly contemptible." Although some South Carolinians and Georgians had represented slave interests, most southerners, and especially Virginians, had then been "opposed to the extension of slavery, opposed to the slave trade, and openly in favor of the policy of emancipation." But in the intervening decades the slave interest had been utterly transformed. For "these six hundred thousand have now increased to four million" while "their value," originally estimated at "forty or fifty million dollars" had "increased to more than two thousand million." Here then was the Slave Power. It was "a vast material interest," an interest "upheld by State law" and it had brought about a revolution in government such that "men in favour of perpetuating and extending this system of slavery over the continent have obtained control of the sovereign States of this Union." One of the Republicans' principal tasks would be to check the aggressions of the Slave Power.[144]

Although no political party in the United States would make such heavy use of it as the Republicans, they were in no sense originators of the term. Resentment of southern power in the Union had been present in the North since the earliest days of the Constitution and had featured strongly in the presidential election of 1812, for example. During the debates over the admission of Missouri the same theme had been sounded repeatedly by northerners who were strongly opposed to the creation of another slave state and deeply resentful of the three-fifths clause. At this time, however, the phrase "Slave Power" had not yet been coined. In the 1830s it came into currency, thanks partly to Senator Thomas Morris of Ohio, who in effect anticipated the Democratic-Republicans by denouncing both the Money Power (the Bank of the United States) and the Slave Power. Also in the 1830s and early 1840s the abolitionists employed the term, again anticipating Republican usage.[145] In the 1840s it became still more widespread and was even used by Whigs like Daniel Webster, whose antislavery convictions were always tempered by his concern for bisectional comity and the preservation of the Union. More typical perhaps were the polemical pamphlets of conscience Whig and Free Soiler John G. Palfrey of Massachusetts entitled *Papers on the Slave Power* and then (in 1852) *Five Years Progress of the Slave Power*. The Free Soil campaign of 1848 gave the theme even wider currency and at a Free Soil convention the following year, for example, Charles Sumner observed that in Massachusetts "the Money Power" had "joined hands with the Slave Power." So its adoption by Republicans from the mid-1850s onwards marked not the birth, but rather the coming of age, of the Slave Power concept. If Jefferson Davis did not understand it clearly by 1860 it cannot have been because it was unfamiliar to him. By then no polemical phrase was more frequently encountered in the nation's political discourse.[146]

When had the Slave Power begun to control the nation? Here there was some diversity of opinion among Republicans. John P. Hale of New

144. *CG*, 36/1, p. 593.
145. Benjamin F. Morris, *The Life of Thomas Morris* (Cincinnati, 1856), p. 181. See the first volume of this study, p. 143.
146. John G. Palfrey, *Papers on the Slave Power first published in the Boston Whig* (Boston, n.d.), [Palfrey], *Five Years Progress of the Slave Power*; "Address by the Free Soil Convention, Sept. 12, 1849," in *Works of Sumner*, II, p. 319.

Hampshire believed that slavery had "ruled this Government, from the adoption of the Constitution," whereas Joshua Giddings and John G. Palfrey, on the other hand, dated the rule of the Slave Power from Jefferson's inauguration in 1801. Jefferson's administration, according to Palfrey, had been "in the slavery interest." Salmon P. Chase, however, on at least one occasion declared that 1820 had been a critical turning point, after which an antislavery era had been replaced by an era of "conservatism." Thereafter "slavery conservatism" had in turn given way in the 1840s and 1850s to an era of slavery "propagandism," when slavery had been on the march into new territories as well as into the federal government. Meanwhile, Democratic-Republicans, who were equally wedded to the concept of a Slave Power tended, as we have seen, to date its dominance from the 1840s.[147]

This uncertainty or imprecision about the genesis of the Slave Power was also apparent when Republicans discussed its composition. In the 1850s the figure normally cited as the membership of the Slave Power was the number of slaveholders listed in the census of 1850: 346,000. But other Republicans claimed that the families and dependants of these slaveholders should also be counted. On the other hand there was some doubt as to whether masters who owned only a small number of slaves should be included and some doubt too as to whether those living in the border South, whose politics were quite different from those of the lower South, merited inclusion. As a result estimates of the numbers comprising the Slave Power varied from as few as a thousand (the largest slaveholders in the Deep South) to more than a million (all slaveholders below the Mason-Dixon Line together with their families and dependants).[148]

Despite these disagreements on the periodisation of the Slave Power's rule or its composition, Republicans were almost at one in their understanding of its nature. A favourite tactic was to examine the nation's history to determine the proportion of offices held by slaveholders since the ratification of the Constitution. Thus Henry Bennett of New York, who made a number of speeches that developed the Slave Power theme comprehensively, noted in 1858 that twelve slaveholders had been president but only six northerners. He then calculated that if their occupancy of the White House had been in proportion to their numbers within the total population, slaveholders would have held the presidency for one year rather than forty-eight. Next he performed similar calculations with respect to the other principal offices of government: the Speaker of the

---

147.  *CG*, 30/2, pp. 207–208; [Palfrey], *Five Years Progress of the Slave Power*, p. 11, *CG*, 33/1, App., p. 140. See also 30/1, App., p. 522; 35/2, p. 343; Foner, *Free Soil*, p. 89.
148.  Leonard L. Richards, *The Slave Power: The Free North and Southern Domination, 1580–1860* (Baton Rouge, 2000), p. 21.

House of Representatives, Cabinet posts, membership of the Supreme Court. In each case the conclusion was the same: slaveholders had enjoyed a hugely disproportionate share of the offices of government. By the 1850s too, representation in the Senate favoured the South in that almost half the states were slave states though their population lagged far behind those of the North. Even in the House of Representatives, which Republicans generally thought least contaminated by the Slave Power, the three-fifths clause had done its work. Bennett estimated that 350,000 slaveholders wielded the equivalent of more than two million votes, thanks to the overrepresentation of slaveholding communities. Instead of three seats they had thirty.[149]

Yet even this did not adequately convey the extent of the power of the slaveholding oligarchy. For their control over the federal government rested upon an absolute power within their own states. Like many Republicans Bennett insisted that the nonslaveholders of the South were utterly powerless. "Who ever heard of any of them," he asked, "being President, Vice-President, a Cabinet officer, a Senator, or member of Congress, or a judge of the Supreme Court, or filling any other important office under this Government?" for "the slaveowners, by their property and political privileges, are made the *ruling class* in those States." "They control the Press," he declared, "and force submission to their will by a system of terrorism and constrained public sentiment." As a result the slaveholders wielded the political power of about eight million people, bond and free.[150]

Little wonder then, that they had been able to control the destinies of the nation. According to Bennett, "with thirty Senators and ninety Representatives, *personally* and *politically* bound to the support of slavery, and without any property representation or union of *interests* at the North," there could have been only one result. Accordingly "there is not an aristocracy in any Government of Europe, that holds the power in it that the slaveholders have held, and now hold, in this free Democratic Representative Republic."[151]

To cement its control over the nation, the Slave Power had been able to rely upon a large, and growing, cohort of northern sympathisers, northern men with southern principles, "doughfaces" who were prepared to sacrifice northern interests to curry favour with the southern elite and thereby secure position and privilege within the federal government. According to Republicans these doughfaces were to be found

149. *CG*, 35/1, App., pp. 236–244. See also Gamaliel Bailey, "The Record of Sectionalism," *Republican Campaign Documents of 1856* (Washington DC, 1856), pp. 1–4.
150. *CG*, 35/1, App., pp. 242–243.
151. *CG*, 34/1, App., p. 699.

at every level in the federal administration, including the very top. Thus Presidents Pierce and Buchanan were roundly condemned for their truckling to southern interests and their indifference to the rights of the North. When the Democratic convention of 1856 at Cincinnati, for example, selected the party's presidential candidate, a northerner, "subserviency to slavery," Republicans charged, rather than "ability, honesty, or integrity" was the decisive criterion: "an avowed determination to extend slavery was the all-important qualification." As a result, slaveholders' influence in Washington could not even be measured by their occupancy of the highest offices.[152]

Yet the fact that southerners and their pawns held a disproportionate share of federal offices, and that slaveholders were equally potent in the governments of the southern states was not the main Republican complaint. It was instead the uses to which this power had been put. Thus Henry Wilson, in his reply to Jefferson Davis, reviewed the history of the preceding thirty years to show the Slave Power's impact. In the 1830s those who, like John Quincy Adams, had presented petitions calling for the ending of slavery had been denounced for it and debate on the subject had been prevented by the gag law, clear violations of republican freedoms. Others like Joshua Giddings had suffered a vote of censure for daring to express the view that international law was hostile to slavery. At the same time the mails had been censored through much of the South and in South Carolina burned. In that state too, coloured citizens of Massachusetts had been imprisoned for no offence, merely because their ships had entered Charleston harbor. These were yet more violations of the liberties that were the birthright of all Americans. In the 1840s the nation had acquired Texas at the behest of the Slave Power, with John C. Calhoun openly avowing that the purpose was to spread slavery. "The aggressive policy of slavery" had then produced the war with Mexico. Although the Democrats in the North had at first been in favour of the Wilmot Proviso with but a tiny number of exceptions, Wilson pointed out, the slave masters had then cracked the whip and "proclaimed that, if the Democracy of the North did not abandon that position, the Democratic party of this country was to be rent asunder and destroyed." As a result, "under the iron rule of this slave power, the Democratic leaders throughout the free States changed their principles, abandoned the doctrine of continuing free the Territories of the United States that came to us free." Next the slave power had resisted the admission of California as a free state, keeping her "for months knocking at the doors of the Union for admission." Texas, on the other hand, had been given fifty or sixty thousand square

152.  CG, 35/1, App., p. 243.

miles of territory and paid some ten million dollars to take it. At the same time the Fugitive Slave Act was passed, which many believed unconstitutional. Such had been the record up to 1850.[153]

Worse was to come. If those who had wished to alert the North to the dangers posed by southern slaveholders had been able in 1850 to write a scenario for the coming decade, they could hardly have found one that more resoundingly confirmed their fears than the actual events that transpired. Apart from disputes over the Fugitive Slave law the first years of the decade were quiet. But then in 1854 came the Kansas-Nebraska Act. In one sense the repeal of the Missouri Compromise came as a bombshell to northerners, since southerners had not demanded it and there had been no forewarning in any election campaign. Yet in a deeper sense it merely confirmed every suspicion, every fear that had been harbored of the South and of the Slave Power for many years. As we have seen, when the Act was being debated, the famous *Appeal of the Independent Democrats* burst onto the scene, written largely by Salmon P. Chase of Ohio, soon to become a prominent radical Republican. Chase did not doubt that the measure had been undertaken at the prompting of the Slave Power. It was for him, for every Free Soiler, for the majority of northern Whigs and for a number of northern Democrats, a measure designed to spread slavery into an "immense region, occupying the very heart of the North American Continent, and larger, by thirty three thousand square miles, than all the existing Free States, excluding California." The fact that the Missouri Compromise had been on the statute book for a third of a century, and had been approved by all Presidents since 1820 seemed to Chase and other future Republicans confirmation that the all-but-insatiable Slave Power was again at work. Moreover when Stephen A. Douglas claimed that the Compromise measures of 1850 had in reality "superseded" the Missouri Compromise, this was dramatic confirmation that a conspiracy had been hatched. For no one had actually made such a claim in 1850. Neither the proponents nor the enemies of popular sovereignty had, at that time, believed that the proposed settlement had any application to the Louisiana Purchase territories. Hence Chase's vehement denunciation of the measure. "Language fails," he thundered, "to express the sentiments of indignation and abhorrence which it inspires."[154]

Although the Nebraska territory was, as originally envisaged, vast enough, Chase and the other signatories of the *Appeal* claimed that the

153. CG, 36/1, pp. 593–594.
154. Salmon P. Chase *et al.*, *Appeal of the Independent Democrats* (Washington, DC, 1854). This is available at http://www.toptags.com/aama/docs/demappeal.htm.

ultimate purpose of the Act and of the Slave Power in general was even more ambitious and far-reaching:

> the first operation of the proposed permission of Slavery in Nebraska, will be to stay the progress of the Free States westward, and to cut off the Free States of the Pacific from the Free States of the Atlantic. It is hoped, doubtless, by compelling the whole commerce and the whole travel between the East and the West, to pass for hundreds of miles through a Slaveholding region, in the heart of the Continent, and by the influence of a Federal Government, controlled by the Slave Power, to extinguish Freedom and establish Slavery in the States and Territories of the Pacific, and thus permanently subjugate the whole country to the yoke of a Slaveholding despotism.

In other words, the Slave Power aimed to take over the entire nation. Little wonder, then, that Chase viewed the Act as "a bold scheme against American Liberty, worthy of an accomplished architect of ruin." "Shall a plot against humanity and Democracy, so monstrous and so dangerous to the interests of Liberty throughout the world," the Independent Democrats asked, "be permitted to succeed?"[155]

Other northerners, later to become Republicans, echoed these charges. According to the Hartford *Courant*, destined to become a Know Nothing then a Republican newspaper, the passage of the Kansas-Nebraska Act had "enabled the slave States to fling off the mask and show what their intentions and determinations are." The goal, it was claimed, was to spread slavery abroad by annexing Cuba, Haiti, and Mexico and, if necessary, making an alliance with slaveholding Brazil. Simultaneously slavery would be extended into the West and southerners allowed to take their slaves into the North, preparatory to a full legalisation of slavery there. Thus even in 1854 some northerners were predicting that the Slave Power would seek to carry slavery into the free states.[156]

This fear became much more widespread three years later with the Dred Scott decision. When the Taney court ruled that neither Congress nor a territorial legislature could exclude slavery from the territories, this did not merely strike at the heart of the Republican programme; it seemed also to presage the next and final claim on the part of the Slave Power: that the state governments could not outlaw slavery either. Francis P. Blair, Jr was one of those who claimed that the arguments used by President Buchanan in February 1858, when he declared that Kansas was as much a slave state as South Carolina or Georgia, were equally applicable to any state of the North. Moreover the Washington *Union*, virtually the official spokesman for the Buchanan administration, made the legal case

155. Chase et al., *Appeal of the Independent Democrats.*
156. Hartford, Connecticut, *Courant*, May 23, June 6, 1854.

for slavery in all the states explicitly, as even Stephen A. Douglas, who himself ridiculed the idea, was forced to concede. Throughout the North Republicans inveighed against the Dred Scott decision, partly because it denied that African Americans could be citizens of the United States, but primarily because it confirmed that the Slave Power was again on the march. No less a statesman than Abraham Lincoln, whilst admitting that there was no direct evidence to confirm the existence of a conspiracy to spread slavery into the North, took pains to explain that the circumstantial evidence was nevertheless conclusive:

> When we see a lot of framed timbers, different portions of which we know have been gotten out at different times and places and by different workmen – Stephen [Douglas], Franklin [Pierce], Roger [Taney], and James [Buchanan], for instance – and when we see these timbers joined together ... or, if a single piece be lacking, we can see the place in the frame exactly fitted and prepared to yet bring such a piece in – in such a case we find it impossible to not believe that Stephen and Franklin and Roger and James all understood one another from the beginning and all worked upon a common plan or draft drawn up before the first lick was struck.

It was thus the ultimate aim of the Slave Power to spread slavery into the North, in effect to nationalise slavery.[157]

By the mid-1850s, therefore, Republicans had come to believe that the Slave Power was bent on further aggressions. What brought home these dangers to the northern electorate, however, were the events in Kansas and their reverberations in Washington. Although it was difficult for anyone in the federal capital to determine with accuracy what was happening in far-off Kansas, Republicans were correct in their fundamental belief that proslavery forces were seeking to impose slavery upon the territory and displaying few scruples about the means employed. As we have seen, the Missourians who flocked into Kansas believed they could not afford either to allow the majority to determine the fate of slavery in the territory or to accord basic civil liberties to any settlers who either exhibited or were even suspected of harbouring, antislavery convictions. Nothing could better have confirmed the fundamentally antidemocratic thrust of the Slave Power. While there was only circumstantial evidence, however strong it might appear to Republicans, about the plan to extend slavery into the North, there was irrefutable evidence, based on incontrovertible fact, that such a plan existed for Kansas, despite the earlier denials of many Democratic champions of the Kansas-Nebraska Act. Yet the Pierce and

---

157. *CG*, 35/1, p. 1282; Basler (ed.), *Works of Lincoln*, II, pp. 465–466. See also New York *Tribune, Jan. 6, 1854*; March 12, 1857. The editorial in the Washington *Union* was Nov. 17, 1857.

Buchanan administrations did nothing to compel the proslavery forces in
Kansas to follow normal democratic procedures; instead they denounced
the northern settlers as agitators and abolitionists and charged them with
ultimate responsibility for the turmoil in the territory. Thus for Republicans a link was forged between the "Border Ruffians" from Missouri and
the Democratic administrations of the 1850s. Once again Henry Bennett
of New York was eloquent in his attack upon the Slave Power and the
Pierce and Buchanan administrations which it controlled:

> *To force slavery into a free Territory, and upon an unwilling peo-
> ple*, all the power of the past and present administrations has been
> exerted. Every species of injustice and oppression has been connived
> at and encouraged; the most outrageous frauds have been sanctioned
> and adopted; criminal prosecutions for political opinions corruptly
> instituted; leading free-State men unlawfully arrested and imprisoned;
> crime left unpunished and criminals protected; and a standing army,
> in violation of law, has been and is now stationed in Kansas, to force
> the people to submission. All this, and much more, has been done to
> make Kansas a slave State. And all in vain.

As Republicans pointed out, there had been an "invasion of five thousand Missourians into Kansas." There had been the "sack of Lawrence."
There had been laws passed making criticism of slavery punishable by
prison sentences and incitement of slaves punishable by death. Worst of
all, perhaps, democratic practices had been violated in order to allow a
proslavery minority to control the territory.[158]

Thus in May 1856 Charles Sumner delivered in the Senate a sustained
assault upon slavery and the Slave Power in a speech subsequently entitled "The Crime against Kansas." In one of its more temperate passages
Sumner accused President Pierce of being "controlled absolutely" by "the
Slave Power" and also referred, less temperately, to Senators Butler and
Douglas, of South Carolina and Illinois respectively, as the Don Quixote
and Sancho Pancha of slavery.[159] Two days later Sumner was assaulted in
the Senate by Representative Preston Brooks, also of South Carolina, who
had taken severe exception to the insults offered to his kinsman Butler.
Once again this was vivid and unmistakable evidence of the Slave Power
and its influence. Northern opinion was outraged. The Portland *Advertiser*, for example, drew the obvious comparison between the intimidation
practised in Kansas and that attempted in Washington. "It would seem,"
its editor observed, "as if the reign of terror and violence which is now
spread over Kansas, is also to be attempted at Washington." For "it looks
as if not only the pens of editors, but the mouths of our Representatives

158. *CG*, 35/1, App., pp. 243–244, 36/1. p. 594.
159. *CG*, 34/1, App. pp. 536, 530.

and Senators, are to be silenced by canes, bowie-knives and pistols." A little later the same newspaper stated that the incident had had a dramatic
effect upon northern public opinion, by vividly illustrating the dangers
presented by the Slave Power to those who had previously been unaware
of it:

> there are many . . . among us whom this ruffianly deed has startled into
> a new train of thought. They either could not see the aggressions of
> Slavery, or they looked upon them as the natural efforts of a system to
> extend itself, and *that* in the domain of politics where all successes are
> fair. Besides, there was an impersonality in the process, which "played
> round the head but came not near the heart." The fatal institution
> was extended – but away from, and out of sight of us. Free labor was
> oppressed – but it was not ours. The whip was wielded – but on distant
> plantations and among another race. All the evils were *thought* of,
> probably deplored – but they were not *felt*. But when free speech, in
> the person of one of our representatives, is punished with cowardly
> and murderous blows, in our Senate Chamber which, of all places on
> earth ought to be the most sacred to every attribute of freedom, we
> cannot but feel ourselves assailed and aggrieved. The blows showered
> upon bleeding Sumner, are blows directed at us, for using rights that
> we have enjoyed every day of our lives. The blows are dealt because
> these rights are hostile to Slavery, and must ultimately give way to, or
> conquer, it. We feel the straightness of the alternative – and we shall
> calmly and resolutely prepare ourselves for it; not with weapons of
> violence, but with earnest and kindly discussion, with dissemination
> of facts and with that freeman's weapon, the *BALLOT-BOX*.

These opinions were widespread within the North. According to the Pittsburgh *Gazette*, Brooks had perpetrated an "outrage upon the dignity of
the American Senate," he had mounted a "ruthless attack . . . on a sitting
and unprotected Senator," and he had "displayed the meanness as well as
the malice of the assassin." The writer concluded that "this one outrage
upon the people in the person of a Senator for words spoken in debate,
has done more to alienate the hearts of the North from the South than
any other one event that has happened since the republic was founded."
When most southerners applauded Brooks for his action, the indictment
was complete. The incident played a key role in the forthcoming presidential election.[160]

For the first two years of the Buchanan administration the affairs of
Kansas and the Dred Scott decision engrossed the nation's attention. By
this time, however, Republicans were becoming aware that in the South

160. Portland *Advertiser*, May 24, June 3, 1856; Pittsburgh *Gazette*, June 11, 1856. Allan
Nevins and Milton H. Thomas (eds.), *The Diary of George Templeton Strong*. 4 vols.
(New York, 1952), II, p. 274.

a campaign was being undertaken for the reopening of the African Slave Trade. This, perhaps the most proslavery of all southern initiatives of the 1850s, again slotted comfortably into the Republican world view and confirmed, if any confirmation were by now needed, that the Slave Power was bent on total control of the nation. And in the late 1850s, partly in response to Douglas's Freeport Doctrine (by which he sought to evade the implications of the Dred Scott decision), southern militants began to demand a federal slave code that would guarantee slavery in every territory, regardless of the wishes of the voters there. As William Seward told an audience at Rochester in 1858 slavery was now out to "extend its sway throughout the whole Union." This was "certain." The strategy would be to spread slavery into all new territories, to "annex foreign slaveholding states" and, ultimately "in a favorable conjecture," to "induce congress to repeal the act of 1808, which prohibits the foreign slave trade," and thus to "import from Africa, at the cost of only twenty dollars a head, slaves enough to fill up the interior of the continent." By this time, when the free states were "sufficiently demoralized to tolerate these designs," slavery would "be accepted by those states themselves." The grand design of the Slave Power would then have been triumphantly fulfilled.[161]

## II

How widespread was the fear of a Slave Power within the Republican party? In fact it united almost all members. Very few Republicans denied that there was an aggressive Slave Power. One who apparently did, how- ever, was Carl Schurz, a major Republican figure in Wisconsin. Schurz acknowledged that while he had heard "much said of the aggressive spirit of the slave power," he was nevertheless "inclined to acquit it of that charge." Yet this departure from Republican orthodoxy was rather less that it seemed. According to Schurz, "all its apparently aggressive attempts" were "dictated by the instinct of self-preservation." Schurz agreed that slavery was an indefensible institution and he merely qualified the standard Republican indictment by arguing that, in order to defend it, southerners were obliged to act in an outrageous manner. This signified only a minor modification of the standard Republican analysis.[162]

More egregious was the attitude of Eli Thayer of Massachusetts. Thayer in 1858 announced in Congress that he "deprecate[d] ... sectional ani- mosity whenever and wherever" he encountered it. Thayer also declared that he had "never been accustomed to speak of the aggression of the

161. Baker (ed.), Works of Seward, IV, pp. 289–294.
162. Bancroft (ed.), Speeches, Correspondence etc. of Schurz, I, p. 127.

slave power," and that he had "no purpose of doing it now or hereafter." This was as outright a repudiation of the Slave Power concept as any Republican offered in the antebellum years but it is important to note that Thayer was a maverick figure within the party, who did not believe that slavery had any chance of spreading into any future territory, whatever the actions of the federal government, and who, because of his heterodoxy, was denied renomination to Congress by his local party. He was in almost every respect an atypical and quite unrepresentative Republican.[163]

For the rest, the Slave Power provided a potent rallying cry. Republicans might disagree as to when its machinations began, their estimate of its numbers might vary and their lists of its northern accomplices might differ (largely, one suspects, as a result of the commentator's previous political affiliation), but the idea of an aggressive slaveocracy or Slave Power was close to the center of the Republican appeal. If only for the sake of convenience, one can classify Republican criticisms of slavery under three headings: the moral, the economic, and the political. The moral arguments were the least frequently voiced, however important they might be for some within the party. The political criticisms, encapsulated in the Slave Power concept, were, along with the economic critique, almost universally endorsed by Republican partisans.

All the major groupings within the party emphasised the Slave Power. The Democratic-Republicans were more likely to stress, and to lament, its hold upon the Democratic party; Whigs instead might hark back to the restrictions of civil liberties introduced in the 1830s and, beyond that, to constitutional compromises like the three-fifths clause. In practice such differences counted for little. Radical Republicans, however much they might stress the moral evil of slavery, were, like abolitionists, utterly convinced that the Slave Power was in control in the South and in Washington; they differed in this respect from conservatives and moderates only in their understanding of the measures needed to combat it. While conservatives felt that the election of a Republican president would itself check the growth of the Slave Power and allow the federal government to attend to more important matters, radicals wished to eradicate it entirely by effecting a complete divorce of the federal government from slavery. Many of them believed, with Charles Sumner, that to destroy the Slave Power would be to destroy slavery itself.[164]

Even this, however, does not convey the full importance of the Slave Power concept in the history of the Republican party and indeed of the nation. For Republicans believed that one of the tactics employed by its agents was the threat of disunion, a threat they almost invariably refused

163. *Six Speeches With a Sketch of the Life of Hon. Eli Thayer* (Boston, 1860), p. 15
164. *Works of Sumner* IV, p. 228.

to take seriously. As we shall see, these and other perceptions concerning the Slave Power would play a vital role in determining Republican policy during the momentous months that followed the election of Abraham Lincoln as the first Republican president of the United States.

## III

The frequent references made by Republicans to the Slave Power and to the successes it had achieved within the South and within the nation as a whole might seem to suggest that they were struck above all by the strengths of slavery. After all an institution which brought such outstanding privileges and benefits to those most closely attached to it had surely provided sufficient evidence of its potency. Moreover some Republicans went out of their way to suggest that claims about the natural unsuitability of certain parts of the West for slavery were wide of the mark. Both Salmon P. Chase and William Seward (in his "Higher Law" speech) declared that slavery was not barred by climate from any part of the West with the latter citing the success of serfdom, first cousin to slavery, in the cold climes of Czarist Russia.[165]

Appearances are, however, deceptive. For the Republican view of slavery contained within it a profound paradox or dualism. Whereas the image of a Slave Power implied that slavery was aggressive and strong, a dangerous and relentless force in the nation, Republicans actually believed that slavery was inherently weak and, since it could not survive alone, parasitical. As we shall see, this view was implicit when they confidently dismissed the threat of secession: slaveholders needed the Union and the North in order to make their system work. Without it the peculiar institution would wither and, many argued, die.

Why and in what sense was slavery weak? Here Republicans emphasised a variety of factors. They considered the dangers posed to the slaveholding aristocracy both by slaves and nonslaveholding whites. They perceived the problem of fugitive slaves and emphasised the role northerners had had to play in legislating against them as well as in capturing them, and thus sustaining the regime. Insurrection was another danger to which the system was vulnerable and in war especially, this might prove a fatal weakness. Thus Carl Schurz concluded that slavery so enfeebled the South militarily that it would be unable to conduct a war either with the North or with a foreign power.[166]

---

165. CG, 31/1, App., pp. 515, 260–269.
166. Bancroft (ed.), *Speeches, Correspondence etc of Schurz*, I, p. 154. See also *Speech of Hon Richard Yates at Springfield, November 20, 1860* (n.p., n.d.), p. 4. Some Republicans thus understood what the slaveholders did not: the slaves were naturally resistant to their enslavement.

Yet whatever the vulnerabilities in the regime that the behavior of the slaves revealed, they were as nothing, most Republicans agreed, compared with the weaknesses that the condition of the nonslaveholding whites illustrated. Partly because, in Republican eyes, slavery denied the nonslaveholding whites all economic opportunity and condemned them to a life of shiftless poverty, their loyalty to the South had to be secured by force. As William Seward observed, "whips, pistols, knives" were used; freedom of speech simply could not be tolerated. "The present show of unanimity at the South in favor of Slavery," according to George Weston, was "a delusion and a sham, and the result of espionage, political and social ostracism, and downright brute violence." Weston himself was a northerner but Republicans had testimony from a small but influential minority of antislavery southerners that an analysis such as this was entirely accurate. One of these was Daniel Goodloe of North Carolina who in 1859 described the reign of terror that existed in the South:

> The people of the South yearn for freedom. They are kept spell-bound and terror stricken by the eternal hue and cry of danger to the State, kept up by a few interested agitators. These demagogues keep up a perpetual reign of terror at the South, so that no man can hope for public favor, or even for private respect, who refuses to join in it. The people look to the State Governments, and they find these agitators in power; and turning to the Federal Government, they find the same men or their creatures ready to crush every inspiration for Liberty.

Hence, as Weston pointed out, the ordinary people of the South, like the slaves, were denied political rights by the Slave Power. The slave regime was too frail, too vulnerable to allow nonslaveholders to enjoy the normal rights or privileges associated with citizenship.[167]

Implicit in this analysis of the weaknesses of the regime was yet another key Republican belief: there was a huge mass of latent support in the South for antislavery, for the Republican party and for the Union. This claim was repeatedly made in the 1850s, and, as we shall see, in the secession crisis and even beyond. In the 1850s Republicans observed the antislavery activities of men like Goodloe and Hinton Helper in North Carolina, of Cassius Clay in Kentucky and of the Blairs in Maryland and Missouri and concluded that their efforts would soon be crowned with success, once the tyrannical grip of the Slave Power was loosened. At this point even the states of the Lower South would exhibit a flourishing Republican party. Thus John J. Palfrey declared that soon after the Republicans won the Presidency there would be "Cassius M. Clays, and tens of thousands

---

167. Baker (ed.), *Works of Seward*, IV, p. 250; Weston, *Who Are Sectional*, p. 5; Goodloe in *Celebration of Jefferson's Birthday*, p. 14.

of voters for them, in South Carolina and Arkansas." John Sherman, the moderate Ohio Republican, addressing an audience at the Cooper Union in New York in 1860, won a round of applause merely by mentioning the name of Cassius Clay and similarly predicted that "such men as these will rise from every hill, every mountain, and every valley throughout the slave States, to take their stand against the iniquity of slavery." Here indeed was an additional reason for resisting the Slave Power, for northern cowardice, according to George Weston, had demoralised the Unionists of the South. "In no part of the country," he claimed, "is the Republican party looked to with more anxious hope than at the South." There were, he declared, vast numbers of southerners by whom a Republican victory would be "hailed with delight." Indeed these southerners would "leap forth into life, and light and liberty, like captives released from their chains." According to Goodloe, "the triumph of the Republican party in the Presidential contest will be the signal for the grandest outburst of the pent-up hopes and aspirations of the people in these States, of which our history furnishes any example." After four years of Republican rule, he predicted, the party would triumph in all the border states and no proslavery presidential candidate would ever again even "take the field."[168]

It is important to note that this highly sanguine view of Republican prospects in the South and the accompanying belief that there was a mass of latent Unionist sentiment there was shared by Republicans of all persuasions. Thus Salmon P. Chase and Owen Lovejoy for the radicals were convinced of it but so too were John Sherman and George Weston, who represented moderate Republicans and former Democrats respectively. This opinion was of enormous importance for, as we shall see, it once again led Republicans seriously to underestimate both the likelihood of secession, since they felt the hitherto-silent Unionists would find their voices and prevent it, and the military potential of a future southern nation, which would be fatally undermined by Unionist enemies within. As we shall see, these errors played a major part in bringing about the final collapse of the antebellum Union.[169]

Despite their depiction of an aggressive and virtually all-consuming Slave Power therefore, Republicans believed that slavery had potentially fatal weaknesses within it. It generated opposition and hostility from both

---

168. [Palfrey], *Letter to a Whig Neighbor, on the Approaching State Election, by an Old Conservative* (Boston, 1855), p. 13; Sherman, *Republican Party*, p. 15; Weston, *The Federal Union It Must Be Preserved* (July 1856), pp. 1–2; Weston, *Who Are Sectional*, p. 5; Goodloe in *Celebration of Jefferson's Birthday*, p. 14

169. *Chase's Letter to Edgerton*, pp. 14–15; CG, 30/2, App., p. 315. See also 35/2, App. p. 197 for the following claim from Owen Lovejoy: "Allow us free access to the minds of the non-slaveholders of the South, and in one year we would have more Republican votes, in proportion in the slave States, than there are Democratic voters in the free States."

slaves, whom it could not adequately pacify, and from the nonslaveholding whites, whose liberties it was forced to abridge and for whose economic aspirations it could not cater. Thus it depended upon the support
of the North and of the Union. These aspects of the slave regime, its
weakness and its strength, were certainly contrasting, but they were paradoxical rather than contradictory. The unifying theme was that slavery
was unnatural and would inevitably, unless counter-measures were taken,
disorganise a community. The weakness of slavery derived from the fact
that it was an unnatural system, which generated a powerful aristocracy,
one which could only survive by constantly disturbing the community in
which it was located. The Slave Power was the product of slavery's disorganising potential. And it is here, in the conviction that slavery was both
unnatural and disorganising, that we encounter the fundamental principle
of the antebellum Republican party.

As we shall see, all Republicans believed that slavery disorganised a
community economically. As we have already seen, many Republicans,
especially but not exclusively the radicals, believed with the abolitionists
that it also disorganised a community morally. The Slave Power was the
political analogue of this process. Abraham Lincoln in a speech in March
1860 observed that slavery was the only threat to the perpetuity of the
Unions and it was for this reason primarily, as we shall see, that as president, he would refuse to compromise on the question of extending it, a
refusal that in effect doomed all hopes of preventing secession,[170]

No Republicans dissented from the view that slavery was a disorganising force. Charles Francis Adams, associated with the radical wing of
the party, in 1855 warned that the Slave Power "as it steadily and surely
increases, deranges more and more the natural operation of a republican
government." He concluded that "from [it] there can be no escape but by
a resolute and persevering system of counteraction." From the opposite,
conservative wing of the party Thomas Corwin complained that slavery
was "a troublesome institution," one that "requires too much law, too
much force, to keep up social and domestic security," while fellow conservative Orville Browning complained that slavery was a question "of
which I am sick at heart, and which I would gladly, if it were possible to
escape it, never hear mentioned again." But Browning's conclusion was
not that the slavery question should therefore be dropped, but rather that
it must be confronted. It was "a great and momentous question" which
swallowed up all others. In other words for conservative Republicans too,
slavery disorganised the nation's political agenda.[171]

---

170. Basler (ed.), *Works of Lincoln*, IV, p. 3.
171. Adams, *What Makes Slavery*, p. 22; Morrow (ed.), *Life and Speeches of Corwin*, pp.
236, 352; *Speech of Browning at . . . Springfield*, p. 3.

The crucial task for the party after the 1856 election was to recruit moderate opinion especially in the key states of the Lower North. The defection of many former Know Nothings to the Republican ranks occurred as they became convinced that the agitation of the slavery question was ultimately a product of slavery itself rather than of northern antislavery extremists, however irresponsible and reprehensible they might be. In other words men joined the Republican party as they too became convinced of slavery's inherently disorganising effects. According to one former Know Nothing "unless the ascendancy of slavery is permanently established or its limits emphatically and definitely defined, there will be no rest from the agitation with which we are now afflicted" and "questions of the greatest moment to our country's welfare" will not "receive any attention whatever." The decision of former Know Nothings to vote Republican in 1860 came when they concluded that action had to be taken to arrest the disorganising effects of slavery in the nation. Just like Republicans who had been in the party from the first they now feared that a movement was underway to establish slavery in the free states. Such were the dangers posed by the Slave Power.[172]

IV

How accurate were Republican fears of a Slave Power? The claim that the South, and more especially slaveholders, had enjoyed a disproportionate share of the nation's offices was incontrovertible. Equally valid was the criticism that southern opinion was becoming increasingly radical on the slavery question, and increasingly removed from the attitude of the Founding Fathers. After all, the attempts to fix slavery upon Kansas, to acquire additional slave territory in the Caribbean and Latin America and to introduce a slave code for the territories together with the proposal to reopen the slave trade were all departures from what Republicans could, with justice, believe to be established tradition. And the attack upon the Democratic party as the vehicle of slavery and slavery extension had, by the mid-1850s, ample justification.

Similarly, the three-fifths clause was indeed of enormous value to the South in many antebellum sectional confrontations.[173] The two-thirds rule employed by Democratic party national conventions functioned in an analogous manner. Moreover, there was no doubt that southerners had interfered with basic civil liberties in the South and in Washington and

---

172.  *The Duty of Americans: Speech of Gen. G. A. Scroggs, and of Hon. Geo. B. Babcock, also of Hon. James A. Putnam* (n.p., n.d.), p. 5. On the Know Nothings and their relationship with the Republicans see pp. 580–590.
173.  Richards, *The Slave Power*, pp. 32–46.

had been able decisively to influence many northern politicians. Equally, Republicans were right to point to the weaknesses of the regime in the South. The problem of fugitive slaves, the danger of insurrection, the abridgement of nonslaveholder freedoms – these were certainly signs of slavery's vulnerability and Republicans accurately identified the counter-measures that the slaveholders had felt impelled to take and the price that had been paid for them. In these respects the Republican view of slavery, of the weaknesses and the aggressions of the Slave Power, was strikingly accurate.[174]

Yet there was also a good deal of inaccuracy in the Republican depiction of the Slave Power. Undoubtedly (as Carl Schurz observed) southerners believed that it was they who were on the defensive, forced to take action against the rising tide of antislavery sentiment in the North. Republicans invariably proclaimed that they were true to the antislavery convictions of the Founding Fathers but in reality men like Jefferson, Madison and Washington had been far more tentative and hesitant in their criticisms of slavery, when they had voiced them at all, than the Republicans allowed. Indeed the attitude of Thomas Jefferson, the figure most frequently cited by Republicans, to slavery extension in 1820 had been in flagrant contra-diction to Republican policies of the 1850s. And the Constitution itself was, on the slavery question, a model not of fervent antislavery sentiment, as Salmon P. Chase and other Republicans had it, but instead of ambi-guity and uncertainty. In other words, although in their attitude towards slavery southerners had moved some considerable distance since the early days of the Republic, so too had northern opinion. This the Republicans did not clearly understand or fully acknowledge.

As we have seen, most Republicans never recognised that southerners genuinely believed they were acting in defence of their traditional and constitutionally sanctioned rights. As a consequence, and as we shall see, Republicans failed to appreciate that for many southerners, and especially those from the Deep South, by 1860 submission to their programme was simply unthinkable. Moreover they greatly overestimated the unity of the Slave Power and believed that it had a master plan, which would come to full fruition with the establishment of slavery throughout the nation. In fact, as we have seen, southerners were seriously divided on many of the issues of the day and had no hope or intention of planting slavery in the North. Finally, although there was indeed some Unionist sentiment in the South that was suppressed, the war years would confirm that, despite important pockets of resistance especially in the Border and Middle South, the slaveholders would be able to count upon a remarkable

174. For a different view, see Chauncey S. Boucher, "In Re: That Aggressive Slavocracy," *Mississippi Valley Historical Review*, VIII (1921), pp. 13–80.

degree of loyalty from the nonslaveholding whites. Though some of these whites might complain that they were enrolled in a "rich man's war but a poor man's fight," the poor men would continue in their tens of thousands and for four long years fighting the rich man's war.

Historians have recognised that the Slave Power concept was of great importance to the Republican party.[175] They have, however, failed to come up with a remotely adequate answer to one key question prompted by their discoveries. Why the misperceptions? Why did statesmen like Lincoln and Seward believe that southerners were far more united than they actually were, that they were acting aggressively rather than defensively and that there was a master plan to spread slavery into the North? Why did they fail to appreciate the danger of secession and why did they exaggerate Unionist strength?

The most conspicuous single mistake concerned the alleged intention of planting slavery in the North. It is tempting to label this as paranoia and some historians have been unable to resist the temptation. But there are at least three problems with this interpretation. First, can a man like Abraham Lincoln be convicted of paranoia without any additional evidence? Most historians find Lincoln a model statesman, blessed with a largeness of vision at least equal to that of any other major figure in American political history. So the idea that he was, in some sense, psychologically deviant is, to say the least, difficult to sustain. Second, while Republicans in some respects exaggerated the dangers to which they were exposed, and discerned conspiracies where none existed, on other occasions they tended to underestimate the dangers facing them (for example during the secession crisis) and overestimated their prospects for success. Can a notion of paranoia do justice to this? Third, application of a label like "paranoid" either tends to forestall further discussion, as though answers have been provided once the label is affixed, or results in a crude reductionism, in which paranoid views are held to be the product of some nebulous process such as rapid social change, or an unusual degree of social mobility. But no one has shown that the Republicans were especially exposed to these social currents any more than that they were psychologically maladjusted.[176]

An alternative explanation has recently been offered in a study of the Slave Power, which is a perfect foil for the paranoia theory. Here the claim is that those who believed in the Slave Power "were no different...than [sic] scores of other groups that historians have studied." Their mistakes

---

175.  I shall assess its overall **importance later**.

176.  For the Slave Power as paranoia, see David Brion Davis, *The Slave Power Conspiracy and the Paranoid Style* (Baton Rouge, 1969). Even Eric Foner, it may be worth noting, describing the belief in a conspiracy to spread slavery into the North as "puzzling," offered no explanation – Foner, *Free Soil*, p. 100.

and misperceptions should be seen as a consequence not of their deviation from normal standards of behavior but instead of their similarity to fallible human beings anywhere and everywhere. Whilst this view adequately refutes the "paranoia" interpretation, it is in reality no answer at all. For, as we shall see, Republican errors were all of a pattern. Moreover they had important social and economic roots and performed a major function within Republican ideology and within the northern social order. In no sense were they random, the mere product of a metahistorical human frailty.[177]

To understand Republican misperceptions it is necessary to recur to Republican ideology. The key Republican belief was that slavery was not simply bad or inferior to free labour, by however wide a margin, but that it was both *unnatural* and inherently *disorganising*. A free-labour system, by contrast, was both natural and, potentially at least, harmonious. From this all the significant Republican misperceptions followed. Since free labour was the natural system, a slave regime could only be maintained by repressing the nonslaveholding whites (to whom it had nothing to offer and whose aspirations were therefore a profound threat). Hence the Republican exaggeration of latent unionism within the South: the non-slaveholders by definition would have established a natural rather than an unnatural system, had they been allowed to voice a preference. Only a small minority, the slaveholders (and perhaps their immediate dependants), whose judgment was warped by the wealth and power slaveholding bestowed upon them (and upon them virtually alone), could fail to choose free labour over slavery.

Since slavery was not only an unnatural system, but self-evidently so, the Founding Fathers were necessarily aware of it and were therefore fully committed to ultimate abolition, however gradually it might be achieved. Hence the claim that southerners had betrayed their legacy whilst Republicans were entirely faithful to it. A natural system, by definition, had appealed to previous generations just as it appealed to the present one.

Based upon an unnatural labour system, the slave regime of the South could only be, in Republican eyes, the product of specific actions taken by slaveholders to shape it, rather than the result of unplanned or organic growth. Only concerted action by the Slave Power could explain the success of a system that ran counter to the most fundamental human needs, aspirations and desires. To spread slavery into Kansas, for example, as the Slave Power had almost succeeded in doing, represented such an extraordinary deviation from the nation's natural course, which was to establish free labour and democracy there, that only a deliberate conspiracy could account for it.

177. Richards, *Slave Power*, p. 26.

So it was with the plan to spread slavery into the North. Southerners utterly repudiated any such intention but they did sometimes insist that slaveholders in transit in the North should have their slave property protected at law.[178] For many Republicans this was enough. Here was the entering wedge. Slavery's record in perverting the natural course of development in the South and West raised the fear that a similar attempt was to be made in the North. This, together with the circumstantial evidence in favour of the plot and a single editorial from the Washington *Union*, was enough to convince so sober and thoughtful a statesman as Abraham Lincoln.

Finally the weaknesses of this unnatural system were so glaringly apparent that even southern slaveholders themselves were aware of them. Although their ambition knew no limits, they surely recognised what was self-evidently true: the South could not afford to secede from the Union.

Thus the errors that Republicans made were all of a piece. They might result in a serious underestimate of the dangers to which the nation was exposed (as a result of the belief in an underlying southern unionism) or they might produce precisely the opposite effect (when a conspiracy to extend slavery throughout the nation was discerned). But in each case the conclusion, though mistaken, followed from the underlying belief: that slavery was a blatantly unnatural system, which could only survive or grow by a whole series of disorganising measures, deliberately taken and carefully orchestrated.

To answer the question about Republican misperceptions in this way is, of course, to pose another: why did Republicans view slavery as unnatural and disorganising, and free labour as natural and harmonious? The political activities undertaken by the Slave Power provide part of the answer but only a part. In addition the economic failures of slavery, as well as its alleged tendency to corrode the morality of those with whom it came into contact, were important. But as significant as the perceived weaknesses of slavery in this process were the assumed strengths of the northern social and political order. If slavery were an unnatural and alien element, free labour was its antithesis, an entirely natural system that was in tune with the most fundamental human desires and aspirations. The Republicans thus conferred upon northern society the ultimate accolade, the most shining badge of legitimacy. Profoundly satisfied with their free society, either as it was, or as it could be, Republicans, as they internalised its values, were sensitised to the dangers, whether real of imagined, presented by the Slave Power.

---

178. See, for example, Lynda Lasswell Crist (ed.), *The Papers of Jefferson Davis* (Baton Rouge, 1985), V, pp. 220–221. On the eve of the Civil War, the Lemmon case, which involved precisely this right of transit, was making its way through the courts and a Supreme Court judgment defending the right was by no means impossible.

## Republicans and capitalism

### I

The third strand in the Republican indictment of slavery emphasised not its moral injustice nor its political shortcomings but rather its economic and social weaknesses and inadequacies. Like the political critique, the economic indictment united virtually all Republicans, whether moderate, conservative or radical, and whatever their former political affiliation. Inevitably the Republican critique of the southern economy and of slavery's impact on it was achieved by means of a comparison, sometimes implicit, more often explicit, with northern society. Hence it will be convenient to combine a discussion of the socioeconomic critique of slavery with an analysis of the Republican view of the northern economy, of northern society and of capitalism in general.

There are three definitions of capitalism employed by historians and used in this study. The first in effect equates capitalism with commerce. A capitalist economy is thus one in which production is for the market. On this view, as subsistence production diminishes in scale and importance so (in the absence of socialised production) "capitalism" expands. Clearly the northern economy by the 1850s qualifies quite easily but so too does the southern. Since slaves were in the United States used in the production of crops like cotton, which were grown exclusively for the market, and primarily for an overseas market at that, it follows that American slavery was itself a highly capitalist form.

A second definition looks not at the purpose of production but instead at the goals and attitudes of the economic actors. According to this definition capitalism emerges when individuals are motivated by acquisitiveness. As far as the economic elite is concerned, this acquisitiveness is likely to find expression in a spirit of enterprise which is deemed to be of critical importance to the functioning of the entire economic system. But even those who are not imbued with entrepreneurial drive will exhibit an acquisitive spirit, in that they will be motivated by the desire either to consume or to better themselves financially. Clearly this definition, focussing on a "spirit of capitalism," is by no means incompatible with the first, since production for the market is an obvious route to material gain and economic betterment.

The third definition, however, is more restrictive. It is derived from Marxism and it suggests that to qualify as capitalist an economy needs to be characterised by a commitment to wage labour. There needs to be, that is to say, a market for labour power. By this definition, American slavery for example, no matter how much it might be oriented towards the market and no matter how acquisitive the slaveholders who presided over it might have been, was not a capitalist system. It is important to note that in western society (and in other societies too) the wage labourer has traditionally been viewed with considerable suspicion on the grounds that he lacked a sufficient stake in, and thus commitment to, the social and political order.[179] Specifically, it was thought that a society in which large numbers of men, and perhaps women too, worked throughout their lives for wages would be disfigured by inequality, in effect by class distinctions and animosities, which would make any polity but especially a democratic one highly vulnerable and unstable. Thus a party which embraced capitalism in this sense might be expected to confront the question of inequality and more specifically to demonstrate that, contrary to traditional assumptions, the inequality that was an irreducible feature of the relationship between employer and wage-earner in fact posed no threat to an egalitarian political system.

Although I have argued throughout the two volumes of this study that the third definition is the most powerful, there is no reason not to employ each in our discussion of Republican ideology.

## II

In fact the first two definitions present few problems. As far as the goals of production are concerned, Republicans simply assumed that the market would be pervasive. They wasted no time lamenting the decline of subsistence production; indeed they simply took for granted that production was and should be for the market. All Republicans agreed that the northern economy was far superior to that of the South and when they deployed their comparisons they frequently used indicators of commercial and industrial development such as banks, factories, railroads. All of these existed, of course, as a result of commodity production: none would have been required in a subsistence economy.

Similarly the Republicans were the enthusiastic champions of the "spirit of capitalism." To be sure, some within the party had their doubts about the acquisitiveness of the rum seller and the tavern keeper but these doubts had receded from prominence along with the temperance movement itself by the mid- and late 1850s. More important, of course, were their doubts about the acquisitiveness of the slaveholder, whose activities they viewed with anything from mild disdain to outright disgust.

Yet these reservations do not alter the fact that the Republicans viewed acquisitiveness and enterprise as engines of growth. The basic satisfaction that most expressed with northern society and the universal belief in its superior performance entailed a warm appreciation of the commercial

179. Christopher Hill, "Pottage for Freeborn Englishmen: Attitudes to Wage Labour," in Hill, *Change and Continuity in Seventeenth-Century England* (London, 1974), pp. 219–238.

values of the age. The Republican party was in any case strongest in the expanding areas of the rural North and there were accordingly few doubts about the need for enterprise and continued development.

Indeed the Republicans here advanced beyond the Whigs. For in the Jacksonian era it had been the Democrats who had been most keen to rest society squarely upon the self-interest of its members.[180] The Whigs, by contrast, had been concerned that appeals to self-interest, which were in any case all too often the trademark of the demagogue, would undermine the commercial infrastructure that they wished to establish. In a sense Andrew Jackson's Bank Veto message had crystallised these fears. But by the 1850s they had largely evaporated. Whereas the Whigs had wished to temper the self-interest of the populace by establishing a paternalist government that would carefully and judiciously balance and harmonise all interests, the Republicans, as we have seen, expressed far more confidence in the populace and were far more confident that self-interest would maintain rather than subvert the economic order. Theirs was thus a more liberal and a more modern outlook and it reflected the greater maturity of American capitalism.

It remains to consider the Republican attitude to wage labour. Here there was no consensus. Instead there were perhaps three views, none of which ever managed to vanquish the others and become party orthodoxy. The small number of Republicans who subscribed to the first view asserted on occasion, though, as we shall see, they seemed to find it impossible to maintain the proposition, that the fewer the wage-earners the better; their goal was a Homestead Act that, by offering free land to actual settlers, would allow more wage workers to become independent farmers. Republicans who held the second view, by contrast, extolled the wages system as an indispensable engine of social mobility and economic growth but also insisted that the labourer, to be fully worthy of respect, must ultimately cease to work for others and become either self-employed or an employer of others in his turn. According to the third view, the wage-earner, even if he remained a worker, was a fully worthy citizen, entirely deserving of democratic rights and a high social status. This range of opinion reflects the transitional nature of the American economy and each of the three positions is worthy of careful consideration.

### III

A small minority of Republicans, whilst continuing to insist that it was far superior to southern society, expressed some considerable dissatisfaction with the northern social order. Some of them did not shrink from asserting

---

180. This should remind us that for the Jacksonian Democrats the self-interest of the masses was invoked to curtail economic development and in defence of the agrarian society.

that in the North labour was being oppressed by capital. These Republicans, however, had only one specific policy to combat this oppression: a Homestead Act.[181] By offering free farms to actual settlers they hoped to relieve the poverty that existed in some northern cities and to ensure that the relations between labour and capital remained or became harmonious.

It was when they discussed the Homestead Act that some Republicans sounded most like Jacksonian Democrats with an implicit or explicit hostility to the wages system. Thus George Julian, who before joining the Republicans was a Whig, argued on classic Jacksonian lines that "a nation will be powerful, prosperous, and happy, in proportion to the number of independent cultivators of the soil." This certainly seemed to imply that the fewer wage labourers there were in the North, or anywhere else for that matter, the better. A homestead bill, he continued, would "weaken the system of chattel slavery, by making war upon its kindred system of wages slavery, giving homes and employment to its victims, and equalising the condition of the people." Julian, who was Indiana's leading radical Republican, displayed a clear concern about conditions in the eastern states when he claimed that it was essential to "check the monopoly of the soil and the exactions of capital in the old States, by withdrawing the landless laborers of the country from their crushing power, and at the same time giving them homes and independence on the public lands." Even more explicitly he claimed that a Homestead Act "would decrease poverty, and the vices and crimes to which it gives birth, by withdrawing its victims from our crowded cities and the slavery of capital, and giving them homes upon the fertile acres of the West." As a result, "the degraded vassal of the rich, who is now confined to exhausting labor for a mere pittance upon which to subsist" would then be able to "find a home in the West."[182]

Although Julian here seemed to equate independence with the ownership of landed property, he also, and in the same speech, explicitly extolled manufacturing. This implied that what was wanted was not the dismantling of the wages system but instead a parceling out of western lands that would encourage migration and thus ease the congestion in the labour market in some parts of the East. In other words there was a tension between his demand that citizens own landed property and his affection for manufacturing.[183]

Other Republicans, when advocating free homesteads, echoed these views and also registered these ambiguities. Like Julian, some of them

181. In the early 1850s some Republicans hoped that passage of a Maine Law would also combat poverty but by the mid- and late-1850s the temperance movement was in full retreat see pp. 494–515.
182. Julian, *Speeches*, pp. 54, 57, 60–61, 65.
183. Julian, *Speeches*, p. 56.

expressed deep concerns about conditions in the East. Thus Galusha Grow, who represented the congressional district in Pennsylvania that had previously been David Wilmot's, spoke in classic Jacksonian fashion about the conflict between labour and capital. "The struggle between capital and labor," he declared, "is an unequal one at best." It was "a struggle between the bones and sinews of men and dollars and cents." "Is it," he asked rhetorically, "for the Government to stretch forth its arm to aid the strong against the weak? Shall it continue, by its legislation, to elevate and enrich idleness on the wail and the woe of industry?" Instead the task should be to promote "the real wealth of a country" which "consists . . . in the bones and sinews of an independent yeomanry and the comfort of its laboring classes." Grow here expressed a preference for agriculture and the agrarian republic that Thomas Jefferson, John Taylor of Caroline and Andrew Jackson would have applauded. Indeed in words redolent of Jefferson's *Notes on Virginia*, he explained that "for purifying the sentiments, elevating the thoughts, and developing the noblest impulses of man's nature, the influences of a rural fireside and an agricultural life are the noblest and the best." According to Grow, it was "in the obscurity of the cottage, far removed from the seductive influences of rank and affluence," that "are nourished the virtues that counteract the decay of human institutions, the courage that defends the national independence, and the industry that supports all classes of the state." And like Jackson, Jefferson and Taylor, Grow left his audience in no doubt that it was the independent freeholder whom he most esteemed, for "the associations of an independent freehold are eminently calculated to ennoble and elevate the possessor." Such a freehold was "the lifespring of a manly national character, and of a generous patriotism."[184]

The implication was that the Homestead Act would maintain the agrarian republic immortalised by Jefferson. "Let the public domain," Grow concluded, "be set apart as the patrimony of labor, by preventing its absorption into large estates by capital, and its consequent cultivation by 'tenants and slaves,' instead of by independent freeholders." The results Grow expected from this single legislative enactment were truly remarkable in extent. The effect would be, he affirmed, "to make men wiser and better, relieve your almshouses, close the doors of your penitentiaries, and break in pieces your gallows." Grow became known as the father of the Homestead Act of 1860.[185]

Yet as he loudly appealed to the dispossessed labourer of the East, Grow quietly addressed his employer. Of course, it could be argued that a

---

184. *Free Homes for Free Men: Speech of Hon. G. A. Grow, of Pennsylvania delivered in the Hourse of Representatives, February 29, 1860* (n.p., n.d.), pp. 4, 5, 7.
185. *Free Homes for Free Men*, pp. 7, 5.

western safety valve would benefit the entire eastern population, employers included, which would otherwise face the threat of bitter class conflict and possible social upheaval. But Grow did not speak only or even primarily to their fears. Instead he argued that the settlement of the West would "increase the consumption of home products and manufactures." In other words, the western farmer would in no sense be a subsistence farmer, or even a semi-subsistence farmer, trading only on a small scale in local markets. On the contrary, he would be a consumer of eastern goods and, therefore, since these goods had to be paid for, a provider of agricultural produce to the East. Here then was the reason that eastern Republicans viewed the Homestead Act with so much enthusiasm. In effect they accepted Grow's claim that "the settlement of the wilderness by a thriving population is as much the interest of the old States as those of the new." Thus, for Grow as for Julian, the agrarian republic would actually be one in which manufacturing would, and should, thrive.[186]

Historians have long recognised, of course, that the Homestead Act in particular, and, more generally, the idea of a western safety-valve for eastern discontent, were highly problematic. Eastern workers all too often lacked the capital, the knowledge or even the inclination to become western farmers, whatever the price of western land. In a sense the so-called overcrowding in the East was less a product of high land prices in the West – in fact land was relatively cheap there even before the Homestead Act – than of other factors such as immigration which was running at unprecedented levels in the late 1840s and 1850s. Yet not even Know Nothings wished to introduce immigration restriction on a significant scale and radical Republicans like Grow and Julian were bitterly opposed to all discriminatory measures against aliens. Indeed the Homestead Bill which Grow introduced in 1860 explicitly authorised aliens to apply for free land in the West. The key fact is that Republicans were united behind the Homestead Act by the late 1850s even though most of them did not share the views of Grow, Julian and others about the oppression of the labourer. This suggests that those more conservative Republicans who believed that the labourer was anything but oppressed had little to fear from a Homestead Act.

An examination of the views of other Republicans lends further support to this proposition. Two Republicans from the newly created state of Minnesota were, on the eve of the Civil War, enthusiastic proponents of homestead legislation. Both expressed a Jacksonian concern for the rights of the labouring many against the privileged few and a Jacksonian insistence on the superiority of agriculture. Thus Morton Wilkinson assumed that it would be "scarcely" necessary to "remind the Senate that the monopoly of land by the few, as against the many, and the parceling

186. *Free Homes for Free Men*, p. 6.

out of the public domain in immense tracts among venal courtiers, have been, all over the world, the most powerful auxiliaries of absolute and despotic power." The result had been that "the monarchies and aristocracies of all ages have been enabled to hold the masses subject to their will." "Millions of the human family," he continued, "have been reduced to penury and degradation, because they were deprived of the right to earn the subsistence from the common earth, which was intended alike for the rich and for the poor." But this was not merely of historical importance; it was still an urgent problem. For in the United States "even now, with all our vast expanse of territory, labor is outweighed by capital, and the rights of the settler are but slightly regarded when brought into comparison with the money of the speculator." Wilkinson claimed that the homestead measure would be directed to "the laboring masses of the country, to those who are so often crushed down by the cruel and unequal conflict between capital and labor; to the poor man, who earns his bread from day to day by the sweat of his brow; to him who feeds upon the uncertain crumbs which fall from the rich man's table." Having painted this bleak picture of the "laboring masses," Wilkinson then focussed upon conditions in the urban North. He exhorted his fellow Senators to "pass through our great cities" and there "see the boys of all ages who swarm around the streets – many of them willing and anxious to labor, but finding nothing for their hands to do." They were "exposed to temptations of every kind; day after day looking upon the equipages of wealth with the hungry and cannibal eye of poverty." A Homestead Act was thus "the measure of the working, suffering class of our people; those who are struggling on from day to day, from week to week, and from year to year, vindicating the dignity of labor against the oppressions and aggressions of capital."[187]

Ironically this picture of conditions in the urban North, where the much-vaunted system of "free labor" was presumably most developed, coincided almost precisely with that offered by the proslavery theorists of the South. Southern senators probably, therefore, found much with which to agree in Wilkinson's speech. Similarly, William Windom, Minnesota's representative in the lower house, claimed, also in classic Jacksonian manner, that "the struggle between capital and labor has ever been a fearful one." It had "caused thrones to crumble, and brought the heads of tyrants to the block." When Windom noted that "too often capital has prevailed in the contest, and labor has been crushed beneath the iron heel of oppression," he was referring to the record of other nations. But he also had in mind the contemporary United States. Who were the representatives of capital? Windom here directed attention, as Republicans often did, to

---

187. *The Homestead Bill: Speech of Hon. M. S. Wilkinson, of Minnesota* (n.p., n.d.), pp. 3–4, 8.

272 The antislavery challenge: The Republicans, 1854–1861

the slaveholders of the South. There was, he contended, an "irrepressible conflict" between "the sons of toil, on the one hand, struggling for food and raiment, and for an humble home beneath whose roof they may shelter their wives and children, and grasping, insatiate capital, on the other, seeking to erect for itself luxurious palaces upon the bones and muscles and heart's blood of those whom it has pleased to designate the 'mud-sills' of society." But in what sense were the slaveholders exploiting northern labour? Only by refusing to allow the creation of free states in the West and by obstructing legislative measures like the homestead. Yet free land in the West was only required because conditions for tens of thousand of labourers in the East were unacceptable, precisely as southerners themselves claimed. So Windom concluded that the task of the Republican party was to pass the Homestead Act and thus "supply the means of subsistence to the hundreds of thousands of needy poor who now throng your Eastern and Southern cities."[188]

Although Windom here referred to southern cities as well as those in the northeast, it was recognised by all that urbanisation had proceeded much faster in the North than in the South. Indeed in most other contexts Republicans prided themselves on the more rapid growth of towns and cities in the North. But both Windom and Wilkinson echoed Jeffersonian agrarianism. Windom explained that whilst he was "proud of our magnificent cities," he was still prouder of the fields and villages of rural America. Indeed he argued that the agrarian influence was essential to maintain the nation's purity. "Your cities," he informed the House of Representatives, "would become intolerable cesspools of vice and immorality, were it not that a better element, from the rural districts is continually pouring into and purifying them." Windom sounded even more like the Jefferson of the *Notes on Virginia* when he argued further that "politically, they would be cancerous sores, which would corrupt the whole nation, were it not that the rabble who so often control elections in them are themselves controlled by the farmers, mechanics, and artisans, of the country." Similarly Wilkinson insisted on the superiority of rural life and, like Jefferson, claimed that the farmer was somehow more independent than other citizens. "Standing upon his own soil," he concluded, "the settler rises to the full dignity of manhood. He is independent from the hour in which he becomes the owner of a free farm – independent of everything, except his country and his God."[189]

Once again, however, the notion of independence proved elusive, for Windom too stressed that the West would supply "a market for the manufactured articles of the East." But if the farmer were to be involved in a

188. *Speech of Hon. William Windom of Minnesota, Delivered in the House of Representatives, March 14, 1860* (n.p., n.d.), pp. 2, 7.
189. *Speech of Windom*, p. 7; *The Homestead Bill*, p. 8.

trading network that spanned hundreds or even thousands of miles then it was far from clear how he would achieve independence of the market and its vicissitudes. After all would an economic recession not bring distress to the rural and urban North alike? And to the extent that demand for manufactured goods was boosted, then there was the danger that yet more labourers would be drawn into the exploitative system that, apparently, prevailed in much of the East. Once again the problem was aggravated by immigration. Yet Windom like virtually all other politicians from the new northwestern states was eager to attract yet more immigrants. He went out of his way to emphasise that homesteads should be available to the foreign born too. Indeed he recognised that immigrants played a key role in developing the nation's commercial infrastructure and in facilitating urbanisation. "Let the immigrant," he exhorted, "come to our shores if he desires to do so. Let him help us to cultivate our lands, build our towns and cities, railroads and canals, and enjoy with us the inestimable blessings of freedom."[190]

Thus the Homestead Act was unlikely to achieve the results expected of it by those who believed capital was able to exploit labour in the East. There were two principal difficulties. One was the problem we have already noted of converting eastern labourers into western farmers. The other concerned agriculture itself. What these Republicans entirely failed to foresee was that farming would soon become an industry or business in its own right. Mechanisation would encourage larger and larger holdings and ultimately doom the small farmer to tenancy, rural poverty, or migration into the cities. But Republicans failed to grasp this development. Thus Lincoln once observed that he "scarcely ever knew a mammoth farm to sustain itself" and Horace Greeley, along with Galusha Grow one of the main proponents of the Homestead Act, explained that the acreage granted under its terms should be "enough for one man to cultivate." For "the end of a homestead bill should be the enabling and encouraging of each man to work for himself." Greeley then explicitly acknowledged that there were "advantages in the use of machinery, &c. which are attained through the employment of many hands together" but the solution, he felt, was for "several farmers" to "combine their labor and means to any extent which their judgment and experience shall dictate." According to Greeley, "to have every man who chooses to be, a farmer, and every farmer a freeholder, is the true design of a Homestead bill."[191]

Republicans like Julian, Grow, Windom and Wilkinson thus all recognised that in the cities of the East labour was severely oppressed.[192] But

---

190. *Speech of Windom*, p. 7.
191. Basler (ed.), *Works of Lincoln*, III, p. 475; New York *Tribune*, July 19, 1854.
192. Greeley sometimes took this view but on this subject (as on others) was not consistent.

their hoped for solution was something of a panacea. The policy of offering free land to actual settlers could not deliver the expected return. But
in a sense this failure was the key to its success. For Republicans united
on the policy and even those who believed that the northern labourer was
in no sense exploited by capital but rather enjoyed the most dazzling economic opportunities supported it. There were two additional reasons for
its appeal. One was the home market argument that we have already
encountered. To the extent that Republicans believed that inadequate
demand for manufactured goods was a problem and was responsible for
reverses such as the Panic of 1857, then it was sensible to encourage the
settlement of the West. More consumers would thus strengthen the labour
system of the North. Equally important was the political motive, the conviction that a homestead law would result in a West dedicated to freedom
rather than slavery. For this reason more than any other the vast majority
of southerners opposed the measure. Thus a Republican campaign tract
of 1860 claimed that the southern attitude derived from the fact that
"homestead laws . . . securing quarter sections of one hundred and sixty
acres to actual cultivators, would amount to a Wilmot Proviso, which
no ingenuity could evade, and which no Supreme Court could nullify."
For the same reason, Republicans, whatever their views on the current
relations between capital and labour in the North, were able to rally to it
wholeheartedly.[193]

## IV

One group of Republicans thus believed, or at least seemed to believe,
that the greater the number of independent freeholders and the smaller the
number of wage earners in the North, the better, though their policies, on
closer inspection, were in reality intended to promote manufacturing too.
Some of these Republicans were on the radical wing of the party and we
should note that their aspirations for the North were extraordinarily high,
considerably higher than those of their more conservative colleagues. But
not all radicals shared these criticisms and within the party as a whole two
other views of wage labour emerged. One of these was to the effect that
employment for wages was highly desirable, meritorious and respectable,
but only if the condition were temporary.

Unfortunately Republican spokesmen were not always entirely explicit
on this subject of wage labour so it is sometimes difficult to determine
which view was being expressed. Thus the *New York Times* in 1857 and
whilst the city was in the grip of the Panic of that year responded to the

---

193. *Homesteads: The Republicans and Settlers Against Democracy and Monopoly, The
    Record* (n.p., n.d.), p. 8. See also *The Homestead Bill – Remarks of Mr Yates of
    Illinois* (n.p., n.d.), p. 2; Sherman, *Republican Party*, p. 11.

taunts of southern proslavery propagandists by asserting that northern liberty was worth twenty thousand starving New Yorkers even if none were similarly afflicted in the slave-ridden South. But then the newspaper claimed that "our best answer to the homilies of our fire-eating friends is that the majority of those who suffer from a panic here are by the time the next one comes round in a position not to fear it." Thus, the writer continued, "the Northern artisans of 1837 ... are the merchants, traders, farmers and statesmen of 1856 and 1857;" "the men who are today, by terrible visitation of Providence, struggling with the bitter pangs of want, will, ten years hence, thanks to the indomitable energy bred and fostered by our institutions, swarm in comfort on the Prairies of the West, own stores, and factories, and steamships, go to Congress, be Speakers of the House, and foreign ambassadors." In other words "our paupers of to-day, thanks to Free Labor, are our yeomanry and merchants of tomorrow" and this was "our glory and our safeguard." The *New York Times* acknowledged that "we have thousands amongst us who now and then suffer, but we have no class doomed to perpetual labor."[194] Here the implication was that the upwardly mobile wage earner was a meritorious citizen and that relatively few wage-workers were outside that category. How that minority of permanent wage-workers should be viewed, the *New York Times* did not say.[195]

Such a view was, of course, fully consistent with the emphasis upon mobility which the Republicans had inherited from the Whigs. In a sense the *New York Times* implied that the prospects for northern labour were, in normal times at least, extremely good, since otherwise the possibility of social mobility would be remote. The *New York Times* inclined to the conservative wing of the party.[196]

Squarely at its centre, however, stood Abraham Lincoln and he, more fully than any other Republican, developed the view that wage labour was highly desirable, indeed essential, glorious even in its effects, but must nonetheless be only a temporary condition.[197] As he told a Milwaukee audience in 1859, "if any continue though life in the condition of the

---

194. *New York Times*, Nov. 18, 1857.
195. But is it not an exaggeration to say, as Eric Foner does, that these workers appeared, even to a Republican source like the *Times* as "almost as unfree as the southern slave"? – see Foner, *Free Soil*, p. 17.
196. The *New York Times* also argued that it was necessary to reduce the numbers of those injured by the economic downturn. The recipe was not western land but instead, in order to combat "ignorance and vice," "the influence of education and its concomitant virtues of frugality and forethought."
197. On Lincoln's thought, see, for example, Gabor S. Boritt, *Lincoln and the Economics of the American Dream* (Memphis, 1978); Bernard Mandel, *Labor Free and Slave: Workingmen and the Anti-Slavery Movement in the United States* (New York, 1955), pp. 56–62; Richard Hofstadter, "Abraham Lincoln and the Self-Made Myth," in Hofstadter, *The American Political Tradition* (new ed., New York, 1973), pp. 118–174.

hired laborer," it could only be "because of either a dependent nature which prefers it, or improvidence, folly or singular misfortune." In the same vein Lincoln tended to repel southern charges of wage slavery not by defending the status of the wage earner as a wage earner but instead by pointing to his opportunities to cease to work for wages.[198]

Thus in 1856 he noted than many southerners were claiming that their slaves were "far better off than northern freemen." Lincoln did not take the modern view and reject the comparison by denying the dependence of the wage earner. Instead he charged southerners with an egregious error: "What a mistaken view do these men have of northern laborers! They think that men are always to remain laborers here – but there is no such class. The man who labored for another last year, this year labors for himself, and next year he will hire others to labor for him." Thus mobility legitimated wage labour. Lincoln also took pleasure in noting how small a proportion of the labour of the North was done for wages. At Cincinnati in 1859 he noted that the wage system entailed "a relation of which I make no complaint." But, he added, "I do insist that the relation does not embrace more than one-eighth of the labor of the country." Though this estimate was far wide of the mark, it may be more important to note Lincoln's defensive tone here. Unlike some of the other Republicans whose views we have considered, Lincoln did not state that there were too many wage earners in the United States; at the same time, however, he was clearly glad that there were not more.[199]

Yet Lincoln also glorified the wage labour, and not merely the free labour, system of the North. We can perhaps best approach this by looking at his view of mobility. More than any previous president, Lincoln emphasised social mobility.[200] As early as 1856 he was attributing American greatness to the fact that in the United States "every man can make himself." For Jefferson and Jackson freedom and equality had necessitated an agrarian society in which the freeholding farmer would, whether or not he migrated to the West, remain a freeholding farmer for his entire life, gradually acquiring a "competence" for his old age. Such a society would be characterised by an equality of conditions, rather than merely an equality of opportunity. Indeed inequalities of outcome, whilst inevitable, would present a danger and would in no sense be necessary to the functioning of the economy. For Lincoln, however, the citizens of the United States, or at least those of the northern states, were engaged in "a race of

198. Basler (ed.), *Works of Lincoln*, III, pp. 478–479.
199. Basler (ed.), *Works of Lincoln*, II, p. 364, III, p. 459; Basler (ed.), *Supplement to Collected Works of Lincoln*, pp. 43–44.
200. The novelty of Lincoln's position, and its break with Democratic tradition, have been underestimated because of the tendency to view Jacksonian Democrats as rising entrepreneurs. See Ashworth, *"Agrarians" and "Aristocrats."*

life." Unequal outcomes are implicit in, indeed the very purpose of, a race. In 1864 he told an Ohio regiment that they were fighting "to secure such an inestimable jewel" as "equal privileges in the race of life." Lincoln's other favourite metaphor also conveyed the idea of mobility and more specifically upward mobility. This involved the image of weights being lifted from shoulders. In February 1861 he told a Philadelphia audience that the unity of the nation had hitherto been maintained by "something in that Declaration [of Independence] giving liberty not alone to the people of this country, but hope to the world for all future time." This was the promise "that in due time the weights should be lifted from the shoulders of all men, and that all should have an equal chance." Thus the Declaration promised liberty and liberty meant equality of opportunity and social mobility.[201]

In the same way, Lincoln stressed that freedom and equality were to be understood in terms of social mobility. Addressing another Ohio regiment in 1864, the President declared that "nowhere in the world is presented a government of so much liberty and equality." As if to define his terms he immediately added: "to the humblest and poorest among us are held out the highest privileges and positions." If opportunities were equal and plentiful then Americans were free and equal. Little wonder then that Lincoln invited Americans to internalise the goal of social mobility, as he himself had done. "I hold the value of life," he once said, is "to improve one's condition."[202]

How was mobility to be secured? Lincoln held that "when one starts poor, as most do in the race of life, free society is such that he knows he can better his condition; he knows that there is no such fixed condition of labor, for his whole life." It was this which distinguished free labour, "which has the inspiration of hope, from slave labor, "which has no hope," for "the power of hope upon human exertion, and happiness, is wonderful." Yet just as free labour was essential for social mobility, so, for Lincoln, wages were essential to free labour. And just as mobility legitimated wage labour, so wage labour was essential for mobility. In all Lincoln's descriptions of mobility the need for wage labour was either explicit or implicit. On one occasion free labour was actually defined in terms of the individual's progress from the rank of wage labourer to that of employer. Thus at Milwaukee in 1859:

> The prudent, penniless beginner in the world, labors for wages awhile, saves a surplus with which to buy tools or land for himself, then labors on his own account another while, and at length hires another new beginner to help him. This say, its advocates, is *free labor* [emphasis

201. Basler (ed.), *Works of Lincoln*, II, p. 364, VII, p. 512, IV, p. 240.
202. Basler (ed.), *Works of Lincoln*, VII, p. 528; Boritt, *Lincoln and Economics*, p. 150.

added] – the just and generous and prosperous system, which opens the way for all – gives hope to all, and energy, and progress, and improvement of condition to all.

Finally, and even more explicitly at Cincinnati the same year Lincoln announced that the very purpose of American democracy was to facilitate the progress of the wage labourer:

> This progress, by which the poor, honest, industrious, and resolute man raises himself, that he may work on his own account, and hire somebody else, is that progress that human nature is entitled to, is that improvement in condition that is intended to be secured by those institutions under which we live, is the great principle for which this government was really formed.

Thus for Lincoln democracy, the Union, freedom, equality, even the Declaration of Independence could not be understood except in terms of mobility, of free labour and of wages.[203] Once again it is important to note that Lincoln did not believe that the conditions facing northern labour were harsh. On the contrary it was because opportunities were unprecedentedly wide that he was able to identify mobility with the North and, since the South was deemed in this respect to be deviant and outside the national mainstream, with the United States itself. Nonetheless Lincoln was a strong supporter of the Homestead measure and was adamantly in favour of free soil. "Free States," he declared, "are the places for poor people to go to and better their condition. For this use, the nation needs these territories."[204] This serves to remind us that the demand that the West be dedicated to freedom and not polluted by slavery united Republicans who held very different views of the conditions currently facing northern labour.[205]

## V

The third attitude towards wage labour was almost certainly the most widespread within the Republican party. Those holding this view believed with Lincoln that wage labour in the North was desirable, indeed essential, but departed from him in denying the need for the wage labourer to become an independent proprietor or an employer of labour in his turn. In other words the employee who remained a wage-earner for life was in no sense degraded or dishonoured as a result.

203. Basler (ed.), *Works of Lincoln*, IV, p. 24, III, pp. 462, 478–479; *Supplement to Works of Lincoln*, p. 44.
204. Basler (ed.), *Works of Lincoln*, II, p. 268
205. A Republican who expressed similar views was Philemon Bliss of Ohio – see *CG*, 35/2, App., p. 241.

It is important to reiterate that these issues were never formally debated. Although the differences between conservatives and radicals on the slavery question were widely acknowledged, there was no recognised division of opinion about wage labour within the party. Thus the differences were never clearly stated, let alone resolved, and it is often necessary to rely upon inference. Nevertheless, northerners were often taunted by southern proslavery spokesman who argued that the white labourers of the North were in effect slaves whatever formal freedoms they might enjoy, and in response Republicans described, sometimes at considerable length, the conditions facing northern labour.

The most famous of these occasions occurred in 1858 when James Henry Hammond of South Carolina claimed in the United States Senate that the "hireling manual laborer" of the North was a slave, a wage slave, whose condition was no better than that of a chattel slave. In response several northern Senators indignantly repelled the accusation and rose from their seats to correct Hammond. Nevertheless several of them conceded that his description might accord with reality in the larger northern cities. James Doolittle, for example, first of New York and later of Wisconsin, acknowledged that "if the honorable Senator had confined his remark to those specimens of misfortune which are to be found in the large cities of the North, I should have given it no notice whatever." Hannibal Hamlin of Maine and Benjamin Wade of Ohio made similar concessions.[206]

The small number of Republicans who, as we have seen, asserted (or who appeared to assert), that wage labour *per se* was to be avoided had also been sharply critical of conditions in the larger northern cities. But the larger group of Republicans whose views we are now considering did not concede that the problems in the cities were in any way inherent in, or characteristic of, a wage-labour system. They at no time acknowledged that such was either the existing condition or the future destiny of wage labour generally in the North. Instead these Republicans believed that the large cities presented abnormal or aberrant conditions which were, perhaps, remediable by the speedy passage of a Homestead Law.

These Republicans did not therefore assert that the fewer wage labourers the better or, in Jeffersonian fashion, that the independent freeholder was the ideal citizen. Instead they were wont to refer approvingly or in a matter-of-fact way to the wage-labourer without implying or stating that he was in any way diminished by his condition, whether permanent or not. Thus William Seward on the eve of the Civil War on occasion referred to the southern states as the capital states and the northern as the labour states. By this he meant that "in the free states, labor being emancipated, seizes upon the democratic machinery of the government, and works out

206.  *CG*, 35/1, pp. 982, 1005, 1113.

the result of political and social equality with great rapidity and success." In this sense, "labor rules in the free states." In the South, on the other hand, "labor being enslaved, the operation of the pure democratic principle is hindered, and the consequence is, that capital is more successful in retaining its ancient sway."[207]

These were highly revealing utterances. It was clear that Seward in no way believed that the conditions facing labour in the North were harsh. On the contrary, they were such as to empower the labourer politically and socially. The wage-worker, of course, lacked the ownership of productive property that previous generations had believed an essential badge of citizenship and guarantor of independence but despite this Seward argued that as the beneficiary of a significant social investment, he was eminently worthy. "The nurture, growth, and education, of a free white laboring man," he declared, "costs not less than one thousand dollars, and so to speak, he estimates himself at that cost, when at the age of twenty-one he offers his labor for hire." In this sense the wage-worker embodied not only labour but, by virtue of this huge social investment in his nurturing and training, capital too, even if he remained a wage earner for life.[208]

Seward also, in common with many other Republicans, subscribed to the classic bourgeois view of the wage relationship, which we have already noted, as one rooted in freedom and equality. He was struck above all by the formal freedom of each of the two parties, employer, and employee, to enter into the contract, or to annul it. Reflecting some of the changes that were currently taking place in the legal status of the employment contract, he affirmed at St Paul in 1860 that the free labourer had "the right to discharge his employer just exactly as the employer can discharge him."[209] Other Republicans made the same point and in so doing underlined the differences between wage labour and slavery. The wage labourer's right to accept or reject a contract of work was, of course, rooted in a political system which promised all citizens equality before the law. Republicans believed that this legal or juridical equality was precious in itself. But they also argued that it served to underpin an equality of esteem in the North that was of at least equal significance. Thus Henry Wilson of Massachusetts, in replying to Hammond, explained that he himself had "been a 'hireling manual laborer.'" Registering astonishment that he

207. Baker (ed.), *Works of Seward*, IV, p. 530.
208. Seward, *Immigrant White Free Labor, Or Imported Black African Slave Labor: Speech of Wm H. Seward, At Oswego, New York, November 3, 1856* (Washington, DC, 1857), p. 4.
209. Baker (ed.), *Works of Seward*, IV, p. 340. On the important developments taking place in labour law at this time see Robert J. Steinfeld, *The Invention of Free Labor* (Chapel Hill, NC, 1991); Steinfeld, *Coercion, Contract and Free Labor in the Nineteenth Century* (Cambridge, 2001); Jay M. Feinman, "The Development of the Employment at Will Rule," *American Journal of Legal History* (1976), pp. 118–135.

should in consequence be classed a slave, he pointed out to southerners that he had been at that time "conscious of my manhood" and "the peer of my employer." At that time he had known that "the laws and institutions of my native and adopted states threw over him and me alike the panoply of equality." In order to appreciate the significance of these utterances, it is necessary to remind ourselves of the low status traditionally accorded to the wage worker. But Wilson's view, and that of other Republicans, was markedly different. "That man is a 'snob,'" he declared, "who boasts of being a 'hireling laborer'; or who is ashamed of being a 'hireling laborer;' that man is a 'snob' who feels any inferiority to any man, because he is a 'hireling laborer,' or who assumes any superiority over others because he is an employer." Such snobbery, according to Wilson, was alien to the people and the culture of the North.[210]

In the same way Senator Daniel Clark of New Hampshire responded to Hammond's taunts by emphasising the rights that the wage "slave" of the North enjoyed. Clark referred not merely to his right to take up or decline an offer of work, important though that was, but also to his wider legal rights and his interests as a consumer. He also referred to the pride and self-esteem which the enjoyment and the exercise of those rights afforded:

> Nine-tenths of all my people are working men . . . and when the honorable gentleman says that they are essentially slaves . . . I tell him he states what is not true. . . . They are in no sense slaves. Why, you can sell your slave. Go and attempt to sell one of those freemen, and what would be the result? You can compel your slave to labor. Go and try to compel one of my countrymen to labor, if you can. You can take from your slave his liberty. Go and take from my countrymen their liberty, if you please – try it. You can feed your slave as you choose. Go and administer food to the laborer of the North. You can clothe your slave as you choose; but the laborer of the North will say, I can clothe myself; I can feed myself; I am master of myself. You say he is a slave because he is poor, because he is obliged to labor. Is that it? Yes, sir; but he can labor where he pleases, where he can find work, and when he pleases; and he can buy what food he pleases, what clothing he pleases; and is, in every sense, a freeman.

In this sense, therefore, the northern states were indeed the home of liberty and equality and the wage-earner, even if he remained in that condition for life, enjoyed both.[211]

In fact Republicans gave at least as much attention to the esteem in which the northern labourer was held as to his formal rights and

---

210. *Speech of Hon. Henry Wilson, of Massachusetts, Senate, March 20, 1858* (Washington, DC, 1858), pp. 13–14.
211. CG, 35/1, App., p. 92.

entitlements. The dignity of labour was a theme to which they returned again and again. One Republican after another emphasised the work ethic which, it was claimed, pervaded northern society, and which, they insisted, guaranteed that labour was honoured. Henry Ward Beecher, for example, told a Rochester audience that "among us and from the beginning, Work has been honorable." In the North, he continued, "it has been honorable to dig, to hew, to build, to reap, to wield the hammer at the forge, and the saw at the bench." Thus, according to Beecher, "a Yankee is a working creature. He is the honeybee of mankind."[212]

Beecher was a radical within the Republican ranks. But the dignity of labour was a theme which united Republicans of all persuasions. Thus the conservative Thomas Ewing in 1858 explained the process by which labour came to be esteemed in the North:

> [It is] the strong will of the man that gives to his muscles vigor and energy and action – when we see and know that intelligence and talents and sometimes genius guides his head – when we see him by the aid of these seizing upon the mightiest physical powers of nature and subjecting them to his will, we grow up habitually in the opinion that labor is not only honourable but ennobling.

Even more strikingly Richard Yates, a moderate Republican, announced that "free labor" was "the great idea and basis of the Republican party." This meant that the party's task was a simple one: "to elevate, to dignify, to advance, to reward, to ennoble labor – to make labor honorable is the object, end and aim of the Republican party."[213]

The Republicans' pride in the northern economy also strengthened their commitment to the work ethic and gave them additional ammunition with which to combat the claim that their labourers were wage slaves or, in Hammond's terminology, "mud-sills." "Who," asked Hannibal Hamlin of Maine, ""are our hireling manual laborers of the North?" In answering his question, he listed their achievements and lavished praise upon them for the part they had played in the economic development of the North:

> Sir, I can tell the Senator that they are not the mud-sills of our community. They are the men who clear away our forests. They are the men who make the green hill-side blossom. They are the men who build our ships and who navigate them. They are the men who build our towns and who inhabit them. They are the men who constitute the great mass of our community. Sir, they are not only the pillars

212. *Great Speech … by Henry Ward Beecher*, pp. 8–10.
213. C. L. Martzolft (ed.), "Address at Marietta, Ohio, 1858 by Thomas Ewing," *Ohio Archaelogical and Historical Quarterly* (April 1919), pp. 186–120, esp. p. 194; *Speech of Richard Yates … Springfield June 7, 1860* (n.p., n.d.), p. 6. See also Evarts (ed.), *Arguments and Speeches of Evarts*, II, p. 449; CG, 35/1, App., p. 298.

that support our Government, but they are the capitals that adorn
the very pillars. They are not to be classed with the slave.

Once again this was a defence of wage-work *per se*, with no hint that
labour should be respected any the less if performed by one who remained
a wage worker for life.[214]
Republicans offered other defences of the northern wage-worker which
also implied a high regard for virtually all forms of wage-labour. One
approach was to demonstrate the nonservile nature of northern labour
by emphasising the amount of property the northern labourer could accu-
mulate and the income that he had at his disposal. Referring to the factory
operatives in his own state, Daniel Clark of New Hampshire acknowledged that "they hire their labor;" but, "he asked, "are they slaves?"
The answer was a resounding no: "Why, they can buy as good a dinner
as the gentleman from South Carolina, and as good a hat or as good a
coat, and supply their wants as well." "In what sense," Clark asked, "are
they slaves?" In the same way Hannibal Hamlin of Maine wanted to know
why, if a labourer lived "by daily manual labor, does that necessarily imply
servitude?" He then answered his own question: It did not: "far from it. I
affirm that the great portion of our laborers at the North own their own
homes, and they labor to adorn them." Similarly Republicans described
the utterly nonservile lifestyle enjoyed by northern wage-labourers, who
had, it was claimed, both the time and the opportunity to educate themselves and refine their tastes and sensibilities.[215]
If the implication here was that the life of the labourer was a pleasant
and comfortable one, other Republicans suggested otherwise. Ironically,
however, both views resulted in the same demand: that labour should be
respected, whether performed for wages or not, and regardless of the per-
manence of the wage labourer's condition. Thus Henry Wilson noted that,
in earning his wages, the labourer might have to face considerable adversity. But this was yet another reason for according him respect. Speaking
in Boston in 1860 Wilson announced that he saw within the audience "the
manly forms of toiling men who, through weary days and sleepless nights
of personal toil, have won for themselves positions of independence, or
who now, by the scanty wages of manual labour, support themselves and
the dear and loved ones of their household." This clearly implied that
their lives were, in some respects at least, harsh. But the reward for this
labour was not only the wage it earned but also the esteem it commanded
within the entire community. "Here," he proclaimed, "the laboring man,
who daily goes forth with a brave heart to toil for his loved ones, wins not

214. *CG*, 35/1, p. 1025.
215. *CG*, 35/1, App., p. 92, 35/1, p. 1025.

only bread by the sweat of his face, but the applauding voice of men who honor labor, who believe the laborer is worthy of his hire." Ironically too, Wilson managed to convert this description of the arduousness of manual labour into a celebration of equality. The Republicans, he proclaimed, were the champions of the toiling masses:

> Accepting as its living faith the creed of the equality of mankind, the Republican party recognizes the poor, the humble, the sons of toil, whose hands are hardened by honest labor, whose limbs are chilled by the blasts of winter, whose cheeks are scorched by the suns of summer, as the equals before the law of the most favored of the sons of men.

The wage-worker could thus enjoy equality before the law and a high degree of esteem within the community, however arduous the labour he performed and however precarious his economic condition.[216]

When Wilson referred to "the dear and loved ones of their household," he touched upon yet another set of rights which the northern wage-worker could enjoy, and which confirmed the nonservile nature of his labour. The celebration of the family which we have already noted in connection with the moral critique of slavery was not merely a source of antislavery sentiment. It was cited to combat the allegation of "wage slavery" in the North. A family that was, in the words of Henry Ward Beecher, "not-marketable" was yet another of the blessings which northern society showered upon the wage labourer. For this reason, among others, it was, according to Hamlin, a grievous error to view northern wage labourers as anything akin to slaves:

> They are not to be classed with the slave. Our laboring men have homes; they have wives; they have little ones dependent upon them for support and maintenance; and they are just so many incentives and stimulus to action. The laboring man, with us, knows for whom he toils; and when he toils he knows that he is to return to that home where comfort and pleasure and all the domestic associations cluster around the domestic hearthstone.

For this reason alone it was wholly mistaken to confuse northern wage labour with southern chattel slavery.[217]

A possible implication of Hamlin's remarks was that the family would function as a consolation for the wage earner. However difficult the material conditions he experienced, and whether he rose in society or not, his family would be a constant source of comfort and joy. And the need

216.  Wilson, *How Ought Workingmen to Vote?*, pp. 2, 8.
217.  Beecher quoted in Amy Dru Stanley, "Home Life and the Morality of the Market," in Stokes and Conway (eds.), *Market Revolution*, pp. 74–96, 1025; *CG*, 35/1, p. 1025.

to provide for wife and child was a major incentive. William Kelley, a Democratic-Republican from Pennsylvania, made a slightly different point when he emphasised that the possibility of his children's mobility was crucially important to the labourer. Indeed Kelley recognised that the conditions in which labourers worked might be extremely difficult and their remuneration poor. In this sense the children's prospects were held to be at once a great consolation and a major stimulus:

> But workingmen, do you value the privileges of free schools, and institutions of learning? While you are at labor in the workshop, do you not feel that, though you have to toil hard for a beggarly subsistence, your children, by the aid of our public schools and public liberties, shall stand the peers of the proudest in the land and may rise, like "the Natick cobbler" [Henry Wilson], to be the great man of the United States Senate?

Kelley emphasised that this was a major difference between slavery and freedom. The loving mother, he claimed, would even contemplate infanticide if her children were to be sent into slavery. Slaves were required to engage in "labor without wages," and they lacked "the right to own their own limbs and their own bodies." "Whereas for you," he told an audience in Philadelphia, "it is different;" you labour "cheerfully" because in your children "your hope lives." Here was a celebration of mobility but it was intergenerational mobility, and it assumed that the father's status as a wage-worker might well be permanent.[218]

Similar assumptions were present when other Republicans discussed social mobility in the North. Thus John G. Palfrey, another Massachusetts radical, argued that "the laboring man in Massachusetts has every reasonable opportunity for improvement and advancement that money could buy, or heart desire." Mobility was thus a real possibility since "every thing there is in him has its fair chance to come out." And he added that here "labor is honorable and honored in all its forms." But this did not mean that all labourers would rise. For when Palfrey went out of his way to argue that the children of every northern labourer would "start from the same level as the richest man in the race for the high prizes of society," he implied that their fathers would still be labourers.[219]

Palfrey's words may serve to alert us to some of the complexities involved in the notion of social mobility, for the greater the opportunities to rise in society, the greater, presumably, the stigma of failure. Indeed it is not too much to suggest that there was a tension between the two

218. *An Address Delivered by Hon. William D. Kelley at Spring Gardens...Sept. 9,* 1856 (Philadelphia, n.d.), pp. 8–11.
219. Palfrey, *Papers on the Slave Power*, p. 51; *Mr Palfrey's Speech* [of 1849 in the House of Representatives], (n.p., n.d), p. 4.

themes, both prominent in Republican rhetoric, of the dignity of labour and social mobility. It is easy to assume that the two are fully compatible and to view the dignity of labour as both cause and consequence of social mobility. But what of the labour of the man who failed to take his opportunities? Republicans occasionally claimed that he had only himself to blame. But they never allowed this to qualify their commitment to the dignity of labour. Virtually all forms of labour, no matter what the labourer made of his opportunities, were honoured. In effect, therefore, the tension between the two concepts was resolved in favour of the dignity of labour. And this resolution also in effect confirmed that the permanent wage earner should be accorded a full measure of respect.

Although Republicans often explicitly discussed the opportunities, the rights and the social standing of the wage labourer, their writings sometimes simply took wage labour for granted, without offering any hint of criticism of those who would experience it throughout their working lives. William Kelley, for example, was one of many Republicans who seemed easily to move from "free labor" to "wage labor" as though the terms were interchangeable. Thus he complained that the southern demand for slavery in the territories threatened to leave the West "shut against the free white laborer – against wages – against the hopes, the enterprise, the prospects of the poor man of the world." Here was the wage system as an engine of prosperity or mobility, though again without any stigma placed against the permanent wage-earner.[220]

The importance of wage labour in the thinking of Republicans is similarly implicit or explicit in some of the speeches of Charles Sumner. Prior to the election of 1860 Sumner began to adopt a shorthand phrase to refer to southern slavery. He began to call it "labor without wages," confident, it would seem, that this phrase would convey to his listeners the enormity of the injustice inherent in the master/slave relation. In June 1860 all the evil effects of slavery were traced to its "single object of compelling men to work without wages." This, he repeated a month later, was its "single motive," its "single object." To appreciate the novelty of this formulation, we should recall that for the greater part of human history labour has been done without wages and for much of that time it would have been grounds for complaint if a system had compelled men to work *with* wages. On the same occasion, Sumner employed a familiar argument against slavery when he claimed that it was contrary to God's intentions for mankind. Less familiar, however, was his assumption about wages. "When God created man in his own image," he declared, "and saw that his work was good, he did not destine his fellow creature for endless ages to labor without wages, compelled by the lash." The rhythm

220. Kelley, *Address*, p. 8.

of this sentence seems to require that a heavy emphasis be placed upon "without wages," perhaps as heavy as "compelled by the lash." The implication was surely that God approves of wage labour. Sumner's attitude was made even more explicit in a rhetorical question which he put to the Senate in 1860. Speaking of "the slaveholder," he asked:

> How can he show sensibility for the common rights of fellow citizens who sacrifices daily the most sacred right of others merely to secure *labor without wages*? With him a false standard is necessarily established, bringing with it a blunted moral sense and clouded perceptions, so that, when he does something intrinsically barbarous or mean, he does not blush at the recital.

Here then is the reason Sumner believed that to refer to slavery as "labor without wages" could convey the enormity of the evil. He seems to have viewed wage labour, properly rewarded, as an anchor of morality. The passage makes no sense unless it is assumed that the wage labourer is worthy of respect or esteem. Gone is the hostility traditionally expressed by Jeffersonians and Jacksonians. And at no point did Sumner ever suggest that the wage-earner lost respect or status if he remained a wage-earner.[221]

In a way Sumner's attitude towards wage labour, and that of the Republicans generally, was only to be expected. Representing Massachusetts, probably the most industrially advanced state in the Union, he was surely aware that it was simply not possible, and perhaps not even desirable, for all wage (or salary) earners to become independent or employers of others in their turn. This applied to a considerable degree to other parts of the Northeast and, to a lesser extent, to the North as a whole. As a result, despite the reservations expressed and the qualifications offered by some of their spokesmen it should be clear that the Republicans displayed a greater enthusiasm for the wages system and for the wage labourer than any major political party the United States had yet seen.

## VI

Entertaining these views of the wages system, of northern society, and of capitalism in general, Republicans were able to develop a thoroughgoing economic critique of slavery in the South. They never found the slightest reason to doubt the superiority of the northern economy in terms of productivity and wealth creation. While a slave-based economy was unnatural, they insisted, since it repressed fundamental human aspirations, the free labour system of the North, they affirmed, catered to those aspirations

---

221. *Works of Sumner*, V, pp. 106, 208, 209, 267. George Julian, later to join Sumner on the radical wing of the Republican party, similarly referred to "that principle of eternal justice, a fair day's wages for a fair day's work" – see Julian, *Speeches*, p. 9,

powerfully, if not quite perfectly, and in any event more fully than any other society the world had yet seen. Southern society in this most literal sense was unnatural, the northern economy and northern society were instead in harmony with fundamental human needs and aspirations

Comparisons between North and South featured strongly in Republican rhetoric and propaganda. According to Henry Wilson, "freedom took the rugged soil, and still more rugged clime of the North, and now that rugged soil yields abundance to the willing hands of free labor." By contrast, "slavery took the sunny lands and the sunny clime of the South, and now it has left the traces of its ruinous power deeply furrowed on the brows of your sunny land." Wilson here compared the aggregate performance of the North with the South. A more common stratagem, indeed a staple of Republican speeches, whether in Congress or on the stump, was a comparison between pairs of states, one northern and one southern, usually states which had entered the Union at the same time or which were in some other way comparable. Invariably the conclusion was that in all important respects the northern state was superior. Thus Charles Hoard of New York declared that Republicans had "noticed the advancement of neighboring States, apparently equal in natural advantages; and in no single instance has the State in which slavery exists kept pace with the States which are free." Like other Republicans who indulged in this exercise, he did not confine himself to narrowly economic criteria but instead broadened the comparison to include what he took to be other indicators of social progress. "In schools, in churches, in libraries, in manufactures, in roads, in canals, in commerce, in domestic peace and security, in agriculture and in wealth, (upon soil where the natural advantages are equal)," Hoard concluded, "the free States uniformly excel."[222]

This view of slavery united all Republicans, indeed virtually every antislavery campaigner in the North (and even the South) from the most conservative Republican at one end of the spectrum to a militant abolitionist like William Lloyd Garrison at the other. In the 1850s when the territorial question was so prominent, it underpinned Republican objections to the spread of slavery into the West. Thus Calvin C. Chaffee estimated that if Kansas became a slave state the value of her lands would be diminished by no less than a half. Chaffee claimed that the census of 1850 had shown beyond any doubt that free labour was twice as productive as slave. Similarly Henry Bennett argued that the soil lost half its value when desecrated by slavery while William Seward claimed that the value of land in a free state was three times that of comparable land in a slave state.[223]

The territorial question almost certainly gave these comparisons additional urgency and perhaps focused attention on the economy of the

222. *Speech of Wilson, March 20, 1858*, p. 7; CG, 35/1, App., p. 273.
223. CG, 35/1, p. 854, 34/1, App., p. 699. Baker (ed.), *Works of Seward*, IV, p. 394.

border states, where slavery was weakest, and where Republicans were gaining a political foothold. Thus Silas Burroughs of New York predicted that if Missourians were to give away all their slaves and adopt a free constitution, then the value of all lands in the state would rise by thirty percent in two years. As Cassius Clay of Kentucky put it, "the aggregate population is always injured, the total wealth always less, by slavery."[224]

The assumption that slavery retarded an economy pervaded Republican ranks. Seward described the southern states as "stationary, or relatively so," and others focused upon the damage that slavery did to the lands upon which the slave worked. According to Thomas Corwin of Ohio, slavery was "an exotic that blights with its shade the soil in which you plant it." "So far from facilitating the increase of individual or national wealth," Horace Mann declared, "slavery retards both, it blasts worldly prosperity." Lafayette Foster of Connecticut observed in Congress that "we of the North . . . oppose slavery because we have seen in the past history of the States which tolerate it, that it is fatal to their prosperity." Foster testified to the ubiquity of this argument when he added that "this view of the subject has been so often and so thoroughly discussed, North and South, that I must refrain from entering upon it in detail at this time."[225]

Why was free labour so much more productive? Many Republicans were driven to reflect on the differences between the two labour systems in order to explain their contrasting economic performances. Natural endowment was immediately ruled out, on the grounds that if anything the South had an advantage in this respect. Few alternatives remained. Although it was technically possible to attribute the failure of the southern economy to the alleged racial deficiencies of its slave labour force, few Republicans took this line. This could only mean that the labour process itself was to blame. And here several arguments were deployed. The first emphasised the structural incentives available within a free labour system and their absence within a slave economy. Thus according to Congressman John Hutchins of Ohio, the reason for the contrasting performance of the two sections was "too obvious to need any argument to show it." Hutchins nevertheless spelled out the argument and the effort was not

---

224. CG, 35/1, p. 815; *The Life of Cassius Marcellus Clay, Memoirs, Writings, and Speeches* (New York, 1886), p. 201. See also *Speeches, Arguments and Miscellaneous Papers of David Dudley Field*. 3 vols. (New York, 1884–1890), III, p. 36; New York *Tribune*, May 24, 1855; Daniel Goodloe, *Is It Expedient to Introduce Slavery into Kansas? A Tract for the Times* (n.p., n.d.), p. 43; CG, 35/1, p. 774.

225. Baker (ed.), *Works of Seward*, IV, p. 417; Morrow (ed.), *Life and Speeches of Corwin*, p. 353. CG, 30/1, App., p. 835, 35/1, p. 1044. The small number of Republicans from the southern states also advanced these arguments – see Benjamin Williams, *Free Soil – Free Labor – Free Speech: Speech of Benjamin F. Williams, of Virginia, before the Republican Association of Washington . . . August 17, 1860* (Washington DC, 1860), pp. 1–3; [Benjamin Hedrick], *Are North Carolinians Freemen?* (n.p., n.d.), pp. 6–7.

wasted since it was in fact by no means an obvious and perhaps not even a persuasive one. Hutchins declared that "slave labor" was "forced and mere hand labor," lacking the motives of reward which stimulate free labor;" as a result "slave labor does not originate; and cannot bring to its aid, the numberless labor-saving inventions which have contributed so much to the industrial enterprise and prosperity of the free states." Yet it was not entirely clear from this argument why slaveholders could not simply copy those labour-saving inventions and thus diminish their need for slaves, just as similar innovations in the North reduced the demand for free labour.[226]

More often, however, Republicans contented themselves with a simpler argument which merely emphasised the lack of incentives offered to the slave himself, as opposed to those which stimulated the free labourer. No Republican articulated these ideas more clearly than Abraham Lincoln, whose views on wage labour and social mobility we have already considered, and who constantly mused upon the differences between northern and southern society. "Free labor," he argued, "has the inspiration of hope" whereas "pure slavery has no hope." The effects were dramatic since "the power of hope upon human exertion, and happiness, is wonderful." Lincoln then presented as an illustration the case of "the slave whom you can not drive with the lash to break seventy-five pounds of hemp in a day." But if the same man were a wage worker then "if you will task him to break a hundred, and promise him pay for all he does over, he will break you a hundred and fifty." Similarly Horace Mann declared that enslavement destroyed a man's "ambition, his enterprise, his capacity." "When the lash is the only stimulant," Thaddeus Stevens concluded, "the spirit of man, revolts from labor." Some Republicans even took the proslavery theorist's claim that the master had an obligation to care for the slave throughout his life and turned it upon its head by arguing that the effect was further to deprive the labourer of incentives.[227]

Not only was the quantity of work carried out by the slave far less than that which a free labourer could perform, the quality too was markedly inferior. Slave labour, it was said, was unproductive because it was uneducated. Both Abraham Lincoln and William Seward believed that slavery reduced the quality of labour performed by the bondsman to that of the brute or the animal. Once again the slave's lack of incentives was held to blame.[228]

Yet however important the financial inducements, the labourer's social standing was a still more important factor in northern economic success.

226.  *Speech of John Hutchins of Ohio in the House of Representatives, May 1860* (n.p., n.d.), pp. 5–6.
227.  Basler (ed.), *Works of Lincoln*, III, p. 462; CG, 30/1, App. p. 835, 31/1, App., p. 142; *Great Speech ... by Henry Ward Beecher* p. 10.
228.  CG, 30/1, App., p. 835; Foner, *Free Soil*, p. 45.

As we have seen, the work ethic, the belief that labour was honoured throughout the North, was a key article of Republican faith. In the South, however, the cultural environment was, according to Republicans, entirely different: labour there, Republicans insisted, was dishonoured because performed by a labour force perceived to be irremediably inferior. Another cardinal tenet of the Republican faith was the conviction that slavery degraded labour. According to the Hartford *Evening Press*, slavery "clearly retards the growth of communities, discourages industry and education and degrades labor." In his *Appeal of the Independent Democrats*, written to combat the Kansas-Nebraska Act, Salmon P. Chase asserted that "labor cannot be respected where any class of laborers is held in abject bondage." For it was "the deplorable necessity of Slavery, that to make and keep a single slave, there must be slave law; and where slave law exists, labour must necessarily be degraded." According to the New York *Tribune*, slavery was "ruinous and degrading to free labor."[229]

The effect of this association of labour with servitude, Republicans reiterated, was not merely to diminish the quantity and quality of the work done by slaves but also to make labour disreputable in the eyes of the nonslaveholding whites too. Having made an elaborate comparison of Virginia and New York, William Howard posed a question to southerners: "do not your own white labourers instinctively recoil from every species of labour performed by slaves and thus lead a life of miserable compromise between degradation and idleness on the one hand, and starvation on the other?" According to Henry Ward Beecher, "the poor white population of the South is degraded. They are ignorant – they are not fertile in thought or labor." Republicans took particular pleasure in finding examples of southerners, and proslavery southerners at that, lamenting the fact that the nonslaveholders of the South were degraded and unaccustomed to labour. Here then was an additional explanation for the poor economic performance of the South.[230]

Here too was the reason that slavery must not be allowed into the new territories. According to Charles Hoard, "slavery degrades labor wherever it exists; and therefore free laborers will not live in a slave State, or emigrate to a slave Territory." Others made the same point. Richard Yates of Illinois was convinced that free labourers "will not go to a State where their labor is to be cheapened and degraded by a comparison with slave labor." In the words of Silas Burroughs of New York, "the white man

---

229. Hartford *Evening Press*, Oct. 25, 26, 1860 in Howard C. Perkins (ed.), *Northern Editorials on Secession*. 2 vols. (Gloucester, MA, 1942), I pp. 61–62; Chase *et al.*, *Appeal of the Independent Democrats*, p. 6; New York *Tribune*, Feb. 4, 1854. See also *CG*, 33/3, pp. 90–91; 34/1, App., p. 636; Horace Greeley (ed.), *The Writings of Cassius Marcellus Clay* (New York, 1848), pp. 204, 390, 523–524.
230. *CG*, 35/1, p. 1277; *Great Speech . . . by Henry Ward Beecher*, p. 11. See also Weston, *Poor Whites of the South*, pp. 1–2.

must be paid for his labor, must be rewarded for his toil, and cannot live in the same community with the unpaid negro slave."[231]

Some Republicans argued that the unfair competition from the labour of slaves operated to reduce the wage level in slave societies. According to George Weston, "whoever makes use of enslaved labor...avails himself of an unfair advantage. The robbery of the slave becomes the robbery of the freeman, with whose labor the slave is brought into rivalry." Thus if unpaid slave labour were available in the territories the effect would be to reproduce the very condition, an excess of labour, that the territories were intended to combat. William Kelley urged his listeners to use their votes to determine "whether the laborer shall walk erect, a freeman, putting his wages in his pocket and spending them at his will, or whether, in the South, white or black, he shall be the mere creature of his owner, and in the North be reduced by the competition of unpaid labour, to a condition scarcely more happy than that of the slave." As far as the settlement of the territories was concerned therefore, the stakes were extraordinarily high.[232]

## VII

To what extent were the Republicans the apologists for northern society and the northern labour system? Although none of them doubted the superiority of their free labour system, some of them, as we have seen, were quite critical of conditions in some parts of the North, and especially in the larger cities. As we have also seen, these concerns on some occasions provoked demands for a Homestead Act. But they were not confined to these occasions. Thus Henry Ward Beecher in 1855 acknowledged that there were many problems in the North. "Selfishness and pride, avarice and cunning, anger or lust," he admitted, "may prey upon the heedlessness of helplessness of many." Indeed in the North, he conceded, "society may be full of evils." It would be an error therefore to assume that Republicans were uniformly complacent about the northern social order.[233]

It would be a still greater error to assume that the Republican antislavery crusade was in any way intended to divert attention from the social problems of the North.[234] Indeed the example of many Republicans (and

---

231. *CG*, 35/1, App., p. 273; *Speech of Hon. Richard Yates of Illinois on the State of Parties* (Washington, DC, 1855), pp. 6–7; *CG*, 35/1, App., p. 62.
232. Weston, *Will the South Dissolve the Union?* (n.p., n.d), pp. 3–4; Kelley, *Address*, p. 13.
233. *Great Speech...by Henry Ward Beecher*, p. 8.
234. This is the argument advanced in regard to Britain by David Brion Davis, or perhaps it would be more accurate to say that it is the argument that many of Davis's readers believed he was advancing. I have commented on these issues at some length in Thomas Bender (ed.), *The Antislavery Debate: Capitalism and Abolitionism as a Problem in Historical Interpretation* (Berkeley, 1992).

abolitionists) suggests that the more fervent the antislavery convictions, the greater the hopes and expectations for the North and the less the tolerance of perceived social evils there. Thus the radical Republican George Julian of Indiana boasted, with some justification, that "anti-slavery men" did not target only the South for criticism. Instead "whilst they wage war against chattel slavery in the South, they wage war against wages slavery in the North." Thus the enemies of slavery were also "the advocates of land reform; of the rights of labor in opposition to the exactions of capital" and were "exerting themselves to the utmost in the cause of down-trodden humanity, whether white or black, or whatever the form of degradation under which it groans."[235]

Nevertheless this should not obscure the fact that the Republicans were indeed the apologists for the northern labour system. Not only were the more conservative and moderate members of the party far less likely to find fault with northern society, even those radicals who did voice criticisms nonetheless made it clear that they believed that the necessary changes could be readily secured if only the will were present. One of the great virtues of Northern society, in contradistinction to that of the South, was that it was eminently improvable. Julian himself boasted that "the free States do not justify the social evils that have grown up in their midst." Here the comparison with the South was glaring. Even if there were indeed "wages slavery" in some parts of the North, it was the task of the conscientious reformer to eliminate it. Unlike the southern states, the states of the North, Julian pointed out, "do not cling to them [their social evils] as to the corner-stone of the Republic. They do not invoke in their behalf the divine sanction, nor threaten to dissolve the Union if they should be abolished." What Julian here left unsaid was as significant as what he said for he assumed, of course, that the evils could be eliminated and, at the same time, he did not fear, indeed he encouraged, the process of agitation that would precede and promote their elimination.[236]

Similarly Henry Ward Beecher, having drawn attention to the social evils within the North, insisted that they should not be seen as inherent in the northern social system:

> But all these things are not consequences of northern doctrines, but violations of them. If sharks in great cities consume the too credulous emigrant, if usurers, like moths, cut the fabric of life with invisible teeth; if landlords suck their tenements and pinch the tenant – all these results are against the spirit of our law, and public feeling, and they that do such things must slink and burrow. They are vermin that

235. Julian, *Speeches*, p. 95.
236. Julian, *Speeches*, p. 95.

run in the walls, and peep from hiding-holes, and we set traps for them as we do for rats and weasels.

Beecher then contrasted the North with the South in this regard. Here the oppression entailed by slavery, "the subordination of man to man, in his earnings, his skill, his time and labor – in his person, his affections, his very children," all this was "a part of the theory of society, drawn out into explicit statutory law, coincident with public opinion, – executed without secrecy." Whereas the evils of northern society were perpetrated by "criminals and reprobates," in the South "a net spread for those guilty of such wrongs against man, would catch States, and Legislatures, Citizens, Courts and Constitutions." North and South were thus fundamentally different: the evils within southern society were inherent in it; those in the North were aberrations, anomalies which could, relatively easily, be eliminated.[237]

Even those Republicans who criticised the North were thus apologists for the northern free-labour society, even if it were the free-labour society that the North might readily become rather than the one it now was. Thus they were the apologists for northern free-labour society with its inherent capacity for improvement. Moreover, as we have seen, the reform upon which they concentrated, the Homestead Act, was one which commended itself to many within the party (and outside it) who had a much more sanguine view of contemporary conditions in the North. It is difficult to avoid the conclusion that even the minority of Republicans who were critical of the existing northern social order in fact posed little challenge to it.

In this way Republican ideology served to legitimate northern society either as it already was or as it would become, the free-labour system upon which it was based, and the wage relationship that was an increasingly integral part of it. Republicans believed that the northern economy, in contradistinction to that of the South, catered to the most fundamental human aspirations and ambitions. The northern labour system, the northern economy and northern society were in, or could easily be brought into, harmony with human nature itself.

## VIII

Although the Republican vision of the North was by no means wholly inaccurate, much was obscured in it. To begin with, it was a highly gendered vision. On most occasions at least Republicans utterly failed to take note of the labour, including the wage labour, performed by women. When faced with southern taunts that northern wage workers were in fact

237.  *Great Speech ... by Henry Ward Beecher*, p. 8.

slaves, Republicans, as we have noted, were ready with their response. Easily overlooked, however, is the gendered nature of that response and it may be appropriate to review some of their utterances in this light. Thus when Hannibal Hamlin in the United States Senate asked who the "hireling manual laborers of the North" were, his answer assumed that all were men. As we have seen, he gave a series of descriptions of these manual labourers, on each occasion terming them "men who," culminating in the description that they had "wives." In this way the wage labour of women, far from being celebrated in accordance with the work ethic, simply disappeared from view. All labour should, according to Republicans, command respect. But some labour was apparently not seen as labour at all.[238]

Even more spectacularly, Senator Daniel Clark, in a passage we have also already noted, made the female population of his state vanish within a single sentence. When northerners referred to their "people," they normally, and quite reasonably, meant men, women and children; when they referred to "working men" they normally and quite reasonably meant only men. From this perspective the statement uttered by Clark, to the effect that "nine-tenths of all my people are working men," was literal nonsense. But it did demonstrate the ease with which wage labour was associated exclusively with men. Ironically Clark himself then specifically discussed the paid employment of women who worked in the mills of New Hampshire and he defended them as "excellent women" whose labor, he had observed, had been able to restore the fortunes of many an impoverished family. Of all wage work undertaken by women in the United States this was perhaps the most conspicuous and it had been in evidence since the earliest days of American industrialism. But Clark implied that even these women sought to be, and were, employed only on a temporary basis, combating a sudden family misfortune.[239]

This neglect of female gainful labour was common among Republicans. In all their descriptions of the northern social order, they discussed the labour of men but rarely the paid labour of women. It was not, of course, that women were supposed to be idle: rather they were assumed to be active as wives and mothers in the household in the manner prescribed by the doctrine of "separate spheres." Men worked outside the home for financial recompense, women worked within it, without financial recompense.[240]

---

238. *CG*, 35/1, p. 1025. See the analysis in Jeanne Boydston, *Home and Work: Housework, Wages, and the Ideology of Labor in the Early Republic* (New York, 1990), pp. 147–160.
239. *CG*, 35/1, App., p. 92.
240. See Nancy F. Cott, *The Bonds of Womanhood: 'Woman's Sphere' in New England, 1780–1835* (New Haven, CT, 1977); Linda Kerber, "Separate Spheres, Female Worlds, Woman's Place: The Rhetoric of Women's History," *Journal of American*

The problem, however, was that this domestic idyll bore little resemblance to the domestic reality. Even in middle class northern families, women were often engaged in money-earning activities of various kinds. In working class households such activities were in no sense marginal but instead were a fundamental necessity of everyday existence. Despite the ideology of separate spheres antebellum northern women were involved in a wide range of commercial activities, such as making shoes, hats, clothes, the churning of butter, street-peddling, as well as taking in lodgers and working as domestic servants. Even the middle-class woman's charitable endeavors often had an unmistakably commercial orientation and could be highly lucrative. Why then were these multifarious activities so badly misrepresented in the social commentaries of Republican (and other northern) statesmen?[241]

There are two possible reasons. First, there was a tendency in the antebellum North to assume that a family's status was enhanced if the wife was not employed for wages, and especially not employed outside the home. Thus a nonearning wife was, it has been suggested, a badge of middle class status. This may have helped obscure the full extent of female employment. Second, wage labour as we have noted had traditionally been associated with dependence,[242] itself viewed as a female trait. Accordingly the doctrine of separate spheres, no matter how poorly it described the social reality, had a key function to play: it allowed wage labour to be legitimated as a thoroughly and essentially masculine activity. Meanwhile the male wage labourer, as we have seen, could be honoured as the head of a family which itself stood outside the world of commerce.[243]

Unable to describe female labour with any accuracy, the Republicans were no more successful in some of their more general observations about northern wage labour. Lincoln's claim that only an eighth of the labour of the "country" was done by wage workers was an extremely nebulous

*History* LXXV (1988), pp. 9–39; Mary P. Ryan, *Cradle of the Middle Class: The Family in Oneida County, New York, 1790–1865* (New York, 1981); Carroll Smith-Rosenberg, *Disorderly Conduct: Visions of Gender in Victorian America* (New York, 1985).

241. Boydston, *Home and Work*, pp. 125–137; Mary Blewett, *Men, Women and Work: Class, Gender and Protest in the New England Shoe Industry, 1780–1910* (Urbana, IL, 1988); Lori D. Ginzberg, *Women and the Work of Benevolence: Morality, Politics and Class in the Nineteenth-Century United States* (New Haven, CT, 1990); Joan M. Jensen, *Loosening the Bonds: Mid-Atlantic Farm Women, 1750–1850* (New Haven, CT, 1986); Alice Kessler-Harris, *A Woman's Wage: Historical Meanings and Social Consequences* (Lexington, KY, 1990); Christine Stansell, *City of Women: Sex and Class in New York, 1789–1860* (New York, 1986).

242. Lincoln's remark, already noted, to the effect that those remaining wage labourers all their lives may well have had "a dependent nature" confirms that this association was still made.

243. This point is made very tellingly by Amy Dru Stanley – see Stanley, "Home Life and the Morality of the Market," pp. 84–85.

one since it was unclear what he meant by "country," unclear whether, in order to be included, such labour had to be performed by those employed for wages throughout their lives and unclear how those who worked part of the year for wages and part on the family farm were to be classified. There is little doubt, however, that his claim was far wide of the mark. The final years before the Civil War saw a large increase in the number of wage workers in the North. The 1850s, it has been argued, more than any other decade "saw the emergence of the wage-earner." By 1860, according to one estimate, the proportion of farm labourers even within the agricultural sector was as high as forty percent in some of the free states. In manufacturing, the proportion was, of course, very much higher and so it is perhaps the case that on the eve of the Civil War a majority of the gainfully employed northern population was working for wages.[244]

Moreover, contrary to the impression given by most Republicans, a significant amount of that labour was performed under the harshest conditions. The men who dug the canals or built the railroads of the North, for example, made a contribution to the northern economy whose importance it would be difficult to exaggerate but their lives did not and could not conform to the notions of middle-class respectability promulgated by Republican social commentators.[245] More generally those who were destitute or nearly destitute and who were driven to the larger cities as they lost their traditional means of support on the land received, as we have seen, a formal recognition in Republican thinking only to have their condition dismissed as aberrant or anomalous. Many Republicans agreed that the plight of thousands in the big cities was lamentable but denied that this was in any sense a necessary feature of a free-labour system.

Nor were the opportunities for social mobility anything like as plentiful as many Republicans believed. Although a few northerners went from rags to riches, the most common form of social mobility was within a specific class. Thus in Newburyport, Massachusetts, for example, in the third quarter of the nineteenth century "by far the most common form of social advance for members of laboring families" was "upward mobility

244. George Rogers Taylor, *The Transportation Revolution, 1815–1860* (New York, 1951), pp. 270–300; Bruce Levine, *Half Slave and Half Free: The Roots of Civil War* (New York, 1992), pp. 56–59; David Montgomery, *Beyond Equality* (New York, 1967), p. 27; Stanley Lebergott, *Manpower in Economic Growth: The American Record Since 1800* (New York, 1964), Lebergott, "The Pattern of Employment Since 1800," in Seymour Harris (ed.), *American Economic History* (New York, 1961), pp. 281–310, esp. 290–291: Lebergott's estimate that forty percent of the nation's workforce was employed for wages assuredly means, given the relatively low numbers of wage-workers in the South, that they were in a majority in the North.

245. There is a large secondary literature on the conditions of labour in antebellum America. For an excellent discussion of these conditions as they affected one group of unskilled workers, see Peter Way, *Common Labor: Workers and the Digging of North American Canals, 1780–1860* (Cambridge, 1993).

*within* the working class." This was an important development in that it allowed many workers to purchase houses or acquire savings, but it was not the movement out of the ranks of wage labour that Lincoln himself was so insistent upon.[246]

In retrospect it is clear that the northern free labour economy of 1860 was one in transition. Ahead, and only a few decades ahead, lay a world of corporate giants, of large labour unions, of factory production and of assembly lines. This was not the world of 1860. When Republicans extolled their society as one in harmony with human nature, it was the small shop, the village artisan and the small-scale manufacturing enterprise with an average of perhaps ten employees, they had in mind. This was the wage labour system as Republicans understood it on the eve of the Civil War.

## IX

As they embraced the wage-labour system of the North and showered praise upon the wage-worker, most Republicans demonstrated that they had left behind them the Jeffersonian identification of democracy with productive and especially landed property. It was no longer necessary to own land or other means of production in order to be a worthy member of a democratic polity. But although Republicans had in practice successfully discarded the older view, they were far less successful in disposing of the arguments that had supported it. In particular they experienced difficulties in refuting the old view that the inequalities inherent in the relationship

---

246. Joseph P. Ferrie, "The End of American Exceptionalism? Mobility in the United States since 1850," *Journal of Economic Perspectives*, XIX (2005), pp. 199–215; David W Galenson and Clayne L. Pope, "Economic and Geographic Mobility on the Farming Frontier: Evidence from Appanoose County, Iowa, 1850–1870," *Journal of Economic History*, XLIX (1989), pp. 635–655; Peter.Gottschalk, "Inequality, Income Growth, and Mobility: the Basic Facts," *Journal of Economic Perspectives*, XI (1997), pp. 21–40; David Bryan Grusky. *American Social Mobility in the 19th and 20th Centuries* (Madison, WI, 1986); Patricia Kelly Hall and Steven Ruggles, "Restless in the Midst of their Prosperity: New Evidence on the Internal Migration of Americans, 1850–2000," *Journal of American History*, XCI (2004), pp. 829–846; Steven Herscovici, "Migration and Economic Mobility: Wealth Accumulation and Occupational Change among Antebellum Migrants and Persisters," *Journal of Economic History*, LVIII (1998), pp. 927–956. Hartmut Kaelble, *Social Mobility in the Nineteenth and Twentieth Centuries: Europe and America in Comparative Perspective* (New York, 1986); J. R. Kearl and Clayne L. Pope, "Wealth Mobility: The Missing Element," *Journal of Interdisciplinary History*, XIII (1983), pp. 461–488; Cornelis A. Van Minnen and Sylvia L. Hilton (eds.), *Nation on the Move: Mobility in U.S. History* (Amsterdam, 2002); Edward Pessen, "The Egalitarian Myth and the American Social Reality: Wealth, Mobility and Equality in the 'Era of the Common Man,'" *American Historical Review*, LXXVI (1971), pp. 1004–1029; Stefan Thernstrom, *Poverty and Progress: Social Mobility in a Nineteenth-Century City* (Cambridge. MA, 1964), pp. 138–165.

between wage-worker and employer, between labour and capital, would subvert the democratic system. They needed to show that the inequalities that were functionally necessary to the operation of a capitalist economy, an economy in which some owned capital and others had no choice but to work for them (or for someone else), would not undermine the equality upon which a democratic polity was based. This was no easy task.

One obvious stratagem was to emphasise social mobility and, as we have seen, Republicans were not slow to adopt it. The esteem in which labour was held together with the incentives which northern society placed before the labourer himself, meant that the opportunities for social advancement in the North were, in Republican eyes, truly astounding. Many would probably have agreed with Henry Ward Beecher that "in the North, if the citizen chooses to walk in it, there is a road from every man's door to the Governor's chair or the Presidential seat." There were thus few if any social or structural obstacles confronting the individual, however poor his origins. According to many in the party, mobility both rested upon and perpetuated a classless society.[247]

Yet this was scarcely a satisfactory solution. As we have seen, most Republicans almost certainly did not believe, and were right not to believe, that all wage-workers could expect to rise into the ranks of the self-employed, still less that all would become employers themselves. Moreover, how could one be sure that superior wealth and income would not bring privileges which would subvert the equality of opportunity and of political rights upon which the northern economy and the northern polity rested and indeed, one might add, were legitimated? In a word, how could democracy survive the class divisions implicit in wage-labour capitalism?

Henry Ward Beecher gave an unusually extended discussion of this question in a speech of 1858 on the differences between North and South and his approach may help to illuminate the Republican attitude to the problem of class, not because all in the party thought precisely as he did, but rather because the very inadequacies of his reasoning demonstrate the difficulties they faced. Ironically these difficulties in effect confirm that those who had traditionally believed wage labour to be incompatible with democracy had been able to deploy some telling arguments.

Beecher claimed that in the North there were "no classes except such as rise out of spontaneous forces." By this he clearly meant that legitimate inequalities separated some groups from others. These would be based upon "wealth, experience, ability." But when Beecher tried to demonstrate that these distinctions were entirely benign, he began to encounter problems. He sought to establish that those with greater "wealth, experience, ability" would only constitute a superior group "as long as there

247. *Great Speech ... by Henry Ward Beecher*, p. 8.

is a *real* superiority." How could this be guaranteed? Beecher now fell back upon two classic bourgeois ideals, while perhaps sensing that neither separately nor together would they quite answer his purposes. One of these was the notion of equality before the law. The deserving social elite, he stressed, occupied its position "not by legal force, not to exercise any legal power, or to have one single privilege or prerogative, which does not belong just as much to every citizen clear down to the bottom." Since the rich did not possess additional political or legal rights, the threat they posed, he claimed, was much reduced.[248]

But this followed only if wealth did not bring social and economic privileges of its own to its holders and especially to their children. Consequently, Beecher at the same time argued that the educational system was crucially important in maintaining a classless society. Schools were vital in re-establishing equality and ensuring that one generation's advantages were not handed down to, and compounded in, the next. Common schools, he argued, were a means "by which every generation is led to a line and made to start equal and together":

> There will be inequality enough as soon as men get into life. Some shoot ahead; some, like dull sailors in a fleet, are dropped behind, and men are scattered all along the ocean. But the *Common* School gathers up their children and brings them all back again to take a new start together. Thus our schools are not mere whetstones to the intellect; they are institutions for evening up society; they resist the tendency to separation into classes, which grows with the prosperity of a community; they bind together, in cordial sympathy, all classes of citizens. For nothing is more tenacious than schoolday remembrances, and the last things that we forget are playmates and schoolchildren.

Here Beecher in effect made two claims. The first was that the school system genuinely equalised opportunities and the second was that, by bringing together those who would end up quite unequal, it bridged the social gulf that might otherwise open up. Both claims have been made many times since he wrote; both are open to severe criticism. In effect two alternative possibilities were left out of the reckoning. The first was that the inequalities of the parents' generation would enable the children of the rich to take greater advantage of the educational opportunities available. The second was that those inequalities would create cultural differences and preferences which would incline those children to associate with others from a similar background, however broadly based the school's intake.[249]

248.  *Great Speech ... by Henry Ward Beecher*, p. 9.
249.  *Great Speech ... by Henry Ward Beecher*, p. 11.

The claims about legal and educational equality, however, ignored a further problem: inherited wealth. Why should the rich not pass on their wealth to their children and thus subvert the next generation's equality of opportunity? This is, of course, a major difficulty for conservative social theorists. Inequality of outcomes, it is claimed, is legitimated by equality of opportunity but how can one be sure that unequal outcomes will not create unequal opportunities for the next generation? Few commentators can have dealt with this problem in a less satisfactory manner than Beecher. Having acknowledged that there were differences based upon "wealth, experience, ability," and that these might even be termed "class" differences, he then dismissed the dangers of inherited wealth in the most cavalier manner:

> All that a class *means* in the North is, that when men have shown themselves strong and wise, men give them honor for it. Death levels it all down again. Their children inherit nothing. They must earn for themselves. There is no diffusion of society into orders, by which some have privilege, and some have not, some have opportunity, and advantages which others have not.

In these remarkable lines Beecher simply brushed aside the problem of inherited wealth and then conflated the issues of legal privilege and economic opportunity. The decreed absence of inherited wealth meant that neither political nor economic privileges accrued to the children of the rich.[250]

In its essence Beecher's argument was quite as unoriginal as it was unconvincing. The notion that American society, and especially northern society, was uniquely fluid had been a recurrent Whig and even Federalist theme, especially in the northern states. Similarly the emphasis on the role of education as a guarantor of equal opportunity had strong Whig antecedents.[251] Yet the frequency with which these arguments were deployed before Beecher wrote is as nothing compared to the service they have performed since. More than a hundred years after Beecher wrote, President Lyndon B. Johnson boosted federal spending on education on the grounds that it would play a vital role in eliminating poverty and in ensuring that class distinctions did not disfigure American society. Beecher, it may be assumed, would have understood perfectly.

These continuities, together with the obvious weaknesses in the underlying social analysis, however, should not obscure the originality of Republican thought. As we have seen, Republicans had left behind them the fear and suspicion of democracy that Federalists and Whigs had so frequently

---

250. *Great Speech... by Henry Ward Beecher*, p. 9.
251. See Rush Welter, *The Mind of America, 1820–1860* (New York, 1975), p. 285.

displayed. They exhibited a confidence that has since become an integral part of mainstream American social and political thought. As they embraced capitalism, and as they recognised that some citizens were to be employers and others, equally worthy, would be wage-workers, perhaps for life, they took a long step towards the reconciliation of democracy and capitalism that has become the hallmark of the modern United States.

X

To the extent that Republicans misdescribed northern society, they could be charged with error. But there is a major question. was more than this involved? When Republicans overestimated the degree of social mobility in the North, for example, they were advancing a view that was of obvious benefit to the northern elites (since it tended to disable opposition to the northern social order). But what was the process involved? This is a question which historians have not yet answered.

One possible explanation might be in terms of a conspiracy by which the elites imposed a set of views which they knew to be false upon the rest of the community. The problem here is that not a shred of evidence exists to support this explanation. No conspiracy has ever been detected; nor has it been shown that the private beliefs of the elites did not match their public utterances Accordingly, historians have generally gone to the opposite extreme and concluded or rather assumed that the misperceptions were simply random and not explicable in terms of the interests of any specific group. Thus any benefit that the northern elites derived from these misperceptions was purely accidental. This view too is incorrect. We can understand the process better if we take an imaginary example.

Consider a newly established community in which for the first time, estimates of its social structure are generated. Two contradictory ones emerge. In the first the social order is thought to be fair and just, offering equal opportunities to all and in harmony with human nature. In the second the same social order is believed to be grossly unjust, denying real opportunities to large numbers of citizens, and at war with human nature. Now there is a tendency for the social elite, in all sincerity, mindful of its own merits, and aware of the effort and sacrifice it has perhaps made to attain its current position, to subscribe to the first view. It also tends to dismiss the other view as the wholly unjustified complaint of those who have lost in a fair contest. Moreover, the elite, by means of the power at its disposal, is able to propagate its preferred view very effectively. Each example of upward social mobility can be highlighted, with perfect sincerity and without any ulterior motive or nefarious intent. This view then becomes hegemonic. In an extreme case, the competing view will disappear entirely and poverty and injustice will be deemed "things of the past."

In this imagined scenario there is no hint of conspiracy or hypocrisy. There is no purposive action, no conscious intention to further the interest of the elite group or class. Yet it is clear that the interest of the elite has indeed been furthered and clear too that the process is not a random one. In this example class interest has actually helped produce the view that the society in question is classless.

Note also that it is scarcely possible to furnish evidence of this process. The historian can show that the idea of classlessness is prevalent in society but there is little else to trace, to detect or to comment upon. Nevertheless, it is rational to prefer this interpretation, which focuses upon the unintended but nonrandom furthering of class interests, to the alternatives. With the conspiracy theory one could point to the kind of evidence that would support it and then adduce the failure to find that evidence as an argument against the theory. No evidence when there can be none is better than no evidence when there could be some. And unlike the third interpretation – which reduces the class effect to coincidence – the view advanced here does not leave us to marvel at the number of times in which social theories, by the most extraordinary coincidence, just happen to benefit the dominant classes in society. Explanations for which there is no direct evidence but which imply a staggering degree of coincidence are weaker than explanations for which there is also no direct evidence but which imply no extraordinary coincidences at all. Although most historians believe they are empiricists whose task is to find evidence for all their claims, one must recognise that sometimes this simply is not possible and one must accept that there are other reasons for preferring one interpretation to another. Although this may be an alarming prospect to the empiricist, it is one from which there is, we may suggest, no escape!

## Secession and war, 1860–1861

### I

The crisis that propelled Abraham Lincoln into the White House simultaneously bequeathed to the new president, as he himself realised, problems greater than those faced by any of his predecessors. His election, of course, quickly triggered the secession of seven states of the Deep South and they had left the Union even before his inauguration. The five months between the election and the outbreak of hostilities were, in some respects, a time of great confusion even within Republican ranks in that on some of the most fundamental questions important differences of opinion were clearly discernible. Nonetheless, the course of the party in these months is readily intelligible in the light of its governing principles. Thus the belief that slavery was inherently a weak foundation for a society and a polity continued to inform Republican perceptions of the crisis, and ironically it underlay the most divergent, indeed contradictory, Republican responses to it. Similarly the confidence in majoritarian democracy and in the northern social system ensured that, despite some initial vacillation on the part of its head, the Lincoln administration would not acquiesce in secession, which was viewed as an explicit threat to that majoritarian democracy and an implicit threat to that social system.

## II

The rise of the Republican party in the North was viewed with trepidation by all other parties in the nation. The reason was simple: the Union might not survive the election of a Republican president. As we have seen, in 1850 many southerners had explicitly and publicly endorsed the Georgia platform, one of whose planks threatened secession in the event that the Wilmot Proviso became law. Since the Republicans' fundamental goal, indeed their *raison d'etre*, was the prevention of the spread of slavery, and since this had been the sole intent of the Proviso, Republican electoral triumphs, it seemed, jeopardised the very existence of the American republic.

This was how most groups viewed it. In 1856 the Republicans fought their first presidential campaign with John C. Frémont their first presidential candidate and they were welcomed into presidential politics by announcements from southerners like Robert Toombs of Georgia, John Slidell of Louisiana, Henry Wise and James Mason of Virginia to the effect that a Frémont victory would mean the end of the Union. The result was that some conservative northerners were intimidated into supporting Buchanan. Moreover former president Millard Fillmore of New York, himself a candidate for the White House that year, offered the same warning. He was only one of many northerners who announced that a Republican victory would imperil the Union.[252]

---

252. William L. Barney, *The Secessionist Impulse: Alabama and Mississippi in 1860* (Princeton, 1974), p. 165; Avery Craven, *The Coming of the Civil War* (Chicago, 1957), pp. 377–380; J. G. De Roulhac Hamilton, *Party Politics in North Carolina, 1835–1860* (Durham, NC, 1916), p. 180; Nevins, *House Dividing*, pp. 494–499; David M. Potter, *Lincoln and His Party in the Secession Crisis* rev ed. (Baton Rouge, 1995), pp. 2–3; Percy L. Rainwater, *Mississippi, Storm Center of Secession, 1856–1861* (Baton Rouge, 1938), pp. 35–38; Henry T. Shanks, *The Secession Movement in Virginia, 1847–1861* (Richmond, VA, 1934), pp. 52–54; Harold S. Schultz, *Nationalism and Sectionalism in South Carolina, 1852–1860: A Study of the Movement for Southern Independence* (new edition: New York, 1969), p. 126; Frank H. Severance

As the presidential election of 1860 approached, these threats and warnings reached a crescendo. According to one historian every governor but one, and almost every senator and representative, from each of the seven states of the Deep South was on record as favouring secession in the event of a Republican victory. This is perhaps a slight exaggeration but it does indicate the degree of danger that the nation now faced. Sometimes these threats were coupled with qualifications, whereby secession would only be adopted as a last resort. In fact many of these warnings were a highly accurate description of what actually transpired after the election of 1860 in that these potential disunionists sometimes made it clear that it would be the Republican programme, from which the victorious party should be allowed to recede, rather than the Republican victory itself, that would trigger secession. Nevertheless the overall message was clear and southerners of all persuasions together with the vast majority of northerners who were not Republican partisans, had no difficulty in deciphering it.[253]

The great majority of Republicans, however, reacted differently to these threats and warnings. They scorned them. Even before the new party was founded, Republicans-to-be dismissed all talk of secession. They were quite unmoved by the threats that southerners had made during the mid-century crisis. As we have already noted, George Julian in 1850, as befitted a radical, announced that he would rather see the Union divided than slavery extended but added that the threat from southerners was an idle one. He believed the real danger emanated not from slaveholders but instead from their northern allies who allowed themselves to be intimidated by wild threats. This was a common reaction. "To be sure," John G. Palfrey declared in 1852, "there is and has been no danger to the Union whatever." Instead the threat of secession was "a political stratagem" on the part of the Slave Power calculated to force the North to make concessions. It was a threat he could only listen to "with utter incredulity."[254]

This became a dominant Republican *motif* whenever secession was threatened. In 1856 prior to the party's first presidential campaign, Henry Wilson of Massachusetts announced in the Senate that the South would under no circumstances leave the Union; just as southerners had acquiesced in the election of a Republican speaker, despite much bluster and many threats, so they would accept a Republican president. In the same year, Hamilton Fish of New York declared that the "jails and lunatic

(ed.), "The Millard Fillmore Papers," *Publications of the Buffalo Historical Society.* 2 vols. X (1907), II, p. 21.
253. Dwight L. Dumond, *The Secession Movement, 1860–1861*(New York, 1931), p. 99. See, for example, Jefferson Davis, Speech at Corinth, Sept. 21, 1860, in Lynda Lasswell Crist (ed.), *The Papers of Jefferson Davis* (Baton Rouge, 1989), VI, p. 365.
254. Julian, *Speeches*, pp. 27, 47; [Palfrey], *Five Years Progress of the Slave Power*, pp. 56–58. CG, 30/2, App., p. 316.

asylums" would prove to be "of sufficient capacity to accommodate" all disunionists while Abraham Lincoln dismissed "all this talk about the dissolution of the Union" as "humbug," partly because southerners would simply not be allowed to break up the nation.[255]

After 1856 the same process continued. In 1858, with a Dickensian flourish, the *Atlantic Monthly* derided the idea of secession as "a threat as hollow as the mask from which it issues, as harmless as the periodical suicides of Mantalini, as insincere as the spoiled child's refusal of his supper." Some southerners at this time were threatening to leave the Union if Kansas were not allowed to enter as a slave state and their failure to carry out the threat almost certainly deepened the Republicans' scorn. By 1860 therefore, southern threats of disunion were entirely familiar to Republicans, and they were greeted with the standard response. Indeed as southern threats became increasingly shrill so the Republican response became, if anything, increasingly dismissive. Thus the leading Republican newspaper in the North, the New York *Tribune* announced that "the South could no more unite upon a scheme of secession than a company of lunatics could conspire to break out of bedlam." Reference to lunatic asylums and mental disorders were common in the final months of the antebellum republic; the *New York Times*, for example, described those northerners who heeded southern threats of disunion as "simpletons." Yet Republicans believed that common sense would reassert itself in the South, provided it were not banished from the North. And this in turn depended upon northerners standing firm. William Seward, until 1860 or perhaps even early 1861 the foremost Republican statesman in the land, offered a commentary on southern attitudes to the Union. "They cry out," he noted, "that they will tear the Union to pieces." But, he asked an audience at St Paul Minnesota in September 1860, "who's afraid?" He answered his own question: "Nobody's afraid. Nobody can be bought." An even more important Republican, Abraham Lincoln, in a letter written some months before his election, explained that the good sense of southerners would, if allowed to reassert itself, ensure the preservation of the Union. "The people of the South," he announced, "have too much of good sense and good temper to attempt the ruin of the government rather than see it administered as it was administered by the men who made it. At least, so I hope and believe."[256]

255. CG, 34/1, App., p. 394; *Frémont the Conservative Candidate: Correspondence between Hon. Hamilton Fish...and Hon. James A. Hamilton* (n.p., n.d.), p. 11; Basler (ed.), *Works of Lincoln*, II, p. 355.

256. *Atlantic Monthly* I (1858), p. 757; New York *Tribune*, July 12, 1860; *New York Times*, July 11, 1860; Baker (ed.), *Works of Seward*, IV, p. 344; Lincoln to John B. Fry, Aug. 15, 1860, quoted in Potter, *Lincoln and His Party*, p. 18. See also CG, 31/1, App., p. 480; *Speech of Richard Yates....Springfield Nov 20, 1860*, p. 4.

For their part, former Democrats within the Republican ranks were equally contemptuous of the threat of secession, which they too viewed as merely a ploy adopted by the Slave Power. The fact that they had repeatedly encountered it from their archenemy, John C. Calhoun, and the fact that their hero, Andrew Jackson, had denounced it unflinchingly made their response as uncompromising as that of the radicals. Timothy Day of Ohio in 1856 was one of many who condemned Millard Fillmore for countenancing and thus effectively condoning southern threats of secession in the event of a Republican victory that year. "It is to such men and their followers," he announced, "that the Union owes whatever of danger it may be in." Once again, as Kinsley Bingham of Michigan pointed out, it was northern timidity rather than southern separatism that actually threatened the Union.[257]

It is of course, clear with hindsight that the Republicans were making a colossal error here. Moreover, the fact that virtually all non-Republicans avoided the error and appreciated the gravity of the threat confirms that it is not only with hindsight that the Republicans can be found wanting. Nor can the fact that southerners had made such threats before be cited in extenuation. Everyone, at all points on the political spectrum, recognised that a Republican victory in the 1860 presidential election was far more portentous than, for example, the refusal to admit Kansas as a slave state in 1858 or the election of a Republican speaker. The Republican victory of 1860, it was all but universally believed, had opened a new era in the politics of the American Republic. Why then did the Republicans make so major an error?

The underlying intellectual process was the one we have already encountered. Lincoln was confident that the South would not leave a Union that, under a Republican president, would be governed according to the historic principles of the founding fathers. Here once again was the Republican assumption that their policies were natural, on this occasion in the sense that they were in harmony with the essential and eternal values of the nation.

There were other assumptions underlying the Republican failure to appreciate the dangers of secession. Foremost among them was the conviction that slavery was inherently weak and needed the Union to survive. This, of course, had long been the position of William Lloyd Garrison, Wendell Philips and some other immediatists, who had then characteristically driven this principle to its logical extreme by actually advocating disunion as a sure route to abolition. Few Republicans went so far but

---

257. *The Humbug and the Reality: An Address of the Hon. Timothy C. Day of Ohio to his Constituents* (n.p., n.d.), p. 4; Fuller (ed.), *Messages of the Governors of Michigan*, II, p. 297. See also Weston, *Who Are Sectional*, pp. 3–4.

many did believe that southerners would not dare to leave a Union whose support was needed to shore up an inherently rickety social system. For the radicals Charles Sumner pointed out that disunion would aggravate the South's problem with fugitive slaves and also cut her off from future territorial expansion. Thus the threat of secession could be discounted. John G. Palfrey went further and echoed the Garrisonian view that disunion would mean abolition, since the slaveholders needed the protection of the North. Similarly Henry Wilson in 1856 claimed that there was not "a mother in the South who would not clasp her babe closer to her bosom if she believed this Union would be dissolved." According to Wilson "the men who fling out this idle threat [of secession] know that they sleep peacefully at night because the Union does stand, and they have the power of this government to protect them."[258]

Many Republicans thus held that the Union was an indispensable support for slavery. William Seward believed it was the slaveholders' greatest defence and hence if they ever left it they would quickly return. Yet Seward, who for the first few months of the secession crisis acted as the Republicans' leader and spokesman, had also believed for many years that southerners wielded an immense and entirely disproportionate influence within the federal government. How had this been achieved? It was not because of slavery's inherent strengths but rather in spite of its inherent weaknesses. "I do not believe," he declared, "there has been one day from 1787 until now when slavery had any power in the government, except what it derived from buying up men of weak virtue, little principle and great cupidity, and terrifying men of weak nerves in the free states." Here was the explanation for the disproportionate southern power and influence in the federal government and here too the way in which it could be eradicated. It was necessary merely to wait and do nothing. Then the danger would evaporate; self-interest would impel southerners to cling to the Union. According to Salmon P. Chase, "all men must see that disunion is no remedy for the slave States." The cry, which had been heard so many times in the past, was thus "to alarm the timid, the sensitive, the unreflecting." For the Democratic-Republicans George Weston reiterated that the North protected the South and concluded that self-interest alone would keep the South in the Union forever. Indeed so great was the support that the Union provided for the slaveholder that the threat of disunion was, in the words of Samuel Foot, "too preposterous to be worthy of the serious notice of a sensible man." This was the reasoning that led so many Republicans to conclude that it was not southern threats of

---

258. *Works of Sumner*, IV, pp. 295–296; [Palfrey], *Five Years Progress of the Slave Power*, p. 56; CG, 34/1, App., p. 394.

disunion that were the danger, but rather northern capitulation to those threats.[259]

When these Republicans talked of the slaveholders' need for the Union they did not always pinpoint the benefits it offered them. Usually they had in mind the threat posed by the slaves themselves because of the dangers of either flight (which would be far easier if the North were a separate nation) or even insurrection (which southerners would then have to quell without any assistance from northerners via the federal government). At the same time, however, Republicans were convinced that there was latent Unionist and even antislavery sentiment in the South which would erupt, if secession were attempted. As we shall see, no belief was more important than this in the final weeks and months before war broke out.

As the presidential election approached, Republicans continued to scoff at the threat of secession. It was, according to the Hartford *Evening Press*, "an empty sham" in that "those who make it have not the remotest intention of fulfilling it, or if a few of them have, their enterprise has as about as good a chance of succeeding as the lunatics in the Retreat at Hartford would have of capsizing the state of Connecticut into Long Island Sound." Such men were simply "too few and too crazy." Election Day was November 6, 1860. On November 12, as the states of the Deep South began their preparations to leave the Union, the Boston *Daily Atlas and Bee* announced that "nobody in the free States need feel any anxiety about secession." "The slave States," the editor observed, "have neither the right, the power, nor the inclination to secede – therefore they will not." On December 13, the New York *Evening Post* expressed doubts whether even a single state would secede. Seven days later South Carolina left the Union.[260]

### III

Even as their predictions about secession were being proved hopelessly wrong, most Republicans shifted their ground only slightly. Many continued to believe that the secession movement would soon collapse, borne down in effect by its own absurdities. According to the Pittsburgh *Gazette*, southerners had threatened secession and now had to appear to be going

259. Baker (ed.), *Works of Seward*, III, p. 248. IV, pp. 344–345; CG, 31/1, App., p. 480; *Will the South Dissolve the Union?*, pp. 6–7; Foot, *Reasons for Joining Republican Party*, p. 7. See also *Works of Sumner*, IV, pp. 295–296.
260. Hartford *Evening Press*, Oct. 25, 26, 1860; Boston *Daily Atlas and Bee*, Nov. 12, 1860 in Howard C. Perkins (ed.), *Northern Editorials on Secession*. 2 vols. (Gloucester, MA, 1942), I, pp. 65–66, 88–91; Kenneth M. Stampp, *And The War Came: The North and the Secession Crisis, 1860–1861* (Chicago, 1950), p. 14.

ahead with it. But "it would be the madness of folly . . . to treat these men as being in earnest," since "in less than a month this farce will be played out." The reason was simple: "within that time the true Union sentiment of the South will develop itself." Here was a vital Republican assumption.[261]

It was shared by virtually all members of the party. According to the New York *Tribune*, "the agitation raised in the South will gradually and surely subside into peace." This was inevitable since "the great majority of Southerners" did not mean to dissolve the Union but rather "simply mean to bully the Free States into concessions." Edward Bates, a conservative within the Republican ranks, was convinced that "the real people" would "rebel against the traitors, and compel a return to allegiance." Republicans differed as to the policy required to revitalise the Union forces in the South. As we shall see, there were four possible courses of action open to Republicans once secession had been attempted. First, they could do nothing, pursue a policy of "masterly inactivity," neither approving secession, nor taking any steps to prevent it, and wait for sanity to return. Second, they could resort to force. Third, they could embark upon compromises and concessions. Fourth, they could simply allow secession to occur peaceably. Each of these strategies had its advocates and ironically each was advocated, in part, as a way of revitalising southern unionism. Hamilton Fish, of New York, for example, believed that concessions to the border states would bring the Cotton States back. William Pitt Fessenden, of Maine, by contrast, argued that secession would have been quashed immediately if the president had done his duty and enforced the laws, while Lyman Trumbull was confident as late as January 1861 that the seceding states would return within a few months if a firm, uncompromising approach were adopted. Thus the apparently contradictory approaches of concession and coercion each, in part, rested upon a shared assumption about the immanent strength of southern unionism.[262]

Some of those advocating force believed with the New York *Tribune* that secession was little more than a bluff and that the secessionists would back down when the bluff was called. Others meanwhile argued that a refusal either to compromise or to accept secession would immeasurably strengthen the Unionist cause within the South. Thus John Sherman was convinced that "in thirty days we could have a large minority or even a majority in every seceding state for maintaining the Union, if the leaders in resisting secession could feel sure of backing." In effect Sherman

261. Pittsbugh *Daily Gazette*, Nov. 14, 1860 in Perkins (ed.), *Northern Editorials on Secession*, I, p. 92.
262. New York, *Tribune*, Nov. 20, 1860; Pease (ed.), *Diary of Browning*, p. 457; Potter, *Lincoln and His Party*, pp. 237–238.

assumed that a resolute Republican president would be able to counteract the Slave Power within the South and thus allow latent (and natural) Unionist sentiment to emerge in triumph.[263]

We shall consider the policy of peaceable secession later. But it is important to note that the other policy, "masterly inactivity," was also calculated to foster Unionist sentiment within the South. In February 1861 the New York *Tribune* announced that since to southerners "the benefits of the Union are really so much greater... than its evils," then "the common-sense of the People will make the runaway States soon beg for readmission into the Old Union, provided that open war can be avoided." Hence a do-nothing policy was entirely appropriate. This serves to remind us that "masterly inactivity" and an opposition to all proposals for compromise was in no sense intended as a policy of surrender to, or acquiescence in, a permanent disruption of the Union. Rather the goal was simply to give time for common sense, the values of the Union and, to a considerable extent, those of the Republican party and of human nature itself, to triumph in the South. Later in the month, the *Tribune* went so far as to announce that the President and Vice-President of the Confederacy, Jefferson Davis and Alexander Stephens "would gladly get back into the Union." This, the *Tribune* assured its readers, was "well known."[264]

William Seward, although heavily criticised by his former ally and *Tribune* editor, Horace Greeley, nevertheless fully shared the *Tribune*'s faith in southern unionism. He proposed some concessions to the South and though, as we shall see, they were extremely limited in scope, they were enough to disappoint and anger Greeley and some other Republicans. But he advocated them on the grounds that they would "open the way for the rising of a Union party in the seceding States which will bring them back into the Union." As a result he too was highly optimistic about the nation's future even after secession was under way. On December 22, two days after South Carolina had seceded, Seward made a major speech to the New England Society in New York city. He displayed a breezy confidence. Seward dismissed the idea of a separate state or separate states existing on the North American continent as absurd; there could be no such thing "in reason," "in philosophy" or (most revealingly, perhaps) "in nature." South Carolina, he announced, might make complaints but these should not be taken too seriously, since "if there were nobody to hear the State of South Carolina when she is talking, she would confess that she liked us tolerably well." Hence her leaders could not "humbug me," could not "humbug you" and "I do not believe... will much longer

263. Sherman to F. P. Blair Jr, Feb. 9, 1861 quoted in Potter, *Lincoln and His Party*, p. 238.
264. New York, *Tribune*, Feb. 1, 14, 1861. As we shall see, however, the *Tribune* sometimes advocated, though with much equivocation, peaceable secession.

succeed in humbugging themselves." Introducing a marital analogy (in an age where divorce was extremely uncommon), Seward observed that every man could "keep his wife if he wants to do so;" he merely needed "to keep his own virtue and his own temper." And this was the approach he intended to adopt with regard to the states of the Deep South:

> If we keep entirely cool, and entirely calm, and entirely kind, a debate will ensue which will be kindly in itself; and it will prove very soon, either that we are wrong – and we shall concede to our offended brethren – or else that we are right, and they will acquiesce and come back into fraternal relations with us.

Thus Seward expected to conduct a harmonious debate with southern secessionists, to redress any reasonable objections to Republican policy, though without any real surrender of principle, and to see all unreasonable ones withdrawn. How could he be so confident? It was "because I know that the necessities which made this Union . . . are stronger to-day than they were when the Union was made and that these necessities are enduring, while the passions of men are short-lived and ephemeral." Thus once again unionism would triumph. Seward concluded by assuring his audience that secession was weaker now than on election night and would become weaker still with each passing day.[265]

As we shall see, Lincoln soon after his inauguration would feel compelled to override Seward, by then his Secretary of State. But this was not because he rejected Seward's assessment of Unionist sentiment within the South. As we have seen, Lincoln too had been confident before the election that secession would not occur. When this had been proved incorrect he continued to believe that it represented the views of an aberrant minority of southerners and even professed to be pleased that secessionists were now attempting to whip up a crisis. When fellow Illinoisan Lyman Trumbull made a speech in Springfield on November 20, Lincoln inserted a passage into it in which he gave assurances that the southern states would not be molested by the incoming administration. Slavery in the states, he promised, would not be attacked. Now that this assurance had been given to the South, Lincoln believed, secessionist sentiment would evaporate. The president-elect went further and announced that it was "extremely fortunate for the peace of the country" that the Republicans could now state their position because this would seal the doom of the disunionists. With the secessionists "'now or never' is the maxim" because "they can not, much longer, maintain apprehension among the Southern

---

265. Seward to Lincoln, Jan. 27, 1861 quoted in Nevins, *The Emergence of Lincoln: Prologue to Civil War, 1859–1861* (New York, 1950), p. 431. Potter, *Lincoln and His Party*, pp. 242–243.

people that their homes, ... and lives, are to be endangered." Lincoln then went still further and explained that he was "rather glad of this military preparedness in the South" since "it will enable the people the more easily to suppress any uprisings there," which the secessionists' "misrepresentations of [Republican] purposes may have encouraged." In other words the people of the South, having understood the true principles and policies of the Republicans, which were after all those to which the nation had been consecrated, would turn the military preparations intended to facilitate secession against the secessionists themselves. This would indeed be a triumphant, in fact the ultimate, resurgence of southern unionism.[266]

Lincoln has been severely criticised by some historians for this huge underestimate of the dangers facing the nation.[267] Undoubtedly the error was of enormous significance, since it necessarily placed the president-elect in opposition to all the most significant compromise proposals that were put forward during the secession winter. But the mistake was common among Republicans and it stemmed once again from the assumption that the majority of southerners would inevitably rally to the values of the Republican party and of the nation, once they understood them and had an opportunity to do so. These were values that corresponded to the most cherished goals and ambitions of free men (and women). How could free men be indifferent to the values of humanity? So strong was this belief that as late as July 1861 (and beyond) Lincoln continued to believe that secession was in essence a *coup d'état*, organised by a small minority who had successfully duped or bullied the majority of southerners. "It may well be questioned," the President announced, in his 4th July Message, delivered after almost two months of war, "whether there is to-day a majority of the legally qualified voters of any State except perhaps South Carolina in favor of disunion." "There is," he declared, "much reason to believe that the Union men are the majority in many if not in every other one, of the so-called seceded States."[268]

By this time war had come. But until the very last, Lincoln and many others had continued to pin their faith on a revival of southern unionism.

266. Lincoln memorandum quoted in Potter, *Lincoln and His Party*, p. 141.
267. Nevins, for example, accuses Lincoln of being "deplorably complacent" regarding the danger of secession – see Nevins, *Prologue to Civil War*, p. 298. See also Potter, *Lincoln and His Party*, pp. 141, 246; Gabor S. Boritt. "'And the War Came'? Abraham Lincoln and the Question of Responsibility," in Boritt (ed.), *Why the Civil War Came* (New York, 1996), pp. 3–30.
268. Basler (ed.), *Works of Lincoln*, IV, p. 438. The historian Daniel Crofts has expressed some doubt as to whether Lincoln really believed this. However, it should be noted that: (a) he was not alone in the belief, (b) it sprang from fundamental attitudes and assumptions that had been in place ever since, indeed even before, the creation of the Republican party, (c) some historians even now think the opinion was correct, (d) there is no evidence for this charge (e.g., private utterances that were at odds with the public ones) – see Crofts, introduction to Potter, *Lincoln and His Party*, p. xxv.

This should serve to remind us that the Republican failure to acknowledge first the likelihood of secession and then the danger that it posed was not primarily a consequence of personal weakness or individual shortcoming. Rather these misapprehensions were a consequence of deeply held beliefs, beliefs that were an integral part of a coherent Republican ideology which, as we have seen, had strong roots in northern society and the northern economy.

## IV

Of the courses of action open to Republicans, inactivity, compromise, coercion, or peaceable secession, one might have thought that the last represented an acknowledgement that Unionist sentiment in the South was, after all, too weak to combat the threat of secession. It appeared to be an admission that the seceding states could and should not be held in the Union against their will and that it was indeed their will to secede. But appearances were deceptive and the policy requires careful examination.

It should be noted at the outset that there was no precedent for using force against a single state. Although Andrew Jackson had prepared to do exactly that against South Carolina in 1832, it had not proved necessary. Accordingly, many Republicans could not imagine a Union whose integrity could be maintained only by force. (This was an even more difficult prospect for northern Democrats, with their deep commitment to state's rights, to entertain.) Thus Greeley's *Tribune* just after the election hoped "never to live in a republic whereof one section is pinned to the residue by bayonets."[269]

Some of those who made such pronouncements and who also followed the *Tribune* in opposing concessions might have been thought to be in favour of peaceable separation, but as we have seen there was in fact a fourth policy open to the Republicans and this was the policy of "masterly inactivity." Historians must therefore not ignore this option and thereby overestimate the number of Republicans who favoured separation. Nevertheless there were those who advocated this policy and at their head stood Greeley's enormously influential New York *Tribune*. "If the Cotton States shall become satisfied that they can do better out of the Union than in it," the newspaper observed after Lincoln's victory, "we insist on letting them go in peace."[270]

Yet this was a highly misleading remark. To begin with, the renunciation of force was in part a tactical matter. As the paper acknowledged, the fear was that force would help the secessionist cause and propel the states of the

269. New York *Tribune*, Nov. 9, 1860.
270. New York *Tribune*, Nov. 9, 1860.

Upper South out of the Union too. More important, the offer of peaceable secession was hedged about with so many restrictions and qualifications that it was virtually meaningless. The *Tribune* insisted that secession be the wish of a settled majority of the people of the states concerned and as late as February 1861 denied that this had been demonstrated even for South Carolina. As for the other states the situation was much clearer: the people did not want secession and until they had had a chance to speak, secession would be "a foul conspiracy." It will be recalled that Republicans were quite convinced that free elections and freedom of expression were in any case impossible in the slave states; hence it followed that they would never really be able to recognise secession as the authentic expression of majority southern opinion. As late as June 1861, almost two months after the outbreak of war, the *Tribune* demanded "a fair chance to disabuse" the people of the South and then "a fair peaceful election." What would be the result? When misrepresentation and intimidation ceased, the South "would give a Union majority tomorrow."[271]

Moreover, the *Tribune*, like other Republican newspapers and spokesmen, sought to distinguish between the use of coercion, which was unacceptable, and the enforcement of the nation's laws, which was entirely legitimate, indeed essential. Again conceding the right to secede (if a settled majority wished it), the *Tribune* then insisted that actions the Confederacy had recently undertaken were nevertheless unacceptable. Robbing arsenals and seizing forts, it was said, made the government "a farce." (Southerners of course, saw these actions very differently, as the legitimate acts of a sovereign government.) Similarly, the *Tribune* passed comment on those in the Upper South who were insisting that there be no coercion of the cotton states. The result was to impose upon us "a Government which cannot be enforced!" and "laws which inflict no penalty in case of their violation." Thus Greeley was willing to contemplate the use of force in certain circumstances, even though he formally repudiated the policy of coercion. Whether a specific action constituted "coercion" or was instead the "enforcement of the laws" was difficult to determine: all too often a secessionist's "coercion" was a Republican's "enforcement of the laws."[272]

Finally, we should note that even when it acknowledged a possibility of peaceable secession, the *Tribune*, in common with other Republican newspapers, argued that the North would be left with a proper government whereas the South, as a result of her inherent weaknesses, would

271.  New York *Tribune*, Dec. 17, 1860, Feb. 23, June 3, 1861 in Perkins (ed.), *Northern Editorials on Secession*, I, pp. 199, 259–260, II, p. 975.
272.  New York *Tribune*, Feb. 23, 27, 1860 in Perkins (ed.), *Northern Editorials on Secession*, I, 259–260, 287–288; Stampp, *And the War Came*, p. 37.

have "an aggregated disintegration, a rope of sand, a tossing, incoherent chaos of petty nationalities." The result would be even now a belated triumph for southern unionism as each slave state would feel itself, for its own interests, compelled to abolish slavery and then limp back into the Union.[273]

Other Republicans who recommended, or seemed to recommend, peaceable secession displayed similar attitudes. And it is striking that those who had argued strongly against force and warned of the dangers of war quickly rallied to the Union banner after the firing on Fort Sumter. Thus although peaceable secession had its advocates within the Republican party, they were very much in a minority and the policy was so heavily qualified and tightly restricted that it was quite unable to effect a lasting settlement between North and South.

The Republican rejection of disunion as a solution to the nation's problems was in a fundamental sense inherent in the party's ideology and outlook. The different groups who made up the party had various compelling reasons to oppose it. As we have seen, the former Democrats came from a tradition in which the Union was utterly sacrosanct. Similarly, conservative Republicans had always placed unionism at the center of their creed; this indeed was the principal legacy of their favourite statesman, Henry Clay. The distinguishing feature of the conservative Republican was his insistence that the Union was even more important than antislavery. Moderates like Lincoln, on the other hand, believed that the Union and antislavery were inseparable, twin ideals, neither of which could be jeopardised for the other. It was the duty of the Republican party to establish, or as they would have put it, re-establish, an antislavery Union. This leaves only the Radicals. This group did indeed put antislavery ahead of the Union and, as a result, had occasionally flirted with disunion. But these dalliances had occurred when the radicals had begun to despair of the Union, when they had believed it hopelessly enthralled to the Slave Power. Such pessimism had surfaced for example when Texas was annexed or when the Free Soil party had gone down to heavy defeat in 1848, or when the Kansas-Nebraska Act had been passed or after Frémont had lost in 1856. In 1860, however, the position was reversed: the Slave Power had been dealt the most crippling blow it had received in sixty years and the Union, it was now hoped, was set fair to become an agent of freedom and emancipation. Hence the secession crisis occurred at the very time the radicals were least prepared to countenance a break-up of the nation. As a result they too were fundamentally opposed to disunion and the policy of peaceable secession.[274]

273.  New York *Tribune*, Feb. 27, 1860 in Perkins (ed.), *Northern Editorials on Secession*,
      I, p. 288.
274.  Foner, *Free Soil*, pp. 138–143.

## V

The rejection of peaceable secession left as active options only coercion or concession. There were various schemes of compromise put forward in the secession winter of 1860–1861 including some which contained only a single provision. But four proposals or sets of proposals came to command most attention and with hindsight it is apparent that it was upon the success of these that hopes of avoiding conflict ultimately rested.[275]

The single most important scheme was put forward by John J. Crittenden of Kentucky, heir of Henry Clay and like Clay a slaveholder, a Unionist and a leading advocate of compromise between North and South. The Crittenden Compromise was amended in the course of discussion but by January 22 it had been finally rejected. At this time a new set of proposals was put forward by a committee of fourteen congressmen from the lower North and the Upper South which became known as the border state plan. Meanwhile the House had set up a Committee of Thirty-Three charged with devising a set of compromise proposals and these were reported in mid-January. They formed the basis of a third prospective settlement. Finally a Peace Conference was convened in Virginia in February and its recommendations constituted a fourth.

The schemes had some features in common. Each of them proposed a new constitutional amendment to protect slavery in the states where it already existed. And all were based in part upon an extension of the Missouri Compromise line at 36° 30' which had formerly marked the boundary between slave and free territory in the lands of the Louisiana Purchase. The proposals nevertheless differed in their approach to the territorial issue. The Committee of Thirty-Three proposed to finesse the question by admitting all existing territory south of 36°30' (which meant New Mexico) as states immediately. (Slavery would thus be allowed in New Mexico, which currently had a slave code though few slaves, but would have no prospects for expansion elsewhere). The Crittenden Compromise (in its amended form) instead explicitly forbade slavery North of 36°30' and also introduced a slave code for all territories south of that line, whether already in existence or to be acquired in the future. The Peace Conference proposal was identical to the Crittenden scheme except that it did not explicitly allow slavery in southern territory acquired later but instead required that at least half the Senators from each of North and South agree to any territorial acquisitions. Finally the border state plan also prohibited slavery north of 36°30' (either by law or constitutional amendment) and also prohibited both the federal government and a territorial legislature from interfering with slavery south of that parallel.

---

275. The best analysis of the different compromise schemes is provided by Crofts, *Reluctant Confederates*, pp. 195–214.

In one variant it also placed restrictions on the acquisition of future territory.

The most important set of proposals was embodied in the Crittenden Compromise. In addition to its clauses on slavery in the states and the territories it denied the power of the federal government to abolish slavery in federal forts and dockyards and in the District of Columbia, it guaranteed compensation to slaveholders who could not recover fugitive slaves and it expressly prevented the federal government from obstructing the movement of slaves over state lines. Finally it stipulated that these clauses were to be incorporated as constitutional amendments and were themselves to be unamendable.

With hindsight it is clear that the secession of the Cotton States could not have been reversed by any of the proposals that came to light after the end of January 1861. Having seceded in December and January these states raced ahead with the formation of the Confederate States of America and showed their scorn for compromise by refusing even to send delegates to the Virginia Peace Conference, which convened on February 4, 1861, the very day delegates met in Montgomery, Alabama to set up the Confederacy.[276] By this time the statesmen of the Deep South had realised that the Republicans were not prepared to give sufficient ground.

Although the crucial questions were those concerning the status of slavery in the territories, even the guarantee offered to slavery in the states where it already existed proved highly controversial among Republicans. This measure finally passed Congress and would have become the thirteenth amendment had other events not supervened. But the proposal obtained the support of only forty percent or so of the Republicans in Congress. The reason was not that they claimed the intention or even the right to abolish slavery where it existed but rather that they objected to the constitution, which as Republicans were fond of reminding themselves contained no explicit mention of slavery, being polluted by direct reference to the institution. (To southerners of course their votes merely confirmed that it was sheer hypocrisy for Republicans to disavow any intention of interfering with slavery in the states). Republicans were also prepared, as their votes on at least one occasion confirmed, to admit New Mexico as a slave state (though almost certainly in the knowledge that slavery was already moribund there). But this was as far as they were prepared to go. The great majority of Republicans refused to countenance an extension of the Missouri Compromise line and this in effect doomed any hope of compromise.[277]

---

276. Arkansas also refused to send delegates.
277. These events may be followed in Crofts, *Reluctant Confederates*, Potter, *Lincoln and His Party*, Stampp, *And the War Came*, as well as many other accounts.

The timing of events during the secession crisis was of some importance here. As we have seen, Republicans were extremely slow to identify the crisis. This might not have mattered if they had then acted quickly. But as we have also seen, the belief in a latent southern unionism was of paramount importance. Many, perhaps most, Republicans believed that it was necessary merely to wait for sanity to return, or alternatively for the forces of unionism to regroup and for secession to collapse. The highest priority was to avoid any precipitate action. This was the rationale for "masterly inactivity." In other words although speedy action was required if a compromise were to be hammered out, Republicans were impelled by their fundamental beliefs to pursue a policy of inaction. The very development that ultimately discredited the policy, the establishment of the Confederacy, meant that it was now too late to offer compromises.

Yet this was not the main reason for the failure of compromise. The key fact was that even if the timing had been right and the opportunity had been present, Republicans did not choose to compromise on the basic issues. This was scarcely surprising. After all a party whose central idea was that slavery should be opposed because it disorganised a community politically, economically and, many added, morally could scarcely be expected to relinquish a major election victory under the threat of an infinitely greater degree of disorganisation. Peaceable secession, as we have seen, would have been the ultimate in political disorganisation but significant compromises, which would have been further evidence of the Slave Power at work, were almost as bad.

The Republicans, it should be noted, were being asked to abandon their most cherished principles. Their party had come into existence to prevent further capitulations on the part of northerners to the slave interest. Now they were being asked, at the very moment of triumph, to capitulate again. In part their refusal was motivated by pride since, as Henry Waldron told the House of Representatives in 1860, "the man who allows a menace to control his suffrage is only fit to be a slave." As we have also seen, Republicans believed that most of these threats were in any case idle and southerners either did not want, or would not be able, to carry them out. But even more important was the conviction that a surrender to these threats would not cure but would instead aggravate the nation's problems.[278]

Here the historian has to contend with the problem of hindsight. It is difficult to imagine any crisis more acute than that into which the nation was plunged between 1861 and 1865 and it is clear that that one was

278. CG, 36/1, p. 1872. See also Ronald P. Formisano, *The Birth of Mass Parties: Michigan, 1827–1861* (Princeton, 1971), p. 326; Robert Cook, *Baptism of Fire: The Republican Party in Iowa, 1838–1878* (Ames, Iowa, 1994), pp. 131–132.

at least in part attributable to the Republicans' failure to offer major concessions to the South. But this was not how the situation appeared to Republicans in the crucial months of 1860 and 1861.

It was not that all compromise was unacceptable.[279] As we have seen, many Republicans were prepared to compromise on the question of a constitutional amendment guaranteeing slavery in the States. One of these was William Seward. Seward was also prepared to allow New Mexico (perhaps joined to Arizona) to enter the Union as a slave state. He would also make concessions regarding fugitive slaves and he favoured laws to prevent armed incursions into the South, such as that attempted by John Brown. But he would not accept the Crittenden Compromise. The sticking point for him and for other Republicans was the possibility of a further extension of slavery, almost certainly into territory subsequently to be acquired. This was the one feature of the Crittenden Compromise that offered southerners the hope that they might escape their doom in a Union otherwise dominated by free states and for precisely that reason it was unacceptable to Republicans. The prospect of further extensions of slavery would simply invite more pressure from southerners for new territory, would then create more northern "doughfaces" and would thus encourage the very processes that the Republican party had been designed to arrest.[280]

This was also Lincoln's view. The president-elect gradually made his opinions known after his election victory. He made it clear that he favoured concessions to the South on some issues. "As to fugitive slaves, District of Columbia, slave trade among the slave States, and whatever springs of necessity, from the fact that the institution is among us," he announced, "I care but little, so that whatever is done be comely, and not altogether outrageous." He also acknowledged that he did not "care much about New Mexico." But then he added the crucial qualification: "if further extension were hedged against." Here was the vital considera- tion. There must be no further expansion of slavery, no further attempts to acquire territory to strengthen the slave interest. It is easy with hind- sight to assume that there could have been no territorial acquisitions from Latin America but this was not the Republican perception in 1860–1861 and there was no reason it should have been. A huge tract of land had recently been seized from Mexico and this was but one in a series of examples of territory acquired primarily at the behest of the slaveholding

279.  Daniel Crofts points out there was considerable feuding within the Republican party between November 1860 and April 1861 and notes that compromise had its support- ers especially in January and February – see Daniel Crofts, *Reluctant Confederates: Upper South Unionists in the Secession Crisis* (Chapel Hill, 1989), pp. 215, 416.

280.  Thus Roscoe Conkling of New York referred to the "folly and disaster of guaranteeing to slavery all possessions hereafter to be required" – *CG*, 36/2, p. 251.

interest. In the 1850s there had been a violent attempt to extend slavery into Kansas and a spate of filibustering expeditions into Latin America, some of them with the covert or open support of prominent Democrats. Leading Democrats north and south had sought to obtain Cuba and in 1860 both wings of the Democratic party had officially committed themselves to the acquisition of additional territory. The Republican fear was therefore well founded.[281]

For Lincoln this issue was conclusive. He announced that he had no desire to abolish slavery in the District of Columbia, nor the interstate slave trade, and that he had never even considered abolition in the federal dockyards and arsenals. But on the extension of slavery he was, he avowed, "inflexible." In a sense all his antislavery principles and attitudes crystallised in a rejection of any and every compromise that would leave open the possibility of a significant further extension of slavery. As we have seen, most Republicans, and almost all secessionists, believed that to prevent the spread of slavery was to preside over its ultimate abolition. Here was the means by which Lincoln would allow "the public mind" to "rest in the belief" that slavery was "in course of ultimate extinction." From this perspective, a compromise that would allow the South to expand into Latin America was anathema. Moreover, opposition to the spread of slavery had been the platform on which he had been elected; to retreat from it would, he avowed, be "dishonourable and treacherous" "Let there be no compromise on the question of *extending slavery*," he wrote to Lyman Trumbull on December 10 1860. "If there be," he continued "all our labor is lost, and, ere long, must be done again. The tug has to come, & better now than at any time hereafter." The Crittenden Compromise, or any such set of proposals, he warned Thurlow Weed, would mean that "filibustering for all South of us and making slave States of it would follow." In January 1861 Lincoln again offered the same warning: "a year will not pass till we shall have to take Cuba as a condition upon which they [southerners] will stay in the Union." For Lincoln, as for other Republicans, a major retreat from the Chicago platform would set a disastrous precedent. "We have just carried an election," he wrote, "upon principles fairly stated to the people." But "now we are told in advance that the government shall be broken up, before we take the offices." Whether such threats were sincere or not, "if we surrender it is the end of us and of the government. They will repeat the experiment upon us *ad libitum*."[282]

Here the president-elect anticipated the argument that he would later present in his Inaugural. Secession, in its denial of the right of the majority to rule, was anarchy. But here he added that a retreat from the principles

281. Basler (ed.), *Works of Lincoln*, IV, pp. 183.
282. Basler (ed.), *Works of Lincoln*, IV, pp. 152, 200, 149, 154, 172.

upon which he had been elected was equally anarchic: "the end of us *and of the government* (emphasis added)." Hence to surrender those principles would be to allow the slave interest to continue on its present course, inflicting incalculable damage upon the political, economic and moral fabric of the nation. It had been precisely to check that process that the Republican party had been formed.

Lincoln made his views known to the public before he took office in March 1861. Inevitably the nation took a keen interest in them. But Lincoln was still an untried Illinois politician and relatively few Republicans probably believed that he had much to teach them. This scarcely mattered however, because here as in so many of his views, the president-elect was in line with dominant opinion within his party. Some Republicans would go further in offering concessions, others would not go so far. Lincoln owed his nomination to the fact he was a quintessential moderate within the party; his views were located at what might be termed the party's ideological center of gravity.

Thus many others echoed his opposition to schemes like the Crittenden Compromise and for similar if not identical reasons. When Thurlow Weed did propose an extension of the Missouri Compromise line as a concession to the South he was violently condemned by his own party and few voices were heard in his defence. This was to be the fate of many Republicans who did waver in these months. In Congress, when opportunities were offered to debate the Crittenden Compromise, Republicans at first refused to take them and then unanimously voted the measures down.[283]

For the radicals the secessionists' protests and threats were precisely what had been expected and provided further evidence that there was indeed an "irrepressible conflict" between slavery and freedom. In their eyes the only solution was to stand firm and resist all calls for compromise. Moreover, they made it clear, as they had in the past, that they would bolt the party rather than acquiesce in a surrender of principles. According to the newspaper associated with Joshua Giddings, if such a surrender occurred, "we will repudiate it with a full heart, and counsel all our friends to do the same." The reason was simple: "we have degraded ourselves enough." The conservative Republicans were of course those most likely to acquiesce in compromise. They had argued that the task of the Republican party was to quell the sectional conflict and thus re-establish unity and harmony in the nation. The events of the secession winter clearly compelled a reappraisal and it was not surprising that some of them began to waver. Yet these Republicans were often subject to a torrent of abuse from their colleagues. As one newspaper in Indiana put it, the compromisers within the party were "engaged in a movement which is calculated

283. Potter, *Lincoln and His Party*, p. 73.

to utterly destroy the Republican party" by committing it to a "truckling pro-slavery policy." Any significant deviation from the Chicago platform would be the party's "death knell."[284]

The problem was that since slavery was a disturbing element in the nation, compromise with it would always prove at best futile and at worst entirely counterproductive. After all, Republicans reminded themselves, the Missouri Compromise had been in existence for a third of a century but southerners had repudiated it when it had suited them to do so. Now they wanted to revive it. As a newspaper in Summit County Ohio put it, "We believe... that we speak the sentiment of every man in Summit county – we know we do our own – when we say that there should be no further compromise of principle, with slavery, whatever may be the result of the present contest." According to the editor the very word "compromise" should be outlawed:

> The truth is, the people have become heartily sick and tired of com-
> promises, and this interminable talk about them; and, after all the
> abuses to which they have given countenance – the enormities that
> have been perpetrated under them, and the utter want of fidelity, that
> has hitherto attended the observance of their most sacred provisions,
> the people would experience great relief, if the very word "compro-
> mise" could be expunged from the English language and the sound
> thereof never heard again – at least upon the American continent."

Another newspaper, this time in Milwaukee, Wisconsin, argued that since the Republican platform of 1860 had been quite moderate there should be no talk of compromise. For there is "no concession we can make in that direction without sacrificing everything. One backward step and the Republican party tumbles from its platform into an unfathomable gulf." "New concessions," wrote an Iowa editor, "will only lead to new demands and new perils," from which it followed that "the issue may as well be met now." Other Republicans pointed out that there were in any event ample opportunities for southerners to reverse the verdict of 1860. They should wait for the next set of elections. Concessions would merely bring "temporary and short-lived repose and a false and treacherous harmony." Nor were Republicans moved by Crittenden's offer to submit his scheme directly to the people. In an open letter to the Kentucky Senator, the New York *Tribune* pointed out that this would in fact be unjust given the absence of free speech in the Deep South. "You are a lawyer and a good one," the newspaper conceded, but "would you like to submit a great case to a jury one half of whom were not allowed to hear your argument, and

---

284. Jefferson (Ohio), *Ashtabula Sentinel*, Feb. 12, 1861 quoted in Stampp, *And the War Came*, p. 156. Muncie (Indiana), *Courant*, Jan. 3, 1861 in Perkins (ed.), *Northern Editorials on Secession*, I, pp. 289–201,

could only give you a verdict at the peril of their lives?" These were the arguments that underlay the Republican refusal to compromise. Although they were faced with an unprecedented set of dangers for which they were quite unprepared, their reactions were in no sense simply *ad hoc* or random. Rather they grew out of the party's most fundamental attitudes and beliefs.[285]

## VI

While some Republicans were prepared to countenance concessions to the South, others from the start demanded the use of force or, as they usually preferred to put it, "the enforcement of the laws." Not all within this group were entirely consistent in their attitudes, with some on occasion recommending a different approach. Moreover some wanted war with a minimum of formalities and delay whereas others instead made it clear that war, though scarcely to be welcomed, was far better than disunion. In the United States Senate John P. Hale and Benjamin Wade announced that they would prefer war to a retreat from the Chicago platform. Former Democrats Lyman Trumbull and Preston King took a similar approach while James Doolittle and James Ashley wanted to raise large numbers of troops even before war had been declared, partly to ensure that the government could go ahead, partly to intimidate the secessionists. The New York legislature similarly offered men and money to President Buchanan as early as January 1861 on the grounds that the secessionists had "virtually declared war." In December 1860 a meeting of Republican Senators and Congressmen agreed unanimously "that the integrity of the Union should be preserved, though it cost millions of lives."[286]

Similar attitudes were struck by many northern newspapers. The New York *Courier and Enquirer* and the Chicago *Democrat* made it clear that force might be necessary. The *Illinois State Journal* in December sent a stern warning to southerners:

> Let the secessionists understand it – let the press proclaim it – let it fly on the wings of the lightning, and fall like a thunder bolt among those now plotting treason in Convention, that the Republican party, that the great North, aided by hundreds of thousands of patriotic men in the slave States, have determined to preserve the Union – peaceably if they can, forcibly if they must.

285. *Akron Summit County Beacon*, Jan. 24, 1861, Milwaukee *Daily Sentinel*, Feb. 4, 1861, *Iowa State Register*, Dec. 12, 1857. *Sandusky Daily Commercial Register*, Feb. 23, 1861; New York *Tribune*, Jan. 7, 1861 in Perkins (ed.), *Northern Editorials on Secession*, I, pp. 254–255, 266, 281–283, 295.
286. Stampp, *And the War Came*, pp. 66–67, 92.

The *Journal* was probably the leading Republican newspaper in Illinois. In Ohio the *Ohio State Journal* occupied a similar position and by mid-January it had concluded that the federal government was being "assailed by a horde of disunion traitors" and that forbearance had now reached its limits. A month later the *Peoria Daily Transcript* complained that the policy of "masterly inactivity" was producing only "national debasement, anarchy, and ruin." Meanwhile the editor in Summit County, Ohio whose dislike of even the word "compromise" we have already observed, explained that he would break his own rule and offer a compromise to the disunionists. If they would repudiate secession immediately, he would compromise, he explained, by not having them all hanged.[287]

## VII

In these months the failure of the Buchanan administration to confront the secessionists with force, the failure of the Republicans to offer a workable compromise and the failure of all parties to negotiate a peaceable secession meant that, if only by default, the policy of "masterly inactivity" in effect held sway. Seward was its main architect. It was built upon two assumptions. The first was that Unionist sentiment in the Middle and Upper South could be relied upon so long as all provocative action against the Deep South could be avoided. The second was that the states of the Deep South, denied the support of these other slaveholding states, would speedily re-enter the Union. The first assumption was quite valid; the second was not.[288]

The problem was that from February 1861 the Cotton States were moving with great alacrity to establish a new nation. They took little note of the attempts at compromise that were still being made. On the other hand, so far as the border states were concerned, Seward's policy was paying dividends. The Union forces there, having withstood the early secessionist pressure, were if anything actually increasing in strength as the weeks and months passed.

The states of the Middle and Upper South showed no sign of wishing to join the new Confederacy. In line with his pacific policy, Seward, now able to speak as Secretary of State for the incoming administration, offered to remove the troops from Fort Sumter, one of the two remaining federal forts that were in government hands within the territory of the fledgling Confederacy. He was not, however, authorised to make this

287. New York *Courier and Enquirer*, Jan. 8, 1861, *Illinois State Journal*, Dec. 20, 1860, *Ohio State Journal*, Jan. 15, 1861, *Peoria Daily Transcript*, Feb. 22, 1861, *Akron Summit County Beacon*, Jan. 24, 1861 in Perkins (ed.), *Northern Editorials on Secession*, II, p. 935, I, pp. 122, 215, 234, 255; Stampp, *And the War Came*, p. 36.
288. See Crofts, *Reluctant Confederates*, for a defence of Seward's approach.

offer. Lincoln himself had not settled on a policy. As we have seen, the president-elect shared Seward's belief in southern unionism, latent or otherwise. But he was also on record as advocating "the enforcement of the laws." In December he had declared that "the very existence of a general and national government implies the legal power, right and duty of maintaining its own integrity." "It is the duty of the President," Lincoln had confirmed, "to execute the laws and maintain the existing government." The problem, of course, was that enforcement of the laws might well result in war.[289]

On the other hand, to abandon Fort Sumter would be seen by many as a shameful capitulation. By the time of Lincoln's inauguration Sumter had acquired huge symbolic importance. Even Buchanan had refused to evacuate it. No sooner had Lincoln been inaugurated, however, than he received word from Major Robert Anderson at Sumter that his provisions were running desperately short. Hence action would be needed. Theoretically there were three courses open to the President. He could certainly evacuate the fort, he could reinforce it with men and provisions, or he could send provisions alone. For a month Lincoln did little while the nation waited

At first Lincoln probably favoured evacuation. This after all, could be construed as being in harmony with "masterly inactivity" in that it avoided provocative action. But the problem was that "masterly inactivity" was producing not peaceable reunion but instead an increasingly viable Confederate States of America. On the other hand to send in reinforcements might be seen as provocation. Many in the North and the border states as well as the Deep South would assuredly see it in this light. This left a peaceful reprovisioning of Sumter as the preferred policy. By the end of March or early April Lincoln had resolved that this would be his approach.

In the month of so of inaction, Lincoln was the object of considerable criticism, even, indeed especially, from within his own party. The *New York Times*, an impeccably Republican paper, on April 3 took the Lincoln administration severely to task:

> It is idle to conceal the fact that the administration thus far has not met public expectations. The country feels no more assurance as to the future ... than it did on the day Mr. Buchanan left Washington. It sees no indication of an administrative policy adequate to the emergency. ... We trust this period of indecision, of inaction, of fatal indifference, will have a speedy end. ... The people want *something* to be decided on – some standard raised – some policy put forward,

---

289. Lincoln quoted in Stampp, *And the War Came*, p. 28; Basler (ed.), *Works of Lincoln*, IV, p. 154.

which shall serve as a rallying point for the abundant but discouraged loyalty of the American heart.

Without doubt these were the sentiments of many within the party, and within the North.[290]

By now too business interests which had been in favour of compromise and concession were demanding a firm policy. The financial markets hated the uncertainty and there were fears that commerce would suffer irreparable damage when, as seemed imminent, the Confederacy introduced tariff duties that were only half those of the Union. The mercantile community had been divided in its political loyalties between Republicans, Democrats and Constitutional Unionists and some Republican merchants, situated on the conservative wing of the party, had been anxious for concessions to conciliate the southern states. But by the time of Lincoln's inaugural there were widespread complaints that business was paralysed and that a bold policy was now essential. Too much, however, should not be made of this. Although the Republican party would become the party of big business in later decades, on the whole such large enterprises as existed in the antebellum North were not yet so closely identified with the party. Nevertheless these interests affected public opinion which in turn may have affected the policies of the incoming administration.[291]

Yet Lincoln's refusal to surrender the forts was, despite the competing approach favoured by Seward, squarely in the logic of the Republican party. It stemmed from the conviction that a stand had to be made against southerners, against the Slave Power and against slavery. To confer legitimacy upon the Confederacy by surrendering the forts would, in the eyes of most Republicans, merely invite further aggressions and further assaults upon the Union and upon American democracy.

It is not possible to know for certain what reaction Lincoln expected his policy to elicit either in the North or in the South. It is virtually certain, however, that he knew that war was highly probable.[292] Moreover he understood that if there were to be a war, opinion in the North, and in some of the border states, would be influenced, and perhaps decisively influenced, by the fact that the Confederacy had fired the first shot. This is not to say, or course, that Lincoln wanted a war, merely that if war

290. *New York Times*, April 3, 1861.
291. Stampp, *And the War Came*, pp. 230–236, 268–269; Foner, *Business and Slavery*, pp. 113–130, 256–258, 277, 307, 319–322; Sven Beckert, *The Monied Metropolis: New York City and the Consolidation of the American Bourgeoisie, 1850–1896* (Cambridge, 2003), pp. 111–113.
292. This point, effectively made by Stampp and others, is conceded by Potter, who had originally offered a different interpretation – see Stampp, *And the War Came*, pp. 280–286, Potter, *Lincoln and His Party*, p. xliv.

could not be avoided, he wanted the Confederacy to be, and to be seen to be, the aggressor.[293] These considerations were indeed vital. The firing at Sumter allowed the new administration to mobilise an extraordinary degree of support, even enthusiasm, for the war throughout the North. The president immediately issued a Proclamation calling for troops to suppress the rebellion. Although four more slave states now left the Union to join the Confederacy, four others did not. Opinion in the North stood overwhelmingly behind the President and over the next four years the Union would benefit enormously from the retention of the slave states of Kentucky, Missouri, Delaware, and Maryland.

It remained for Lincoln to present the war to the northern public. His chance came three months later when he delivered a 4th July Message to Congress. In a few lines he explained that the war was a momentous test of democracy, not simply in the United States but the world over:

> And this issue embraces more than the fate of these United States. It presents to the whole family of man the question whether a consti-tutional republic or democracy – a government of the people by the same people – can or cannot maintain its integrity against its own domestic foes. It presents the question whether discontented indi-viduals, too few in number to control administration according to organic law in any case, can always, upon the pretences made in this case, or on any other pretences, or arbitrarily without any pretence, break up their government, and thus practically put an end to free government upon the earth. It forces us to ask: Is there in all republics this inherent and fatal weakness? Must a government, of necessity, be too strong for the liberties of its own people or too weak to maintain its own existence?

Here was a ringing affirmation of the majoritarian principle, now explic-itly threatened by a minority of the people (and the states) of the Union.[294]

Lincoln made it clear, however, that democracy was far more than a principle of government, however important that might be. For the pur-pose of democracy, he explained, once again employing his favourite metaphors, was to secure equal opportunity and to promote social mobility:

> This is essentially a people's contest. On the side of the Union it is a struggle for maintaining in the world that form and substance of government whose leading object is to elevate the condition of men – to lift artificial weights from all shoulders; to clear the paths of laud-able pursuit for all; to afford all an unfettered start, and a fair chance

293. See Richard M. Current, *Lincoln and the First Shot* (Philadelphia, 1963), pp. 190–203; Richard J. Carwardine, *Lincoln* (Harlow, 2003), p. 156.
294. Basler (ed.), *Works of Lincoln*, IV, p. 426.

in the race of life. Yielding to partial and temporary departures, from necessity, this is the leading object of the government for whose existence we contend. . . .

Thus the war was being fought to vindicate American democracy, and the capitalist economy of the North.[295]

## VIII

Like their counterparts in the South, Republicans were convinced that the war would be of short duration. According to the *Tribune*, "it would only be necessary for the Government of the North to concentrate at New York a small fleet of seagoing steamers and an army of 20,000 to 30,000 men to hold the entire South in perpetual check." The *New York Times* thought a month sufficient to quell this "local commotion" and other equally eminent newspapers made similar predictions. Republican statesmen were equally confident. Some had actually been looking forward to war, which they anticipated would be both brief and glorious.[296]

Implicit here was a familiar Republican belief: the South was inherently weak and, denied the support of the North and the Union, likely to collapse. The reasoning of the Republicans was the inverse of that of the Confederates: slavery was inherently unstable and parasitical; therefore, in a conflict with a social system that was in harmony with human nature itself, it could only fail. The logic was impeccable but although Republicans were right about the outcome of the war and right too that slavery was indeed a weaker foundation for a society than free labour, the margin was not so great, and the South not so feeble, as they believed. It would be four years before Americans would find that truth to be self-evident.

## Conclusion

### I

If the election of the first Republican president precipitated the nation into a Civil War, then the exigencies of that war in turn helped propel the Lincoln administration, despite the reassurances that had been given to the slave states before the outbreak of hostilities, into abolition and the emancipation of more than three million slaves. It thus fell to the Republicans, who had ironically espoused a milder form of antislavery

295. Basler (ed.), *Works of Lincoln*, IV, p. 438.
296. Nevins, *Prologue to Civil War*, p. 413; Nevins, *The Emergence of Lincoln: The Improvised War 1861–1862* (New York, 1959), p. 75; Potter, *Lincoln and His Party*, p. 234; Stampp, *And the War Came*, p. 261.

than abolitionists or members of the Liberty party or perhaps even the Free Soilers of 1848, to accomplish the destruction of slavery in the United States.[297]

The precise nature of Republican antislavery has therefore seemed to historians a matter of considerable significance. As we have seen, Republicans offered three sets of criticisms of the peculiar institution. One centred on the suffering of the slaves and stressed the moral evils of human servitude. A second, which crystallised around the concept of the Slave Power, emphasised the political threat which slavery and slaveholders were deemed to pose to American democracy and the American Republic. The third focussed upon the weaknesses of the southern economy, weaknesses that were unhesitatingly attributed to slavery. All these lines of attack featured strongly in Republican utterances, both public and private, in the years preceding the outbreak of war. This does not mean, however, that each was necessarily of equal importance.

Which indeed was most important? Some historians have argued that this distinction belongs to the political critique.[298] If they are correct, the conclusion might be, given the Republican role in the final destruction of slavery, that political rather than economic (or moral) forces were paramount at this decisive moment in the nation's history. In other words, economic or class forces must here take second place to politics; northerners who rallied beneath the Republican banner were confirming that on some occasions human beings respond to political imperatives rather than economic ones. This would suggest that interpretations which *a priori* accord primacy to the economic realm are arbitrary and dogmatic and that historians who subscribe to them are guilty of finding what they wish to find in the historical record rather that what is actually present.

Yet this conclusion is unwarranted. It assumes that the most important objections to slavery were those that were most frequently voiced or most widely held. As we shall see, this assumption, whatever its apparent plausibility, is unfounded. However, even if were valid, the conclusion is still questionable. There is no doubt that all, or virtually all, Republicans endorsed the view that slavery posed a political threat to the nation. There is no doubt that this political critique was voiced more frequently than the moral objections to slavery, which as we have seen, did not feature strongly among former Democrats or the more conservative Republicans. But there is little reason to believe that the economic criticisms of slavery did not command as wide a measure of acceptance within the party as

---

297. This is not to say, however, that the slaves played no part in it. See pp. 628–649.
298. William E. Gienapp, "The Republican Party and the Slave Power," in Robert H. Abzug and Stephen E. Maizlish (eds.), *New Perspectives on Race and Slavery in America* (Lexington, 1986), pp. 51–78; Michael F. Holt, *The Political Crisis of the 1850s* (New York, 1978), pp. 189–190.

the political. Which criticisms were more often expressed? This is diffi-cult to determine. After all, the entire controversy over the extension of slavery raised issues that were at once political and economic. Slavery in the West, (as in the South), was denounced so vehemently precisely because it simultaneously impaired political freedoms and blighted eco-nomic opportunity. Political and economic objections were thus fused. On straightforward empirical grounds therefore, it is not clear that the political critique of slavery should be privileged over the economic.

This separation of the economic, the political, and the moral, however, whilst highly convenient as a heuristic device, threatens to disguise their profound but asymmetric interdependence, to obscure the dynamics of historical change and to conceal the primacy of the economy. Moreover the fact that the Republicans presided over the dismantling of the southern labour system threatens to misrepresent the role of the abolitionists in the entire process. One cannot determine the relative importance of the three sets of criticisms of slavery simply by totalling the number of occasions each was voiced by Republican partisans, whatever the intuitive appeal of such an approach.

Instead one must incorporate a notion of causal depth. Rather than a one-dimensional listing of causal factors, we must recognise that some factors underlie others and operate, consequently, at a deeper level. If we take this approach, we will find that the political critique of slavery dimin-ishes in importance, whereas the economic factors, with class differences at their core, emerge as paramount.

To see this we need to remind ourselves of the origins of the political critique. Resentment of southern power, as promoted by for example the three-fifths clause, was virtually as old as the Constitution itself. Although it had briefly flared up at the time of the Missouri Compromise, at most times prior to the 1830s it had provoked relatively little controversy. In the 1830s, however, a new era opened. Southerners now moved to pre-vent discussion of slavery both in Congress via the Gag Law and in the states by restrictions on freedom of speech. They also sought to prevent the circulation through the federal mails of antislavery pamphlets in the South. Slaveholders took these actions in response to three underlying fears: (1) fears of the slaves themselves (who might be induced to rebel or flee), (2) fears of the nonslaveholding whites of the South (who might challenge the privileged role of the slaveholder), and (3) fears of north-ern antislavery sentiment (which had entered a new and menacing phase with the emergence of the abolitionist crusade). As I have noted through-out the two volumes of this study, southerners believed that the threat from the North underlay the others. As I have also argued throughout these volumes, however, they were mistaken and in reality the primary threat came from their slaves and was generated in the final analysis by the slaves' refusal to embrace their chains and passively accept their own enslavement.[299]

Thus the initial southern actions, which gave rise to the Slave Power concept, were themselves the product of the weaknesses of southern slavery and the growth of abolitionism (which, it should be noted, stressed the moral rather than the political case against slavery). In the 1840s and 1850s, southerners, as we have seen, took a further series of actions intended to protect themselves against the threats which surrounded them. The demand for Texas, the drive to plant slavery in Kansas, the proposal to reopen the slave trade and the pressure for a slave code for the territories – all were an attempt to compensate for the weaknesses of slavery. All, moreover, reflected not merely the growing strength of antislavery sentiment in the North, but also the obvious fact that the South was being outpaced by the North, in terms of both population and States. Here the economic weaknesses of slavery came decisively into play. If the South had been able to keep pace with the North then the growth of northern antislavery sentiment would have been of far less importance, and the actions taken to combat it – actions which fuelled the fear of the Slave Power – would not have seemed so necessary.

Thus the political critique was derivative of the other criticisms slavery attracted and of the weaknesses of slavery itself in the South. We should note, moreover, that one cannot reverse this equation. The weaknesses of slavery, its vulnerability to the resentment of the slave and its failure to keep pace with the free labour system of the North scarcely derived from the political objections raised against it. Thus while there was an interdependence between the economic and political critiques of slavery, it was not a symmetrical interdependence. This suggests the primacy of the former.

What of the moral criticisms? These were in fact more important than might be suggested by the relative infrequency with which they were voiced. Southerners responded very strongly to this moral onslaught, in part because they were convinced that compromise with what they deemed fanaticism would prove futile. It is thus probable that the moral absolutism of abolitionists and radical Republicans had an impact that was disproportionate to their numbers, and disproportionate to the relative infrequency with which moral criticisms were expressed within the antislavery movement generally. Moreover, the initial actions taken by southerners in the 1830s, the actions which fuelled the accusations concerning the Slave Power, were taken in response to the abolitionist critique of slavery, a critique in which moral considerations were uppermost. This

299. See the first volume of this study, esp. pp. 281–285.

too suggests a greater role for the moral critique than might as first be assumed.

Yet these moral arguments, which revolved around the violence that slavery did to both the individual conscience and the family, were themselves a function of the changes taking place within northern society and the northern economy. Southern slavery had not become in itself more immoral as the years passed and even its enemies did not bother to make this claim; rather northern society became increasingly intolerant of slavery's long-standing moral shortcomings. Within northern society the increasing separation between work and home generated a view of the home as a refuge from the wider world and of the family as an irreplaceable, almost sacred, source of virtue and stability. Meanwhile the growth of wage labour (which was a prerequisite of the separation between home and work) meant that increasing numbers of northerners lacked the ownership of land or other means of production that had previously been thought necessary for inclusion in a republican or democratic polity. Abolitionists and many Republicans, however, insisted that the individual conscience could instead perform this role. The conscience would operate as an anchor for individual morality and a guarantor of social harmony. The implications for slavery, which scorned the conscience of the slave and denied him the right to a family, were obvious: slavery was simply intolerable and must be abolished, by means of an appeal to the conscience of the nation, or at least of the North.

Thus if we are explaining the growth of antislavery in the North we should certainly not ignore the political critique of slavery that found expression in the concept of the Slave Power. Nor should we fail to note the almost certainly disproportionate impact of the minority of northerners, within Republican and abolitionist ranks, for whom the moral indictment was paramount. Nevertheless this should not obscure the fact that economic and class factors were of primary significance. Economic changes in the North operated in a number of ways. First, they produced the belief, universal among Republicans and abolitionists alike, that the northern economy was superior in productive potential and in the opportunities it provided to individual citizens. As we have seen, this was a cardinal tenet of the Republican political faith. Second, they played a decisive role in generating the moral critique of slavery which focussed upon the impact of enslavement upon the family and the conscience. Third, they gave rise to an increasing imbalance in political power between North and South. Faced with this moral and economic challenge from a region whose political power, both relative and absolute, seemed to be ever-increasing, southerners took, in the political arena, what they hoped would be preventative action and in so doing fuelled the fears of the Slave Power.

At this point the weaknesses of the slave regime itself, and the conflict between master and slave that was at its core, were, in their turn, decisive. Unable to diversify economically (and thereby weaken the northern economic critique of slavery), unable to match the growth of the free-labour system (and thus ignore the threat from the North), and unable to loosen the controls they held over their slaves by, for example, legalising slave marriage (and thus begin to blunt the moral critique), southerners, as we have seen, took a series of actions in the 1830s, 1840s and 1850s that were intended to make the Union safe for slavery. These actions, however, merely served to fuel the political critique of the institution, the claim that the nation was being ruled by a Slave Power. In 1860–1861 southerners took the ultimate step of withdrawing from the Union, a step which in Republican eyes offered confirmation, if any were still needed, that slavery posed a deadly threat to American democracy.

It is clear therefore that a whole series of factors, some economic, some political and some moral, generated the antislavery movement, a movement which culminated in the creation of the Republican party and in its triumph in 1860. It is also the case, however, that not all these factors were of equal importance and it is a principal conclusion of this study that the economic and class forces were primary.

## II

As we have seen, the wage-worker had traditionally been viewed with suspicion as someone who lacked a sufficient commitment to, or stake in, the social and political order. Antebellum northern society saw a very considerable increase in the numbers of such workers and yet made a relatively painless adjustment. It was possible to point to the advantages and benefits that he (and only rarely she) enjoyed in the North. Thus the wage-earner benefited from unprecedentedly wide opportunities for social mobility, was free to enter, on an "equal" basis, into a contract with his employer, was able to purchase goods and services on a significant scale, had the inestimable benefits of the family, could enjoy political and legal rights and was free to follow the dictates of his conscience. Antebellum Republicans gave considerable attention to these features of northern society and, while sometimes warning against complacency, invited the northern electorate to share their satisfaction with them. Yet the inevitable effect was to increase northern hostility to southern slaveholders who denied each of these rights to their slaves and threatened to deprive whites both north and south of the Mason-Dixon Line of many of them.

In effect the accommodation with wage labour was achieved within the North with relative ease, but only at the cost of an increasing dissatisfaction with the South and an increasing hostility towards slavery and slaveholders. Hence northern perceptions of the South, of slavery and of slaveholders were deeply coloured by the changes taking place in northern society.

A similar process also governed some northern misperceptions of the South, of slavery and of slaveholders. As we have seen, the Republicans held that northern society either was in, or could relatively easily be brought into, harmony with the essential qualities of human nature. The result, as we have seen, was a number of misperceptions about both North and South. Thus many Republicans believed that there was a conspiracy on the part of southerners to spread slavery into the North and that there was in the South a huge mass of latent support for the Union. As we have also seen, these views played an extremely important role in the sectional controversy.

Of all schools of thought on the origins of the Civil War, it is of course the "revisionists" who have given most attention to the misperceptions or, as they preferred to term them, the "blunders" of the statesmen of the Civil War era.[300] In fact revisionism has rather more to recommend it than modern-day historians usually allow. There can be no doubt that major errors were made by Republicans and no doubt either that they played a highly significant part in bringing about the war. As we have seen, they were very prominent during the critical months of the secession crisis, for example. But the revisionists were guilty of a fundamental error themselves. They in effect assumed that politicians' mistakes or blunders were divorced from material interests: to the extent that war was attributable to errors, they assumed, it could not be explained by reference to the clash of economic (or class) interests. To demonstrate the errors of the politicians was thus to suggest that the war was needless, since less error-prone statesmen would presumably have been able to resolve the conflict without recourse to arms.

What is wrong with this argument? The flaw consists in the failure to appreciate that the most important of these errors were themselves the product of economic or class forces. Republicans believed that the society of the North was harmonious and above all "natural." As a consequence they were led to believe that southern society was unnatural and that its successes could only be explained by reference to a conspiracy. But the belief that northern society was "natural" and classless itself bore the imprint of particular economic interests: the injustices within northern society were obscured, underestimated or mystified by this analysis.

---

300. Avery Craven, for example, referred to Lincoln's "House Divided" speech as an "extreme partisan appeal to unfounded fears," one which resulted in "a political contest" being "elevated to the eternal conflict between right and wrong." – see Craven, *Coming of the Civil War*, p. 392.

Although there was no conspiracy involved by which a dominant class deliberately indoctrinated the dominated groups, there were vested interests which stood to gain enormously by this characterisation of northern society as "natural." As we have seen, it is scarcely satisfactory to attribute this gain to coincidence.

In this way, economic and class interests in the North helped produce a particular image of the North, which in turn led directly to the misperceptions of the Slave Power, for example. The process involved was complex and highly mediated, but in this way class interests generated misperceptions and "errors." To the extent that these errors contributed to the process of sectional polarisation and ultimately war itself, class interests (however complex the process of mediation), rather than mere human frailty, were responsible. Thus in their discussion of the Slave Power and of antislavery generally, the revisionists were right to draw attention to the errors of the Republicans and right too to stress their role in the coming of the War. But their mistake was to assume a dichotomy between misperceptions, on the one hand, and material interests on the other. The Republican assault upon slavery, the Slave Power and the slaveholders of the South confirms that the two are often intimately related.

# PART II

# Polarisation and Collapse

# 3

# The disintegration of Democratic hegemony: Northern Democrats and their southern allies, 1850–1861[1]

## Introduction: The Kansas-Nebraska Act (1)

### I

On January 4, 1854 Stephen A. Douglas, Senator from Illinois and Chairman of the Senate Committee on Territories, reported his bill for the organisation of what was then called the Nebraska territory. The bill went through many modifications, in the course of which the single territory became instead two. Douglas sought to employ the principle of popular sovereignty, by which the inhabitants of the two territories, Kansas and Nebraska, would be allowed to determine whether slavery would or would not be authorised. This principle had been central to the Compromise measures of 1850, measures with which Douglas himself had been closely identified and indeed for which he could claim considerable credit. Now, therefore, he determined that popular sovereignty, apparently a winning formula, should once again be applied.

The crucial difference, however, was that the Nebraska territory, acquired by Thomas Jefferson as part of the Louisiana Purchase,[2] lay above the line of latitude at 36° 30′ and was thus, according to the Missouri Compromise of 1820–1821, barred to slavery. So Douglas's bill seemed to be at odds with the Missouri Compromise. Although he did not

---

1. This chapter deals with the ideology and the politics of the Democratic party up to the outbreak of war in 1861. It is primarily, but not exclusively, concerned with northerners. When appropriate and where there was a genuine convergence, I consider also those southerners who at the time (though not necessarily subsequently) shared their views as well as northerners like Presidents Pierce and Buchanan, who held national office but were disproportionately dependent upon southern support. Almost all the southerners I consider were moderates. It should be noted, perhaps, that there is no adequate treatment of the northern Democrats, though there are, of course, important insights in a number of works. These are cited in this chapter when appropriate.
2. A very small portion of the territory was outside the Louisiana Purchase, but this did not affect the debate over the Act.

initially wish to be explicit, under pressure from other Senators he finally took the crucial step. He inserted a clause into his bill which declared that the Missouri Compromise, "being inconsistent with the principles of non-intervention by Congress with slavery in the States and Territories, as recognized by the legislation of 1850, is hereby declared inoperative and void." On May 30, 1854, after protracted and bitter debate in both Houses of Congress, President Franklin Pierce signed the bill. Perhaps the most portentous legislative measure in the history of the United States had been enacted.[3]

As we have seen, the repeal of the Missouri Compromise provoked an outburst within the North that exceeded in intensity any previous display of antislavery sentiment. The possibility that slavery might now be established in Kansas (Nebraska being universally held to be climatically unsuited to it) caused a storm of protest. As we have also seen, antislavery opponents of the bill heaped abuse not only upon the Kansas-Nebraska Act but also upon its author, whom they accused of conspiring to spread slavery into the Northwest. Although a northerner, Douglas was, in the eyes of these antislavery militants, merely a pawn in the hands of the aristocrats of the South, a tool of the Slave Power.

Although Douglas had expected his bill, and in particular the repeal of the Missouri Compromise, to be controversial, he was himself astonished and outraged by the flood of vituperation and personal abuse that now engulfed him. Of all the charges leveled against him, the one that he found most baffling was that he desired to extend slavery. In truth the purpose of the bill was not to strengthen the South but to develop the West. Although he was compelled to spend much of his career grappling with the slavery question, Douglas actually would have been delighted never to have discussed it at all. A yawning gulf existed, therefore, between his actual motives and those imputed to him. And just as his political enemies mistrusted his purpose, so he was equally critical of theirs and equally unable to understand it. He believed them motivated by the most sordid considerations. "The cry of the extension of slavery," he wrote, "has been raised for mere party purposes by the abolitionist confederates and disappointed office seekers." The debate over the Kansas-Nebraska bill, like so many of the twists and turns in the sectional conflict, was characterised by misunderstanding and mutual incomprehension.[4]

3. *United States Statutes at Large: Treaties of the United States of America* (Boston, 1855) X, p. 277.
4. *Letter of Senator Douglas in Reply to the Editor of the State Capital Reporter, Concord New Hampshire* (Washington, DC, 1854), p. 7. Robert W. Johannsen, *Stephen A. Douglas* (New York, 1973), p. 420; Mrs Archibald Dixon, *The True History of the Missouri Compromise and its Repeal* (Cincinnati, 1899), pp. 445–47.

## II

However acrimonious the debates over the Kansas-Nebraska bill, they were a model of harmony and restraint in comparison with the events following its passage. For attention now switched to Kansas itself where, as we have seen, settlers from the North, most of whom wanted the state to be free, clashed with settlers from the South, and with temporary migrants or "invaders" from Missouri, who were equally adamant that it should be slave. With skirmishes between the two sides, rival governments established each claiming to represent the territory, and Congress occupied with the animosities that every piece of news from Kansas seemed to generate, the slavery controversy now entered a new era.[5]

The Democratic party too entered a new era. In 1852 Franklin Pierce had carried every northern state but two. But in the elections of 1854 the northern Democrats suffered crushing defeats and in 1856, although James Buchanan won election to the White House he lost every northern state except California, Illinois, Indiana, Pennsylvania, and New Jersey. It was the passage of the Kansas-Nebraska Act, the subsequent events in Kansas, and their impact in Washington, which did most to end Democratic hegemony in the North and hand the region instead to the Republicans. Four years later the election of Lincoln would confirm that the Democrats were in a minority in the North and that they could no longer speak for, and harmonise the interests of, the nation as a whole.[6]

In 1860–1861, therefore, regime and party crashed together. Although northern Democrats with relatively few exceptions were enthusiastic defenders of the Union in the aftermath of the attack on Fort Sumter, they were nonetheless highly critical of many Republican actions. Most of all they detested the Republicans' Emancipation Proclamation. They yearned for the Union that had existed before the War, rather than the new nation that Lincoln and his party seemed to be forging. But another defeat in 1864 confirmed the degree to which they had lost the initiative in American politics. The introduction of the Kansas-Nebraska bill had thus inaugurated a decade of crisis and disaster for the Democratic party, as for the nation itself.[7]

---

5. See pp. 63–66.
6. Some historians have, of course, argued that this effect was achieved in large part by the ethnocultural issues of temperance and nativism. This subject is a principal theme of Chapter 4 in this volume.
7. Roy F. Nichols, *The Disruption of American Democracy* (New York, 1948), p. 506. For a reminder that the northern Democrats retained some force in the 1860s, see Joel H. Silbey, *A Respectable Minority: The Democratic Party in the Civil War Era, 1860–1868* (New York, 1977). As he notes, however, the party's chairman, August Belmont described the 1860s as "the most disastrous epoch in the annals of the … party" – see p. xv.

## III

Not surprisingly, therefore, the Kansas-Nebraska Act has attracted the attention of historians seeking to understand the causes of the Civil War. Those who have endorsed the so-called "revisionist" view, according to which statesmen's errors were the crucial factor, have found much ammunition in the early history of Kansas. It has been tempting to blame Douglas for the introduction of the bill. After all, the slavery controversy had been in abeyance in 1853; the Compromise measures of 1850, resoundingly reaffirmed in the Democratic platform of 1852, having apparently settled the sectional controversy. Prior to the introduction of Douglas's bill there was no concerted southern pressure for a repeal of the Missouri Compromise. So should Douglas not be blamed for being impervious to antislavery sentiment and thus blind to the consequences of his actions? Alternatively, one might blame his opponents. Since they entirely misunderstood his motives, and since their language was extreme, uncompromising and inflammatory, should they too not receive censure?[8]

Yet here, as elsewhere, the revisionist emphasis is misplaced. It is true that each side in the debate entirely failed to understand the actions of the other, and equally true that these failures had the most momentous political consequences. But the misperceptions are themselves explicable by reference to factors which go far beyond the lapses and errors of individual statesmen. Two suggestions may be offered. First, Douglas, the committed Democrat, knew that his purposes were quite unconnected with slavery and that he was party to no conspiracy to extend the institution. Second, his opponents nevertheless knew that once again the Democratic party was furthering a slaveholding interest, that this effect was not a random one even though it was not acknowledged or avowed by Douglas or the other northern Democrats with whom he acted. Superficially contradictory, these two propositions can be reconciled, once we recognise that the Democratic party had always borne the imprint of the slaveholding interest, that even its most distinguished and committed members, especially in the North, were not necessarily aware of the fact, and that actions which seemed to them merely inspired by democracy or party tradition in fact

8. Allan Nevins, *Ordeal of the Union: A House Dividing 1852–57* (Boston, 1947), pp. 109, 112; Michael F. Holt, *The Rise and Fall of the American Whig Party: Jacksonian Politics and the Onset of the Civil War* (New York, 1999), p. 815; Avery Craven, *The Coming of the Civil War* (Chicago, 1966), p. 327. It may be appropriate to add here that the question of slavery in Kansas has seemed to some historians to have been a mere abstraction. If Kansas were, in any case, as unsuited to slavery as Nebraska then the entire controversy over its future was unnecessary, or, in the language of revisionism, "needless." See, for example, Charles W. Ramsdell, "The Natural Limits of Slavery Expansion," *Mississippi Valley Historical Review*, XVI (1929), p. 171.

often confirmed the privileged status of the slaveholder in the antebellum Republic and the hegemonic control he wielded via the Democratic party.[9]

Only by re-examining the traditions of the party and by treating its ideology with the utmost seriousness can this process be understood. Here is one of the two main reasons for considering the beliefs of the northern Democrats in the final antebellum years. The other is, ironically, a consequence of the party's failures and its declining appeal in the North in these years. For while mainstream Democratic ideology – even as expounded by its northern phalanx – had served as a functional but covert defence of slavery, in the 1850s this process was severely disrupted. In effect that ideology was now asked to bear too much and it buckled under the strain. So long as antislavery sentiment in the North was within manageable proportions, it could be tempered, undermined or disabled in various ways by Democratic ideology, by Democratic tradition and by Democratic partisanship. But as northern hostility to slavery deepened, a subtle shift occurred. Instead of the Democratic party successfully discrediting and disabling antislavery, antislavery now increasingly discredited and disabled the Democratic party. Its southern orientation became ever more apparent as the southern wing, desperate to find a way of reconciling slavery and the Union, asked more and more of its northern allies. Thus what had been an implicit or covert defence of slavery and the South now became increasingly (though not in the North fully) explicit and overt.

One consequence was a dramatic hemorrhaging of electoral support in the North. Throughout the 1850s the party retained in the North an appeal among those closest, whether ethnically, culturally or economically, to the South: merchants in the cities connected with the cotton trade, rural residents who had migrated from the South into the lower Northwest, immigrants and particularly Roman Catholic immigrants, who welcomed the party's stance against an evangelical reform impulse that seemed to threaten their cultural identity and thus their equal rights. Even as late as 1860 the Democrats had not become an entirely southern party. Nevertheless the 1850s saw an extraordinary diminution in its appeal in the North, one which marked a seismic shift in the American political landscape. Its main cause was the slavery controversy.

9. There is an important theoretical issue involved here. Many historians assume that what is not intended by anyone is therefore, by definition, random. But this is not so. For a discussion of these issues see John Ashworth, "Capitalism, Class and Antislavery," in Thomas Bender (ed.), *The Antislavery Debate: Capitalism and Abolitionism as a Problem in Historical Interpretation* (Berkeley, 1992), pp. 280–284. For additional discussion of the relationship between Democratic ideology and slavery, see the first volume of this study, *Slavery, Capitalism and Politics in the Antebellum Republic: Commerce and Compromise, 1820–1850* (Cambridge, UK, 1995).

This process found a reflection in the party's ideology. The decade of Democratic failure inaugurated by the introduction of the Nebraska bill would leave the party increasingly dislocated in the North, unable, as we shall see, to compete with the Republicans in articulating the aspirations, relieving the anxieties or affirming the hopes of millions of northerners. Although Douglas did not know it when his bill passed Congress, at this his moment of apparently greatest success, catastrophe awaited his policy, his party and his nation.

## Democracy, the nation, and the Democratic party

### I

Some of the most important utterances made by Democrats in the 1850s were those which, to a modern ear, might sound the least worthy of attention. All modern political parties which aspire to control a nation seek to clothe themselves in the mantle of nationalism and to inspire patriotic devotion on the part of their actual or potential supporters. A successful identification of nation and party is a proven route to electoral triumph; if voters can be persuaded that a party somehow embodies the deepest, most cherished values of the nation, its success is assured. Thus in most countries where representative and popular institutions are established, these strategies are so obvious as not to call for comment or discussion.[10]

In the United States before the Civil War, however, the same strategies were less familiar, more controversial and thus less widely adopted. Federalists and Whigs, for example, generally eschewed them.[11] The Democrats, on the other hand, were in this sense at least a modern political party, for many of them displayed an exuberant patriotism that knew no bounds or, as we shall see, territorial boundaries.

The United States was still, in the 1850s, a new nation and the temptation to review its progress was irresistible – to Democrats. Thus the Governor of Indiana in 1852 reported progress "in all the elements of moral, political, and intellectual greatness." Although this seemed to

10. A good treatment of the views of northern Democrats in the 1850s is to be found in Bruce W. Collins, "The Ideology of the Ante-Bellum Northern Democrats," *Journal of American Studies*, XI (April 1977), pp. 103–121. See also Jean H. Baker, *Affairs of Party: The Political Culture of Northern Democrats in the Mid-Nineteenth Century* (Ithaca, NY, 1983); Roy F. Nichols, *The Democratic Machine* (New York, 1923); Nichols, *Disruption of American Democracy*; Stephen E. Maizlish, "Race and Politics in the Northern Democracy: 1854–1860," in Robert H. Abzug and Stephen E. Maizlish (eds.), *New Perspectives on Race and Slavery in America* (Lexington, 1986), pp. 79–90.
11. John Ashworth, *"Agrarians" and "Aristocrats": Party Political Ideology in the United States, 1837–1846* (London, 1983), pp. 55–60. Whigs remained suspicious of the exuberant nationalism championed by the Democrats; for them the political party was a means to an end rather than the embodiment of eternally valid principles.

voice a wide-ranging approval, he was nevertheless restrained in comparison with many of his colleagues. When James Buchanan in 1850 was
unable to accept an invitation to attend a public meeting, he followed
standard practice in offering some observations on the current political
scene. One of his injunctions was to "Preserve the Union!" "And what a
Union this has been!" Buchanan exclaimed. "The history of the human
race presents no parallel to it." Some years later, in Georgia, Governor
Herschel Johnson, destined to be Stephen A. Douglas's running mate in
1860, expressed similar sentiments. "The growth of the United States,"
he told his audience, "in wealth, population and power, under the operation of this government, is an example in the history of the world." Once
again the review was wide-ranging: "in everything that adorns and dig-
nifies society; in everything that elevates and ennobles humanity, we have
attained a height scarcely ever reached by any former nation."[12]

It is easy to overlook what was surely a key phrase in Johnson's
encomium. The inclusion of the words "under the operation of this government" was no accident. For nothing came more easily to antebellum Democrats than the assumption that progress in all spheres, and
not merely the political, was attributable to the nation's republican and
democratic institutions. In 1853 August Belmont delivered an address
to a group of merchants in New York. His theme was the enormous
improvement in the national economy since the Panic of 1837. At that
time, he reminded his audience, "we had but a few straggling railroads
on the Eastern borders of our country," while "not a single American
sea-steamer had yet left our ports." Similarly, "the few works of internal
improvement begun by our infant Western States had to be abandoned
and left unfinished, involving discredit and ruin to their projectors, while
the vast produce of the fertile West, unable to find a market, added but
little to the wealth of those . . . communities." But "what," Belmont asked,
"is our condition now?" The answer was delivered with an undisguised
triumphalism:

> Our mighty empire, stretching from the rolling surf of the Atlantic to
> the placid waves of the Pacific, comprises a Confederacy of thirty one
> States, each containing in itself the germs of national prosperity and
> greatness, and each adding to the brilliancy of the whole constellation.
> Our steamers, after having successfully striven for supremacy with
> those of England, carry to every sea the proud flag of our country,
> bearing witness to American progress. The far West is brought to our
> very doors by a net of railroads, carrying the products of its virgin soil
> to our sea ports, from thence to provide the marts of the world. And

12. *Documents of the General Assembly of Indiana . . . 36 Session, Convening Dec. 1,
    1851.* Part 1 (Indianapolis, 1852), p. 165; John Moore (ed.), *The Works of James
    Buchanan.* 12 vols. (Philadelphia, 1908–1911) VIII, p. 390; Herschel Johnson,
    *Address Delivered . . . At Milledgeville, 4 July 1857* (Milledgeville, 1857), p. 18

the time is near at hand when, either by the energies of our private citizens or by the action of Congress, our possessions on the Pacific will be united to their sister States on the Atlantic by a public work, which, in grandeur of conception and execution, will outstrip any human enterprise the world has yet seen.

Belmont looked forward to a day when the United States would "command the trade of the world."[13]

For Belmont, however, these commercial triumphs were to be explained in essentially political rather than economic terms. For "these amazing results, which make the calmest eye grow dizzy at the prospect of a future empire lying before us," he had no doubt, "we owe, under God, to the American system of government." The key was "our beneficent Republican institutions" which "foster the energies of individuals and masses; bring to our shores the producing classes of Europe, flying from oppression and want; . . . protecting and cherishing every citizen with equal solicitude," and which "inspire us all with that deep devotion to our country and that love of liberty which are the surest guarantees of national prosperity and renown." Economic progress thus had political and indeed democratic roots.[14]

This mode of analysis, in which complex economic, political or moral processes were simply and unproblematically attributed to democratic forms and practices, came easily to Democratic partisans. Thus Horatio Seymour of New York baldly asserted that the nation's political institutions "give promise in the future of such greatness and civilization as the world has never seen." Stephen A. Douglas, meanwhile, offered an even more enthusiastic celebration of American democracy. In a sense he offered a challenge to the entire world:

> If another form of government can be shown to exist, to ever have existed, upon the face of the globe that has done more to elevate the condition of the people – to render them intelligent, peaceable, and happy – that has done more for the cause of civilization, religion, and morality, in the same space of time, than this, let that country be pointed out, and my word for it, we will be willing to receive its government as the model.

Thus religion, civilisation, morality, economic growth and even happiness were reducible to politics.[15]

13. *Letters, Speeches and Addresses of August Belmont* (n.p., 1890), p. 6.
14. *Letters . . . of Belmont*, (n.p., 1890), p. 6.
15. Thomas M. Cook and Thomas W. Knox (eds.), *Public Record: Including Speeches, Messages, Proclamations, Official Correspondence, and Other Public Utterances of Horatio Seymour* (New York, 1868), pp. 3–4; *Speech of Mr. Douglas, of Illinois, at the Democratic Festival at Jackson Hall January 8th, 1852*, (n.p., n.d.), pp. 6–7. See

## II

Antebellum Democratic thought exhibited not one but instead two spectacular feats of intellectual reductionism. For if commercial, moral, cultural and political progress could be painlessly attributed to the nation's democratic institutions, so the development of democracy itself, at least since the 1790s, could be effortlessly ascribed to a single unmistakable cause: the Democratic party. As they reviewed the past, Democratic partisans dwelt fondly upon the history of political parties within the nation. Ironically perhaps, they paid considerable attention to their opponents.[16] The editor of the *National Democratic Review* in 1856 declared that he hoped "never to see the time when a powerful opposition will not contest the palm of victory with the Democratic Party." Fortunately, perhaps, this was not, according to other Democratic partisans, a likely prospect. Senator John B. Weller of California expressed what had been a characteristically Democratic view since the time of Andrew Jackson when he declared that a two-party system was a permanent feature of the American political landscape. "We know," he reminded a New England audience in the mid-1850s, "that there always have been, and always will be, two great political parties in this country, so long as the government retains its present form. These were "the Democratic and the Anti-democratic parties." Taking an even more expansive view of the past, and encompassing not merely the United States but instead the entire world, Joseph Holt of Kentucky declared that "as far back as the light of history or tradition conducts us, two great political parties have been found to exist in all ages and countries, claiming to be at all civilized." Indeed, according to Holt, "these parties stand out from the pages of history, as distinctly and boldly as do any mountain peaks from the undulating plains on which they cast their shadows." Like Weller, he believed the two parties "in their nature and mission, essentially antagonistic." What then did they represent? Holt was emphatic: "the one is the party devoted to power – the other the party devoted to the people." Whereas "the one responds to the conservatism of the nineteenth century," "the other" instead reflected "its democracy." In this sense, if in no other, the experience of the United States resembled that of the rest of the civilised world.[17]

also *Journal of the House of Representatives of the State of New Hampshire...1847* (Concord, 1847), p. 10.
16. I have discussed Democratic attitudes to the political party and to the role of an opposition in the first volume of this study (p. 293) and in my *"Agrarians" and "Aristocrats,"* pp. 205–219.
17. *National Democratic Review*, 1 (Jan. 1856), p. 15; *Speeches of Messrs. Weller, Orr, Lane, and Cobb Delivered in Phoenix and Depot Halls, Concord, New Hampshire, At a Mass Meeting of the Demcoratic Party of Merrimac Country* (n.p., n.d.), p. 2; *Speech of Joseph Holt, Louisville, Oct. 19, 1852* (Louisville, 1853), p. 3. See also

Although it was not unreasonable to trace the history of the Democratic party to the 1790s, (identifying the Democrats with the Jeffersonian Republicans and ignoring the rupture in the party's history between Monroe and Jackson), it was, at first glance at least, more difficult to find a comparable continuity in the history of the opposition. After all, the Federalist party had gradually disintegrated following the War of 1812 and only a small minority of Jackson's enemies had sought to identify themselves with or defend its principles and record. By the mid-1850s the Democrats (and their Jeffersonian forebears) had been faced by not only Federalists but also National Republicans, Whigs, Know Nothings and Republicans, together with a host of smaller parties. Nevertheless, these complexities posed no problems to Democratic theorists. For changes in nomenclature could not, they proclaimed, disguise continuities of principle, of intent, and even, in many cases, of personnel and policy. Joseph Holt acknowledged that the names of great parties had "changed with the tastes, the caprices or the necessities of the times," and he admitted that "their forms have been modified by the pressure of surrounding circumstances." But it was necessary to focus upon more fundamental characteristics, for "the animating temper and purpose of each, have ever remained the same." More succinctly, Weller declared that while "you may call ... [the opposition] by whatever name you will, it is the representative of the anti-democratic principle."[18]

The inevitable and thus permanent presence of an opposition did not mean, however, that its role had been in any way an honourable one. The anti-Democrats, it was recognised, had "occasionally held power." With presidential elections like that of 1840 presumably very much in mind, Weller asserted that these victories had been achieved "by fraud, by misrepresentation, by demagoguism." Nevertheless such periods of enemy rule had been mere aberrations. The crucial fact was that "during nearly the whole period of our national existence the government has been in the hands of the Democratic Party."[19]

Thus the nation's political triumphs were in fact Democratic triumphs. The role of the anti-Democratic party was important but only in a negative sense: its destiny, in the United States at least, was to suffer one crushing defeat after another. Democratic spokesmen delighted in listing the policies favoured by Federalists and Whigs that had now been discredited,

---

*Works of Buchanan*, VIII, p. 434, for the assertion that the principles dividing the Democrats from their opponents "from the very nature of the Federal Constitution, must continue to divide us from them until the end."

18. *Speech of Holt*, p. 3; *Speeches of Weller, Orr, Lane, and Cobb*, p. 2. See also the 1849 tract *To the People of Pennsylvania* (n.p., n.d.), p. 1 for a characteristic tracing of Federalist principles among the opposition.
19. *Speeches of Weller, Orr, Lane, and Cobb*, p. 2.

or those espoused by Democrats that had been permanently enshrined in the statute book, in order to confirm the especial suitability of democratic and Democratic principles to the American social and political environment. Thus James Buchanan referred to the controversies over the Bank of the United States, the Independent Treasury, distribution of the proceeds of land sales and the presidential veto as questions which had all been settled in favour of the Democracy. Similarly Daniel Dickinson in the late 1840s noted with some glee that the Whigs were now silent on the previously vital questions of a national bank and a protective tariff. Weller for his part cited the Bank of the United States, a high tariff, the bankruptcy laws and going back to the Jeffersonian era, the Alien and Sedition Laws, as legislative enactments effectively expunged by the Democrats. He even conceded that men of towering intellect, like Webster, Clay and Adams, had been ranged against the party; their brilliance merely underscored the inappropriateness of the policies and principles they had championed.[20]

This meant that in the history of the nation the Democratic party should be accorded a unique and privileged place. Alongside the triumph of Democratic financial policies relating to banks, tariffs, the sale of public lands and internal improvements should be placed the party's enlightened attitude towards immigrants, from which the nation had derived, it was held, incalculable benefits. And as if all this were not enough, there was also the Democratic record in defending the nation in the international arena, and, most importantly of all perhaps, in expanding her territory.[21]

As a result, for the Democrats party and nation had fused. As John Weller argued, "none of the acquisitions [of territory] which have so much increased the power and wealth of the Republic would have been made if the policy of the anti-democratic party had prevailed." Indeed party spokesmen shuddered at the thought, however improbable, of what a succession of Federalist or crypto-Federalist rather than Democratic victories would have produced. "Suppose," the editor of the party's campaign newspaper at Washington in 1852 wrote, "that the doctrines of the Whigs had been adopted, and their principles had been acted upon in this country since the day when, under another name, they passed the Alien and Sedition laws, and clamored for a strong central government and an executive clothed with almost regal attributes." "What," he asked, "would have been our position now?" He then answered his question

20. *Works of Buchanan* VIII, p. 433; John R. Dickinson (ed.), *Speeches, Correspondence, etc. of the Late Daniel S. Dickinson, of New York.* 2 vols. (New York, 1867), I, pp. 270–271; *Speeches of Weller, Orr, Lane, and Cobb*, p. 2; *National Democratic Review* I (Jan. 1856), p. 46. See also New London (CT) *Democrat*, March 1, 1855.
21. See pp. 371–375 and 389–399 for a discussion of immigration and of territorial expansion.

with a further series of rhetorical questions that reviewed virtually the entire political history of the nation:

> where the countless myriads of our patriotic naturalized citizens? – where, indeed, our native liberties? Where would now be our national character and dignity – where the glory won upon the ocean's wave – the laurels gathered on the land, from where Niagara thunders in the North down to the sunny South, where Jackson saved the mighty valley of the Mississippi – where the freedom of the seas – if Whig or federal counsels had prevailed, and the arrogant pretensions of Great Britain been submitted to in 1812? Where would be our financial independence – where our national prosperity – where our solvency – had the efforts of the Whigs to sustain the Bank of the United States been successful, and the weight of that incubus been permitted longer to burden the industry and commerce and control of the legislation of the country? In whose possession – under whose control – would now be Louisiana, Florida, Texas, New Mexico, and California? What despotic, or monarchical, or semi-barbarous powers would have dominated over those rich States and territories, now the happy homes of myriads of free men and the sources of incalculable wealth – where would be the credit of the splendid diplomacy by which some, and the high renown of the martial valor by which others of these vast domains were acquired – had the timid, selfish, narrow-minded opposition and remonstrance of the Whigs been heeded?

These questions were then followed by yet more interrogatives, whose cumulative effect was to emphasise, once again, to contemporaries the majestic role that the Democratic party had played and to make intelligible to modern-day historians the extraordinary loyalty that it had traditionally been able to command:

> Who first tore down and trampled underfoot the wall of separation which aspiring power had interposed between the people and itself? Who threw open wide the gates, and welcomed first the fugitive and the oppressed? Who, with open hearts and arms, received the thousands flying to escape from foreign wrongs and outrage, and gave them homes and shared with them their rights and privileges? To whom do we owe the incalculable benefits, the vast increase in power, in wealth and strength, which we have gained by foreign emigration? Who, upon the very threshold, met the arrogant pretensions of Great Britain, hurled defiance in her teeth, repulsed her legions, braved her naval power, and broke down her empire over and proclaimed the freedom of the Seas? Who delivered us from financial vassalage, and freed us from the bonds of monetary power? Who enlarged our bounds, until from the Gulf of the St Lawrence to the Gulf of Mexico, from the Atlantic to the Pacific, over the mountain and the

valley, the forest and the plain, the crowded city and the quiet hamlet, the flag of freedom floats fair and free, and her sons roam masterless and unrestrained?

This time, however, the editor gave a succinct answer to his questions: "the democracy."[22]

These attitudes were widespread within the party. Spokesmen reiterated that the Democratic party was responsible for the successes of democracy and that democracy was responsible for the extraordinary progress that the nation had made. Again and again this double reduction occurred. Thus Daniel Dickinson of New York in 1848 declared that the principles of the party had produced success "in all that goes to make up advancement in civilization, as never before attended the career of any people." James Buchanan similarly boasted of a lifetime "devoted to the defence & promotion of the great principles of the Democratic party" for the simple reason that "their ascendancy in the Legislative & Executive branches of the government has secured to us liberty, order, & unexampled prosperity at home, and has elevated us to a high and enviable rank amongst the most powerful nations of the earth." It was therefore essential, he continued, to adhere to "the line of public policy which has been pursued by successive Democratic administrations." The rewards would be immense: "should this policy continue to be our guide, we shall soon surpass every other nation in wealth, power, & prosperity." "The day will not then be distant," he concluded, "when to be an American citizen will constitute as proud a title and command as much respect throughout the world as ever did the name of a Roman citizen."[23]

By the 1850s, therefore, the Democratic party was able to command an exceptional degree of loyalty from its members. This did not mean that its unity was assured, for the same decade would witness a series of disastrous schisms that would facilitate the Republican triumph of 1860. But contemporaries recognised that it was difficult to entice even disgruntled Democrats away from their party and those who did abandon it were concerned to take their old principles with them. Meanwhile those who remained continued to assert that their party bore a unique responsibility for realising the hopes and fulfilling the destiny of the entire nation[24]

In a sense, however, the role of the Democratic party in the antebellum republic was more unprecedented and exceptional than party spokesmen

---

22. *Speeches of Weller, Orr, Lane, and Cobb*, p. 2; *The Campaign*, June 19, 1852, p. 23. See also *Proceedings of the Banquet of the Jackson Democratic Association, Washington 8 Jan. 1852* (n.p., n.d.), p. 6.
23. *Speeches, etc. of Dickinson*, I, p. 269; *Works of Buchanan*, VIII, p. 356.
24. Joel H. Silbey, "'There Are Other questions Beside That of Slavery Merely'" in Silbey, *The Partisan Imperative: The Dynamics of American Politics Before the Civil War* (New York, 1985), p. 93.

themselves even knew. The 1850s would be the last decade in which these boasts would be possible. In the 1860s the Republicans would be able to claim center stage in the nation's political drama and no longer would even the most committed Democratic partisans be able to relegate their opponents to the marginal role to which they had been consigned before the War. Indeed the position of the Democrats in the antebellum years was anomalous. Rarely can a single party have been able to claim, with plausibility and after many decades of bipartisan conflict, that its principles are so closely identified with the nation. It was indeed true that most of the policies of the Federalists and Whigs had been discarded and discredited. It was indeed true that Democrats had offered the warmest welcome to immigrants. It had indeed been their policies that had resulted in the huge accessions of territory that had taken place as a result of the Louisiana Purchase and the Mexican War. Thus Edson B. Olds, addressing an Ohio audience, confirmed that, to a Democrat, the triumphs of nation and party were inseparable. Once again the premise was that the opposition had contributed nothing positive to the history of the nation. "You may search your national statute books, and the history of parties in the country," Olds challenged, "but you will look in vain if you expect to find a single measure of national policy, opposed by the Democracy, but advocated and put into operation by the opposition, which has not been signally condemned by the American people." From this a familiar set of claims was derived, expressed in the familiar rhetorical style. Olds posed three questions. The first focused upon territorial expansion: "am I, then," he asked, "claiming too much ... when I say that it is the democracy who have unrolled the map of Empire, until the American Union extends from the waters of the Gulf of St Lawrence to the Gulf of Mexico, and from the Atlantic to the Pacific oceans?" The second turned to international relations: "am I claiming then too much when I say that it is the Democratic Party who have maintained your national honor during the prosecution of every war since the days of the Revolution" and "that to the democracy we are indebted for the higher position we have taken among the nations of the earth?" The third switched to domestic policy: "am I claiming then too much when, after searching the past records of the country, I say that to the Democratic party we are indebted for those measures of internal policy," measures "which have made us not only the most prosperous people upon the face of the globe, but the envy and admiration of all whole world?" It was obvious both that Olds did not believe he was claiming too much, and that he expected his audience to accept his claims.[25]

---

25. *Speech of the Hon. Edson B. Olds At ... Circleville, Ohio, 9 Feb 1856* (n.p., n.d.), p. 3. See also *Letter of ex-President Van Buren, June 28 1856* (n.p., n.d.), pp. 3–4; *National Democratic Review*, I (Jan. 1856), pp. 14, 19.

## III

Although it is tempting to assume that Democrats' claims about their party were mere electoral froth, it would be an error to do so. Instead they were, for many in the 1850s, key articles of democratic, as well as of Democratic, faith. Indeed it may even be appropriate to compare the Democratic creed with a religious faith and to suggest that the Democratic party in the ante-bellum years was akin to a church. Many evangelicals within the Whig party (especially in the North) believed in carrying into politics the religious and moral principles which they promoted within their churches. Democrats were generally, as we shall see, resistant to these efforts but for them their party itself had a quasi-religious mission. There was a widespread belief that its founders and its chief spokesmen had identified principles, moral and ethical, as much as political or economic, which were eternal, and to which both party and nation had been consecrated. It followed from this that just as no event could disprove the existence of God, and none should be allowed to destroy individual faith, so no processes could develop which could not be illuminated and explained by Democratic modes of thought and to which Democratic principles would not prove applicable. The glorious past would provide a compass which the committed Democratic would employ as an infallible guide to the future. This was a cosy assumption, and by virtue of its very cosiness, one which would bring ruin upon the party.

Yet though Democratic claims about the past were plausible, they were not, on closer inspection, entirely convincing. The official analysis omitted much. Although it was true that Whig and Federalist economic policies had been abandoned, even as these committed Democrats spoke, Whig and Federalist visions of the Good Society were being in good part realised, in good part too at the expense of the agrarian idyll championed by Jefferson and most of the other founders of the Democratic church. Indeed it was primarily because the economy was developing in the way that the principal enemies of the Democrats had visualised that tariffs and banks had ceased to be demanded. To some extent, therefore, the Democrats had won the battles and were loudly proclaiming their victories, oblivious to the fact that they were losing the war.[26]

Similarly, the Democrats' account of the past ignored many factors. The nation's economic growth was in fact far beyond the control of any political party and especially of one which, as we shall see, claimed that *laissez-faire* was the appropriate model for government. The United States did indeed in the nineteenth century experience enormous economic change and had achieved international economic pre-eminence by its close. But the role of democracy in this success story is one which economic

26. See pp. 436–457 and 478–485.

historians have not even begun systematically to consider. None, however, believes that the relationship was as direct or straightforward as contemporary Democrats held. And the role of specific Democratic policies is even more difficult to determine; once again, however, it is safe to assume that their impact was far less than Democratic spokesmen believed.[27]

Yet the major deficiency of the Democratic analysis lay elsewhere. The Democratic account of the past ignored a critical factor. As I have already argued, the reason the party of Jefferson and John Taylor and of Jackson and Van Buren was able to employ egalitarian rhetoric and seek to empower the white male was that they were not, in so doing, posing a challenge to the slaveholders of the South. Indeed on many occasions they were actually furthering the interests of that group.[28]

Here, as we shall see, was the explanation for some of the greatest of Democratic triumphs, even though party spokesmen were largely oblivious to it. But in the late 1840s and 1850s the social and political power of the slaveholders would itself be subjected to an unprecedented series of challenges. A party which had built its successes upon foundations of which it was not even properly aware would be in difficulties when those foundations began to shake. The Democratic solution, to build even higher upon the same foundations, could only end in disaster.

## A constricted universalism: Race and ethnicity

### I

One of the paradoxes of the United States under its present constitution is that it has proved, in general, extraordinarily hospitable to immigrants, particularly Caucasians who have come to its shores voluntarily. At the same time the history of African Americans, brought to the country under duress, has been one of egregious oppression. This pattern was strikingly evident and was indeed firmly established in the antebellum era; the paradox reached a culmination in the thinking of antebellum Democrats. In these years no group was more welcoming to the immigrant, none so infected with racial prejudice against the African American.[29]

The rise of nativist sentiment in the 1850s, manifested most conspicuously in the Know Nothing party,[30] elicited a firm and uncompromising

---

27. Jeremy Atack and Peter Passell (eds.), *A New Economic View of American History*, 2nd ed. (New York, 1994), pp. 1–25.
28. It is perhaps worth repeating that I am not suggesting here that mainstream Democratic ideology was overtly proslavery. But neither was the benefit that it accorded to the slaveholding interest merely a random outcome. See the first volume of this study.
29. These attitudes were present among Democrats in the Jacksonian era, and earlier. See my *"Agrarians" and "Aristocrats,"* pp. 190–193, 221–223.
30. For a discussion of the nativist movement and its impact on party politics in the 1850s see pp. 515–592.

response from Democratic leaders and spokesmen. The *National Democratic Review*, for example, was extremely hostile. In the first issue after its launch in 1856 it called the Know Nothing party "a foul and infamous blot upon the fair horizon of America." Here was a "a crusade against the rights of man, rivaling any to be met in the darkest annals of human depravity." Its history was "a history of riot, of bloodshed, of unexampled corruption." Other newspapers and magazines were equally critical. In Connecticut the New London *Democrat* announced that no genuine Democrat should countenance "secret political societies, whose influences are so obviously pernicious and detrimental to true Republicanism." Indeed "Democrats cannot, for a moment, tolerate their existence, much less a connection with them." Similarly in Boston, a hotbed of nativist sentiment, the *Ledger* denounced the Know Nothings of Massachusetts as "a party based upon professions and assertions, of bigotry and intolerance, in politics and religion, which are hostile to the genius and spirit of our government, and deeply repugnant to every principle of justice and equality."[31]

In the same way Democratic state parties across the nation, but especially in the North, where immigration was concentrated, placed their opposition to the Know Nothings firmly on the record book. Although Indiana was a nativist stronghold, the Democratic party did not shrink from an official condemnation of the Know Nothings. The Democracy of Indiana, according to the platform of 1854, "openly and avowedly condemn any organisation, secret or otherwise, that would aim to disrobe any citizen, native or adopted, of his political, secular, or religious liberty." This was a clear reference to the proscriptive policies advocated by some nativists and directed against the foreign-born. Such proscription, "founded on bigotry and ideas of intolerance," was "tyrannical." The major nativist demand, however, was for a change in the naturalisation laws. Indiana's Democrats passed a formal resolution against this proposal:

> Resolved, That our naturalization laws, our republican institutions, our marvelous growth of national greatness and the happiness of our people, have been and are irresistible inducements and invitations to the inhabitants of less favored lands to become citizens of ours; and that past experience, injustice, sound policy, and national pride, all concur to favor the continuation of our present naturalization laws; that if any abuses have grown up under these laws, they have sprung from that imperfect execution alone, and not from inherent defects in the laws themselves, and that we are in favor of that policy which will soonest assimilate naturalized citizens with the mass of

31. *National Democratic Review*, I (Jan. 1856), p. 16, II (Feb. 1856), pp. 102–104; New London *Democrat*, Jan. 27, 1855; Boston *Ledger*, Oct. 31, 1857.

our people, and opposed to that anti-American and illiberal policy which proscribes the foreign born citizen for the accident of birth, and drives him to self-defence, to antagonism with our native-born citizens in feeling, political opinions and conduct.

The resolution captured the hostility of the Democrats to the nativist groups.[32]

## II

Democrats offered many reasons for encouraging immigration and welcoming immigrants. Not least among them was the economic benefit which, they contended, the nation had received in the past and could expect to obtain in the future. Reviewing the economic progress already witnessed, the *National Democratic Review* applauded the contribution made by immigration. "It has been," the editor asserted, "the bone and sinew of our independence." In rhapsodic language he described immigration's "voice," "heard in the clatter of every factory and in the shriek of every steam whistle;" immigration "bade the forests sink; and lo! In place of darksome woods, the harvests are waving in the sunbeam, and, where the panther roved, now grazes the peaceful herd." Moreover immigration "stood upon the beach of the sea and upon the margins of broad rivers; and cities sprang from beneath its creative feet." And finally "it endured the noisome vapors of the marshes; and millions of acres were won to culture."[33]

Nativists frequently drew attention to the presence of paupers among the immigrant population. But the *National Democratic Review* brushed aside these objections. Even if the occasional pauper or vagrant landed on the nation's shores, the editor asked, "does not the immeasurable good compensate for the petty evil?" More prosaically but no less extravagantly, Louis Shade in a pamphlet entitled,*The Immigration into the United States* set out to calculate the impact of immigration. He concluded that if Know Nothing policies had been adopted in 1790 the nation's population would have grown by only a third as much as it actually had. Turning to the more recent past, he also claimed, again without burdening his readers with

---

32. William E. Henry (ed.), *State Platforms of the Two Dominant Political Parties in Indiana, 1850–1900* (Indianapolis, 1902), pp. 10–11, 18. See also *Proceedings and Address of the Democratic State Convention Held at Syracuse...Jan. 10, 1856* (Albany, 1856), pp. 23–26; Michael W. Cluskey, *Buchanan and Breckinridge, The Democratic Hand-Book...Recommended by the Democratic National Committee* (Washington, DC, 1856 ), pp. 30–32; *To the People of Connecticut: The Extension of Slavery: The Official Acts of Both Parties in Relation to This* (n.p., n.d.), pp. 6–7; *Washington Campaign*, Oct. 27, 1848, p. 374.

33. *National Democratic Review*, I (April 1856), p. 292.

statistical details or discussions of methodology, that the great increase in national wealth and power obtained between 1850 and 1855, was owing "chiefly to immigration" and the role played by the immigrant in the construction of railroads and canals, and the peopling of the newer states. A less precise but equally grand claim was offered by Horatio Seymour of New York who, boasting of the extraordinary achievements made by "the commercial men of the United States, or by its artisans and agriculturists," explained that they were, in no small part, attributable to immigration. Thus "no Alexander or Caesar in the height of his conquests, ever made such acquisitions of power as immigration brings to us." He concluded that it was imperative that the nation continue to welcome immigrants, lest they instead be diverted to other regions of the New World.[34]

Although Seymour specifically mentioned the contribution of immigrants to the nation's commercial life, Democrats more commonly emphasised their value as a source of labour. Since the nation had "immense resources undeveloped for the want of labor," it was sound policy to "let the downtrodden and oppressed of the Old World come here," so that they could "strengthen the government by increasing its wealth." Here was perhaps the primary economic rationale for the Democratic policy on immigration.[35]

Yet in the 1850s nativists did not seek to restrict immigration (except that of paupers and criminals) and did not dispute the need for an additional supply of labour. The thrust of antebellum nativism was instead political: it sought a reduction in the political power wielded either by the immigrants themselves, or by those unscrupulous demagogues, usually Democrats, who marshaled and controlled their votes. Hence the desire, manifested by some political nativists, to bar foreigners from holding office and also the desire, displayed by virtually all, to extend the naturalisation period. Since Democrats benefited electorally from the immigrant vote, it was scarcely surprising that they defended the existing naturalisation laws and insisted on the equal right to office of all citizens, whether native or foreign-born. But this electoral windfall was at least as much the effect as the cause of Democratic liberalism on this issue. As we have seen, and as Democratic spokesmen loudly and proudly proclaimed, their party had a record of support for the immigrant that went back to the time when the Jeffersonians had inveighed against the Alien Act.

As a result, Democrats took pains to present a host of arguments in defence of the political rights of immigrants. Some were slightly unexpected. Thus J. F. Dowdell of Alabama argued that it was "a matter of no

---

34. *National Democratic Review*, I (April 1856), p. 292; Louis Shade, *The Immigration into the United States* (n.p., n.d.), pp. 6, 12; *Speeches . . . of Seymour*, pp. 12–13.
35. *Speeches of Weller, Orr, Lane, and Cobb*, p. 3.

small moment, either in political or moral results, whether the door to citizenship shall be practically closed to our neighbors in the Old World," for "the effect upon us at home, and the popularity of our Republic abroad, should be seriously considered." It was evident that "we already have the enmity of the crowned heads of Europe." "Shall we lose," he asked, "the sympathy of the masses of their subjects – that most salutary check upon despotic diplomacy and tyrannical interference – that silent power that holds the kingly arm, and thwarts the combinations of despotism against free government?" For "who doubts that our Constitution is read and admired, our national airs sung, by thousands in the Old World?"[36]

It was, however, comparatively unusual for Democrats to concern themselves with the opinions of Europeans. Their main task, in combating nativist propaganda, was rather to show that the more immediate domestic interests of the United States were not jeopardised by the rapid enfranchisement or the election to office of the recently naturalised immigrant. The key question was a simple one: could he be trusted? Know Nothings doubted it, Democrats did not. Dowdell himself quickly returned to this theme. "Who believes," he demanded, "that when these suffering sons of toil, by self-denial and frugality, save enough to bring them across the ocean, and they come among us, swearing allegiance to this government and fidelity to our Constitution, that they will prove faithless to the land of their choice?" This was a rhetorical question but Dowdell left his audience in no doubt as to the appropriate answer: "it cannot be; it has not been; the charge is groundless; the history of the past refutes it."[37]

Yet when Know Nothings voiced their doubts about the immigrant's suitability for political rights, they did not merely express a concern that he had been born and brought up in a foreign land. Thus English immigrants encountered little hostility from them. The ethnic group to bear the brunt of their resentment was undoubtedly the Irish. One reason was that many Irish immigrants were extremely poor. Democrats were therefore required to show that poverty was an irrelevance. Thus Howell Cobb of Georgia restated a view that had been prevalent in earlier decades when he insisted that poverty, so far from being a disqualification, could actually be construed as a recommendation. Since economic impoverishment was all too often a function of political disfranchisement, it followed that the poor (but honest) immigrants "of all others . . . most fully recognize the blessings of our free institutions, and will be among the last to surrender them." Though poor, the immigrant was still a worthy Democrat.[38]

36.  *Speech of Hon. J. F. Dowdell of Alabama at the Democratic Ratification Meeting at City Hall, Washington, June 18th, 1856* (Washington, DC, 1856), p. 5.
37.  *Speech of Dowdell*, p. 5.
38.  *Speeches of Weller, Orr, Lane, and Cobb*, p. 29.

The most potent charge against the Irish, however, concerned not their economic condition but instead their religious affiliation. It was their Roman Catholicism, in general, and the power of the Pope, in particular, which caused most disquiet among nativists. Democrats accordingly spared no effort in rebutting their charges. Thus one anonymous "Adopted Catholic," writing to a Democratic Association in Kentucky, avowed that he owed "no allegiance to any prince, Pope, or potentate, inconsistent with the fullest allegiance of my adopted country." More specifically, and more implausibly perhaps, he considered the possibility that the Pope might "come as an invader." In this event the author reassured his fellow Democrats that he "would oppose him as I would any other usurper."[39]

Other Democrats denied that the Pope possessed any temporal power. Roman Catholics, it was noted, had fought in wars alongside Protestants, and, when required (as in the recent war with Mexico) against a Roman Catholic enemy. Many partisans thus dismissed fears that the Church of Rome could overwhelm the Protestant sects as grossly unrealistic. The Catholics were heavily outnumbered, both in terms of clergy and laity and if the disparity were being reduced then the solution was for the Protestant denominations to redouble their efforts – but outside the political arena. In other words, they should "look to their internal organizations, and not political action, for the desired remedies." Protestantism, according to some party spokesmen, simply did not need any advantages; it should rely instead upon reason and persuasion, upon common sense and upon free discussion.[40]

## III

Although Democrats were fully aware of the economic benefits that immigrants brought to their nation, and equally mindful of their political contribution to both nation and party, it would be an error to ignore or underestimate the moral fervor animating the crusade against nativism. Once again Democratic memories were long. Party spokesmen even harked back to the original founding of the colonies. Thus John B. Weller reminded his New Hampshire audience that "your ancestors left their native land, crossed the boisterous ocean, and came to a howling wilderness because religious freedom was denied to them." Now, however, they were being urged by the Know Nothings "to engage in this same work of

---

39. *Letter of an Adopted Catholic, Addressed to the President of the Kentucky Democratic Association of Washington City* (n.p., n.d.), p. 5.
40. *Speech of Olds*, p. 7; *National Democratic Review* I (Feb. 1856), p. 104; *Speeches of Weller, Orr, Lane, and Cobb*, pp. 2–3.

persecution which compelled them to abandon their homes and seek an asylum upon this Continent!" "Are you ready to do this?" he asked.[41]

A more common injunction, however, was to look for inspiration to the early decades of the Republic. For no immediately obvious reason, Edson B. Olds compared the Know Nothings with the tories of the revolutionary era. He also made the more obvious reference to the Federalists' Alien Act. The temptation to identify the Know Nothings with now-vanquished political enemies was clearly irresistible. Many referred to the Federalists and at least one party spokesman, again for no obvious reason, invoked the specter of those Federalists who, with treasonous intent, had conspired at the Hartford Convention of 1814.[42]

More fundamentally, however, Democrats insisted that any restriction of freedom of opinion and religious liberty was at odds with the national ethos. According to James Orr of South Carolina, the Know Nothings were making "war ... upon the freedom of religion." This was "unholy, unjust and violative of the spirit of the Constitution and the genius of our institutions." In New York in 1855, when nativist unrest was close to its peak, the Democratic party did not hesitate to condemn Know Nothing policies as "not only a violation of the Constitution, but also as subversive of personal liberty." Such policies undermined, it was claimed, the individual's right to his religious beliefs, a right that was not only enshrined in the American constitutional tradition but also "heaven born, the gift of God." And in a more general sense, the proscriptive policy was "a cold and selfish policy, at war with the spirit of the age and the large liberality of a Christian people."[43]

There was an unmistakable idealism here. Democrats frequently suggested, and no doubt believed, that theirs were the values of humanity, eternally and universally valid. Once again it was easy to equate the Democratic party with democracy itself. On this reasoning the *National Democratic Review* was able to proclaim that democracy "ignores all the wretched distinctions of blood and clime, which have degraded the conventionalities of the old world; it opens its heart to receive the oppressed of every land."[44]

Yet however sincere the sentiments might have been, the words were not strictly accurate. As with many Democratic utterances, the editor had on this occasion omitted to offer an important qualification. For democracy

41. *Speeches of Weller, Orr, Lane, and Cobb*, p. 3.
42. *Speech of Olds*, pp. 5–6; *To the People of Pennsylvania*, p. 1; Michael W. Closkey, *The Democratic Hand-Book* (n.p., n.d.), p. 32.
43. *Speeches of Weller, Orr, Lane, and Cobb*, p. 17; *Proceedings of the State Convention of the National Democracy of the State of New York, August 23, 1855* (New York, 1855), pp. 10–12; *Speech of Olds*, p. 7; *Speech of Dowdell*, p. 5–7.
44. *National Democratic Review*, I (Jan. 1856), p. 17.

did not in fact ignore "all the wretched distinctions of blood and clime" and did not open "its heart to receive the oppressed of every land." The apparent universalism of the Democratic creed was belied or undercut by the deepest racial prejudice, as a result of which democracy would in fact rigidly observe at least some of "the wretched distinctions of blood and clime" and resolutely ignore the "oppressed" of some lands. Among these were the lands of Africa, from where the ancestors of several million Americans had been forcibly removed, and, closer to home, much of the land of which the United States itself was now made up, acquired in often dubious fashion from the Native American population. Neither group would be esteemed by Democrats. Both groups, African Americans and Native Americans, would remain irretrievably beyond the Democratic pale.[45]

## IV

In 1858 the Democratic party of Indiana, the same party which had over the preceding few years boldly set its face against the persecution of the immigrant, passed a resolution concerning race. It was again a model of clarity but this time of illiberality too. "We hereby denounce and hold up to the universal execration and scorn of all loyal American citizens," these Democrats proclaimed, "the loathsome doctrine of 'Negro equality.'" In the antebellum United States there were relatively few who believed the races were equal. But there were even fewer who were as strident or vehement as the Democrats in their denunciations of African Americans (and to a lesser extent, Native Americans) or as fervently committed to the principle of Caucasian superiority.[46]

Racist utterances litter the record of antebellum Democrats. According to the *National Democratic Review* the black race was unlike any other in that it was always in servitude when in contact with another race. "The cause . . . of this unvarying condition of the African, through every age, can only be found," the editor concluded, "in *an inherent, ineradicable mental inferiority to every other people.*" Whereas every other race had furthered the course of civilisation in certain eras, blacks had failed to produce a religion, a literature or a history. The *Review* also noted the

---

45. On another occasion the same journal did, by implication at least, enter the necessary racial (and racist) caveat: "it was not for the benefit of the Anglo-Saxon alone, that our fathers left this brilliant legacy; they looked forward to a nobler destiny; they wished to open a reservoir, in which the blood of *all the tribes, that boast the title of Caucasian man* [emphasis added], might mingle their currents, and thus form a race that should rise superior to the physical and moral effeminacy of present generations" – *National Democratic Review*, I (April, 1856), p. 293.
46. *State Platforms of . . . Parties in Indiana*, p. 14.

discrimination practised in the North against free blacks – which it then cited as further proof of their inferiority. Similarly, Daniel Dickinson of New York echoed many southern comments on racial differences when he declared that it was impossible for blacks and whites to coexist on equal terms. And New York Democrat John Van Evrie published books and tracts purporting to demonstrate the reduced size and diminished capacity of the negro brain.[47]

Once again tradition weighed heavily upon Democrats. Once again they looked back to revolutionary times. Once again their own attitudes were traced back to the fathers of the Republic. Thus Franklin Pierce, in his 1855 Annual Message to Congress, praised "the wise and brave statesmen" of revolutionary times who, "being engaged in no extravagant scheme of social change," left "the subject races, whether Indian or African, of that day," precisely "as they were." It was important, he insisted, to recognise the magnitude of this achievement for the policy "preserved themselves and their posterity from the anarchy and the ever recurring civil wars which have prevailed in other revolutionized European colonies of America."[48]

Yet of all northern Democrats of the 1850s it probably fell to Stephen A. Douglas to make the most significant statements about race and racial differences. Like others in his party he was generous in his attitude towards Caucasian immigrants, condemning Know Nothing proscription as "subversive of all our ideas and principles of religious freedom" and "revolting to our sense of justice and right."[49] But when he discussed racial, rather than ethnic, differences his attitude abruptly shifted. "This government," he declared at New Orleans in 1858, "was made by white men, for the benefit of white men and their posterity for ever, to be administered by white men, and no others." In his celebrated debates with Lincoln that year Douglas repeatedly returned to this theme. "This nation," he told a Chicago audience, "is a white people – the people composed of European descendants – the people that have established this government for themselves and their posterity." Moreover he was "in favor of preserving not only the purity of the blood, but the purity of the government from any mixture or amalgamation with inferior races." Douglas then referred, as

47. *National Democratic Review* I (March 1856), pp. 185–193; *Speeches etc. of Dickinson*, I, pp. 299, 354; J. H. Van Evrie (M.D.), *White Supremacy and Negro Subordination; or Negroes a Subordinate Race and Slavery its Normal Condition* (New York, 1868), pp. x, xi, xiii, 121–128, 176–177, 228, 283.
48. James D. Richardson (ed.), *A Compilation of the Messages and Papers of the Presidents 1789–1897* (Washington, DC, 1899), V, p. 341.
49. *Speech of Senator Douglas at the Democratic Celebration of the Anniversary of American Freedom, in Independence Square, Philadelphia, July 4, 1854* (Philadelphia, 1854) quoted in Johannsen, *Douglas*, p. 446. See also Johannsen, *Douglas*, pp. 457, 470.

Pierce had done and as other Democrats were wont to do, to the experiences of Latin America, confirming that he had "seen the effects of this mixture of superior and inferior races – this amalgamation of white man and Indians and negroes." And the result?: "degeneration, demoralization, and degradation below the capacity for self government."[50]

Douglas was impelled to make these statements in part as a result of the Dred Scott decision, which he supported and which denied that African Americans could be citizens of the United States. But while the Supreme Court decision may have brought the question under the political spotlight, Douglas's racist utterances antedated it by many years. Thus in 1850, speaking at Chicago in defence of the Compromise that he had played so large a part in securing, he offered a racist's perspective on virtually the whole of human history. "The history of the world," he asserted, "furnishes few examples where any considerable portion of the human race have shown themselves sufficiently enlightened and civilized to exercise the rights and enjoy the blessings of freedom." Douglas first glanced at "Asia and Africa," where "we find nothing but ignorance, superstition, and despotism." Then he noted that "large portions of Europe and America can scarcely lay claim to civilization and Christianity; and a still smaller portion have demonstrated their capacity for self-government." These were the perceptions that would allow him to endorse the racism of the Dred Scott decision.[51]

Douglas's racism was itself part of a long Democratic tradition. In the 1850s, however, Democratic racism was pushed further than ever before. As the question of America's black population came to the fore, it became necessary to enquire into the relationship between racial minorities and the key symbolic acts of American history. The Constitution was, of course, heavily implicated in this, as it always had been, but in the 1840s and 1850s the Declaration of Independence too came under unprecedented scrutiny. Here a spectrum of opinion is identifiable. At the two extremes lay William Lloyd Garrison, who venerated the Declaration even as he derided the Constitution (and the Union), and Calhoun who venerated the Constitution (and even the Union if it could only be administered according to the Constitution!) and derided the Declaration. At this point (as at others) the two men's reasoning converged in support of a single proposition: the Declaration, in contrast to the Constitution, was

---

50. *Speeches of Senator Stephen A. Douglas on the Occasion of his Public Reception by the Citizens of New Orleans, Philadelphia and Baltimore* (Washington, DC, 1859), p. 5; *Political Debates Between Hon. Abraham Lincoln and Hon. Stephen a Douglas ... Including The Preceding Speeches Of Each, At Chicago, Springfield, etc.* (Columbus, 1860), p. 12.

51. *Speech of Hon. Stephen A. Douglas on the "Measures of Adjustment" ... Chicago, Oct. 23rd, 1850* (Washington, DC, 1851), p. 29.

at odds with slavery. More moderate views, meanwhile, were expressed by Republicans like Lincoln and Democrats like Douglas. For Lincoln the principles enshrined in the Declaration were a set of ideals constantly to be striven for, goals which Americans should never lose sight of however far they might yet be from fully attaining them. But Douglas's view was quite different. It was also very simple: the Declaration was not antislavery. It applied only to white Americans.

"No one," said Douglas in his first major speech after the Dred Scott decision, "can vindicate the character, motives and conduct of the signers of the Declaration of Independence, except upon the hypothesis that they referred to the white race alone, and not to the African, when they declared all men to have been created equal." This statement was another model of clarity but Douglas nevertheless began to encounter problems. For the Declaration, of course, did not actually specify that white men alone were created equal. For this reason perhaps, he felt himself compelled to describe the context and the purpose of the document. In so doing, however, he experienced even greater difficulties. The signers, he argued, "were speaking of British subjects on this Continent being equal to British subjects born and residing in Great Britain." Their object had been to show that American colonists were "entitled to the same inalienable rights, and among them were enumerated life, liberty, and the pursuit of happiness." Thus, he concluded, "the Declaration was adopted for the purpose of justifying the colonists, in the eyes of the civilized world, in withdrawing their allegiance from the British Crown, and dissolving their connection with the mother country."[52]

The problem here was not that his account was factually erroneous but rather that it left the Declaration, the enunciation of which was one of the great symbolic acts of the young Republic, a severely diminished or shrunken document. Carl Schurz, the Republican leader and orator, in the late 1850s made Douglas's career, principles and policies a special target and subjected them to the most searching analysis and criticism. With great acuity, he fastened upon Douglas's attitude to the Declaration and denounced it with the most withering scorn:

> There is your Declaration of Independence, a diplomatic dodge, adopted merely for the purpose of excusing the rebellious colonies in the eyes of civilized mankind. There is your Declaration of Independence, no longer the sacred code of the rights of man, but a hypocritical piece of special pleading, drawn up by a batch of artful

52. *Remarks Of The Honorable Stephen A. Douglas On Kansas, Utah And The Dred Scott Decision, Delivered At Springfield, Illinois, June 12th, 1857* (Chicago, 1857), pp. 9–10. See also *Debates between Lincoln and Douglas*, p. 37; *Speeches of Douglas at New Orleans, Philadelphia and Baltimore*, p. 5.

pettifoggers, who, when speaking of the rights of man, meant but the privileges of a set of aristocratic slaveholders, but styled it "the rights of man," in order to throw dust into the eyes of the world, and to inveigle noble-hearted fools into lending them aid and assistance. These are your boasted revolutionary sires, no longer heroes and sages, but accomplished humbuggers and hypocrites, who said one thing and meant another.

Schurz concluded that Douglas had brought the signers of the Declaration down to his own level.[53]

This, however, was not the only, or even necessarily the most important, way in which Democratic ideology came under pressure as a result of the sectional conflict and the increasingly urgent need to address the race issue. From the era of Jefferson to the 1840s the Democrats had led in proclaiming the virtues of democracy, in glorifying the nation's democratic practices and in boasting of their global significance. As we have seen, they did not in any way abandon these practices in the 1850s but they were now, for the first time, being challenged and, in a sense, outbid by a rival party. For the radical Republicans had now overtaken them as the most enthusiastic proponents of the rights of man, not only in the United States (where their more inclusive view of the American population comprehended its racial minorities too) but also in the world as a whole. Racism had always blinded Democrats to the plight of African Americans and Native Americans but now it was hardening into a creed with significant international implications.

Once again the thought of Stephen A. Douglas, the most popular northern Democrat of the late antebellum era, illustrates this tendency. A comparison between his views and those advanced by Democrats in previous decades is instructive. In the 1840s Democrats had announced to the world that it was the nation's "Manifest Destiny" to take control of the American continent, with some spokesmen confining their ambitions to North America but others embracing Latin America too. It is not necessary to deny the role of economic factors in this drive for territorial aggrandisement to recognise that there was also a strong dose of idealism present. One aim had been to further the global advance of democracy. As we shall see, these territorial ambitions were still very much intact in the 1850s and an idealistic rationale in terms of democracy was still present. But Democrats like Douglas now held a much harsher and less compassionate view of the international order than Democrats had previously espoused. "It is a law of humanity," Douglas announced in 1858, "and a law of civilization, that whenever a man, or a race of men, show themselves

53. Frederic Bancroft (ed.), *Speeches, Correspondence and Political Papers of Carl Schurz.* 6 vols. (New York, 1913), I, pp. 94–95.

incapable of managing their own affairs, they must consent to be governed by those who are capable of performing the duty." Douglas then employed a telling comparison. "It is on this principle," he claimed, "that you establish those institutions of charity, for the support of the blind, or the deaf and dumb, or the insane." This had immediate applications in the case of the United States for "in accordance with this principle . . . the Negro race, under all circumstances, at all times, and in all countries, has shown itself incapable of self-government."[54]

If this argument served to justify the enslavement of African Americans, it also justified other forms of control over allegedly inferior races, even when employed by nations whom Democrats had traditionally tended to convict of the most deplorable tyranny. Since the time of Jefferson Democrats had generally been Anglophobes and Douglas himself had been, and continued to be, no exception. But the rules of international conduct that he enunciated now seemed suddenly and unexpectedly to justify the British Empire's oppression of other peoples. "The civilized world," he argued, "have always held, that when any race of men have shown themselves so degraded, by ignorance, superstition, cruelty, and barbarism, as to be utterly incapable of governing themselves, they must, in the nature of things, be governed by others, by such laws as are deemed applicable to their condition." But this doctrine was more perilous than Douglas himself realised. It led him towards wide-ranging and unexpected conclusions, conclusions he almost certainly did not wish to reach. "It is upon this principle alone," he noted, "that England justifies the form of government she has established in the Indies, and for some of her other colonies," "that Russia justifies herself in holding her serfs as slaves, and selling them as a part of the land on which they live," "that our Pilgrim Fathers justified themselves in reducing the Negro and Indian to servitude, and selling them as property," and "that we, in Illinois and most of the free States, justify ourselves in denying the Negro and the Indian the privilege of voting, and all other political rights." As if this were not enough, he then cited a final example. This was the doctrine used in "many of the States of the Union," in order to justify . . . depriving the white man of the right of the elective franchise, unless he is fortunate enough to own a certain amount of property."[55]

The final example was in one sense appropriate since those denied the franchise at all times in history have indeed been deemed unworthy of self-government. But Douglas had said too much. He himself acknowledged that he did not agree with some of the practices that he had cited but in so doing he undercut his own argument. In effect the principle he had

---

54. *Speeches of Douglas at New Orleans, Philadelphia and Baltimore*, p. 5.
55. *Speech of . . . . Douglas on "Measures of Adjustment,"* p. 29.

invoked to justify the exploitation of the nation's racial minorities was one to which he could not actually give his own assent. For neither the first nor the last time, racism and democracy were proving to be uncomfortable bedfellows.

V

Democrats normally kept their views upon race separate from their statements on immigration and ethnicity. This was perhaps advisable since there were serious tensions between them. It was extremely difficult to sustain a view of immigrants which refused to deduce their potential from the conditions they experienced on their native soil whilst doing precisely that for African Americans (and Native Americans).

Occasionally these tensions became outright, but still unrecognised, contradictions. Thus a favourite argument employed by Democrats against the abolitionists concerned the impact that freed African Americans would have upon white labour in the North. The freedmen would then, Daniel Dickinson warned, degrade "the white laborers of the North by mingling with them and competing for their employment." For it was evident that blacks and whites "cannot exist together upon terms of equality without detriment to both." This was inevitable: "heaven has so ordained and men cannot subvert the decree – one [race] will not be elevated while the other will be degraded." Similarly James W. Bradbury, a former Democratic Senator from Maine declared that emancipation "would kill the North." "The slaves," he predicted, "would be here competing with them, lowering labor and degrading the working man."[56]

These were common enough fears, perhaps expressed by all northern Democrats who remained in the party throughout the 1850s and by no means novel then. But occasionally Democratic spokesmen, in discussing immigration, contradicted themselves. Thus the *Albany Argus*, one of the foremost Democratic papers in New York, set out to repel a nativist charge that immigration led to an oversupply of labor and thus reduced wages. Immigration, the editor retorted, so far from depressing wages actually "elevates labor." The reality was that "it lifts up the whole fabric of humanity, the laboring classes and all, and adds to the comforts of all, their power, their intellectual pleasures, and even lengthens...the term of life." How were these results obtained? The editor explained that "the great hordes of foreign laborers have displaced the American workman only to elevate him to the condition of an artisan" They "do the rough and massive work upon the canals, and the railroads, and the houses, so that he [the native-born laborer] may find in them the exercise of

56. *Speeches etc. of Dickinson*, I, p. 299; *Boston Ledger*, Oct. 31, 1857.

his higher handicraft, and more varied employment." Thus "the foreign laborer releases his domestic brother from mere manual drudgery."[57]

This argument bore some resemblance to the southern proslavery notion of a "mud-sill" class, supposedly necessary in all advanced societies. But more fundamentally the *Argus* had unwittingly supplied the perfect racist rationale for emancipation, which, of course, it most fervently opposed. It had supplied a powerful antidote to Democratic fears of migrating freedmen. And it was one that was entirely consonant with Democratic racism. If blacks were indeed inferior, why should they not admirably perform the tasks now carried out by the unskilled immigrant, and to the benefit of all?

These problems illustrated some of the tensions within Democratic ideology in the 1850s. Yet the logical inconsistencies should not be allowed to obscure a more fundamental coherence. Why, after all, could Democrats afford to be generous towards the immigrant but then in the next breath give vent to hostility to the African American? It may be tempting to pose the answer in terms of "tradition" and it is, as we have seen, quite true that these attitudes were very much part of Democratic tradition by the 1850s. But to recognise this is merely to displace the question: why were Democrats traditionally hostile to African Americans but traditionally hospitable to immigrants? It would be equally unsatisfactory to reply that national economic interest dictated these attitudes. Even if it could be shown that all white Americans gained from immigration and from slavery, not all were so sympathetic to the immigrants or so unsympathetic to the nation's racial minorities. So a different answer must be sought.

It is to be found in the relationship between slavery and Democratic ideology. The Democratic creed, as established by Thomas Jefferson, John Taylor of Caroline and Andrew Jackson, was able to espouse some extraordinarily egalitarian and liberal principles, but only so long as they did not challenge the social, economic and political power of the slaveholding class. The rapid enfranchisement of immigrants did not traditionally pose such a challenge, a concern for the welfare of enslaved African Americans most assuredly did. It was as though an invisible filter existed, blocking those egalitarian ideals that threatened the slaveholding elite, but allowing the rest to pass through. Of course, the Democrats themselves did not see the issue in this light. By the 1850s they were in effect trapped by the traditions which their predecessors had established and to the preservation of which they were utterly dedicated. But to acknowledge this is merely to confirm that individuals are not fully aware of the

---

57. *Albany Argus*, Sept. 24, 1858. The editor added that immigration created "new markets for the sale of the products of native skill" – again precisely as emancipation was expected (by its proponents) to do.

forces operating upon them. Whether the Democrats knew it or not, their ideas were fundamentally shaped by the needs, the fears, and the interests of southern slaveholders.

Yet by the 1850s, the dualism that placed ethnic and racial minorities in entirely different categories was itself becoming increasingly problematic. As the debate over the Declaration of Independence showed, Democratic universalism was in partial retreat and for the first time the party was being outflanked in its commitment to democratic ideals and the rights of man. This was to cost the Democrats dear in the North. Meanwhile although the presence in the North of large numbers of immigrants was not in itself a threat to the southern elite, particularly if they continued to vote Democrat in disproportionate numbers, a new problem was emerging. As immigrants flocked into the North, they increased its political weight within the nation. So long as antislavery sentiment in that region was of limited strength and intensity, this augmentation of northern power did not matter. But as northern hostility to slavery deepened, this process itself was yet another source of danger for the increasingly beleaguered slaveholders. It was a danger which not even Democratic ideology, Democratic traditions or the Democratic party itself would be able to remove.[58]

## State's rights and limited government

### I

The interests of the slaveholding class of the South had thus left an indelible imprint on Democratic attitudes towards race but at the same time had not prevented party leaders from embracing the newly arrived immigrant. The same interests were again discernible, though once again partly obscured, in Democratic views on government. Here the key issues were first, the role and power of the states in the federal system ("state's rights") and second, the need to restrain governments at every level from interfering in the economic development or determining the moral standards of the community (limited government). In both areas Democrats believed that they were, as ever, simply being faithful to the glorious traditions of the party. The reality, however, was more complex.

Since the 1830s (and earlier) Democrats had been devout believers in *laissez-faire*. The Washington *Globe*, Jackson's quasi-official newspaper, had had as its motto, "the world is too much governed," while the *Democratic Review*, the party's monthly magazine, had proclaimed on its

---

58. It is perhaps necessary to remind ourselves that immigration, disproportionately into the North, was what opened up the gap between the two sections in terms of population. They had begun with roughly equal numbers and the rates of natural reproduction were not dissimilar.

masthead that "that government is best which governs least." In the 1850s Democrats endorsed these opinions wholeheartedly, and sometimes with explicit reference to the slogans of the 1830s. The Indiana Democrat State Platform of 1852, for example, demanded "the least possible amount of legislation," while in St Paul, Minnesota some years later the *Pioneer and Democrat* announced that "the truth is, men legislate too much; they make too many laws." Indeed, "the people of these United States are especially a law-ridden people." Then in words that would have gladdened the heart of John L. O'Sullivan or Francis P. Blair, editors of the *Democratic Review* and the *Globe* respectively in the 1830s, the *Pioneer and Democrat* concluded that "the laws of nature are better than the laws of men." In 1856 George Buell, editor of the *National Democratic Review*, went so far as to claim that it had been the nation's unique achievement to have enunciated correct principles concerning the role of government. It was "upon American soil" that "it was first proclaimed that law is a restraint of the natural liberties of men, and that the great care of legislators should be to confine this restraint within the bounds of absolute necessity." Democrats thus continued to desire as little government as possible.[59]

On this premise the Jacksonian Democrats had, in the 1830s, launched a crusade against "partial legislation," laws that benefited only a minority of the community at the expense of the rest. The veto of the Bank of the United States had been the most spectacular display of Democratic intent but the veto of the Maysville Road (which threatened to arrest the involvement of the federal government in the creation of a carefully planned national road network) had also dramatically illustrated Democratic priorities. A little later in the decade the struggle against the banks had shifted into the states, where once again a primary goal had been to remove the government from the banking system. As a result, in the late 1830s and early 1840s withdrawal of governmental support from banking was the most explosive issue in state politics. At the same time Democrats sought to end or at least dramatically curtail the involvement of state governments in the building of roads and canals. And by the mid-1840s the Democrats were also identified with the principle of free (or freer) trade, tariffs too being denounced as devices for the benefit of the favoured few at the expense of the many. Thus at both federal and state levels, the party had become increasingly committed to *laissez-faire*. It was the party of limited government.[60]

59. *Address and Correspondence of the Democratic State Convention of Pennsylvania* (Philadelphia, n.d.), p. 6; *State Platforms of ... Parties in Indiana*, p. 5; St Paul *Pioneer and Democrat*, Jan. 14, 1858; *National Democratic Review*, 1 (Jan. 1856), p. 11. Ashworth, *"Agrarians" and "Aristocrats,"* pp. 17–20.
60. Lawrence Frederick Kohl, *The Politics of Individualism: Parties and the American Character in the Jacksonian Era* (New York, 1989); Rush Welter, *The Mind of*

In the 1850s these attitudes persisted. Yet the context had now significantly altered. As we shall see, banks, tariffs and internal improvements all ceased to be matters of great concern[61] and even when they did generate controversy Democrats rarely articulated the social philosophy with which they had been identified in previous decades. By the 1850s they rarely denounced the rich and powerful in the way that Andrew Jackson had done and no longer feared government intervention in the economy as a threat to the agrarian society, in part because party members were now increasingly reconciled to the industrial and commercial sectors. For a number of reasons, therefore, democratic government and the Democratic society were, it was apparent, no longer under so serious a threat from the "aristocratic" minority that favoured an active government.

## II

In fact the Democratic commitment to *laissez-faire* now generated most controversy not when economic policy was being considered but when legislation designed to promote moral reforms was under discussion. Here, with the obvious exception of the slavery question (a moral as well as an economic and political concern), the most important issue of the 1850s was temperance. Indeed even though exclusively a state and local matter, this issue probably generated more controversy in the early 1850s than the economic questions of the day. It was not at that time an entirely new subject and Democrats had confronted it previously. But in the late 1840s and early 1850s the goals of temperance or even prohibition received an unprecedented degree of support within the community. The prohibitionist Maine Law of 1851 became the model for temperance reformers in other states and equally, of course, the specter that haunted their enemies.[62]

The new popularity of temperance was reflected in the cautious attitude of many Democrats. Whereas party members had traditionally objected to such legislation, some now clearly felt that the standard Democratic response needed modification. Thus Daniel Dickinson sought a middle position on the question. The party, he declared, was "not for fanatical temperance principles." But it was not "for unbridled and unlicensed traffic in liquor" either. Instead it was "for correcting and adjusting all abuses as they may appear." In Indiana, Governor Paris C. Dunning announced that he favoured "such stringent laws, for the prevention of the sale of ardent spirits, as will arrest the vice of drunkenness, which stalks over

---

America, 1820–1860 (New York, 1975); Ashworth, *"Agrarians" and "Aristocrats,"* pp. 34–47.
61. See pp. 436–457 and 478–485.
62. For a discussion of the temperance issue, see pp. 494–515.

the fairest portion of our country with a worse than pestilential march."
Nevertheless like Dickinson, Dunning also announced that he could not
endorse "the ultra views" of some. Drunkenness, however, was clearly
an intractable problem for four years later his successor as governor was
also drawing attention to the phenomenon. "Its haggard victims," Governor Joseph Wright announced, "meet us everywhere. They crowd our
almshouses, hospitals, jails and penitentiaries. They throng upon every
avenue of life chilling us with an overpowering sense of their wretchedness." His proposed solution – to make drunkenness an offence – may
have denoted a lack of sympathy with its victims, but it also fell far short
of the reforms demanded by the prohibitionists.[63]

This cautious attitude persisted. The following year the Indiana Democratic party passed a resolution which recognised a need for legislation
but at the same time warned that excessive zeal might result in still greater
abuses:

> [resolved:] that intemperance is a great moral and social evil, for the
> restraint and correction of which legislative interposition is necessary
> and proper; but that we can not approve of any plan for the erad-
> ication or correction of this evil that must necessarily result in the
> infliction of greater ones; and that we are therefore opposed to any
> law upon this subject that will authorize the searching for or seizure,
> confiscation, and destruction of private property.

Here was an endorsement not merely of temperance but also of legal coercion in order to help bring it about. Nevertheless, Indiana's Democrats
were here repudiating the more coercive and draconian features of the
original Maine Law. Finally, two years later, Governor Wright again
emphasised the need for legislation but now noted, without apparent
regret, that "we may, in many places, see the evidences of a re-action in
public sentiment, apparently unfavorable to the cause of temperance."[64]

Yet while these Democrats had reached a partial accommodation with
the temperance reformers, others within the party retained and gave vent
to the traditional hostility. In New York, where the issue was extremely
contentious, a Democratic State Convention in 1855 announced its

63.  *Speeches etc. of Dickinson*, I, p. 499; *Journal of the Indiana...State Senate...34
     Session...Commencing Dec. 3, 1849* (Indianapolis, 1848), p. 28; *Documents of the
     General Assembly of Indiana...37 Session, Convening Jan. 6, 1853 Part 1* (Indi-
     anapolis, 1853), p. 30.
64.  *State Platforms of...Parties in Indiana*, p. 9; *Journal of the Indiana State Senate...39
     Session...Jan. 5, 1857* (Indianapolis, 1857), p. 60. For another Democratic warning
     against extreme measures see *Journal of the House of Representatives of the State of
     New Hampshire...1853* (Concord, 1853), p. 54, while for a neutral, noncommittal
     response to the temperance question see *Journal of the House of Representatives of
     the State of New Hampshire...1852* (Concord, 1852), pp. 39–40.

opposition to "all attempts at creating and then forcing statutory standards of temperance or morality by experimental legislation." Many prominent Democrats shared this view and some elaborated upon it. Thus Horatio Seymour, who as Governor vetoed a prohibitory law, acquired a reputation as a leading "wet." When justifying his stance, he staked out classic Democratic ground. First he reaffirmed the Democratic commitment to *laissez-faire*: "we have but one petition to our law-makers – it is to be let alone." Then he explained that since governments, or at any rate democratic governments, were the creatures of popular opinion, they could not, and should not, be expected to control that opinion. For governments "emanate from the people and merely represent their morality or intelligence." From this he concluded that "the folly that looks to governments to evolve the virtues is like the ignorance which regards the thermometer as a regulator of temperature, or the barometer as the controller of the weather." Seymour acknowledged that the motives of these reformers might be admirable but he warned too that "good motives and wrong principles have lain at the root of almost every evil which has oppressed and afflicted mankind." Indeed history taught that precisely the opposite approach was required: "the progress of civilization, morality, and virtue, has been marked by the extension of education and religion, and the contraction of coercive laws."[65]

Other Democrats employed similar reasoning. Samuel J. Tilden, also of New York, in 1855 wrote a public letter spelling out many of the objections Democrats harbored towards prohibition. "Such legislation," he asserted, "springs from a misconception of the proper sphere of government." It was simply "no part of the duty of the State to coerce the individual man except so far as his conduct may affect others, not remotely and consequentially, but by violating rights which legislation can recognize and undertake to protect." The contrary approach, he argued, "leaves no room for individual reason and conscience, trusts nothing to self-culture, and substitutes the wisdom of the Senate and Assembly for the plan of moral government ordained by Providence." Like Seymour, Tilden then identified this voluntary, noncoercive approach with the unfolding of civilisation itself. "The whole progress of society," he concluded, "consists in learning how to attain, by the independent action or voluntary association of individuals, those objects which are at first attempted only through the agency of government, and in lessening the sphere of legislation and enlarging that of the individual reason and conscience." The

65. *Proceedings of State Convention of National Democracy of New York*, pp. 24–25; *Speeches . . . of Seymour*, pp. 5, 10–11; Holt, *Whig Party*, p. 897. See also *Proceedings and Address of the Democratic State Convention Held at Syracuse . . . Jan. 10, 1856* (Albany, 1856), p. 26.

progress of civilisation was thus inversely proportional to government activity.[66]

Although these views were more frequently expressed in the North, where the temperance movement itself was far more conspicuous, they were also developed by some southern Democrats. Thus Howell Cobb of Georgia, addressing a New England audience, drew attention to a widespread "disposition to intermeddle with matters in which we have no concern, and about which we have no right to act." It had, he claimed, "led to legislation equally wrong and indefensible." Cobb denounced what he took to be the principle underlying such activity, the "self-righteous idea that one man is called upon to be the conscience-keeper of another." Cobb then referred directly to the Maine Law:

> It is illustrated in your Maine Liquor Law. One class of the people seek to take charge of the morals of another, and the strong arm of the law is invoked to aid in the work of moral reform. The seared consciences of political prostitutes are awakened to a tender sensibility about their neighbor's moral condition. The convincing argument of the philanthropist, and the persuasive appeals of good men, teaching both by precept and by example, are thrown aside for the more effective weapon of legislative power. The idea of this class of reformers seems to be that men are not to be reformed by appeals addressed to their hearts and judgments, but that the work can be more successfully carried forward by penal enactments. Bad men are to be made good men by law.

Like many who opposed the Maine Law, Cobb insisted that he was "no enemy of the temperance reform." He felt, however, that reformers should rely on moral suasion rather than legislative enactment and that their recent entry into politics would actually retard the cause "for the next quarter of a century." The conclusion was simple: men would "best promote the cause of justice and morality by placing sentinels over their own consciences, instead of becoming the general conscience keepers of their neighbors."[67]

Cobb's words were delivered in the context of a speech or a set of speeches devoted to the slavery question. And it is not difficult to detect in his references to "the seared consciences of political prostitutes," an implicit reference to abolitionists and their claim that slaveholding inflicted moral damage upon the slaveholder as well as the slave. On occasion, however, northern Democrats explicitly linked temperance and

66. John Bigelow (ed.), *The Writings and Speeches of Samuel J. Tilden.* 2 vols. (New York, 1885), I, p. 282.
67. *Speeches of Weller, Orr, Lane, and Cobb*, p. 26.

antislavery.[68] Thus Nicholas Hill of New York, again at a State Convention, expressed standard Democratic views when he declared that the party was designed "as a means of influencing the course of public or governmental affairs, by the concentrated action of political opinion; leaving all other matters to the free and unbiased choice of the citizens." This meant that "it was not organized, as some of its former friends seem to have assumed, to keep watch and ward over the entire domain of taste and sentiment, thought and duty, or to act as a spy upon the private opinions or pursuits of men, or sit in judgment upon their consciences, or control their actual conduct, except through the rightful action of government." But Hill then lumped together temperance advocates, Know Nothings (because of their hostility to Roman Catholics) and antislavery enthusiasts, all of whom had, he asserted, mistaken the true role of government.[69]

## III

This explicit identification of moral reform with abolitionism hints once again at the relationship between limited government and slavery. Yet that relationship was extremely complex. The Jacksonian rationale for limited government was to allow individuals to retain the full fruits of their labour (rather than have them filched by an "aristocracy") and to allow them to determine for themselves the moral principles by which they would be guided (rather than have them dictated by a self-righteous and self-designated moral elite). At first glance it would seem difficult to find two principles that could be more effective in combating slavery. After all, the slave more than anyone was denied the fruits of his labour and more than anyone was denied the right to live according to his own moral standards.[70] But here Democratic tradition and Democratic racism came decisively into play. For the Democrats, African Americans were not only not citizens, they were scarcely human at all. This had been the attitude of Thomas Jefferson and of John Taylor of Caroline. Just as Jefferson, when celebrating "those who labor in the earth" as "the chosen people of God," conspicuously ignored the slaves, Democrats ignored them when demanding economic and moral autonomy for Americans. By the 1850s, this ideological practice had been familiar for more than half a century; it was an essential part of the Democrat's political heritage.[71]

---

68. This link was, of course, made still more frequently by southern militants who wished to condemn the North for its "isms."
69. *Albany Argus*, Jan. 14, 1856.
70. Indeed these were two of the favourite arguments employed by abolitionists.
71. See the first volume of this study, pp. 21–32.

Ironically, once racism excluded slaves from the freedom and equality that Democratic ideology promised, those same principles operated to promote the interest of their masters. For the demand that all should receive the fruits of their labour was extremely beneficial to the slaveholder, since he would be allowed to receive, without restriction, the fruits of not only his own labour but also that of his now-invisible slave. Similarly the demand for moral autonomy for all men offered, once African Americans males were deemed not to be men, a powerful rejoinder to abolitionism, which was undoubtedly (among other things) an attempt to impose one group's moral standards upon another.

It is important to recognise that there was no conspiracy here. Democratic demands for "equal rights" and limited government had roots in the radical thought of early modern Europe where there had been no slaves. Similarly, the insistence upon moral autonomy was part of a long anticlerical tradition, linked once again to early-modern religious radicalism with its emphasis upon the right of all to achieve a direct and unmediated relationship to God. But in the United States these ideals had acquired such extraordinary power because, provided that slaves were excluded from the reckoning, they did not challenge and in some cases actually augmented the social and political power of the slaveholding class. Once again the filtering process was at work, allowing those egalitarian doctrines that did not disrupt the power of the slaveholders to pass through, blocking those that did.

Thus while the protection offered by Democratic ideals to the southern slaveholder was not the result of a conspiracy, nor was it mere coincidence. Democrats were vulnerable in the 1850s to the charge that they were the dupes of the Slave Power but in reality their principles had always offered at least covert support to the dominant class of the South. As we shall see, one of their favourite retorts in the 1850s was to claim that antislavery militants, so far from benefiting the slave, had merely "riveted the chains" that bound him. What they utterly failed to understand was that this was precisely the effect of the principles, the time-honoured and glorious principles, of Democracy, which they themselves espoused.

IV

The principle of limited government, when applied at federal level, implied a concern with the rights of the states. Indeed the much-trumpeted demand for a "strict construction" of the Federal Constitution implied both state's rights and limited government, since all powers not explicitly granted to the federal authorities were to be reserved to the states. In effect, therefore, strict constructionism, state's rights, and limited government were indissolubly linked in Democratic thought. Thus Herschel Johnson of Georgia reminded an audience at Milledgeville that a strict construction of the constitution was necessary to maintain the rights of the states, while James Buchanan observed that high federal expenditures would offer an inducement to unscrupulous and avaricious individuals to extend federal authority still further and in the process ride roughshod over the rights of the states.[72]

All three principles had by the 1850s been Democratic orthodoxy for many decades. When asked for his thoughts on recent political developments Buchanan in 1852 told the party faithful that it was essential to "fall back...upon those fundamental and time-honoured principles which have divided us from our political opponents since the beginning, and which from the very nature of the Federal Constitution, must continue to divide us from them until the end." This meant that "we must inscribe upon our banners a sacred regard for the reserved rights of the States – a strict construction of the Constitution – a denial to Congress of all powers not clearly granted by that instrument and a rigid economy in public expenditures."[73]

The doctrine of state's rights was thus integral to Democratic thought. The relationship of the doctrine to slavery is both complex and important but it would be a grave error to assume that it was only southern Democrats who enthused about state's rights. The Governor of Ohio, for example, in 1856 announced that the maintenance of the Union and "the success of the great republican experiment in progress among us, require the inflexible application of the doctrine of state's rights, limiting the interference by federal authority to those few objects of national interest which are specifically enumerated in the Constitution." In part he was motivated by the need to respect the rights of southern states, which might otherwise contemplate disunion, but it is also important to note the more general fear of power, the same fear that produced the emphasis upon limited government. "Centralization," he pointed out, "is the greatest danger of Republics."[74] This was a widespread fear among Democrats and a key reason for their dedication to state's rights. According to the *National Democratic Review*, "wherever administration is consolidated – under whatever name – is tyranny." It did not matter "whether all power is centered in one man, in one senate, in one parliament, or in one plebeian body: where it is undivided, there can be no liberty." The editor of the

72. Herschel Johnson, *Address...At Milledgeville*, p. 20; *Works of Buchanan*, VIII, pp. 434–435.
73. *Works of Buchanan*, VIII, p. 434.
74. *Journal of the House of Representatives of the State of Ohio...52nd General Assembly...Commencing Jan. 2, 1854* (Columbus, Ohio, 1856), p. 31

*Review* explained that the powers of the state were extremely wide and far-reaching:

> the individual members of each State of the Union enjoy the right at all times to remodel the laws and Constitution of that State – to enlarge or restrain their own privileges – to regulate their own policy, and do everything *in their own midst* which absolutely independent powers may do. The States in their sovereign capacity sustain the same relation to the federal government which the individual members of the States do to the States respectively. The . . . indestructible privilege of private judgment belongs to every State of the Union just as it does to every member of the human family.

Other Democrats went so far as to claim that the states resembled independent nations in their relations with one another.[75]

The other common thread running though discussions of state's rights was the assumption that people in a given locality knew best how to regulate their own concerns. Here Democrats repudiated the traditional conservative argument, associated with James Madison in particular, which had seen government, and especially the federal government, as a harmonising agency, an institution through which the natural aristocracy, whose vision would transcend that of the particular class from which they sprang, would promote the collective good and balance the various competing interests. Indeed at the time of the ratification of the constitution, a Federalist priority had been to create a government that was at some remove from the people, in order to afford greater scope to the talents of this elite. It was also a Federalist belief that, to secure election in an extended republic, a candidate for office would have to demonstrate true statesmanship: the demagogue might triumph at local, but scarcely at national, level.

Democrats had long since rejected this line of reasoning. If one primary reason was the fear of the power which such a governing elite would wield, another was the belief that those most affected by government were best placed to direct it. As Horatio Seymour argued, the people of a town, a county or a state were "more intelligent about their own affairs than the public of any other locality."[76]

---

75. *National Democratic Review* 1 (Jan. 1856), pp. 2, 13; *Journal of the House of Representatives of the State of Ohio . . . 51th General Assembly . . . Commencing Jan. 2, 1854* (Columbus, 1854), p. 61. See also *State Platforms of . . . Parties in Indiana*, pp. 12–14. It should be noted, however, that northern Democrats' attachment to state's rights did not in any way weaken their attachment to the Union. In effect they continued to subscribe to the views Andrew Jackson had set forth during the nullification crisis. Southern Democrats, meanwhile, were moving some way away from this position – see Chapter 1 above.
76. *Speeches . . . of Seymour*, p. 4.

It would thus be an error to claim that the doctrine of state's rights was merely a cloak for the defence of slavery. On the other hand, it would be an even greater error to deny any connection between the two. Southerners, of course, frequently declared that if the constitutional rights of the states were violated, they could not be expected to remain in the Union. Here they often acknowledged – but often did not need to acknowledge – that it was the protection of slavery that was uppermost in their minds. Northerners, and especially northern Democrats, often adopted this reasoning. As we have seen, James Buchanan in 1852 exhorted his fellow Democrats to exhibit "a sacred regard . . . for the reserved rights of the States." He had employed identical terminology a few years earlier but had then made the link with abolition explicit. To prepare for "the approaching storm," he had announced in 1847, Democrats' "best security in the hour of danger is to cling fast to their time-honored principles." The highest priority was to maintain the rights of the states since "this has saved us from the inroads of abolition." Here was "the immovable basis on which the party can alone safely rest." The doctrine of state's rights was thus employed to disarm abolitionists and protect slaveholders.[77]

To understand fully the relationship between the doctrine of state's rights and slavery it is necessary to identify the different arguments adduced in favour of those rights. All exponents of the doctrine agreed that to preserve the rights of the states was to prevent a dangerous engrossment of power in the federal government, which could then be used on behalf of some groups and at the expense of others. Similarly all agreed that the citizens and officeholders of the states were best placed to understand and promote their own interests. This was common ground. But beyond this, there were important differences of opinion, some subtle and some very basic.

There were in fact by 1850 three important arguments in favour of state's rights. The first was identified with Andrew Jackson. Classic Jacksonian theory emphasised the danger of the power wielded by a minority, either the elite political minority who actually held office in the federal government, or the social elite in whose interests those officeholders would, if left unchecked, legislate. State's rights would thus curtail the freedom of movement of these minorities and consequently safeguard the interests of the majority. A second approach, however, was linked with John C. Calhoun. Where the Jacksonians emphasised the rights of the majority and voiced their fears of the minority, Calhoun instead stressed the dangers posed by the majority (which by its control over the federal government might encroach upon the states) and sought to safeguard minority rights. From this came the doctrine of the "concurrent majority,"

77. *Works of Buchanan*, VII, p. 386.

designed to prevent mere numerical majorities from trampling upon the rights of certain key minority groups.

In each case there was a link with slavery. Calhoun made no secret of the fact that the key minority group was the slaveholders of the South; indeed he wasted little time dealing with any other minority. Jackson's version of state's rights, however, despite his own status as a slaveholder, made no reference to slavery and indeed in the eyes of many of its supporters, no connection existed. Once again, however, this majoritarianism, directly descended from Jefferson and from John Taylor of Caroline, had much to do with the covert interests of slaveholders. The faith in the democratic process upon which it rested was, as I have already suggested, highly congenial to an elite whose power derived from the exploitation of a group excluded from that process.[78] Thus each of the two versions of state's rights owed much to slavery, one avowedly and overtly, the other in a more subtle manner that was unrecognised even by its adherents.

In the 1850s the more militant southern Democrats who enlisted under the banner of "Southern Rights" and who, with varying degrees of enthusiasm, were ready to contemplate secession, espoused a state's rights philosophy that owed much to Calhoun. They echoed his fear of the majority and made explicit the link with slavery (even if they largely ignored the theory of the "concurrent majority"). Northern Democrats, however, were caught between the two theories. Their fear of the minority – bankers and industrialists – had greatly diminished. Officeholders remained a potential threat, and logrolling, to which, as we have seen, James Buchanan referred, remained a source of concern. But much of the old urgency had gone. Nevertheless, as northerners, they could not repudiate majoritarianism outright, despite the lead taken by the increasingly dominant southern wing. So once again, northern Democratic thought suffered. Unable to boast of their attachment to the majoritarian principle at federal level, northern Democrats found it equally difficult to embrace the minoritarian views of their southern colleagues. It was thus easier to leave the issue unresolved, and merely reiterate the abstract commitment to state's rights.

In the 1840s, however, a third rationale for state's rights had presented itself. The crusade to realise America's "Manifest Destiny," by making the United States a continental power, with possessions on the Pacific, once again raised the old question whether republican governments could preside over a huge expanse of territory. The federal system now came to the rescue. If the rights of the states were preserved, it was claimed, there would be virtually no limit to the territorial expansion possible. State's rights thus offered the promise of a huge nation with all the democratic practices and sensibilities traditionally associated with a small one. Little

---

78. See the first volume of this study, esp. pp. 21–32.

wonder that it had proved so attractive to expansion-minded Democrats. In the 1850s Democrats, as we shall see, continued to favour territorial expansion, even though they were unable to secure the colossal gains of previous decades. The doctrine of state's rights continued to serve this purpose. And here too, as we shall see, the interests of slavery were heavily implicated.[79]

## V

In the 1850s, however, a fourth and a new argument for state's rights emerged. Its principal, and perhaps its only,[80] exponent was the North's leading Democrat, Stephen A. Douglas. In effect Douglas took as his starting point the standard claim, made by almost all defenders of state's rights, that the inhabitants of a state were better placed to legislate for themselves than any other group of people. Implicit here was the idea that they were better informed and more knowledgeable. This notion, in turn, rested on the assumption that there might be significant differences between the states: legislation that was suitable for one might be entirely inappropriate in another.

In the 1850s, therefore, Douglas emphasised the differences between the states. But he did not claim that these differences had recently manifested themselves. On the contrary, he insisted, the Federal Constitution had been drawn up by wise statesmen who had been fully aware of them. This was one of his major arguments in his famous encounters with Lincoln in 1858. Thus at Springfield (before the debates had begun) he asked why it was that the Founding Fathers "did . . . not blot out State Sovereignty and State Legislatures, and give up all the power to Congress, in order that the laws might be uniform?" He then answered his question: "for the very reason that uniformity in their opinion, was neither desirable or [sic] possible." Two years later he restated this argument with still greater force. "The framers of our Constitution," he asserted, "knew that in a country as broad as this, with such a variety of soil, climate and productions, there must necessarily be a corresponding variety of interests requiring different laws and different institutions." Here was the unshakeable foundation upon which the creed of state's rights was built, for "it was supposed at that day that each state had interests different from every other one, and accordingly would require different legislation and institutions." "The Federal Constitution," Douglas concluded, "was made on this theory."[81]

---

79. This is a principal theme of the first volume of this study.
80. See, however, *Speeches etc. of Dickinson*, I, p. 232.
81. *Debates between Lincoln and Douglas*, p. 46; David R. Barbee and Milledge L. Bonham, Jr, "The Montgomery Address of Stephen A. Douglas," *Journal of Southern History*, V (Nov. 1939), pp. 527–552, esp. p. 530.

This emphasis upon "variety" allowed, or appeared to allow, Douglas to score a telling point against the Republicans. Lincoln had argued that a "house divided" between slave and free states could not stand, rather as William Seward identified an "irrepressible conflict" between those states. But Douglas brought his notion of variety strongly to bear upon these Republican declarations. Fortunately, he noted, the Founding Fathers had not espoused such blasphemous opinions. They had been prepared to tolerate diversity. Indeed had they done otherwise, he pointed out, the nation would have had only slave states, since these were at that time in the majority. Instead, however, these wise patriarchs had left the matter of slavery to the states. For "they knew," he claimed in 1858, "that variety and dissimilarity of local and domestic institutions was an essential element in a Confederated form of government."[82]

Here, however, a slippage had occurred in Douglas's reasoning. From claiming that variety required state's rights, he had jumped to the conclusion that state's rights required variety, a very different proposition. Previous exponents of the doctrine had not made this claim. The Jacksonian variant had not in any way required dissimilarity between the states; state's rights for Andrew Jackson were a matter of majority control and of limited federal government. Indeed Jacksonians, like Thomas Jefferson before them, had wanted a largely undifferentiated economy made up of yeoman farmers. There was no emphasis on variety here.[83] While the Calhounite position had assumed "variety," the logic was again that this variety necessitated state's rights, rather than the reverse. And those who proclaimed the nation's "Manifest Destiny" had also sought, in the main, to retain the largely undifferentiated agrarian society.[84]

Nor was this merely a careless lapse on Douglas's part. At Chicago in 1858 he expressed the same idea but with even greater clarity. Again emphasising "variety," he warned that it could only be ended by establishing a consolidated government, which would then obliterate the rights of the states. "From this view of the case," he announced, "I am driven irresistibly to the conclusion that diversity, dissimilarity, variety in all local and domestic institutions, is the great safeguard of our liberties." In other words, without "variety," the rights of the states would be trampled on and American liberty would be at an end.[85]

---

82. *Speeches of Douglas at New Orleans, Philadelphia and Baltimore*, p. 4.
83. Indeed the differences between plantation slavery and free farming were entirely obscured in this ideology – see the first volume of this study.
84. In a sense Madison's pluralism was a precedent for Douglas's argument. Yet the contrasts between the theories are at least as striking as any similarities. After all, Madison was making a case for a more powerful central government. Its thrust was thus against state's rights.
85. *Debates between Lincoln and Douglas*, p. 10.

Once again, however, the Republican Carl Schurz was lying in wait for Douglas. Once again he dissected, and then shredded, Douglas's logic. First he noted that state's rights in no sense required "variety." "This ramification, division, and subdivision of political power," he reminded an audience at New York in 1860, "is carried out no less where there is a uniformity of domestic affairs and local institutions, than where there exists variety." For Schurz, as for Jackson before him, state's rights was a means of achieving a more direct exercise of sovereignty, regardless of the social and economic composition of the state. Then Schurz made a still more telling point. What, he asked, did Douglas mean by "variety"? According to Schurz, there was already a remarkable degree of variety within the North itself. Here was a multiplicity of interests and of occupational groups embracing agriculture, manufacturing, mercantile pursuits, mining. All that was lacking in the North was, of course, slavery. So was Douglas claiming that slavery was necessary to "variety" and thus to liberty?[86]

In effect Schurz had impaled Douglas on a dilemma. If democracy required states rights and states rights required "variety" and "variety" required slavery, then Douglas was in effect advancing a proslavery argument: democracy required slavery. But if this reasoning was flawed and "variety" did not require slavery, then what had it to do with the sectional crisis and why was Douglas placing so much emphasis upon it? For Douglas there was no easy way out, and Schurz's challenge went unanswered.

## VI

The creed of state's rights and the accompanying belief in limited government each had by the 1850s a distinguished pedigree in the United States. Both harked back to Thomas Jefferson, both had been cardinal tenets of the Jacksonian Democratic faith. Between them they had, it seemed, served the nation well, encouraging the dismantling of the American System of national bank, protective tariff and federally sponsored internal improvements, and facilitating the expansion of the Republic's territory to the Pacific. It was little wonder, therefore, that Democrats in the 1850s, even outside the slave states, were fervently committed to both ideals.

Yet neither doctrine had its old appeal in the North. With the greater fiscal stability of the 1850s the demand for a strict construction of the federal constitution no longer had the enormous political and social implications that it had had in Jackson's era. To raise questions about the power of the federal government was no longer, as it had been for leaders on

---

86. Carl Schurz, *Speeches of Carl Schurz* (Philadelphia, 1865), pp. 201–203

both sides of the political divide in the 1830s and early 1840s, to draw attention to the distribution of wealth and social power in the nation or the basic character of its economy. In other words, whilst the political creed remained, it had been emptied of much of its former social significance.[87]

At the same time, however, the relationship of both doctrines to slavery became more and more apparent. Despite the prominence of the temperance question, the ideal of limited government, in the sphere of moral legislation, functioned even more conspicuously to disable opposition to slavery and, in the charged atmosphere of the 1850s, left its northern adherents even more exposed to the charge that they were "doughfaces," northern men with southern principles. Meanwhile the doctrine of state's rights, as it lost much of its old Jacksonian rationale, found an alternative place in the social and political philosophy of Stephen A. Douglas. But just as Douglas himself experienced enormous difficulty in coping with the political polarisation brought about by slavery and the sectional controversy, his defence of state's rights proved highly fragile and intellectually vulnerable. The economic expansion of the late 1840s and 1850s drained the older issues that had separated the political parties of their former significance and at the same time, by confirming the attachment of each section to its labour system, intensified the sectional conflict. The twin Democratic ideals of limited government and state's rights, as they were subtly adapted, modified, or redefined, reflected both aspects of this process.

### Territorial expansion: Extending the area of freedom (and slavery)

#### I

When Franklin Pierce was inaugurated President of the United States on March 4, 1853 he announced that "the policy" of his administration would "not be controlled by any timid forebodings of the evil from expansion." Although events would quickly overtake the Pierce administration so that it would be dominated by entirely unforeseen controversies over Kansas, the new President was as good as his word. In 1853 he purchased from Mexico some 45,000 square miles of land south of the Gila River. This act would be known, after the name of the envoy sent to Mexico City, as the Gadsden Purchase.[88]

---

87. That these were indeed the issues involved in the party struggles of the 1830s and 1840s is the theme of my "*Agrarians*" and "*Aristocrats*."

88. Richardson (ed.), *Messages and Papers of Presidents*, V, p. 198. The indispensable work on territorial expansion in the 1850s is Robert E. May, *The Southern Dream of a Caribbean Empire* (Gainesville, 2002).

This, the first and by American standards rather modest, territorial acquisition of the decade, was, unfortunately for Pierce perhaps, also to be the last. But as we have seen, many southerners continued to agitate for additional territory and they were joined by significant numbers of northerners. Most of these southerners were Democrats, an even higher proportion of the northerners were. Thus the Democratic party continued to be as vociferous in urging expansion as it had been in the 1840s.[89] Once again, it was claimed that it was the nation's "Manifest Destiny" to possess more territory in the Americas. In the 1840s the *Democratic Review* and its editor, John L. O'Sullivan, had led the crusade for "Manifest Destiny" and as late as 1859 the same journal, albeit with a different editor, was still sounding the same theme. "At no former period since the foundation of the government of the United States," the editor remarked (rather implausibly given the other events that were in train), "has the public mind been so thoroughly and pointedly awakened to a comprehensive sense of the mission and duty of the American Republic, in extending our Democratic system over this entire Continent." Indeed this was no less than "a great duty" that "devolves on the American people in connexion with the spread of free institutions."[90]

Thus to extend American territory was to spread self-government and freedom. "Every barrier," the *Review* declared, "erected by foreign powers against the extension of our theory of government will speedily disappear." Indeed "it cannot be otherwise," since "despotism cannot long continue to chain down and crush out freedom, especially within sight of our Republic." It followed that "the children of Cuba, Central America, and Mexico, must fraternize with those of the United States." On this occasion the writer implied that expansion would occur only in Latin America, with Canada apparently untouched. But here a degree of uncertainty crept in for, in the same article, he declared that "every foot of this continent is destined for the occupancy of freemen, and to its utmost limits it must be dedicated to Democracy." This implied that the destiny of Canada too was manifest.[91]

Other Democrats echoed these sentiments. Buchanan and Douglas were each ardent expansionists and publicised their views on many occasions. Buchanan was a signatory of the so-called Ostend Manifesto, which, as

89. Frederick Merk and Lois B. Merk, *Manifest Destiny and Mission in American History: A Reinterpretation* (New York, 1963); Frederick Merk, *Slavery and the Annexation of Texas* (New York, 1972); Thomas R. Hietala *Manifest Design: Anxious Aggrandizement in Late Jacksonian America* (Ithaca, 1985); Charles G. Sellers, *James K. Polk, Continentalist, 1843–1846* (Princeton, 1966). Only a small minority of Whigs voiced a matching desire to expand the nation's territory.
90. *Democratic Review*, XLIII (April 1859), 1, p. 32
91. *Democratic Review*, XLIII (April 1859), 1, p. 32

we shall see, explicitly called for the acquisition of Cuba. Douglas for his part believed it so obviously "our destiny to have Cuba," that "it is folly to debate the question" and "its acquisition is a matter of time only." He added that the same was true of Mexico and the whole of Central America. In 1860 both the Douglas and Breckinridge platforms would contain a plank calling for the annexation of Cuba[92]

As always, Democrats were mindful of the traditions of their party. As they reviewed its record, the familiar self-congratulatory tone re-emerged. "Empire after empire," the *Democratic Review* boasted, "has been added to the original territory occupied by our ancestors, through the expansive policy of the Democratic party." This was a story not only of political but also of commercial and economic triumph for "millions upon millions of mineral treasures have been reclaimed from the bowels of the earth, and millions after millions of acres of land made to teem with more than golden harvests." Of course Democrats recognised that other nations had also, in the past, risen to greatness. Yet American success was, according to Democrats, fundamentally different. For "while the history of every other nation on the globe is written in letters of blood, amidst the groans of suffering humanity," the United States had instead grown "through a policy embodying the Divine sentiment of 'peace and good will towards all men.'" American expansion had been, and would continue to be, exceptionally altruistic and benign.[93]

Some Democrats, having absorbed the gains of the 1840s both politically and intellectually, now detected a pattern in American territorial expansion. In 1853 the *Democratic Review*, on the again rather dubious premise that "all the world knows and says, that it is the manifest destiny of our political system to extend itself until it embraces the entire North American Continent," referred to the key role played by the Monroe Doctrine. Here was a "grand and prudent declaration," forbidding further European colonisation in the Americas and enunciated "in order that this [manifest] destiny may be peacefully accomplished." The Doctrine had in effect guaranteed "peace and security" to all the fledgling Republics of Latin America and thus "covered, and, if we may so speak, republicanized the entire continent." In fact, as the *Review* later claimed, it seemed that an evolutionary process or cycle was becoming discernible. "Has not destiny manifested here," the editor asked rhetorically, "on this

92. *Works of Buchanan*, VIII, p. 387; *Speeches of Douglas at New Orleans, Philadelphia and Baltimore*, p. 9. See also Douglas's autobiographical notes in Robert W. Johannsen (ed.), *The Letters of Stephen A Douglas* (Urbana, 1961), p. 473.
93. *Democratic Review*, XLIII (April 1859), pp. 34–35, 2. Once again the temptation to gloat over their opponents was irresistible: "all of this land would have remained blank and barren under the policy of the Opposition, whose theory has ever been to restrain and prohibit the progressive spirit of the age."

continent, such order, such sequence as this, in political development – first colonies, next republics, and, in the ultimate, United States of America?" With hindsight it was therefore clear that the previous expansion of the nation had followed a preordained pattern. The advocates of 'Manifest Destiny' projected this pattern into the future. The nation, embodying and promoting the values of democracy, would take over the remainder of the American continent and thus bring "peace and good will towards all men."[94]

## II

It was relatively easy for Democrats to proclaim the nation's "Manifest Destiny" and easy too to find precedents for territorial expansion. But it was much more difficult to specify the exact processes that would occur, to relate them to the acquisitions already made and to associate them with the idealism that "Manifest Destiny," on some occasions at least, conveyed. One possibility was that future expansion would come about merely by example. After all, something like this had, perhaps, happened in the past. The *Democratic Review* declared that the Republics of South and Central America "assuredly seem to owe their origin to our example." And they would soon, thanks to the breathtaking spectacle of progress and improvement presented by the United States, complete their journey into the Union. The *National Democratic Review* described the process:

> The spirit of our republicanism is progressive; our policy and our civilization have already accomplished wonders in the diffusion of liberal principles. Wherever they have gone, as if by magic, peace and prosperity have quietly supplanted anarchy and ruin. Other nations of the continent, already in their decadence, begin to look forward to a day when they too can fraternize with us, and be received as part of our own great Republic. When we review the past, and see the rapid and sure progress of our institutions, when we behold the force of commercial, political and social interests gradually drawing these nations towards us, and binding us together with ties far stronger than those of nationality; the possibility of a Continental Republic seems no longer either a wild dream, or a monstrous absurdity. Gorgeous as is the vision, more glorious will be the reality. It needs no prophetic inspiration to predict its accomplishment, for – it is our 'MANIFEST DESTINY.'

94. *Democratic Review*, XXXII (March 1853), p. 199, LXII (Aug. 1858), p . 110. It was even claimed that the doctrine was entirely consonant with the principles of nonintervention and state's rights, since the purpose was "to establish the rule of nonintervention, and the doctrine of State rights, for the benefit of all the North American Republics" – *Democratic Review*, XXXII (March 1853), p. 199.

Thus the United States, merely by continuing in its present course, and setting an example to the rest of the nations on the Continent, would achieve its "Manifest Destiny."[95]

This strategy, or nonstrategy since it required the United States to do nothing but attend to its own affairs and wait, had much to recommend it. It could antagonise no one and it offered the prospect of an expansionary process fully in accordance with the wishes of the peoples concerned. But it also had serious flaws. In the first place and despite what was sometimes implied, it had not hitherto resulted in the acquisition of any territory at all, since the other Republics on the continent, however much inspired by the U.S. example, had not yet applied to join the Union. Nor, more importantly, was there a prospect of their doing so in the foreseeable future: none of the nations of North, Central, or South America were currently queuing up for entry into the Union. Finally, the waiting policy necessitated inactivity and this did not suit the Democratic temper of the 1850s.

This left three alternative means of acquiring territory, each of which had been successfully employed in the past, but none of which was so easily reconciled with democratic values. The first was the Texas model. At first glance it seemed that the people of Texas had simply asked to join the Union because of the example of democracy and freedom it offered. Yet the Texas precedent was perhaps not as "democratic" as it first appeared. Even if we ignore for the present the question of slavery, it is important to note that the "democratic" majority in favour of annexation in Texas had been manufactured as a result of the (at times illegal) migration of Americans into what had been juridically a foreign country. Having arrived there in sufficient numbers, they were then able to outvote or overpower the original inhabitants. Thus the acquisition of Texas had been achieved not by example but by the migration of large numbers of American citizens.

Democrats, however, viewed this as a spontaneous and entirely "natural" process, legitimated, if legitimation were needed, by the improved economic productivity achieved by the American migrants to Texas. At any rate, it was now a useful precedent. Just as Texan land had attracted American farmers and planters, so Mexican silver now beckoned. "The painful scarcity of silver which at present afflicts the entire trading and agricultural community," one Democrat announced in 1853, "can only be removed, as the scarcity of gold was removed, by the application of American enterprise to the mines of Mexico." The simple fact was that "silver coin will never be abundant in the United States, until the boundary of the South includes the mineral fields of Central Mexico, now occupied

---

95. *Democratic Review*, XLII (Aug. 1858), p. 110; *National Democratic Review*, 1 (Feb. 1856), p. 143.

by a people who have no knowledge, or no appreciation of their value." The writer then proclaimed that "the time is not far distant when the enterprise of the South will direct itself upon those regions." Then came the truly remarkable assertion that these lands actually "belong to it [the South], not by any fictitious and barbarous claim of conquest, but by the well-founded and legitimate rights of industry and intelligence." In other words if southerners went to Mexico and mined silver successfully, annexation would rightfully follow. The writer then compared this with the course of events that had taken place in Texas: "this was the same [right] that made Texas, first a free State and then a free member of the Union." Indeed it was "the same that confirms the title of every free people to the soil upon which they stand." In effect the Democrats here reversed the standard relationship between annexation and exploitation of natural resources: exploitation of resources justified annexation and ownership.[96]

Similar hopes were entertained of Nicaragua. As a result of an American presence there, the *National Democratic Review* predicted, "a young and active spirit" would be "at work." As a result, "eager enterprise will lay the rail, and bore the mountain, and build the city; industry will open the neglected mine; and the axe of the hardy woodman will startle the solitude of primeval forests." Thus "under a mild and equitable rule, untold resources will be tested and approved." This, however, would be only the beginning for neighboring provinces would grasp at similar opportunities and "Central America will be ours." As if this were not enough, the writer added that eventually Canada too would follow suit.[97]

This strategy, which required the movement of large numbers of Americans to the desired territory, was quite compatible with democratic practices if the Americans, having arrived there, merely sought to persuade, again by example, the existing inhabitants of the benefits of joining the Union. But this was a remote prospect. If, on the other hand, their task was to set aside the wishes of the original peoples, this would be a more questionable triumph for the forces of democracy and would need to be justified, or at least explained. As we shall see, explanations were attempted but they were not wholly successful.

The second strategy was to purchase territory. This had been effected on several occasions, most conspicuously when Jefferson had acquired Louisiana, and most recently when Pierce had obtained the territory south of the Gila River. Since it did not involve conquest, it was relatively easily justified and it was the option that President Buchanan favoured for the acquisition of Cuba. Endorsing this plan, the *Democratic Review* observed that the "proposition" was in accordance with "past usages"

96. *Democratic Review*, XXXII (Feb. 1853), p. 106. See Hietala, *Manifest Design*, p. 193.
97. *National Democratic Review*, 1 (March 1856), p. 256.

which were in turn "established . . . by the magnanimity of our own government, and never practised by any other nation." One advantage of this approach was that it underlined the difference between American and European expansionism. For "they invariably extend their dominions by the power of conquest, while we extend ours by purchase, or by peaceful annexation." Moreover, this approach seemed to offer the promise of quick returns.[98]

Yet there were some insuperable problems here too. The first was that there were no sellers. Thus Spain did not wish to sell Cuba at any price. Nor, after the Gadsden Purchase, would Mexico bring her land to market. But this difficulty, as we shall see, was not seen as necessarily fatal to the enterprise. An even more important obstacle, in theory at any rate, was the wishes of the inhabitants of the territories to be acquired. If they wanted to be annexed then democratic procedures could be followed and democratic honour satisfied but without this the question would again present itself: how could annexation be depicted as a triumph for democracy if it actually ran counter to the wishes of the peoples concerned? It was, theoretically at least, a thorny question.

The third strategy was simply to resort to force. Despite Democratic rhetoric there was a precedent here. The land acquired from Mexico by the treaty of Guadeloupe Hidalgo had been obtained by force, even though Mexico had been paid "compensation" for her loss of territory. This precedent, however, was never cited since, as we have seen, it conflicted with the expansionists' claims about previous territorial acquisitions and discredited their version of history. Nevertheless, as we shall see, the use of force to acquire territory, however undemocratic or even antidemocratic it might be, was by no means ruled out.

## III

When Democrats sought to purchase territory or to acquire it either by force or as a result of popular migrations, a question arose about the desires of the native peoples. After all, it was difficult to depict annexation as a triumph for democracy while at the same time flouting their wishes – difficult, but not impossible. Without a trace of irony, the *Democratic Review* pointed out that "the first objection, and the only one of weight, that suggests itself to the mind of the statesman, to the proposed purchase of Cuba," was "the possibility that her people might not be willing to consummate the transfer." As a result, to the untutored eye, "the appearance of the transaction partakes too much of a sordid financial business arrangement, and not sufficiently of that spirit of liberty and

98. *Democratic Review*, XLIII (April 1859), p. 19.

independence which should have long since severed the unnatural and cruel connexion subsisting between Cuba and Spain." Here was a problem indeed. Yet the solution was easily found, for "regarded in its true light, the proposition to purchase Cuba is merely a proposition to purchase from Spain the governmental right she claims to exercise over that island." Whereupon this right would be vested "in a free sovereign people," the people of the United States, "in which the community of Cuba would thus become merged." So because the United States was itself free and democratic, any acquisition of territory would be in the name of freedom and democracy, no matter what the wishes of the people concerned. It was an arresting argument.[99]

Despite its obvious appeal, however, other Democrats preferred to claim that, whatever the outward appearance, public opinion in the territories to be acquired actually favoured annexation by the United States. In 1856 the *National Democratic Review* scrutinised the history of the states of Central America and concluded that there could be "no doubt" that in the 1820s, "and since that time," they had "sincerely desired an amalgamation with our Republic." Again without any irony, the *Review* acknowledged that "they have never, directly and unanimously, proposed such a Union." Yet they had "at least, given unmistakable proofs of their willingness to accept it soon." It was not entirely clear, however, what these "proofs" comprised. For "their leaders, their soldiery, their officeholders have, of course, deemed it more consonant with their own interests, to maintain a sickly nationality." The views of these elites could therefore be safely ignored. Far more important was the fact that "the hearts of the masses are with us." How did the writer know this? This too was not entirely clear since although "their voices" had in the past been "for us," unfortunately "oft-repeated disappointment" had "struck than dumb." The silence of the masses thus demonstrated their desire to join the United States and afforded a democratic legitimation for their incorporation into the Union.[100]

An additional reason for the rapid acquisition of territory, whether by force or purchase, was the existing disorder in the nations in question. In 1858 the *Democratic Review* predicted that the unrest in Mexico might compel that nation to "come to us for consolation in its distresses." The alternative was, apparently, for Mexico to "die – perish for ever." But whereas the *Review* was waiting and hoping for overtures from the Mexicans, Stephen A. Douglas was not so hesitant. "If experience shall continue to prove," he told an audience at New Orleans, "what the past may be considered to have demonstrated, that these little Central American powers

99. *Democratic Review*, XLIII (April 1859), p. 19.
100. *National Democratic Review*, 1 (March 1856), p. 250.

cannot maintain self-government," then no less than "the interests of Christendom require that some power should preserve order for them." Given the Monroe Doctrine, it was not difficult to deduce which Christian power Douglas had in mind. And the *Democratic Review* explained that an extension of American power in Mexico was permissible whereas the involvement of a European nation would be an instance of entirely unacceptable interference:

> If any power is extended over Mexico, it must be that proceeding from the government of the United States, and founded upon principles characteristic of the republicanism and democracy of this Union. All efforts to this end, by any foreign league or alliance, must be regarded in the light of a usurpation, as transcending their legitimate functions, and derogatory to the sovereignty of the United States. Our purposes, in the event of such a contingency, are well known to every European nation, by the negotiations and diplomacy of our government in the past. It will be for Congress to declare the precise conditions of a National American Protectorate to be established over Mexico in case of a continuance of the present state of disintegration and the difficulties now notoriously obtaining throughout that republic.

Thus even if the people of Mexico did not wish to be taken over by the United States, such action would be entirely legitimate and honourable.[101]

By this point Democratic assumptions about the nation had resulted in a paradox, one that would become more familiar in the twentieth century. Since the United States embodied democratic values, and since it was clearly desirable for democracy to advance, then whatever was in the American national interest was in fact in the interests of democracy too, no matter what the wishes of the peoples concerned. Partly on this reasoning, Democrats often abandoned the claim that annexation was in the interests of those annexed and simply asserted that it was in the interests of the Republic.

This meant that almost any territory in the Americas might now be up for grabs. According to the *Democratic Review*, Central America lay "in such a relation to the two extremes of this Union, that our own interests and safety impose it upon us as a national necessity – a simple law of self-preservation – to exercise exclusive control over the right of transit." For example "the Isthmus of Panama especially is necessary to us, as the connecting link between our Atlantic and Pacific Empire." By now all concern for the peoples being taken over had evaporated. After all, it was "the manifest destiny of North Americans to colonize and control this

101. *Democratic Review*, XLII (Aug. 1858), p. 110; *Speeches of Douglas at New Orleans, Philadelphia and Baltimore*, p. 10; *Democratic Review*, XLII (Nov. 1858), pp. 369–370.

continent" and "this necessity is of so imperious a nature as to override all minor considerations of policy, and even of right." At this point the writer played the race card. For the peoples concerned were racially inferior and "the destinies of thirty millions of people [Americans], and such a people, must not and can not be jeopardied [sic] for the sake of a handful of mongrel half-breeds." From this it followed that "if the isthmus he indispensable to us as a means of national cohesion, we must occupy it – and we will." Democratic ideals had now, it seemed, been left far behind.[102]

## IV

As the *Democratic Review*'s sentiments imply, however, racism had not. Indeed it was a prominent feature of Democratic expansionism. Yet here the Democrat encountered a cruel dilemma. The most racially desirable people, the Canadians, were also the least available. The Canadians did not wish to be incorporated into the United States. Moreover, behind Canada stood the might of the British Empire. Mexicans, Cubans, and other Hispanics, on the other hand, were a considerably softer target, but they were, in the eyes of American expansionists, also racially dubious, not least because of the racial mixing that had occurred throughout much of Latin America.

In the 1850s there were many filibustering activities in Central America, some of which proved in the short term, highly successful. Thus William Walker enjoyed a remarkable career as a filibuster culminating in his gaining control of Nicaragua, until he met his end at the hands of a firing squad in 1860. Walker's activities won the plaudits of many, especially Democrats, and especially southerners. Nevertheless expansionists concentrated their energies, rhetorically at least, upon Cuba. This was despite the alleged racial deficiencies of the Cubans. For yet again the key factor in determining Democratic priorities was slavery. Cuba contained many slaves and it was feared that, without the intervention of the United States, they might be freed.[103]

It is important to remind ourselves that this was never the sole justification for annexing Cuba. In addition to the wider imperative to "extend the area of freedom," Democrats in the North as well as some in the South emphasised the economic case for annexation. This case centered on the potential market for American goods. Thus one Connecticut Democrat announced that his party regarded Cuba as "Gibraltar to the American

---

102. *Democratic Review*, XXXVII (June 1856), p. 513.
103. As we have already seen, there was a parallel hope that the South might obtain in Cuba one or more slave states and thus offset the ever-increasing preponderance of the free states in the federal government – see Chapter 1 above.

Mediterranean; as destined by the irresistible *fiat* of the CREATOR, to be a constituent part of the government which shall have in hand the destinies of this Continent." He claimed that the principal beneficiary of the annexation of Cuba would be not the South but instead the New England states, which would then find a large additional export market. Meanwhile the *Democratic Review* in 1859 believed it "certain that no hope can be entertained for a revival of commerce, to any considerable extent, between this country and Cuba while Spain retains the control of the latter." But if possession of the island were instead transferred to the United States, an immediate transformation would occur, for "there is scarcely any article produced by Cuba that could not be imported to advantage and consumed by us, while almost all the products of agriculture and manufactures of the United States could be profitably exported to that island."[104]

As always, however, the interests of slavery were never far from the surface. Ironically they sometimes resulted, once again, in the invisibility of the slave. The rhetoric of "Manifest Destiny" led its supporters to announce that they "claim no subjugated territory by the brute right of conquest, nor court the forced allegiance of any reluctant race or country." Yet in the case of Cuba the "forced allegiance" of its African population was precisely what was desired. In a somewhat different context Democrats invoked the doctrines of popular sovereignty and state's rights to describe the future form of the American Republic with territory extending not only over the continent but over the entire world:

> The nation owes to the Democratic party its greatness, progress, and prosperity, and through its irresistible power will yet be planted upon every quarter of this vast continent, and ultimately throughout the globe, the American theory of local and independent sovereignty of States, with dissimilar social organizations, existing and prospering in political union and brotherhood, each moving harmoniously in its own sphere, and all revolving with unerring precision within the orb of our *Magna Charta* – the Constitution of the United States.

Here a key phrase was "dissimilar social organizations," which was almost certainly intended to denote dissimilar labour systems, with slavery very much included.[105]

In such statements slavery was merely implicit. On other occasions, however, Democrats explicitly cited the dangers facing the slaveholders

---

104. *The Union: Present and Future, A Speech Delivered by Hon W. W. Eaton... Hartford March 3, 1860* (n.p., n.d.), pp. 12–13; *Democratic Review*, XLIII (April 1859), p. 9. See also *Boston North*, Feb. 5, 12, 1859. On Walker's impact on southerners, see May, *Southern Dream of a Caribbean Empire*, pp. 77–134.
105. *Democratic Review*, XLIII (April 1859), p. 37.

of Cuba. Thus the *National Democratic Review* announced that Cuba longed to throw off the yoke of Spanish despotism but was restrained by her fears of a servile rebellion. But if the United States were able to calm those fears, then she would seek to join the Union within three months.[106] A more immediate threat, however, was that of emancipation in Cuba. Such a prospect provoked a high degree of moral indignation. Once again the nefarious influence of the British Empire, now militantly antislavery, was discerned. But, according to the *Democratic Review*, "it must not be supposed that emancipation is possible in Cuba." For, fortunately, the slaveholding United States offered a shining example to the Cuban slaveholders. "We do not believe that the people of Cuba," the writer continued, "with our example before them, will ever permit the Spanish Government to yield to England in this respect." Such action by Spain would be, the writer continued, "a despotic interference by force and fraud against the rightful sovereignty of a neighboring people" and in such circumstances "the Government of the United States would be bound to enforce its rule of non-intervention in the affairs of this continent by European powers, to shield the people of Cuba." But if, despite this protection, "Spain should succeed in treacherously declaring bound labor abolished in Cuba," all would not be lost. For the United States, with its ideals of popular sovereignty and state's rights to the fore, would then come to the rescue of the Cuban slaveholders. In this eventuality "under our well established and defined principle of local sovereignty," "the people," and here the writer was referring exclusively to the Caucasian people of Cuba, would "be entitled to institute or re-establish whatever domestic institutions, consistent with the constitution of the United States, they might think best calculated to promote their prosperity as a State." In other words in a spectacular vindication of American democratic values, they could then triumphantly re-establish slavery in Cuba.[107]

## V

The desire to annex Cuba produced one of the most extraordinary documents in the history of American foreign policy. The Ostend Manifesto was an initially confidential memorandum, drawn up in October 1854 by Pierre Soulé of Louisiana, James Mason of Virginia and James Buchanan of Pennsylvania and addressed to Secretary of State William Marcy of New York. Following leaks, however, it had to be made public. The result was that although Democrats, as we have seen, continued to press for expansion in general, and into Cuba in particular, for the rest of the

106. *National Democratic Review*, I (Feb. 1856), p. 138.
107. *Democratic Review*, XLIII (April 1859), p. 15

decade, the cause of "Manifest Destiny" was largely discredited within the North and would not regain a widespread appeal there until the 1890s.[108]

The three statesmen, representing the nation at London, Madrid and Paris, urged that Cuba be acquired with all possible speed. In effect the document encapsulated the boasts and the fears, the circumlocutions and the rationalisations of "Manifest Destiny" in the 1850s. It began by asserting that Cuba "naturally" belonged to the United States: "Cuba is as necessary to the North American republic as any of its present members, and . . . it belongs naturally to that great family of States of which the Union is the providential nursery." Indeed there was such an affinity between the two that the two peoples (here the slaves of both countries had once again disappeared) "now look upon each other as if they were one people and had but one destiny."

Having taken the wishes of the Cuban people fully into account, the ministers were then able to recommend that the United States offer to purchase the island from Spain. Clearly it would be very much in the interests of Spain to accept this offer and the three diplomats did not hesitate to inform her ministers where the money could be spent. But the most remarkable part of the document came when they considered the possibility that Spain might stupidly refuse the offer. What was to be done "if Spain, dead to the voice of her own interest, and actuated by stubborn pride and a false sense of honour, should refuse to sell Cuba to the United States?"

At this point the Ministers resorted to a straightforward assertion of national interest. "Self-preservation," they argued, "is the first law of nature, with States as well as with individuals." Recognising that the principle was very much open to abuse, they nonetheless insisted that it "has always been recognized." To annex Cuba solely on these grounds, they conceded, would be a departure from American tradition since all previous territorial acquisitions, including those obtained after the war with Mexico had been made "by fair purchase, or, as in the case of Texas, upon the free and voluntary application of the people of that independent State, who desired to blend their destinies with our own." Thus "our past history forbids that we should acquire the island of Cuba without the consent of Spain," unless – and here the crucial qualification was entered – "justified by the great law of self-preservation." In such circumstances, other nations, it was true, might condemn the United States but this was of no consequence: "whilst pursuing this course we can afford to disregard the censures of the world, to which we have been so often and so unjustly exposed."

---

108. The Manifesto may be found in *House Executive Documents*, 33/2, X, pp. 127–136.

So the critical question was whether Cuba "in the possession of Spain, seriously endanger[s] our internal peace and the existence of our cherished Union?" If this question were "answered in the affirmative, then, by every law, human and divine, we shall be justified in wresting it from Spain if we possess the power." The ministers now introduced a telling analogy. In such circumstances a resort to force would be justified "upon the very same principle that would justify an individual in tearing down the burning house of his neighbor if there were no other means of preventing the flames from destroying his own home." But still the question remained: did the present condition of the island justify such measures?

The Ministers then produced an apparently anticlimactic answer: "we forbear to enter into the question." Here, however, they were perhaps guilty of some disingenuousness for they had already asserted that "considerations exist which render delay in the acquisition of this island exceedingly dangerous to the United States." Yet the next sentence left no room for doubt and at the same time raised the specter of emancipation, first hinted at in the analogy with the burning house:

> We should, however, be recreant to our duty, be unworthy of our gallant forefathers, and commit base treason against our posterity, should we permit Cuba to be Africanized and become a second St. Domingo, with all its attendant horrors to the white race, and suffer the flames to extend to our own neighboring shores, seriously to endanger or actually to consume the fair fabric of our Union.

The danger was thus acute: "we fear that the course and current of events are rapidly tending towards such a catastrophe." The Ministers concluded that "the Union can never enjoy repose, nor possess reliable security, as long as Cuba is not embraced within its boundaries."[109]

This extraordinary document, which effectively urged a resort to naked force in the event that Spain refused to sell Cuba, was immediately denounced by Republicans (and those who were soon to become Republicans). According to the New York *Tribune*, it was "a buccaneering document," which set out "to grasp, to rob, to murder, to grow rich on the spoils of provinces and the toils of slaves," while the Republican platform of 1856 denounced "the highwayman's plea," that "might makes right," as "in every respect unworthy of American diplomacy." It was a document which "would bring shame and dishonor upon any Government or people that gave it their sanction." Even many Democrats were shocked, with Secretary of State William Marcy, for example, immediately disavowing

---

109. It should perhaps be added that like other Democrats, the authors of the Manifesto took account of the existence of the slave trade in Cuba and argued that annexation by the United States would result in its suppression.

it. The acquisition of Cuba for them was indeed desirable but it needed a sounder justification. Yet the Ostend Manifesto did nothing to prevent James Buchanan, along with Soulé one of its two prime movers, from receiving the Democratic nomination for President a little more than a year later. Indeed it probably helped his cause.[110]

## VI

The fate of the demand for additional territory illuminates many of the weaknesses in the Democratic world-view. The Ostend Manifesto revealed once again the extent to which democratic ideals were being subordinated to, or reshaped and modified by, the need to protect slavery. In the 1840s it had been possible to furnish a patriotic appeal to northerners and southerners alike on behalf of "Manifest Destiny." By the 1850s this was no longer possible, partly because northerners, it was realised, having had to stomach the Kansas-Nebraska Act, were disinclined to welcome other projects that might result in the extension of slavery.

Another factor, partly related, was that easy pickings were no longer to be had. Expansion in the 1840s had taken advantage of the military and economic weakness of Mexico and the sparseness of the population living on the land acquired. By the 1850s no such tracts of land were available (apart from the Gadsden Purchase). Additional lands to the South now contained large numbers of Mexicans, who, as far as Democrats were concerned, had never adequately demonstrated their capacity for self-government and whose incorporation into the Union was accordingly viewed with distaste. Although Democratic ideology viewed previous waves of expansion as divinely ordained, such an analysis obscured these more mundane factors. Meanwhile Canada offered no hope at all to expansionists, though it continued to be the subject of many wistful thoughts.

This left other Latin American countries such as Nicaragua, which was the object of many filibustering expeditions in these years, and Cuba. But here an even more glaring weakness in Democratic ideology became apparent. Cuba was attractive because, like Texas, it had the combined allure of additional territory for the nation as a whole, and additional slaves and slaveholders, for the South. But whereas in the 1840s it had been possible to balance the admission of Texas with the acquisition (or "re-occupation") of Oregon, no such counterweight was available in the 1850s.

---

110. New York *Tribune*, March 8, 1855; Donald B. Johnson (ed.) *National Party Platforms: Volume I 1840–1956* (Urbana, IL, 1973), pp. 27–28. May, *Southern Dream of a Caribbean Empire*, p. 72.

Similarly the desire for additional territory in the 1850s revealed the failure of Democrats to understand the nature of the sectional controversy that now threatened to overwhelm them. By the mid-1850s an alternative perspective on the nation's territorial expansion might have suggested itself. The Louisiana Purchase had, after all, generated a deep sectional crisis over the admission of Missouri. In the 1840s the Mexican cession had brought the nation closer than it had ever been to dissolution. In the mid-1850s the attempt to organise another area of the Louisiana Purchase, Kansas and Nebraska, had raised sectional animosities to a still higher pitch. Yet Democrats continued to believe that territorial acquisitions would strengthen nationalistic feeling and even serve as an antidote to sectional animosity. By the 1850s a huge weight of evidence to the contrary had accumulated. But once again Democratic principles had become dogma. Experience counted for little when it challenged the orthodoxies of the Democratic faith.[111]

## Slavery and antislavery

### I

In 1856 a Democratic Convention in Illinois passed the following motion:

> *Resolved*, that the democratic party is neither a pro-slavery, nor an anti-slavery party. It allows every man to be fully persuaded in his own mind upon that vexed question. It does not recognize slavery as a national question, but restricts its discussion and the question of its continuance to the people of the States where it exists, and who are responsible for it, confident that they will settle it wisely, and if it be an evil, abolish it in good time.

These attitudes were characteristic of northern Democrats in the 1850s. Although the slavery question in that decade became the primary focus of political debate and a source of unprecedented controversy, northern Democrats would have preferred otherwise. Their stance was, they believed, a neutral one in that the party was, as Daniel Dickinson reiterated, "neither a slavery nor an antislavery party." While some individuals might be able to pass some favourable comments on the South's "peculiar institution," and others might instead express their dislike, these opinions were not, and should not become, Democrats affirmed, the policy of the party.[112]

111. Charles Sellers, *The Market Revolution: Jacksonian America 1815–1846* (New York, 1991), p. 414.
112. Democratic Convention quoted in Columbian (New Haven, CT) *Register*, Dec. 5, 1856; *Speeches etc. of Dickinson*, I, pp. 518.

Dickinson's professed neutrality did not therefore mean that he had no opinion concerning slavery, still less that he would have tolerated its reintroduction into the North. "The people of the North," he correctly observed, were "uniformly opposed to slavery." Indeed no northern Democrat who aspired to federal or state office ever proposed that slavery be introduced or reintroduced into his state. Moreover even a Democrat like Dickinson, who before the Civil War was as sympathetic to the South as any senior figure in the party, went out of his way to stress that he did not favour the extension of slavery into the West either. In 1849 he declared that he had "never favored the institution of slavery nor its extension, either immediately or remotely." He then added, and in so doing confirmed the hostility of the northern people, that "whoever charges or insinuates the reverse, originates a base and deliberate, and, unless he is ignorant of my sentiments, a willful calumny." Clearly Dickinson recognised the dangers of being identified as an advocate of slavery.[113]

If northern Democrats did not recommend the extension of slavery, they were still more opposed to the plan, hatched in the 1850s by southern militants, to reopen the African slave trade. President James Buchanan, also renowned for his generosity to southerners, made it clear that he would have none of it. His arguments were those normally presented by northern and southern opponents alike and focussed on the dangers to be apprehended from newly arrived "heathens," and on the impact upon Africa itself, where slave catching would become rampant. This, perhaps the most extreme proslavery initiative of the decade, won no support in the North.[114]

Many northern Democrats went a little further than merely opposing the slave trade, or disclaiming a desire to see slaves in the new territories of the West, or professing neutrality towards the peculiar institution. The anonymous author of a James Buchanan campaign tract in 1856 acknowledged that Democracy "looks upon slavery as an evil" while a Minnesota Democrat conceded that there were "great abuses in slavery." Yet such utterances were generally followed by qualifications and caveats, whose effect was always to undermine any opposition that might have been aroused by the initial assertion and, in effect, to bring the

---

113. *Speeches etc. of Dickinson*, I, p. 303; see also I, p. 279, II, p. 18. For other examples of Democrats disclaiming any desire to see slavery spread, see Columbian *Register*, Oct. 18, 1856; *To the People of Connecticut: The Extension of Slavery: The Official Acts of Both Parties in Relation to This* (n.p., n.d.). pp. 3–4; Peoria *Weekly Democratic Press*, Sept. 30, 1854; *Illinois State Register*, Jan. 31, 1854; Cincinnati *Enquirer*, April 28, May 25, 1854.

114. Richardson (ed.), *Messages and Papers of Presidents*, V, pp. 557–558. On the campaign for reopening, see the first volume of this study, pp. 262–279.

spokesman back towards the neutrality professed by others. Thus the writer of the pro-Buchanan tract announced that slavery was "to be removed by improvement in condition." It was "a condition incident to humanity," "no people have been exempted from its momentous and painful requisitions," and "no age has been spared from the heavy burdens which it ever imposes upon society where it prevails." The Minnesota Democrat similarly insisted that reform of slavery rather than its destruction was the order of the day. Since he then claimed that emancipation (even if followed by colonisation) was inimical to the interests of even the African American, it followed that slavery, whether or not it were "reformed," and however full of "abuses" it might be, was destined to persist for some considerable time in the United States.[115]

In the meantime other northern Democrats took pains to remind the voters that, despite its overall inferiority to free labour, slavery brought considerable benefits. John Weller of California assured a New England audience that, having travelled widely in the South, he had found the slaves to be "better provided for in sickness and in health, better fed and better clad, than the laboring classes in any country in Europe." Moreover slave labour had generated great prosperity in parts of the Southwest which otherwise "would have been howling wildernesses to this day." The *National Democratic Review* endorsed these views and added that while the races coexisted and blacks were so numerous in the South, slavery was the best possible labour system there. Edmund Burke of New Hampshire similarly noted that "the toil of the Negro directed by the intelligence of the white man, caused those regions which would otherwise be as benighted as the wilds of Africa...to blossom as the rose."[116]

Many Democrats thus agreed that slavery had been a source of economic strength to the South. But in benefiting the South it had also benefited the nation. Northern Democrats insisted that the two sections were not, in reality, in conflict or competition: "their interests are not inimical, as is often falsely asserted; but identical and mutually dependent on each other." Thus "the agriculture of the South and the manufactures and shipping of the North are the natural allies and sustainers of each other." The prosperity of each depended upon the other. These were not the only

115. *Plain Facts and Considerations Addressed To The People Of The United States....In Favor of James Buchanan...by an American Citizen* (Boston, 1856), p. 26; D. A. Robertson, *The South and the Democratic Party* (St Paul, 1857), pp. 9–10.
116. *Speeches of Weller, Orr, Lane, and Cobb*, pp. 6–7; *National Democratic Review*, I (March 1856), p. 193; Edmund Burke, *An Important Appeal to the People of the United States* quoted in Murray E. Heimbinder, "Northern Men with Southern Principles: A Study of the Doughfaces of New York and New England," (Ph.D. dissertation, New York University, 1971), pp. 25–26.

arguments adduced in favour of slavery in the South. As we have seen, Democrats warned northerners that emancipation would produce a huge migration of former slaves into the North, to the detriment of northern workers. More simply, they pointed out that several billion dollars of property were at stake.[117]

Yet there was one argument that in the final antebellum years was rarely used by northerners. In the 1830s and 1840s it had not been uncommon for northern radicals to assert that northern workers were in reality more severely oppressed than southern slaves. Their views had thus converged with those of the early southern proslavery publicists. And in the 1830s and 1840s these northern radicals had found the national Democratic party a congenial home. But the return of prosperity in the mid-1840s produced an inevitable reaction and Democrats, as we shall see, no longer complained so vigorously about the dangers posed by banks and tariffs and no longer delivered warnings about deepening inequalities within northern (or southern) society. The result was that few northerners now claimed that the plight of northern labourers was worse than, or even comparable to, that of southern slaves. Such an attitude might have implied that an acute crisis existed in the North if not that slavery should be reintroduced there.[118]

Northern Democrats were thus neither explicitly proslavery nor actively antislavery. They could express misgivings about slavery but could also find reasons to acquiesce in its preservation in the South. If these misgivings set them apart from the southern proslavery theorists, in the 1850s this acquiescence similarly differentiated them from most other northern groups. By that time the other political parties of the North, Whigs, Republicans, even Know Nothings, each displayed far deeper antislavery convictions. Accordingly it followed that, north of the Mason-Dixon Line, the Democrats were the South's principal allies. They themselves knew it. As James Buchanan told future Vice President William King in 1850, "beyond the limits of the Slave States themselves the slaveholders have no friends or allies to stand by their constitutional rights except the Democracy of the North." Daniel Dickinson implicitly endorsed this view when, in apportioning blame for the sectional unrest of the day, he assigned the greater part to the North, and to northern anti-Democrats. A

---

117. *Letter from Hon. Harry Hibbard to Stephen Pingry and Other Citizens of New Hampshire* (n.p., n.d.), p. 8; James W. Bradbury quoted in Boston *Ledger*, Oct. 31, 1857; *The Agitation of Slavery – Who Commenced and Who Can End it?* (n.p., n.d.), p. 1. See also Robertson, *South and the Democratic Party*.

118. One who came very close to this was James Lynch of New York. See *State Rights: Speech of Hon. James Lynch, Delivered in Assembly, State of New York, March 6, 1858* (n.p., n.d.). Note that it was far more common, and far more politic, to claim that the workers of *other* nations were worse off than the slaves of the South.

similar purpose, engendering sympathy for the South, was apparent when northern Democratic publicists reminded their readers that some of the greatest figures in the American past, men like Washington, Jefferson and Jackson, had been slaveholders. Plainly the ownership of slaves could in no sense be a sign of wickedness or degradation.[119]

When northern Democrats expressed their solicitude for the South, however, it was neither to the conditions of the slaves, nor to the economic contribution made by slave labour but rather to the Constitution that they most frequently turned. Here, they believed, the right of southerners to hold slaves was guaranteed and here the obligation, reaffirmed in the Compromise measures of mid-century, of northerners to return fugitive slaves was spelled out. As James Buchanan pointed out, "northern Democrats are not expected to approve slavery in the abstract." Yet "they owe it to themselves, as they value the Union & all the political blessings which bountifully flow from it, to abide by the compromise of the Constitution & leave the question, where that instrument has left it, to the States wherein slavery exists." The Constitution, according to Buchanan, thus guaranteed slavery in the States where it existed. "Our fathers," he affirmed, "have made this agreement with their brethren of the South & it is not for the descendants of either party in the present generation to cancel this solemn compact."[120]

These were Buchanan's sentiments in 1847. A decade later, when as President he was delivering his first annual message to Congress, they had not changed. "The relations between master and slave," he declared "are 'domestic institutions,' and are entirely distinct from institutions of a political character." In a sense Buchanan was following in the footsteps of previous Democratic presidents like Jackson and Polk, who had assumed that there was little or nothing to discuss about slavery, so long as the Constitution in general and the rights of the states in particular were respected.[121]

Indeed the doctrine of state's rights meant, as Buchanan argued as late as 1860, that the northern people were no more responsible for, and had no more right to interfere with, slavery in the South than with slavery in Brazil or serfdom in Russia. His predecessor in the White House, Franklin Pierce, was similarly unequivocal. In his Annual Message of 1855 Pierce noted with "painful regret" that some northern states now went so far as to "disregard their Constitutional obligations." To the President as to many other Democrats, North and South, such defiance was as futile as it

119. *Works of Buchanan*, VIII, p. 371; *Speeches etc. of Dickinson*, I, p. 341; Robertson, *South and the Democratic Party*, p. 8.
120. *Works of Buchanan*, VII, p. 386.
121. Richardson (ed.), *Messages and Papers of Presidents*, V, p. 452. See the first volume of this study, pp. 333–350.

was dangerous and pernicious. It demonstrated a foolish refusal to establish priorities or recognise realities. For there was within every northern
state ample scope for the genuine reformer, the reformer who concerned
himself only with the affairs of his own state and who refused to meddle
in the affairs of another. Yet, Pierce complained, "although conscious of
their inability to heal admitted and palpable social evils of their own, and
which are completely within their jurisdiction," some northern states nevertheless "engage in the offensive and hopeless undertaking of reforming
the domestic institutions of other States, wholly beyond their control and
authority." Like many other Democrats Pierce simply could not understand such activities. For "in the vain pursuit of ends by them entirely
unattainable, and which they may not legally attempt to compass, they
peril the very existence of the Constitution and all the countless benefits
which it has conferred."[122]

The Constitution thus superseded, so far as northern Democrats were
concerned, any abstract or personal opinion about slavery. John B. Weller
of California avowed that "whatever my opinion upon the abstract question of slavery may be, it is enough for me to know that it is constitutional," while Howell Cobb of Georgia, despite holding opinions on
slavery that were very different from Weller's, agreed that constitutionality was indeed the key issue. "On the subject of slavery," he announced,
"there is but one question and one answer." The question was "not
whether slavery is right or wrong; or whether it is a blessing or a curse; or
whether it should be increased or abolished." Instead "the only question"
was "what says the Constitution?" and "the only answer" was "I will
do what the Constitution requires to be done."[123]

This was without doubt the principal argument used by Democrats in
response to those who urged action against slavery, whether abolitionists, Free Soilers, or Republicans. Thus Edson Olds declared that he did
not need to defend slavery, he merely followed the Constitution. Even
when northern Democrats expressed their desire to prevent slavery going
into the territories, they emphasised that this could only be done within
the boundaries set by the Constitution. At the beginning of the decade,
when expressing their distaste for the Fugitive Slave law, they recognised
that their constitutional obligations required that they enforce it. Similarly at the end of the decade those same constitutional obligations were
in part responsible for the horror with which they viewed the Brown raid.
"The morality of servitude," according to a Pennsylvania Democrat, was
"not an open question, for we are bound by the legal and moral obligation of the compact of the Union, under which we have been brought
into existence, and preserved as independent States." As if to underline

122. Richardson (ed.), *Messages and Papers of Presidents*, V, pp. 627, 344.
123. *Speeches of Weller, Orr, Lane, and Cobb*, pp. 6, 25.

his commitment to state's rights, and in order to suggest that the states were actually akin to nations, he added: "as well as by the principles of international law."[124]

This understanding of their constitutional obligations thus operated to prevent northern Democrats from advocating action against slavery, even when they were unwilling explicitly to defend or recommend the peculiar institution. But if their attitude was, compared to other northern groups, apparently noncommittal and even bland, this did not seem to them to constitute a weakness, even in the fevered political atmosphere of the 1850s. In part they prided themselves upon being moderates or conservatives where sectional questions were concerned and did not hesitate to claim the greater part of the credit for the compromises that had been achieved with the South. But more fundamentally, they believed that slavery was, or should be, a minor question even in federal politics, let alone in the politics of northern states. For this reason Stephen A. Douglas in 1852 announced that he had "determined never to make another speech on the slavery question." Douglas avowed himself "heartily tired of the controversy," and added that "the country is disgusted with it." Within less than two years, of course, the Kansas-Nebraska Act had doomed these hopes but Douglas had not changed his priorities. It was the southern insistence on repeal of the Missouri Compromise and the ensuing northern outrage that compelled him, reluctantly, to return to the subject. But by 1855 the same hope resurfaced. In September of that year he declined to give an address on the subject of slavery. The reason was, he explained, that he regarded slavery "as a domestic regulation which derives its existence and support from the local laws of the several States where it prevails and with [which] neither the federal government nor the citizens or authorities of other States have any right to interfere, except to perform their Constitutional obligations in reference to the rendition of fugitives." From this it followed that it was in no sense his "duty as a citizen of a nonslave holding state, to discuss the supposed advantages or evils . . . [of] the domestic institutions of Sister States; with which, under the Constitution and laws of the land, I have no right to interfere, and for the consequences of which I am in no wise responsible." The statesman, Douglas believed, had other and worthier subjects than slaves and slavery to occupy his attention.[125]

124. *Speech of Olds*, p. 11; Message of Governor Wood in *Documents Made to the 50th General Assembly of the State of Ohio* (Columbus, 1852), p. 27; Message of Governor Samuel Dinsmoor in *Journal of the House of Representatives of the State of New Hampshire . . . 1850* (Concord, 1851), p. 36; Message of Governor William F. Parker in *The Legislative Record: Proclamations of the General Assembly of the Commonwealth of Pennsylvania for the Session Commencing Jan. 1860* (Harrisburg, 1860), p. 9. See also *Works of Buchanan*, VIII, p. 403.
125. Stephen A. Douglas to the editor of the Washington *Union*, March 19, 1852 in *Letters of Douglas*, p. 243; Stephen A. Douglas to James W Stone, Sept. 11, 1855 in *Letters*

II

Although many northern Democrats were willing to express an abstract dislike of slavery, their concern for the constitutional rights of the South took precedence. Thus Daniel S. Dickinson of New York, once again confirming both his and his section's disapproval of slavery, announced that he experienced "high gratification" when he saw "a new state, in founding her political organization, adhere to what I regard as true principles of economy, and reject an institution which, sooner or later, must bring more of embarrassment and evil than ever it can even of imaginary good." But then came the inevitable qualification. "It is," he insisted, "a question of Constitutional right" and "each political community should, on the principles of self-government, decide for itself."[126]

Yet the emphasis upon constitutional rights and obligations was itself largely a product of an even deeper concern. For if southern rights were not observed and the constitution were violated, the ultimate catastrophe of disunion would, Democrats feared, almost certainly ensue. So however desirable it might be for the territories of the West to become free states, this objective was for many Democrats of trivial importance and should be sacrificed, if it conflicted with the paramount goal of maintaining the Union. Thus Dickinson, for example, declared that rather than risk the break-up of the Union, he would "see every member of this unfortunate race, bond and free, well provided and provisioned for the journey, in one dark and mighty cloud, march from the old States to the new Territories, or any other section of the Union, there to reside, if the inhabitants would permit them." For this reason he condemned all attempts to agitate the slavery question even when constitutional rights were not at issue. Thus almost all northerners agreed that Congress had jurisdiction over slavery in the District of Columbia and, until the mid-1850s, it was generally agreed that the same applied to slavery in the territories. But Democrats like Dickinson insisted that agitation of these issues was foolhardy in the extreme.[127]

Similarly northern Democrats refused to condemn southerners for taking action in their own states to prevent discussion of the slavery issue. While Republicans complained that the sacred principle of free speech was being violated in the South and bitterly resented the disproportionate share of offices held by slaveholders in the southern states (as in the federal government), Democrats were either blind to these issues or were happy to acquit southerners of ultimate responsibility. They vented their

*of Douglas*, pp. 340–341. See also *Congressional Globe*, 32nd Congress, 1st Session, Appendix., p. 65 (hereafter cited in the form *CG*, 32/1, App., p. 65).

126. *Speeches etc. of Dickinson*, I, pp. 342–343.
127. *Speeches etc. of Dickinson*, I, pp. 343, 297–298, 316.

spleen instead upon the "agitators," most of whom came from the North, who had compelled southerners to rally to the defence of their "peculiar institution."[128]

Thus however desirable the removal of slavery from the South might be, or its exclusion from the territories, these goals should be wholly subordinate to the maintenance of the Union, on which so much depended. As we have seen, the Union to northern Democrats symbolised democracy itself and its destruction would therefore mean the end of freedom not merely in the nation but in the entire world. It followed that the Free Soilers, for example, of the late 1840s were, as Dickinson pointed out, engaged in "an agitation which for a purpose comparatively trivial, sports at a game where the destiny of the world's freedom is the hazard." "Shall we," he asked, "experiment upon our institutions because they, like all that is human, have not attained perfection?" Dickinson made the same identification of slavery with the continuance of the Union more succinctly when he insisted that there was one, and only one, crucial question: "whether we should have a Union with slavery, or slavery without a Union."[129]

These sentiments were frequently expressed by northern Democrats. Franklin Pierce in his last Annual Message to Congress denounced antislavery militants as "agitators" who were risking the best government ever for a purpose only attainable by civil war, while John B. Weller asked his New Hampshire audience whether they would be "willing, after your ancestors have conferred on you the best government the wisdom of man ever devised – a government which has made you the freest and happiest people on earth – to sacrifice all to appease the demands of infatuated, lying abolitionists?" Another Democrat asserted that if by antislavery agitation you "destroy this government" then, in so doing, "you put out the light of the world."[130]

Democrats did not, however, merely claim that the promulgation of antislavery doctrines jeopardised the Union and American democracy. Their utter inability to understand those who agitated against slavery in the South came in part from an insistence that such agitation had been, even for the slaves themselves, wholly counterproductive. Northern Democrats reviewed the history of slavery and of antislavery in the United States and found in it confirmation of their assumptions, beliefs and priorities. Thus James Buchanan condemned the "abolitionists," for having "by their efforts...arrested the natural progress of emancipation and done great injury to the Slaves themselves." They had, he later claimed,

128. In precisely the same way, northern Democrats had been more likely in the late 1830s and 1840s to defend the gag law.
129. *Speeches etc. of Dickinson*, I, pp. 359, 255, see also pp. 274, 289.
130. Richardson (ed.), *Messages and Papers of Presidents*, V, pp. 398–399; *Speeches of Weller, Orr, Lane, and Cobb*, p. 7; *Speech of Olds*, p. 22

delayed emancipation in Virginia, Maryland, Kentucky, and Missouri. Similarly Harry Hibbard, a New Hampshire Congressman, claimed that, far from freeing the slave, the agitation had instead made "his yoke heavier, and his chain tighter," and accordingly delayed emancipation by half a century.[131]

Democrats did not always explain the process by which antislavery agitation served only to "rivet the chains" of the slave. Clement C. Vallandigham of Ohio claimed quite plausibly that, faced with the abolitionist onslaught, southerners had developed the proslavery argument, with the implication that but for that attack, they would have continued to view slavery as a "necessary evil." More questionable, however, was his assumption that this shift had actually delayed emancipation. Other Democrats, meanwhile, identified a very different mechanism. According to James Buchanan the slave states in 1860 faced an "immediate peril," which was the result neither of events in Kansas nor of the possibility of slaves fleeing from their masters. Instead "the incessant and violent agitation of the slave question throughout the North for the last quarter of a century" had "produced its malign influence on the slaves." It had "inspired them with vague notions of freedom," as a result of which "a sense of security no longer exists around the family altar." In other words a "feeling of peace at home" had "given place to apprehensions of servile insurrections," and the masters had accordingly been forced to tighten their control. Again it was assumed, without much discussion, that these fears made emancipation less rather than more likely.[132]

The Democratic reading of the past thus confirmed the futility of political agitation against slavery. Again Stephen A. Douglas exemplified Democratic thinking not only when he too denounced abolitionists for their utter failure to improve the plight of the slave but when he then claimed that the alternative approach, which left every state in the full possession of its constitutional rights, was in fact more likely to result in a process of gradual, voluntary, and peaceful emancipation. Indeed this was one of Douglas's constant refrains in the 1850s. In defence of the Compromise of 1850 he pointed out that states which had abolished slavery had done so "of their own free will." Thus the Northwest Ordinance of 1787, he insisted, had not in fact made the states of Indiana and Illinois free; this had been achieved instead by "the voluntary action of the people" directly concerned. In 1854 he reiterated that it was essential to leave the question to the people most directly concerned, a policy which had resulted in slavery's disappearance from the entire North and from California. Douglas

---

131. *Works of Buchanan*, VII, p. 386, VIII, p. 397; *Letter from Hibbard to Pingry*, p. 7.
132. James C. Vallandigham, *A Life of Clement L. Vallandigham* (Baltimore, 1872), pp. 55–59; Richardson (ed.), *Messages and Papers of Presidents*, V, pp. 626–627.

then expressed the hope that "whenever, in God's Providence, it shall cease in the States where it now exists, it may cease under the operation of this principle, and NONE OTHER." Finally in 1858, during his debates with Lincoln, he drove home the same message: six of the original twelve states that had once allowed slavery had abolished it but abolitionism had led to a reaction, as a result of which the process had been halted. Thus for Douglas, as for many Democrats, slavery would ironically be perpetuated by antislavery, whereas its demise would be hastened if full respect were accorded to the South, if southerners were allowed to enjoy without restriction their constitutional rights, and if antislavery agitation ceased.[133]

### III

Yet however loyal to the Union or dedicated to the constitution, Democrats could claim no monopoly on these sentiments. Many abolitionists (apart from the Garrisonians) and almost all Republicans were equally committed to both Union and Constitution. But they did not reach the same conclusions regarding slavery or the South. What distinguished the northern Democrats from these groups was not their concern for the Union or the constitution but rather their understanding of slavery itself. As the controversy over the territories unfolded in the late 1840s and the 1850s so northerners of all persuasions were compelled to address key questions about southern slavery and about the northern response to it. The answers to these questions then formed the core of the differences between northern Democrats and Republicans.

The northern Democrats held that slavery would be established in an area, state, or region if, but only if, it were profitable there. In such circumstances indeed its establishment was virtually inevitable. And profitability, in turn, was a function of climate and soil. Thus August Belmont of New York as late as 1860 spoke of new slave territory being added only "where climate and soil render it more profitable than Free Labor," while Caleb Cushing of Massachusetts in the same year remarked that population, soil and climate had led southerners to defend slavery and northerners to eliminate it. A decade earlier, Daniel Dickinson had fully anticipated these observations.

> Slave labor, as existing and organized in a portion of our country, like every other department of human affairs, founded in pecuniary

133. Barbee and Bonham, "Montgomery Address of Douglas," p. 548; *Speech of.... Douglas on 'Measures of Adjustment'*, p. 7; Stephen A. Douglas to Twenty Five Chicago Clergymen, April 6, 1854 in *Letters of Douglas*, p. 321; *Debates between Lincoln and Douglas*, p. 31. See also *Speeches etc. of Dickinson*, I, p. 518.

considerations, is controlled in its movements by the principles of profit and loss, of demand and supply. Like free labor, it will eventually be found where there is the greatest demand and where it pays the best profit. It may linger in an old settlement, where it has long been, after it has ceased to be profitable; but it will not go to a new one unless invited by reward. So long as the spirit of cupidity is inseparable from man it will go where a majority of the people desire it, and not elsewhere; and since it is tolerated by our fundamental law, a majority who favor it will soon be found where it is greatly to their advantage.

As if to reinforce his argument and to demonstrate that slavery was reducible to dollars and cents, Dickinson pointed out that California's Constitutional Convention had recently voted to exclude slavery. The exclusion had been unanimously agreed, despite the large number of southern-born delegates in attendance. Abstract or prior attachment to slavery or to free labour thus counted for nothing if it conflicted with the fundamental force of economic self-interest.[134]

Once again, however, it was Stephen A. Douglas, who, despite his stated preference for other topics, both most clearly set out and most fully elaborated the northern Democratic view of slavery. Douglas was, of course, the principal architect of the party's policy on slavery in the 1850s and even though later in the decade his views were repudiated by most southerners, he remained by far the most popular Democrat in the North. As we have seen, Douglas would have preferred to discuss other subjects rather than slavery but this hope had proved illusory. He was sometimes criticised by his enemies for ignoring the moral aspects of the slavery question and it is true that he rarely discussed these matters. In fact he made a strong, almost a moral, principle out of his amoral approach to slavery, denying that there was "any tribunal on earth that can decide the question of the morality of slavery or any other institution." Instead it was his duty, as a statesman "to deal with slavery as a political question involving questions of public policy." This was classic Democratic doctrine, a refusal to allow moral questions to intrude into politics.[135]

Douglas was similarly candid when discussing the conditions under which slavery would take root. And here a profound consistency emerged. He insisted that morality would play no part when the inhabitants of a new territory themselves decided whether or not to allow slavery. In other

134. August Belmont to Stephen A. Douglas, Dec. 31, 1860, in *Letters . . . of Belmont*, pp. 44–49; Heimbinder, "Northern Men with Southern Principles," p. 20; *Speeches etc. of Dickinson*, I, p. 345. See also *Official Proceedings of the Democratic National Convention, Held in 1860, at Charleston and Baltimore* (Cleveland, 1860), p. 187.
135. Ohio *Statesman*, Sept. 20, 1859 quoted in Johannsen, *Douglas*, p. 712.

words his amoral approach precisely mirrored that which he expected and desired the inhabitants of a state or territory to display.

Douglas maintained this attitude throughout the 1850s. In 1851, defending the Compromise measures of the previous year, he observed that California had been destined to become a free state regardless of the actions taken by politicians or statesmen. "The whole of California," he claimed, "– from the very nature of the country, her rocks and sands, elevation above the sea, climate, soil, and productions – was bound to be free territory by the decision of her own people, no matter when admitted or how divided." Much later in the decade Douglas embarked on a triumphal tour during which he spoke at Baltimore and New Orleans. At New Orleans he reiterated that "this question of slavery is not a question of legislation at all, but of climate, soil, and self-interest" and even went so far as to suggest that if the people of his own state of Illinois "had lived further South, in the districts which produce sugar, and cotton, and rice," then "we would have seen just as much virtue in slave labor as you do in Louisiana." Self-interest ruled. And, according to Douglas, the states of New England had only abolished slavery when it had been in their interest to do so. Thus it was easy to see where slavery would, and even should, exist. It would be "in those latitudes and climates which adapt it to the profitable production of rice and sugar and cotton, and where slave labor will be remunerative." Douglas concluded that "slavery will exist wherever soil, climates, and productions demand it, and it will exist nowhere else" He then asked why, "if climate, and soil, and self interest will regulate this question," Americans should "quarrel about it?"[136]

Two years later and immediately prior to the presidential election of 1860 Douglas went, at some personal risk, to Montgomery Alabama. By now he almost certainly knew that Lincoln would win the election. His message, however, in a state that was a hotbed of secessionist sentiment, was unchanged. Indeed he was still more emphatic. "Slavery," he argued, "will exist wherever the people want it, and it will not exist anywhere else." Popular opinion would thus determine whether a state or territory should allow or forbid slavery. But public opinion would itself be determined by self-interest: "the people will want it wherever the climate and soil render it necessary and profitable." It followed that if "the climate is such that slavery is neither necessary [n]or profitable," then "the people will not have it, and no power in Christendom can force it on them." Thus "this question of slavery is one of political economy depending upon the laws of climate, production and self-interest." Douglas now went out of

---

136. *Speech of .... Douglas on "Measures of Adjustment,"* p. 9; *Speeches of Douglas at New Orleans, Philadelphia and Baltimore,* pp. 6–8.

his way to ensure that his southern audience understood this point. "You cannot," he insisted, "compel slavery to exist in a cold, northern latitude any more than by an Act of Congress you can make cotton grow upon the tops of the Rocky mountains." To underline the absurdity of any such attempt he asserted that "whenever you make up your minds to maintain slavery in those cold northern regions, where the people do not want it and will not have it, you must first get an act of Congress compelling cotton, rice, sugar and tobacco to grow there, and then you can have negroes."[137]

It followed that slavery was not, and should not become, a moral question. If southerners migrated to a region where slavery was not profitable, then they would be opposed to it. If northerners moved to a region where slavery was "necessary under the climate and profitable," then they would "protect it." Douglas even claimed that abolitionists and Republicans would themselves advocate slavery if they inhabited a region where it was suitable: Lincoln, Sumner and Seward, he claimed, if they lived in Cuba would soon acquire a plantation. Indeed he went so far as to suggest that in such circumstances they would not only establish slavery but also urge the reopening of the African slave trade. For "it does not matter where a man comes from when he settles in a country, he will advocate that line of policy and legislation which he thinks the good of the community in which he lives, his own Interests, and those of his children require." Self-interest would thus overwhelm abstract moral commitment.[138]

Throughout the 1850s Douglas prided himself on being able to propound the same principles throughout the nation, and on being able to appeal to northerners and southerners alike. Even though by 1860 his appeal to the South was greatly diminished, he continued to seek southern support for the principles with which he had been identified for more than a decade. Like most northern Democrats he had been in the North a defender of the South; now in the South, he took pains to defend the North. As a committed nationalist he did not hesitate to challenge the southern stereotype of the Yankee. Once again he referred to the force of self-interest operating upon all (white) men, Yankees included, and explained that in this lay the security of the South:

> But the fire eaters tell you that if you allow the people to do as they please, under the limitations of the Constitution, that the Yankees will just swarm into the New Territories and out-vote the Southern men. Well, I have not as bad an opinion of the Yankee as some people have; but I have not so good an opinion of him as to believe that he will carry his antislavery sentiments with him wherever he goes. My

137. Barbee and Bonham, "Montgomery Address of Douglas," p. 543.
138. Barbee and Bonham, "Montgomery Address of Douglas," pp. 544–551

opinion of the Yankee is the same as my opinion of the Southern man, that whenever he goes into a new state or territory he will vote according to the opinions which prevail in the country in which he lives, and not according to the notions he brought with him from Yankee land.

The fate of slavery depended upon climate and soil, rather than morality or legislation.[139]

## IV

Northern Democrats believed therefore that the slavery question did not, of itself, possess the potential to disturb the Union. After all, if it were a mere question of dollars and cents, involving only the people directly concerned, why should the security of the nation be at risk? This reasoning led them to a conclusion that was of the first importance: it was not slavery but slavery agitation, and especially antislavery, that threatened the Union. The root of the problem was, as Franklin Pierce put it, "the inflammatory agitation," which "has for twenty years produced nothing save unmitigated evil, North and South." This view was Democratic orthodoxy in the North in the 1850s. When the furore over Kansas was at its height, Pierce complained bitterly that the controversy was entirely needless. For "climate, soil, production, hopes of rapid advancement and the pursuit of happiness on the part of the settlers themselves, with good wishes, but with no interference from without, would have quietly determined the question which is at this time of such disturbing character." In the absence of agitation therefore, "the character of the domestic institutions of the future new state would have been a matter of too little interest to the inhabitants of the contiguous States, personally or collectively, to produce among them any political emotion." In other words, the laws of supply and demand, operating in conjunction with the state's climatic and topographical endowments, would have quietly settled the slavery question in Kansas.[140]

Occasionally Democrats lumped together southern and northern extremists and denounced both as "agitators." Thus Daniel Dickinson in 1850 complained that it was "the political agitators in both sections who have made all the mischief." He then claimed that if one could "take a small number of men out of the northern and also out of the southern sections of this Union, or silence their clamor," then "this accursed agitation could be settled in less than a single week." But in their own states it was northern antislavery agitators with whom northern Democrats had

139. Barbee and Bonham, "Montgomery Address of Douglas," p. 543.
140. Richardson (ed.), *Messages and Papers of Presidents*, V, p. 359

to contend, and consequently they were usually, as we have seen, driven to defend the South. As a result, before the firing on Fort Sumter they more often attacked northern antislavery militants than southern secessionists.[141]

In so doing, they gave particular attention to the more celebrated Republican and Whig utterances. When William Seward declared that slavery violated a "higher law" than that made by human legislators or constitution makers, he could scarcely have found a formulation better calculated to arouse the wrath of northern Democrats. First, it encouraged violations of constitutional rights and thus risked disunion, civil war and, in their eyes, democracy itself. Second, the invocation of a "higher" or "divine" law seemed to invite individuals to indulge their own enthusiasms without restraint. Could any government survive such an invitation to fanaticism? As one Indiana supporter of Buchanan in 1856 put it, "with such ideas in the ascendant in any country, no government is practical, and anarchy and confusion, and brute force, must inevitably 'rule the hour.'" Groups or individuals would become "maddened by sectional or party prejudices" and would "never want an excuse for the violation of unpalatable laws, so long as they are permitted to substitute the vagaries of their own distempered intellects as having a stronger claim to their obedience than the Constitution of their country." Alternatively, if anarchy were to be avoided, it could only be, Stephen A. Douglas claimed, by empowering a single individual "to be the prophet to reveal the will of God and establish a theocracy for us."[142]

William Seward's invocation of a "higher law" was followed later in the decade by equally celebrated utterances by Seward himself and by Abraham Lincoln. While Seward spoke of an "irrepressible conflict" between North and South, Lincoln delivered essentially the same message when he insisted that a "house divided" into slave and nonslave areas could not stand. Again Douglas was quick to respond. He pointed out that if such a view had been held in 1787, when only a minority of states was free, the effect would have been to spread slavery throughout the nation. Why, he asked, if the Union had had both free and slave states since the Revolution, could it not continue to have them? In 1859 Douglas complied with a formal request from a party supporter for his autograph and added the inscription "that this Union can exist forever divided into

---

141. *Speeches etc. of Dickinson*, I, pp. 330–331.
142. *Frémont – His Supporters And Their Record By an Indianian* (n.p., n.d.), p. 4; *Speech of.... Douglas on 'Measures of Adjustment'*, p. 30. See also *Proceedings and Address of the Democratic State Convention Held at Syracuse...Jan. 10, 1856* (Albany, 1856), p. 26. Douglas also added, rather pointedly, that any individual who believed the Constitution to be in violation of the laws of God should refuse to take office or exercise any function of citizenship under it.

free and slave States, as our fathers made it, if the Constitution be preserved inviolate."[143]

Northern Democrats gave particular attention to these, the more dramatic Republican (and Whig) utterances because they believed they exemplified the agitation that threatened the Union. But they did not simply
disagree, however fervently, with the Republicans or Free Soilers on the
slavery question. Instead they refused to credit their opponents with even
a semblance of sincerity. Political antislavery, they held, was mere political
posturing, devoid of genuine principle. Thus Daniel S. Dickinson repeatedly warned that the Free Soilers were using the slavery question merely
for partisan purposes. This agitation was "solely to furnish a hobby for
demagogues to ride." A similar perception, as we shall see, underlay the
Democratic rationale for the Kansas-Nebraska Act and indeed these attitudes would persist throughout the decade.[144]

Douglas also explained how it was that agitators were able to manipu-
late popular sentiment. The problem, he pointed out, was that the citizens
of the Upper North and the Lower South simply lived too far apart to
know one another. At the time of the Compromise of 1850 and again
after Lincoln's election a decade later he observed that "ultra" opinions
on the slavery question were to be found in the geographical extremities of
the nation. "The war [over slavery] rages," he told the Senate "furiously
between these extremes, whose positions preclude the idea of their having
any real grievances involved in the struggle, or being able to comprehend
the true merits of the controversy." Hence he had "always noted that
those men who are so far off from the slave States that they did not know
anything about them, are most anxious for the fate of the poor slave."
Indeed "those men who are so far off that they do not know what a negro
is, are distressed to death about the condition of the poor negro." On the
other hand, in the border South and the lower North there was harmony:

> But, sir, go into the border states, where we associate across the line,
> where the civilities of society are constantly interchanged; where we
> trade with each other and have social and commercial intercourse,
> and there you will find them standing by each other like a band of
> brothers. Take southern Illinois, southern Indiana, southern Ohio,
> and that part of Pennsylvania bordering on Maryland, and there
> you will find social intercourse, commercial intercourse, good feeling;
> because these people know the condition of the slave on the opposite

143. *Speeches of Douglas at New Orleans, Philadelphia and Baltimore*, p. 4; Stephen A.
Douglas to George H. Hull, February 10, 1859 in *Letters of Douglas*, p. 437. See
also *The Legislative Record: Proclamations of the General Assembly of the Commonwealth of Pennsylvania for the Session Commencing Jan. 4, 1859* (Harrisburg,
1859), p. 10.
144. *Speeches etc. of Dickinson*, I, pp. 279, 255, 259.

> side of the line; but just in proportion as you recede from the slave
> states, just in proportion as the people are ignorant of the facts, just
> in that proportion party leaders can impose on their sympathies and
> honest prejudices.

This perception informed Douglas's understanding of the entire sectional
controversy.[145]

## V

Although Democratic traditions were often a source of strength to the
party's leaders and supporters, they were also a source of weakness. So far
as slavery and antislavery were concerned, the Jeffersonian legacy proved
highly damaging. Undoubtedly the inability of northern Democrats to
respect, or even comprehend, antislavery sentiment owed much to the old
Jeffersonian equation of antislavery with Federalism. Jefferson had himself viewed the crisis over Missouri as "a mere party trick," perpetrated by
Federalists who could not hope to win office by normal, respectable means
and more than thirty years later Democrats, as we shall see, continued to
view antislavery in general, and the opposition to the Kansas-Nebraska
Act in particular, in the same light.[146]

Thus although Democrats sincerely believed themselves to be neutral
on the slavery question, their attitude was in reality far more complex.
On the one hand, they were not at all neutral concerning slavery in the
North. To this they were adamantly opposed.[147] Similarly, as far as the
West was concerned, they were still not neutral, since, as we shall see,
most of them had a decided preference for free labour in the territories,
even though they assigned a much lower priority to this goal than the
Republicans. On the other hand, in their attitude to slavery in the South
a quite unneutral sympathy emerged. Not only did they sometimes find
benefits in slavery for the slaves, the South and the nation as a whole, they
were also slow to criticise any of the restrictions placed by southerners
on antislavery activity within the South and within the nation. Here the
doctrine of state's rights, constitutionally underwritten as they believed,
allowed them to defend practices which appalled many northerners.

This, however, was only one of the ways in which the Democratic creed,
in shaping their view of slavery, came to the aid of the slaveholder. Their
dedication to state's rights and limited government, their reluctance to

---

145. *CG*, 31/1, App., p. 371, 36/1, p. 558, 36/2, p. 52.
146. See the first volume of this study, pp. 71–75. See also *Address and Proceedings of the Democratic State Convention, August, 1849* (Albany, 1849), pp. 4–6.
147. It should, however, be added that while Republicans like Lincoln believed that there was a conspiracy to extend slavery into the North, no northern Democrat – or at least no northern Democrat who did not defect to the Republicans – entertained these fears.

allow moral questions (like temperance or antislavery) to be carried into politics, their intense racism and their perception of antislavery as "Federalism," all operated as bulwarks behind which the slaveholder could enjoy the fruits of not only his own but also his slave's labour. All were time-honoured articles of the Democratic faith; all persisted into the crisis decade of the 1850s. But all were coming under great strain in the 1850s.

The principal difference between northern Democrats and Republicans in the 1850s lay in their understanding of the slavery controversy itself. While Republicans believed that slavery was the root cause of the sectional controversy, on the grounds that it disorganised a community politically, economically and, many added, morally too, the Democrats instead found the source in antislavery. However much they might for the North prefer free labour to slavery, they simply did not accept that slavery in the South must pose a threat either to their own section, to the West, or to the nation as a whole. Some southern extremists might earn their censure but they saw no inevitable conflict between free labour or freedom, in the North or West, and slavery in the South. Hence they tended to see northern antislavery groups as the aggressors and easily found reason to acquit militant southerners of ultimate responsibility even when disapproving of their specific actions. For this dramatic departure from neutrality they would pay, as the 1850s wore on, a heavy electoral price.

### The Kansas-Nebraska Act (2): Popular sovereignty

#### I

The passage of the Kansas-Nebraska Act can only be fully comprehended with reference to the principles of the Democratic party, which had traditionally functioned, as they were about to function again, to serve the interests of the slaveholders. This has not been recognised sufficiently by historians, who have understood that northern Democrats had a straightforward political motive for pleasing or conciliating their southern allies but who have been much slower to find ideological links between popular sovereignty and traditional party themes.[148] Nor was it recognised by Democrats like Stephen A. Douglas. But historians have also failed to grasp what Douglas himself did not miss: the status quo after the Compromise of 1850 was itself highly unsatisfactory and could not endure. For while the Compromise measures were hailed by their supporters as a final solution of the slavery question, with the status of all existing territories now defined, they actually left the nation in a highly anomalous

---

148. These ideological and electoral pressures were in no sense opposed. They reinforced one another.

condition. As a result of the admission of California into the Union there were, on the one hand, states in the East and what would now be regarded as the Midwest and, on the other hand, there was one state on the Pacific (with others anticipated). But between the two lay a huge tract of territory, ruled free by the Missouri Compromise, but as yet both unorganised and, without southern acquiescence, unorganisable. If Douglas and his fellow Democrats had believed the territory to be truly unorganisable, they would have had to conclude that the nation was in crisis.[149] After all the ability to establish and maintain the rule of law over national territory is a crucial attribute of sovereignty. But Democratic pride and Democratic tradition ruled out such a conclusion. It was simply unthinkable that the nation had reached an impasse, and inconceivable that Democratic principles would be found wanting.

Douglas, whose prime concern was the development of the West, was convinced of the need to organise this territory. Indeed he had been seeking to organise Nebraska since 1844, even before the Mexican cession. After 1850 he redoubled his efforts and was able to show that it would be absurd to allow present conditions to persist. In 1852 he claimed that it would be "utterly impossible to preserve this Union," – by which he meant retain the loyalty of the Pacific states – "if you are to keep a wilderness of two thousand miles between you."[150]

Here was a primary reason for the organisation of the Nebraska territory. In 1853 Douglas tried once again and once again failed. His object, he declared, was "to form a line of territorial governments extending from the Mississippi Valley to the Pacific ocean, so that we can have continuous settlements from the one to the other." Yet again he reminded the Senate that "we cannot expect, or hope even, to maintain our Pacific possessions unless they can be connected in feeling and interest and communication with the Atlantic States." For "that can only be done by continuous lines of settlements, and those settlements can only be formed where the laws will furnish protection to those who settle upon and cultivate the soil." The bill failed, however, partly because there was insufficient congressional time available but more fundamentally because southerners, mindful of the restriction on slavery imposed by the Missouri Compromise in this territory, had little reason to facilitate the creation of more free states.[151]

For Douglas, however, the slavery question was, at this time as always, of relatively minor importance. Like many Americans his imagination was seized by the prospect of a transcontinental railroad, a project that

149. Other groups, like the Whigs, escaped this conclusion because they had traditionally not desired territorial expansion and had little desire to organize new territories in the West.
150. *CG*, 32/1, p. 1760.
151. *CG*, 32/2, p. 1116.

appealed to northerners and southerners alike, whatever their views of slavery. Although some historians have claimed that this was a hidden motive in the introduction of the Kansas-Nebraska Act,[152] it in fact reflected Democrats' clearly stated concerns and was one of Douglas' openly avowed aims. "I do not think," he told the Senate in 1853, "that there is any question that can come before us more worthy to occupy attention than that of a railroad to the Pacific." For Douglas this goal, of paramount importance to the West, transcended the slavery question; it was one for which he would continue to agitate even after Kansas and Nebraska had been organised.[153]

In 1854, therefore, Douglas tried again. Although his enemies claimed that no action was in fact necessary and that Nebraska did not need to be organised, he retorted by asking whether they supposed that "you could keep that vast country a howling wilderness in all time to come, roamed over by hostile savages, cutting off all safe communication between our Atlantic and Pacific possessions?" "You must," he reiterated, "provide for continuous lines of settlement from the Mississippi Valley to the Pacific Ocean." So the territory had to be organised.[154]

In effect Douglas now employed a syllogism. "In making this provision," he noted, "you must decide upon what principles the Territories shall be organized." There were only two: either the principle of 1820, which allowed Congress to make the crucial decision about slavery, or that of 1850, popular sovereignty, which instead authorised the people of the territory to make it. But even though it ran afoul of the Missouri

---

152. David Potter, *The Impending Crisis, 1848–1861* (New York, 1976), pp. 145–176; Roy F. Nichols, "The Kansas-Nebraska Act: A Century of Historiography," *Mississippi Valley Historical Review*, LXIII (1956), pp. 187–212.

153. *CG*, 32/2, p. 507. All three candidates in the presidential election of 1856, for example, were committed to a Pacific railroad. Douglas's enthusiasm for the scheme persisted, quite independently of any legislation to do with Kansas. See *CG*, 35/1, p. 1645. In 1853 Douglas wrote a letter in which he again explained the importance of the Nebraska territory and which exemplified his hopes and ambitions for the West: "to the States of Missouri and Iowa, the organization of the Territory of Nebraska is an important and desirable local measure; to the interests of the Republic it is a national necessity. How are we to develop, cherish and protect our immense interests and possessions on the Pacific, with a vast wilderness 1500 miles in breadth, filled with hostile savages, and cutting off all direct communication? The Indian barrier must be removed. The tide of immigration and civilization must be permitted to roll onward until it rushes through the passes of the mountains, and spreads over the plains, and mingles with the waters of the Pacific. Continuous lines of settlement with civil, political and religious institutions all under the protection of law, are imperiously demanded by the highest national considerations. These are essential, but they are not sufficient. No man can keep up with spirit of this age who travels on anything slower than the locomotive, and fails to receive intelligence by lightning. We must therefore have railroads and Telegraphs from the Atlantic to the Pacific." – see Douglas to J. H. Crane etc., in *Letters of Douglas*, p. 270

154. *CG*, 33/1, p. 337.

Compromise, only the second could command the necessary southern support. Hence it followed that if Nebraska were to be organised, the Missouri Compromise would have to be somehow evaded or negated. Any other course of action would leave the nation in crisis, unable to govern a huge swathe of its own territory. Any other course of action would mean an acknowledgement of the bankruptcy of Democratic principles.

As soon as they realised that the Missouri compromise was to be either ignored (the early Nebraska bill) or "superseded" (the later versions), Douglas's enemies were able to embarrass him by fastening upon some statements he had previously made. As recently as October 1849 he had described the Missouri Compromise as "a sacred thing which no ruthless hand would ever be reckless enough to disturb." Its main achievement, he had then declared, was that it had "allayed all sectional jealousies and irritations." The previous year, indeed, he had urged its extension to the Pacific. Here, it seemed, was irrefutable evidence that Douglas lacked principle and consistency.[155]

Moreover, his enemies drew attention to, and ridiculed, his claim that the nonintervention policy of 1850 had itself been intended to apply to all territories subsequently to be organised rather than merely to those under discussion that year. Here they were also, it seemed, on firm ground, since the opponents of the policy in 1850 would certainly have made much of any apprehended impact on the Missouri Compromise. But neither northerners nor southerners, whether supporters or enemies of the Compromise, had discussed its application to the Missouri Compromise, almost certainly because, in the vast majority of cases, they believed it had none.[156]

Nevertheless, Douglas was by no means vanquished by these arguments. In 1850 he and others had insisted that it was wrong to divide the nation's territory up between North and South and, in so doing, had asserted the superiority, *as a general principle*, of congressional nonintervention or popular sovereignty. He was also able to show that both he and the Illinois state legislature had declared that popular sovereignty was to be the policy when dealing with all future territories (though whether this included the already acquired but still unorganised lands of the Louisiana Purchase was certainly questionable).[157] Undoubtedly

---

155. *Illinois State Register*, Nov. 8, 1849
156. This claim, made in the bill itself, was also made by other northern Democrats. See, for example, Detroit *Free Press*, Jan. 27, 1854.
157. CG, 31/1, App., 369, 33/1, App., p. 327. In other words it was unclear whether future territories denoted territories to be acquired in the future or existing territories to be organized in the future. The Illinois resolutions are to be found in *Illinois State Register*, Feb. 11, 1854.

Douglas like other Democrats in 1850 had not suggested, and had probably not believed, that his efforts on behalf of popular sovereignty for New Mexico and Utah had any implications for the Missouri Compromise, not least because the crisis of that year had fully absorbed their attention. Yet it was not entirely inappropriate to believe that a possible precedent had been set.[158]

II

For a Democrat, indeed, there were many reasons to prefer popular sovereignty for the territories to congressional involvement, some of which had no direct connection with the slavery question. Indeed congressional involvement had only two advantages. One was its obvious value to the North as a means of bringing the power of the numerical majority to bear upon slavery. But this advantage was also a disadvantage since the same logic would impel southerners to resist the exercise of that power. Thus the policy might be expected to generate controversy rather than the harmony it was designed to create, with the settlement and development of the West the principal casualty. The other advantage was simply its long pedigree, stretching back to the Missouri Compromise, and even to the Northwest Ordinance of 1787. Yet if it could not harmoniously resolve the territorial question, then just how valuable was this pedigree? It is not clear when Douglas reached the conclusion that the Missouri Compromise had to be repealed or set aside but without doubt he had many valid reasons for entertaining the scheme.

In fact popular sovereignty was square in the logic of Democratic thinking. Undoubtedly the main argument adduced in its favour was that it empowered the people most directly concerned. Throughout the 1850s and until the secession crisis, Douglas and other Democrats sought to show that to allow the people of the territory to decide whether they would or would not have slavery was simply to extend democratic rights to them. "My idea," Douglas declared in 1860, "is that a people, if they are capable of self-government, should be permitted to decide for themselves what laws are good and what laws are bad." It followed that "you have no more right to force a good thing on an unwilling people then you have to force a bad thing on them." The underlying principle was that the people "are the best judges of what institutions will suit them and what

---

158.  President Pierce similarly claimed, though again after the event, that the Kansas-Nebraska Act "was the natural and legitimate, if not the inevitable, consequence of previous events and legislation that the same great and sound principle which had already been applied to Utah and New Mexico, should be applied to them – that they should stand exempt from the restrictions proposed in the act relating to the state of Missouri." This was a standard Democratic claim by the mid-1850s – see Richardson (ed.), *Messages and Papers of Presidents*, V, p. 348.

will not" and the corollary was that "slavery will exist wherever the people want it, and will not exist anywhere else." Thus the people were better judges of what was appropriate for their community than Congressmen. A decade earlier, when defending popular sovereignty for Utah and New Mexico, Douglas had made this point explicitly. To an audience in his home city of Chicago he explained, with mild but unmistakable irony, that the inhabitants of a territory, "after their arrival in a country, when they had become familiar with its topography, climate, productions, and resources, and had connected their destiny with it," were then "fully as competent to judge for themselves what kind of laws and institutions were best adapted to their condition and interests, as we were who never saw the country, and knew very little about it." Indeed Douglas noted that "to question their competency to do this, was to deny their capacity for self-government."[159]

Other Democrats emphasised, time and again, that popular sovereignty was synonymous with faith in the people, that it allowed the inhabitants of a territory to determine their own destiny and that it accorded with the fundamental American democratic principle that each community should govern itself.[160] These arguments proved difficult to rebut in a society where the rights of racial minorities were at a discount[161] and hence were advanced very frequently before, at the time of, and after the passage of, the Kansas-Nebraska Act. As early as 1850 David Disney of Ohio asserted that "under our Government, the right of each community to make its own laws, is of the very essence of our institutions." He then concluded that it was absurd to contemplate any policy for the territories other than popular sovereignty:

> We assert that all just power is derived from the consent of the governed; that the people have the right to abolish their government; that all men are born free and equal; that there are certain natural and inalienable rights; and yet declare that the people in our territory, composed, too, as they may be, principally of our own native born citizens, have no rights whatever, but such as the benevolence of Congress may confer.[162]

159. Barbee and Bonham, "Montgomery Address of Douglas," p. 543; *Speech of.... Douglas on "Measures of Adjustment,"* p. 6.
160. *Speeches etc. of Dickinson,* I, pp. 241, 351; *Speeches...of Seymour,* pp. 16–17; *Speech of Olds,* p. 17; CG, 33/1, App., pp. 249, 514, 608; Detroit *Free Press,* Jan. 15, 27, 1854.
161. Douglas himself complained that the enemies of the Kansas-Nebraska Act invariably referred to the Missouri Compromise rather than challenging the principle of popular sovereignty itself – see CG, 33/1, App., p. 28.
162. CG, 31/1, App., p. 302. Clearly Disney's argument meant that a repeal of the Missouri Compromise, even if not yet intended, implied or even sought, would effect a major

Democrats also demanded to know why, when moving from a state to a territory, the emigrant should have his rights curtailed: why should a man be unable to wield the influence in a territory that he had previously exerted in a state? Indeed many went so far as to argue that, by denying the inhabitants of a territory the right to pronounce upon such an important question as slavery, the federal government was perpetrating the injustices of which the British had been guilty in the eighteenth century and which had provoked the Revolution.[163]

This concern for popular government, however exaggerated some of its expressions may now appear, was undoubtedly deeply felt.[164] Two years after the passage of the Kansas-Nebraska Act, when Kansas was itself in crisis, opponents of the act claimed that their fears had been justified and their objections sustained. Senator Charles Stuart of Michigan, however, retorted that to proclaim the Act a failure was to denounce American democracy itself:

> What, sir, the idea which lies at the very basis of American freedom throughout all the States a failure! – the right, and authority, and the ability of a people to legislate for themselves – that is the Kansas-Nebraska act; and that is all of it – that a failure! That principle an experiment that was born, so far as this country is concerned, with the Revolution, which is so resplendent this day as to command the admiration of the civilized world!"

Stuart insisted that the blame lay not with the policy but instead with the irresponsible agitators (on both sides) who had flocked into Kansas intent upon mischief.[165]

There can be little doubt that these ideas were sincerely held. In the Jacksonian era the Democrats had held views of sovereignty and of democracy itself that had been sharply at odds with those espoused by the Whigs. The Democrats had been far more enthusiastic about a democratic government (for adult white males) than their opponents. Moreover, as episodes like the Dorr war in Rhode Island had in the early 1840s revealed, the Democrats had traditionally held a far more populistic view

improvement in the nation's policy for the territories. For other statements at this time, see *CG*, 31/1, App., pp. 514, 841.

163. *CG*, 31/1, App., pp. 560, 675, 841, 33/1, App., pp. 249, 514, 607–608, 1132; Douglas, *Speech on "Measures of Adjustment,"* p. 6; Detroit *Free Press*, Feb. 10, 1854; *Democrats Against Black Republicanism* (Washington, DC, 1856), p. 4. The anonymous author of this pamphlet also argued that it was unfair to withhold rights from the territories of Kansas and Nebraska that had been given to New Mexico and Utah – see p. 4.

164. This point is made very effectively in Michael A. Morrison, *Slavery and the American West: The Eclipse of Manifest Destiny and the Coming of the Civil War* (Chapel Hill, 1997), pp. 122–146.

165. *CG*, 34/1, App., p. 859.

of sovereignty. At that time the reform party, backed by all Democrats apart from the Calhounites, in Rhode Island had dramatically invoked the original rights of the people to rule and set aside the existing constitution entirely on the grounds that it violated those inherent rights. The Whigs, however, had denounced the Rhode Island reformers as revolutionaries. Democrats in effect assumed that liberty "springs spontaneous in the human breast" and that laws were not, as most Whigs charged, to curb or restrain the power of the people so much as to give it expression. In the 1850s they engaged in fewer discussions of what might be called political theory, partly because the gap between southern and northern Democrats on these matters was widening. But in the early 1850s, the doctrine of popular sovereignty, though never advanced in the Jacksonian era, clearly owed much to the legacy of previous decades.[166]

Thus one Boston newspaper declared that "popular sovereignty in this country is *original* – not *derivative*." It did not "come of Congress or of state legislatures," but rather was "*inherent in the people*." The editor then asserted that "the right of each distinct political community to govern itself" was "an American right." It followed that "a territory derives its rights from the same source that a State derives its rights, from the sovereignty of the people – and not the one solely from the act of organization, and the other from the act of admission into the Union." This argument, which might have been employed a decade earlier with reference to the Dorr controversy, allowed the editor to reach an important conclusion. If, as some claimed, Congress had power over slavery in the territories, it should immediately delegate it. If not then "it belongs, upon every principle of our republican theory of government, to the people of the territories, for all power is inherent in the people." In either case, the right of the territory to self-government was beyond dispute. Similarly Stephen A. Douglas as early as 1850 as we have seen had advanced an argument that was designed to show that the Missouri Compromise had in fact had little impact on the northwest. Douglas argued that "in free countries laws and ordinances are mere nullities, unless sustained by the hearts and intellects of the people for whom they are made." Even though its application to the territories was new, this was classic Democratic doctrine.[167]

Just as popular sovereignty reflected Democratic enthusiasm for democracy itself, so it derived considerable authority from the theory of state's rights to which, as we have seen, Democrats were also deeply devoted. To stress the rights of the states was, of course, to seek to diminish or restrain the powers of the federal government, and this was in fact the

---

166. On the Dorr war see Ashworth, *"Agrarians" and "Aristocrats,"* pp. 225–231.
167. The Boston *North*, Feb. 5, 1859; CG, 31/1, App., p. 370.

*raison d'être* of the Kansas-Nebraska Act. Indeed popular sovereignty, as most northern Democrats understood it, was intended to clothe the territories with many of the powers of states.[168] According to Franklin Pierce, the repeal of the Missouri Compromise "was the final consummation and complete recognition of the principle that no portion of the United States shall undertake through assumption of the powers of the General Government to dictate the social institutions of any other portion." This, of course, was one of the standard rationales for state's rights. Other Democrats noted that, since Congress' power over a territory abruptly ceased when it joined the Union, any legislation on slavery could, at that point, be overturned. By contrast, if the territory exercised the power, its decision could be expected to continue after statehood. "How perfectly" therefore, exclaimed the Detroit *Free Press*, did the stipulations of the Kansas-Nebraska Act "assimilate with the principles of State rights." Popular sovereignty and state's rights had, it seemed, a natural affinity.[169]

Similarly Democratic racism informed the defence of popular sovereignty. Douglas castigated his antislavery enemies for believing "that it requires a higher degree of civilization and refinement to legislate for the negro race than can reasonably be expected the people of a territory to possess." Instead he insisted that if the people "have the requisite intelligence and honesty to be entrusted with the enactment of laws for the government of white men," then he knew "of no reason why they should not be deemed competent to legislate for the Negro." Was it, one Indiana Democrat asked rhetorically, that "the rights of the black man" were "too sacred?"[170]

In fact most of the tenets of the Democratic creed were quite compatible with, if they did not actually enjoin, the shift from congressional intervention to popular sovereignty. When their enemies complained that the repeal of the Missouri Compromise marked a breach of faith, Democrats were ready with the classic Jacksonian rejoinder that no statute was, or should be, irrepealable. Here their views were reminiscent of those expressed in the 1830s and 1840s when the party had mounted a more concerted and wide-ranging challenge to the force of precedent. Whereas Whigs had sought to use precedent as a means of access to the accumulated political wisdom of the ages, Democrats had instead adopted the

---

168. It may be worth noting that the Act conferred on the territories concerned somewhat wider powers of self-government than territories normally enjoyed, and made them rather more like states so far as, for example, the Governor's veto was concerned – see New Hampshire *Patriot*, May 31, 1854.

169. Richardson (ed.), *Messages and Papers of Presidents*, V, p. 348; Detroit *Free Press*, Jan. 13, 1854. See also *Speeches etc. of Dickinson*, I, p. 520; Detroit *Free Press*, Jan. 27, Feb. 10, 1854.

170. *Letter of Douglas to the State Capital Reporter*, p. 3; *Speech on "Measures of Adjustment,"* pp. 6–7; CG, 33/1, App., p. 212.

Jeffersonian dictum that "the earth belongs to the living." In 1856 the *National Democratic Review* complained that "*precedent* has been the apology for the most outrageous and intolerable governmental oppression of modern times," a view which might have been expressed twenty years earlier and without reference to the slavery question. Indeed the editor asserted that he had "ever contended ... that one Congress has no power to bind a future Congress" and then, with a telling analogy, announced that the Missouri Compromise could be no more sacred than the bill for the recharter of the Bank of the United States had once been. In each case precedent had been set aside. The way was clear for the triumph of popular sovereignty.[171]

### III

By the mid-1850s the northern Democrats had a distinctive reading of the American past and their own understanding of the history of the slavery controversy. It is possible to recreate the past as seen by devotees of popular sovereignty. Before 1820, it was held, Congress had rarely tried to interfere with slavery either in the States or territories and as a result "there was peace between the North and the South, and harmony between the free and slave States." But in 1820 "the first time that it attempted to touch the question anywhere with the view of controlling it a sectional strife arose which came very near dissolving this glorious Union." The cause was the attempt by the discredited Federalists to introduce the slavery question into federal politics, a potentially catastrophic strategy as Thomas Jefferson had himself pointed out at the time. Thus the all-seeing Sage of Monticello had been opposed to the Missouri agitation and to congressional intervention and had foreseen that it would be a bone of contention in the decades to come.[172]

So it proved to be. In 1848 northerners refused to vote to extend the Missouri compromise line to the Pacific, thereby demonstrating that the policy of congressional intervention could not resolve the controversy over slavery. (Southerners at this time, in supporting the proposal, showed themselves willing to set aside the doubts they harbored about its constitutionality.)[173] As a result the policy of nonintervention or popular

171. Ashworth, "*Agrarians*" *and* "*Aristocrats*," pp. 59–60; *National Democratic Review*, I (April 1856), p. 349. See also Richardson (ed.), *Messages and Papers of Presidents*, V, p. 402; Major Wilson, *Space, Time, and Freedom: The Quest for Freedom and the Irrepressible Conflict* (Westport, CT, 1974).
172. Barbee and Bonham, "Montgomery Address of Douglas," pp. 532–533; *Address and Correspondence of the Democratic State Convention of Pennsylvania* (Philadelphia, n.d.), p. 9; Closkey, *Democratic Hand-Book*, p. 5.
173. Closkey, *Democratic Hand-Book*, p. 8; Barbee and Bonham, "Montgomery Address of Douglas," p. 534. It is worth noting Douglas's belief that "if the Missouri line had

sovereignty was taken up and in 1850 was applied to the territories of New Mexico and Utah. This policy, together with the other Compromise measures of that year, was extraordinarily successful. It was endorsed by every single state in the Union and public opinion forced extremists in both North and South to acquiesce in the measures of that year. Indeed after the Compromise those agitators whose stock-in-trade was the slavery question were compelled to recognise that the approach taken in 1850, which for the territories meant popular sovereignty, had been entirely successful. By 1851, New Mexico and Utah were being settled quietly and peacefully and, much to the chagrin of the abolitionists and Free Soilers, who wanted the sectional agitation to continue, proceedings in Congress had been "dull and quiet." So, applied in 1850 in the Compromise measures, resoundingly confirmed thereafter by all the states and emphatically proclaimed in the election of 1852 by both the major parties, popular sovereignty had by 1854 become the tried and tested policy for the territories. Hence the introduction of the Kansas-Nebraska Act in 1854.[174]

As far as Democrats were concerned, popular sovereignty was in one sense novel but in another not. Perhaps mindful of the affinity between popular sovereignty and the traditional Democratic views of sovereignty itself, of race and of state's rights, they insisted that it was scarcely a new doctrine at all. Thus John Appleton of Maine told Congress in 1852 that it was not a creed but "only the fruit of certain old and established Democratic principles, applied to a serious exigency in affairs," while William English of Indiana, when the Kansas-Nebraska bill was under consideration, declared that "the principle of non-intervention, on the part of Congress, with the domestic concerns of the States and organized Territories, is no interpolation upon the Democratic creed." Rather "in one shape or other," it was "as old as the creed itself."[175]

As a result it was easy for Democrats to place the controversy over the Act within the ideological framework which they employed to make intelligible almost all political controversy. Was it not true that there were, and always had been, two parties in the nation, one contending for the power of the federal government, and the other striving to maintain the rights of

been adhered to, and extended to the Pacific Ocean, there would have been an end to the controversy forever, so far as the territories were concerned." – see p. 535.

174. Barbee and Bonham, "Montgomery Address of Douglas," pp. 537–538; Closkey, *Democratic Hand-Book*, p. 10; Detroit *Free Press*, Jan. 6, Feb. 2, 1854; *Illinois State Register*, Jan. 31, 1854; *New Hampshire Patriot*, February 1, 1854. Stephen A. Douglas to Thomas Settle, Jan. 16, 1851, in *Letters of Douglas*, p. 207. Douglas said northern antislavery enemies of the Compromise all agreed that prior to the Kansas-Nebraska Act there was complete calm in the nation – see CG, 33/1, App., p. 326.
175. CG, 32/1, App., pp. 317, 33/ 1, App., p. 609.

the states and the liberties of the people? "That," English announced in a speech on the Kansas-Nebraska Act, "was the leading division between the Federal and Republican parties, is to some extent an issue between the parties of the present day, and is certainly involved in the bill now under consideration." Similarly the Detroit *Free Press*, discussing the Kansas-Nebraska Act observed that "the democrats say that the people shall legislate for themselves in the Territories – the whigs say that Congress shall usurp such legislation." Thus "the battle" was "between popular constitutional rights on the one hand, and the encroachments of the central power on the other." The issue was therefore, the editor explained, "not new:"

> In all the contests between the two parties since the organization of the government the same material principle has been at stake. Jefferson was in favor of a liberal government – Adams desired a strong government. Jackson attacked the great monster which federalism had built up – his opponents sought to renew the life of the monster – Cass evolved the doctrine of universal sovereign rights – the whigs and abolitionists of to-day, true to their natural instincts, are hostile to the establishment of those rights. The parallel started at the formation of the constitution – it will continue as long as the Union stands

Popular sovereignty was therefore merely the latest in a long line of Democratic initiatives that aimed to curtail centralised power.[176]

As such its ultimate success was assured. Douglas himself knew that the repeal of the Missouri Compromise would be highly controversial but, as he informed Georgia Democrat Howell Cobb, he was confident that tranquility would soon be restored:

> [The Kansas-Nebraska Act] will triumph & impart peace to the country & stability to the Union. I am not deterred or affected by the violence & insults of the northern Whigs & abolitionists. The storm will soon spend its fury, and the people of the North will sustain it when they come to understand it. In the meantime our southern friends have only to stand firm & leave us of the North to fight the great battle. We will fight it boldly & will surely triumph in the end. The great principle of self government is at stake & surely the people of this country are never going to decide that the principle upon which our republican system rests is vicious & wrong.

Since the Act was in essence merely a straightforward reapplication of democratic principles and procedures to newly organised territories,

---

176. *CG*, 33/1App., p. 609; Detroit *Free Press*, Feb. 18, 1854

history suggested that it would ultimately be crowned with complete success.[177]

At this point it is important to remind ourselves of the Democratic view of the Democratic party itself and its history. Democratic innovations had frequently met with great opposition but had ultimately been triumphantly vindicated and become the established policy of the nation. Daniel Dickinson in 1856, after two years of intense controversy over the affairs of Kansas, easily fitted the struggle into this pattern. Referring to the Kansas-Nebraska Act, he began with the standard Democratic claim that "every great and beneficent measure which has been instituted in the halls of the government has been of Democratic origin" and that "every considerable abuse which has been checked, every considerable reform which has been practiced have been the fruits of Democratic administrations." And yet," he continued, "every leading democratic measure in its progress has been resisted with the same systematic virulence, every proposed reformation has been characterized as mad and revolutionary," and "every attempt to check abuses has been denounced with as much noisy zeal and ill-tempered vehemence as signalize the denunciation of the present day and present hour." But, he continued, history demonstrated that these controversies were short-lived. For "not a single leading democratic measure, from first to last, has failed to meet the approbation of the people; and if our opponents had the power, there is not one of them which they would venture to disturb." Thus although a storm of protest might be expected, the record seemed to indicate that it would be short-lived and that the opposition would ultimately embrace the proposed changes, precisely as those opposed to popular sovereignty in the Compromise of 1850 had come to accept it. In this connection, Democrats also cited the struggle over the United States Bank. Just as there had been a great body of opinion in favour of the Bank and specifically affirming its constitutionality, so a similar weight of opinion favoured the Missouri Compromise. But just as, after a period of intense controversy and strife, all had come to accept, or at least acquiesce in, the destruction of the Bank, so, it was held, the policy of popular sovereignty would ultimately generate a similar consensus.[178]

## IV

If popular sovereignty had its affinities with Democratic political theory and the views held by Democrats on race, it was also a direct product of their attitude towards slavery itself. As we have seen, Democrats argued

177. Douglas to Howell Cobb, April 2, 1854 in *Letters of Douglas*, p. 299.
178. *Speeches etc. of Dickinson*, I, p. 511.

that soil and climate would determine whether slavery would exist in a territory (or a state). As we have also seen, Douglas himself, in denying that the Missouri Compromise had had any effect upon slavery in the northwest, had argued that all laws should reflect public opinion. The prohibition of slavery in Illinois, for example, had accordingly resulted from the popular preference for free labour there. And this in turn had been determined by soil and climate. Hence "the Missouri compromise," he informed the Senate, "had no practical bearing on the question of slavery – it neither curtailed nor extended it one inch. It did the South no harm and the North no good."[179] It followed that its repeal under, or supersession by, the Kansas-Nebraska Act would not result in the introduction of slavery into Kansas or Nebraska. Douglas himself made this assertion and many other Democrats echoed it.[180]

Some contended (very plausibly) that there were far superior opportunities for slaveholders in Florida or the southwestern states, where rice, cotton or sugar could be grown and William English of Indiana calculated that since far more northerners than southerners would emigrate to Kansas, and since immigrants from Europe would also go there, not one in ten of the territory's inhabitants would vote for slavery. Indeed with remarkable prescience English announced that he could "see nothing which slaveholders are to gain under this bill – nothing but an unequal and vexatious contest, in which they are to be the losers."[181]

English added that if the people of Kansas did in fact adopt slavery, then it would be their responsibility and not his. It was in this connection that Douglas later made his famous utterance to the effect that he did not care whether slavery was voted up or down in Kansas.[182] As far as that territory was concerned he had perhaps then reached the conclusion, after the attempt had been made to establish slavery there, that it lay in an intermediate zone between regions where slavery was impossible to establish and areas where it would inevitably take root. Thus in 1859 he explained that there was a line, a natural geographical line based upon

179. *CG*, 31/1, App., p. 369.
180. Thus Senators and Representatives like John Weller of California, John Pettit of Indiana, Lewis Cass of Michigan, and James C. Allen of Illinois, all declared that Kansas was unsuited to slavery – see *CG*, 33/1 App., pp. 200, 212, 270, 255. For Douglas's view, see p. 371; Douglas, *Letter of Douglas to the State Capital Reporter*, pp. 6–7; *Debates between Lincoln and Douglas*, p. 34. For other such statements, see Detroit *Free Press*, Jan. 15, 27, 1854; *Illinois State Register*, Jan. 31, 1854; *Speeches etc. of Dickinson*, I , p. 494.
181. *CG*, 33/1, App., pp. 247–248, 607, 610.
182. *CG*, 35/1, App., p. 559. This was an accurate but misleading statement. Douglas meant that he would take no action to prevent slavery from being established in Kansas, nor criticise her citizens for introducing it. It did not mean that he would not prefer to see Kansas, like his native Illinois, become a free state. In other words, it was in his capacity as a national political leader that he did not care.

soil and climate, which marked out the areas where slavery would, would not, or might exist. It was in areas close to that line, where its viability was uncertain, that popular sovereignty would be most needed and where it was especially appropriate:

> When you arrive at a certain distance to the North of the line there can not be any doubt of the result: and so when you go a certain distance South the result will be equally certain that the other way. But in the great central regions, where there may be some doubt as to the effect of natural causes, who ought to decide the question except the people residing there, who have all their interests there; who have gone there to live with their wives and children.

This left open the possibility that slavery would be established in some of these areas, although Douglas almost certainly believed that Kansas was not one of them.[183]

Thus Democrats were willing to acknowledge that slavery might spread to some territories (particularly any which might in future be acquired in the Caribbean) and even to promise that they would not intervene in Kansas or condemn her voters if slavery were properly established there. Such observations implicitly reaffirmed the priorities of northern Democrats. For the introduction or exclusion of slavery from the territories was less important than the establishment of the principle of popular sovereignty. The actual planting of slavery was less to be feared than the agitation of the slavery question. The Detroit *Free Press*, having predicted that slavery would not enter the new territories, declared that this was nevertheless "not the question," for it must be "left to the people, whom we must learn to trust." Indeed, as the editor observed a little later, "in settling the fundamental principle . . . it is of infinitesimal consequence whether or not a few miserable negroes shall go into Nebraska." The principle of popular sovereignty, acceptable to the South, would allow the nation to settle and develop the great West. Hence Douglas's measure offered, it seemed, the irresistible combination of westward expansion and sectional harmony.[184]

The problem, however, was the unscrupulous agitator, and especially the northern antislavery agitator. Although Douglas's enemies accused him of agitating the slavery issue by repealing the Missouri Compromise, his intention was precisely the opposite. The Kansas-Nebraska Act was specifically designed to remove the potential for slavery agitation by withdrawing the subject from Congress. According to the wording of the Act, its purpose was "in all time to come," to "avoid the evils of . . . agitation,

---

183. *Speeches of Douglas at New Orleans, Philadelphia and Baltimore*, p. 8.
184. *CG*, 33/1, App., p. 610; Detroit *Free Press*, Jan. 27, 1854; *Illinois State Register*, Jan. 31, 1854.

by withdrawing the question of slavery from the halls of Congress and the political arena, and committing it to the arbitrament of those who were immediately interested in and alone are responsible for its consequences." Although the results were entirely at odds with this goal, there was an internal logic in Douglas's thinking. As we have seen, he and other northern Democrats did not believe that there was any inherent reason for North and South to quarrel about slavery. As we have also seen, they believed that the main protagonists in this conflict represented the nation's geographical extremities, the Upper North and the Deep South. But these groups had little contact with one another, except in Congress. Hence it followed that, as Douglas repeated in his closing speech on the bill, it would "have the effect to destroy all sectional parties and sectional agitations." With congressional interference at an end, there would be "nothing left out of which sectional parties can be organized."[185]

Even though the Act almost immediately stirred up an extraordinary degree of conflict and controversy, Democrats ironically attributed this to its potential to end conflict. In so doing they postulated a conspiracy on the part of abolitionists who, they claimed, were using the slavery controversy to destroy the Democratic party and even to break up the Union (precisely as the Federalists had done a generation earlier). The Act was fatal to the personal ambitions of the abolitionists and thus must be resisted. Hence the sudden discovery – by men who believed the constitution itself should be subordinated to a "higher law" – that the Missouri Compromise, whose extension they had resolutely voted against, was sacred and irrepealable.[186]

Historians have not generally found these charges at all credible and there is no doubt that they represented a serious misunderstanding of the motives of antislavery leaders. But this is not to say that the allegations were insincere.[187] Certainly they were made many times. Indeed one Democratic editor after another explained the process. Thus the Detroit *Free Press*:

> We do not wonder that Mr. Douglas' Nebraska bill encounters the fierce and imbittered [sic] opposition of the abolitionists and northern whigs in Congress. Its passage will be the death-knell of their future hopes. They well know that by no means, save a continuation of

185.  CG, 33/1, App., p. 337. For other statements to the effect that the removal of congressional power over the territories would end conflict see *Speeches etc. of Dickinson*, I, pp. 228, 554–555; Cincinnati *Daily Enquirer*, May 24, 1854; CG, 33/ 1, App., p. 514; Detroit *Free Press*, Feb. 2, 1854.
186.  Richardson (ed.), *Messages and Papers of Presidents*, V, p. 403.
187.  The charges were no more unfounded than the allegation, made by Republicans (including Lincoln), that Democrats like Douglas were conspiring to spread slavery even into the North.

slavery agitation, can they divide and conquer the democratic party. They know that, united, it is impregnable. For these reasons, as well as to establish for all time a great and correct principle of government, should Mr. Douglas' bill have the willing and cordial concurrence of democrats every where. For these reasons should it become a law. Once passed – its principles once finally adopted as the settled policy of the country – and the Spirit of agitation may hang its harp upon the willow. – Peace and concord, union and harmony, will be its consequences. Then, indeed, will there be no north, no south, but one common country.

Similarly the Washington *Union*, noting that the opposition had "come forward so promptly to denounce the measure," claimed that this was "conclusive that his [Douglas's] proposition is regarded by abolitionists as a death-blow to their hope of making the slavery question available for future political excitement." As a result "the democracy now have it in their power to drive the last nail into the coffin of abolitionism." And the New Hampshire *Patriot* argued that, since Kansas and Nebraska were the only territories now unorganised, they offered "the last chance for these agitators." Hence they were forced to play "a desperate game." But passage of the Act would "give a death-blow to abolitionism." It would create sectional harmony and would thus provoke from antislavery agitators, in the words of the Cincinnati *Enquirer*, a "howl of rage over the result, which, to them, is so calamitous."[188]

## V

Yet however sincere these allegations might have been, and whatever grounds history might have been afforded for optimism at the time of the Kansas-Nebraska Act, Democratic hopes for sectional peace were soon to be shattered. The fact that they did not modify their analysis and continued to believe, despite apparently overwhelming evidence to the contrary, that popular sovereignty was a winning formula testifies to the strength of their convictions. But it also prompts the historian to ask how they could have been so fundamentally and so catastrophically mistaken.

To some extent Douglas and the northern Democrats were simply unfortunate in that parts of Kansas would prove attractive to a relatively small number of slaveholders. In other words Kansas would be in that zone where the ultimate victory of free labour would not be certain and both northerners and southerners could entertain hopes for the territory. Yet this cannot in itself explain the failure of Democratic policy. For one thing,

188. Detroit *Free Press*, Feb. 9, 1854; Washington, DC, *Union*, Jan. 15, 1854; New Hampshire *Patriot*, Feb. 1, 1854; Cincinnati *Daily Enquirer*, May 24, 1854.

when the Kansas-Nebraska Act was being debated, its enemies pointed this out again and again. Why did the Democrats not heed the warning? Moreover it was, according to Douglas, precisely in these areas, where the ultimate outcome was uncertain, that popular sovereignty was most needed. When there was no chance of slavery being established, or where its introduction was a certainty, then according to Douglas the laws of supply and demand would operate automatically and democratically arrived at decisions on the part of those in the territory would scarcely be required. Thus popular sovereignty failed in one of the very cases for which it was specifically designed and for which it was held to be quintessentially suitable.

The reasons for Democrats' blindness to the weaknesses of popular sovereignty are to be found in the relationship between Democratic ideology and slavery. As we have seen, that ideology bore the imprint of the slaveholding interest. Democratic insistence on devolved forms of government for whites only, together with Democratic indifference to the plight of African Americans, Democratic resistance to the intrusion of moral issues into politics and Democratic perceptions of antislavery as Federalism – all this worked to promote the interests of the slaveholders of the South. The effect was to diminish northern Democratic resistance and hostility to slavery.

Thus however much they might minimise the effects of the Kansas-Nebraska Act on slavery, there was no doubt that it did leave open the possibility of slavery spreading into areas from which it had previously been barred. Democrats like Douglas might reply that this was not the goal of the Act, that they were confident that it would not be the result either, and that even if it were the outcome then the responsibility would lie with the inhabitants of the territory in question. The cumulative effect of these rejoinders was enough to persuade a small but critical number of northerners to support the measure. So once again, and despite the heavy electoral price paid, the Democratic party had shown its functional but still partly unacknowledged support for slavery and the slaveholding interest.

As we have seen, Democrats utterly misunderstood the motives of those northerners who opposed popular sovereignty in general and the Kansas-Nebraska Act in particular. It was relatively easy to dismiss them as antidemocratic Federalists. Douglas argued that if the people of a territory were "sufficiently enlightened to make laws for the protection of life, liberty, and property – of morals and education – to determine the relations of husband and wife, of parent and child," then he was "not aware that it requires any higher degree of civilization to regulate the affairs of master and servant." Slavery was simply another issue. Similarly in a public letter to a group of Chicago clergymen he insisted that the effect of slavery entering a new territory would be on the other inhabitants of that territory and on them alone:

> his [the slave's] presence in the new Territory could not in any mode or degree affect or injure any human being in any other territory or State. If his presence should be offensive or injurious to anybody it would be to the people of the territory or state where he was located.... It is purely a question of domestic concern, which, for weal or for woe, affects the people of such Territory or State and nobody else.

The conclusion was that slavery was, to the nation as a whole, a relatively unimportant matter.[189]

Here was Douglas's cardinal error. He himself came out of a tradition where slavery was indeed relatively unimportant. As we have seen, for a Democrat the nation had a glorious past and its legitimation was in terms of popular government, the welcome it afforded to immigrants, the equal rights it offered to all, the successful wars it had waged, the territory it had annexed and the prosperity it had secured. Northern Democrats, like their southern allies, had their own economic outlook and economic policies.[190] When they debated these questions, they discussed banks and paper money, internal improvements and western lands, matters that had traditionally been of considerable importance both north and south of the Mason-Dixon Line. But by the 1850s northern Democrats lacked an analysis of the northern labour system. Whereas Republicans talked of social mobility, of the dignity of labour, of incentives as key features of a free labour system, Democrats had little to say on these matters. Their tolerance for slavery in the South was both cause and effect of their lack of understanding of, or even interest in, these subjects. Hence they missed a development in the North whose significance can scarcely be exaggerated. Northerners were coming to believe, in ever-increasing numbers, not merely that the values of free (and wage) labour were of great importance but that they were the defining values of the nation as a whole. In effect the legitimation of northern society was, for these northerners, increasingly in terms of free labour. If its values were those of the nation then the spread of slavery into new territories was a subject of the profoundest importance to every American, and not merely to those who lived in those territories.[191] Indeed, as we have seen, many northerners were coming to identify democracy itself with the values of

---

189. Douglas, *Speech on "Measures of Adjustment,"* p. 6; *Letters of Douglas*, p. 320.
190. See pp. 436–457.
191. Similarly, as Eric Foner points out, those who did not live, or intend to live, in the territories, were interested in the development of western markets as well as the lure of the West to potential competitors who would otherwise have remained in the East – see Foner, *Free Soil, Free Labor, Free Men*, p. 58.

free and of wage labour. The crisis which engulfed Kansas would be, in large part, a consequence of this identification, just as the events there operated to confirm it. Thus the northern enemies of popular sovereignty were not in reality unreconstructed Federalists in disguise; rather they were the representatives of an emergent northern social order, one which celebrated free labour in the North and which was profoundly hostile to slavery in the South. Far from being anti-democrats, they were the spokesmen for a newly emerging American democratic ethos, one which threatened to overwhelm the party of Franklin Pierce, James Buchanan and Stephen A. Douglas.

## Democrats and the economy

### I

On August 24, 1857 news hit New York City, the nation's financial capital, that an Ohio insurance company was about to collapse. The news triggered a sudden financial crisis. Stocks fell, banks failed, land and commodity prices collapsed. Although the event that precipitated the crisis was unexpected and concerned embezzlement by one of the company's cashiers, the crisis itself was not. Journalists both at home and in Europe had been warning for some time that a speculative bubble was forming. In August and September of 1857 the bubble burst.[192]

The Panic immediately reminded contemporaries of the comparable crisis that had struck just twenty years earlier. And just as that event had deepened the already existing hostility of many Democrats to the nation's banking institutions, so once again the banks were the object of severe criticism leveled by Democrats from the President downwards. In his first annual message to Congress, delivered in December 1857, James Buchanan argued that despite possessing "all the elements of material wealth in rich abundance," the nation was "in its monetary interests . . . at the present moment in a deplorable condition." The Panic, the President noted, had not only caused banks to suspend specie payments but had also resulted in unemployment on a large scale, as manufacturing enterprises were compelled either to close or to cut back their output. But whilst the pressures had been felt far beyond the financial community, it was, in Buchanan's view, there that they had originated. Moreover, if the crisis was attributable to financial weakness, the cause of that weakness in turn was, the President insisted, excessive issues of paper money. In words

192.  Allan Nevins, *The Emergence of Lincoln: Douglas, Buchanan and Party Chaos, 1857–1859* (New York, 1950), pp. 187–197; William Shade, *Banks or No Banks: The Money Issue in Western Politics 1832–1865* (Detroit, 1972), p. 201.

that Andrew Jackson or Thomas Hart Benton would have applauded, Buchanan declared that the banks bore full responsibility:

> It is apparent that our existing misfortunes have proceeded solely from our extravagant and vicious system of paper currency and bank credits, exciting the people to wild speculations and gambling in stocks. These revulsions must continue to recur at successive intervals so long as the amount of paper currency and bank loans and discounts of the country shall be left to the discretion of fourteen hundred irresponsible banking institutions, which from the very law of their nature will consult the interest of their stockholders rather than the public welfare.

This was classic Jacksonian doctrine.[193]

Buchanan then reviewed the financial history of the nation over the preceding forty years. Once again his conclusions would have warmed the heart of any Jacksonian Democrat, however radical:

> It has been a history of extravagant expansions in the business of the country, followed by ruinous contractions. At successive intervals the best and most enterprising men have been tempted to their ruin by excessive bank loans of mere paper credit, exciting them to extravagant importations of foreign goods, wild speculations, and ruinous and demoralizing stock gambling. When the crisis arrives, as arrive it must, the banks can extend no relief to the people. In a vain struggle to redeem their liabilities in specie they are compelled to contract their loans and their issues, and at last, in the hour of distress, when their assistance is most needed, they and their debtors together sink into insolvency.

What then was the solution? Again Buchanan showed his Democratic colours by insisting that the federal government could do little other than pass a bankruptcy law for banks that suspended specie payments. A national bank, he was certain, would only make things worse. Within the states, however, there was scope for much more action. Here all notes below first twenty and subsequently fifty dollars should be outlawed. In addition banks should be required to maintain one dollar in specie for every three of paper. Then all banks which suspended specie payments should be immediately liquidated and each should be compelled to publish a weekly statement of its finances. These measures together, the President believed, "would go far to secure us against future suspensions of specie payments."[194]

193. Richardson (ed.), *Messages and Papers of Presidents*, V, pp. 436–437.
194. Richardson (ed.), *Messages and Papers of Presidents*, V, pp. 439–441.

These impeccably Jacksonian recommendations did not, however, end there. Buchanan conceded that "the existence of banks and the circulation of bank paper are so identified with the habits of our people that they can not at this day be abolished without much immediate injury to the country." Hence the task was to "confine them to their appropriate sphere and prevent them from administering to the spirit of wild and reckless speculation by extravagant loans and issues." In these circumstances "they might be continued with advantage to the public." Here was a reluctant acquiescence in banking. But then the President delivered an extraordinary threat to the banks:

> But this I say, after long and much reflection: if experience shall prove it to be impossible to enjoy the facilities which well regulated banks might afford without at the same time suffering the calamities which the excesses of the banks have hitherto inflicted upon the country, it would then be far the lesser evil to deprive them altogether of the power to issue a paper currency and confine them to the functions of banks of deposit and discount.

Thus Buchanan threatened to deprive the banks altogether of the power to increase the supply of money within the community, traditionally their most important function. The President in effect was contemplating an entirely specie currency.[195]

Under the leadership of Andrew Jackson and Martin Van Buren, the Democratic party's prime concern had been with the nation's banks. But neither President in the 1830s had gone further than Buchanan in the 1850s. Indeed James Buchanan in the 1850s went considerably further than James Buchanan had in the 1830s, for as a Pennsylvania Senator he had, without ever leaving the party, after the Panic of 1837 distanced himself from its dominant hard-money wing.[196]

Whether the President would have placed himself at the head of an antibank crusade in the 1850s remains unclear, however. For unlike twenty years earlier, the nation's economy recovered fairly rapidly. At that time the country had been gripped by a recession which lasted for several years; this time there was to be no repetition. Instead in his second annual message, the President, whilst again recommending a bankruptcy law for banks, and again noting the unemployment of many workers, was now able to report that "the effects of the revulsion are now slowly but surely passing away." Capital had "again accumulated in our large cities" and "confidence" was "gradually reviving." As a result the crusade

195. Richardson (ed.), *Messages and Papers of Presidents*, V, p. 441.
196. Ashworth, *"Agrarians" and "Aristocrats,"* p. 145.

against the banks never acquired the momentum that it had achieved two decades earlier.[197]

Within the states a similar pattern obtained. By the time the Panic struck, the Democrats were powerful primarily in the lower North,[198] with Pennsylvania and Indiana their most important strongholds. In each the President's antibank sentiments were echoed. In Pennsylvania Governor William F. Parker voiced opposition to small notes and to any increase in banks or banking capital within the state. He insisted that the legislature possessed and should exercise the power to alter or annul the charter of any banks deemed to be injuring the public. In January 1859 he observed that while the "financial pressure of the past eighteen months" might be the product of "many causes," nevertheless it was "too plain to admit of doubt that our banking system has been one of the most prominent." Like Buchanan he recognised that the power of banks to issue paper money was so well-established as to be no longer "an open question." But like Buchanan too he pointed out that it had been "greatly abused" and had resulted in "evils of the most alarming character." In words redolent of Andrew Jackson's bank veto message Parker observed that when a bank failed the greatest sufferers were "always" "the humble and the ignorant." Nevertheless the Governor conceded that in Pennsylvania, one of the states hardest hit by the financial troubles of 1857–1858, the majority of the state's banks were safe. For that reason, perhaps, an antibank crusade failed to materialise in Pennsylvania.[199]

Indiana was perhaps in the 1850s the strongest Democratic state in the North and was unique among northern states in throughout the decade electing only Democratic governors. Unlike in Pennsylvania, where the banking controversy had been dormant since the early 1840s, Indiana's Democrats, or at least a large portion of them, had continued to espouse antibank doctrines since the 1830s. In the Constitutional Convention of 1850 a large number of Democrats had tried to outlaw banking altogether but the familiar alliance of Whigs and conservative Democrats blocked this attempt. Shortly thereafter a free banking law was passed. A typical Democratic attitude was that of Governor Joseph Wright who in 1853 adopted a middle course on banking, on the one hand acknowledging that there been in the past too little banking capital in the state but, on

197. Richardson (ed.), *Messages and Papers of Presidents*, V, pp. 520–521.
198. In addition one should mention the Pacific States of California and later Oregon together with the infant state of Minnesota.
199. *Legislative Record ... of Pennsylvania ... 1859*, p. 8. See also *Address and Correspondence of the Democratic State Convention of Pennsylvania* (Philadelphia, n.d.), p. 8 and, for Democratic enthusiasm for the state's recent free banking law, *The Legislative Record Containing the Debates and Proceedings of the Pennsylvania Legislature for 1861* (Harrisburg, 1861), p. 7.

the other, lamenting the failure of the Constitutional Convention to prohibit all banknotes under five or ten dollars. In subsequent messages to
the state legislature he anticipated Buchanan's recommendation that all
banks suspending specie payments should automatically be wound up and
also insisted that all paper money should be convertible to specie at all
times – or else "we can never have steadiness, and permanent prosperity
in the business of the country."[200]

Since it met only biennially, the Indiana Legislature did not address the
question of the Panic until the beginning of 1859. At this time the new
Governor voiced a preference for specie but at the same time recognised
that there was no possibility that all the states would outlaw paper money
and consoled himself with the thought that "Indiana has established as
safe systems of banking as any other state in the Union." By 1859 the
state's financial system could indeed boast an impressive record since only
one bank had failed in the preceding four years. As in Pennsylvania the
abstract preference for specie had to be subordinated to existing and by
now time-honoured commercial practice.[201]

In other northern states a broadly similar pattern emerged, with minor
differences from one state or even locality to another. Even in their heyday
hard money Democrats had often been frustrated by temporary coalitions
between Whigs and conservative Democrats so that even if the party was
in control it by no means followed that antibank legislation would ensue.
The loss of support the party suffered in the North in the 1850s thus left
no chance for antibank radicals to implement their favoured reforms.[202]
(This remained true despite the presence of antibank Democratic Republicans, whose activities we have already noted.) Thus in most northern
states the banking controversy had subsided by the mid-1840s and, a
decade later, with the Republicans now dominant in the North as a whole,
the Panic did not permanently alter the political landscape.

There were of course, some exceptions. In Ohio the war with the banks
reached a crescendo only in the early 1850s but once again hard money
Democrats were frustrated by conservatives within their own party as well
as by the Whigs. In 1851 Democratic Governor Reuben Wood denounced,
in classic Jacksonian manner, "all special legislation for the benefit of
capital, at the expense of labor" but the war with the banks was about

200. *Documents of the General Assembly of Indiana ... 1853*, pp. 21, 23, 25, 29; *Journal
     of the Indiana State Senate ... 38 Session ... Jan 4, 1855* (Indianapolis, 1855), pp. 18,
     22–23; *Journal of the Indiana State Senate ... 1857*, pp. 52–55; Shade, *Banks or No
     Banks*, pp. 147, 177, 186–197.
201. *Journal of the Indiana State Senate ... 40th Session ... Jan. 6, 1859* (Indianapolis,
     1859), p. 22; Shade, *Banks or No Banks*, pp. 202, 211.
202. These losses were partly offset, of course, by gains in the South, where the party was
     stronger than ever, but the South was in any case less severely affected by the Panic.

Democrats and the economy 441

to subside in Ohio. When the Panic of 1857 struck, the Democrats had acquired control of the state legislature and they managed to impose some additional restrictions upon the state's banks. But the system survived the turbulence of the following months largely intact. A typical Democratic attitude of the 1850s was struck by the Democratic Governor of New Hampshire who, in 1853 warned against extending the banking system too far but, at the same time, conceded that it was "sound."[203]

Perhaps the strongest denunciations of banking in the North in the late 1850s came from the infant state of Minnesota whose first Governor was the former Ohio radical Democrat Samuel Medary. Medary and his successor, H. H. Sibley, denounced the banks with Sibley referring to paper money as "the great curse of the West, and indeed of the entire nation." Similarly the St Paul *Pioneer and Democrat* in January 1858 blamed the Panic squarely upon the banks and condemned "the whole paper money system" as "a sham and lie from beginning to end." The analysis of the cycle of boom and bust which the newspaper then presented was identical to those which radical Democrats had offered twenty years earlier:

> The current value of money is depreciated below its just and real value, and the value of property, and commodities, are appreciated above their proper and true value. Fictitious facilities of credit are afforded, debts are incurred, and transactions are entered into without any valid basis; speculation is unduly and unnaturally stimulated; all sorts of wild schemes for rapid gains are inaugurated; splendid fortunes are realised with the dazzling suddenness of the events of an Arabian Nights Tale, and with no more elements of reality. The expansion of credit and the multiplication of business transactions and enterprises, continue, with increasing rapidity, until the extreme tension of the fictitious and unnatural system is reached; then come the break, the crash, the panic and disaster and ruin follow. At the very first movement caused by the falling fabric, of course all the unreal bubbles of fortune instantly vanish. But, unfortunately, innumerable solid edifices go down in the general ruin; the late order of things becomes suddenly reversed, property and labor are depreciated below their true value, and money, or the medium of exchange, is appreciated beyond its real worth; credit is destroyed, transactions cease and enterprise is paralyzed.

The conclusion was that "these monetary cycles will continue to mark the commercial history of our country as long as it shall be cursed with

203. *Documents Made to the 49th General Assembly of the State of Ohio* (Columbus, 1851), pp. 24–25; *Journal of the House of Representatives of the State of New Hampshire . . . 1853* (Concord, 1853), pp. 44–45; *Journal of the Indiana State Senate . . . 1847*, p. 100.

a paper currency." It was one with a long and distinguished Democratic pedigree.[204]

Nevertheless even in Minnesota a sustained antibank movement failed to materialise. In most of the northern states the effects of the Panic were relatively short-lived and recovery came too quickly for the widespread political radicalism of the late 1830s to become entrenched. Part of the problem, for doctrinaire enemies of banks and paper money at any rate, was that for a variety of reasons the nation's financial system was far more stable than it had been in earlier decades. California gold together with the rising tide of British investment into the United States meant that both the money supply and the specie reserves of banks in the early 1850s had increased sharply. As a result, even when the Panic of 1857 struck, the banks were able to weather the crisis far better than twenty years earlier. By the middle of 1858 most had resumed specie payments and, although there would be severe dislocation in the financial markets in the following years, this would be as a consequence of secession and war rather than underlying fiscal instability. By the late 1850s even the demand for an exclusively specie currency no longer carried such hugely deflationary overtones. Despite the crisis of 1857 the new maturity of the northern economy, coupled with the more stable international environment of the 1850s, prevented the banking controversy from recovering its former prominence in either federal or state politics.[205]

## II

The tariff controversy followed a similar pattern. Whigs had fiercely opposed both the reintroduction of the Independent Treasury and the Walker tariff, the key financial reforms of the Polk presidency. But the economic boom of the late 1840s and early 1850s had falsified their predictions of imminent financial collapse. Democratic policy on the tariff insisted that revenue-raising be the primary objective, though it allowed for a modicum of "incidental protection" to American manufactures.

---

204. *Journal of the Senate during the First Session of the Legislature of the State of Minnesota . . . 2nd Dec. 1857* (St Paul, 1858), p. 38; *Journal of the House of Representatives during the Second Session of the Legislature of the State of Minnesota . . . 2nd Dec. 1859* (St Paul, 1860 ), p. 20; *Pioneer and Democrat*, Jan. 14, 21, 1858. William Shade points out that in Illinois there was also a marked revival of antibank sentiment in these years, though it produced relatively few tangible effects – see Shade, *Banks or No Banks* , pp. 212, 218.

205. Thomas D. Willett, "International Specie Flows and American Monetary Stability, 1834–1860," *Journal of Economic History*, XXVIII (March 1968), pp. 28–50; Jeffrey G. Wilkinson, *American Growth and the Balance of Payments, 1820–1913* (Chapel Hill, 1964), p. 111.

When, despite the passage of the Walker tariff, American manufacturing boomed, it seemed as though the tariff was ceasing to be a controversial question.[206]

For the Democrats to have revived the tariff as a major issue, therefore, required the Whigs to agitate against the Walker tariff of 1846. But even by 1848 they were disclaiming any desire to do so and indeed the decision to run Zachary Taylor for the presidency that year owed something to the fact that he was not clearly identified with the traditional Whig economic programme. By now it took economic reverses for the party to reopen the tariff question. Although President Millard Fillmore spoke publically of the need for tariff revision, he himself realised that this was a hopeless quest. Indeed in 1853 Robert J. Walker himself was able to boast that "the result of the existing system" had been "to double our exports and imports and also our revenues." Although it might have been possible to challenge the causal relationship that Walker imputed, it was difficult to arouse the electorate on behalf of tariff revision. Not until the Panic of 1857 would there be any sustained pressure for additional protective duties.[207]

In that year the Democrats had reduced the tariff still further, with relatively little dissent from their opponents. But when the Panic struck, renewed calls for protection emerged in the states where the tariff had traditionally been most popular: New York, Pennsylvania, New Jersey, and Massachusetts.[208] In the spring of 1858 Senator John J. Crittenden, partly in an attempt to revive the now moribund Whig party, urged a return to the protective principle. But the Republican party, as we have seen, was unable wholeheartedly to embrace the protective tariff, largely owing to the presence within its ranks of a large and important contingent of former Democrats, many of whom were doctrinaire free traders. As a result there was little need or opportunity for the Democrats to emphasise the issue or to campaign upon it.[209]

In a strong Democratic state like Indiana the result was that the party simply congratulated itself on having passed the Walker tariff which, it was "confidently believed," would place "the permanent prosperity of the toiling millions of our population" upon "a durable basis." Indeed Governor James Whitcomb in 1847 argued that since there had been a "great increase" in manufacturing in the State over the previous year, it

206. Holt, *The Political Crisis of the 1850s* (New York, 1978), pp. 48, 74.
207. Holt, *Whig Party*, pp. 246–247, 286–287. Holt points out that Taylor privately thought the tariff a dead issue – see p. 272. Nevins, *The Emergence of Lincoln: Prologue to Civil War* (New York, 1950), p. 222.
208. Holt, *Political Crisis*, pp. 201, 207–208.; Nevins, *Prologue to Civil War*, p. 220.
209. See Chapter 2.

was clear that "these interests are in a most flourishing condition." But rural Indiana had never been a centre of protectionist sentiment.[210]

Pennsylvania, the other Democratic northern stronghold, however, was the strongest protariff state in the Union. In a sense, therefore, the very strength of the party there testifies to the relative unimportance of the tariff in the North as a whole, and even, in some years, in Pennsylvania herself.[211] This did not mean, however, that Democrats were enthusiastic free traders in Pennsylvania. In 1844 Polk had been presented, rather disingenuously, as a friend to the tariff there and the reduced rates introduced by his Secretary of the Treasury, Robert J. Walker, had been a huge disappointment to many Pennsylvanians. That year James Buchanan stated that he frankly preferred the higher duties of the Whig tariff of 1842 and, like the Whigs, predicted that the reduced rates would "to a great extent, be ruinous to our mechanics & artisans who work up foreign material for use." Nevertheless, he acknowledged that an overtly protective tariff could not be enacted. Two years later Lewis Cass was presented to the people of Pennsylvania as a statesman who would promote the welfare of the whole country. This meant that "the proprietors of iron and other manufactures, and of the inexhaustible coal mines of Pennsylvania have nothing to fear at his hands," for "if he finds they need additional protection to enable them to secure a fair profit on their investments, he will listen like a kind parent to their appeals, and recommend with all his strength and power that justice be done." But the anonymous writer did not straightforwardly endorse protection. "At the same time," he assured his readers, Cass would "keep a vigilant eye upon the interests of the farmer – the tiller of the soil – and other industrial classes, and see that they shall not suffer injury by any wild and reckless scheme introduced under the specious name of' 'protection to American industry!'" This was a typical straddle for the Democrats of Pennsylvania.[212]

By the 1850s even in Pennsylvania protectionist sentiment was waning. A major revival came only with the Panic of 1857 and the difficulties that followed it. At this time Pennsylvania was probably the hardest hit of any state and so it was scarcely surprising that Governor William F. Parker at the beginning of 1859 should point out that if the state's demands for higher duties had been heeded, much of the distress of the preceding months would have been avoided. Yet even he stuck to the established Democratic formula, demanding a tariff that "would not only produce revenue, but furnish the largest incidental protection to the great mineral,

210.  This is not to say, however, that rural areas had no motive to support the tariff, rather that the more industrial areas had traditionally been its strongest supporters.
211.  *Journal of the Indiana State Senate…1849*, p. 12.; *Journal of the Indiana State Senate…1847*, pp. 98–99.
212.  *Works of Buchanan*, VII, pp. 43–47, 117; *To the People of Pennsylvania*, p. 13.

manufacturing and industrial interests of the country." In other words the revenue principle was to prevail.[213]

Despite the unquestioned popularity of a protective tariff in Pennsylvania in these years,[214] Democrats in the nation as a whole were able to maintain ranks on the issue. The Whigs had a long history of support for the tariff but when they were the Democrats' main challengers in the first half of the decade economic conditions were not conducive to a revival of the issue. But then after 1857 they had been replaced by the Republicans who were deeply divided on the question. Thus when economic conditions were at last more favourable to a renewed debate over the tariff, the political will was missing and the triumph of Democratic policy was not challenged.

In a deeper sense, however, the eclipse of the tariff, like the retreat of the banking question, was the result of the greater maturity and strength of the American economy. The admission that the Walker tariff had not had the catastrophic effects predicted was itself a reflection of that strength and stability. Indeed, as historians have noted, larger textile firms by now often opposed high duties on the grounds that they would encourage smaller and less efficient companies to compete with them. The protective tariff had always been justified primarily as a temporary measure to allow infant American industries to compete with those already established in Europe and especially in Great Britain. Once established, they would no longer require protection. Those manufacturers who now denied the need for a higher tariff were, in effect, announcing that, in international terms, and by the standards of the time, their companies were reaching maturity.[215]

## III

In the heyday of Jacksonian Democracy the Democrats had been able, despite the reluctance of their conservative wing, to translate antibank attitudes into concrete policies or at least specific proposals. When those policies were introduced into the state legislatures or debated in constitutional conventions, the party had been able to maintain a reasonable degree of unity. So it was with the tariff, except in those northeastern states where protectionist sentiment had been strongest. As far as the third great financial issue was concerned, internal improvements, the pattern had usually been somewhat different. Here local pressures had typically

---

213. *Legislative Record...of Pennsylvania...1859* (Harrisburg, 1859), p. 9. See also Holt. *Political Crisis*, p. 111.
214. The tariff was also still popular with some New England Democrats but the party was so weak there by the late 1850s that they had little impact on national party policy – see Nevins, *Prologue to Civil War*, pp. 402, 455–457.
215. Holt, *Whig Party*, pp. 686–687.

produced a splintering of the party vote, both at Washington and within the states, with representatives from areas that stood to benefit from new roads, canals or railroads often finding the temptation to support them irrresistible, despite the promptings of official Democratic theory. In the late-1840s and 1850s, especially at state level, this splintering continued and Democrats found it even more difficult to maintain their official position of hostility to government sponsorship of schemes for internal improvements.[216]

Nevertheless there were distinct echoes of traditional Democratic principles. At federal level Democratic Presidents Pierce and Buchanan dealt with many internal improvement bills as the hallowed Jacksonian tradition dictated, but again without arousing the controversy that the Old Hero had provoked. Thus, after using the veto in 1853, Pierce quietly announced that the constitution did not confer upon the federal government a general power to construct internal improvements. Some years later Buchanan expressed the same opinion and buttressed it with reasoning that Jackson himself might have applauded:

> What a vast field would the exercise of this power open for jobbing and corruption! Members of Congress, from an honest desire to promote the interests of their constituents, would struggle for improvements within their own districts, and the body itself must necessarily be converted into an arena where each would endeavor to obtain from the Treasury as much money as possible for his own locality. The temptation would prove irresistible. A system of "logrolling" (I know no word so expressive) would be inaugurated, under which the Treasury would be exhausted and the Federal Government be deprived of the means necessary to execute those great powers clearly confided to it by the Constitution for the purpose of promoting the interests and vindicating the honor of the country.

Here was the classic Jacksonian fear of special interests controlling the legislature and employing the power of government for their own narrow ends.[217]

Yet this was not followed by a denunciation of a social elite, an "aristocratic" minority, that was purportedly seeking to control the destinies of the nation. Such rhetoric was now alien not only to the president but also to his party. Moreover, Buchanan could not even maintain his own hostility to federally sponsored improvements. He, like almost every other American of his generation, was entranced by the largest project of all:

---

216.  Herbert Ershkowitz and Willam G. Shade, "Consensus or Conflict: Political Behavior in the State Legislatures during the Jacksonian Era," *Journal of American History*, LVIII (1971), pp. 591–621.
217.  Richardson (ed.), *Messages and Papers of Presidents*, V, pp. 260, 604–605.

a railroad link to the Pacific. Whigs and Democrats, Republicans and proslavery enthusiasts, found this prospect difficult to resist.

The Democrats, however, found it hardest to justify, at least in terms of fundamental party principle. Thus Buchanan was driven to advocate federal involvement in the project on the dubious grounds that it was justified for military purposes. In his second annual message to Congress, the President tried to resuscitate classic Democratic doctrine when he argued that Congress should not be directly involved since this would lead to too much patronage and corruption. But Buchanan clearly found the project as irresistible as everyone else because he claimed that the states could incorporate the companies which would build the railroad and congress would offer financial subsidies or land grants. Was this constitutional? By Democratic lights, it almost certainly was not but the President again, and equally implausibly, cited the federal government's warmaking power. Which war he had in mind, Buchanan did not say.[218]

The main controversy over the Pacific railroad concerned its route. Not surprisingly, southerners wanted a southern route, and northerners wanted a northern one. Stephen A. Douglas, as ever anxious to conciliate the South, proposed that no fewer than three railroads spanning the continent be built. This, however, struck many observers as altogether too ambitious and extravagant. Some Democrats, especially southerners, did display constitutional scruples but the failure to begin the railroad under the Democratic administrations of Pierce and Buchanan owed more to sectional rivalries than to traditional Democratic sensibilities. In this sense warmaking was indeed linked to the construction of a Pacific railroad, but it was an anticipation of the war that was soon to erupt between North and South.[219]

Within the states a similar erosion of traditional Democratic policy occurred. Before the Panic of 1837 many states had begun internal improvement schemes which they found they could not properly fund when the economic climate worsened. This strengthened Democratic commitment to limited government and *laissez-faire*. In the 1840s and, to a lesser extent, in the 1850s party spokesmen continued to exercise some of the caution and display some of the suspicion that had been in evidence in the 1830s. Thus Democratic Governors in states like Pennsylvania and Indiana reminded their legislatures of the need to keep the government

---

218. *Works of Buchanan*, X, p. 110; Richardson (ed.), *Messages and Papers of Presidents*, V, p. 526.
219. See Nevins, *Douglas, Buchanan and Party Chaos*, pp. 440–444, *Prologue to Civil War*, pp. 195, 448, *House Dividing*, pp. 82–87. Traditional Democratic reservations about internal improvements at federal expense did, however, surface occasionally, as when Pierce vetoed a project that was to remove impediments to navigation of the Great Lakes.

removed from schemes of internal improvement. Yet for most of the 1850s and in most of the states the Democrats offered warnings and reminders rather than radical changes of direction.[220] The prosperity of the era simply did not lend itself to a full restaging of the dramas of the Jackson-Van Buren years.[221]

Indeed the return of prosperity in the mid-1840s and the railroad boom that was a feature of the capitalist world in the 1850s placed great strain upon traditional Democratic policy. Democratic enthusiasm for the projects grew and, although the railroads of the era were private corporations rather than the public-private enterprises of previous decades, they received much support from government in the form of corporate charters and financial inducements. Democrats were scarcely less enthusiastic than Whigs in the early 1850s or than Republicans in the middle of the decade. Moreover, their new-found affection for internal improvements was almost as apparent in the South as in the North with even Andrew Johnson of Tennessee, as doctrinaire a Jacksonian as could be found anywhere, announcing in 1855 that he favoured a "judicious system" of internal improvements. The Panic of 1857, however, produced yet another reaction, though milder than that seen twenty years earlier, and government activity in many states was somewhat curtailed. Yet these developments attracted relatively little interest; since the issues at the top of the political agenda, those involving slavery and the sectional controversy, were so very different.[222]

## IV

Alongside the traditional Democratic commitment to a low tariff and the traditional Democratic hostility to banks and internal improvements lay the equally traditional Democratic desire for the rapid settlement of the West. In Jackson's day the Democrats had striven to grant pre-emption rights to settlers on the public domain and to graduate the price of public lands. Both policies had been opposed, however inconsistently, by the Whigs. In the 1850s, however, a reversal took place. The Republicans

220. The canal question in the state of New York provides the most important exception. Here the old feud between Democrats and Whigs continued, with conservative Democrats, as formerly, siding with the Whigs in support of the canals.
221. *Legislative Record ... of Pennsylvania ... 1859*, p. 7; *Journal of the Indiana ... State Senate ... 32nd Session ... Commencing Dec. 6, 1847* (Indianapolis, 1848), p. 108.
222. Paul H. Bergeron, *Antebellum Politics in Tennessee* (Lexington, 1982), p. 124; Clarence C. Norton, *The Democratic Party in Antebellum North Carolina, 1833–1861* (Chapel Hill, 1930), p. 126, 130, 156, 174; Joseph Gregoire de Roulhac Hamilton, *Party Politics in North Carolina, 1835–1860* (Durham, NC, 1916.), pp. 125, 186. Anthony Carey, *Parties, Slavery and the Union in Antebellum Georgia* (Athens, GA, 1997), p. 137.

with their demand for Homestead legislation now took the lead in promoting the settlement of the West. For the Democrats the issue brought considerable embarrassment. In the North they gave real support to the Homestead but the problem was the party's increasingly dominant southern wing. Apart from a few individuals like Andrew Johnson of Tennessee or Albert Gallatin Brown of Mississippi, southern Democrats were hostile to the Homestead bills that were introduced into Congress in the 1850s. Their fear was, of course, that such legislation would simply spur the emigration of free labour into the territories to the exclusion of slavery and the slaveholder. As the decade wore on the issue became a thoroughly sectional one, with almost every northern Representative and Senator in favour and almost every southern opposed.[223]

This caused acute problems for the Democratic party. The Republicans, as an exclusively northern organisation, were able, especially by the end of the decade, to display almost total unanimity on the Homestead issue but northern Democrats were increasingly encumbered by their southern wing. In 1852 Pierce maintained a discreet silence on the question and no bill passed Congress. Buchanan was not so lucky. In 1859 a somewhat watered-down Homestead Act passed Congress. As ever southerners were ranged against it. Buchanan knew that he owed his position to the South and accordingly vetoed it. In his veto message the President offered a whole host of objections, which ranged from its alleged unconstitutionality to the injustice which it apparently perpetrated upon various groups in American society. Ironically, Buchanan here resurrected some of the arguments that Whigs had previously advanced in order to delay westward settlement. The President claimed the measure was unfair to the eastern states (which would derive no immediate benefit from it), unfair to the native-born (who were not favoured over immigrants), and, most remarkably, unfair to the nonagricultural classes (who would be required in effect to subsidise a hand-out to farmers of potential government revenues). None of these arguments was novel; all had been made previously – by the enemies of the Democratic party. Buchanan's list of objections to the Homestead bill was a long one but it did not include the one which was almost certainly decisive: its antislavery impact.[224]

The veto came in June 1860 and it provided valuable ammunition for the Republicans, especially in the Northwest, in the coming elections. In a broader sense, however, the veto illustrated the problems that confronted the northern Democrats. Although by now they needed their southern wing if they were to have any chance of national success, such support,

223. Nevins, *House Dividing*, pp. 33, 334–335, 501, *Douglas, Buchanan and Party Chaos*, pp. 402–403, 444–445, *Prologue to Civil War*, pp. 189, 253.
224. Richardson (ed.), *Messages and Papers of Presidents*, V, pp. 611–614

it was clear, would come only at a high price. Southern objections to the Homestead principle, together with the southern demand for a slave code in the territories, inflicted incalculable damage upon the party in the North and especially the Northwest, and paved the way for the historic Republican triumph of 1860.

## V

When Buchanan cited as one reason for his veto of the Homestead bill the benefits the bill would confer upon the farming interest (to the detriment of other groups), he showed how far his party had moved from the principles that it had enunciated in the days of Andrew Jackson and Martin Van Buren. These principles were never formally renounced and, as we shall see, here and there they made vestigial appearances. Nevertheless, the party that Buchanan led, or tried to lead, in 1860 was very different in its social philosophy from that headed by Martin Van Buren just twenty years earlier.

The main difference in economic outlook was the most obvious one. Whereas the dominant wing of the party in the Jackson-Van Buren era had sounded a note of alarm, a protest against the dominant economic developments of the time, by the 1850s the tone had altered dramatically and most northern Democrats announced themselves, in general and with the exception of the months that followed the Panic of 1857, highly satisfied with economic conditions. In Indiana, for example, Democratic governors repeatedly invited their citizens to congratulate themselves on what was termed in 1853 an "unprecedented degree of prosperity." A year later the Governor of Ohio announced that "there has never been a period in the history of the State when industry and enterprise were more adequately and liberally rewarded." In New England the Governor of New Hampshire similarly declared in 1853 that his state was "in a prosperous condition beyond any former period of her history" and even in Pennsylvania, where the Panic of 1857 had struck hard, Governor William Parker in 1859 was able to proclaim that "health and reasonable prosperity prevail." This self-congratulatory note was characteristic of northern Democrats throughout the 1850s.[225]

The Democratic party, both north and south, had traditionally extolled the merits of agriculture and had not hesitated to open fire upon the nonagricultural sectors of the economy, where privilege and exploitation were

225. *Documents of the General Assembly of Indiana... 1853*, p. 17; *Journal of the House of Representatives of the State of Ohio... 52nd General Assembly... Commencing Jan. 2, 1854* (Columbus, OH, 1856), p. 30; *Journal of the House of Representatives of the State of New Hampshire... 1853* (Concord, 1853), p. 40; *The Legislative Record... of Pennsylvania... 1859*, p. 6.

held to reside. Similar attitudes were occasionally struck in the late 1840s and 1850s. Thus Jeremiah Black, later to serve in Buchanan's cabinet, developed a neo-Jeffersonian theme when he insisted that "the fruits of the farmer's labour support the industry of all other classes," and Stephen A. Douglas, with whom Black would later clash over the intricacies of popular sovereignty, agreed that agriculture was "the parent and supporter" of every type of industry. Douglas resembled the Sage of Monticello even more closely when he announced that "as long as the great body of our population is composed of owners and cultivators of land, we shall remain true to our republican institutions." In the western states, especially, it was frequently asserted that agriculture must remain the primary economic activity.[226]

This preference for agriculture occasionally spilled over in the late 1840s and 1850s, as it had in Andrew Jackson's day, into an attack on manufacturing. In 1848, for example, the author of the *Democratic Text Book* warned that "one of the most dangerous features of this system of manufacturing protection" was "the horrible tyranny to which it gives rise," for "the operative has, indeed, become the bondsman of the capitalist." In the same way some Democrats revived the old Jacksonian assault upon legislation that was "partial" or that was designed to benefit capital at the expense of labour. Thus Jared Williams as Governor of New Hampshire in the late 1840s announced that "in all legislation there is, perhaps, an improper tendency in favor of capital rather than labour; to benefit the few rather than the many" while a decade later the mechanics of Harpers Ferry lauded Buchanan on the grounds that he was "never the representative of capital or associated wealth."[227]

Yet these were no longer typical utterances in the North. More representative was the enthusiasm for manufacturing that was displayed by Democratic Governors throughout the North. The Governor of Indiana in 1852 actually welcomed the introduction of manufacturing capital into Indiana on the grounds that "the more manufacturing capital there is introduced, the lighter will be the burthens of each individual, the more the taxable wealth of the state." The result would be "a division of labour, so indispensable to the agricultural, and so important to all interests." Similarly, despite sporadic references to the dangers of "associated wealth,"

---

226. Chauncey F. Black, *Essays and Speeches of Jerremiah S. Black* (New York, 1885), p. 35; *Address of the Hon. Stephen A. Douglas at the Annual Fair of the New York State Agricultural Society, September 1851* (Albany, 1851), pp. 7–9;. *Documents of the General Assembly of Indiana...35th Session, Convening Dec 30 1850 Part 1* (Indianapolis, 1851), p. 106.
227. *The Democratic Text Book* (New York, 1848), pp. 65–66; *Journal of the House of Representatives of the State of New Hampshire...1847* (Concord, 1847), p. 23; Cluskey, *Buchanan and Breckinridge*, p. 25.

northern Democrats did not voice any sustained protest against existing or even anticipated future social conditions. Thus Daniel Dickinson in 1848 went out of his way to assure an audience that even though the Democrats were "opposed to monopoly," they were not "the foe, as has been charged, of capital." Dickinson emphasised that far from being a danger, "associated wealth has, in numerous instances, been of great public service, in furnishing profitable employment to labour; in constructing works of internal improvement of immense national and individual advantage, and in aiding enterprise in numberless ways in developing the resources of the country." This contrasted sharply with the warnings that Martin Van Buren had delivered in the late 1830s about "associated wealth." Although Dickinson had always inclined to the conservative wing of the Democratic party, his views were echoed by those who had impeccably radical credentials. Thus John A. Dix, the former Barnburner and Van Burenite, was now equally explicit in acknowledging the benign influence of accumulated wealth.[228]

Far from objecting to the economic environment of the 1850s then, most (though not all) northern Democrats went out of their way to express their satisfaction and contentment. They were highly gratified with the economic expansion that was underway and whose signs seemed everywhere visible. Thus the Governor of New Hampshire in 1853 contemplated with evident satisfaction contemporary economic and social trends:

> Our plains and valleys are covered with a network of railways; the cars rush along upon their tracks freighted with human and animal life, and all kinds of merchandise with almost inconceivable velocity; manufacturing and mechanical establishments adorn and make useful our waterfalls, the hum of the machinery, the voices of the cheerful operatives... enliven the daily toil of intelligent and well paid industry; Meeting houses, Common School houses and academies bedeck our towns and villages, and workshops, mercantile stores, tasteful, comfortable dwellings and well cultivated farms, everywhere attest our progress in useful arts, industrial pursuits, morals and civilisation.

This was a far cry from the protests which Democrats had entered only a decade earlier.[229]

228. *Documents of the General Assembly of Indiana... 1851*, p. 173; *Speeches, etc. of Dickinson*, I, pp. 268–269; John A. Dix, *Speeches and Occasional Addresses* (New York, 1864), p. 359.
229. *Journal of the House of Representatives of the State of New Hampshire... 1853* (Concord, 1853), p. 40. Michael F. Holt, *Forging a Majority: The Formation of the Republican Party in Pittsburg, 1848–1860* (New Haven, CT, 1969), p. 202.

This macroeconomic success translated, Democrats believed, into individual well-being on an unprecedented scale. James Buchanan in 1851 invited his fellow Americans to rejoice in the opportunities available to them. "In this country," he claimed, "every man of industry and economy, with the blessings of Providence upon his honest labour, can acquire a freehold for himself, and sit under his own vine and his own fig tree, and there shall be none to make him afraid." This too was a message very different from that which Democrats had previously sought to convey and it serves to confirm that the party of Douglas and Buchanan was very different from that which Andrew Jackson and Martin Van Buren had led in the none-too-distant past.[230]

## VI

The Democratic party of the 1850s had thus undergone fundamental changes since the 1830s. Both North and South it had largely ceased to voice the criticisms of the existing social order that had so often been heard at the time of the bank war. On each side of the Mason-Dixon Line, many prominent Democrats expressed their approval of their section's labour system. In the South, as we have seen, more and more party members embraced a fully fledged proslavery that did not shrink from proclaiming the superiority of slavery to free labour. In the North meanwhile, as we have also seen, Democrats continued to believe the converse: their free labour economy was in all respects superior.

Since the two parties were agreed on the superiority of the northern labour system, some historians have been led to conclude that Republicans and northern Democrats were equally dedicated to the ideology of "free labor."[231] On this view, northern Democrats and Republicans differed not in their attachment to, or perceptions of, the northern social order but rather in their contrasting attitudes towards immigrants for example, or towards the political challenge posed by the South, perhaps in the form of the Slave Power.

Yet this is a mistaken view. To understand its inadequacy we need to recur to the distinction between free labour and wage labour. Democrats in the North undoubtedly agreed with Republicans that free labour was

---

230. *Works of Buchanan*, VIII, p. 410.
231. As William Gienapp has put it, "the ideology of free labor may have distinguished northerners from slaveowners, but that it divided Republicans from northern Democrats is questionable." For "all northerners and not just Republicans, shared a belief in the values associated with free labor" – see Gienapp, "The Republican Party and the Slave Power," in Abzug and Maizlish (eds.), *New Perspectives on Race and Slavery in America*, pp. 51–78, esp. p. 58. Gienapp provides no evidence for the claim but instead cites Collins, "Ideology of the Ante-Bellum Northern Democrats." Collins, however, provides no evidence for the claim either.

superior to slavery. But they did not share the Republican view of the wages system. In the Jacksonian era Democrats had expressed strong reservations about wage labour on the traditional grounds that the wage worker lacked autonomy. His excessive dependence on his employer undermined both his own liberty and the equality required in a democratic republic.[232] In the 1850s these attitudes occasionally resurfaced. Thus Theophilus Fisk claimed that free soilism and abolition distracted northern workers from "their own grievous wrongs and intolerable oppressions." More significantly, Fernando Wood, campaigning for Breckinridge in 1860, insisted that "until we have provided and cared for the oppressed labouring man in our own midst, we should not extend our sympathy to the labouring men of other states." As mayor of New York city in 1857 Wood set out a view of the condition of northern labour that both revived Democratic radicalism of previous decades and revealed a jaundiced view of the condition of northern wage workers:

> In the days of general prosperity they [the working classes] labor for a mere subsistence whilst other classes accumulate wealth, and in the days of general depression they are the first to feel the change, without the means to avoid or endure reverses. Truly it may be said that in New York those who produce everything get nothing, and those who produce nothing get everything. They labor without income, whilst surrounded by thousands living in affluence and splendor who have income without labor.

As we have already noted, these views were distinctly uncommon within the Democratic party in the 1850s. They were more common, however, than the celebrations of wage labour in which Republicans like Abraham Lincoln indulged. Indeed on some occasions Democrats went out of their way explicitly to reject Republican claims about the extent of social mobility in the nation. Thus the Chicago *Times* in 1859 protested that only one in ten labourers might rise to become an employer of labour – contrary to the claims made by the Illinoisan who was soon to enter the White House. But these contrasting attitudes were never brought into sharp focus and there was no clear party alignment on them as there had been in the 1830s and early 1840s. Many northern Democrats now took an intermediate position, in which they quietly recorded the condition of the wage worker and affirmed that he had no cause for complaint. The key point is that, unlike most Republicans, Democrats did not privilege the role of the wage labourer or the relationship between employer and worker; nor did they dwell on the opportunities for social mobility that were so dear to

232. See the first volume of this study, pp. 307–309.

the Republican heart Such had not been Democratic practice in the past; such was not Democratic practice in the 1850s.[233]

Instead most Democrats abstained from a close analysis of the northern labour system. One reason was perhaps the support they received from the Irish, especially in the larger urban centres. Whether they were being attacked or defended, the Irish were rarely identified with upward mobility. In the 1850s Irish Catholic immigrants in particular were under assault from Know Nothings and other nativists and, as we have seen, the Democratic defence was in terms of religious pluralism (which functioned to legitimate the Roman Catholic Church), of cultural diversity (which functioned to legitimate the tavern), and of political inclusiveness and equality (which functioned to legitimate the immigrant's rapid enfranchisement). Beyond this the Irish were applauded for the contribution their labour had made to the construction of American roads, railroads, canals for example, but far less frequently for their success in ceasing to be employees and becoming employers in their own right. Traditionally, of course, Democrats had been hostile to the political and social influence of the larger towns and cities, on straightforward Jeffersonian grounds. But in part owing to the patterns and the pace of immigration, in the 1850s the party received disproportionate support from the Irish and from the cities in which they resided. (Only a quarter of the Irish made their way onto the land.[234]) The result was to leave Democratic ideology largely shorn of its traditional antiurbanism but unable or unwilling to offer any positive affirmation or celebration of the city. As we have seen, Democrats still occasionally reiterated Jeffersonian pieties about the need to make every citizen a freeholder but it was difficult to see how this squared either with the experience of the Irish, who flocked to the nation's urban centres, or with the party's difficulties (thanks to its southern wing) in supporting Homestead legislation.

This hints at a deeper reason for the lack of engagement with the key features of the northern free labour economy. It is perhaps best seen by comparing the foremost northern Democrat, Stephen A. Douglas, with the foremost Republican, Abraham Lincoln. Lincoln as we have seen, had a clearly articulated vision of northern society, one which emphasised the honoured role of the wages system in creating social mobility and the still more honoured role of social mobility in inspiring the Declaration of

---

233. *The National Crisis* I (Washington, DC, 1860), pp. 10, 13. *Speech of Fernando Wood, Delivered before the Meeting of the National Democratic Delegation to the Charleston Convention, at Syracuse, Feb. 7, 1860* (New York, n.d.), p. 5; Gabor S. Boritt, *Lincoln and the Economics of the American Dream* (Memphis, 1978), p. 179. See also Wood in the *New York Times*, Oct. 23, 1857.
234. Bruce Levine, *Half Slave and Half Free: The Roots of Civil War* (New York, 1992), p. 67.

Independence, the Union and American democracy itself. No matter that Lincoln grossly exaggerated the degree of social mobility in the northern states in the 1850s and no matter that his description of the social philosophy of the nation's founders was somewhat inaccurate. Lincoln had articulated a set of beliefs that resonated with the electorate in his own times and which, to a remarkable extent, would continue to resonate with the American electorate for decades to come.

Douglas, however, had no such analysis of the northern social system. And the reason was, quite simply, the need to defend slavery or at any rate the need to oppose the antislavery movement and counteract or deflect criticisms of the South. There was little he could say on the subject of mobility, for example, even if he had wished to do so, without either claiming that the South exhibited similar degrees of mobility or implicitly criticising slavery and thus undercutting his own neutral approach to its extension into the territories. But southerners themselves did not claim that their social system was especially conducive to social mobility. They knew what historians have since often overlooked: the relationship between master and slave was fundamentally different from that between employer and worker and so long as manumission was ruled out, there could be no real prospect of social mobility for the slave. But the defence of the wages system relied heavily upon claims about social mobility, as indeed it had to in a nation which gave the vote to its wage-workers. Douglas was silent on the question of social mobility in the North, silent on the extent to which it existed and silent on the mechanisms which promoted it.

The Democracy's southern wing brought great success in the 1850s to the party in national and especially presidential elections. In this respect northern Democrats benefited from their party's increasingly dominant position in the South. But they paid a heavy price. Not only were they forced to swallow measures like the Kansas-Nebraska Act that were repudiated in the most dramatic manner by the northern electorate, they were also driven away from their traditional ideological terrain. The need to defend southern slavery was ultimately responsible not only for electoral catastrophes but also for the increasingly dislocated ideology that they propounded. They might on occasion reaffirm Jeffersonian agrarianism, but their party now blocked the rapid settlement of the West. They might genuinely prefer free labour to slavery but they were unable to tell the voters why. They might enjoy the support of large numbers of Irish wage-earners but they had nothing to say about wage labour itself. In all these areas, the ideology of the northern Democrats lacked clarity. By these and other criteria the party in the North compared unfavourably with the Republicans. By the end of the decade the voters were on the verge of telling the northern Democrats so and in the most dramatic manner imaginable.

## Secession and war, 1860–1861

### I

If the Panic of 1857 had turned into a fully fledged economic recession, as had occurred twenty years previously, the agenda of American politics might have been significantly altered. If banks and tariffs had become dominant issues, then it might have been considerably more difficult for either section to achieve the degree of consensus that was in place by the time war broke out in April 1861. But the economic revival of the late 1850s together with the Brown raid meant that the sectional issues were never displaced from their privileged position at the top of the national political agenda.

For the Democratic party in the North these were years of frustration and division. Although one of their own occupied the leading position in the federal government, this gave, as all discerning observers realised, a misleading impression of their strength within the nation. Buchanan owed his position to southern votes and southern power. A better indication of northern Democratic influence was the fate of Stephen A. Douglas in these years. It was an unhappy one indeed. In the interests of party unity, Douglas had generously withdrawn his presidential candidacy in 1856 in favour of Buchanan.[235] More than anyone else, he had been responsible for the passage of the Kansas-Nebraska Act. For this conduct he might have expected to be rewarded, and in particular he might have expected to continue to enjoy the gratitude of southern Democrats. In fact he secured the presidential nomination in 1860 only after the bitterest wrangling and at the cost of a ruinous split within the party. Although he had supporters, some of them extremely influential, in the South, he was by that time vilified by the main body of southern Democrats, repudiated by Buchanan, and finally defeated by Abraham Lincoln.[236]

The principal cause of this rift was, of course, the events in Kansas. As we have seen, Douglas had hoped and expected that Kansas would become a free state. But he had assumed that his would be achieved peacefully and uncontroversially. These hopes, however, had been frustrated, as he saw

---

235. Johannsen, *Douglas*, p. 519; Nevins, *House Dividing*, p. 458.
236. Douglas enjoyed some support even after the Lecompton controversy from southerners, for example in his battle against Lincoln in 1858. A larger number of southerners were initially at least highly reluctant to condemn him. See Johannsen, *Douglas*, pp. 600, 651–652, 740–741, 762–764.

it, by the creation of the Emigrant Aid societies which had encouraged, as Douglas termed it, a bogus "armed and forced emigration." "All the troubles of the territory," he later claimed, "grew out of this armed and forced emigration"; "there would have been no trouble if emigration had been left to its natural causes and course." This was a standard Democratic claim, made both north and south of the Mason-Dixon Line, and it did not distinguish Douglas either from Buchanan or southern mainstream opinion.[237]

Very different however, was Douglas's response to subsequent events concerning Kansas and the status of slavery in the territories. The Dred Scott decision exposed the gulf; the crisis over Lecompton made it unbridgeable. When the Supreme Court handed down the Dred Scott decision in 1857 two of its three main conclusions were uncontroversial within the Democratic party. Douglas, as we have seen, was able to welcome its pronouncements on the rights, or the lack of rights, of African Americans. He could also applaud the Court's denial of the constitutionality of the Missouri Compromise and of the principle of Congressional restrictions upon slavery. But its denial of the right of a territorial legislature to exclude slavery was a very different matter. As we have seen, Douglas sought to accept the judgment but evade its consequences by means of the Freeport doctrine which asserted that while a territorial legislature could not prohibit slavery directly, it could achieve the same result indirectly by refusing to pass the policing regulations necessary in any slave community. Even though the doctrine had been anticipated in many of Douglas's earlier speeches, going back as far as 1842,[238] it nonetheless brought him into bitter opposition not merely with most southern Democrats but also with the Buchanan administration, now more clearly than ever under southern control. Similarly when Douglas opposed the Lecompton constitution not on the grounds that it promoted slavery in Kansas but instead because it had been adopted undemocratically,[239] the breach with the administration

---

237. J. Madison Cutts, *A Brief Treatise Upon Constitutional And Party Questions, And the history of Political Parties, As I Received It Orally From The Late Senator Stephen A. Douglas, Of Illinois* (New York, 1866), p. 97

238. Johannsen, *Douglas*, pp. 570, 656, 670. Douglas himself, on one occasion, claimed he had maintained the position as early as 1850 – see *Letter Of Judge Douglas In Reply To The Speech Of Dr Gwin* (n.p., n.d.), pp. 1–4. Douglas supporters also took pains to demonstrate that some of his current enemies within the Democratic party had previously advanced similar views themselves – see *Popular Sovereignty in the Territories: The Democratic Record* (n.p., n.d.), pp. 5–12; *Speech of the Hon. Reverdy Johnson of Maryland, Delivered before the Political Friends of Hon. Stephen A. Douglas... Faneuil Hall... June 7, 1860* (Baltimore, 1860), p. 11.

239. Lecompton, according to Douglas, "should be repudiated by every Democrat who cherishes the time-honored principle of his party, and is determined, in good faith, to carry out the doctrine of self-government and popular sovereignty" – see Stephen A. Douglas to John W. Forney *et al.*, Feb. 6, 1858," in *Letters of Douglas*, pp. 409–410.

and with mainstream southern Democrats became irreparable. To combat the Freeport doctrine southerners then demanded a slave code, that is, congressional protection for slavery in the territories. Douglas and the overwhelming majority of northern Democrats refused to accept it. Not only would it have meant electoral annihilation in the North (since it would have confirmed every Republican charge relating to the encroachments of the Slave Power), it would have utterly destroyed Douglas's cardinal principle, for which he had been striving for a decade and upon which he had built his entire reputation, of congressional nonintervention. But Buchanan, despite initial misgivings, bowed to the southern demand for a slave code, just as he had bowed to the demand for the Lecompton constitution. The scene was set for the climactic split in the party in 1860.[240]

By now, as we have seen, southern militants heaped opprobrium upon Douglas and his supporters. They were not infrequently denounced as being no better than abolitionists or free soilers. Equally bitter was the antisouthernism of many northern Democrats. Their view was quite simple: they had been asked to make huge sacrifices on behalf of the South, they had made them and suffered the most humiliating electoral punishment as a consequence. There was simply no more room for concession. As one Democrat put it, "we have essayed to vindicate their [southerners'] rights under the Constitution, we grant to them all we claim for ourselves." He concluded that "we are not in a condition to carry another ounce of Southern weight"[241]

During the Buchanan years the Douglas Democrats repeatedly warned southerners that too much was being asked of them. Not only had they had to absorb the Kansas-Nebraska Act itself, with its devastating consequences for the party in the North but also the further pressures placed on them by the Dred Scott decision and the Lecompton controversy. Moreover the lack of real support for the administration in the North meant that its supporters had resorted to bribery and corruption; the Buchanan administration was tainted by corruption to a greater degree than any in the entire history of the antebellum Republic. All of this the Douglas Democrats in the North had had to bear but they drew the line at a slave code in 1860 and insisted upon Douglas's nomination on a platform which endorsed congressional nonintervention.[242]

The delegates to the Democratic convention at Charleston were thus unable to agree on a nomination or a platform. Many southerners held

---

240. Johannsen, *Douglas*, p. 698. For a defence of Buchanan's actions, see Philip S. Klein, *President James Buchanan: A Biography* (University Park, PA, 1962).
241. James W. Singleton to Douglas, Feb. 20, 1859 quoted in Johannsen, *Douglas*, p. 698. See also CG, 35/1, p. 1307.
242. See *Letter of Hon. Whitney Griswold, In Reply to the Speech of Hon. Benjamin F. Butler, May 15, 1860* (n.p., n.d.), pp. 14–15.

that not a single state in the Deep South could be carried on the basis of Douglas's policy; northerners retorted that not a single state in the North could be carried with a platform that incorporated a slave code. Under these circumstances there was no hope for unity unless a deliberate resort to ambiguity could be made. This the southerners refused to accept.[243]

Douglas, in common with some other Democrats, held that there was in fact a conspiracy afoot to break up the Union using the slavery issue as a mere pretext.[244] He also insisted that the Republicans, however much they might disavow the Brown raid, were actually responsible for it because they had fed antislavery fanaticism.[245] Hence they must disavow their doctrines too. In one sense it was natural that Douglas should open fire upon extremists on both sides and denounce them both in unmeasured terms. He also made it clear in the course of several campaign speeches in the South (most famously at Norfolk, Virginia), that the election of a Republican would in no way be grounds for the secession of any state of the Union and that seceders should be treated precisely as Andrew Jackson had treated the nullifiers of South Carolina – as traitors.[246] In this sense, therefore, he engaged, as one might expect from a moderate in politics, in an even-handed condemnation of both sets of extremists.

On the other hand there was surely a tension, if not an outright contradiction, between his views on each set of political enemies. If there was indeed a conspiracy to break up the Union, did this not confirm many of the Republicans' claims about the South and the Slave Power? Moreover, if the Republicans were indeed responsible for the Brown raid, could one blame southerners for wanting to leave a Union which the Republicans had taken a long step towards controlling? Douglas was a pugnacious and highly effective adversary but his immoderate attacks upon his enemies sometimes jarred with the politics of moderation which he professed and upon which his career had been built.[247]

---

243. The actions of the Democratic convention at first Charleston and then Baltimore have been analysed in great detail. However, by then the split was inevitable, given that neither side could back down on the question of a slave code and that southerners would not accept a fudge. Moreover, if the northern wing had given way, the Republican triumph would have been even greater and the southerners would have had at least as much reason to secede as they did. See, on the convention, *Official Proceedings of Democratic National Convention, 1860, at Charleston and Baltimore*; Nichols, *Disruption of American Democracy*, pp. 288–322; William B. Heseltine (ed.), *Three Against Lincoln: Murat Halstead Reports the Caucuses of 1860* (Baton Rouge, 1860).

244. Barbee and Bonham, "Montgomery Address of Douglas," p. 551; Johannsen, *Douglas*, pp. 94, 790, 813, 867–868. See also George Bancroft to Dean Milman, August 15, 1851 in M. A. De Wolfe Howe, *Life and Letters of George Bancroft*. 2 vols. (New York, 1908), p. 135; *Letters . . . of Belmont*, pp. 23–24.

245. Harpers Ferry, he declared in the Senate, "was the natural, logical, inevitable result of the doctrines and teachings of the Republican party" – see *CG*, 36/1, p. 553.

246. Barbee and Bonham, "Montgomery Address of Douglas," pp. 551–552; Johannsen, *Douglas*, pp. 788–789.

247. Historians have not, perhaps, given this point sufficient attention.

II

The presidential election of 1860, extraordinary by any standards, saw Stephen A. Douglas break with tradition by actively campaigning throughout the nation. Such a move was thought by many to denote a vulgar hankering for office but Douglas justified it on the grounds that the nation was facing unprecedented dangers. Here he was surely correct. While Republicans, as we have seen, made light of the threat of secession, Douglas had a far more realistic appreciation of the gravity of the situation.

Douglas in fact carried only the single state of Missouri.[248] He ran well throughout the North in that he garnered some forty-three percent of the popular vote in the northern states. But Lincoln of course was still more successful there. In the South, Douglas could make no inroads and Breckinridge swept the cotton states. The vagaries of the American electoral system meant that Douglas's 1.4 million popular votes, about thirty percent of the total, translated into only twelve, or four percent, of the electoral votes. In much of the North, and especially the Northwest and the Upper North, Breckinridge's support – and he the candidate endorsed by the sitting, northern President – was derisory.[249]

Within a few weeks of the election South Carolina had seceded, to be followed by six more states of the Deep South. Douglas had threatened to hang all secessionists as traitors but for the present he and other northern Democrats urged compromise and concession, first to prevent secession then, when that failed, to woo the cotton states back into the Union. With

248. He also got a portion (three) of New Jersey's electoral votes. Some of the arguments presented by Breckinridge campaigners in the North can be found in *Speech of Gen. Benjamin F. Butler, in Lowell, August 10, 1860* (Lowell, 1860), esp. pp. 8–11; "Who Are the Disunionists? Breckinridge and Lane, The True Union Candidates," *Breckinridge and Lane Campaign Documents, No. 16* (n.p., n.d.), esp. pp. 1–5, 9–14; *Speech of the Hon. William B. Reed, on the Presidential Question, delivered before the National Democratic Association, Philadelphia, Sept. 4, 1860* (n.p., n.d.), esp. pp. 3, 5, 11; "Biographical Sketches of Hon. John C. Breckinridge and General Joseph Lane," *Breckinridge and Lane Campaign Documents, No. 8* (Washington, DC, 1860), esp. p. 18; "The Doctrines and Policy of the Republican Party," *Breckinridge and Lane Campaign Documents, No. 13* (Washington, DC, 1860), esp. pp. 3, 5, 8, 10; "The Great Issues To Be Decided in November Next," *Breckinridge and Lane Campaign Documents, No. 19* (Washington, DC, 1860), esp. pp. 12–15, 19–21; *Speech of the Hon. B. F. Hallett, Before the National Democratic State Convention of Massachusetts . . . Sept. 12, 1860* (Boston, 1860), esp. pp. 5, 8–12; *Speech of the Hon Caleb Cushing . . . Oct. 2, 1860 Before the Democracy of Maine* (n.p., n.d.), esp. pp. 3, 11–12, *The National Crisis* 1.(1), pp. 4–16; *Address of the National Democratic Volunteers* (New York, 1860), esp. pp. 3–7.

249. An exception here was provided by the Pacific states of California and Oregon, then of course very small in population. Otherwise Breckinridge ran creditably only in Pennsylvania. Lincoln of course would have been elected, other things being equal, if all the other candidates' votes had been combined against him, Whether he would have defeated Douglas if he had been the sole Democratic candidate is less sure, however, given that the election (and other events) would then have been very different.

this in mind but also to conciliate the border states, many Democratic newspapers, most of which had supported Douglas, urged that the federal forts in the South be given up. With few exceptions they endorsed the Crittenden Compromise. Douglas himself did so, even though it sought to restore the principle of congressional control over slavery in the territories, the very principle against which he had fought for so long.[250]

At this time many Democrats were simply at a loss. They experienced an intellectual paralysis. It was not that they found it difficult to offer suggestions for conciliation and compromise but rather that they were at a loss when those suggestions did not bear fruit. On the one hand, they could not contemplate the break up of the Union. On the other hand, they found it impossible to see how the Union could exist if it were maintained only by force. What would become of the cherished principle of state's rights, for example, if a state were in the Union only because of federal power and federal armies? One after another northern Democratic newspapers and statesmen explained either that the South could not be conquered by force or, alternatively, if it were, that the Union would not then be worth maintaining. "This Union," said Douglas himself, "cannot be preserved by war." Others added that the Union would be no more than a "mockery" in such circumstances.[251]

Douglas himself listed the alternatives; first, compromise and reunion, second, peaceable secession, third, war. He unequivocally asserted that the first would be the best and the last the worst. This seemed to imply that, if compromise failed, the seceding states should be allowed to depart. This seemed hopelessly at odds with his position as stated during the election campaign at Norfolk, Virginia (and elsewhere), a position which, it is safe to assume, had cost him much southern support. But Douglas was too much a Jacksonian Democrat and too fervent a nationalist to allow the Union to be broken up. Although he and his allies could not conceive of a war to maintain the Union, still less could they conceive of a fragmented nation. Apart from anything else, as Douglas himself pointed out, the idea of a "foreign power" (such as the Confederate States of America) controlling the mouth of the Mississippi river was quite intolerable. Democrats, like Republicans, observed that if one rival confederacy

250. Pittsburgh *Post*, March 18, 1861; Providence *Daily Post*, April 13, 1861 in Howard C. Perkins (ed.), *Northern Editorials on Secession*. 2 vols. (Gloucester, MA, 1942), II, pp. 648, 711–712; Silbey, *Respectable Minority*, p. 36; Kenneth M. Stampp, *And The War Came: The North and the Secession Crisis, 1860–1861* (Chicago, 1950), pp. 21, n39, 131. 210; *CG*, 36/1, App, p. 39; *Speeches . . . of Seymour*, p. 31.
251. *CG*, 37/4, p. 1438; Chicago *Times*, April 9, 1861, Providence *Daily Post*, Nov. 8, 1860, Trenton *Free Press*, March 11, 1861, Concord *New Hampshire Patriot and State Gazette*, April 17, 1861 in Perkins (ed.), *Northern Editorials on Secession*, II, p. 675, I, pp. 83, 361, II, 778; Cincinnati *Enquirer*, Dec. 27, 1860; Stampp, *And the War Came*, p. 209.

were established, others might follow, with catastrophic consequences for the political stability and economic development of the entire continent. Abhorrent though war might be, disunion was still worse. According to the Peoria *Daily Democratic Union* it was "a moral, physical and financial impossibility."[252]

At this point Democratic concerns for state's rights and a limited federal government came into head-on collision, as they had never done before, with Democratic attachment to the Union. Although Democrats could respect the rights of the states and could allow each local community to determine its stance on slavery, most of the northern phalanx could not allow their nation to be broken up.

Some northern Democrats had previously criticised Buchanan for failing to act against the secessionists. But when the South Carolinians opened fire on the relief expedition sent by Lincoln to Fort Sumter, northern Democrats overwhelmingly (though not unanimously) rallied to the government. Douglas himself responded to Lincoln's call for 75,000 volunteers by proposing a figure of 200,000 instead. "We must fight for the country," he declared, "and forget all differences." One of his most influential (and wealthy) supporters, August Belmont of New York, at that time acknowledged that a few months previously he had favoured peaceable secession. But, he added, things had "changed very materially." The Confederacy had gone ahead and committed "lawless acts," (probably Belmont had in mind the seizure of federal property) and had launched its attack on Fort Sumter. This had left "every loyal citizen" with "the choice between a firm and manful support of our Government or a disgraceful drifting of our nationality into a state of anarchy and dissolution similar to the fate of Mexico and Central America."[253]

This was the dominant Democratic reaction. Some criticised Lincoln for having pursued a policy calculated to induce the southerners to fire the first shot. But even these critics did not necessarily oppose the War or Lincoln's Proclamation calling for volunteers. The Chicago *Times*, for example, announced that the attack on Sumter had done "what Mr Lincoln hoped it would do"; "it gave to the loyal states a rallying point." But if the implication was that Lincoln had been guilty of warmongering the *Times* quickly changed tack and referred to "that majestic outburst of patriotism which astonished the world, and has placed the security of the Union beyond a doubt." Many northern Democrats now reacted bitterly to what they saw as a southern betrayal. The sacrifices they had been asked to

252. Johannsen, *Douglas*, pp. 850–852; Stephen A. Douglas to Charles H. Lanphier, Dec. 25, 1860, in *Letters of Douglas*, p. 504; Peoria *Daily Democratic Union*, Oct. 5, 1860 in Perkins (ed.), *Northern Editorials on Secession*, I, p. 49.
253. Johannsen, *Douglas*, pp. 859–860; August Belmont to Lionel de Rothschild, May 21, 1861, in *Letters . . . of Belmont*, p. 49,

make and had made for more than a decade seemed to have been for naught. Even Douglas acknowledged that he had probably conceded too much to the South, an assertion that would have astonished those of his southern critics who now quite sincerely believed him no better than a Republican or abolitionist.[254]

For many Democrats the intense patriotism that had led them, in the name of national unity, to surrender much to the South, now produced precisely the opposite reaction. Although some urged that secessionists be treated even in war as brethren, others did not shrink from the bitterest condemnation. Secessionists were "traitors who seek to destroy the Republic." "Let our enemies," it was said, "perish by the sword"[255]

One by one influential northern Democrats swung behind the war policy after the attack on Sumter. Newspapers like the Pittsburgh *Post*, the Detroit *Free Press*, the Rochester *Daily Union and Advertiser* and the *Boston Herald* fell into line, indeed in many instances became ardent supporters of the war.[256] Horatio Seymour, after counseling compromise and concession, dramatically changed tack after Sumter while individuals like Daniel Dickinson, Caleb Cushing and Fernando Wood who had only a few months earlier even been prepared to swallow the slave code, now came out for war and the Union. New Jersey was one of the few northern states where the Democrats were in control at the time of the secession crisis. But the legislature now unanimously agreed that "the most certain and speedy mode of restoring peace is by the most vigorous prosecution of the present war." Although one or two individuals, like Clement Vallandigham of Ohio and Jesse Bright of Indiana, still harbored sympathies for the secessionists and although many northern Democrats insisted that the War should be solely to preserve the Union and not to further the antislavery cause, the reaction of the great mass of northern Democrats ensured that the northern war effort would be launched with the support of the overwhelming majority of the northern people.[257]

254. Chicago *Daily Times*, June 12, 13, 1861; see also Buffalo *Daily Courier*, April 16, 27, 1861, in Perkins (ed.), *Northern Editorials on Secession*, II, pp. 848, 722–723, 716–717, 1068
255. Philadelphia *Press*, April 16, 1861, Madison *Daily Patriot*, April 24, 1861, see also Boston *Herald*, March 4, 1861, in Perkins (ed.), *Northern Editorials on Secession*, II, pp. 742, 749, 1010.
256. Pittsburgh *Post*, April 15, 1861, Detroit *Free Press*, April 29, May 30, 1861, Rochester *Daily Union and Advertiser*, May 2, 1861, Boston *Herald*, April 15, 1861 in Perkins (ed.), *Northern Editorials on Secession*, II, pp. 738, 754, 1025, 818–819, 730–731.
257. *Speeches ... of Seymour*, pp. 33–36; *Speeches, etc. of Dickinson*, II, *passim*; Silbey, *Respectable Minority*, p. 39, Stampp, *And the War Came*, pp. 208–209, 212, 289; Richard J. Carwardine, *Lincoln* (Harlow, 2003), pp. 160–162.

## III

And Buchanan himself? The old man who sat in the White House retained responsibility for the fate of the nation in the days and months following secession. Lincoln was elected in November but did not take office until March. Buchanan was initially paralysed. He made it clear that he regarded secession as unconstitutional but he made it equally clear that he felt the constitution gave him no powers to combat it. Like other Democrats he could not conceive how the nation could survive on the basis of coercion. "It may be safely asserted," he announced in his final Annual Message delivered at the beginning of December 1860, "that the power to make war against a state is at variance with the whole spirit and intent of the constitution." If such a war resulted in victory over a state that had seceded, he continued, "how are we to govern it afterwards? Shall we hold it as a province and govern it by despotic power?" Like other Democrats he could not envisage even a war that was militarily successful, let alone one that ended in defeat:

> In the nature of things, we could not by physical force control the will of the people and compel them to elect Senators and Representatives to Congress and so perform all the other duties depending upon their own volition and required from the free citizens of a free State as a constitutional member of the Confederacy.[258]

By now Buchanan's cabinet was hopelessly divided with its southern members either supporting secession or at any rate opposing any measures against it, and northern members like Lewis Cass advocating a much firmer response. Buchanan would not have the forts strengthened, on the grounds that this was too provocative. Major Robert Anderson, who was in command of the Union forces in Charleston harbor had been occupying Fort Moultrie. When under cover of darkness on December 26, he moved to Sumter, on the grounds that it would be more easily defended, southerners put pressure on the President to order Anderson out of Sumter. Perhaps Buchanan would have bowed to southern pressure, as he had done so many times before, if Moultrie had not been quickly taken by the Confederates. But by December 31 Buchanan had announced that he would not comply with the southerners' request. The President now reorganised his administration and brought into it some inflexible Unionists like John A. Dix, the old New York Barnburner. For a time Buchanan was in unfamiliar territory, unpopular in the South, popular in the North. Only the southern attitude endured.[259]

258. Richardson (ed.), *Messages and Papers of Presidents*, V, p. 636.
259. Stampp, *And the War Came*, pp. 46, 62, 71–101; David M. Potter, *Lincoln and His Party in the Secession Crisis* (Baton Rouge, 1995), pp. 253–254.

Nothing illustrates the bankruptcy of the northern Democrats so much as Buchanan's policy, or rather the lack of it, in these weeks. Believing that both secession and coercion were unacceptable he was left with a political agenda that was almost entirely blank. Inertia ruled and it was this inertia which caused his newfound popularity in the North to evaporate. The President could propose nothing other than a settlement on the basis of the slave code, the very policy which every northern state and thus a majority of the nation had just repudiated. More generally, the northern Democrats were now bit players in a great national drama, perhaps for the first time in their history.[260]

Buchanan refused to surrender the forts, however, and he bequeathed them to Lincoln as the new president's most pressing problem. When Lincoln sent his relief expedition to Sumter, however, Buchanan, now in retirement, supported the move. And when war broke out, he supported that too. "The assault upon Fort Sumter," he declared, with only slight exaggeration, "has made as unanimous throughout the North." It was a strange ending to a career that had been based upon the conciliation of the South and upon a dogged insistence, made over decades, that the North was primarily to blame for the sectional controversy. But the fact that few people cared what the former president believed was perhaps a fitting commentary on the fate of the northern Democrats in the spring of 1861.[261]

## Conclusion

During his famous debates with Abraham Lincoln, Stephen A. Douglas, like many other northern Democrats, repudiated the notion that a "House Divided" into free and slave states could not stand. According to Douglas it could stand "for ever." He and other northerners saw no reason to believe that the "House" to which Lincoln referred, the nation, or the other "House" with which they so fervently identified, the Democratic party, could not continue to accommodate both slavery and free labour indefinitely. In his view, both the federal government and the Democratic party had traditionally been neutral or impartial between free states and slave states. They could and should continue in the same vein.[262]

Douglas was wrong, however, both in his understanding of the past and in his prognosis. The Democratic party had never been neutral on the question of slavery and since it was the dominant force in national politics, nor was the nation itself. Instead the party was for over half a century the

260. Richardson (ed.), *Messages and Papers of Presidents*, V, pp. 634–666.
261. *Works of Buchanan*, XI, p. 187; see also p. 181.
262. Roy F. Basler (ed.), *The Collected Works of Abraham Lincoln*. 9 vols. (New Brunswick, 1953–1955), III, pp. 286–287.

principal institution which secured the hegemony of slaveholders in the antebellum Republic.

It is important to note, however, that the principles of the party were in no sense reducible to the class interests of slaveholders, in that many of them had their roots in the European past and had been highly visible in societies that had no slaves. Yet they operated in the United States to maintain the slaveholders' hegemony. What were they? First, Democratic insistence upon limited government, and especially on the limited extent of federal power, operated to reduce the threat from antislavery sentiment generated outside the South. The doctrines of state's rights and limited government had other important functions and had a genuine appeal to many who were in no way concerned to protect slavery in the South. Nonetheless both benefitted the slaveholders enormously. Second, the emphasis on agriculture and agrarian virtue, themes which went back deep into Antiquity, permitted the slaveholders to reach out into areas of the South in which slaveless farms predominated, as well as into the North, and launch a powerful appeal on the basis of shared interests and values. Third, the stress on racial differences, which had always characterised the Democratic tradition, operated to disable the forces of abolition and to cement loyalty to the slaveholders' governments in the South. Fourth, the Democratic emphasis on individual moral autonomy – provided once again that blacks were excluded – served to empower each individual to choose whether or not to hold slaves, uncoerced by the views of others. Again the effect was to disable opposition to slavery. In none of these strands of Democratic ideology, state's rights, limited government, agrarianism, racism, and moral individualism, did slavery need to be explicitly defended. As men like Stephen A. Douglas recognised, the ideology was not explicitly proslavery. But as the antislavery militants who opposed the Kansas-Nebraska Act were aware, it furthered the interests of slaveholders in a nonrandom way and was thus, as men like Stephen A. Douglas were unable to recognise, functionally proslavery,

The Democratic party, implicitly the champion of slaveholding interests, had been at the same time explicitly the champion, indeed the virtual embodiment, of American democracy. Although the equality it preached was for adult white males only, the party nevertheless had been home in the days of Andrew Jackson to those who were willing, indeed eager, to appeal to and mobilise public opinion in ways that shocked traditional elites. Moreover, important and sometimes dominant sections of the Democratic party, especially in times of financial disturbances and dislocations, had been willing to denounce the privileges of the commercial and manufacturing elites of the nation. Such had been the character of "Jacksonian Democracy" in the 1830s and early 1840s.

Even in these years, however, the slaveholding elite had enjoyed a unique status. Whilst merchants, manufacturers and bankers had been the targets of Democratic radicalism, the wealth and power of the slaveholder, since it was not derived from "partial" legislation, had alone been immune. In the democratic tradition of the antebellum Republic, exemplified by Thomas Jefferson, John Taylor of Caroline and Andrew Jackson, slavery and slaveholding played a vital role.[263]

Even in the heyday of Jacksonian Democracy, however, some southerners had entertained serious doubts as to whether the Democratic party could provide sufficient protection to slaveholders. Observing the growth of abolitionism in the 1830s, John C. Calhoun had come to feel that northern opinion could not in the long term be trusted and he demanded overt recognition of the rights of southern slaveholders. He demanded, in effect, cast iron constitutional guarantees for slaveholders rather than the loose, hegemonic control afforded by Jacksonian Democracy. In the 1850s this was the approach, or one of the approaches, that southerners in general took. In the final antebellum years it would culminate in the demand for a territorial slave code.

The difficulty for the Democratic party was that northern society was generating an ever deeper hostility towards slavery, even as southerners' confidence in their peculiar institution was soaring to new heights. The economic growth of the final antebellum years operated to confirm each section's attachment to its labour system. In the North it strengthened the commitment to free labour and deepened the hostility to slavery; in the South it confirmed that the prosperity of the region was, to an even greater degree than hitherto, dependent upon its slave labour foundation. These processes operated to pull the Democratic party apart, to strip the party of its intellectual *accoutrements* and expose its slaveholding base, as never before. The result was that by 1860 the party enjoyed unprecedented power in the South. But equally apparent was its chronic weakness in the North. As of 1860 the Democrats were reduced to fewer than thirty percent of the North's seats in each house of Congress, and in the states controlled a similar percentage of legislatures and occupied a similar proportion of Governors' mansions.[264] Although Democratic support for the War would, in the next four years, be important in the North, it was clear that the struggle was one in which Republicans would play the main part

---

263. To recapitulate an argument from the first volume of this study: a precapitalist radical tradition had come to prominence in the United States because it was quite compatible with the maintenance of the rights of an extraordinarily powerful and determined social group: the slaveholders of the South. Only the emphasis on race, not found in its European antecedents, betrayed the social character of the dominant class – see p. 347.

264. Silbey, *Respectable Minority*, p. 18.

throughout. Rather than initiating, Democrats now reacted. When the War became a war to end slavery, even the War Democrats reacted badly. Thus the party's southern sympathies continued to be in evidence.

The Act that Stephen A. Douglas introduced in January 1854 was the last great measure of the antebellum Republic for which the Democrats could claim responsibility. With the benefit of hindsight it is clear that the Kansas-Nebraska Act did much to destroy the party, not merely by virtue of its immediate electoral impact, but also because of the sequence of events that ensued in Kansas, the impossibility of maintaining a policy on slavery in the territories that was acceptable to both the northern and the southern wings, the furore that accompanied the Lecompton constitution and the Dred Scott decision. But it is important not to leap to the conclusion (as some of his enemies did and as some historians have) that Douglas and his supporters had foolishly brought on the Civil War. At the start of 1854 it had been impossible to organise the nation's territory on the basis of the *status quo*: southerners had effectively had a veto on the settlement of the northern part of the Louisiana Purchase and only the repeal (or perhaps the circumvention) of the Missouri Compromise would induce them not to employ it. It is quite true that Douglas underestimated the impact in the North of the repeal. But despite the relative youth of congressional nonintervention, the policy, as we have seen, had deep roots in Democratic party tradition and Democratic ideology. At the start of 1854 the traditional Democratic need to open up the West clashed with the traditional Democratic need to conciliate, and further the interests of, slaveholders in the South. This was an impasse that by the start of 1854 had proved beyond the capacity of any statesman, even one as resourceful as Stephen A. Douglas, to remove. It was difficult for Douglas, or for other northern Democrats, to acknowledge the existence of this impasse. Nevertheless he implicitly understood what historians have ignored: a nation which could not properly govern the territory it had acquired was in severe difficulties, perhaps even in crisis. But, if the Kansas-Nebraska Act was his way of resolving the crisis, its passage instead merely deepened it.

By the final antebellum years the Democratic party in the North was in a woeful condition. It was a party committed to territorial expansion in order to extend the area of freedom but on inspection it was apparent that the only territory to be annexed would be slave territory. It was a party committed to Jeffersonian agrarianism but it was could not match its opponents in facilitating the settlement of the West. It celebrated the Declaration of Independence but could only depict it in curiously shrunken form. It insisted on the superiority of free labour to slavery but had no sustained analysis that could articulate the conditions facing northern labourers. Benefiting from the support of southerners, it ended the decade by resorting to an unprecedented degree of bribery in the North to win support for its policies. By the time of the secession crisis, its national leader, himself a northerner, confessed from the White House his inability to deal with the issue. A few months later, in June 3 1861, Stephen A. Douglas, its best loved statesman since Andrew Jackson, died. The death of the one and the obscurity into which the other had by then sunk confirmed the reality which recent events had suggested: the Democratic party, like the Republic itself, was in utter disarray. Like Stephen A. Douglas himself both were casualties of the conflict over slavery.[265]

265. Douglas died aged 48, almost certainly prematurely as a result of his endeavours on behalf of national unity.

# 4

# Political realignment: Collapse of the Whigs and neo-Whigs, 1848–1861

## Introduction: Whiggery, neo-Whiggery and their discontents

On June 29, 1852 Congress assembled and then immediately adjourned. The reason was that one of its most illustrious members, Senator Henry Clay of Kentucky, had died. Over the next days and months eulogies were pronounced on Clay, one of them, thought by some to be the best, by New York's Senator, William H. Seward, another by Abraham Lincoln, the little known, single-term Congressman from Illinois. By 1860 more than forty towns and counties had been named after the Kentuckian and there were monuments to his memory in cities north and south, east and west, a testament to his popularity throughout the nation. On his death Clay became the first American to be honoured by having his body lie in State in the Rotunda of the Capitol.[1]

Almost four months later the nation heard that Clay's long time Whig ally and rival, Daniel Webster of Massachusetts, had died too. Again there were outpourings of grief across the nation. Webster had by the time of his death won considerable respect and admiration in the South. Elsewhere in the nation he had long been venerated as, with Clay and John C. Calhoun, one of the greatest statesmen of his age, an orator of unsurpassed power and an adornment to the nation.

Clay and Webster were acknowledged as the great leaders of the Whig party, even though neither had realised his all-consuming ambition of winning the presidency. At the time of their deaths, there was peace between the sections and public opinion gave almost all of the credit to the Compromise settlement of 1850, and much of it to these two Whig leaders who had played such prominent roles in securing it. This surely strengthened the possibility that the Whig party would be able to survive their demise. Moreover, in 1852 a Whig president occupied the White House. Here was additional cause for Whig optimism.

---

1. Merrill D. Peterson, *The Great Triumvirate: Webster, Clay and Calhoun* (New York, 1987), pp. 487–498.

Yet there were fundamental and chronic problems within the Whig party. It was deeply divided. Although never on friendly terms, Clay and Webster had seen eye to eye on the principal issues of their era, from the Bank of the United States and the protective tariff to the sectional controversy and the Compromise of 1850. But with William Seward's brand of Whiggery they had clashed repeatedly. Whilst Seward might pronounce a eulogy on Clay, both Clay and Webster had been anything but eulogistic towards Seward's claim in 1850 that there was a "higher law" than the Constitution, one which enjoined opposition to slavery. But most northern Whigs had followed Seward in viewing the Compromise with deep misgivings. In the South meanwhile, although the course taken by Clay and Webster might earn them the gratitude of moderate opinion, their supporters were repeatedly told that the party image was tarnished and its very survival threatened by the presence within its ranks of antislavery zealots like Seward. Clay and Webster suffered the fate of many moderates in politics, they were attacked from both directions, and for opposite reasons.

This was not the only cause of division. Although they never joined nativist organisations, both Clay and Webster had reservations about the political power of immigrants. Seward, however, had none and his was the approach that prevailed. Even as the two leaders were expiring, the Whig party was attempting to appeal to the immigrant vote as never before. The effect would be to leave the party vulnerable to a nativist backlash, should one occur. Similarly, by 1852 the temperance question, in which neither Clay nor Webster had ever taken much interest, was highly prominent in some areas of the North. The state of Maine had the previous year passed a prohibitory law, known throughout the nation as the "Maine Law." This too would create problems for the Whig party.

When the Whigs won their second presidential victory in 1848, few would have guessed that it would be their last. Indeed the presidential contest of 1852, the outcome of which neither Clay nor Webster lived to see, was the last which the party even contested. By 1856 two of Clay's northern eulogisers, Lincoln and Seward, had joined the Republican party; by that date their southern supporters had also found new homes. The second party system, which had pitted Democrat against Whig and which had been in existence since the time of Andrew Jackson, was no more.

Nonetheless Whig ideals were not themselves defunct. In 1860 the Constitutional Union party emerged to challenge for the presidency and, as we shall see, it espoused an almost letter-perfect Whiggery. Moreover the two political movements which came to prominence in the early or mid-1850s, whose existence we have already noted, and which in fact played a part in bringing about the Whig collapse, were ironically themselves vehicles through which Whiggish ideas and aspirations were expressed. The temperance reformers in the 1850s (and earlier) espoused views many of which were in full accord with Whig priorities and the same was true of the so-called Know Nothing party, the overtly anti-immigrant or nativist organisation which burst onto the political scene in the summer of 1854. Although it was not only erstwhile Whigs who were members of temperance societies, supported the Know Nothings or rallied to the Constitutional Unionists in 1860, an analysis of the ideology of these organisations suggests that it is legitimate to refer to them as "neo-Whig" in attitude and orientation.[2]

Nevertheless there were important points of difference between Whigs and Know Nothings, and between Whigs and temperance reformers. Moreover the continuities should in no way obscure a basic discontinuity. The Whigs had been for a little more than twenty years a major political party; around 1854 they collapsed and neither temperance reformers nor nativists proved to have the popular appeal and the staying power to replace them in the long or even medium term. And the Constitutional Union party of 1860 would prove even more transient and even less able to shape the future of the nation. Thus the neo-Whigs of the 1850s and 1860 ended by being as powerless as the regular Whigs had become.

The collapse of a major party is an exceptional event in the history of the United States. Indeed the collapse of a mass party might be said to be a unique event, since some have questioned whether the Federalists or the National Republicans, the only other major parties to suffer extinction, were ever truly mass organisations. Moreover, the collapse of the Whig party and its replacement by the Republicans clearly marked a stage in the escalation of the sectional controversy which was to erupt with such extraordinary ferocity in 1861. The Whig demise was part of the realignment of the 1850s which would by 1860 pit an almost solidly Democratic South against an equally solidly Republican North. For these reasons it has attracted the attention of many historians.[3]

Until comparatively recently there was a well-established orthodoxy on this question. It held that the Whig party was the victim primarily of sectional conflict which was detonated in 1854 by the introduction of the Kansas-Nebraska act. When southern Whigs supported this essentially Democratic measure, northern Whigs, who were among its bitterest

---

2. For a discussion of the similarities (and differences) between Whigs and Republicans see pp. 205–234.
3. Undoubtedly the main attempts to explain this have been offered by Michael Holt, whose contribution cannot be questioned. See Holt, "The Mysterious Disappearance of the American Whig Party," Commonwealth Fund Lecture University College London, Feb. 16, 1990 (to which I was respondent) and, more recently, *The Rise and Fall of the American Whig Party: Jacksonian Politics and the Onset of the Civil War* (New York, 1999), which I reviewed in *Reviews in American History*. See "*The Whigs, the Wood and the Trees,*" *Reviews in American History*, XXVIII (2000), pp. 215–222.

enemies, announced that they could no longer associate with them. As a result the Whig party died. Of course historians always recognised that sectional stresses had existed within the party for some time but they laid great emphasis upon the Kansas-Nebraska act as the primary factor in the party's collapse.[4]

This interpretation had certain historiographical characteristics. First, it placed a heavy emphasis upon federal politics; the role of events in Washington was accorded primary causal significance. Second, it assumed that the voters were motivated by factors which can be identified relatively easily from sources such as newspapers, manuscripts, legislative debates, and political speeches. And third, it downplayed the cultural diversity which existed within the sections and especially within the North and which helped bring about, in the final years of the Whig party, the emergence of the temperance question (which was entirely a local and state issue) and the recrudescence of the nativist movement (whose energies focussed upon local and state as much as, if not more than, federal issues).

Beginning in the 1960s, however, a reaction against this interpretation began. Much influenced by contemporary work in the social sciences, its exponents took their cue from the claim that "at least since the 1820s...ethnic and religious differences have tended to be *relatively* the most important sources of political differences in the electorate." This approach implied a shift away from federal politics to local politics, where such ethnic and religious conflicts were most likely to be played out. More important, it also implied that, whereas historians had frequently assumed that economic or class differences underpinned party conflict, the real sources of disagreement lay elsewhere. It was argued that Americans had been since the Jacksonian era at least, in agreement upon the "fundamental" values of the nation. These were in essence, the values of democracy (for adult white males) and capitalism. Yet that very agreement on fundamentals, it was said, was such as to "permit almost every kind of social conflict, tension, and difference to find political expression." In this sense therefore, ethnocultural tensions were seen to be operating within a consensus on more fundamental values and to have derived their political potency precisely because such a consensus existed.[5]

---

4. A succinct statement of this view was made by Eric Foner in an essay published in 1974. "We can date exactly the final collapse of that [second party] system – February 15, 1854 – the day a caucus of southern Whig Congressmen and Senators decided to support Douglas's Nebraska bill, despite the fact that they could have united with northern Whigs in opposition both to the repeal of the Missouri Compromise and the revival of sectional agitation" – see Eric Foner, *Politics and Ideology in the Age of the Civil War* (New York, 1980), p. 45. In fact Foner's view was far more nuanced than that of his predecessors – see note 21 on p. 210.

5. Lee Benson, *The Concept of Jacksonian Democracy: New York as a Test Case* (Princeton, 1961), pp. 165, 275.

These claims were advanced for various different eras in the American past. Thus it was argued, for example, that partisanship in the second half of the nineteenth century "was not rooted in economic distinctions" but rather "mirrored irreconcilably conflicting value conflicts emanating from divergent ethnic and religious subcultures"[6] As far as the political upheaval of the 1850s was concerned, scholars who wrote within this framework and whose work was quickly dubbed the "new political history," dissented sharply from the old orthodoxy. They argued that in the 1850s ethnocultural conflicts reached new heights. The temperance cause, for example, enjoyed unparalleled success in some of the states of the Union, while the nativist movement, whose most visible agent was the Know Nothing (later known as the American) party, enjoyed in the mid-1850s a series of electoral triumphs which must rank as among the most extraordinary in all of American history and which left even the most seasoned contemporary observers bemused and uncomprehending. Some scholars have argued that these ethnocultural factors – the divisions within the electorate over religious issues, the conflicts over moral questions like temperance, the animosities between different, traditionally hostile ethnic groups, some of them only recently arrived in the United States – were the driving force behind political change in general in the 1850s and behind the collapse of the Whig party in particular.[7]

As we shall see, it is easy to acknowledge that the "new political history" has deepened our understanding of American politics in the nineteenth century and of the collapse of the American Whig party. As we shall also see, however, it is important not to exaggerate the success or the significance of this revisionism. There are two major problems. First, it is doubtful whether ethnic and religious conflict can be separated from economic and class issues in the way that the new political history assumes. For, as we shall see, it was when ethnocultural factors converged with economic and class issues and with traditional concerns about the suitability of the lower orders for inclusion in a democratic polity that they came to the fore. In other words "ethnocultural" conflicts over temperance and immigration did not derive their potency because of agreement upon the "fundamentals"; instead they represented a disagreement about political

---

6. Paul Kleppner, *The Third Electoral System, 1853–1892: Parties, Voters and Political Culture* (Chapel Hill, 1979), p. 144. See also Kleppner, *The Cross of Culture: A Social Analysis of Midwestern Politics, 1850–1900* (New York, 1970).

7. Other important works emphasising the role of ethnocultural factors in the upheaval of the 1850s include Ronald P. Formisano, *The Birth of Mass Parties, Michigan 1827–1851* (Princeton, 1971); William E. Gienapp, *The Origins of the Republican Party 1852–1856* (New York, 1987); Michael F. Holt, *Forging a Majority: The Formation of the Republican Party in Pittsburg, 1848–1860* (New Haven, CT, 1969); Joel Silbey, *The Partisan Imperative: The Dynamics of American Politics before the Civil War* (New York, 1985).

democracy and an attempt to reform the lower orders and render them fit members of American society. Class issues were thus at the heart of these movements, however vociferously (and sincerely) their supporters might claim that the United States was (or should be) a classless society.

Second, there is ample reason to doubt whether, even in this larger sense, ethnocultural factors played the key role in the collapse of the Whig party and the realignment of the 1850s that has been claimed. In other words, although those historians who asserted that sectionalism was the primary factor in the Whig collapse can be criticised on some significant counts, their overall causal schema needs relatively minor modification rather than total abandonment. As we shall see, the 1850s witnessed a large expansion in the supply of land, labour, and capital in the United States and this expansion unleashed sectional animosities and economic reconfigurations that would prove fatal to Whigs and neo-Whigs alike.

## The Whigs, 1848–1852

### I

When the Compromise measures of 1850 were finally hammered out, the nation breathed a huge sigh of relief. Although there were many dissidents, both North and South, who felt that the package was unacceptable, it soon transpired that within the nation as a whole the settlement was popular. The objections that were voiced on both sides of the Mason-Dixon Line to specific items led some to condemn the settlement outright but a larger number to acquiesce in the measures they did not like and to rejoice in those of which they approved. As we have seen, most supporters of the Compromise hailed it as a final settlement of the sectional controversy.

The Whig party had played a full part in this achievement. Although a majority of northern Whigs were opposed to the Compromise, the great body of southern Whigs with Henry Clay at their head were among its strongest supporters.[8] Moreover even in the North the support of conservative Whigs like Daniel Webster and Millard Fillmore had been enormously important. Fillmore, upon entering the White House in July 1850 on the death of President Zachary Taylor, had thrown the weight of the administration behind the settlement. Webster's famous conciliatory speech of March 7 1850 had convinced many southerners that northerners were indeed prepared to heed the voice of reason.[9] Although the

8. The fact that southern Whigs (and northern Democrats) were the most loyal advocates of compromise has been noted by many historians, explained by almost none. I have attempted an explanation in the first volume of this study – see pp. 476–492.
9. This is disputed in Holman Hamilton, *Prologue to Conflict: The Crisis and Compromise of 1850* (New York, 1964), p. 82 but the southern Whigs' admiration for

Compromise owed much to Democrats also, especially in the North, and especially to the heroic efforts of Stephen A. Douglas, there seemed no reason to expect that the Whigs would be disadvantaged by the events of 1849–1851. And since they had actually won the presidency itself, for only the second time, in 1848, it appeared at first glance that the party's future was assured. If the sectional question had indeed been removed from politics, why could Whig and Democrat not continue to battle as they had since the 1830s with each party strong in both North and South, each frequently able to win the presidency outright and each regularly able to enact at least significant portions of its legislative programme at federal, state and local levels?

In fact the years following the midcentury crisis saw not a revitalisation but rather a gradual disintegration and a final collapse of the American Whig party. To explain these developments it is essential to recall the origins and the subsequent development of the second party system. The Whig party had been formed in 1833–1834 as a result of President Andrew Jackson's decision to remove the federal deposits from the Bank of the United States. But it was not until Jackson himself had left the White House in 1837, perhaps not until the great victories of 1840 that the Whigs achieved real cohesion. The Panic of 1837 reopened deep divisions within the American political community over the nature and role of government. In addition it drove many to ask whether the nation's agrarian traditions and egalitarian values (as applied to adult white males) were being eroded by the process of commercial development which it had been experiencing but which had come to an abrupt halt with the financial dislocation of the late 1830s and the early 1840s. In these years and prior to the recovery which began around 1843, the Democratic party had been increasingly the party of antibank radicalism, with the more militant Democrats voicing opposition to banks at local as well as federal level (and also to manufacturing and the tariff and to internal improvements, whether sponsored by federal or state governments). Moreover the very successes of Democratic radicalism and the electorate's apparent enthusiasm for attempts to dismantle the nation's financial structures reawakened in the minds of most Whigs concerns about popular government itself. Although the Whigs were, of course, committed republicans, many of them were in no sense committed to the highly populistic politics of conflict championed by Andrew Jackson. These concerns too fed into the party conflicts of the late Jacksonian era.[10]

---

Webster and his role in the Compromise was illustrated by, among other things, their willingness to see him nominated for the presidency in 1852.

10. John Ashworth, *"Agrarians" and "Aristocrats": Party Political Ideology in the United States, 1837–1846* (London, 1983).

It was therefore no coincidence that the zenith of the two-party system came at a time of fiscal and commercial instability. Economic distress made for partisan conflict which in turn, insofar as it cut across divisions over slavery and related issues, ironically made for sectional harmony and, in this sense, national unity. This causal relationship persisted after economic recovery began in the mid-1840s. Now economic stability blunted Democratic radicalism and steadily removed the threat to the nation's commercial infrastructure. Moreover, the same process of economic advancement in the North weakened the influence of those (primarily conservative Whigs) who had a direct tie and a major interest in southern plantation slavery. The effect was to remove a constraint on the growth of antislavery sentiment there, to the obvious detriment of a party which aspired to maintain an appeal on each side of the Mason-Dixon Line. In the South meanwhile, economic growth deepened confidence in the southern economy, and steadily removed the rationale for the programme of economic diversification that had been the hallmark of southern Whiggery. Thus the extraordinary growth of the final antebellum years strengthened each section's commitment to its labour system, and widened the gap between the sections even as it narrowed the gap between the parties.

The economic expansion that began in the mid-1840s thus had an enormous impact upon the political system and upon the Whig party in particular. Not only did it ease Whiggish fears of democratic populism and democratic radicalism but, in more concrete terms, it deprived the Whig economic programme of its rationale. First to abate was the banking controversy. James K. Polk's victory in the presidential election of 1844 virtually ended controversy over a national bank. Polk instead reintroduced the Independent Treasury, first established in the Van Buren years, by which the nation's finances were to be separated from its banking system. The result was to remove the question of a central bank from American politics for almost twenty years. Not until the Civil War would there be sustained or even significant pressure for the federal government to involve itself in the nation's banking system. Within the states an analogous process occurred, though here it was inevitably untidier and less complete. Within almost every state of the Union in the late 1830s and early 1840s the Democrats had sought to reform or even destroy banks. Often they had been unsuccessful with a combination of Whigs and conservative Democrats often managing to block the radicals' reforms. But in almost every state an entrepreneurial reaction accompanied the return of prosperity and a more stable banking system, sometimes the stronger because of Democratic reforms, evolved. The result was that by the late 1840s, in all but a small number of states, banking was not an issue of fundamental importance. Except for a relatively brief interlude following the Panic of 1857, this situation would also persist until the Civil War.[11]

The period from 1843 to 1861 was indeed one of extraordinary economic expansion. American economic success was closely related to the triumphs of the world economy, even though the world boom began a few years later and was not significantly interrupted by the Civil War. It owed much to the huge increase in international trade and international investment as the capitalist world created a new network of global interdependencies. This was the age of the railroad boom, enormously important in the United States, and of even greater significance in Great Britain, still the leading industrial power. Prior to 1850 the United States could boast 10,000 miles of railroad track; by 1860 the figure was 30,000. In the first forty years of the century world trade had not even managed to double; between 1850 and 1870 it increased by 260 percent.[12]

The banking systems of the more advanced economies inevitably benefited from this economic boom. Moreover the discovery of gold in California (and in Australia) fuelled the growth process still further and weakened antibank radicalism at its very source. In the 1830s and early 1840s, the dash for economic growth had left many banks overexposed and highly vulnerable to even a modest economic downturn. But now specie freely flowed into the banks. British industrialists were willing to invest in American enterprise and entrepreneurs as never before and the American financial infrastructure benefited accordingly. In effect the shortage of fixed capital, from which the nation had chronically suffered, was now largely, if not entirely, a thing of the past.

Yet ironically the Whig party, which had been the enthusiastic proponent of American economic diversification, industrialisation and development generally, was to be a casualty of this process. The Whigs had championed a public-private cooperation exemplified in the charter of the second Bank of the United States. Just as the new fiscal stability robbed Democratic radicalism of its targets, so it removed the rationale for the Whig economic programme. In short, the banks did not need defending, nor did the federal or even the state governments need to play so direct a role in supporting the financial system. A curious paradox had resulted. Democratic policy, by which *laissez-faire* would be enshrined, would result in the realisation of Whiggish aspirations for the national

11. James Roger Sharp, *The Jacksonians versus the Banks: Politics in the States after the Panic of 1837* (New York, 1970).
12. Eric Hobsbawm, *The Age of Capital, 1848–1875* (London, 1975), p. 49. There were in fact economic downturns in 1851 and 1854, but these were both mild and short-lived.

economy. But in the process the Whig programme could itself be discarded.

Thus the tariff, second only in importance to a national bank in Henry Clay's American System, itself the embodiment of Whiggery's economic programme, gradually shrank in importance. As we have seen, in 1846 the Polk administration introduced the Walker tariff which reduced rates from the relatively high levels established by the Whigs in 1842. Predicting ruin, the Whigs sat back in anticipation of substantial political dividends. But the downturn never materialised and even the costs incurred by the war with Mexico did not destabilise the government's fiscal policy. In Ireland the potato famine stimulated grain sales to Europe while the rapid increase in specie circulation set in train a mild inflation which had benign effects upon both profitability and investment. American manufacturing itself entered upon a period of unprecedented progress. Its predominant sector was probably farm machinery where the United States in any case had a technological lead and where there was in consequence little need for a protective tariff.

It is possible that the American economy would have performed even better behind a tariff wall but the weight of political opinion in favour of a tariff for revenue alone together with the demonstrable economic triumphs of the era meant that there was little pressure for change. The Panic of 1857 would, once again, introduce new considerations but by then the Whig party had been disbanded.

Ironically the Whig retreat from the protective tariff began only a short time after the party had achieved real unity on the question. The conversion of many southern Whigs to the tariff their party had passed in 1842 occurred after, rather than at the time of, its passage; a majority of them had initially opposed it. This was especially true in the states of the Deep South, in most of which the Whigs were in any case chronically weak. Here the important exception was Georgia where the Whigs were indeed able to compete effectively. By 1844, when the entire national party united behind the presidential candidacy of Henry Clay, the Georgians were, as a leading Whig put it, "becoming more and more convinced of the advantage of a division of labor." Robert Toombs of Georgia at this time reported that southerners now "very generally considered" free trade to be "an obsolete idea." In Mississippi a similar shift took place while in the border and upper South the effect was still more pronounced. Here the tariff was championed by prominent figures like William Graham of North Carolina and the principle of protection formally endorsed by the Whig state party in Tennessee for example. Although there was never complete unity within the Whig party across the entire nation on this question, the states where there was most dissent (South Carolina, Missouri, Arkansas, Mississippi, and Alabama) were those in which the party was weakest and consequently unable to exercise much influence on national policy.[13]

As far as the South was concerned, outside states like Louisiana and Kentucky (where it was welcomed by sugar and hemp producers respectively) the tariff was most popular when it could be viewed as a possible salvation from the evils of a monocultural economy. Weakness in the agricultural sector, and especially in cotton, therefore was, to a considerable degree, conducive to support for the tariff. It followed, however, from this logic, that if the principal staple crops of southern agriculture, and especially cotton, revived, then the pressure for diversification and consequently support for the tariff, would diminish. This was precisely the process that occurred with the economic recovery of the mid-1840s. In Mississippi, for example, where the Whigs had fallen into line on the tariff question in 1844, the subject received far less attention after 1846. In the North meanwhile the very successes of manufacturing industry meant that there was simply less need, outside certain sectors like iron production, for protection. Thus economic success ironically spelled political difficulty for its foremost champions, the Whigs, in both North and South.[14]

Some of this difficulty had already become apparent by 1848. Although the presidential election of that year was one of only two in which the Whigs were ever victorious, it was in many respects a curious victory. Not only did it utterly fail to resolve the sectional crisis that was steadily assuming crisis proportions, it did not even herald the triumph of Whiggish economic policies. For the retreat from those policies had already been signalled. In April 1848 Meredith Gentry of Tennessee told Daniel Webster that "a combination of circumstances at home and abroad" had made the (Democratic) Walker tariff of 1846 "eminently successful as a revenue measure and less destructive to our home manufactures than was anticipated." The conclusion was that it would be unwise to tamper with it. Indeed this was one reason Zachary Taylor became the Whig candidate that year. Not linked with Henry Clay's American system, the General possessed, or at least appeared to possess, the essential quality of "availability." Moreover during the campaign Taylor publicly

---

13. John J. Berrien, *Speech on the Tariff* (Washington, DC, 1844), p. 16; William W. Freehling, *The Road to Disunion: Secessionists at Bay, 1776–1854* (New York, 1990), p. 436. J. G. De Roulhac Hamilton, *Party Politics in North Carolina, 1835–1860* (Durham, NC, 1916), p. 85; Holt, *Whig Party*, p. 267. See also Robert H. Tomlinson, "The Origins and Editorial Policy of the *Richmond Whig and Public Advertiser*, 1824–1865," (Unpublished Doctoral Dissertation, Michigan State University, 1971), pp. 105–116; Robert N. Elliott, *The Raleigh Register, 1799–1863* (Chapel Hill, 1955), p. 83; *Congressional Globe*, 26th Cong., 2nd Session, Appendix, p. 356 (hereafter cited in the form *CG*, 26/2, App., p. 356).
14. David N. Young, "The Mississippi Whigs, 1834–1860," (Unpublished Doctoral Dissertation, University of Alabama, 1968), pp. 114–132.

refused to answer questions concerning the classic Whig economic policies (banks, tariffs and internal improvements) and made it clear at least
in private that these issues were dead and buried.[15]

The next four years, in which he and then his Vice President, Millard
Fillmore occupied the White House, merely confirmed this diagnosis.
There were occasional murmurings of interest in the tariff. For example
in late 1848 in response to a fall in coal and iron prices, some Pennsylvanians reverted to type and began to call for a rate increase. But by now the
largest textile firms no longer needed high tariffs and indeed even opposed
them on the grounds that they encouraged unwelcome competition from
smaller and otherwise less efficient firms.[16] Taylor's death brought to the
White House a northerner who had always been strongly committed to
the tariff. In his first Annual Message of December 1850 Fillmore claimed
that the Walker tariff had "prostrated some of our most important and
necessary manufactures." He also claimed, as a good Clay Whig, that
the effect of a protective tariff would be to stimulate production so that
prices would "finally" be lower than those obtaining under a system of
free trade. Fillmore continued to insist, as Whigs had done for twenty
years (and National Republicans before them), that agriculturists needed
a home market for their produce and that this would be secured by a
protective tariff. But in 1851 he himself acknowledged in a public message that the inflow of gold from California had removed, in the popular
mind at least, the need for tariff revision. And in 1852 the Whig platform made little mention of the tariff, and none at all of the banking
question.[17]

This left only internal improvements. Here the old Whig dream of a
carefully planned federal network of transportation facilities, roads and
canals, had never really recovered from the battering it had received from
Andrew Jackson twenty years earlier. Although there was great interest in
the construction of a Pacific railroad after the acquisition of California,
this was a bipartisan issue, among the greatest supporters of which was
Illinois Democrat Stephen A. Douglas. At state level the same effect was
discernible. In the years following the Panic of 1837 insolvency had prevented most state legislatures from continuing with the schemes that had
been hatched earlier. Economic recovery in the 1840s brought a fresh surge
of activity, this time focussing upon railroads, but as so often happened,
internal improvements within the states tended to pit one locality, rather
than one party, against another. Moreover the railroads of the era were

15. Meredith P. Gentry to Daniel Webster, April 13, 1848 quoted in Holt, *Whig Party*, p.
    247, see also p. 272.
16. This point is made very effectively in Holt, *Whig Party*, pp. 686–687.
17. James D. Richardson (ed.), *A Compilation of the Messages and Papers of the Presi-
    dents, 1789–1897* (Washington, DC, 1899), V, pp. 84, 169–170.

essentially private corporations rather than the public or public-private enterprises of previous decades.[18]

The problems with the traditional Whig economic policies were reflected in somewhat different ways in the different states. In Arkansas, for example, the *Arkansas Whig*, from its first issue in 1851 developed some classically Whiggish ideas on the need for government intervention in the economy. The editor argued, rather questionably, that the Founding Fathers had favoured tariffs and internal improvements for the purpose of "fusing together, as it were, the populations of the different States into one mind, one interest and one sentiment: making them dependent mutually upon one another, and, by consequence, rendering them independent of foreign nations, for the necessaries of life." These were sentiments that Henry Clay might have uttered in the mid-1830s. The newspaper continued in the same vein:

> The result of their experiment is visible now, in the vast increase of human manufacture and the rapid progress of mechanics in every department of industry. A country like this, possessing every variety of climate, the richest soils and boundless facilities for internal commerce, they knew, in a natural and agricultural point of view, would grow and prosper of itself. But they felt the want of legislative aid for the protection and advancement of other branches of human industry.... They thus introduced the protective system, a system, we deem, of vital importance to the people of the Union.

The *Whig* similarly complained that the South was too dependent upon cotton and warned of the "general colonial dependency into which producers of the raw material, in a remote and half-civilised community, depending on the one profit of production for their wealth, and without manufacturing resources, must necessarily fall." Here was letter-perfect Whig doctrine.[19]

This enthusiasm for the protective tariff was accompanied by a matching warmth for internal improvements. In 1852 the *Whig* lamented that Arkansas was the only state in the Union without a single mile of railroads. But Arkansas was, as the Whigs knew only too well, a banner Democratic state and in that year the *Whig* admitted that there was no real point even in putting up a Whig candidate. The state was "hopelessly

18. Thomas B. Alexander, *Sectional Stress and Party Strength: A Computer Analysis of Roll-Call Voting in the United States House of Representatives, 1836–1860* (Nashville, 1967), pp. 77–84; Joel H. Silbey, *The Shrine of Party: Congressional Voting Behavior, 1841–1852* (Pittsburgh, 1967), pp. 121–136; Michael F. Holt, *The Political Crisis of the 1850s* (New York, 1978), p. 115, *Whig Party*, pp. 687, 1108.
19. Material for this and the following paragraph is from the *Arkansas Whig*, May 22, 1851, Feb. 5, May 13, 1852, May 24, 1855. See also April 15, June 3, 1852, July 21, 1853, July 20, 1854.

democratic." Moreover in that year too the Democrats relaxed their traditional hostility towards internal improvements so that by 1855 the *Whig* was able to report a change in that the spirit of improvement, in the form of schools, academies and railroads, had at last come to Arkansas. But the Democrats could claim much of the credit and by then the Whig party was in total disarray. Thus the isolated voice of the *Arkansas Whig* could not disguise the unpopularity of Whig views on the tariff or the party's inability to exploit the internal improvements issue.

In Kentucky a somewhat different situation obtained. Kentucky was one of the strongest Whig states in the Union but party leaders there proved unable to exploit the traditional issues. By 1849 these issues were clearly diminishing in importance and some Democrats were modifying their party's traditional hostility to banks. State aid to internal improvements, however, resulted in some rather unsuccessful projects and in 1850 the new state constitution virtually prohibited the practice. As in other states, enthusiasm for railroads was unmistakable but as in other states too, support tended to be local and bipartisan. The result was once again to weaken the traditional Whig appeal.[20]

In Virginia the Whigs were stronger than in Arkansas, weaker than in Kentucky. Here the Richmond *Whig* in the 1850s continued to call for economic diversification, and for internal improvements and on some occasions at least, to announce the superiority of the Whig tariff of 1842 to that of 1846. On some occasions too the newspaper deplored the lack of industry in the South. John Minor Botts, one of Henry Clay's staunchest supporters, continued to advocate protection and even took the unusual step of defending a national bank. In North Carolina, traditionally one of the strongest Whig states in the South, William Graham, Whig vice-presidential candidate in 1852, and Edward Stanly, closely identified with the most conservative Whiggery, advanced almost identical arguments with some regularity in the 1850s. And similar views occasionally found expression in other states.[21]

Yet it was all on a modest scale. No presidential election turned on the issues of either the tariff or internal improvements, still less on the banking

20. Harry A. Volz, III, "Party, State and Nation: Kentucky and the Coming of the Civil War," (Unpublished Doctoral Dissertation, University of Virginia, 1982), pp. 62–68.
21. Richmond *Whig*, Jan. 31, Sept. 19, 27, Oct. 3, Dec. 16, 1850; *Speech of the Hon. John M. Botts...at Newark, New Jersey, 19 Sept. 1853* (Newark, NJ, 1853), pp. 13–14; *Speech of the Hon, John Minor Botts, of Virginia, Delivered at the Academy of Music, New York, 22 Feb. 1859* (New York, 1859), p. 21; *Speech of Edward Stanly of N. Carolina, Exposing the Consequences of the Slavery Agitation, Delivered in the House of Rrpresentatives, March 6, 1850* (Washington, DC, n.d.), pp. 6, 16; William Graham to James Graham, Jan. 6, 1851 in J. G. De Roulhac Hamilton and Max R. Williams (eds.), *The Papers of William Alexander Graham*. 6 vols. (Raleigh. NC, 1957), III, p. 270.

question. In areas where the tariff, for example, was most popular, such as Pennsylvania, the practice was for both Whigs and Democrats to favour the protective principle, as indeed they had since the inception of the second party system. Thus although the classic issues which had set Democrats against Whig did not entirely disappear in the late 1840s and 1850s, their impact, at least until 1857, was extremely limited.

The result was that the years immediately following the midcentury crisis were years when relatively little seemed to separate the major parties. Contemporaries recognised this. Of course it was natural that those who wished to see the slavery question at the centre of political debate, whether to defend or to denounce it, should point to the irrelevance of the Jacksonian issues. In some cases their careers were dependent on a reordering of the political agenda. Far more striking were the attitudes of those who had in the past been committed to Whig economic policies. Thus William Graham of North Carolina acknowledged in 1851 that there was "but little party feeling manifested as between old parties" while Meredith Gentry of Tennessee admitted the following year that the old questions and issues that had formerly divided the parties "are practically obsolete." These sentiments continued to be expressed into the mid-1850s. In 1856 they helped send many Old Line Whigs, as they were known, to the aid of James Buchanan, the old Democratic party warhorse, in the presidential contest of that year. These Whigs were primarily motivated by the fear of sectional conflict but the obsolescence of the Jacksonian issues undoubtedly cleared the way for them to vote for a party they had traditionally scorned.[22]

## II

By 1852 therefore, if not earlier, the traditional issues that had separated Whigs and Democrats had lost most of their salience. This was a major long-term factor in the collapse of the Whigs party. But at the same time sectional differences within each party continued to take their toll and for a variety of reasons the Whigs were the primary victims of this process. In the years prior to and immediately after the midcentury crisis, the Whig party was subjected to a degree of internal conflict, pitting northerners against southerners, that was quite unprecedented.

22. William Graham to James Graham, Jan. 6, 1851 in *Papers of Graham*, IV, p. 3; *Speech of M. P. Gentry of Tennessee, Vindicating His Course in the Late Presidential Election...Delivered...at Franklin, Tennessee, Nov. 20, 1852* (Washington, DC, 1853), p. 28; Charles Gayarré, *Address to the People of Louisiana on the State of Parties* (New Orleans, 1855), pp. 2–3; *Speech of Josiah Randall Esq. of Philadelphia, Chambersburg, August 6, 1856* (n.p., n.d.), pp. 1–2. See also "Letter from Thomas G. Pratt" in *Letter from the Hon. James Alfred Pearce, Senator from Maryland, On the Politics of the Day* (Washington, DC, 1856), p. 8.

Yet if the depth of conflict was new, the conflict itself was not. Since the earliest days of the second party system, indeed since the time of John Quincy Adams and even of Thomas Jefferson, the anti-Democratic (or, in the 1790s, anti-Republican) party had always tended to be anti-Southern. From the inception of their party northern Whigs had usually been more antislavery than northern Democrats and this pattern persisted throughout the era of the party system. The result was to leave southern Whigs chronically vulnerable to the charge that their party, or at least its northern wing, posed a threat to the South and to the peculiar institution. In the 1830s and the early 1840s these charges had been frequently heard but they had not usually been sufficiently potent to destroy Whig prospects in the South. The classic rejoinders for the Whigs had been either to claim (erroneously) that there was as much antislavery in the northern Democracy or (much more plausibly) that in the South the Whigs were the party of the Union, battling against the sectional extremists who were disproportionately ranged within the southern Democracy. This strategy continued to be implemented in the late 1840s and early 1850s and it was not without success. Yet for a variety of reasons its effectiveness dwindled and then finally ebbed away.[23]

The Whig party had been under pressure in the South, and especially in the Deep South where proslavery sentiment was most intense, since its very inception. In 1836 the problems of reconciling proslavery southerners like John C. Calhoun, then acting in concert with northern Whigs like Daniel Webster in opposition to the Jackson administration, had been resolved only by running different candidates in different sections of the Union. In 1840 this problem had been addressed by running a military hero, William Henry Harrison whose views on most issues were not so widely known. But even Harrison had been accused of harbouring antislavery sentiments. The General's success throughout the nation, however, suggests that these accusations had had only limited impact. In 1844 the charges were revived when Henry Clay was the Whig standard bearer, even though Clay was himself, of course, a southerner and a slaveholder. In 1844 the Whigs were pilloried in the South and especially the Deep South for betraying southern interests by opposing the immediate annexation of Texas. Clay himself found it necessary, in order to maintain ranks in the South, to announce that he was an enemy to abolition and to abolitionism, but this did not prevent his party suffering an electoral hemorrhage in the Deep South, where the Whigs did not carry even a single state.[24]

---

23. This theme of loyalty politics is especially emphasised in William Cooper, *The South and the Politics of Slavery, 1828–1856* (Baton Rouge, 1978).
24. See Charles G. Sellers, *James K. Polk: Continentalist, 1843–1846* (Princeton, 1966), "The Election of 1844" in Arthur M. Schlesinger and Fred Israel (eds.), *A History of American Presidential Elections*, Vol. 1. (New York, 1971); Michael J. Heale, *The*

In 1848 similar problems surfaced. The Whig strategy that year was in effect a synthesis of the approaches taken in 1836 and 1840. As in 1840 a military hero was selected, but as in 1836 the appeal to the voters was strikingly different on each side of the Mason-Dixon Line. In the North Taylor was lauded as a patriot who would not veto the Wilmot Proviso and the electorate was invited to support Whig congressmen in order to ensure the Proviso went through Congress. Meanwhile in the South Taylor was hailed as a southerner who could be trusted to veto the Proviso in the event that it should pass Congress. Clearly Whig unity was proving difficult to maintain.

Prior to the election, Henry Clay, with an eye as always upon the White House, had acknowledged that slavery was an evil and must not be extended. However advantageous it might have been in the North, this declaration, in conjunction with his other liabilities, had been enough to convince many southerners that Taylor should instead be their candidate. As a result, at the Whig national convention, Clay failed to command the support of a majority of delegates from a single southern state. Indeed by this time many southerners were stating, quite openly, that the nomination of an avowedly antislavery northerner would ruin the party. Since the Whigs were traditionally stronger in the North than in the South, and since most northern Whigs had strong objections to slavery, the party's vulnerability to the slavery question was exposed once again.

The state of Georgia was again of particular importance. Alexander Stephens and Robert Toombs, her leading Whigs, were convinced that their party must run Taylor, who, it was felt, could be trusted to veto the Wilmot Proviso, should it be approved by Congress. Indeed, according to Toombs, Clay's stance on slavery meant that his election "posed the greatest possible danger to the South." Yet Taylor was to prove a bitter disappointment to these southerners. They were appalled at his plan to admit California into the Union as a free state, bypassing the territorial phase, and outraged when they learned that he did not favour the extension of slavery at all. Moreover, the influence of William Seward, now widely regarded as the most dangerous politician in the land, was all too obvious within the Taylor administration. Disillusionment came relatively quickly after Taylor's election.[25]

Southern Whigs by now had emerged as strong defenders of the mid-century Compromise measures, as their votes in Congress demonstrated. And with only trivial exceptions they conspicuously absented themselves

---

*Presidential Quest: Candidates and Images in American Political Culture, 1787–1852* (Harlow, 1982).

25. Ulrich B. Phillips (ed.), "The Correspondence of Robert Toombs, Alexander H. Stephens, and Howell Cobb," *Annual Report of the American Historical Association 1911*, Vol. 2. (Washington, DC, 1913), p. 105.

from the two Nashville Conventions of 1850, where southern militants had assembled (though to little purpose). Despite, or perhaps because of this moderation on sectional issues, they were being pressured as never before by southern Democrats and compelled to demonstrate their loyalty to the South and to slavery. In Alabama Henry Hilliard, the state's leading Whig, had opposed the Mexican war. In so doing he had been in step with the Whigs nationally but out of step with most of his colleagues in Alabama. Now he was denounced for being too northern in his sympathies. Perhaps for this reason, in 1849, and to demonstrate his loyalty to the South, along with Stephens and Toombs of Georgia and three other southern Whigs, he walked out of a Whig caucus when the northern majority refused to repudiate either the Wilmot Proviso or a proposal for the abolition of slavery in the District of Columbia. The reason was simple. The dominance of the party's northern wing, as he explained with great frankness, "leaves those of us who come from heavy slaveholding Districts under the necessity of maintaining just now an independent course – lest we should seem to sanction the course of the caucus on that dangerous question." In other words the danger of seeming too sympathetic to the North here fractured Whig unity, as it had before and would again.[26]

It was thus increasingly difficult for Whigs from the Deep South to maintain their ranks. They were caught between the demands of the northern wing of their own party and the attacks of (mainly Democratic) southern militants at home. As the midcentury crisis unfolded, they sometimes seemed to be in danger of succumbing to the politics of sectional loyalty. A fellow Alabama Whig, Arthur Hopkins, recalled in 1852 that those southerners who opposed the Compromise had in 1850 "charged, in advance, all the citizens of the Slave-holding States, who might turn out to be supporters of the Compromise, with being submissionists, & traitors to the South." Their plan had been "to make it necessary for every man to prove his patriotism by denouncing the Compromise as they did, & uniting with them in their opposition to it" and the hope had been that "by the constant repetition of these charges, they . . . would be the only accusers, & the friends of the Union the only subjects of accusation." As Hopkins' remarks indicate, it was by now not easy for Alabama Whigs to reconcile the conflicting pressures placed upon them.[27]

---

26. Arthur C. Cole, *The Whig Party in the South* (Gloucester Mass, 1962), p. 161–169; Cooper, *South and Politics of Slavery*, p. 293; Carlton Jackson, "A History of the Whig Party in Alabama, 1828–1860" (Unpublished Doctoral Dissertation, University of Georgia, 1962), pp. 109–131; Henry Hilliard to Nathan Appleton, Dec. 4, 1849 quoted in Holt, *Whig Party*, pp. 468–469.

27. Arthur F. Hopkins to William Graham, April 6, 1852 in *Papers of Graham*, IV, p. 284; Holt, *Whig Party*, p. 467.

In Mississippi pro-Compromise Whigs had similar experiences. Charles C. Langdon, editor of the Mobile *Daily Advertiser*, a major Whig newspaper, was challenged by other Mississippians to state his views on the sectional controversy. The implication was, of course, that his opinions were unsound. Langdon then explained that he would advocate resistance to the North in the event of the Wilmot Proviso being passed or slavery abolished in the District of Columbia. He also denounced the abolitionists in terms that must have pleased his interrogators. But he was equally critical of the "ultras" of the South, the southern militants concentrated in the Democratic party who, he claimed, had by their very extremism "magnified the influence of the Abolitionists." Indeed Langdon insisted that without these southern "disunionists" (as he termed them) abolitionism would have "died out of itself long ago." Nonetheless Langdon felt it necessary to assure other Mississippians that if southern rights were indeed violated he would "unite with you in any measure of resistance that the people of the South may devise." Here were yet more signs of the pressures facing southern Whigs.[28]

In Kentucky meanwhile, the strongest Whig state in the entire South, the Whigs made it clear that they would embrace the Union even with the Wilmot Proviso. Yet even here the Democrats, whose strength was in any case increasing, sought to make political capital from the charge that the Whigs were disloyal to slavery and to the South.[29]

Despite this example, however, in the early 1850 southern Whigs experienced far less discomfort in the Upper South, their traditional heartland, than in the Cotton South, traditionally the home of southern militancy. In states like Kentucky, Tennessee and North Carolina (as well as Maryland and Delaware) the pro-Union stance could be maintained relatively easily. In the Deep South it was different. In three states, Alabama, Mississippi, and Georgia, the defence of the Compromise brought about a realignment of parties with a huge majority of Whigs combining with a portion of the Democrats to defend the Union against so-called "Southern Rights" parties. In no state was this a straightforward battle between Unionists and Secessionists, still less between unconditional Unionists and immediate secessionists. Rather the Southern Rights parties rejected the Compromise not because it spelled immediate doom for the South but instead because it sent the wrong signal to the North and would merely encourage further aggressions, in response to which secession might well at some stage become imperative. This was the position of Jefferson Davis,

28.  Charles C. Langdon, *Reply to the Twenty Seven* (Mobile, 1850), pp. 5–7, 11–13, 23–24.
29.  As Harry Volz observes, "The Democrats would pick up on these themes over and over again in the next few years, throwing the Whigs onto the embarrassed defensive"– see Volz "Party, State and Nation," p. 62.

for example, in Mississippi. In the same way most Unionists espoused a
highly conditional unionism which centred, as we have seen, upon the
Georgia Platform and which spelled out quite clearly the conditions under
which "resistance" and even secession might have to take place.[30] When
the Compromise measures had passed through Congress, it soon became
apparent that the Southern Rights parties faced defeat in each of the
three states. In Georgia, Howell Cobb easily defeated Charles McDonald,
the Southern Rights candidate, in the gubernatorial election of 1851. The
Union party also won almost all Georgia's seats in Congress and in addition sent Robert Toombs to the United States Senate. The outcome was
similar in Mississippi with Jefferson Davis defeated in the gubernatorial
election of 1851 by Henry Foote, and in Alabama where the Union candidates were victorious in the legislative elections of the same year.[31]

The result was to damage the prospects of southern militants throughout the South. Yet the Whigs did not benefit from this development as
much as might have been expected. In the three states where realignment had occurred, the Union Whigs did not return to the fold, not even
when their Democratic partners rejoined their former party around 1852.
Undoubtedly the reasons were the ones we have already encountered. First
there was no incentive to support the Whigs given the obsolescence of the
traditional issues that had separated the two parties. Second, there was
the danger of being tainted by association with the northern wing of the
party, which was always a greater liability in the Deep South than in the
Upper South. These problems came to a head as the presidential election
of 1852 approached.

## III

Although the struggles within the South over the Compromise had apparently ended in victory for the moderates there (disproportionately found
within the ranks of the Whig party), their success was rather less that it
seemed. Pressure from southern Democrats had been successfully resisted
but at a high price. Its defenders held that the Compromise was, and had
to be, a final settlement. The South, it was acknowledged, had conceded
much and these concessions could only be justified if they were to be
the last. It may be that some southern Whigs would have been prepared
to concede more if they had been given a free hand but the presence of
southern militants meant that they were constantly in danger of being
outflanked and of being denounced, yet again, as faithless to the South.
Thus William Graham of North Carolina received a highly revealing letter

30.  See Chapter 1.
31.  Holt, *Political Crisis*, p. 92.

from former Senator William Archer of Virginia in February of 1851 in which Archer described the tactics employed by anticompromise southerners (whom he dismissed as "factionists"). Archer observed that the Fugitive Slave Law, the one major northern concession secured in 1850, must at all costs be enforced in the North and especially in Massachusetts:

> There is . . . a very sensitive chord responsive to mischief pervading the South, on which the factionists play, the fear of *seeming* to *submit* to Northern insolence and aggression. You know as well as I do, the peril which threatens from this source. There is but one way to keep it down. It is to have strict enforcement of the Fugitive Bill, and especially in the State of Massachusetts. No Body cares much for Vermont. Her proceedings are held in contempt. Not so New York and especially Massachusetts.

Maintenance of the Compromise as a finality was thus essential to the careers of many southern Whigs and to the viability of many southern Whig state parties in the early 1850s. Almost certainly, some of them believed that the South should not in any case make any further concessions but pressure from within their states meant that many of the least militant among them simply could not afford to concede more, even if they had been willing to do so. In short they now had little freedom of manoeuvre.[32]

What made these difficulties insuperable was the attitude of northern Whigs, most of whom had opposed the Compromise on the grounds that it had surrendered too much to the South. And they themselves in the North were under pressure from Free Soilers and Liberty party veterans who, without a southern wing to propitiate, could press their antislavery convictions and demands much further. On some occasions even Democrats in the North were seeking to bid for antislavery votes. In the absence of any major economic policies with which to woo the voters, it was impossible for northern Whigs to abandon antislavery, even between 1851 and 1853 when the Compromise had been confirmed and sectional hostilities were much abated.

The situation resembled that in which in which the Whigs had run their Janus-faced campaign of 1848. A clear policy on slavery in the territories would break the party in two. Robert Winthrop of Massachusetts had feared in 1850 that any decisive congressional action either for or against

---

32. William S. Archer to William Graham, Feb. 4, 1851 in *Papers of Graham*, IV, p. 25. For the travails of one southern Whig at this time, see *Speech of Hon. Charles James Faulkner of Virginia at Reading, Pennsylvania, Sept. 4, 1852* (Washington, DC, n.d.), pp. 1–15; *Speech of Hon. C. J. Faulkner of Virginia in the House of Representatives, August 2, 1852* (Washington, DC, 1852), pp. 5–15.

slavery in the territories would "kill Whiggery at one end of the Union."[33]
Yet in 1852 northern Whigs did not in fact demand a repudiation of the
Compromise; on the contrary they would have been willing to ignore the
slavery question altogether.[34] But this neutrality was simply not enough
for southerners. They demanded both a candidate and a platform that
unequivocally endorsed the Compromise as a finality. And this they did
not get. Fearing defections to the Free Soilers or even the Democrats, most
northern Whigs could not endorse finality. They could be silent on the
slavery question in the hope that time would allow antislavery sentiment
to make itself felt and somehow further the antislavery cause. But they
could not endorse the measures of 1850 as a permanent settlement.

Southern Whigs were keen to see Millard Fillmore, closely identified
with the Compromise, become the candidate in 1852. Failing that, they
would have been pleased to take Daniel Webster, now, thanks in part to
his Speech of 7th March 1850, viewed as highly moderate on the slavery question. But northern antislavery elements within the party regarded
both as anathema, indeed as traitors to the antislavery cause. Instead
Whig leaders wanted General Winfield Scott who, like Harrison and
Taylor before him, was not clearly identified with Whig policies and who
might be expected to appeal to both pro- and anti-Compromise groups
in the North. Northerners therefore wanted a discreet silence from Scott.
But for many southerners this was simply inadequate. They feared that
Scott, like Taylor before him, was under the influence of William Seward.
In Congress attempts to pass a finality resolution and to commit the party
to it failed, with no fewer than seventy percent of the northern Whigs
opposed to the move.[35] As one Tennessee Whig complained, southerners had "no evidence whatever that a faithful adherence to the compromise" or a determination to "proclaim" it "as a final settlement ... would
henceforth be considered as part of the Whig creed." Accordingly many
southerners, including Stephens and Toombs of Georgia, Alabama's two
Union Whigs and many from the southern Whig heartland of the Upper
South, refused to attend or else walked out of the party caucus. Only a
small number of southern Whigs now remained. The plight of the party
was dramatically illustrated when a southerner warned that if it hoped to
carry even a single slave state the party must commit itself to finality. This
elicited a spectacular rejoinder from a northerner who retorted that those
supporting Scott would "never consent that the finality of the compromise measures shall be made a part of the Whig creed." The reason was
that "any candidate, whether he be General Scott or any other man, who
insists upon that, or who is nominated by a convention which affirms it,

33. Holt, *Whig Party*, p. 483.
34. A point which Holt makes very effectively.
35. Holt, *Whig Party*, p. 703.

cannot ... obtain the vote of a single northern State – not one." It seemed
that there was for the hapless Whigs no escape from this impasse.[36]

The result was a compromise that left many highly dissatisfied. A finality
resolution was incorporated into the Whig platform, as southerners had
wanted, but Winfield Scott was nominated, whom southerners believed
insufficiently committed to that plank. The attitude of Meredith Gentry
of Tennessee typified that of many southerners who were unhappy with
Scott's candidacy. Gentry refused to vote for Scott and announced within
a few days of the election that he would have supported Democratic candidate Franklin Pierce if he had thought it would have prevented Scott
carrying Tennessee. The Whigs of Tennessee had announced in 1851 that,
if forced to choose, they would prefer a pro-Compromise Democrat to
an anti-Compromise Whig and Gentry claimed that the finality resolution had been added to the platform as a sop, a purely cynical attempt to
prevent a southern bolt. He simply could not support a candidate who
failed to commit himself wholeheartedly to the Compromise of 1850 and
who was instead the choice of an antislavery Whig like William Seward.
The same view was taken by Stephens and Toombs of Georgia, who
endorsed Webster instead of Scott, and by a number of other prominent
southerners.[37]

Southerners were thus happy with the platform, unhappy with the candidate. Most northern Whigs by contrast liked the candidate but deeply
disliked the platform. They thus found it impossible to match the unity
of the Democrats whose platform and candidate endorsed finality. The
election was a catastrophe for the Whigs. Although Scott's total of popular votes was respectable, he carried only four states: Massachusetts,
Vermont, Kentucky and Tennessee. Moreover the party won only three
of the twelve gubernatorial elections held that year and by 1853 had only
five governorships (out of a total of thirty one states). In Congressional
elections the results were equally dramatic. In 1848 the party had won
fifty-seven percent of the seats contested. This had fallen to forty-two percent in 1850 and now slumped to twenty-nine percent. Although support
for the Free Soil party in the North and for a Southern Rights party in
the South was virtually negligible this did not mean that sectional animosities had played no part in the Whig debacle. In the Deep South Scott
had polled a mere thirty-eight percent of the vote.[38] Undoubtedly many

---

36. Holt, *Whig Party*, p. 703–705; Phillips (ed.), "Correspondence of Toombs, Stephens,
    and Cobb," pp. 304, 369.
37. *Speech of Gentry*, pp. 3, 5, 14–17, 25. See also Herbert J. Doherty, *The Whigs
    of Florida* (Gainesville, FL, 1959), pp. 50–55. Phillips (ed.), "Correspondence of
    Toombs, Stephens, and Cobb," p. 216. For the reaction of other Whigs to this bolt,
    see the Whig campaign sheet *The Signal*, July 10, 1852, p. 24.
38. This excludes South Carolina where there was still no popular election for presidential
    electors.

had concluded there, as throughout the nation, that if the goal were to maintain the Compromise as a final settlement, Franklin Pierce was the candidate and the Democrats were the party.[39]

In truth there was in 1852 little reason to vote Whig. There were no traditional economic policies at issue. Nor did the Whigs have anything to contribute to the debate over slavery. Little wonder therefore that many Whigs believed, when they saw the election results, that their party was dead. This was the attitude of some major figures within the party. Newspapers like the *New York Times* and the New York *Tribune* believed the party finished while Robert Toombs rejoiced in the Whig debacle and merely regretted that the party had carried Kentucky and Tennessee. His verdict illustrated the attitude of many southern Whigs, especially in the Deep South. "We can never have peace and security," he wrote, "with Seward, Greeley & Co in the ascendancy in our national councils and we can better purchase them by the destruction of the Whig party than of the Union." If the party could not rise "to the same standard of nationality as the motley crew which offers it under the name of Democracy," then, he concluded, "it is entitled to no resurrection – it will have none."[40]

By the end of 1852 therefore two distinct processes had taken their toll upon the Whigs. On the one hand, the party's traditional policies had been rendered largely superfluous by the economic boom now underway. On the other hand, the differences between the party's northern and southern wings, even at a time of relative quiescence on the slavery issue, made co-operation across the Mason-Dixon Line almost as difficult as it had been in 1850. The Whigs were without doubt at a low point. The party was not, however, dead. Instead it would linger on for a few more years. And its death would be the product of a combination of factors, some of which had been barely glimpsed at the end of 1852.

## Temperance

### I

One of these factors was the temperance movement although by 1852 this was highly visible and in fact entering upon its era of greatest success, at least prior to the twentieth century. The years 1851–1855 saw many

39. Paul Murray, *The Whig Party in Georgia* (Chapel Hill, 1948), pp. 165–168; James M. Woods, *Rebellion and Realignment: Arkansas's Road to Secession* (Fayetteville, AR, 1987), p. 57; Cooper, *South and Politics of Slavery*, pp. 342–343; Cole, *Whig Party in South*, pp. 225–227.
40. Phillips (ed.), "Correspondence of Toombs, Stephens, and Cobb," p. 322; Allan Nevins, *Ordeal of the Union: A House Dividing, 1852–1857* (New York, 1947), pp. 36–37.

states enact stringent laws prohibiting the sale of alcohol and temperance as an issue now proved as volatile as the beverages whose influence it sought to combat.[41]

The temperance movement originated in the early nineteenth century and had begun as a series of quite restrained actions on the part of a Federalist or quasi-Federalist elite in the northeast and especially in New England. Rather than advocate total abstinence, temperance reformers at this stage tolerated the use of wine and other alcoholic beverages. The movement in its earliest phase was clearly intended to reform the habits of the lower orders and to achieve this result its leaders characteristically believed they needed only to set an example of temperate drinking rather than teetotalism. In some parts of the northeast temperance in the late 1820s quickly became a major issue, though as yet at local rather than state level. By now the movement was broadening in scope and membership and major shifts in strategy, outlook and membership were becoming evident. In the early and mid-1830s total abstinence became the official goal (though not all reformers were prepared to embrace it). Here the principal arguments were to the effect that, first, the example of the moderate drinker encouraged others to turn to alcohol who themselves might subsequently become drunkards or alcoholics and second, that all drunkards began as moderate drinkers. By now the hostility to alcohol was so deep among some reformers that they believed, with Lyman Beecher, that to talk of the prudent use of alcohol was akin to recommending the prudent use of the plague.[42]

Another shift came when many reformers concluded that moral suasion would not be enough to defeat the demon rum (or the demons whiskey, wine and beer) and began to demand the legal prohibition of all, or almost all, alcohol. As we shall see, the demand for prohibition was brought about by the need to change the behaviour of groups who were not easily reached through normal channels. At first this demand was voiced at local or county level and local prohibition triumphed on a piecemeal basis in

41. On the temperance movement the work to which I am most indebted is Ian R. Tyrrell, *Sobering Up: From Temperance to Prohibition in Antebellum America, 1800–1860* (Westport, CT, 1979), an excellent study. See also Alice Felt Tyler, *Freedom's Ferment: Phases of American Social History From the Colonial Period to the Outbreak of the Civil War* (Minneapolis, 1944), pp. 308–350; John A. Krout, *The Origins of Prohibition* (New York, 1925); Joseph R. Gusfield, *Symbolic Crusade: Status Politics and the American Temperance Movement* (Urbana, IL, 1963); Jed Dannenbaum, *Drink and Disorder: Temperance Reform in Cincinnati from the Washingtonian Revival to the WCTU* (Urbana, IL, 1984).
42. Tyler, *Freedom's Ferment*, pp. 313–315, 319; Whitney R. Cross, *The Burned-Over District: The Social and Intellectual History of Enthusiastic Religion in Western New York, 1800–1850* (New York, 1950) pp. 130, 136; Gusfield, *Symbolic Crusade*, p. 212; Lyman Beecher, *Six Sermons on the Nature, Occasions, Signs, Evils and Remedy of Intemperance* (Boston, 1827), p. 38.

the 1830s and 1840s across much of the Northeast and especially in New England where it was aided by the region's strong traditions of community and town government.[43]

Despite these successes, however, the illegal selling of alcohol continued and the enforcement of local laws was often lax or nonexistent. Moreover, if a dry county or town were in close proximity to one in which alcohol was allowed, it was easy for the dedicated drinker to frustrate the reformers' efforts. By midcentury reformers began to realise that coordinated action at state level would be necessary.[44]

In the 1840s this demand was voiced increasingly frequently in the North by organisations such as the American Temperance Union. At the same time, however, (in 1840) a new temperance organisation was born, the Washingtonian movement. Washingtonian societies sprang up in many states and were more plebeian and artisanal in composition than previous reform organisations had been and in their period of greatest strength (the early and mid-1840s) they relied upon moral suasion rather than legal prohibition. They concentrated upon reforming the drunkard, and indeed gave reformed drunkards a prominent position in their organisations and at their meetings, a tactic which would have appalled the earliest temperance reformers. Nevertheless, some Washingtonians were prepared to join forces with the temperance regulars and by the 1840s the drink issue could not be ignored in the politics of many of the states of the North. The first real state-wide triumph came in 1846 in Maine when a prohibitory law was passed. This was tightened up in 1851 in a law which won fame or notoriety throughout the nation and which was dubbed the "Maine Law." By 1855 no fewer than thirteen states or territories had passed Maine Laws.[45]

Beneath these legislative achievements lay an impressive recruitment drive. As early as 1834 it was claimed that no fewer than five thousand local societies existed, with more than a million members. The Sons of Temperance, the Society established by the Washingtonians, in 1849 alone claimed more than two hundred thousand members. When the temperance reformers entered politics, therefore, the established parties were compelled, sometimes against their will, to take note.[46]

From the mid-1850s, however, and for a variety of reasons which we shall explore subsequently, an abrupt decline set in and within a couple

43. Rev. Marcus E. Cross, *The Mirror of Intemperance, and History of the Temperance Reform*, 2nd ed. (Philadelphia, 1850), p. 60.
44. Krout, *Origins of Prohibition*, p. 276.
45. Tyrrell, *Sobering Up*, pp. 151–215; Mary P. Ryan, *The Empire of the Mother: American Writing about Domesticity 1830–1840* (New York, 1982), p. 75; Tyler, *Freedom's Ferment*, p. 345.
46. Tyler, *Freedom's Ferment*, p. 325; Tyrrell, *Sobering Up*, p. 212.

of years temperance was dead as a political issue in a majority of states. The movement had experienced a remarkable, almost meteoric, rise and fall in the politics of a majority of the states of the North.

## II

The first task for the historian of temperance is to explain its growth and in particular its growth to a point at which it could exert a major political influence. The problem is the more acute since the consumption and purveying of alcohol in the colonial and early national eras had been seen as important and, on the whole, quite respectable activities, valuable since alcohol was viewed as both an aid to physical labour and a source of social conviviality. Although regulations had been in force to prevent excessive consumption, usually via local licensing restrictions, the idea that liquor was in itself sinful was quite new to Americans (and indeed to Christians generally). Nor did the temperance crusade represent a response to increased consumption of alcohol since the evidence is strong that per capita consumption was actually falling in the decades in question.[47]

In fact the temperance crusade cannot be understood without reference to class interests and class differences but it is important to note that this was not the reformers' own understanding of their movement. As we shall see, most of them denied the existence of major class differences or distinctions within American society and in any event believed that their cause was primarily a holy and spiritual one. The reformers were convinced that they were doing God's will and were convinced too that the removal of alcohol would be a means to an end; it would do no less than clear the way, many believed, for a millennialist triumph in the young nation. Here we encounter one of the key features of the temperance movement: its links and affinities with the religious revivals which were sweeping the United States from the 1820s onwards.[48]

Temperance indeed had much in common with the revivals. Both offered the opportunity to all believers or converts to renounce sin, either sin generally by means of a spiritual rebirth, or a specific sin by a formal signing of a pledge of abstinence from alcohol. Indeed indulgence in drink was seen as the master symbol of the sinner's fall from grace just as the pledge came to denote the new life into which he or she had been reborn. Both the revivals and the temperance crusade offered an equality of spiritual opportunity that was remarkably consonant with the

---

47. Tyrrell, *Sobering Up*, pp. 4, 16–21. Tyler, *Freedom's Ferment* pp. 309–311.
48. Richard J. Carwardine, *Evangelicals and Politics in Antebellum America* (New Haven, CT, 1993); pp. 61–102; Cross, *Burned-Over District*, p. 211.

wider political and cultural values of antebellum and especially northern society.[49]

Yet however deeply felt these spiritual concerns, it was the earthly blemishes disfiguring American society that had clearly inspired them. And here the reformers spared no pains in alerting the nation to the scale of the social problems they detected. Sometimes reformers made general claims about the role of alcohol, as when the Sons of Temperance in New York in 1842 declared "the use of alcoholic liquids" to be "the prolific source (directly or indirectly) of nearly all the ills that afflict the human family," or when the Reverend Marcus E. Cross in a work published at midcentury claimed that intemperance was "at this time, the master sin of the civilized world." On other occasions the indictment was more specific. Lyman Beecher, who had been a pioneer in the shift to total abstinence in the 1820s, had set the tone by arguing that alcohol bred both crime and ignorance; indeed he had claimed that "almost the entire extent of national ignorance and crime is the offspring of intemperance." Beecher's words were echoed many times in the following decades. Other reformers added a third evil to those Beecher had cited. Poverty completed the trinity and its existence clearly alarmed many reformers. Thus the Reverent Albert Barnes insisted that alcohol was "the fruitful source of poverty, wretchedness and crime!" According to Barnes, it had "been proved that three-fourths of all these evils result from its use." In the same vein, Neal Dow, the leading temperance reformer of the entire antebellum era, when delivering his inaugural message as Mayor of Portland, Maine in 1851, announced that "the traffic in intoxicating drinks tends more to the degradation and impoverishment of the people than all other causes of evil combined." "There is," the Mayor affirmed, "no fact better established than this."[50]

Indeed poverty or economic hardship was probably the social problem to which temperance writers most frequently alluded and which temperance, or better still prohibition, was designed to combat. The Massachusetts Society for the Suppression of Intemperance, for example, went out of its way to emphasise the link between intemperance and pauperism and this was by now a common refrain of charitable organisations, especially in the Northeast where they were most numerous and influential.

49. Tyrrell, *Sobering Up*, p. 67; Gusfield, *Symbolic Crusade*, p. 168. See J. G. Adams and E. H. Chapin (eds.), *The Fountain: A Temperance Gift* (Boston, 1847), p. 239 for the argument that religious enthusiasm would make up for the loss of intemperate drinking via "enchanting visions."
50. Cross, *Mirror of Intemperance*, pp. 130, 11; Beecher, *Six Sermons*, p. 57; Samuel Flary, *The National Temperance Offering, and Sons and Daughters of Temperance Gift* (New York, 1850), p. 289; Neil Dow, *The Reminiscences of Neil Dow* (Portland, ME, 1898), p. 331.

When Massachusetts in 1839 introduced a law prohibiting the sale of alcohol in quantities less than fifteen gallons, the Special Committee of the state legislature that was responsible for the bill explicitly argued that three-fourths of the pauperism in the state was attributable to alcohol. Similarly Neal Dow later commented on the poverty that was apparent in his own state of Maine and observed that in the 1830s "no thoughtful person could fail to connect cause and effect, and to see that much of this poverty was the direct result of the general distribution of the traffic in liquor."[51]

From this it followed, of course, that the renunciation of alcohol by its members would inevitably augment the prosperity of any community and Dow himself, surveying the effects of the temperance reform after the passage of the Maine Law, reported that businessmen throughout the state "confirm that prohibition has allowed Maine to combat periods of business depression better than anywhere else." Many temperance advocates added that temperance would bring important benefits to a community simply by reducing the need for locally funded relief; the improved material condition of the teetotaller would reduce the likelihood, or even eliminate the possibility, that he would require support from the local community. The result would be, as many temperance organisations did not hesitate to point out, that local taxation would be cut. Indeed some pressed this argument further and actually denounced the drunkard as a "robber" who filched the wealth of the sober citizen by subjecting him to unnecessarily high levels of taxation.[52]

The belief that moral and material progress went hand in hand was of course quintessentially Victorian and temperance reformers did not shrink from proclaiming it. In conjunction with its spiritual premium, therefore, prohibition promised an important economic pay-off.[53] It was at this point that temperance reformers began to betray their class bias. But before examining the role of class consciousness, whether acknowledged or not, and class conflict, whether real or potential, in motivating the reformers, we need to note that ethnic differences and ethnic tensions also played their part. The rapid increase in immigration of the late 1840s and early 1850s brought into the nation large numbers of foreigners,

51. Krout, *Origins of Prohibition*, pp. 96–97, 262–264; Dow, *Reminiscences*, p. 176.
52. Dow, *Reminiscences*, p. 176; Beecher, *Six Sermons*, p. 56; Cross, *Burned-Over District* p. 36; Mary P. Ryan, *Cradle of the Middle Class: The Family in Oneida County, New York, 1790–1865* (Cambridge,UK, 1981), pp. 122–139; Krout, *Origins of Prohibition*, p. 235; Tyrrell, *Sobering Up*, p. 273.
53. As one temperance journalist put it: "we think it quite likely that the moral world is to be changed and elevated, as the physical has been, by means and instruments as simple and old-fashioned as the long neglected steam power" – quoted in Tyrrell, *Sobering Up*, p. 128.

particularly Irish and Germans, whose fondness for alcoholic beverages was widely noted and, by temperance advocates, equally widely deplored.

As a result immigration began to bulk large in temperance literature around midcentury. Some reformers proposed restrictive legislation aimed specifically at the immigrant but the more general response was simply to exhort temperance supporters to ever greater sacrifices for the cause. As the Secretary of a Total Abstinence Society in New Jersey put it in 1847, "every political convulsion, every famine that visits Europe, will drive to our shores, and mingle with our people, a mass of population quite unacquainted with temperance arguments, accustomed to drink freely, and unaccustomed to think for themselves: thus the *work is perpetually to be done anew.*" As we shall see, in the case of the Irish and, to a lesser degree the Germans, hostilities that were grounded in ethnic differences also had a religious dimension. Anti-Catholicism often accompanied nativism and temperance reformers were by no means immune.[54]

It was therefore the all-too-visible social problems, with which immigrants were identified (though by no means exclusively), that drew the ire of temperance reformers. Once again, however, their strictures against the immigrant betrayed their class bias. Although highly sensitive to the damaging effects of alcohol, reformers dismissed or even failed to see the important role played by drink in some immigrant communities and cultures. For the Irish, the supplying and selling of liquor was an important means of advancement within their own communities. Moreover the infrastructure of the liquor industry and especially the tavern was a source of political power and control for some immigrants. More important, many taverns functioned as informal labour exchanges for native born and immigrant alike, where transactions of vital importance to the wage-earner might take place. Most important of all perhaps, the tavern provided, again for native born and immigrant alike, a refuge both from the elements and from the rigors of the working day. Those who had jobs that were unpleasant, perhaps dirty, probably physically demanding and almost certainly entailing periods of unemployment or irregular employment found solace in the conviviality of the tavern and in the effects of alcohol. Such considerations, however, usually escaped the notice of the antebellum temperance reformer entirely.[55]

Changing employment patterns and practices in fact played a central role in promoting the temperance movement. In the colonial and early national eras liquor had been widely viewed as a stimulus to labour, a

54. J. Henry Clarke, M. D., *The Present Position and Claims of the Temperance Enterprise* (New York, 1847), p. 8; Cross, *Burned-Over District*, p. 163 Gusfield, *Symbolic Crusade*, pp. 69–70; Tyrrell, *Sobering Up*, pp. 267–268.
55. Tyler Anbinder, *Nativism and Slavery: The Northern Know-Nothings and the Politics of Antislavery* (New York, 1992), p. 145. Tyrrell, *Sobering Up*, pp. 297–305.

protection against the elements and also a source of diversion and conviviality during the workday. It had not been uncommon for the master craftsman and his employees or apprentices to relax together and enjoy an alcoholic drink. But the changing pattern of work, with larger units of production, more expensive machinery and stricter market discipline, placed a premium on regular and predictable output achieved by sober and disciplined workers during the working day, even as periods of paid employment themselves became, for many, less regular and predictable.

Accompanying this process was an increasing separation between employer and employee. The booming towns of the North experienced greater residential segregation as employees ceased to live with employers. In a parallel development, leisure time became increasingly distinct from time spent at work. As a result a cultural and spatial gap opened up between employer and worker, and the rowdiness of the working class neighbourhoods in which the taverns and grog shops were usually located seemed to the temperance reformer not merely an affront to decency but also an impediment to moral and material progress, in short to everything that he or she held dear. In this sense temperance was, in part, an attempt on the part of employers and their allies to re-establish their former influence over the lives and pastimes of their workers.[56]

Itinerant workers aggravated these problems. Those who dug the canals and built the railroads, (the Irish were disproportionately represented here) necessarily made up a transient population that was largely immune to traditional appeals for temperance on the basis of moral suasion. One advocate of prohibition referred to "the floating population" who "comprise a class that cannot be reached by local efforts at moral reform." These workers were difficult to integrate into local communities and the demand for a statutory, statewide ban on alcohol owed much to their presence.[57]

The temperance reformers never for a moment believed that the costs of the economic changes which the nation, and especially the Northeast, was undergoing were too high. On the contrary they were enthusiastic proponents of these changes and the temperance movement was, in part, an attempt not to reverse them but rather to remove the conspicuous evils which accompanied them. In effect temperance flourished not only because it directed attention to many authentic ills within American society but also because it did not challenge the underlying economic processes which had spawned them.[58]

---

56. Tyrrell, *Sobering Up*, pp. 275–276. Paul Johnson, *A Shopkeeper's Millennium* (New York, 1978), pp. 55–61.
57. Tyrrell, *Sobering Up*, p. 275.
58. Tyrrell, *Sobering Up*, p. 6. Tyrrell notes that temperance was not in this sense a defensive movement opposed to the changes taking place in American society. However,

Thus temperance reformers were convinced that American society offered extraordinary opportunities for social betterment. The United States, according to a Convention of Young Men of Massachusetts "favourable to temperance," was "a country where every thing invites and stimulates to honorable enterprise and effort, where the road to the highest eminence and most enviable distinctions is thrown open equally to all." Alcohol, however, blocked the individual's advancement or, worse still, led directly not to riches or respectability but instead to moral and financial ruin. Abstinence would therefore clear the path either to social mobility, or at least the acquisition of a "competence." The typical temperance tale (of which there were a great many in these years) drove home the link between temperance or teetotalism and prosperity by describing, often in graphic detail, the impact of alcohol upon the drinker's material as well as moral welfare. Similarly the Washingtonians' public recounting of individual experience reinforced the assumption that poverty was the result of individual shortcomings while Neal Dow, for his part, in 1834 announced that he did not "remember a single instance of suffering in the families of sober and industrious people."[59] Thus although temperance literature and temperance propaganda recognised and even dwelt upon the poverty that afflicted significant numbers of Americans, the effect was to reinforce the view that this was the result of individual moral shortcomings rather than weakness in the socio-economic system.[60]

The two groups to whom most temperance literature was addressed were wage workers and employers (together with their wives); very little was directed to the freeholding farmer, for example, who worked his own land with only his own or his family's labour at his disposal. Thus Neal Dow in his autobiography recalled that he had been "brought into contact with many who depended upon daily manual labour for support, and to whom, therefore, health, strength, and continuous employment were all important." He had been struck by "the evident inability of workmen to provide for the pressing necessities of their families when spending so much as was their habit for intoxicants." But prohibition, he insisted, would leave them with far more to spend and would allow them to save when in work and thus escape all reliance upon charity when out of

temperance reformers, like Whigs in general, were indeed opposed to many of the *political* changes taking place within the nation, not least because they felt that the Democratic enthronement of the common man hindered the moral progress they so desired.

59. Tyrrell, *Sobering Up*, pp. 141, 170; Gusfield, *Symbolic Crusade*, p. 50; Dow quoted in Frank L. Byrne, *Prophet of Prohibition: Neil Dow and His Crusade* (Madison, WI, 1961), p. 22.

60. Temperance reformers occasionally recognised that poverty was a genuine cause, rather than a consequence, of alcoholism but this was rare – see, for example, Moses Ballon in Adams and Chapin (eds.), *The Fountain*, pp. 220–224.

employment. Moreover, the intemperate man, it was announced, would be the first to lose his job in a time of recession. Abstinence was thus a form of unemployment insurance.[61]

According to Lyman Beecher, every experiment had shown that getting rid of drink was conducive to the material betterment "both of the laborer and his employer." Temperance reformers gave as much attention to the benefits the reform would bring to the employer as to the gains it offered to the worker. John R. Gough, the popular temperance writer, insisted that alcohol was responsible for no fewer than ninety nine percent of business failures. Neal Dow meanwhile spared no effort to demonstrate the link between abstinence and productivity. Again the assumption was that enlightened employers could see the impact alcohol was having upon their workers (rather than upon themselves) and hence upon their own profits and profitability: This had been clearly visible, Dow later recalled, to those who had formed one of Maine's temperance organisations:

> Its members had unusual opportunities to see the evil effects of the liquor traffic and the drinking habits of the day. Through them most of the labouring men of the town found employment. They put out a large portion of the money distributed in wages for skilled, as well as unskilled, labor, and they had constantly before them the evidence that no inconsiderable portion was expended for liquor. They saw, too, in the resulting indisposition to work in the loss of time for drinking, and the impairment of energy, capacity and health by debauch that the money thus spent was more unwisely used than if thrown into the sea.

These men, Dow continued "were practical men of affairs" who "knew that their own success depended in great measure upon the capacity, skill and faithfulness of their employees." They thus had the clearest motive to promote temperance because "they were often compelled to pay for untrustworthiness and incapacity caused by drink where they had contracted for better service." It was little wonder therefore that when elected mayor of Portland in 1851 he recommended prohibition to local legislators. For "as a question of domestic and political economy, of earnings and savings, of annual accumulating wealth to the city, this subject demands the highest consideration."[62]

In the same way temperance reformers stressed that industrial machinery, which was of increasing complexity and sophistication with every passing decade, must be manned and maintained by a sober workforce, one which could ensure regularity of work and output. Here the primary

61. Dow, *Reminiscences*, pp. 205–207; Krout, *Origins of Prohibition*, pp. 236–238.
62. Beecher, *Six Sermons*, pp. 87–88; Ryan, *Empire of the Mother*, pp. 63–75; Dow, *Reminiscences*, pp. 207–208, 331.

emphasis was on manufacturing but temperance reformers also pressed the advantages of prohibition for the farmer who employed labour and for whom mechanisation was becoming increasingly possible, especially in the 1850s. Elaborate arguments were offered to demonstrate that farmers should no longer, as they had in the past, offer alcohol as a fringe benefit for wage-earners. As early as 1825 Justin Edwards, in a work entitled *The Well Conducted Farm* cited the example of a farmer who ceased to supply alcohol and instead paid a dollar more in wages per month. The result was that men worked better and saved more; even more important, the land became more productive than ever.[63]

Temperance advocates thus offered to those who would sign the pledge, and abide by it, far more than a change of personal consumption habits. They repeatedly drew attention to the benefits, both moral and material, that an entire community would reap if it prohibited the sale of alcohol. A typical description was offered by one of the authors of a work revealingly entitled *The Fountain: A Temperance Gift* and published in 1847:

> Every house is in repair; no one with broken windows, shattered doors, or rickety gates and well-curbs. You see no fences out of repair, and your ears are not pained with the shouts of men and the barking of dogs, running and storming to drive the hogs and cattle out of the corn or the wheat field. Walk over the farms. You find the owners, their sons, and their hired men, at work, – health, contentment, and happiness beaming on their countenances.

In such a town "All are happy, and all are prosperous." "Why?" the author asked. He gave a simple reason: "It is a temperance town."[64]

Temperance was thus, to a considerable degree, a response to the problems caused by an expanding manufacturing sector and an increasingly commercialised agriculture. Although highly successful for a short time, it was never, as we shall see, unchallenged, even in the northeast, its heartland. Ironically the resistance offered by many immigrants and low income workers may, for a time at least, have increased its attractions to the middle-classes and those who wished to join them. For temperance increasingly became a badge of middle-class status, a requirement for those who wished to attain respectability and enjoy the advantages that it brought. Perhaps an upbringing which ensured that sons would be tee-total began to function as a substitute for the transmission of productive property that was now increasingly difficult in New England and other regions of the northeast. In this sense temperance (together with other

---

63. Krout, *Origins of Prohibition*, pp. 236–238. Tyrrell, *Sobering Up*, pp. 167–168.
64. Adams and Chapin (eds.), *The Fountain*, pp. 100–101.

related virtues), was a form of moral capital that could be bequeathed to a new generation.[65]

Temperance thus helped the community to distinguish between the worthy and the unworthy, between those to whom credit should be given and those from whom it should be withheld, between those who were fit employees and those who were not. The temperance crusade was in this sense unmistakeably middle class in orientation, not because all its proponents or converts were middle class but because it enshrined values that have been identified with middle-class groups across the developed world. "I saw," Neal Dow recalled in his Autobiography, "that, as a rule, neither industry, thrift, prudence, saving, nor comfort was to be found, where indulgence in intoxicants prevailed."[66]

As we have seen, the temperance movement was blind to some of the problems that drove lower income groups, whether native born or immigrant, to seek solace in alcohol and the tavern. It also harboured suspicions of those among the traditionally wealthy, for example the merchant princes of Boston, who insisted upon their right to wine, the gentleman's drink, and who, as we shall see, began to denounce the temperance movement when prohibition became its goal.[67] Above all the movement aimed to address the problems posed by wage earners in communities whose very survival in a market economy needed steadiness of work and unprecedentedly high levels of productivity.

In a sense the reformers' goal was social control but this was not the social control which the Federalists had sought. Whereas the earlier Federalist temperance advocates had set out to impose, from on high as it were, a code of behaviour upon the lower orders, the middle-class reformers who followed Neal Dow at midcentury wanted in the first instance to reform themselves and those who thought like them and then, by means of legislation, to embrace the entire community in their uplifting endeavour. The Federalists believed themselves an elite and wished to govern as an elite, regulating the conduct of their inferiors. The later temperance reformers also believed that they constituted an elite but they offered membership in that elite to all who were prepared to sign the pledge. Their fondest wish was to raise the morals of the entire society and in that way make themselves indistinguishable from the community at large.

The temperance and prohibition movements of the antebellum years represented above all a search for order, an attempt to find a new

65. Johnson, *Shopkeeper's Millennium*, pp. 58–61; Gusfield, *Symbolic Crusade*, p. 45; Ryan, *Cradle of the Middle Class*, pp. 139–141: Charles G. Sellers, *The Market Revolution: Jacksonian America, 1815–1846* (New York, 1991), p. 266.
66. Gusfield, *Symbolic Crusade*, pp. 4–5, 45; Daniel Walker Howe, *The Political Culture of the American Whigs* (Chicago, 1979), p. 159; Dow, *Reminiscences*, p. 206.
67. Adams and Chapin (eds.), *The Fountain*, p. 128.

foundation for individual morality in a society that was undergoing rapid changes and where traditional social bonds were losing their strength. Ironically, although temperance reformers insisted and sincerely believed that the United States was a uniquely classless society, their vision was bounded by the assumptions of one class and their movement may even have served to strengthen that class's sense of separate identity.

III

We are now in a position to assess the impact of temperance upon the political parties and the politics of the 1850s. First we should note the political geography of prohibition. Between 1851 and 1855 thirteen states or territories enacted prohibitory laws. No fewer than eight were in the East.[68] Only one was a slaveholding state and that one, Delaware, had so few slaves that it scarcely counted as part of the South. The reason for this uneven performance was simply that the groups which most favoured temperance were both most numerous and most powerful in the North and especially the Northeast. The weakness of the movement in the South was partly owing to its identification with antislavery but also and more fundamentally to its lack of appeal to the planter elite. Most planters were extremely keen to impose total abstinence upon their slaves but not at all keen to embrace it themselves. Hence the movement was even weaker in the Deep South, where planter power was greatest, than in the border regions and the middle South. The problems posed by wage-earning were at the heart of the temperance crusade and such problems, though not absent, were far less in evidence in the South.[69]

In the North, however, temperance had a major impact upon politics and upon the political parties. Although, as we have seen, the reformers soon concluded that legal action, and indeed legal action at state level, was necessary, they did not form a distinct party. Instead they sought pledges of support from existing parties. This, of course, gave each of those parties at least a potential dilemma, since prohibition was as unpopular with some groups as it was popular with others. The parties responded, however, in different ways.

As we have already seen, the Democrats found prohibition least attractive. Although many Democrats favoured temperance themselves, the

68. These were the New England states together with New York and Delaware. The other states and territories were Michigan, Indiana, Iowa, Nebraska and Minnesota. Prohibition came close to success in New Jersey, Pennsylvania, Ohio, Wisconsin and Illinois.

69. Ian R. Tyrrell, "Drink and Temperance in the American South: An Overview and Interpretation." *Journal of Southern History*, XLVII (Nov. 1982), pp. 485–510, esp. pp. 497–498.

tradition of Jefferson and Jackson simply had no point of contact with the attempt to prohibit alcohol by legislative statute. Nevertheless many Democrats supported temperance and even legal prohibition; indeed five of the state legislatures which enacted prohibition laws had Democratic majorities. But in so doing they were breaking with the traditional values of their party and it may be significant that the states where Democrats did support prohibition were, for the most parts, states in which Democratic control was soon to be eroded. Moreover the continuing and indeed increasing identification of the Democratic party with the immigrant vote, especially in the larger cities, tended to strengthen Democratic resistance to antiliquor legislation in many regions and localities.[70]

For the other parties, however, the Know Nothings, the Free Soilers and Republicans and the Whigs, temperance had far more to offer. When the Know Nothings burst onto the political scene in 1854 as an avowedly nativist organisation, there was much for temperance advocates (if they had not already joined the Order) to ponder. As we have seen, temperance reformers had long complained of the influence of the foreign born, especially the Germans and the Irish, whose predilection for liquor was frequently noted and whose votes had often been mobilised to defeat attempts at prohibition. Moreover, as we have also seen, some of the social problems which exercised the temperance reformers were ones with which immigrants were closely identified. For these reasons many temperance advocates welcomed the nativist movement and hoped to use it to further their aims.[71]

Yet there were other factors which complicated the relationship between nativism and temperance. There was in reality no reason the dedicated nativist could not be a dedicated drinker too, and this possibility was vividly confirmed by many artisans who joined the Know Nothings. Moreover, in New York, for example, the nativist Order of United American included many who were involved in the liquor trade. Finally many patricians were sympathetic to nativism but were decidedly hostile to a movement that might deprive them of the fine wines they so enjoyed. Thus although temperance had a real appeal to many nativists, there were other considerations which prevented the two movements from fusing in the way the teetotal nativist might have wished.

The relationship between antislavery groups and temperance supporters was, initially at least, much clearer and less ambiguous. There were many important affinities between temperance and antislavery, particularly the morally charged antislavery espoused by abolitionists and those

70. See pp. 371–375.
71. For material in this and the following paragraph, see Tyrrell, *Sobering Up*, pp. 265–269; See also Anbinder, *Nativism and Slavery*, pp. 43–44, 60, 106, 144–145.

who remained in the antislavery movement in the quiet years between 1851 and 1854 (and who would subsequently occupy the radical wing of the Republican party after 1854). As we have seen, antislavery placed a heavy emphasis upon the impact of slavery upon the conscience and the soul both of the slave (who was not at liberty to obey his or her own conscience) and of the slaveholder (whose conscience was polluted by the enormity of trading in the consciences and the souls of his fellow men and women). As we have also seen, antislavery enthusiasts were confident that to follow the path to virtue, one must listen to, and obey, the voice of the conscience within.[72]

By these lights intemperance was as morally reprehensible as slaveholding. Indeed the temperance reformer sometimes referred to alcohol in terms identical to those the abolitionist employed when describing slaveholding. Sellers of liquor were, according to the author of one temperance tract, "men who traffic in other men's souls." Thus no Christian should "contaminate his hands and his soul with this most destructive and demoralizing commerce." Even more important were the effects upon the conscience of those who consumed alcohol. Lyman Beecher declared that it made men "slaves"; the drunkard was, as another reformer put it, a "slave of intemperance." With the drinker, as with the chattel slave and the slaveholder, "conscience loses its power" resulting in "the extinction of all the finer feelings and amiable dispositions of the soul." Alcohol "obliterates the fear of the Lord and a sense of accountability, paralyses the power of conscience, hardens the heart, and turns out upon society a sordid, ferocious animal." It was no less than a "poison" which "hardens the hearts, breaks down the conscience, quickens the circulation, goads up every passion to a high pitch of excitement, makes men disregard law and right, and prepares them for the commission of any crime." Intemperance thus "obliterates the moral sense, destroys all shame, all perceptions of character, all feelings of integrity." Alcohol "tortures" or "stupefies" the conscience.[73]

Temperance crusaders, together with antislavery militants and other religiously inspired reformers believed that the conscience should be one of society's strongest pillars. It was therefore imperative that individuals should heed her voice. But alcohol was the means by which the

---

72. See the first volume of this study, pp. 168–173.
73. Delia A. Hudson, *The Temperance Token* (Whitehall, NY, 1853), p. 10; Adams and Chapin (eds.), *The Fountain*, pp. 105, 26–29; Beecher, *Six Sermons*, pp. 19, 16, 35, 52–53; Cross, *Mirror of Intemperance*, p. 40; Leonard Bacon, *Total Abstinence from Ardent Spirits: An Address Delivered, By Request of the Young Men's Temperance Society of New Hampshire . . . June 24, 1829* (New Hampshire, 1829), p. 11; Heman Humphrey *Parallel Between Intemperance and the Slave Trade: An Address Delivered at Amherst College, July 4, 1828* (Amherst, 1828), p. 14; Krout, *Origins of Prohibition*, p. 301.

unrepentant sinner was able, though at a frightful cost, to silence that voice. "What tormenter," it was asked, "was ever so fierce and relentless as a guilty conscience?" Although it might be "possible to silence her voice for a season," the drunkard nevertheless "subjects her to the slow process of crucifixion" in the course of which "she, in most cases, maintains a long and deep struggle in his bosom." In this sense therefore alcohol, just like slavery, sapped the moral foundations of American society.[74]

In the same way temperance reformers, once again like antislavery crusaders,[75] dwelt upon the threat they perceived to the home and the family. Just as Harriet Beecher Stowe, for example, believed the worst evil of slavery to be its effect upon the family, temperance reformers drew attention to the plight of the drunkard's wife and children. Some temperance writers and lecturers did not hesitate to proclaim that woman was the principal victim of intemperance, not because she partook of alcohol herself (an almost unimaginable prospect), but rather because of her husband's drinking. For this reason among others, perhaps, women joined the temperance movement in large numbers. Once again the middle class assumptions of the reformers came to the fore when they described the role of the home and of the wife whose domain it was:

> The appropriate sphere of female life is comparatively a narrow and restricted one. The little sanctuary of home, which they seem made to adorn and bless, comprises the field from which they must reap the harvest of most of their earthly enjoyments. Most of their happiness, that this world has the power to give and take away, must here have its source.

This of course was a description of women's life and of the middle class home as they ought to be rather than of the realities that confronted hundreds of thousands of families throughout the nation. This, however, did nothing to abate the reformers' zeal; on the contrary, the greater the gap between the domestic idyll and the reality, the greater the need to war against alcohol. Thus alcohol once again was blamed for the imperfections in American society and women were targeted as its victims. "How awful must be their condition, then," it was claimed, when the "sanctuary" that was home was "profaned by the drunkard's revels." Like the slave-trade, it was said, intemperance would break up and ruin families.[76]

Temperance reformers believed with abolitionists that the home should serve as a refuge from the world outside; it should be a place of repose

74. Humphrey *Parallel Between Intemperance and Slave Trade*, p. 20.
75. For a discussion of abolitionists' view of home and family see the first volume of this work, pp. 174–181.
76. Cross, *Mirror of Intemperance*, p. 180; Adams and Chapin (eds.), *The Fountain*, pp. 63–65;

and tranquillity where the incomparable joys of the family circle could be experienced. But alcohol, like slavery, denied its victims these precious comforts. It made the father a curse to his family and destroyed the influence that the virtuous mother would otherwise exert over her husband and children. Drunkenness, one writer concluded, was "the serpent that enters this blissful Eden."[77]

It was no coincidence that the many northerners who came to view the family in this light should be driven to embark upon crusades against both slavery and intemperance. Hence the close links between prohibition and antislavery. "The one group in the state on which the Prohibitionists could count," Neal Dow recalled in his *Autobiography*, "was the anti-slavery element" and historians have confirmed that this pattern existed across much of the North in the early 1850s, when the prohibition movement was at its peak.[78]

It was, however, on the Whig party that the temperance movement had its greatest impact. Many Whigs rallied to the cause of temperance and for good reasons. Once again there were strong affinities between reform movement and political party; indeed virtually every tenet of the temperance creed struck a Whiggish chord. Like temperance reformers, Whigs had always, and especially in the North, placed great emphasis upon the harmony of interests between labour and capital, and had insisted that the labourer had unprecedented opportunities to rise in society. Whigs too had welcomed the economic changes of the era and had firmly believed that material and moral progress went hand in hand. The idea that drink might explain the poverty that still scarred American society appealed to Whigs just as it did to temperance reformers while hostility to immigrants had been expressed by Whig partisans for many years. Moreover the idea that underlay the prohibition crusade, that government could and should be used to promote both cultural homogeneity and the moral improvement of the people, was one which Whigs had always embraced, especially in the North.[79]

Furthermore, some temperance reformers shared with some Whigs, a profound suspicion of the populistic tendencies of American democracy. Such concerns had been particularly evident in the early years of the temperance movement. Lyman Beecher, for example, who was closely identified with the Federalist party, and who had played a major role in the

---

77.  Flary, *National Temperance Offering*, pp. 129–140, 185–201. Temperance reformers insisted that the full extent of the damage wreaked by alcohol upon the family had never been exposed: "Oh, my friends," one of them lamented, "back of all the visible outward evils of intemperance, there lies a field of devastation, which has never been fully explored. – It is the wasted realm of the social affections – the violated sanctuary of domestic peace," see Cross, *Mirror of Intemperance*, p. 37.
78.  Dow, *Reminiscences*, p. 289; Krout, *Origins of Prohibition*, pp. 176–177; Tyrrell, *Sobering Up*, p. 264.
79.  The ideology of the Whig party is a main theme of the first volume of this study.

temperance movement in the 1820s, had fretted that "in proportion to the numbers who have no right in the soil and no capital at stake and no moral principle, will the nation be exposed to violence and revolution." Beecher noted that "in Europe, the physical power is bereft of the right of suffrage, and by the bayonet is kept down." But, he warned, "in this nation, the power which may be wielded by the intemperate is tremendous." For Beecher the temperance movement would counteract the decline of ecclesiastical control in American society and remove the danger that the intemperate would gain political power and threaten the rights of property.[80]

Such concerns had receded by the mid-1840s. Nevertheless, they still surfaced occasionally. The Whigs continued to see themselves as the party of respectability and, as we have seen, respectability often denoted abstinence from alcohol. Thus the New York *Tribune* in 1844 compared the traits of working men who supported the Whigs with those who voted for the Democrats: "Upon those Working Men who stick to their business, hope to improve their circumstances by honest industry, and go on Sundays to church rather than the grog-shop," the *Tribune* announced, "the appeals of Loco-Focoism [i.e., the Democratic party] fell comparatively harmless, while the opposite class were rallied with unprecedented unanimity against us." Thus the middle-class aura which surrounded the temperance movement was highly congenial to Whig partisans.[81]

For these reasons Whigs proved more receptive than Democrats to temperance and prohibition in virtually every state and locality. From the 1820s, before the birth of the Whig party, temperance had tended to attract anti-Democrats. In the late 1830s the Massachusetts Fifteen Gallon Law had been a Whig measure, and prominent temperance campaigners like Neal Dow were Whig supporters. More generally, throughout the period of the second party system, many Whigs advocated temperance or prohibition.[82] Some of them made no secret of the electoral benefits they believed would then accrue to their party. "Intoxicating drink," it was said, "has long been one of the most formidable engines of the Democratic party." Hence "destroy it and the spell of Democracy is half broken."[83]

80. Beecher, *Six Sermons*, pp. 58–59; Gusfield, *Symbolic Crusade*, p. 39.
81. New York *Tribune*, Dec. 21, 1844 quoted in Benson, *Concept of Jacksonian Democracy*, p. 199.
82. See Ashworth, *"Agrarians" and "Aristocrats,"* pp. 198–202; Herbert Ershkowitz and William G. Shade, "Consensus or Conflict? Political Behavior in the State Legislatures during the Jacksonian Era," *Journal of American History*, LVIII (Dec. 1971), pp. 591–621; Gusfield, *Symbolic Crusade*, p. 52. See also Table 2.4 in Gienapp, *Origins of Republican Party*, p. 488; Carwardine, *Evangelicals and Politics*, p. 102.
83. J. A. Chestnut to Richard Yates, June 18, 1853 quoted in Gienapp, *Origins of Republican Party*, p. 47. A further point of contact between Whiggery and the temperance movement was the Whiggish hostility to labour unions evinced by, for example, the New York *Organ*, newspaper of the Sons of Temperance.

Unfortunately for the unity of the Whig party, however, there were also powerful reasons for members to view the temperance cause with grave misgivings. Whigs on both the liberal and conservative wings of their party had ample reason to question the wisdom of an unequivocal endorsement of prohibition. The conservative Whigs, who were the closest it was possible to be at midcentury to the old Federalists, were as suspicious of temperance zealotry as they were of other political enthusiasms. Edward Everett, for example, although favouring temperance himself, nevertheless regarded prohibition as an "ascetic Utopian vision." Religious conservatives both within the party and outside it confessed themselves unable to find any scriptural authority for the pledge; it rather strained credulity to depict Jesus Christ as a committed teetotaller. Moreover, for all the emphasis placed by prohibitionists on the conscience, could it not be said that the pledge itself was a surrender of self-control and a subjection of the conscience to external forces? Calvin Colton, friend and biographer of Henry Clay and as ardent a Whig as any in the land, had as early as the 1830s denounced prohibition as inquisitorial and hostile to the spirit of American freedom. These Whigs were also mindful, as many southerners were, that prohibition was closely allied to antislavery in terms both of personnel and fundamental assumptions and joined their southern allies in condemning it. Finally, as we have seen, some conservatives made no secret of their enjoyment of alcoholic beverages, and did not doubt their ability to control their own consumption of it. Thus William King, a former Whig Governor of Maine, believed wine "essential to the intercourse of gentlemen." Such men frowned upon drunkenness, of course, but they looked askance at the enthusiastic temperance reformer, who himself seemed intoxicated by the ardour of his cause.[84]

Meanwhile, Whigs on the opposite wing of their party were alarmed that an endorsement of prohibition would simply alienate large numbers of voters and especially immigrant voters. Such a strategy would run directly counter to that employed in 1852 when the party made direct overtures to immigrants, who were now of course entering the nation in record numbers.[85]

Finally there was a consideration which united all Whigs. Although temperance reformers wanted to establish or re-establish order in their

---

84. Tyrrell, *Sobering Up*, pp. 149–150; Tyler, *Freedom's Ferment*, p. 326. A good illustration of one conservative Whig's ambivalence to prohibition can be found in Allan Nevins and Milton H. Thomas (eds.), *The Diary of George Templeton Strong*. 4 vols. (New York, 1952), II, p. 165. See also Horace Greeley to Thurlow Weed, April 18, 1852, in Harriet Weed (ed.), *Memoir of Thurlow Weed* (New York, 1970), p. 216.

85. Holt, *Whig Party*, pp. 686–687. It was also said that the attempt to use the power of the law to enforce temperance would lead to a backlash against the movement – see *The Great Fraud Upon the Public Credulity in the Organization of the Republican Party, An Address to the Old-Line Whigs of the Union* (Washington, DC, 1856), pp. 3–18.

communities, many Whigs wondered whether the injection of so hugely controversial a subject into politics would not generate additional political strife and social conflict. As we shall see, these fears were in good part borne out and the result was to hasten the demise of the temperance movement. It was not surprising therefore, that many Whigs were strongly opposed to a formal endorsement of prohibition. Whenever temperance has been agitated, one Whig warned, "the Whig party has always lost ground."[86]

The result was that although more Whigs supported prohibition than Democrats, the party was unable to maintain a consistent stand on the question. The fact that temperance was exclusively a local and state rather than a federal issue meant that it was possible for each state party to go its own way. Some endorsed prohibition, others opposed or ignored it. The result was almost certainly to increase the sense of alienation from politics, or at least from the established parties, that observers and commentators noted from 1851 onwards. Thus temperance contributed greatly to the political chaos of these years.

IV

As we shall see, however, by 1856, a political realignment was well under way. By this time, for reasons still to be explored, the Whigs had disappeared as a significant political force and been replaced in the North as the major anti-Democratic organisation by the nascent Republican party. Among the Republicans' most enthusiastic recruits were the various anti-slavery groups who had not been absorbed, or re-absorbed into the main parties after 1850 and whose support for temperance we have already noted. Yet this did not result in a formal Republican commitment to prohibition across the entire North. The Kansas-Nebraska Act of 1854, which above all precipitated the formation of the new party, broadened the anti-slavery cause immensely and the Republicans received the support of other groups whose priorities were different from those of the original antislavery agitators and who often lacked any commitment to the temperance cause. Thus former Democrats in the Republican ranks were as suspicious of the temperance crusade as Democratic regulars had traditionally been while many former Whigs brought with them the ambivalence or even hostility to the movement that some in their party had previously displayed. Even radical Republicans, the group most likely to share the moral fervor of the temperance agitators, feared that the reform might prove a distraction from the party's main task, which was to defeat slavery and the Slave Power. For these reasons, from the mid-1850s onwards

86. Robert Morris to Hamilton Fish, Feb. 10, 1852 quoted in Gienapp, *Origins of Republican Party*, p. 47.

in areas where it had once been a plank in their platform Republicans generally abandoned prohibition.

This process was both cause and effect of the decline of the temperance movement, a decline which was unmistakeable by late 1855 or 1856. What had gone wrong? In part the slavery controversy, fuelled by the sensational events in Kansas, had simply overshadowed prohibition, as it also overshadowed nativism and every other issue. But there were other factors at work. First were the legal challenges to prohibition. The Maine Laws enacted by many states and territories contained search-and-seizure clauses, which conferred wide powers upon officials charged with finding violators of the law. In 1854 in Massachusetts and in New York in 1856 these clauses were stuck down by the Courts on the grounds that they destroyed property rights without due process. Also in 1854 the Michigan Supreme Court ruled that the state's recent referendum on prohibition (which had resulted in its enactment) had been an unconstitutional delegation of the power of the state legislature. Rulings like these were not consistently made across the entire North but even where they were not seen they fuelled controversy and provoked sometimes violent public resistance.[87]

Nor was it easy to enforce prohibition even when its legality was confirmed. Public opposition made enforcement extremely difficult and in any event many states and localities simply lacked effective policing agencies. Moreover, the law was powerless to prevent interstate trading in liquor and this continued or even increased in extent. Even more important was the disorder that sometimes accompanied prohibition. Its advocates had made much of the threat that alcohol posed to public order and decency and, as we have seen, had promised that prohibition would effect a revolution in crime levels In 1855, however, in Maine, the very heartland of prohibition, Neal Dow, newly elected Mayor of Portland and the virtual embodiment of the temperance crusade, was faced by an angry mob. Dow instructed the militia to open fire upon the mob and one death ensued. A few weeks earlier an anti-prohibition riot in Chicago had also resulted in casualties. This was the antithesis of the orderly society that temperance crusaders had promised.[88]

Yet these local confrontations were a symptom rather than the fundamental cause of prohibition's failure. Temperance initially took root because it did not challenge the fundamental economic processes at work within northern society whilst addressing some of their attendant evils. But it promised what it could not deliver. Although prohibition may well

87. Tyrrell, *Sobering Up*, pp. 282, 290–293.
88. Tyrrell, *Sobering Up*, pp. 293–307. Dow's account of the riot can be found in his autobiography.

have alleviated some of the problems associated with the consumption of alcohol, it was a blunt instrument with which to combat poverty and crime for example. Indeed it took on some of the qualities of a panacea. Although the reformers' middle-class perceptions blinded them to the fact, intemperance had always been far more a symptom than a cause of poverty. It may be imagined that many of those who resisted the reform reasoned that renouncing alcohol would not bring the material (or even the moral) rewards that were promised. This factor alone made prohibition immensely controversial and served to prevent it from producing the harmony and tranquillity for which its supporters yearned.

These concerns underlay the Republicans' retreat from prohibition. In late 1855 even in Maine party leaders attributed a statewide defeat in the autumn to the drink question. Gradually, and at different times in different states and localities, Republicans concluded that the drink issue would, on balance, both lose them votes and deflect attention from the antislavery cause, which alone united all elements within the party. Although the votes of immigrants bulked large here (and especially the votes of the many Germans in the Midwest), it is important to note that it was the opposition of the native-born, who vastly outnumbered the immigrants in every state, which doomed prohibition.[89]

As a result by 1857 the crusade for the Maine Law was over. Some temperance reformers now reverted to the old emphasis upon moral suasion and by the late 1850s the issue was politically dead. Twenty years later only three states were still dry. All were in New England.[90]

What then was the role of the temperance movement in bringing about the collapse of the Whigs? Before this question can be answered, we need to examine the part played by another of the movements that flourished at this time. The Know Nothing crusade, which sought to combat the injurious effects of mass immigration into the United States, was even more important than the temperance movement in the highly complex, indeed chaotic, political environment of the mid-1850s.

## Nativism: The Know Nothings

### I

The era which opened around the middle of the nineteenth century witnessed the greatest and most dramatic migration of peoples the world

---

89. There were simply not enough immigrants to prevent prohibition, if the native born had desired it. On the Republican abandonment of prohibition, see Eric Foner, *Free Soil, Free Labor, Free Men: the Ideology of the Republican Party Before the Civil War* (New York, 1970), pp. 241–242.
90. Tyrrell, *Sobering Up*, pp. 307–316.

had yet seen. This was a migration often, though not exclusively, from rural areas to urban centres, often between countries, sometimes across oceans. The United States was a huge beneficiary of this migration and indeed the most popular destination of these migrating millions. Although some emigrants were attracted by the prospects of political and religious freedoms, a larger number were fleeing from hunger or from the pressure of population on the land.[91]

The attitude of native-born Americans, or at least of many of them, to this influx was curiously ambivalent. In the South slavery nourished a distinctive set of anxieties. While the growing imbalance in the populations of North and South was itself, as we have already seen, a cause for the deepest concern and a reason to welcome immigrants into the region, there were at the same time even more powerful reasons to discourage them. Could immigrants be trusted to be loyal to slavery and even if they could, did the South want to see the expansion in her cities that might well result from mass immigration? Many southerners were doubtful and, partly as a result, the overwhelming majority of immigrants went to the free-labour North, though significant numbers did settle in the larger cities of the South like New Orleans, Baltimore and St Louis.[92] But in the North there was also ambivalence for while virtually everyone here wanted immigrants they did not want *all* immigrants. Even more important, those whom they did want for economic reasons, might prove difficult to assimilate culturally, might prove themselves unsuitable politically and might espouse religious opinions that were distasteful or threatening.[93]

Such reservations were likely to be expressed in any nation at any time but in the United States it was possible for immigrants to exercise full political rights within a few years, sometimes within a few months. Thus for some Americans whilst the capitalist economy required or at any rate benefited from the presence of immigrant labour, the democratic polity might be threatened by it. This dilemma reached painful levels in the mid-1850s when the Know Nothings, an anti-immigrant party, suddenly rose

91. On immigration, see, for example, Marcus Lee Hansen, *The Atlantic Migration, 1607–1860* (Cambridge, 1940); Kerby A. Miller, *Emigrants and Exiles: Ireland and the Irish Exodus to North America* (New York, 1985); Oscar Handlin, *Boston's Immigrants: A Study in Acculturation* (New York, 1959); Mack Walker, *Germany and the Emigration, 1816–1885* (Cambridge, 1964).
92. In 1860 only about ten percent of the nation's immigrants were located in the South. They totalled about ten percent of the nation's population in 1850 but only five percent of that of the South – see Fred Bateman and Thomas Weiss, *A Deplorable Scarcity: The Failure of Industrialization in the Slave Economy* (Chapel Hill, 1981), p. 91.
93. See the first volume of this study, pp. 272, 280, 499–500, 504–510.

to political prominence and, for a brief period, dominated the political landscape.[94]

For a generation or so after the ending of the Napoleonic wars, immigration into the United States remained at relatively low levels. Between 1815 and 1845 fewer than a third of a million immigrants arrived. But then came an extraordinary increase. In the next ten years almost three million entered the United States, with no fewer than 400,000 in the peak year, 1854. The two largest groups were the Irish and the Germans, both of whom migrated primarily in search of enhanced economic opportunities. In both Ireland and Germany overpopulation on the land was a key "push" factor and for both immigrant groups the promise of greater material well-being was the decisive "pull" factor.

The Irish comprised the largest group of all. From the mid-1830s an important shift in the migratory pattern became evident. Previously Irish Protestants or relatively prosperous Roman Catholics had been most likely to uproot themselves and move to the New World; the poorer elements, often unable to finance the transatlantic crossing, remained tied to the land. But Irish agriculture was at this time entering its most difficult era. Overpopulation and the scarcity of land made many holdings unviable. One solution was to institute primogeniture, but this of course only increased the pressure on younger sons to leave. A decline in agricultural living standards had already set in when in the mid-1840s the potato blight struck. Millions died of starvation and an even larger number, encouraged by the now sharply reduced cost of the transatlantic crossing, resolved to emigrate. The United States was the preferred destination for a million and a half of them in the era of the famine.

Most of the Irish who now arrived in the United States were Roman Catholic, poor and unskilled. Tens of thousands of them could not speak English. Although they had had experience only of agriculture, that experience had been so calamitous that their preferred destination within the United States was the large cities, and specifically the large cities of the Northeast. This increased their visibility and made them an obvious target

94. There is a large literature on the Know Nothings. The best book by far on the Order in the North is Anbinder, *Nativism and Slavery* (which also contains an excellent bibliographical essay); for the South there is no modern equivalent but see W. Darrell Overdyke, *The Know Nothing Party in the South* (Baton Rouge, 1950). See also Ray Allen Billington, *The Protestant Crusade, 1800–1860: A Study of the Origins of American Nativism* (Chicago, 1938); Dale T. Knobel, *Pdddy and the Republic: Ethnicity and Nationality in Antebellum America* (Middletown, 1986); Leonard and Robert Parmet, *American Nativism, 1830–1860* (New York, 1971). There are statewide studies of the Order in many states, some of which are cited below. I should also like to acknowledge my gratitude to Bruce Levine for some invaluable and expert observations he made after reading an ealier version of this chapter.

for those among the native born who doubted whether a republican government could cope with the enfranchisement of such a large and seemingly unassimilable group.[95]

The Germans, on the other hand, although also fleeing from economic adversity, had not been so scarred by their experience in agriculture. When they did not settle in midwestern cities like Cincinnati and Milwaukee they tended to go to agricultural areas of the Midwest. Though most German immigrants were Roman Catholics, there were significant numbers of Protestants. Moreover, their preference for agriculture made them somewhat less conspicuous, despite differences of language. On the other hand a small minority of Germans (especially the so-called Forty Eighters) had fled from political persecution and had brought radical ideas with them into the United States. This would earn them the lasting enmity of many American nativists in the 1850s.[96]

The unprecedented surge in immigration was, it is hardly necessary to observe, the indispensable condition of the eruption of nativist feeling that occurred in the mid-1850s. By that time immigrants outnumbered the native born in a host of Midwestern cities (Chicago, Detroit, Milwaukee) and were close to that mark in many in the East (New York, Brooklyn, Buffalo). But the growth in nativist sentiment had other causes too. In 1846 Pius IX became Pope and he adopted a highly reactionary position on almost all political and moral questions. Pius resurrected the notion of papal infallibility, opposed all the revolutions of 1848, no matter what their character, and did not hesitate to speak out against liberty of conscience and of the press.

Meanwhile in the United States American Catholic Bishops in 1852 formally resolved that Roman Catholic children should be educated exclusively in parochial schools but at the taxpayer's expense, a move which rekindled previous controversies about the funding of education. By now, however, the numbers involved were so great that the issue became highly charged in many areas of the North. Similarly there were attempts to prevent the reading of the King James Bible, which the Catholic hierarchy viewed with suspicion, in schools and, even more important, debates about the ownership of church property as bishops sought to gain title to, and control over, the property of the Catholic Church. This involved a

---

95. Miller, *Emigrants and Exiles*. Only a quarter of the Irish, as opposed to forty percent or fifty percent of British or Scandinavian immigrants, made their way onto the land – see Bruce Levine, *Half Slave and Half Free: The Roots of Civil War* (New York., 1992), pp. 56–59;

96. Walker, *Germany and the Emigration*, pp. 46–48; Bruce Levine, *The Spirit of 1848: German Immigrants, Labor Conflict, and the Coming of the Civil War* (Urbana, 1992).

struggle within the Church, as rebels were to be excommunicated if they resisted. But such moves also awakened Protestant fears of the temporal power of the Church and an equally traditional Protestant fear of papal power in Rome.[97]

Partly to settle these disputes, the Vatican sent an emissary, Archbishop Gaetano Bedini to the United States. Bedini, like Pius IX, was deeply reactionary and some nativists were alarmed when he remained in the country far longer than had been anticipated (from June 1853 to February 1854). Another source of concern was President Franklin Pierce's decision to appoint a Roman Catholic to the position of Postmaster General. The appointee, James Campbell, himself had a large number of offices at his disposal and this compounded fears of Catholic influence. Although the appointment of Campbell was unrelated to it, there was without question a new assertiveness in the Catholic Church at this time, both in the United States and elsewhere. Archbishop John Hughes, for example, openly expressed the desire to make the United States a Catholic country. Since many of the American Protestant sects were themselves proselytising and outward looking, a collision in the United States between two aggressive creeds was, in the early 1850s, highly likely.

With the upsurge of the 1850s anti-immigrant sentiment in the United States reached new levels, but it was by no means itself a new phenomenon. Hostility to the Church of Rome was as old as, indeed far older than, the Republic itself and it re-emerged in the 1830s and again in the 1840s. In 1843 the American Republican Party was created in New York City from where it spread to some other cities, primarily on the eastern seaboard, and succeeded in electing a small number of Congressmen. In New York City too Thomas Whitney and James Harper established the Order of United Americans, one of a number of fraternal organisations which espoused anti-Catholic and often anti-immigrant sentiments, while in Philadelphia Jacob Broom set up the United Sons of America. In 1850 Charles B. Allen founded the Order of the Star Spangled Banner, an organisation which attempted to maintain a high degree of secrecy. After a couple of years of very slow growth its membership suddenly surged when the rank and file of the OUA joined in very large numbers. In late 1853 this organisation became the Know Nothings and in 1854 the Know Nothings entered politics, with rapid and extraordinary success. The Know Nothings were formally named the American Party but the Know-Nothing label was used by friend and foe alike.[98]

97. Formisano, *Birth of Mass Parties*, pp. 219–224 contains a good account of these events.
98. Ashworth, *"Agrarians" and "Aristocrats,"* pp. 182–183; Anbinder, *Nativism and Slavery*, pp. 20–21.

For a variety of reasons many Whigs had been sympathetic to the nativist agenda. Henry Clay's defeat in the presidential election of 1844 was widely attributed to the immigrant vote and Clay himself acknowledged at that time that "with the Natives, we have strong sympathies and ought to cultivate amicable relations." Daniel Webster, perhaps the second most important Whig leader, at the same time expressed a "deep and strong conviction" that a reform of the naturalisation laws was "a deep and strong necessity," on which nothing less than "the preservation of the Government depended." Webster added that he had "seen the pernicious influence of these foreign votes for the last thirty years." Although the defeat of 1844 saw an increase in Whig hostility to the immigrant, the attitudes underlying it had been present earlier and would persist after it.[99]

Yet in 1852, and partly because of the huge increase in immigration, the Whigs had made a deliberate attempt to court the immigrant vote. After all, to hand the Democrats this growing block vote seemed foolhardy, especially since there was no evidence that an overtly nativist appeal would bring electoral rewards. As early as 1850 the Whigs in states like Michigan had begun to woo the Roman Catholics, despite the misgivings of some within the party and this tendency was subsequently strengthened by the temporary subsidence of the slavery issue. In 1851, for example, Zachariah Chandler did not hesitate to flatter the Irish in his successful campaign to become Mayor of Detroit, and he repeated the strategy in the Michigan gubernatorial election of the following year. These became the tactics of the party nationally that year. The Whig campaign sheet, the *Signal*, blatantly tried to appeal to Roman Catholics and Pierce, the Democratic candidate, was denounced for not having attempted to remove the religious tests that were still on the statute book of his home state, New Hampshire, and which had excluded Roman Catholics from certain offices there. Scott's running mate, William Graham, for his part, went out of his way to demonstrate that he had never been anti-Catholic while Scott himself took pains to disavow some previous utterances that were nativist in tone and, on a lengthy tour of the West, made purportedly complimentary remarks about Irish and German accents, remarks which embarrassed even some of his own supporters.[100]

99. Henry Clay to John M. Clayton, Dec. 2, 1844 quoted in Richard A. Wire, "John M. Clayton and the Search for Order: A Study in Whig Politics and Diplomacy," (Unpublished Doctoral Dissertation, University of Maryland, 1971), p. 186; J. W. McIntyre (ed.), *The Writings and Speeches of Daniel Webster*. 18 vols. (Boston, 1903), VIII, pp. 303, 321.
100. Formisano, *Birth of Mass Parties*, pp. 198, 203–205; *The Signal*, July 10, 17, 24, 1852; William Graham to W. E. Robinson, Aug 10, 1852 in *Papers of Graham*, IV, pp. 369–370; Gienapp, *Origins of Republican Party*, p. 25. See also Thurlow Weed to Fitz Henry Warren, Aug. 14, 1852 in *Papers of Graham*, IV, p. 373.

The strategy was an abject failure. Not only did the Catholic vote almost certainly remain Democratic but nativists within the party and within the wider electorate were alienated. The result was to deepen the widespread disaffection with both parties, but especially with the Whigs. In courting the Catholic and immigrant vote, the Whigs had erased yet another set of issues which had traditionally differentiated them from the Democrats. Moreover, the timing could not have been more unfortunate. Just as religious controversies were beginning to escalate to levels not seen for many decades the Whigs, it appeared, had ensured that they would be unable to benefit from any Protestant, nativist backlash that might develop. That backlash would come in 1854 and it would indeed bring no benefit to the Whigs.[101]

## II

What did the Know Nothings believe? Here the historian encounters certain major difficulties. First, the movement in its early stages sought secrecy. Although it had official publications, not many have survived. Moreover, it is impossible to know how widely these official views were shared within the membership; indeed it has proved extremely difficult to establish who the members were, especially in the early stages. In addition to these problems, however (which face the historian of any nineteenth-century political party), there are others which are unique to the history of the Know Nothings. There were major differences in personnel and support from one year to another; the party's composition changed with extraordinary rapidity. By 1856 when Millard Fillmore was running for President as the official Know Nothing or American Party candidate, the party's nativist principles, while by no means absent, had clearly been subordinated to its unionism: Fillmore was the candidate who sought to reconcile North and South on the basis of compromise and moderation, precisely as he had as a Whig in 1850. But just one or two years earlier, in 1854 and 1855 in the North the party had been the home of many who were ardently antislavery. By the time of the presidential election of 1856 indeed, sectional tensions had undermined the Know Nothings and within a few short months would destroy their party entirely.[102]

101.  Gienapp, *Origins of Republican Party*, p. 31; *Whig Party*, pp. 742–746.
102.  Before and after the great upsurge of 1854–1855 the principles of the nativists are more easily determined; in those crucial years, the problems are greatest. Undoubtedly the secrecy of the movement helped it become all things to all men. Electoral victories, however, and the pressures of office, inevitably resulted in a clarification of the party's appeal. The analysis of Know Nothing ideology offered here relates to these core nativists, rather than to those who joined and then quickly abandoned the Order.

There is a further problem. In some localities the Know Nothings sought to infiltrate other parties and were sometimes in turn infiltrated by groups who did not share and might indeed repudiate outright their professed principles. It is never easy to reconstruct the ideology of a long-gone political party but in the case of the Know Nothings the task is especially difficult.[103]

Nevertheless, it is clear that at its core lay a hostility towards foreign-born Roman Catholics, and especially Irish Catholics.[104] Some of the criticisms levelled against the Church of Rome in the United States in the 1850s were new or at least the product of distinctively American conditions. Others, however, went back to the time of the Reformation. Their lack of novelty did nothing to reduce the vehemence with which they were advanced.

At the heart of the opposition to Roman Catholicism lay the centuries-old objection that it placed obstacles between man and God. Whereas Protestantism, or at least most Protestant sects, sought an unmediated relationship between man or woman and the deity, the Church of Rome emphasised ritual, ceremony and image worshipping, all of which, it was held, prevented true spirituality and piety. Protestantism instead laid stress upon the individual conscience and upon personal responsibility. The author of a tract which sought to define the purpose and explain the goals of the Know Nothings offered a succinct statement of what he took to be the essence of the Protestant faith:

> *Salvation by faith in the Bible, not in flesh and blood – freedom of conscience and of judgment, and personal responsibility for the proper exercise of the conscience and the mind* constitute the vital principle of Protestantism. And this principle is the germ of *civilization*, as well as of religious liberty.[105]

A key theme here was individual responsibility. But it was not merely the rituals of the Roman Catholic Church which, it was held, diminished that sense of responsibility It was also, and even more alarmingly, the power of the priest within Catholicism. Thomas Whitney explained that whereas Protestantism required the individual to be guided by the voice of

103. A very good survey of Know Nothing thought is Jean G. Hales, "The Shaping of Nativist Sentiment, 1848–1860," (Unpublished Doctoral Dissertation, Stanford, 1973). See also Anbinder, *Nativism and Slavery*, pp. 102–126 and an excellent article by Bruce Levine, "Conservatism, Nativism, and Slavery: Thomas R. Whitney and the Origins of the Know Nothing Party," *Journal of American History*, LXXXVIII (2001), pp. 455–488.
104. Not all scholars agree with this assertion, however. See, for example, Hales, "Shaping of Nativist Sentiment," p. 106.
105. George Robertson, *The American Party: Its Principles, Its Objects, and Its Hopes* (Frankfort, KY, 1855), p. 16.

conscience, Roman Catholics instead abdicated that responsibility and transferred control to the priest. "The individual who places his conscience in the keeping of another," declared Whitney, "divests himself of all responsibility and becomes the creature, the very slave of his conscience-keeper." Such an individual, according to Whitney, becomes "in every sense, moral, social, and religious," a "mere instrument." The result was that "his successes and defeats, his condition and circumstances, all are made dependent on the will or caprice of another." The contrast between the Protestant and Catholic faiths, Whitney concluded, could not be sharper for "he who gives his conscience and faith to a principle may retain and exercise his judgment; whereas he who gives his conscience to a human being creates a visible and present master over his judgment."[106]

This abandonment of the conscience resulted, nativists believed, in an absence of restraint. "Parson" William G. Brownlow of Tennessee claimed that Roman Catholicism "lays no restraint on [men's] lusts, and gives a loose rein to all their unsatisfied passions and desires." Looking at Catholic countries around the world, Justin Fulton concluded that "religion, with the inhabitants of Catholic countries" was "a matter of habit more than conviction." In consequence "their religion exerts no restraining influence upon them."[107]

At the heart of this indictment of Catholicism lay an implacable hostility to the confessional. It was a "startling fact" that "the awful secrecy of the priest's closet supersedes and extinguishes all *moral obligations*, as well as every duty due from the citizen to the state." An even more alarming expose of the confessional was provided in 1854 by a Know Nothing newspaper published in Boston:

> The CONFESSIONAL. It is a bad branch of a bad institution. It heeds, sanctions, makes crime commendable. It tells vice that it is virtue – that to steal is honest – that falsehood is truth – that sin is religion – that to injure neighbour, violate friendship, and ruin character is all right – that to oppose one's country, its good institutions, its laws, its customs, all that has made it great and beautiful, is patriotism – that the sanctity, the privacy, the genius of the family circle is nothing – that female purity and innocence, and sacredness are of no account – that obligations to a fellow-man, to country, to God are mere words, without force [or] meaning.

106. Thomas R. Whitney, *A Defence of the American Policy* (New York, 1856), p. 329.
107. William G. Brownlow, *Americanism Contrasted with Foreignism, Romanism, or Bogus Democracy* (Nashville, TN, 1856), p. 5; Justin D. Fulton, *The Outlook of Freedom: Or, The Roman Catholic Element in American History* (Cincinnati, 1856), p. 170.

This, the writer concluded, "is your Confessional – the Confessional of the Roman Church." To leave the reader in no doubt, he summarised its effects: "it ruins men and women – it ruins society – it ruins all it touches." These were the charges that the enemies of Catholicism had been levelling since the Reformation.[108]

Although such a degree of vehemence by no means characterised all nativist attacks upon Catholicism, the concern with the power of the priest and with the Confessional was undoubtedly widespread in the 1850s, as indeed it had been throughout Europe since the birth of Protestantism. Often nativists detected conspiracies, as when Anna Carroll, virtually the high priestess of American nativism before the Civil War, claimed that priests "confess and forgive weekly, the sins of each other." Furthermore, the confessional gave the priest an extraordinary degree of power which could then be used for the most nefarious purposes. Once again the 1850s saw a revival of traditional anti-Catholic motifs when the sexual power of the priesthood, and the sexual proclivities of monks and nuns, were examined. Although this was by no means a principal theme in the 1850s, it was one which continued to attract attention.[109]

Yet the anti-Catholicism of the Know Nothings did not simply resuscitate charges that had been made for centuries. It also bore a clear imprint of mid-Victorian prosperity and economic expansion as well as the characteristic Victorian belief in progress. When examined by these lights, the Catholic Church was again found woefully inadequate, indeed deeply threatening. According to *The American's Text Book* image-worshipping and the attention given to relics and tombs resulted not in advancement and enlightenment but instead in superstition and ignorance. The effect was to stifle all progress and stunt all improvement. It was indeed "the chief objection to Roman Catholicism . . . that it never improves." As Justin Fulton observed, the "traditions and ceremonies" of Catholicism operated so as to "enslave the believer, entomb thought and shackle limb." Thomas Whitney was convinced that Roman Catholicism resulted in power for the clergy and ignorance for the masses.[110]

When they reviewed the history of Europe, nativists found that periods marked by the ascendancy of the Roman Catholic Church were periods "in which there were no inventions, there was no progress." Similarly, a

108. *Startling Facts for Native Americans* (New York, 1855), p. 109; *The Know Nothing and American Crusader*, Aug. 19, 1854.
109. Anna E. Carroll, *The Great American Battle* (New York, 1856), p. 301; *The American's Text Book: Being a Series of Letters Addressed by "An American" to the Citizens of Tennessee* (Nashville, TN, 1855), pp. 75–76.
110. *American's Text Book*, pp. 77–78, 60. The author even revived the old charge made by Martin Luther that the Church of Rome sold indulgencies at prices determined by the recipient's ability to pay – see Fulton, *Outlook of Freedom*, p. 369; Whitney, *Defence of American Policy*, p. 70.

comparison of present-day Protestant countries like England, the United States, and Switzerland with Catholic nations like Italy or Spain yielded the same conclusion: Roman Catholicism invariably produced poverty, servitude, and intellectual torpor.[111]

This was the context in which contemporary Roman Catholic criticisms of the nation's free schools were viewed. If, as Anna Carroll believed, education was no less than "the instrument of liberty, property and security to America," those criticisms were ominous indeed. Did they not illustrate a priestly fear of education and confirm that Roman Catholicism was hostile to individual reflection and improvement? Moreover, the Catholic hostility to the King James Bible, thought to be far clearer and more accessible than the Catholic version, seemed yet more evidence that Roman Catholicism was inherently obscurantist and reactionary. Finally, the control over education wielded by nuns and priests seemed deeply alarming to Protestant nativists. For how could "these miserable specimens of human nature esteem the domestic, social, and civil virtues, when they have renounced them forever and are incessantly teaching others to do so?" Any state in which such practices prevailed was inevitably "closed to all liberal cultivation of the mind, to all high moral illumination, to ennobling freedom, to human felicity, to industrial development, thrift, and fortune – to the highest destination of man."[112]

Despite these manifold criticisms of Roman Catholics, nativists in the 1850s did not usually seek to prevent them from entering the United States. Although the immigration of criminals and paupers was roundly condemned,[113] even in the peak years of immigration there were no proposals to prevent the Catholics of Ireland, Germany or any other nation from coming in large numbers into the United States. Justin Fulton supplied a rationale for this attitude when he explained that in the United States Catholicism would simply be unable to withstand the competition

111. *Mass Meeting of the Citizens of Washington, Sept. 27, 1854* (n.p., n.d.), p. 18; Fulton, *Outlook of Freedom*, pp. 375–377.

112. Carroll, *Great American Battle*, p. 57; Whitney, *Defence of American Policy*, p. 66; Fulton, *Outlook of Freedom*, p. 259; Hales, "Shaping of Nativist Sentiment," pp. 43, 47; *American's Text Book*, pp. 74–75. Thus the *Know Nothing and American Crusader* demanded that a "*free bible*" be taught in schools "and not the riddled, and patched, and disjointed, and unchristianized Jesuit botch-potch" – Aug. 19, 1854.

113. See, for example, *Speeches of Millard Fillmore at New York, Newburgh, Albany, Rochester, Buffalo, etc Also Evidence of Frémont's Romanism* (n.p., n.d.), p. 10; *Mass Meeting of Citizens of Washington*, p. 30.; *American's Text Book*, p. 27; Samuel Busey, *Immigration: Its Evils and Consequences* (New York, 1856), pp. 110–120; John Sanderson, *Republican Landmarks* (Philadelphia, 1856), pp. 26–38. *Speech of William R. Smith of Alabama in the House of Representatives, January 15, 1855* (n.p., n.d.), p. 6; *The Republic: A Monthly Magazine of American Literature, Politics and Art*, IV (Oct. 1852), pp. 210–212; *The Know Nothing and American Crusader*, Aug. 19, 1854.

from Protestantism. It was, he held, America's destiny to be Catholicism's gravedigger, "to give the principle which has beggared Europe an appropriate burial upon the forest continent of America." "The hum of commerce," he predicted, "shall be its requiem – happy and enlightened millions its pall-bearers – the Bible its disease, and an untrammelled liberty its epitaph." On this logic Protestantism had nothing to fear from Catholicism.[114]

Such logic, however, assumed that the incoming Catholics would be exposed to the healthful influences of Protestantism. Hence the importance of public schooling. More important, it assumed that there would be a transitional period during which the prejudices of Catholicism should not be given artificial stimuli. And this in turn meant that the nation's politicians must not pander to those prejudices and thus prevent the proper assimilation of the Catholics, many of whom would then freely convert to Protestantism. Here we encounter the major policy aim of the Know Nothings: a lengthening of the period of naturalisation. Most nativists wanted twenty-one years, rather than the current statutory requirement of five, to elapse before the immigrant was naturalised. In this way, they reasoned, just like the native born, the immigrant would have twenty one years to familiarise himself with American society, with American mores and with the American polity.

It was not always entirely clear how an extension of the naturalisation period would address some of the evils for which the nativist held the immigrant responsible. Many nativists argued that immigrants committed a disproportionate amount of crime and that their poverty in effect levied a tax upon the native born (who had to supply them with charity or fund local relief). Although the exclusion of paupers and known criminals was clearly aimed at this problem, nativists argued that a lengthening of the naturalisation period for the remainder would indirectly play a similar role. The reason was that involvement in politics "tempts immigrants to become the tools of corruption, enters them into habits of dissipation, converts honest mechanics and labourers into lounging loafers and pillars of pot-houses, and finally leads them to ruin and the penitentiary." The exclusion from politics of recently arrived immigrants was thus to their advantage as much as to the advantage of the native born.[115]

The same logic impelled many, though not all, nativists towards a second major goal. Many believed that the foreign born should be excluded from political offices. In some respects this was a more radical proposal than the extension of the naturalisation period and for this reason could

---

114. Fulton, *Outlook of Freedom*, p. 392.
115. Gayarré, *Address to the People of Louisiana*, p. 26.

not command universal support, even among confirmed nativists. Nevertheless, these were the twin political objectives of the Know Nothings, as they had been of previous nativist movements. Neither was attained in the antebellum years but this did not prevent nativists from expending considerable time and effort upon them.

Many nativists held that at present the foreign born were in control politically as a result not only of the offices they directly held but also because there was an immigrant block vote, cast in the many elections where they held the balance of power. Hence many Know Nothings believed that they had embarked upon a crusade which aimed at nothing less than the recovery of American government from alien forces. This goal was expressed in their frequently repeated slogan: "Americans should rule America."[116]

## III

When nativists looked upon contemporary American politics, they did not like what they saw. In effect they offered an indictment of American political life, which, they believed, was scarred by a multiplicity of abuses. But more fundamentally, many of them voiced a profound concern about democracy itself and the nation's populistic political culture. They doubted whether large numbers of Americans were fit to be members of the political community. Political rights and privileges, they fretted, were being cheapened. Thus much of the impetus behind the drive for a longer naturalisation period came from the belief that liberty and political rights within the United States were privileges which not every human being, even if adult, white, and male, was necessarily equipped to enjoy. There was thus an explicit repudiation of the claims made for all adult white males by Democrats (and some Whigs). Thomas Whitney, for example, rejected the principle of universal white male suffrage and rejected too the idea that all men "without regard to the intelligence, the morals, the principles of the man" had a right to "take part in the control of the State." At a time when Democrats were steadily reducing the qualifications needed (for adult white males) for the suffrage and claiming that an "enlightened self-interest" was sufficient, Know Nothings instead clung to the older view that emphasised freedom, judgment and restraint rather than license, passion or mere "impulse."[117]

116. *Mass Meeting of Citizens of Washington*, p. 10. Hales, "Shaping of Nativist Sentiment," p. 202.
117. Whitney, *Defence of American Policy*, p. 126. See also Jacob Broom, *An Address Delivered at Castle Garden, Feb. 22, 1854* (New York, 1854), p. 8; *The American Text Book for the Campaign of 1856* (Baltimore, 1856), p. 14. It is important to note that the temporary upsurge in nativist support in 1854 and 1855 may well have been in response to a less elitist appeal than the one I am analysing here – see, for

These were precisely the qualities which immigrants, particularly Roman Catholic immigrants, were thought to lack. Those who had been brought up in Europe, and especially in Roman Catholic Europe, were simply unfamiliar with the practices, mores and attitudes that were appropriate in republican America. Millard Fillmore, when running for president as the American Party candidate in 1856, confirmed that "as a general rule, Americans should govern America." The reason was that "men who come fresh from the monarchies of the old world are prepared neither by education, habits, or thought, or knowledge of our institutions, to govern Americans." And it was important to note that, as another nativist put it, "there could be no ingenious and sudden process by which you can transform the sluggish elements of ignorance and stupidity into the scintillations of wit, the inspirations of genius, or the carefully hoarded acquisitions of learning." Such people simply could not "be expected to understand the complicated machinery of our political system."[118]

This reference to the complexity of the American political system betrayed a key tenet of the nativist faith: American liberty was itself a delicate plant which had been nourished over centuries and which could not be tended by immigrants, and especially Roman Catholic immigrants, without considerable time and effort. It was simply not the case that all individuals were entitled to the rights enjoyed by native-born Americans. Americans themselves had served a long apprenticeship. According to Thomas Whitney, the United States on the eve of Independence "had been prepared for the transition by the training of a century and a half in the school of self-reliance."[119]

To this delicate constitutional fabric, foreign influence was therefore a profound threat. As the author of the *American's Text Book* put it, there was an urgent need to guard "our most delicate and beautiful flower of constitutional liberty" against the "withering blight of *foreign* influence." The ignorant simply could not understand "the science of government" which was in fact "the greatest of all sciences." Even seven years were not enough to understand the American system of government, a system "so intricate, yet so nicely adjusted, with its admirably arranged checks and balances."[120]

example, the argument advanced in John R. Mulkern, *The Know Nothing Party in Massachusetts: The Rise and Fall of a People's Movement* (Boston, 1990). But, as Mulkern notes, no sooner had the Know Nothings won office in Massachusetts, and elected elitists like Henry Gardiner, than their populism evaporated.

118.  *Speeches of Millard Fillmore*, p. 10; Gayarré, *Address to the People of Louisiana*, p. 11.
119.  Whitney, *Defence of American Policy*, pp. 14–16.
120.  *American's Text Book*, pp. 7–8; Whitney, *Defence of American Policy*, pp. 126–127; Busey, *Immigration*, pp. 5–6.

Roman Catholicism, nativists believed, rarely equipped men for inclusion in a republican polity. If Catholics lacked the necessary restraint to govern even themselves, it surely followed that they were not fit to play a part in the governance of others. "Men who are lax in principle," Thomas Whitney argued, "will make laws and elect lawgivers in conformity with their own notions of right and wrong." Whitney concluded that "the utmost prudence should be observed in granting or extending the right of suffrage." Indeed in a Fourth of July Address delivered in 1851 before the Order of United Americans he compared "the right of suffrage in the hands of an ignorant populace" with "a magazine in the keeping of a lunatic."[121]

The problem was that the immigrant, brought up in tyranny, was unable to appreciate the subtleties of American freedom. He was all too likely to parrot terms like "democracy" and "freedom" without really understanding them. Upon his arrival in the United States "the flood gates of passion and desires long pent up, and closed by unnatural restraints, are now thrown apart." The result was that "the individual, having conceived a false estimate of liberty, rushes forth to the opposite extreme." As Henry Winter Davis observed, all too often the immigrant could not distinguish liberty from anarchy, freedom from license.[122]

Many of these arguments marshalled against the recently enfranchised immigrant were comparable to the antidemocratic utterances of the Federalists in the 1790s directed against the "lower orders." They had also been the refrains of the more conservative Whigs in the 1830s and 1840s. More generally, they resembled contemporary conservative thought throughout Europe. In effect the older hostility towards the masses, openly avowed by the Federalists, and more cautiously expressed by large numbers of Whigs, had been displaced into an antagonism towards a number of large and growing ethnic minorities, themselves to be found disproportionately in the ranks of the poor and powerless. Like Federalists and the most conservative Whigs, many conservative nativists embraced democracy with some reluctance, if at all. Like Federalists and conservative Whigs they preferred the values of republicanism with their emphasis upon restraint, upon order, and upon unity.[123] According to John P. Sanderson, the American government was "not a democracy . . . subject to every fickle change

---

121. Whitney, *Defence of American Policy*, pp. 126–127; Whitney, "An Oration Delivered before the Order of United Americans, and Citizens of New Haven, Connecticut, July 4, 1851," in *The Republic*, II (July 1851), p. 92.

122. Whitney, *Defence of American Policy*, p. 131; Henry Winter Davis, *The Origin, Principles, and Purposes of the American Party* (n.p., n.d.), p. 24. See also *Speech of William R. Smith*, p. 4.

123. Whitney, *Defence of American Policy*, pp. 131–133. Whitney argued that the suffrage was the shield of liberty but only "where an unequivocal patriotism pervades the masses of the people."

and caprice of the people, without constitutional restraints, balances and counterbalances, and incapable of keeping to any course but that of the popular current." "Our system," he concluded, "is a *Republic*, as contradistinguished from *Democracy*."[124]

Perhaps because of their doubts about democracy and their concern with the stability of a popular government, some nativists were convinced that the nation required of its citizens not merely residence within its boundaries or naturalisation after a fixed period, but also attachment to a distinctive set of attitudes, mores and habits. These shared attributes would be, as John Sanderson explained, a source of cohesion and unity:

> Race, kin and kindred, training and tradition, devotion to country, knowledge of its institutions, history, trials, progress and achievements, an aggregation of men that have a country and love it, feel that they have nationality and place a value upon it, have ancestral graves and ancestral toils to look and dwell upon, an ancestral spirit to be inspired with, precepts to respect, examples to imitate, and an inheritance to glory in, as well as a present blessing to be enjoyed – all these are requisite to make an American and constitute an American nationality.

This emphasis upon the qualities needed for the franchise or for officeholding derived in part from an evaluation of the political regimes in existence elsewhere in the world. Just as Catholic nations were denounced for their lack of economic progress and vitality so they were condemned for their inability, as nativists believed, to sustain stable representative government. In Europe there was merely "tyranny and misery" while in Latin America "our Southern Sister Republics" exhibited "ceaseless insurrections, massacres and proverbial instability." Moreover, the failure of the revolutions of 1848 seemed to confirm this analysis. Some nativists drew attention to the case of France, where republic had once again been supplanted by empire. "Why," asked one Know Nothing, "has she not been able to become free?" The answer was simple: "because she is not Protestant." In nativist eyes liberty was as precarious as it was precious.[125]

It was not, however, merely the personal inadequacies of the Catholic immigrant which alarmed the nativist. There was also the question of his

---

124. Sanderson, *Republican Landmarks*, pp. 236–237. For the claim that the premature enfranchisement of immigrants undermined the Constitution's checks and balances, see *American's Text Book*, p. 10.
125. Sanderson, *Republican Landmarks*, p. 333; *Mass Meeting of Citizens of Washington*, pp. 3, 18; Whitney, *Defence of American Policy*, pp. 23–35; *Speeches of Millard Fillmore*, p. 10. Whitney also argued that the recent experience of France showed that universal suffrage could be "easily converted into an instrument of despotism" – *The Republic*, III (Jan. 1852), p. 45. See also Hales, "Shaping of Nativist Sentiment," pp. 219–255.

loyalty to his adopted nation. Here the power of the priesthood once again loomed large. By means of the confessional, it was feared, the priest could compel obedience to a set of values different from those of an enlightened patriotism. "The subjects of the priest," according to Frederick Anspach, Lutheran Minister from Maryland, "have less freedom of will than the slaves on our plantations, and are, therefore, totally incompetent to exercise intelligently the elective franchise." But behind the priest stood, of course, a still more sinister figure: the Pope. The Roman Catholic immigrant's allegiance to the Pope placed an immediate obstacle between him and his adopted country, much to the chagrin of the nativist. Anna Carroll voiced the most strenuous objections to the Pierce administration on the grounds that it had favoured the Roman Catholic element within the population. Carrroll referred to those "aliens among us, whom ... in virtue of their imperishable allegiance to the Pope, cannot, whether gone through the forms of naturalization or not, ever become American citizens." This implied that even a twenty-one year wait might not be enough for these immigrants.[126]

Some nativists pressed this analysis still further. They claimed not only that the Roman Catholic Church was injurious to the American Republic but that there was an orchestrated conspiracy on the part of the Pope and perhaps European heads of state, against republican America. There was a plot, as "Parson" Brownlow put it, "to overturn the civil and religious liberties of the United States." Others, without going so far, claimed that the influence of a prominent Roman Catholic leader such as Archbishop John Hughes of New York was so vast that he had "made and unmade, governors, legislators and presidents." Thus the very structure of the Roman Catholic Church served to undermine the principles of representative government in America.[127]

Yet even as they rallied to the defence, nativists displayed their own dissatisfaction with contemporary American politics. Much of their indictment of contemporary political life was in effect a commentary, not merely upon certain ethnic and religious groups, but also on the populistic forces unleashed by the Democratic party especially since the time of Andrew Jackson. Most Know Nothings were both anti-democratic and

---

126. Frederick R. Anspach, *The Sons of the Sires: A History of the Rise, Progress, and Destiny of the American Party*, (Philadelphia, 1855), p. 169; Anna E. Carroll, *A Review of Pierce's Administration* (Boston, 1856), p. 127. See also *American's Text Book*, p. 41. A minority of nativists did indeed believe that immigrants should never receive political rights; such privileges would be extended only to the second and subsequent generations.

127. Brownlow, *Americanism Contrasted with Foreignism*, p. 5. See also Robertson, *The American Party*, p. 15; *The Republic* I (Jan. 1851), p. 38; *The Dollar Times* (Cincinnati, OH), March 1, 1855; Fulton, *Outlook of Freedom*, p. 227; [Anspach], *Sons of the Sires*, pp. 46, 169.

anti-Democratic in their core values. They had little respect for Thomas Jefferson, still less for Andrew Jackson and his successors at the head of the Democratic party. Instead they venerated Washington, Madison, and, more recently, Henry Clay.[128]

Alongside their emphasis upon the qualities required for voting, nativists stressed the qualities needed for office. In common with those in the Federalist tradition and like conservative Whigs in the 1830s, 1840s, and 1850s, they believed that true statesmanship required qualities possessed by only a small minority within the population. As Frederick Anspach of Maryland put it, "not all are born to govern, and comparatively few possess the high attributes that should characterize a ruler or law-maker." Yet it was "of the highest moment, to have wise and able statesman," a fact which, he claimed, "both the old parties had lost sight of... altogether." Instead, nativists believed, the present age had seen the replacement of the statesman with the demagogue. And the demagogue was crucially dependent upon the immigrant vote, for the untutored immigrant "has all the passions of humanity" which "may be inflamed by designing men, to a pitch bordering on insanity." The result was that "whole classes of frantic enthusiasts may be marshalled by thousands to the polls, and with their unreflecting votes bear back the calmer judgment of the nation." The demagogue would appeal to the prejudices of the ignorant and, as all good citizens knew, "an appeal to a single prejudice, like a spark of fire in a magazine, is alone sufficient to produce the direst results." Here was the link between immigration and the decline in political leadership that had become unmistakeable in recent years, especially at national level. As George Robertson concluded, Roman Catholic immigration "breeds *demagogues* and banishes *statesmen.*"[129]

In much the same way Charles Gayarré of Louisiana drew attention to what he took to be an alarming decline in the quality of statesmanship currently in evidence within the nation. According to Gayarré "the veriest jackasses in the land, those who had the longest ears, and who were saddled with the heaviest bags of putrefaction" had been "transformed into the highest officers of the land." There had been "a complete inversion of the social body, and its lowermost extremities raised to that point of elevation where alone the majestic forehead should have been." Indeed the mere possession of office suggested that the officeholder had made "some degrading sacrifice." How had this arisen? Gayarré concluded that

128. See, for example, [Anspach], *Sons of the Sires*, pp. 46, 85, 169; Carroll, *Great American Battle*, pp. 354–355.
129. [Anspach], *Sons of the Sires*, p. 46; Whitney, *Defence of American Policy*, p. 41; Robertson, *The American Party*, pp. 2–3. See also *The Republic*, I (Jan. 1851), p. 43; *The Dollar Times* (Cincinnati, OH), March 1, 1855; Jean M. Baker, *Ambivalent Americans: The Know Nothing Party in Maryland* (Baltimore, 1977), p. 77.

foreign influence, the scope offered to the demagogue by the enfranchised immigrant, was at the heart of the problem.[130]

If immigration were linked with demagoguery, then both were associated with the tyranny of the political party. Once again political charges that had been levelled in previous decades were revived. In the heyday of Andrew Jackson, conservatives had argued that party loyalty resulted in the elevation of unfit party hacks and demagogues rather than wise and sagacious statesmen. Nativists now added a further twist when they insisted that party loyalty itself encouraged, and was encouraged by, demagogic appeals to the immigrant. Antiparty sentiment and nativism thus merged in the minds of many Know Nothings, even as they were in the processes of founding their own political party. The close relationship between the two is apparent from a description of the American party offered by Percy Walker of Alabama. The party, according to Walker,

> was composed of men who, believing that the constant and unceasing influx of foreign and distracting elements into the country was pregnant with danger to the purity of the ballot box, and destructive of that earnest and enlightened patriotism which is the life and soul of our institutions, were determined, if possible, to effect a change in the system of naturalization; of men who were convinced of the demoralization of old parties, and their inefficiency for the general good; and who, moved by the suggestions of a high and solemn duty, were anxious to weaken the force of *partyism*, which had so long degraded political associations, lowered the character of men, and detracted from the dignity of the Government, and who were emulous of achieving the great work of restoration to the pure conduct and lofty, patriotic aims of their fathers.[131]

Some Know Nothings were willing to concede that until the 1840s or even perhaps until 1852 there had been conflict between the parties over real and significant issues. But from the early 1850s at the latest, decline had set in. Spoilsmen and demagogues had finally triumphed and they had been unscrupulous in employing the votes of the immigrant to achieve their goals. The decision of the Whigs in 1852 to appeal to the Roman Catholics and to immigrants bulked large in this indictment since it meant of course that both major parties were now complicit in the debasement of political life.[132] For some nativists the desire to dampen the spirit of

---

130. Gayarré, *Address to the People of Louisiana*, pp. 4–5, 11–13.
131. *Letter of Hon. Percy Walker, of Alabama, To His Constituents, In Reference to the Election of Speaker* (Washington, DC, 1856), p. 3.
132. Know Nothings were alarmed at the riotous nature of election days and complained about "excitements, riots, affrays, bettings, buying up of votes, illegal voting, drunkenness, debauchery, and other iniquities" – for all of which immigrant voting was held responsible – see *American's Text Book*, pp. 31–32.

party was perhaps even more important than the need to restrain the immigrant (though of course the two were intimately related). According to Henry Winter Davis of Maryland, it was no less than "the purpose of the American party" to "redress these evils by substituting government by the *people* for government by a *party*."[133]

## IV

Although the Irish Roman Catholic immigrant was the principal target for nativists' criticism, he was not, of course, their sole concern. Other immigrants were also viewed with great suspicion. In fact one problem for the Know Nothings was to find a principle which would justify the disproportionate attention given to Irish Catholics. This was perhaps what George Robertson had in mind when he lamented the fact that "foreigners cannot be classified by law so as to make any legal discrimination as to their naturalization." Thus "we must naturalize all or none." In other words, it was not easy to find a governing principle on which to base one's prejudices or with which to make them properly consistent.[134]

Among the most difficult groups for the nativist to classify were Protestant immigrants. Many Germany and Irish Protestants were themselves deeply hostile to Roman Catholicism and some nativists were clearly reluctant to lose them as allies in what was, in large part, a Protestant crusade. Thus one Know Nothing editor announced that theirs was "emphatically an Anti-Catholic movement" which therefore "claims the support of every Protestant." Similarly Anna Carroll, though a bitter critic of Catholic immigrants, had a very different view of Protestants. "Whoever heard," she asked, "of an Irish or other foreign Protestant disturbing the peace or voting fraudulently at elections?" On the contrary, she continued, "we find them worthy, useful, respectable, and industrious in all the pursuits of American citizens." As a true enemy of the Catholic Irish Carroll attributed the good conduct of these Protestants to the Bible teaching they had received in their youth. Yet these immigrants often had no

---

133. [Davis], *Origin, Principles, and Purposes of American Party*, p. 15. Davis believed that 1850 had marked, or should have marked, the end of the second party system – see pp. 18–19. As these remarks make clear, the antiparty animus of many nativists owed much to their conviction that there was, by 1854, little or nothing to choose between the major parties. In this respect therefore, they arrived at the same ideological destination as their predecessors who had formed the nativist parties of previous decades and who had also complained of the tyranny of party. Yet ironically, they had taken a very different route. In the 1830s and 1840s nativists had complained that the foreign vote had promoted Democratic radicalism and hence unnecessarily widened the gulf between the major parties – see Ashworth, *"Agrarians" and "Aristocrats,"* pp. 186–187.

134. Robertson, *The American Party*, p. 18

more experience of politics than their Catholic counterparts with the result that many of the same criticisms could be levelled against them. Moreover, nativists trumpeted their belief that religion and politics must be kept separate. This made it difficult to find ways of discriminating, as far as office holding and naturalisation were concerned, between immigrants on the basis of religious affiliation.[135]

An additional consideration prevented nativists from discriminating against Roman Catholics, regardless of their ethnic background. If Protestant immigrants were difficult to come to terms with, some of the native-born Roman Catholics were even more troublesome – precisely because they were not troublesome. Unfortunately for the nativist, in states like Maryland and Louisiana there were well-established Roman Catholic families who by Know Nothing yardsticks measured up very well. Hence it was extremely difficult for nativists to attack Roman Catholics indiscriminately. "I acknowledge with pleasure," one Know Nothing announced, "that American-born Roman Catholics are generally as intelligent and patriotic as any other class of citizens," while another distinguished between those who accepted the temporal power of the Pope (in effect the immigrants) and those who did not (in effect the native-born). As staunch a nativist as Thomas Whitney went out of his way to praise the Roman Catholics of Louisiana, who were not, since they rejected the Pope's temporal power, "Papists."[136]

The problem was most acute in Louisiana. New Orleans was one of the few southern cities which attracted immigrants in large numbers but with its French roots and cultural traditions, it was also home to many highly affluent Roman Catholic families. These families were in danger of falling foul of any religious test for officeholding such as that put forward at the Know Nothing National Convention held in Philadelphia in June 1855. The purpose of the test was clear: it was intended to proscribe the Catholic immigrant, and especially the Irish Catholic. But it inevitably caught the "good" Catholics too. Charles Gayarré, himself in this category, denounced the test in the most uncompromising manner:

> It was conceived in the womb of ignorance, fathered by prejudice, nurtured by fanaticism, and pushed into the place which it now occupies by the efforts of narrow brained bigots and shallow politicians, who thought it would be an element of success, when appealing to the worst instincts of the human heart.

135. *The Dollar Times* (Cincinnati, OH), March 1, 1855; Carroll, *Great American Battle*, p. 315.
136. *Mass Meeting of Citizens of Washington*, pp. 5, 14; Whitney, *Defence of American Policy*, pp. 104–105. See also (on the subject of "good" Roman Catholics) Robertson, *The American Party*, p. 21; Gienapp, *Origins of Republican Party*, p. 196; Baker, *Ambivalent Americans*, pp. 45–46.

Thus the native-born Roman Catholic was as awkward to classify as the foreign-born Protestant. And just as nativists welcomed the Protestant immigrant, so some of their organisations, such as the Order of United Americans, allowed Roman Catholics to join. Thus neither religious affiliation nor ethnicity was entirely satisfactory as a basis for discrimination.[137]

Most of the criticism of immigrants focussed upon their religion or their ethnic loyalties. But there was another category of immigrant whom Know Nothings roundly condemned. These were the radicals who had entered the United States, often in the wake of the failed revolutions of 1848. Small but vociferous groups of European radicals were by the early 1850s demanding fundamental changes in the political and social systems of the host nation. Indeed they now subjected the Republic to a searching critique. The political and social conservatism of most nativists meant that these radicals attracted their ire. They were therefore believed to be little better than Irish Catholics.

Nativists prided themselves on a political heritage which, they believed, was untainted by the radical excesses of continental Europe. Percy Walker in his description of the American Party in 1856 recalled that the goal had been to establish a party "that had in it no admixture of the vague, speculative Germanic theories of Government" nor of "Red Republicanism, belched forth by unstable France in her heavings and throes of her revolutionary spirit." Hence the activities of radical immigrants within the United States were greatly to be deplored. As Frederick Anspach pointed out, "it is not from Catholics alone that danger is to be apprehended." Also to be feared were "socialists and infidels," "men who would tear our noble charter into fragments" and "shiver our social structure to atoms." Thomas Whitney warned of these "Red Republicans," "men who were "red with the blood of the innocent," men who would "gladly abolish law and Gospel at a single swoop." In the United States they were to be found advocating the abolition of the Senate, the Presidency and of landed property.[138]

Although utterly different in almost all respects from the Roman Catholic immigrants, these radicals, nativists were convinced, resembled them in having no true appreciation of American liberties. Indeed the United States offered them "more liberty than they are capable of employing and enjoying rationally." Thomas Whitney explained that their

---

137. Gayarré, *Address to the People of Louisiana*, p. 33; Hales, "Shaping of Nativist Sentiment," pp. 106–110.
138. *Letter of Percy Walker*, p. 3; Anspach, *Sons of the Sires*, pp. 103–104; Whitney, *Defence of American Policy*, pp. 171–174.

experience in Europe, like that of the Roman Catholics, had simply not equipped them to cope with American political life.

> Bred to a hatred of their own home-government, they have acquired an almost instinctive hostility to all government. Taught by sad experience to regard the rulers of their native land as tyrants, they do not realize the possibility of a government of equal and liberal laws. Never having seen liberty, they know not what it is, and with the first tastes of its sweets, all restraints, civil and religious, become alike irksome to them. They soon begin to regard all laws as oppressive, whether they emanate from the edict of a despot, or the openly-declared will of a free people.

The European-born radical thus took his place alongside the Roman Catholic immigrant as a target of nativist hostility.[139]

## V

As we have seen, the political outlook of the most highly committed nativists – Thomas Whitney, Jacob Broom, Frederick Anspach, Anna Carroll, for example – was strongly Whiggish. Moreover it was, in many respects, the outlook of conservative Whiggery. It is not therefore surprising to find that nativists espoused a social philosophy that was also akin to that to which Whigs and especially northern Whigs had been committed for more than two decades. Indeed many nativist comments about American society are indistinguishable from those which Whigs had been wont to make.

At the heart of their beliefs lay the assertion that American society was inherently fair and just. Thus William Smith announced that he never yet "saw an honest, healthy man, that could not earn his daily bread; who could not, with the labor of his own right arm, get enough for himself, his wife and children." From this much followed. Nativists embraced a holistic view of American society which stressed mutual interdependence between different groups. There should be no conflict between labour and capital, rich and poor, agriculture and manufacturing. All should progress together.[140]

It followed that the politics of conflict advocated by radicals and, in previous years at any rate, by many Democrats, was utterly inappropriate.

---

139. Whitney, *Defence of American Policy*, p. 179; Carroll, *Great American Battle*, pp. 309, 355–361; *The Republic*, II (Oct. 1851), p. 118. A revealing objection to the German radicals was voiced by John Sanderson who complained that their goal was to convert the American republic into a democracy – see Sanderson, *Republican Landmarks*, p. 236.

140. *Speech of William R. Smith*, p. 6. See also *The Republic*, I (June 1851), p. 32.

Thomas Whitney expressed a fear of the levelling tendencies of democracy that had been the hallmark of Whiggery since the days of Andrew Jackson. He complained bitterly of the tendency to array rich against poor. Similarly he insisted that in the United States labour occupied a position utterly different from that which it held in Europe. The American mechanic, he argued in classic Whig fashion, was "morally, socially, and politically, on a par with his fellow citizens of every calling." Whitney nevertheless recognised that there were currently problems facing American labour. Yet these were entirely the product of immigration. Supply had simply exceeded demand. He painted a picture of the conditions facing the labourer before the onset of mass immigration, a picture that might have been drawn by a northern Whig of the Webster stripe:

> Before the unequal competition of immigrant labor cast its shadow over the industrial interests of our country, every American journeyman mechanic was enabled, by the force of his industry, to maintain a financial position equal to that of his social, moral and political position. He was sure of employment, at wages adapted to the dignity of his franchise; to the necessities of the present, and the vicissitudes of the future. He could dwell in his own cottage, supply his family with comforts and luxuries, rear his children respectably, find time for his own mental improvement, and lay by a little of his earnings each week for a rainy day. Neatness and cleanliness pervaded his home, and the cheerful hearth was to him the ever-welcome refuge from toil.

But with mass immigration had come, for many labourers, a catastrophic decline in living standards. Although "many an American mechanic still lives in the enjoyment of his just privileges," yet "how great the proportion of those who, from want of employment, or reduced compensation, or both, have been alienated from their homes, their comforts, their ambitions." The problem was that the native-born worker was being undercut by the immigrant; he "cannot live upon the pittance demanded by his European competitor."[141]

This was the reasoning that led many nativists to demand an end to pauper immigration. This single act, it was felt, would restore the labour market to its former equilibrium and allow workers to receive, once again, high wages. Thus the nativist assumed that the fundamental structures of the American economy were entirely sound. There was nothing wrong in working for wages and American society would esteem its wage-earners and reward them appropriately, so long as the evils of mass immigration were ended. Indeed some nativists pushed these arguments still further and, as they did so, reform of the naturalisation laws became something

141. Whitney, *Defence of American Policy*, pp. 132, 308–309.

of a panacea. Know Nothings frequently commented upon the crime that disfigured many American cities. This too they laid at the door of the immigrant: "to immigration alone," Thomas Whitney declared, "we are indebted for the vast excess of crime which so often startles the moral sense of our communities."[142]

Once again the underlying assumption was that American society was essentially good and harmonious. It is important to stress that this social philosophy closely resembled that of the Whigs. Not only were many Whigs, as we have seen, sympathetic to nativism, they too had emphasised the essential fairness of the American and especially the northern social order, and the uniquely advantageous position of the American labourer. They too had warned that the American worker could not compete with his European counterpart. The difference was that the Whig warning had usually been delivered with reference to the protective tariff (which was advocated in part as a measure that would boost American wages) rather than to immigration. But a similar social and political conservatism underlay the attitudes and policy demands of Whig and nativist alike.[143]

## VI

The evils for which the immigrant was, in the eyes of nativists, responsible were many and varied. The immigrant vote had debased the political system by promoting the demagogue at the expense of the statesman and the party at the expense of the nation. The presence of large numbers of immigrants had undermined the position of American labour and brought crime and pauperism on a huge scale to American shores for the first time. Know Nothings believed that their movement alone could prevent the social and political decline of the Republic.

There was, however, an additional concern. Nativists insisted that immigrants bore a heavy responsibility for the growth of sectionalism within the United States. Historians have long recognised that by 1856 the Know Nothings were strongly Unionist. They were by then sectional moderates hoping to steer a course between the extremes of North and South. But these attitudes in fact underlay the movement from the first,

---

142. Whitney, *Defence of American Policy*, pp. 183.
143. There was, as with the Whigs, occasionally some criticism of the capitalist class in the United States. Once again, however, the assumption was that the social order was essentially just and benign so that these evils could be corrected merely by the ending of pauper immigration – see Whitney, *Defence of American Policy*, p. 311; Busey, *Immigration*, p. 81. And like the Whigs many nativists were prepared to champion reforms such as the abolition of child labour – see Hales, "Shaping of Nativist Sentiment," pp. 139–142.

even though at times when sectional issues were not so prominent they inevitably received less attention.

The Know Nothings were powerful both north and south of the Mason-Dixon Line and, accordingly, were never able to achieve anything approaching unanimity on the question of slavery. Nevertheless the range of opinion within the party was far narrower than that within the nation as a whole. Although there were members who defended slavery as a going concern in the southern states, there were no proslavery theorists, southerners who were prepared to assert that slavery was inherently (rather than in certain localities at certain times) a more stable foundation for an economy and a society than free labour. A common attitude in the South was that of George Robertson of Kentucky. Robertson believed that slavery was "probably more harmful to the master than to the slave" but at the same time insisted that southerners must be left to deal with the issue themselves. Interference would merely "rivet the chains" of the slave. Most southern Know Nothing leaders had previously been Whigs and this had been the mainstream southern Whig opinion on slavery.[144]

The absence of southern proslavery ideologues within the party was matched by a corresponding dearth of Garrisonian abolitionists. The typical northern nativist was in no sense a defender of slavery in the abstract; on the contrary he was likely to voice a clear disapproval of the institution. But however little sympathy northern party members might have for slavery, most went out of their way to dissociate themselves from abolitionism in all its variants.[145]

Thus most Know Nothings rejected sectional extremism whether northern or southern in inspiration. They took pride in the fact that the American party contained no southern secessionists and no northern disunionists. Instead Know Nothings, as Frederick Anspach pointed out, were utterly dedicated to maintaining the integrity of the Union. George Robertson argued that "foreign influence and domestic faction" had "progressed to such an extremity as to bring the constitutional Union of the States, and the Constitution itself, to a trial of their strength, more severe and perilous, than any to which they have ever been subjected." The antidote however, was easily administered. In order to safeguard both Union and Constitution, one merely needed to support the Know Nothings: "to maintain the integrity of the one, and the supremacy of the other, is the ultimate object of our American Organization."[146]

---

144. Robertson, *The American Party*, pp. 27–28.
145. Whitney, *Defence of American Policy*, pp. 203–204. *The Republic*, II (Oct. 1851), p. 179.
146. Anspach, *Sons of the Sires*, p. 142; Robertson, *The American Party*, p. 25.

From here it was but a short step to the conclusion that the controversy between North and South was needless and groundless, artificially stimulated, and stirred up by politicians who were themselves under the sway of foreign influence. In 1850, Thomas Whitney claimed, opinion in the North and South alike had been "outraged by the course pursued by the national representatives and eager for a cessation of the dangerous controversy." The Order of United Americans, he further maintained, had striven to restore order to the nation. Indeed the Compromise of 1850, he claimed, rather implausibly, "*was the work* of the OUA." By the time the Know Nothing membership was beginning to grow in the early 1850s, party loyalty had been ebbing and the parties "were gradually dissolving into a sectional slime, whose stagnant and fetid odors would have been poisonous to the national health." The threat to the nation was obvious: "the current of political fraternity had ceased to flow across the geographical line, dividing the Northern from the Southern States, and as a result of estrangement, sectional hostilities were being engendered in their most noxious form." But the American party had stepped into the breach and its advent "opened a new avenue to intersectional harmony." It "broke down the imaginary line of Mason and Dixon," it "re-established political inter-course between the North and the South" and it "fearlessly stood forth the advocate of State sovereignty, and the foe of the spirit of disunion."[147]

Know Nothings believed therefore that in combating foreign influence they were simultaneously removing the causes of sectional strife. They accepted that northerners and southerners inevitably differed over slavery but they could see nothing to prevent peaceful co-existence between the sections, nothing that is, except the baleful political influence of the immigrant.[148]

Some Know Nothings accordingly went out of their way to blame antislavery upon immigrants, though often on the basic of highly dubious reasoning. The author of *The American's Text Book*, for example, claimed that "*foreignism*" was "the prolific source of *Abolitionism*" on the grounds that immigrant labourers felt degraded by working alongside slaves and were thus attracted to antislavery doctrines and parties. The problem here was that there were few immigrants in the South anyway and it was surely absurd to attribute abolitionism to them.[149] Edwin G. Reade of North Carolina, on the other hand, argued that President

147. Whitney, *Defence of American Policy*, pp. 275–277, 286–287.
148. *Letter of Hon. Edwin G. Reade, of North Carolina, To His Constituents* (Washington, DC, 1856), p. 3.
149. *American's Text Book*, p. 21. There was a link between immigration and abolition but it operated to make slaveholders hostile to immigrants and thus reduce the number of immigrants in the region.

Franklin Pierce, controlled by the foreign vote, had appointed Free Soilers to office and thus promoted abolitionism. Reade invited his fellow countrymen to "join the American party and strike down foreignism, which is the main cause of abolitionism." But it was difficult to claim that the Pierce administration, which probably tried to do as much for the slaveholding South as any in the nation's history, was fundamentally antislavery. When it appointed Free Soilers to office this was the consequence rather than the cause of antislavery sentiment; few antebellum presidents were more hostile to the principles of free soil or abolition than Pierce.[150]

An alternative link between antislavery and immigration was discerned by Charles Gayarré of Louisiana. Gayarré referred to the pernicious influence of "higher law" men like antislavery Senator William Seward of New York and sought to rally southerners in opposition to him. Seward was the *bête noire* of Know Nothings for his attempts to appeal to Roman Catholics and to immigrants but if he combined antislavery with the bitterest attacks on nativism this was, as far as historians have been able to determine, not a particularly common attitude within the electorate as a whole. Many immigrants, and especially the Irish Catholics, the largest and most despised immigrant group of all, were notoriously hostile to antislavery in all its forms as well as being indifferent to the plight of the slave. In no direct sense therefore could an appeal to Irish Catholic immigrants be said to further the cause of antislavery.[151]

Thus Know Nothings found several links, however tenuous they might now appear, between immigration and antislavery and denounced both in the name of sectional harmony and of the Union. In a much vaguer sense, however, they linked sectionalism and immigration by claiming that the former was caused by the degeneration of the political parties and the disappearance of true statesmanship, which were themselves the product of the latter. Thomas Whitney referred to "the demagogues who have taken the lighted torch of discord from the hands of foreign agitators, and waved the scorching flame across the land." The demagogue thrived on the votes of the immigrant and the discussion of slavery, a subject on which passions were easily aroused. Whitney indeed believed that many designing politicians had espoused free soil and abolition doctrines purely to retain power and office.[152]

150.  *Letter of Reade*, pp. 5–6; *Letter of Percy Walker*, p. 8.
151.  Gayarré, *Address to the People of Louisiana*, p. 10. Gayarré also claimed that when sectional conflicts were most bitter, the exclusion of foreign influence became of even greater importance. It was imperative "to exclude naturalized citizens from political power, as long at least as this awful crisis may last" – see p. 28.
152.  Whitney, *Defence of American Policy*, pp. 208, 225; *The Republic*, I (March 1851), p. 131. For further examples of the association between foreign influence and sectional discord, see *The Republic*, II (Oct. 1851), p. 231.

It followed that if true statesmen rather than demagogues and principled political parties rather than gangs of unprincipled spoilsmen were placed once again in control of the Republic then sectional conflicts would soon be quieted. If the American party were supported, Charles Gayarré claimed, "we shall soon have in office throughout the land the purest and most enlightened of our patriots; and then, all the discrepancies, the diversity of opinions, feelings, interests and prejudices which may exist among us, would be reconciled."[153]

In this sense too therefore the Know Nothings were the heirs of the Whigs. In the party's heyday, many northern and almost all southern Whigs had believed that sectional animosities could be curbed by wise statesmen and prudent voters. Daniel Webster and Henry Clay had each maintained that the differences between North and South were eminently compromisable and each had dreaded an appeal to passion, whether made by northern abolitionists or southern militants (or radical Democrats). These were precisely the attitudes adopted by most Know Nothings.

There was, however, a major difference which was a source of both weakness and strength to the Know Nothings. In taking their opposition to the immigrant much further than the Whigs, Know Nothings were able to tap into the resentments of native-born Protestants more directly than the Whigs had ever done. This perhaps gave the Know Nothings a slightly more plebeian character, or at least a more plebeian appeal, than mainstream Whiggery had been able to generate. At the same time, however, the desire for moderation, for elite leadership and for harmony within American society and the American polity did not sit easily alongside potentially explosive denunciations of Catholics and foreigners. This problem might have become acute if the Know Nothings had lasted longer as a major political force.

Instead nativism proved to be the casualty of the very forces it was in part designed to resist. As we have seen, hostility to immigrants and to Roman Catholics was intended to unite native-born Americans and to serve as, among other things, a counterweight to sectional animosities. The intensification of those sectional animosities provided the final spark in 1854 that the American party needed and it accordingly entered its period of most rapid growth. But from that point onward Know Nothings would be called upon to redeem their promises. They would then be called upon to demonstrate that an appeal to the native-born could indeed counteract sectional loyalties. Instead, when the moment of truth came, they were to find that sectional loyalties were too deep and would instead overwhelm the ethnic, religious and national appeal that they had sought

153. Gayarré, *Address to the People of Louisiana*, p. 36.

to make. Instead of nativism uniting the sections, sectionalism would divide and destroy, as a political force, the nativists.

## Collapse of the Whigs and Know Nothings, 1852–1856

### I

In October 1853 former President Millard Fillmore wrote a letter to his fellow conservative Whig, John P. Kennedy, in which he speculated about the future course of national politics. Fillmore hoped, as conservative Whigs had intermittently hoped for twenty years, that a new Union party might be formed which would eschew sectional extremism and proscribe sectional extremists. Fillmore offered a penetrating analysis of the process by which new parties might be formed. "Parties," he asserted, "are broken up by local causes and that centrifugal force which throws individuals and masses beyond the attraction of the central power." Local factors might thus prove decisive in the destruction of old parties. But the creation of a new party, he believed, was a different matter: "new parties of a national character can only be gathered from these fragmentary *nebula* of dissolving systems by the magnetism of some great national and centripetal force at Washington."[154]

There was much truth in this analysis, more in fact than Fillmore himself knew. The disintegration of the second party system was indeed well advanced at the time he wrote and local causes, particularly temperance and the religious controversies of the preceding years, had played a significant part. But Fillmore's prediction that a great national event was needed proved entirely correct. That event was the passage of the Kansas-Nebraska Act in 1854. Yet ironically while the former president had been hoping for an act or event that might precipitate the formation of a Union party, composed of sectional moderates, it set in motion a sequence of events that would result instead in the death of not one but two organisations in which many sectional moderates (including Fillmore himself) had been enlisted and in their replacement by a new one whose very existence would signal a new deepening of the sectional divide. Over the next three years the Whig party would dramatically collapse, the Know Nothings, after a period of extraordinarily spectacular growth, would collapse even more dramatically, and, most dramatically of all, the Republican party, explicitly antislavery in a way that no other major party had yet been, would emerge as the main challenger to the Democratic party in the North and consequently in the nation as a whole. In so doing the Republicans

154. Millard Fillmore to John P. Kennedy, Oct. 14, 1853 quoted in Holt, *Whig Party*, p. 802.

would rapidly jettison the temperance cause, towards which, as we have seen many antislavery spokesmen had shown considerable sympathy. The next three years would therefore witness a dramatic transformation in the American political landscape.

In early 1854, however, when the Kansas-Nebraska bill was introduced into Congress, these developments still lay in the future. At that time, as we have seen, the Whigs had been damaged by the obsolescence of the issues that had traditionally separated them from the Democrats and by their inability to cope with the sectional pressures that had generated the controversy about "finality" in 1852. The temperance movement had cut across party lines and injured both parties while the Whig pro-immigrant stance of 1852 had removed yet another source of interparty conflict. And waiting in the wings were the Know Nothings, who, it is apparent with hindsight, stood ready to exploit any eruption of nativist sentiment.

Yet as late as 1854, it has been estimated, the total Know Nothing membership was a mere 50,000. The composition of the organisation was precisely what one would have expected of a group espousing conservative Whig values. Know Nothings as yet tended to be town dwellers and a disproportionate number of them were manufacturers and merchants. But from June 1854 the membership soared and by the end of the year was perhaps as high as a million. Yet no new religious controversies had emerged in the interim. The reason for the spectacular increase was that many saw the new organisation as a means to pursue goals that were as important as, or even more important than, nativism. For some this meant temperance, which as we have seen, had some clear links with nativism. For a larger number it meant antislavery. And the trigger for the resurgence of antislavery was, of course, the Kansas-Nebraska Act, which became law only at the end of May 1854.[155]

## II

The Kansas-Nebraska Act was emphatically a Democratic measure. This was true not simply because it was introduced by Stephen A. Douglas, already a pre-eminent Democrat, but also because it was, as we have noted, quite consonant with Democratic values. The two major parties had traditionally clashed over the West, with Whigs generally suspicious of attempts to expand the nation's territory and, in general, advocating the improvement of existing land rather than the opening up of new areas.

---

155. Anbinder, *Nativism and Slavery*, pp. 31–36. The analysis that follows is indebted to Anbinder who in turn interprets the political upheaval of the 1850s broadly along the lines suggested by Eric Foner in *Free Soil, Free Labor, Free Men*. Michael Holt and William Gienapp do, of course, advance a very different view.

Cheap land too had traditionally been a Democratic priority. Moreover, the repeal of the Missouri Compromise and the surrender of congressional control over slavery in the newly created territories, while in one sense departures from past practice, were nevertheless square in the logic of the traditional Democratic preference for decentralisation and for state's rights.

The identification of the Kansas-Nebraska Act with the Democratic party was further strengthened by the overwhelming opposition it elicited from northern Whigs. Nevertheless the measure did not bring about a revival of the two-party conflict. Not only were many northern Democrats deeply disturbed by it and indeed, as it transpired, unable to stomach it, but southern Whigs could not maintain their ranks in opposition. On the contrary, as we shall see, the great majority of them rallied to it, though with varying degrees of enthusiasm. As a result, far from reviving the party system, the Kansas-Nebraska Act, as historians have generally recognised, marked a key stage in its disintegration.

In fact southern Whig complicity in the Act went even beyond the support they provided. When the legislative manoeuvrings were still at an early stage it was not clear whether Douglas's bill would actually repeal the Missouri Compromise or not. At this point it was a Whig, Archibald Dixon from Kentucky, who intervened and sought an amendment that would remove all ambiguity and thus allow slavery into the territory. This was an example of a southern Whig seeking to outdo Democrats as a defender of slavery. Other southern Whigs had occasionally used this ploy in the past with other issues, only to find their party subsequently outbid by the Democrats. All Whig attempts to ratchet up the politics of loyalty, in other words, had previously ended in failure. The Kansas-Nebraska Act would prove no exception.[156]

Although some northern Democrats were deeply hostile to the Act, the greatest outcry against it came from northern Whigs, not a single one of whom proved willing to vote for it in either house. The attitude of southern Whigs was thus of critical importance. Some northern Whigs warned them that the party would be destroyed as a national force if they supported it. Moreover, there was, when Douglas first introduced the bill in January 1854, no pressure within the South for a repeal of the Missouri Compromise. Such an initiative was simply not expected.[157]

Still more important, there were principled reasons for the southern Whigs to reject the bill. The Missouri Compromise had been one of Henry Clay's greatest accomplishments and it represented a victory for the

156. See Mrs Archibald Dixon, *True History of the Missouri Compromise and Its Repeal* (Cincinnati, 1898), pp. 437–449.
157. Holt, *Whig Party*, p. 814.

enlightened statesmanship which he was believed to have embodied and which Whigs had always celebrated. To destroy it was thus to betray the Clay legacy. It was, furthermore, a denial of the prescriptive force of the past which Whigs had always cherished as a counterweight to Democratic radicalism. Democrats might scorn the force of precedent, Whigs did not. Thus John Minor Botts of Virginia, who had long been one of Henry Clay's greatest admirers, denounced the Act as "the most mischievous and pernicious measure that has ever been introduced into the halls of Congress." What force would future congressional acts have if the most time-honoured of them could be so easily overturned? In this most general sense, some southern Whigs thus objected to the bill as a repudiation of a precious heritage and an invitation to set aside the accumulated wisdom of the past.[158]

More specifically, some southern Whigs pointed out that the Compromise of 1850 might soon meet the same fate. "If a Compromise which has stood the test of one-third of a century is no longer available or operative," Botts asked, "how long can the Compromise of three years duration be expected to last?" The danger was that the Act would reopen the entire slavery question, which had been settled in 1850. And had southern Whigs not been insistent that the settlement of 1850 should indeed be final? But northern opposition to Douglas's bill made it apparent that a new storm of controversy was gathering. Thus the Raleigh *Register*, most influential of all Whig newspapers in North Carolina, warned that the bill would have the direst consequences. "The proposition to repeal the Missouri Compromise act," the newspaper predicted, "will not fail to awaken the smothered fires of political anti-slavery from Maine to Iowa, with all its fearful consequences to the peace and happiness of the country."[159] And Botts along with John J. Crittenden of Kentucky, William Graham of North Carolina and newspapers like the New Orleans *Bee*, the Savannah *Republican* and the Louisville *Journal* all reminded southerners that they were pledged to oppose all attempts to reopen the slavery controversy.[160]

Finally southern Whigs were by no means convinced that slavery would go into Kansas (or Nebraska). The Arkansas *Whig* complained that the Act "opened to slavery no territory to which slavery would ever go, while it reopened the slavery agitation, which has, in every instance, resulted unfavourably to the South." There was therefore considerable logic in the conclusion of Sion H. Rogers of North Carolina "I doubt very much,"

158. *Letter of John Minor Botts, of Virginia, On the Nebraska Question* (Washington, DC, 1853), p. 3.
159. *Letter of Botts on the Nebraska Question*, pp. 3–4, 8; Raleigh *Register*, Feb. 1, 1854.
160. Savannah *Republican*, Jan. 28, 1854; Cole, *Whig Party in South*, pp. 295–300; Holt, *Whig Party*, p. 814; Nevins, *House Dividing*, p. 134.

Rogers wrote, "the propriety of repealing the Missouri Compromise, without effecting by it some practical good to the South."[161]

Rogers carried his principles into action by voting against the bill when the critical moment came. But other southern Whigs took the opposite course. The problem for the party as a whole was that many southern members found even stronger reasons to support the new bill. As we have seen, it proved irresistible to almost all southern Democrats. It appeared to offer an entirely unexpected but hugely beneficial windfall. As we have already noted, there were several possible gains. For one thing, slavery might go into Kansas. Even many southern Democrats doubted this but others, including neighbouring Missourians, thought otherwise. Even if this did not happen, the principle of popular sovereignty might perhaps facilitate the acquisition of slave territory elsewhere. Since northerners had refused to extend the Missouri Compromise to the Pacific in the late 1840s it was not clear how else southerners could obtain more slave states. Finally the denial of congressional power over slavery in the territories was clearly of benefit as a precedent. The ever-growing numerical power of the North meant that constitutional bulwarks, precedents to protect slavery from northerners, were not to be scorned. These were the reasons that brought southern Democrats almost unanimously in favour of the Act.[162]

These advantages, or potential advantages, enabled southern Democrats to place extraordinary pressure upon southern Whigs. The attitude of the *Mississippian* was typical. The *Mississippian* was the foremost Democratic newspaper in Mississippi and it vilified, as traitors to the South, those who did not vote for Douglas's bill. Those southern Whigs who opposed the bill were denounced for being "ready to sacrifice the true interests of the country and the rights and honor of the slaveholding States upon the altar of party." In the same way the Milledgeville *Federal Union* warned that there were "some men," by which it meant, of course, southern Whigs, "in whose bosom the hatred of Democracy is even stronger than the love of country." As the struggle over the bill forced northern Democrats onto the defensive, southerners were urged not to betray them. "On this subject," according to the *Federal Union*, "there should be but one party at the South."[163]

Many southern Whigs took up this refrain. The Richmond *Whig*, as influential as any Whig newspaper south of the Mason-Dixon Line,

161. Arkansas *Whig*, June 1, 22, 1854; Sion H. Rogers to William Graham May 11, 1854 in *Papers of Graham*, IV, p. 514. Rogers later added: "I think I can show myself a much better Southern man, than those who voted and spoke for the bill" – Rogers to Graham, May 25, 1854 in *Papers of Graham*, IV, p. 516.

162. Sam Houston of Texas was an exception. But he was, as a direct result of his vote against it, driven out of the Democratic party.

163. *Mississippian*, March 17, April 21, 1854; Milledgeville *Federal Union*, Feb. 14, 1854.

insisted that southern congressmen must leave no doubt about "the soundness of Southern Whigs upon the questions involving the peculiar institutions of the South" and supported the Act. The Raleigh *Register*, ended by doing likewise despite expressing the objections we have already noted. In Kentucky, where pro-Union sentiment was extremely strong, the Whigs nevertheless took the same course.[164]

Part of the problem was that southern Whigs were, as ever, tainted by the antislavery attitudes of their northern colleagues. As in the past, Democrats could score heavily in the South by claiming that the Whigs not only harboured, but were actually controlled by, northern antislavery extremists. The Democracy, by contrast, in adopting the Act and making it no less than a test of party loyalty, was far less vulnerable to this charge.

As controversy over the bill raged, so many southern Whigs felt themselves placed under intolerable pressure. Alexander Stephens and Robert Toombs of Georgia, who had in effect separated from the party some time earlier, had no difficulty in supporting it; indeed Stephens played a vital role in ushering it through the House of Representatives. But they were unusual in being quite indifferent to the fate of the Whig party. For most others the experience was far more painful.

Of particular importance was the course taken by John Bell, now representing Tennessee in the Senate. Bell's political career was a long and distinguished one culminating in his bid for the presidency in 1860. But his finest hour perhaps came when the Kansas-Nebraska Act was being debated in Congress. Bell understood that the measure was an extremely difficult one for southerners to resist but with great prescience he warned that slavery would not in fact be established in Kansas, that the opposition to the repeal of the Missouri Compromise in the North would be so intense as to remove the possibility of any future territorial gains for the South, and that the overall effect would be to leave opinion on the slavery issue polarised as never before. In all these predictions he was proved correct.[165]

Yet Bell also reported in the Senate that some of his fellow southern Whigs who had initially been hostile to the bill had, under pressure from

---

164. Richmond *Whig* quoted in Cooper, *South and Politics of Slavery*, p. 354. As Volz observes, "although there were many Kentucky Whigs who had opposed the passage of the bill, and there remained some who would have privately acquiesced in its repeal, most understood that they could not maintain their supremacy within the state if they advocated repeal. The Democrats would at last be able to convict them in the court of public opinion of being untrue to the state and the South" – see Volz "Party, State and Nation," p. 173.

165. *CG*, 33/1, App. pp. 940–943. Bell did not, however, address the conundrum that had impelled Douglas to repeal the Missouri compromise in the first place: to leave the land in question unorganised was clearly absurd in an era where so many Americans dreamt of a transcontinental railroad; yet support for the organisation of that land could not be had with the Missouri Compromise intact.

their constituents or their colleagues, capitulated. He acknowledged too that he himself had been told again and again that his career as a public man in the South would be over if he opposed it: "I ran a great risk," he wrote in August 1854, "of losing standing in the South & at home in going against the Nebraska bill." This was an accurate reflection of the pressures which southern Whigs now faced. "I did not ask for it," said Senator John M. Clayton of Delaware, "I would not have proposed it; and I may regret that it was offered, because I do not believe that it will repay us for the agitation and irritation it has cost." "But," Clayton asked, "can a Senator, whose constituents hold slaves, be expected to resist and refuse what the North thus freely offers us as a measure due?"[166]

In the event few southern Whigs managed to vote against the Kansas-Nebraska Act. In the Senate Bell was alone; apart from Democrat Sam Houston he was the only southerner to oppose it. Nine southern Whigs were in favour. In the House, where the success of the bill had always been less certain, thirteen southern Whigs supported it and seven opposed it. (Four others did not vote.) The measure had been from first to last a Democratic one but when the final vote was taken and it was passed by 113 to 100 the votes of those thirteen southern Whigs had clearly proved decisive.[167]

The impact of the Kansas-Nebraska Act, the controversy accompanying it as well as the final vote, on the Whig party as a national organisation was immense. In the North, many Whigs at first had felt that they had been handed a huge vote-winner. It may be that some of them even felt that they could repeat the strategy of 1848 and run different campaigns north and south of the Mason-Dixon Line with northerners denouncing the bill and southerners defending it. Thus William Seward later claimed that he had himself encouraged Dixon to offer his amendment in order to make the bill as objectionable as possible in the North, while allowing southern Whigs to gain some of the credit for it in the South. If the objective were indeed to make the measure as offensive as possible in the North, then Seward assuredly succeeded but the rest of his strategy, if such it were, came badly unstuck. As a party the Whigs got little credit in the South but the contradictory responses of northern and southern members played a huge role in discrediting their party as a national organisation. Indeed it soon

---

166. CG, 33/1, App., pp. 940–943; Bell to William B. Campbell, Aug. 10, 1854 quoted in Cooper, *South and Politics of Slavery*, p. 356; Cole, *Whig Party in South*, p. 293. See also Paul H. Bergeron, *Antebellum Politics in Tennessee* (Lexington, 1982), p. 106; Nevins, *House Dividing*, p. 117.

167. Richard W. Sadler, "The Impact of the Slavery Question On the Whig Party in Congress, 1843–1854," (Unpublished Doctoral Dissertation, University of Utah, 1969); Holt, *Whig Party*, p. 821. Of the eight dissident southern Whigs, five were from Tennessee, two from North Carolina and one from Louisiana.

became apparent that the Kansas-Nebraska Act, together with the events in Kansas that directly followed its implementation, would preclude the possibility of any further union between northern and southern Whigs.[168]

This effect was produced by a process of action, reaction, and counterreaction which involved intraparty as well as interparty struggles. In the North the Whig opponents of the Kansas-Nebraska Act fell into two categories. One group, made up essentially of moderate or conservative Whigs of the Webster stripe, objected to it for reasons that were similar, even identical, to those advanced by those southern Whigs who also opposed it. They objected to it as essentially wrong-headed and imprudent and their views were expressed by Edward Everett of Massachusetts in a Senate speech on the bill.[169] Unfortunately for the Whig party and its future prospects, however, this was not the predominant attitude of northern party members. Instead the measure was, as we have seen, excoriated by antislavery Whigs (as well as Free Soilers and abolitionists) as confirmation of the predatory instincts and unscrupulous tactics of the Slave Power. Anticompromise Whigs now seemed vindicated in that, as they had predicted from the first, southern proslavery groups had simply failed to respect the Compromise of 1850 as a final settlement of the slavery controversy. What hope could there be, it was asked, of them respecting any future bisectional agreement? In other words the Kansas-Nebraska act gave a tremendous boost to the antislavery cause within the northern Whig party and in the North as a whole.

In fact within northern Whig ranks the plight of the conservatives was quite pitiable. In New York, for example, the Silver Grays, as the conservatives were known, with Millard Fillmore as their unofficial leader, had been fighting the more radical antislavery elements, led by William Seward, for many years and had staked much on both the Compromise in particular and on the trustworthiness of the South in general. The Kansas-Nebraska Act ruined them. One of their number, Solomon Haven, described its impact. Announcing that he was bitterly disappointed by the actions of "Whigs and moderate men of the South," he acknowledged that in 1850 the South had merely asked for what she had a right to. Not so in 1854. The result was that those northern Whigs who had defended her were now "placed in the equivocal position of having defended her in reference to a covenant she now shows she had no intention to keep." By the same token the "extreme men" in the North, by whom he meant Seward and his supporters, now occupied a position that was "impregnable."

168. Seward's role remains controversial and there is simply insufficient evidence on which to base any firm conclusion. A succinct summary of the evidence, for and against, is to be found in Cooper, *South and Politics of Slavery*, p. 379.
169. See CG, 33/1, App. pp. 158–163.

They could say "'I told you so.'" In this way Douglas's bill threatened to cut off "all communion" between Silver Grays and the South.[170]

Nor was the experience in New York in any way unusual. Edward Everett himself, though enjoined on all sides to present the conservative case against the Kansas-Nebraska Act, actually remarked subsequently that it might have been termed a measure "to annihilate all conservative sentiment in the non-slaveholding states." From Maine Edward Kent, himself a conservative Whig, reported that in his state "the feeling is intense & bitter, & the National Whigs as they are called are beyond all others mortified, enraged and determined." What had mortified Kent himself had been the actions of southern Whigs. In determining their stance on the Kansas-Nebraska Act they had at one point (February 15, 1854) held a meeting at which they had rejected the recommendations of the *National Intelligencer*, which advocated opposition. This meeting, according to Kent, had marked "the funeral of the national Whig party – or rather the choking and stabbing – preparatory to the funeral on the last night of the Nebraska bill."[171]

Other northerners also announced the death of their party, at least as a national organisation. Horace Greeley's *Tribune* reviled the southern Whigs and even William Seward (though he subsequently changed tack) warned that "we no longer have any bond to Southern Whigs." Benjamin Wade, Senator from Ohio, announcing himself an "abolitionist at heart," declared that "we certainly cannot have any further political connection with the Whigs of the South" while Truman Smith of Connecticut resigned his Senate seat and heaped scorn upon the southern Whigs. "Further cooperation with them will be impossible," he declared, "the break is final. We could not heal it if we would & would not if we could."[172]

The hostility of northern Whigs to the Kansas-Nebraska Act, together with their disgust at the course followed by most southern Whigs, was thus highly corrosive. Moreover it now produced a corresponding, retaliatory antagonism on the part of southern Whigs themselves who deeply resented the attacks and lack of sympathy of their northern colleagues. In the summer of 1854, stung by northern Whig denunciations of the South, and especially of the southern Whigs, the *Florida Sentinel* announced that "the Whigs of Florida have already *waived* their party affinaties [sic]

170.  Lee H. Warner, "The Silver Grays: New York State Conservative Whigs 1846–1856," (Unpublished Doctoral Dissertation, University of Wisconsin, 1971), pp. 251–256. Warner concludes that "the Kansas-Nebraska Act effectively killed the Silver Grays in New York" – see pp. 251–252.
171.  Letter from Edward Everett, Oct. 31, 1857, quoted in Nevins, *House Dividing*, p. 141; Edward Kent to Israel Washburn March 9, 1854 quoted in Holt, *Whig Party*, pp. 811, 819.
172.  Gienapp, *Origins of Republican Party*, pp. 86–87, CG, 33/1, App., pp. 763–765; Holt. *Whig Party*, p. 818.

and allegiance with Northern Whigs until they shall give unmistakable signs of repentance." This was especially worrying for the party in the South since the Whigs of Florida had been relatively successful in recent years. Similarly the Milledgeville *Southern Recorder* claimed in March 1854 that the hostility of northerners showed that it was in fact they who had repudiated the Compromise of 1850 as well as the Whig platform of 1852 and demonstrated that they were not prepared to treat their southern brethren as equals. And "we will have no party association that will not admit and treat us as equals."[173]

As a result some southern Whigs now announced that their party should cease to exist. This was the message of such important and influential party newspapers as the Savannah *Republican*, the Milledgeville *Southern Recorder*, the *Florida Sentinel* and the Petersburg *Intelligencer*. Of course, it was not unheard of for partisans to make such declarations in the heat of battle and then subsequently retract them. In this light the attitude of the Louisville *Journal* in Kentucky deserves attention. Its editor, George D. Prentice, announced that the Kansas-Nebraska Act had killed the Whig party. A little later (July 1854) he announced that the party might survive as long as the Kansas-Nebraska Act did not become a test of party orthodoxy.[174]

If the Kansas-Nebraska Act had operated as Stephen A. Douglas, for example, had hoped and expected, its impact on the Whig party might have been greatly diminished and Prentice's optimism might have been justified. If there had been intense controversy during debate on the bill, coupled with intense disappointment on the part of northerners upon its passage, but then no further disturbance of the sectional peace, continued collaboration between northerners and southerners would have been infinitely easier. Some southern Whigs hoped that northern resentment would subside when it became evident that slavery could not in fact go

---

173. Tallahassee *Florida Sentinel*, June 20, July 4, 1854; Milledgeville *Southern Recorder* March 14, 1854 quoted in Cooper, *South and Politics of Slavery*, p. 358.

174. Holt, *Whig Party*, p. 823; Volz "Party, State and Nation," pp. 168–173. It should perhaps be noted that on this point there is some confusion in Holt's account. Noting that the elections of 1854 in most southern states continued to see battles between Whigs and Democrats, he argues that "by itself that fact undermines assertions that sectional anger stirred up by the Nebraska debates, and especially southern Whigs' fury at northern Whig assaults on their support for the Nebraska measure, instantly caused southern Whigs to desert the Whig party. Southern Whigs instead gave every indication that they hoped to perpetuate the national Whig organization" – see p. 850. One wonders, however, how this is to be reconciled with the following statement: "Incensed by the anti-southern posture many northern Whigs assumed to win the elections of 1854, most southern Whigs by the end of that year renounced allegiance to the national Whig party" – see p. 838. Is the point simply that the traditional interpretation, stressing slavery and sectionalism, is correct but that it took a few months for the full effects of the Kansas-Nebraska controversy to make themselves felt? If so, this marks only a modest revision.

into Kansas. Others subsequently regretted the support they had given to the Act.[175]

But the antagonisms aroused by the Act simply did not abate after its passage. Northern Whig attacks upon slavery and the South instead increased to a crescendo during the state, congressional and even local elections of 1854. Not only did they feel that their worst fears about the South and the Slave Power were being realised, Whigs in the North had to compete with other parties (Free Soilers, Know Nothings) who were themselves not slow to denounce the Kansas-Nebraska Act. Moreover, in response to the passage of the Act, which seemed to demonstrate the perfidy of the South, some northern states (Connecticut and Rhode Island in 1854, Michigan, Maine and Massachusetts in 1855) in effect nullified the Fugitive Slave Act by enacting Personal Liberty laws. Only Democrats and the now hopelessly weakened national Whigs in these states offered effective resistance. Finally by 1855 events in Kansas were themselves causing uproar and would continue to do so for the next few years. In such circumstances the antagonisms unleashed by the Kansas-Nebraska Act, far from abating, actually intensified.[176]

This left southern Whigs with little reason to remain in their party. Already a minority within it, they had little to gain by a continued association. Even those who regretted their support for the Kansas-Nebraska Act realised that to repeal it was impossible. Repeal would look like abject surrender in the face of northern attacks. Moreover by 1855 hopes were running high in the South that Kansas might actually become a slave state. In the summer and early fall of 1854 elections were held in half a dozen southern states. These came in the context of an almost unbroken series of Whig defeats in the South since 1852 and the most important of them took place in Florida and North Carolina. Both resulted in crushing defeats for the Whigs. In September 1854 the Richmond *Whig* pronounced an epitaph for southern Whiggery. However much we might like the Whig party, the editor declared, "we love the South more." The *Whig* blamed the party's demise on northern hostility to slavery. There were to be no more statewide campaigns in the South for the Whig party and by the end of 1854 in all but one or two states the party was dead there.[177]

175. Holt, *Whig Party*, pp. 824–825.
176. Don E. Fehrenbacher, *The Slaveholding Republic: An Account of the United States Government's Relations to Slavery* (New York, 2001), pp. 236–238.
177. Richmond *Whig*, Sept. 26, 1854 quoted in Cooper, *South and Politics of Slavery*, p. 356. Ironically, the Whigs ran quite well in Missouri, where they had traditionally been weak. This was partly, one suspects, because there was considerable hostility to the Kansas-Nebraska Act within both the major parties. The alignment in Missouri was thus unusual. On these election results, see Holt, *Whig Party*, pp. 850–855.

This enables us to offer some preliminary observations about the collapse of the Whig party and the role of sectional antagonisms in bringing it about. The Democrats, it was clear, could survive after 1854 as a national party despite the substantial losses they incurred in the North as the northern electorate punished them for the Kansas-Nebraska Act. However, the experience of the Whig party suggested that it was not possible for an anti-Nebraska party, given the continued controversies over slavery in the territories, to gather support from both North and South. Thus sectional hostilities, unleashed by the Act but continuing up to and well beyond the presidential election of 1856, made a national Whig party, one which was strong both north and south of the Mason-Dixon Line, unsustainable. As we shall see, the same pressures would also undermine and finally destroy the Know Nothings. We need still to assess the role of ethnocultural issues in the upheaval of 1854–1856, but it is important to note that Whig experience suggests the inability of any party in these years to house both large numbers of southerners and committed northern enemies of slavery. In this respect therefore, the Whig experience underlines the importance of sectional forces in the political realignment of those years.

### III

For approximately two and a half years after the passage of the Kansas-Nebraska act, American politics assumed an extraordinary character. Few new issues now arose, other than those which grew out of events in Kansas, themselves the product of the Kansas-Nebraska Act. But remarkable changes nevertheless took place. As we have seen, at the start of the period several political movements were jostling for supremacy. In many states the temperance crusade was still extremely potent, in many states too, the Know Nothings were entering their period of most rapid growth, while in the North there was a widespread revulsion against the Kansas-Nebraska Act. Throughout the nation the disdain for established political parties that had been apparent since at least 1851 remained highly visible. The result was a bewildering array of parties and coalitions between parties.[178]

In these years the Democratic party was the only one that maintained its status. It suffered huge losses in the North, partially compensated by

---

178. There is no satisfactory synthesis of the politics of these years though there are many very fine histories of individual parties or states. Part of the problem is that those scholars who have immersed themselves in the political minutiae of these years have found it difficult to do justice to the trends that underlay these events and which transcended state boundaries – see Ashworth, "The Whigs, the Wood and the Trees," *passim.*

gains in the South, and in the process its character and composition were significantly modified. But, despite often intense factional infighting, it remained a single party, still able to win elections both north and south of the Mason-Dixon Line. The other political groupings had very different experiences. By November 1856 it was clear that the Whig party was dead. The results of the November 1856 elections also indicated that the Know Nothings were in a precipitous and irreversible decline. The temperance movement had also passed the peak of its popularity. In most states of the North the coalitions that had united temperance devotees, nativists and antislavery men in different combinations in different states and even localities had given way to a much simpler political alignment. By 1856 it was apparent that rather than Whigs, Know Nothings, Free Soilers or Republicans battling against the Democrats, in most of the North there would once again be a two-party system, this time pitting Democrats against Republicans, whereas across most of the South there would be the Democratic party and various ill-defined Opposition parties, none of which could easily challenge its hegemony.

Several factors made the politics of these years extremely complex, indeed chaotic. In the first place the issues being considered found expression at different levels within the political system. Opposition to the Kansas-Nebraska Act was primarily a federal matter, opposition to liquor was exclusively a state and local matter and opposition to immigration was federal, state and local. This enhanced the likelihood of split tickets with voters favouring say temperance at the local level, but antislavery nationally and thus supporting different parties during elections that might even be held on the same day. Sometimes the parties ran independently, sometimes there were instead attempts at "fusion" though not always with the same groups fusing and only rarely in the same proportions. Moreover there were affinities between all the movements vying to become the main anti-Democratic force in the North. Many nativists, for example, were, as we shall see, strongly antislavery while many temperance men, as we have already noted, blamed drunkenness on immigrant influence. On the other hand these movements were also partly in competition with one another and they produced sometimes conflicting alignments. We have seen that Know Nothings had difficulties with Protestant immigrants and with some of the Roman Catholic native born. Similarly German Protestants although anti-Catholic tended to dislike temperance. Many antislavery radicals despised nativism as both a distraction from the real issues and an unwarrantable attack upon the rights of immigrants and Roman Catholics. Finally the political situation was confused by the evolution of the Know Nothings. As we have also seen, they began with the attitudes to slavery characteristic of conservative Whigs. By 1856 this would again be their orientation on sectional and other questions. But in the intervening months their extraordinarily decentralised structure for a time allowed them in some, though not all, states in the North to express and to exploit much more radical antislavery sentiment.

In so highly decentralised a polity as that of the United States, the result was that almost every state in the North followed a distinctive path as the realignment of the mid-1850s unfolded.[179] Nevertheless certain patterns emerged, and at least five tendencies transcending state boundaries can be discerned.[180] First, in a majority of states the Know Nothings grew considerably in popularity and entered politics in the later part of 1854 (Maine, Massachusetts, Michigan) or the first months of 1855 (Iowa). The degree of success varied, however from state to state. In Massachusetts their achievements were extraordinary. They won for example the entire congressional delegation, every single seat in the state senate and ninety-nine percent of those in the lower house in 1854. In some other states (Vermont, Wisconsin) they made little impact. The result was that in several states they controlled the elections (Indiana, Pennsylvania, Massachusetts) but in only one did they manage to win independently (Massachusetts). Elsewhere either the Democrats hung on (Illinois), or, more often, they were defeated by combinations, sometimes coalitions, of anti-Democratic parties.[181]

179. The realignment had, however, begun earlier in the decade in the Deep South with the reorientation of politics in Alabama, Georgia and Mississippi– see James L. Huston, *Calculating the Value of the Union: Slavery, Property Rights. And the Economic Origins of the Civil War* (Chapel Hill, 2003), pp. 153–189, esp. p. 184.
180. The following paragraph makes mention of parantheses of some of the states to which these generalisations can be applied. These are intended to be examples, rather than exhaustive lists, of the states affected.
181. The generalisations in this and the following paragraphs are based upon (in addition to works already cited) Dale Baum, *The Civil War Party System: The Case of Massachusetts* (Chapel Hill, 1984); Carl F. Brand, "The History of the Know Nothing Party in Indiana," *Indiana Magazine of History*, XVIII (1922), pp. 47–81,177–206, 266–306; Arthur C. Cole, *The Era of the Civil War, 1848–1870* (Chicago, 1922); John F. Coleman, *The Disruption of the Pennsylvania Democracy, 1848–1860* (Harrisburg, 1975); Robert Cook, *Baptism of Fire: The Republican Party in Iowa, 1838–1878* (Ames, IA, 1994); Thomas J. Curran "Seward and the Know Nothings," *New York Historical Society Quarterly*, LI (1967), pp. 141–159; William E. Gienapp, "Nativism and the Creation of a Republican Majority in the North before the Civil War," *Journal of American History*, LXXII (1985), pp. 529–559; Stephen L. Hansen, *The Making of the Third Party System: Voters and Parties in Illinois, 1850–1876* (Ann Arbor, 1980); Michael F. Holt, "The Antimasonic and Know Nothing Parties," in Arthur M. Schlesinger Jr (ed.), *A History of U.S. Political Parties*, Vol. 1. (New York, 1973), pp. 575–737; Holt, "The Politics of Impatience: The Origins of Know-Nothingism," *Journal of American History*, LX (1973), pp. 309–331; James L. Huston, "The Demise of the Pennsylvania American Party," *Pennsylvania Magazine of History and Biography*, CIX (1985), pp. 473–497; Stephen E. Maizlish, "The Meaning of Nativism and the Crisis of the Union: The Know Nothing Movement in the Antebellum North," in Stephen E. Maizlish and John J. Kushma (eds.), *Essays on American Antebellum Politics, 1840–1860* (College Station, 1982); Stephen E. Maizlish, *The Triumph of Sectionalism: The Transformation of Politics in Ohio,*

Second, there was a clear tendency for states in the Upper North to display more antislavery zeal than those in the Lower North, as they had done for many years and would continue to do after 1856. Thus elections in the upper North tended to result in a victory for strongly antislavery candidates (Maine, New Hampshire), in contrast to the situation in some of the states of the Lower North, where lack of antislavery radicalism helped delay the formation of the Republican party (Pennsylvania, Indiana). These differences were also very visible within certain individual states. Thus the southern counties of Ohio, Indiana, Iowa and Illinois were far more moderate than the northern counties on the slavery question and far more likely to support Democratic candidates. Once again this phenomenon had existed before the 1850s and would persist beyond the Civil War.

Differences between East and West produced a third pattern. In the states of the West concern over the extension of slavery tended, other things being equal, to be more pronounced than in the East and for this reason, in part, the formation of the Republican party occurred quickest here (Michigan, Wisconsin). By contrast, nativist sentiment tended to be stronger in the East (where most Irish Catholics were located), and this both strengthened the Know Nothings and delayed the formation of the Republican party (Massachusetts, Connecticut, New Hampshire, New Jersey, Pennsylvania). This sectional pattern was sometimes visible even within a single state. Southern and eastern Pennsylvania, for example, displayed relatively less interest in the slavery issue, relatively more in nativism, than the northern and western parts of the state.

A fourth factor that transcended state boundaries concerned the prior strength of the Whig party. Where the Whigs were strong (Massachusetts, New York), they could sometimes block the formation of the Republican party whereas in weaker Whig states, the way was cleared either for the Know Nothings or the Republicans (Maine, Indiana). And finally there was a tendency for Whigs, as their party faced unprecedented challenges

*1844–1856* (Kent, OH, 1983); C. J. Noonan, *Nativism in Connecticut* (Washington, DC, 1938); Thomas H. O'Connor, *Lords of the Loom: The Cotton Whigs and the Coming of the Civil War* (New York, 1968); Louis D. Scisco, *Political Nativism in New York* (New York, 1901); Joel Silbey, "'The Undisguised Connection: Know Nothings into Republicans: New York as a Test Case," in Silbey *The Partisan Imperative: The Dynamics of American Politics before the Civil War* (New York, 1985), pp. 127–165; Kevin Sweeney, "Rum, Romanism, Representation and Reform: Coalition Politics in Massachusetts, 1847–1853," *Civil War History*, XXII (1976), pp. 116–137; Sister M. Evangeline Thomas, *Nativism in the Old Northwest, 1850–1860* (Washington, DC, 1936); John B. Weaver, "The Decline of the Ohio Know Nothings, 1856–1860," *Cincinnati Historical Society Bulletin*, XL (1982) pp. 235–246; John B. Weaver, "Ohio Republican Attitudes Towards Nativism, 1854–1855," *Old Northwest* IX, (1983–84), pp. 289–305.

from other groupings, to divide according to the liberal/moderate split that had existed in most states virtually since the party's birth. In some states (Massachusetts) the more conservative among them remained longer within the party, though in New York the opposite happened as they *en masse* joined the Know Nothings.

These were some of the principal patterns transcending state boundaries that influenced state politics in these years of extraordinary flux. But of course, some other factors were unique to particular states. Thus in New York William Seward came up for re-election to the Senate in early 1855 and his manager and *alter ego* Thurlow Weed did not want to disband the Whig party (if it were to be disbanded at all) until that re-election had been secured. This almost certainly delayed the formation of the Republican party in New York. Similarly the course of events in Massachusetts was almost certainly influenced by the rejection of the work of the 1853 Constitution Convention, a rejection for which the Irish were heavily blamed. In other states other unique considerations also made themselves felt. Nevertheless these factors accelerated or retarded the pace of realignment rather than decisively affecting the final outcome, by which the Republicans emerged as the major anti-Democratic force in the North.

In effect, therefore, the combination of events at Washington relating to the slavery controversy, the obsolescence of Whig economic policies at federal and state levels, and the simmering controversies within the states over temperance and nativism meant that state politics were, to some extent, cut loose from national and even regional developments, But only to some extent. Although each state followed its own path through the political turmoil of the mid-1850s, the outcomes were remarkably similar throughout the North and many of the paths, as we have seen, displayed important common characteristics.

The crucial question, however, concerns the relative importance of nativism (and temperance) and antislavery in the upheaval of these years. It is clear that the political chaos that characterised this brief period precludes any easy answer to this question. Indeed the question is even more difficult than even recent scholars have realised. Although there is little doubt that in most states in the early months of this realignment the Know Nothings exhibited greater strength than the Republicans, one cannot thereby conclude that nativism played the major role in the entire process. But to understand why such a conclusion is unwarranted, it is necessary to examine in more detail the relationship between the Know Nothings and the Kansas-Nebraska Act.[182]

---

182. This vital point is made with great force in Anbinder, *Nativism and Slavery*, pp. 66–67.

IV

The months that immediately followed the passage of the Kansas-Nebraska Act were precisely those in which the Know Nothing party grew most quickly. This was no coincidence. Even veteran nativists, those who had been in the party from the start and who would remain in it when its popularity waned, recognised that the repeal of the Missouri Compromise had provided a major fillip. Thus Frederick Anspach referred to "another cause which has contributed to the rapid diffusion of the principles of the new order, we rank as very efficient – the abrogation of the Missouri Compromise." More generally the Kansas-Nebraska Act was viewed by many nativists, even those who after its passage were not prepared to seek its repeal, as a clear illustration of the low level of statesmanship which the Republic now exhibited and against which the nativists intended to battle. Thomas Whitney, while opposing repeal, believed the Act was "not difficult to characterise as a gross and wanton violation of national integrity." The reason was that "so foul a wrong" as the repeal of the Missouri Compromise had led to needless agitation of the slavery question. Whitney, in common with many other nativists might have liked to restore it but like many others too he recognised that its restoration might only serve to increase the level of agitation and deepen the controversy still further.[183]

Nevertheless for the rest of the decade even those nativists who did not voice antislavery sentiments were often strongly critical of the Act as a threat to the peace and security of the Union, a reckless attempt to intervene in matters that were best left alone. Thus the Kansas-Nebraska Act confirmed the antiparty convictions of many nativists. Henry Winter Davis of Maryland argued that the Know Nothings were utterly opposed to the tyranny of party, as a result of which sectional tensions had been needlessly aggravated. Davis referred to recent "tampering with the peace of the country" and "the trifling with dangerous sectional passions."[184]

In the North, however, the Kansas-Nebraska Act did not merely confirm nativists' antiparty sentiments, it also generated a resentment of slavery from which the Know Nothings at first derived immense benefit. In other words it produced a huge but, as it would turn out, temporary accession of strength as many for whom antislavery was as important as, or more important than, nativism flocked into the Order.

183. [Anspach], *Sons of the Sires*, p. 142; Whitney, *Defence of American Policy*, pp. 218–219.
184. [Davis], *Origin, Principles, and Purposes of American Party*, pp. 13–15. Davis criticised both major parties for whipping up sectional animosity. In the North, he claimed, each courted the abolitionists; in the South each condemned the other for doing so.

These antislavery nativists sometimes stressed the similarities between slavery and the Roman Catholic Church. Thus Massachusetts Congressman Anson Burlingame claimed that the two were allied: "one denies the right of a man to his body, and the other the right of a man to his soul. The one denies the right to think for himself, the other the right to act for himself." Similarly the Hartford *Courant*, a newspaper which boasted a long record of commitment to the nativist cause, announced in March 1856 that it was "as hostile to the march of the slave oligarchy as we are to the control of a foreign potentate over free America." Henry Wilson, another antislavery Know Nothing, claimed that the Roman Catholic Church naturally sympathised with the oppressor while Thomas Spooner, president of the Know Nothings in Ohio, similarly argued that "Americanism and Freedom" were "synonymous terms" while "foreignism and slavery are equally so." Here the notorious opposition on the part of Irish Roman Catholic immigrants to the entire antislavery movement bulked large. Some Know Nothings even lumped antislavery together with both nativism and antiparty sentiment when they argued that, in order to resist the usurpations of the Slave Power, the North must cease sending to Congress "doughfaces" (northern men with southern principles), elected by Roman Catholic influence.[185]

These nativists took pains to explain the links between nativism and antislavery. Others, however, did little more than pay lip service to nativist principles. They were motivated by antislavery zeal and had come to the conclusion that neither the Whigs, because of their southern wing, nor the Republicans, because in most states they were still too weak in 1854, could meet their needs. Of course the secrecy of the Order helped them move out of their old parties and into new ones but the uncertainty which surrounded the Order could not last. Sooner or later a stand would have to be taken on sectional issues and if the Know Nothings could not meet northern antislavery expectations they could expect a collapse in their membership every bit as dramatic as the Whig collapse and every bit as rapid as their own rise.

Reflecting the influence of antislavery on the movement, in many northern states Know Nothings, when they won power, did everything possible to promote the cause of antislavery. In Massachusetts the legislature, dominated by Know Nothings, passed resolutions that demanded the restoration of the Missouri Compromise and the repeal of the Fugitive Slave law. It was at this session that a Personal Liberty law, effectively nullifying the Fugitive Slave act, was passed. More important, in Massachusetts as in almost every state, when the Know Nothings were in control they elected or re-elected antislavery Senators: in Massachusetts Henry Wilson,

185. Anbinder, *Nativism and Slavery*, pp. 45–46.

in Connecticut James Dixon, in New Hampshire, John P. Hale and James Bell. Some of these men endorsed nativist principles too but often in a cursory manner. Hale for example had been identified with antislavery for many years and his nativist credentials were scarcely convincing. Most remarkable of all, however, was the re-election of William Seward of New York, partly owing to the votes of Know Nothings. Authentic nativists detested Seward perhaps more than any politician in the land. He had had a lifelong and highly conspicuous hostility to their cause (which he would continue to display as a Republican) and it was he, more than anyone else, to whom the nativists attributed the recent Whig attempts to court the immigrant vote. Moreover, his re-election was secured despite the pleas of southern Know Nothings who feared it would damage them in the South. A major reason for his triumph was, of course, the slavery question, constantly in the public eye as a result of events in Kansas. "The American party in New York," announced a Know Nothing newspaper, "is Anti-Nebraska to the backbone.... It would be difficult to find a dozen members of the Order in any one Council who are not." Hence its members helped send Seward, the arch antinativist, back to Washington as their Senator.[186]

The antislavery zeal of so many nativists thus renders it difficult to ascertain the relative importance of nativism and antislavery in the nation during the early stages of the northern realignment of the 1850s. Contemporaries understood what a number of historians have not: anti-Nebraska sentiment was pervasive, especially in the Upper North, and it benefited the Know Nothings considerably. It followed that one could not and cannot determine the relative strength of nativism and antislavery by comparing Know Nothing and Republican voting strength in 1854 and 1855. Thus Henry Wilson, when elected as a Know Nothing to the United States Senate, replied to questions about the new party and explained that no-one could represent Massachusetts in Congress unless he were opposed to the Kansas-Nebraska Act. "Men of all parties," Wilson declared, "are opposed to it." In Massachusetts "we have no controversy there about it" since "Massachusetts is anti-Nebraska" – "nearly the whole population."[187]

Yet if the election of Know Nothings tells us little about the relative strength of nativism and antislavery, an examination of the legislative record at Washington is more instructive and allows some tentative

186. Anbinder, *Nativism and Slavery*, pp. 145–154, 185. In Pennsylvania no Senator was elected because it was impossible to agree on a candidate who satisfactorily combined nativism with antislavery.
187. CG, 33/2, App., p. 216.

conclusions to be offered. The elections for the Thirty-Fourth Congress which assembled in December 1855 resulted in victories for large numbers of Know Nothing candidates. Although the party affiliations of some Congressmen are extremely difficult to ascertain, it is likely that about 120 were Know Nothings in a house of 234 members. These Know Nothings can be classified into three groups. One group of about thirty were southerners, often referred to as Southern Americans. A second group of about ten or twenty was of northerners, National Americans who were in most respects the heirs of Clay and Webster. But the largest group of Know Nothings, comprising about seventy or eighty congressmen, were northern antislavery Know Nothings. Their attitudes present an opportunity to assess the relative importance of nativism and antislavery within the North.[188]

Unfortunately there was the usual gap of some twelve months between the date at which representatives were elected and the convening of the new Congress. These were months in which politics especially in the North were in a state of rapid flux. As a result it is difficult to know whether priorities had shifted in the intervening months.[189] However what is abundantly clear is that by the time Congress met antislavery was of far greater importance to these northern Know Nothings than nativism. Unlike the other two subgroups, they gave very little attention to nativist issues and rarely even spoke upon them. A detailed analysis of the *Congressional Globe* for the first session of this Congress confirms a clear difference in the priorities of the Southern and National Americans, on the one hand, and the antislavery northern Know Nothings, on the other. All groups found themselves obliged to give more attention to Kansas and to slavery than to nativism but this was done reluctantly by the Southern and National Americans who continued to put forward nativist proposals and to engage in nativist criticism of Roman Catholics and immigrants. The antislavery nativists, on the other hand, had a different agenda. At the top was the need to restore the Missouri Compromise and to prevent the further extension of slavery. As one of them put it, the passage of the Kansas-Nebraska Act had destroyed the North's faith in the South and had unleashed a "storm" that "has not yet subsided, and *it never will*, until that faith is restored in form or in fact." In short, they were far more antislavery than they were nativist. Perhaps the experience of

188. Here I am following the analysis of Owen Butler, "American Party Representatives in the Thirty-Fourth Congress" (Unpublished Masters of Research dissertation, University of Nottingham, 2002), undertaken under my supervision.
189. There was some controversy about the relative importance of antislavery and nativism in the elections even within a single state. Thus in the case of Pennsylvania contradictory claims were made – see *CG*, 34/1, pp. 39, 46.

major figures like Nathaniel Banks and of Anson Burlingame was typical. According to one historian they had taken "note of the early signs of support for the mysterious new order and rushed out to join the crowd so that they might lead it." And when the opportunity came they were quick to abandon it.[190]

Many of these antislavery Know Nothings were in the process of becoming, or had already become, Republicans. Consequently in the Thirty Fourth Congress they expressed views that would be widespread, in many cases universal, within the Republican party. For example they argued that the Constitution was an essentially antislavery document, that the Fathers of the Republic disliked slavery and wished to put it on the road to ultimate extinction and that legislation in the nation's early years had been entirely consistent with this goal.[191] They then identified a concerted movement on the part of the South or, as they often termed it, the Slave Power, to frustrate those goals. The Compromise of 1850 had marked the partial success of this movement, the Kansas-Nebraska Act marked a further step upon the slaveholders' road to national domination and events like the caning of Charles Sumner graphically illustrated the threat posed to the North and her statesmen.[192] Finally these antislavery nativists denounced slavery as a threat to the dignity of labour and to social mobility, as a fruitful source of aristocracy in the South and in the nation and, in some cases, as a moral evil imposed on millions of defenceless African Americans. This was letter-perfect Republicanism.[193]

It should be noted that most of these antislavery nativists did not repudiate nativism. Instead they ignored it. Undoubtedly the sequence of events that took place in 1856 in Kansas (together with the beating of Charles Sumner consequent upon those events) helped ensure pride of place for antislavery. But it is striking that even when the Congress first convened there was a bitter and protracted battle over the Speakership which resulted, after 133 ballots, in the election of Banks, himself an antislavery Know Nothing. Banks' election was secured because antislavery Know Nothings would not vote for a Know Nothing like Henry Fuller of Pennsylvania. Fuller was a confirmed, indeed a veteran, nativist but he was committed against the repeal of the Kansas-Nebraska Act and thus could not unite the whole strength of the Know Nothings. If the election of Nathaniel Banks to the Speakership in February 1856 represented the triumph of an antislavery nativist, it also demonstrated the triumph of antislavery over nativism.

190. CG, 34/1, App. p. 907; Mulkern, *Know-Nothing Party in Massachusetts*, p. 69.
191. CG, 34/1, p. 1588, App., pp. 35, 471, 677, 887, 907, 955, 1160.
192. CG, 34/1, p. 224, App., pp. 292, 677, 872–875, 907–908, 1196.
193. CG, 34/1, App., pp. 194, 294, 681–682, 906–907, 951, 954, 1165, 1201, 1215–1216, 34/3, App., p. 166.

## V

Although historians have scarcely recognised the fact, the Know Nothings who went to Congress for the session that opened in December 1855 closely resembled the Whigs whom as a party they had effectively replaced. The National Americans were Whigs of the Webster cast, the South Americans were ideologically akin to the southern Whigs and even represented similar regions and constituencies while the antislavery Americans had views and priorities that closely resembled those of antislavery Whigs. Of course not every Whig had become a Know Nothing, nor had every Know Nothing been a Whig but there was an unmistakeable similarity in personnel as well as in principle. The major difference between Whigs and Know Nothings was, of course, over nativism itself but even here the gap was narrower than might be imagined. As we have noted, many Whigs had traditionally held nativist sympathies; many Know Nothings, as we have seen, subordinated nativism to other goals, goals that had been shared by the Whig faction they most closely resembled. It is not therefore surprising that the Know Nothings, after their great triumphs of 1854–1855 should rapidly go the same way as the Whigs. In fact their demise was even more obviously the product of sectional divisions than that of the Whigs.

At first, however, slavery did not pose a problem for the Order. The Know Nothings were perhaps the most decentralised political party ever to emerge in the highly decentralised polity of the antebellum Republic. The secrecy of the Order together with its organisational structure meant that it sprang up in local communities throughout the nation from the early 1850s. There was therefore no pressure, scarcely even an opportunity, to produce a single consistent policy on slavery. The Order's very successes, however, resulted in its members beginning to covet control of the federal government and raised hopes that even the presidency might be within reach. This required a national organisation and, much more problematically, a policy, however vague or nebulous, on the sectional questions that in the aftermath of the Kansas-Nebraska Act, were agitating, indeed convulsing, the country.

Here was a problem of vast proportions. Prior to the reopening of sectional hostilities in early 1854 nativists had generally avoided the slavery question. On this basis they might have continued to unite Americans north and south of the Mason-Dixon Line. But the Kansas-Nebraska Act shattered these possibilities even as it spread disillusionment with the existing political parties and helped send men into the Order in their hundreds of thousands. Nativists might agree that the decision to repeal the Missouri Compromise had been an act of poor statesmanship. But beyond this it was difficult to go. Indeed over the next two years the Know

Nothings would again and again find it impossible to become more explicit on the slavery question whilst retaining members on the scale necessary to control the federal government.

The first significant Know Nothing national convention took place in November 1854 and it attempted to address the growing crisis over slavery. The ritual that accompanied membership of the Order was altered with a view to strengthening Unionist sentiment among members and in the nation as a whole. A new Union or Third Degree was appended to the ritual and platform which called on all members to "maintain and defend" the Union "against all encroachments and under all circumstances, and to put under ban of proscription any and all men who might be engaged in impairing its vigor or resisting its authority." This was the Order's first real attempt to address the sectional controversy within a national arena.[194]

It failed just as all subsequent attempts were to fail. The problem was to define and identify the enemies of the Union. Who were its enemies and who its friends? In fact in the 1850s everyone from Abraham Lincoln on one side to Jefferson Davis on the other could claim to be a friend of the Union, battling earnestly against its foes. For Lincoln, and the great mass of antislavery northerners, for example, the threat to the Union came from slaveholders, ultimately from slavery itself. It followed that the Union was to be defended by crushing southern disunionists. For southerners like Davis, by contrast, the threat to the Union came from antislavery fanatics, who, trampling upon southerners' rights, left the South with no option consistent with honour but disunion. In their eyes the Union was to be defended by demonstrating that southerners would not tolerate these assaults and thus forcing northerners to see reason and cease their aggressions. In this sense, the vast majority of southerners were Unionists until the election of Lincoln in 1860.

Nativists therefore faced a painful dilemma. The Third Degree could either be left vague and unspecific, in which case it would have little or no impact, or it could be defined more sharply, in which case it would inevitably alienate one group of the other. Thus Henry Wilson of Massachusetts believed that the Third Degree should be directed against southern disunionists but complained that it was in fact being used against antislavery forces and thus against freedom itself.

Another national convention met in June 1855 and here there was renewed pressure from both sides to define the Order's position on the slavery question. Delegates from Massachusetts, where anti-Nebraska sentiment was all but universal, refused to accept the Third Degree and Wilson presented a series of antislavery demands that, as a package,

194. Anbinder, *Nativism and Slavery*, pp. 162–163.

resembled what would become the programme of the radical wing of the Republican party. But the Order could not even agree to repeal the Kansas-Nebraska Act. The convention established a platform committee but the divisions between North and South were so deep that two versions of the key plank, Section Twelve, were submitted. The pro-Southern majority version was finally accepted and this reaffirmed the Kansas-Nebraska Act as a final settlement of the slavery question and denied that Congress could prohibit slavery in either a territory or the District of Columbia. This was very much the southern Know Nothing position on the slavery question. Kenneth Rayner of North Carolina, for example, perhaps the leading Know Nothing in the South, declared that while he would not have supported the Kansas-Nebraska Act, he would not seek its repeal.[195]

When this became official national policy, a large majority of the northern delegates repudiated the official party platform outright. Some had by now given up hope and were acting either overtly or covertly with the nascent Republican party. Others hoped to change the policy subsequently. Unfortunately in seeking to put pressure on southerners to abandon Section Twelve they often took action that had precisely the opposite result. For southern Know Nothings themselves had grievances. The antislavery resolutions and policies of northern legislatures that were under Know Nothing control incurred the hostility and resentment of southern members, themselves under pressure at home from generally more militant southern Democrats. In Virginia, for example, Henry Wise rode to victory in the gubernatorial election of May 1855 by denouncing the Know Nothings as a party dominated by northern "abolitionists" and accordingly disloyal to the South on the slavery question. In this respect, as in so many others the experience of southern Know Nothings replicated that of southern Whigs.[196]

Under these circumstances it was impossible for southerners to countenance the repeal of the Kansas-Nebraska Act, even if they had wished to. In retaliation, the Know Nothing State Councils of several northern states repudiated the national policy and in some cases (Massachusetts and Indiana) severed ties with the national organisation. Moreover northerners now sought to put pressure on southerners to effect a change in national policy by demonstrating the importance of antislavery in the North. For example in Ohio Republican Salmon P. Chase was elected Governor on a platform that largely ignored nativism but as part of a ticket which featured many Know Nothings. But if the intention was to demonstrate the power of antislavery in the North and thus force a reform of Section

195. Hales, "Shaping of Nativist Sentiment," pp. 270–283.
196. William A. Link, *Roots of Secession: Slavery and Politics in Antebellum Virginia* (Chapel Hill, 2003), pp. 126–135.

Twelve, the effect was once again to weaken southern Know Nothings by allowing their enemies to identify them still more closely with antislavery. By this stage the Know Nothings were as divided over slavery as the Whigs had ever been.

Even when the party ran well in the North (as in New York) it was because Section Twelve was either repudiated or ignored. In most of the North nativism continued to be combined with antislavery, despite the growing strength of the Republican party. In November 1855 northern Know Nothings met at Cincinnati and agreed to seek a change of national policy on the slavery question. They hoped (though there was little justification for this optimism) to persuade southerners to agree to a restoration of the Missouri Compromise. In February 1856 another national convention met, this time charged with the task of finding a presidential nominee. By now the divisions within the party were beyond repair. Southerners were threatening to bolt if Section Twelve were rejected; northerners did bolt when it became apparent that a commitment to restore the Missouri Compromise could not be obtained. With northerners gone, the nomination went to ex-President Millard Fillmore. By now in most of the states of the North, Know Nothings were entering the Republican party in droves; those who remained were conservative Whigs for whom maintenance of the Union took primacy over nativism and antislavery alike.

Meanwhile events in the Thirty Fourth Congress offered further proof of the deep divisions within the Know Nothings. Although possessing a majority of the seats in the House of Representatives (by many estimates at least), they did not manage to pass a single piece of nativist legislation. Instead they showed themselves hopelessly split over the most pressing issues. During the Speakership contest South Americans proved willing to vote for even a Democrat, traditionally the *bête noire* of the nativist, rather than an antislavery Know Nothing. These Know Nothings made it clear that they would not tolerate any repeal of the Kansas-Nebraska Act. They both denied the power of Congress to legislate upon slavery in the territories and rejected the Douglas version of popular sovereignty, which allowed settlers in the territorial stage to take the crucial decision on slavery. In other words they rejected the two policies which together commanded the support of almost the entire North. Moreover these South Americans offered defences of slavery in the abstract which, while falling far short of the proslavery polemics of a George Fitzhugh, would nevertheless have been perfectly acceptable within the southern Democratic party.

Finally, like orthodox southern Democrats, the South Americans took the standard southern position on the most pressing issues of 1856. They proved willing to defend the actions of the Missouri "border ruffians," as they were known. Mordecai Oliver, for example, a Know Nothing from Missouri, defended those who had ridden from his state into Kansas "for the purpose of maintaining law and preserving the peace and order of that Territory" from murderous abolitionists.[197] Similarly when Preston Brooks made his violent assault upon Charles Sumner in the United States Senate, one southern Know Nothing went a long way to excusing the attack. "While we may not approve the act," Charles Ready of Tennessee announced, "we cannot condemn the warm and generous impulses of his heart, without feeling that icicles have gathered around our own."[198] Most of the South Americans accordingly voted against censuring Brooks.[199]

In this way slavery divided the Know Nothings at what should have been their moment of greatest triumph.[200] The problem was that in the North and the South they were in constant danger of being outflanked by more radical groups. In the North the Republicans put them under pressure to demonstrate that they were not merely pawns in the hands of the Slave Power, while in the South Democrats constantly challenged them to display their southern credentials and their antipathy to the antislavery movement. Perhaps these pressures would have eased and become containable if events in Kansas had followed a different course. But wave after wave of controversy in the territory, together with events like the "sack" of Lawrence and the beating of Charles Sumner meant that, far from easing, pressure actually increased as the months passed. As one Know Nothing lamented: "it is conceded, I believe, that the difficulty at the foundation of all our troubles is the one question of slavery." By mid-1856 it was clear that the Know Nothings were in decline. The elections to be held later that year, and especially the presidential election, would demonstrate how far that process had advanced.[201]

## VI

By the time of the election the Know Nothing, or as it now preferred to be known American, party had become primarily the party of the Union. In nominating Millard Fillmore for the presidency, it had adopted one who had only recently joined the Order, who had done little or nothing for the

197. *CG*, 34/1, App., p. 154.
198. *CG*, 34/1, App. p. 922.
199. *CG*, 34/1, App., pp. 1642–1643.
200. They also received much criticism for the delay in electing a Speaker. See the attempt at a defence in, for example, *Letter of William R. Smith, of Alabama On the Circumstances Which Have Prevented an Organization of the House of Representatives of the Thirty-Fourth Congress* (n.p., n.d.).
201. *CG*, 34/1, App. p. 54.

nativist cause during his presidency and who now had other priorities. Fillmore's main appeal was that of a conservative Whig. He was running, his supporters liked to believe, as the heir of Henry Clay.

Fillmore himself was not reticent during the campaign and enunciated his conservative principles on several occasions. "I am free to admit," he remarked, that "I regard this conservatism as the proudest principle I have ever been able to sustain." Although he endorsed the maxim that "Americans should rule America," and reminded audiences that Clay's defeat in 1844 had been attributable to the immigrant vote, he made it clear that his party stood above all for sectional moderation. The American party, he claimed, "alone, in my opinion, of all the political agencies now existing, is possessed of the power to silence this violent and disastrous agitation, and restore harmony by its own example of moderation and forbearance."[202]

Fillmore made much of his record in the White House and presented it in terms that would endear him to conservative Whigs. Stressing the qualities they had always valued, he explained that he had at that time "felt it my duty to rise above every sectional prejudice, and look to the wellfare [sic] of the whole nation." He had been "compelled to a certain extent to overcome long cherished prejudices, and disregard party claims." This was the ideal of disinterested statesmanship that conservative Whigs had long cherished. Rising far above the party spoilsman or the rabble-rousing demagogue, the statesman would carefully consider the interests of every section of the nation, rather than merely reflect the opinions of the one from which he had himself sprung, before formulating a policy or deciding upon a course of action. This had been the approach recommended by Clay and Webster and even, decades earlier, by the Federalists.[203]

Fillmore condemned the repeal of the Missouri Compromise in precisely these terms. Acknowledging that the disturbances of midcentury had been the unavoidable consequence of the acquisition of new territory, he contrasted them with the recent troubles over Kansas. "It is for you," he told one audience "to say whether the present agitation, which distracts the country and threatens us with civil war, has not been recklessly and wantonly produced by the adoption of a measure to aid in personal advancement rather than in any public good." Although inviting his listeners to reach their own conclusion, he left them in no doubt that he believed the Kansas-Nebraska Act to have been the product of utterly defective statesmanship.[204]

202. Frank H. Severance (ed.), "The Millard Fillmore Papers," 2 vols., *Publications of the Buffalo Historical Society*, X (1907), II, p. 7. *Speeches of Millard Fillmore*, pp. 1–5.
203. *Speeches of Millard Fillmore*, p. 11.
204. *Speeches of Millard Fillmore*, pp. 11–12.

On the other hand, what he left unsaid was as important as what he said. On one occasion Fillmore opposed a restoration of the Missouri Compromise but did not explain what his policy would now be for the territories. His supporters meanwhile gave contradictory answers. In the North it was claimed that Fillmore would repeal the Kansas-Nebraska Act; in the South it was announced that he would not. Anna Carroll of Maryland declared that "every patriot should know with how much heart and soul Millard Fillmore would delight to see that Compromise of 1820 restored," as a result of which the Union would be "blessed with the peace and prosperity which pervaded every section of the country when he resigned the government into the hands of Franklin Pierce." Yet the policy of the National Americans in Congress, the group to whom Fillmore was obviously closest, it had emerged during the Speakership contest, was to acquiesce in the Kansas-Nebraska Act, whilst disavowing responsibility for it, and withholding approval from it. One of Fillmore's supporters, sensing these and other difficulties, observed that the candidate had no need of a specific platform since his record in the White House should be platform enough.[205]

Rather than dwell on specific policies, therefore, his supporters celebrated his personal qualities. "Since the death of Henry Clay," William Graham of North Carolina declared, "no man has more eminent fitness to heal the disorders of the times." Graham, the Whig vice-presidential candidate in 1852, endorsed Fillmore when he addressed the small number of Whigs who attended their national party convention in September 1856 (and in so doing confirmed the futility of a separate Whig organisation). Fillmore's main quality, nativists and Whigs alike confirmed, was his ability to transcend personal prejudices, sectional loyalties and narrow party interests and thus restore tranquillity to the nation.[206]

For many of those in the conservative Whig tradition the election of 1856 should be decided after a careful assessment of the qualities of the statesmen nominated by the three parties. Congressman Oscar F. Moore of Ohio, for example, heaped scorn upon Republican candidate John C. Frémont as "a man, whose only merit, so far as history records it, is in the fact, that he was born in South Carolina, crossed the Rocky Mountains, subsisted on frogs, lizards, snakes and grasshoppers, and *captured* a

---

205. *Speeches of Millard Fillmore*, p. 24; Anna Ella Carroll, *Which? Fillmore or Buchanan?* (Boston, 1856), pp. 21–22. Contrast the North Carolina *Whig* of July 1856 with *The Duty of Native Americans in the Present Crisis* (n.p., n.d.) which tried to claim that Fillmore would be a more effective opponent of slavery than Frémont.
206. William Graham, "Notes For A Speech" and "Speech at the Whig National Convention" in *Papers of Graham*, IV, pp. 647–649, 654–657; Carroll, *Which? Fillmore or Buchanan?*, p. 20. See also Carroll, *The Union of the States* (Boston, 1856); *Letter of Reade*, p. 13.

woolly horse." Moore clearly found it extraordinary that Frémont had been "chosen as the person to control the destinies of this great nation" and he explained that if it were a two-horse race he would support the Democratic candidate James Buchanan. But fortunately for the entire nation Fillmore was also a candidate and Moore's endorsement of his candidacy read like a profile of the ideal conservative Whig statesman:

> There is still another candidate in the field – a gentleman also of emi-
> nent ability, or experience, and of integrity; Union loving, fearless in
> the discharge of public duty, watchful of the rights of all and regard-
> less of none: – one who could, even in these times, administer this
> government with the same scrupulous care as it was administered by
> the early Presidents.

Such were Millard Fillmore's elevated qualities.[207]

Events would show, however, that they were not elevated enough either to win the presidency or even to capture the support of all those in the conservative Whig tradition. The problem of course was sectionalism. His supporters sometimes tried to claim that a man who was attacked as an abolitionist in the South and reviled as a tool of the Slave Power in the North was precisely the man needed to reconcile the two extremes. He occupied, it was said, "exactly that noble, moderate, conservative position towards which the eyes of all true lovers of their country may turn with confidence in this hour of trial." But if this was Fillmore's strength, it was also his weakness. Both north and south of the Mason-Dixon Line it was too easy to present a vote for him as a vote for the enemy. Fillmore's can-didacy thus foundered on the problems that had beset the Know Nothings since the heady days of their initial success. They were the same problems that the Whigs before them had experienced.[208]

Although William Graham himself endorsed Fillmore in 1856, his cor-respondence indicates a widespread fear that those who supported him might be inadvertently aiding the Republicans. Fillmore himself, in an understandable bid for support in the North, claimed that southerners would not submit to Republican rule and some of his supporters echoed the warning. Yet this was a dangerous ploy. As with most centrist strate-gies at this time it ended by alienating both sections rather than uniting them. Those northerners who were in any case concerned about the Slave Power thought this a disgraceful capitulation, nothing less indeed than a surrender of the franchises of northern freemen to southern bullying and intimidation. But southerners and Union-loving northerners often drew the opposite conclusion. Many agreed that the Republicans should be stopped but was it not far easier to achieve this goal by supporting

207. *Letter of Hon. O. F. Moore of Ohio, To His Constituents* (n.p., 1856), p. 5.
208. *Is Millard Fillmore an Abolitionist?* (Boston, 1856), p. 2.

James Buchanan, the Democratic candidate? The Fillmore camp hoped that, though their candidate might not be able to win outright, he might nonetheless emerge victor if the election were thrown into the House of Representatives. But this too was a hazardous strategy. The Speakership contest had shown that such a process might end in a Republican triumph. Surely it was safer therefore to vote for Buchanan.[209]

Such was the conclusion of more than one conservative northern Whig. Rufus Choate, for example, one of the Webster circle of "Cotton" or now "Old Line" Whigs, whilst maintaining a distance from the Democratic party, nevertheless supported Buchanan, while Joseph Randall, another Old Line Whig from Pennsylvania, also championed Buchanan on the grounds that his election would end the danger of secession and re-establish harmony between the sections for at least a generation.[210]

In the South such considerations were still more prominent. Here the fear of a Republican victory was intense and one southerner after another, many of them potential Fillmore supporters, pressed Buchanan's case. Some of them pointed to the antislavery activities of the national Know Nothing organisation. At the last conference, one "Old Clay Whig" from Tennessee noted, Section Twelve, "the only plank in their platform upon which the party could hope to stand in the South," had been "ruthlessly stricken down." The same author even espied a conspiracy by which the American party would divide the South and thus let the Republicans in. In Missouri, where the Whig party had enjoyed a brief revival, the splits in the ranks of the American party, together with the attempts made in some northern states to effect alliances between Know Nothings and Republicans provoked deep concern. Samuel Caruthers, in order to demonstrate the futility of seeking to revive the Whig party, reviewed the anti-Southern record of northern Whigs in regard to the Wilmot Proviso, the Fugitive Slave Law and the Kansas-Nebraska Act. And as the possibility of Republican victory loomed, it seemed to pose a huge threat to the continued existence of the nation. "Who is it," Caruthers asked, "that does not know the Union," in such an eventuality, "would not survive an hour?" As another Missourian put it, after noting the splits in the American ranks, "nationality inheres in the Democratic party alone."[211]

209. See, for example, William W. Morrison to William Graham, June 19, 1856, in *Papers of Graham*, IV, p. 641; *Speeches of Millard Fillmore*, p. 21.
210. *The Life and Writings of Rufus Choate* 2 vols. (Boston, 1862), II, p. 388; Nevins, *House Dividing*, p. 492; *Speech of Joseph Randall, Esq of Philadelphia, Chambersburg Aug. 6, 1856* (n.p., n.d.), p. 3; *Great Fraud Public Credulity . . .*, pp. 31–32.
211. *Reflections and Suggestion on the Present State of Parties By An Old Clay Whig* (Nashville, 1856) pp. 12–13; *Letter of Hon. Mordecai Oliver of Missouri To Robert H. Miller Esq* (n.p., n.p.), pp. 4, 6; *Letter of Samuel Caruthers to His Constituents* (Washington, DC, 1856), pp. 9, 14–15. J. Mills Thornton III, *Politics and Power in a Slave Society: Alabama 1800–1860* (Baton Rouge, 1978), p. 359.

Throughout the Whig and American heartland of the Upper South, the message was the same. Even in Maryland, which would prove the most fertile soil for the American party in 1856, these sentiments were widespread. United States Senators James Pearce and Thomas Pratt, previously staunch Whigs, argued that the real choice was between Frémont and Buchanan, since the northern wing of the American party was acting so closely with the Republicans. Even more damaging, perhaps, was the attitude of James B. Clay of Kentucky, son of the great man himself. Announcing that he had lived and would die a confirmed Whig, Clay acknowledged that he preferred Fillmore's personal qualities. But he nonetheless felt impelled to support Buchanan: Fillmore simply could not win and it was imperative that the Republicans be defeated.[212]

The problem for Fillmore and his party was that many in the North, as his defenders acknowledged, condemned him for being irresolute on slavery. Although the Republican party's national organisation was in its infancy in 1856 and failed to match the Democrats' campaign efforts (or funds), Republicans were nevertheless quick to seize upon evidence of Fillmore defections and to publicise the reasons for them. Ephraim Marsh of New Jersey had actually been the presiding officer at the Convention which had nominated Fillmore. He nevertheless defected to Frémont. In common with so many northerners Marsh was clearly motivated, in large part, by the events in Kansas. The repeal of the Missouri Compromise had been "perfidious" but the subsequent events in Kansas, involving robbery, murders, electoral frauds and other "outrages" had demonstrated the folly of seeking to appease the Slave Power. Marsh explained that he had looked to Fillmore for an explicit condemnation of these acts, but had looked in vain. Instead "there was a studied and significant avoidance... of the question upon which he knew, as we all know, the Presidential election is to be decided, either in favor of, or against slavery extension." Fillmore's problem of course was that he wished to clear the slate, to start afresh in 1857 with the events in Kansas firmly in the past or at least on their way to a resolution. He simply could not afford to take sides and, in the process, antagonise one section or the other. But events had overtaken him and this attempt at neutrality or even-handedness was perceived as itself highly partisan. Thus the great wrongs done by the proslavery elements in Kansas, "though arousing the just indignation of freemen, have elicited no word of reproof from Mr Fillmore." Moreover, the platform, even without the odious Section Twelve, still failed to repudiate, indeed tacitly approved, the Kansas-Nebraska Act. Just as the absence of Section Twelve antagonised many southerners, so northerners now objected to the failure

---

212. *Letter from Pearce*, pp. 2–3; "Letter from Thomas Pratt" in *Letter from Pearce*, p. 11; *An Appeal for the Union* (Washington, DC, 1856), p. 15.

to condemn the Kansas-Nebraska Act. Marsh claimed that southerners had been willing to take Fillmore as their candidate only on terms that drove most northerners out. Indeed "they aimed, with Americanism as a cover, to extend slavery."[213]

Moreover southern defections from the Fillmore camp to Buchanan led directly to northern defections to Frémont. "Shall we of the North," Marsh asked, "be required to adhere to a nomination which has been deliberately abandoned by the South?" Marsh believed that a vote for Buchanan would merely perpetuate "the encroachments and usurpations of the Slave power" and announced that "in a contest which is to determine whether Slavery or Freedom is to be the governing principle of the Republic, I choose to cast my vote where it will tell for freedom." This was an apt illustration of the polarisation that was increasingly evident within the nation, and of which the Fillmore candidacy would ultimately prove a casualty.[214]

In fact the hopes of the Know Nothings, so high in 1855, were to be dashed by the elections of 1856. The biggest disappointment was in the presidential canvass. Fillmore polled only twenty-one percent of the total popular vote and carried only the state of Maryland. The election produced a victory for James Buchanan but it was clear that the Republicans had made enormous inroads into the North. Whether the results should have brought greater satisfaction to Democrats or Republicans was a moot point. What was clear was that they could bring nothing other than gloom and disappointment to the American party. The nativist moment had passed. Like the Whigs before them the Know Nothings were destined for oblivion.

## VII

The collapse of the Know Nothings was clearly the product of sectional antagonisms. It was not merely the Kansas-Nebraska Act itself which did the damage but also the events which subsequently occurred within Kansas, unleashed of course, by the passage of the Act. Moreover it is difficult to see how any course of action undertaken by the statesmen in the American party could have allowed them to escape their dilemmas.

213. *Letter of Judge Ephraim Marsh, of New Jersey, who Presided at the Convention which Nominated Millard Fillmore, Giving His Reasons for Supporting Col. J. C. Frémont* (n.p., n.d.), pp. 2–4. Chauncey Shaffer of New York, another former American, was even more critical of Fillmore. Dismissing the Know Nothing nominating convention as "a convention for the Propagation of Human Slavery," he dubbed Fillmore "a most subservient instrument of the Slave Power" – *Chauncey Shaffer's Reasons for Voting for John C. Frémont* (n.p., n.d.), p. 1.
214. *Letter of Judge Ephraim Marsh*, p. 2.

As we have seen, against the backdrop of Kansas it was impossible to find a viable middle way; indeed the middle way they found ended by antagonising the extremes rather than reconciling them.

The death of the Whig party is a more difficult and complex matter. Yet a list of causal factors is not difficult to draw up. There are four. First we need to consider the growing obsolescence of Whig economic policies, which clearly deprived the party of its traditional rationale. Second, and most obvious, we need to take account of the sectional animosities which characterised the final years. Third, we cannot ignore the growing antiparty sentiment of these years, since the growing disillusionment with parties plainly gave encouragement to the new political organisations that challenged and then replaced the Whigs. And finally we need to assess the role played by the so-called ethnocultural factors, specifically immigration and temperance.

The more difficult task is to rank these factors. However, at least one of them is relatively easily disposed of. Antiparty sentiment was real, pervasive, and profound in the final years of the Whig party but it was clearly a function of the other three factors. The disillusionment with the parties sprang from a feeling that they were simply unresponsive. In other words the real issues that were exercising voters were ones with which the parties could not properly deal. As we have seen, it was extraordinarily difficult to find a policy on slavery that could be a vote-winner on both sides of the Mason-Dixon Line. Although it has been claimed that the strategies for dealing with this, either deliberate ambiguity (the Democrats' espousal of popular sovereignty) or a resolute refusal to enunciate a national policy at all (the Whigs in 1848) was beneficial to the party system, there is no evidence for this claim. On the contrary there is every reason to believe that it promoted cynicism and indifference. Similarly ethnocultural issues cut across party lines and made the party organisations seem out of touch and irrelevant. Finally the obsolescence of the older issues, ones which the parties could have dealt with, obviously reinforced this tendency.[215]

Before leaving the question of antiparty sentiment, we should note an additional point. Antiparty sentiment had traditionally been stronger among Whigs than Democrats. The Whigs themselves had recognised that they lacked the internal discipline possessed by their rivals. Moreover the Democrats were able to cloak themselves in the mantle of nationalism to an extent and in a manner that the Whigs never managed or even desired. As we have seen, Democrats believed that their party was synonymous with American democracy, American freedom, and the American nation.[216] For these reasons, the various factors that weakened the two party system took their heaviest and earliest toll upon the Whigs.

---

215. This is the argument in Holt, *Political Crisis*.
216. See pp. 344–354.

Although it is easy to see that antiparty was a derivative and thus secondary cause of the Whig collapse, it is much more difficult to rank the other factors. Although some historians have unhesitatingly done so, it is particularly difficult to claim primacy for ethnocultural factors. As we shall see, there are several reasons to question these claims. But first we should note that even if they are valid, they amount to rather less than is sometimes supposed. Since the so-called new political history appears to acknowledge that sectional factors overtook ethnocultural ones by 1856, it is not clear that the implications for our understanding of the Civil War itself, and its origins, are as dramatic as is sometimes assumed. Even if it could be shown that ethnocultural factors in general and the rise of the Know Nothings in particular destroyed the Whig party, the fact that the Know Nothings were themselves destroyed by the slavery controversy diminishes the novelty of the new political historians' claims. There is no major challenge to existing interpretations of the Civil War unless it is claimed that the American party was an *essential* stepping stone from the second party system to the sectional alignment of the later 1850s. But this, it should be noted, is a highly determinist assumption for which no evidence has ever been provided. Indeed the fact that many, including, for example, such important figures as William Seward or Abraham Lincoln, went straight from Whig to Republican confirms that it was not necessary for Whigs to use the American party as a halfway house. So the overall impact of the ethnocultural issues on the origins of the Civil War, even if the claims made for their impact in the mid-1850s are accepted, seems surprisingly limited. Is it claimed that overall they accelerated the pace of realignment, or that they retarded it? In what way did they even decisively shape the final outcome? In what way was the great crisis of 1860–1861 affected by the fact that many Republicans had once been Know Nothings? In this context the ethnocultural impulse of the early and mid-1850s seems of only marginal importance.

In fact there are reasons to question the claim made for the primacy of ethnocultural factors even in the upheaval of the mid-1850s. First, the other factors – sectionalism and the decline of the traditional issues – were long term and had done part of their work even before the upsurge of nativist and temperance sentiment. Ethnocultural factors may have helped deliver a knock-out blow to the Whigs but the blow fell upon an already severely weakened fighter and it is arbitrary to emphasise the blow rather than the prior weakness. But – and this constitutes a second reason – it is not even possible to demonstrate that ethnocultural factors were primarily responsible for the blow. As we have seen, one cannot draw inferences about the relative strength of nativism or temperance compared with slavery from the votes cast for Know Nothing candidates in 1854 and 1855. The record merely shows that voters usually preferred candidates who combined the various appeals to those who had only one.

In the process of events that actually occurred there is no reason to single out one of these three factors and accord it primacy.

We might, however, advance a counterfactual argument. Is there any reason to believe that a single one of these factors, *had it been operating alone*, had the capacity to destroy the Whig party? One cannot of course offer definitive answers and there is no procedure by which a hypothesis can be subjected to rigorous testing. However some tentative suggestion may be offered. It is surely likely that the obsolescence of the traditional issues could not alone have destroyed the party. The actual record suggests that the Whigs could carry on, albeit without generating much enthusiasm within the electorate, without their economic programme. In the late 1840s and early 1850s this was precisely what happened. And the political history of the United States confirms that it is perfectly possible for a two-party system to continue even when the ideological differences between the parties are quite narrow. It took the additional factors to bring the party to ruin.

If, however, we ask whether the party might have withstood the ethno-cultural challenge if that had been the only one with which it had had to contend, the answer is more difficult. Yet there had always been an ethnocultural dimension to the party system and one suspects that if the two parties had been vibrantly competitive in the early 1850s and untroubled by sectional animosities, an adjustment might have been made. If they had had strong reasons to vote Whig because of the economic policies on offer, and because of the respite the Whigs offered from Democratic radicalism, the voters might not have flocked to the temperance and nativist crusades. This claim becomes increasingly plausible when we recall that both before and after the mid-1850s these issues were indeed far less prominent. It is possible to claim that the very prominence of the ethnocultural factors in the mid-1850s was itself, in part, a consequence of other factors. Traditional economic policies were on the wane and sectional alignments were not as clear-cut as they would become by say 1856.

This leaves the sectional question. Although the proposition cannot be demonstrated empirically, there is reason to believe that this factor, had it been operating alone, could indeed have destroyed the Whigs.[217] After all it destroyed the Know Nothings, who, as we have seen, in many respects resembled them very closely. Finally we should remind ourselves once again that even if, as is claimed, ethnocultural factors had alone destroyed the Whigs, all scholars agree that by 1856 sectional considerations had in turn overwhelmed ethnocultural factors. This also suggests the primacy of the slavery question.

217. In making this claim I do not contradict the previous point that voters preferred candidates who combined several appeals to those who offered only one.

This is not to claim that ethnocultural factors were of no importance in explaining the political upheaval of the 1850s. There can be no return to the older historiographical tradition in which these factors were simply read out of the story. But the reaction against the older tradition has surely gone too far. There is every reason to believe that the slavery question should still have primacy in explaining the realignment of the 1850s, a realignment whose importance for the future of the nation can scarcely be exaggerated.

## Realignment completed, 1857–1860

### I

The presidential election of 1856 showed that the Republican candidate, John C. Frémont, had carried eleven of the sixteen free states (the exceptions being Indiana, Illinois, California, Pennsylvania and New Jersey). The Republicans had thus triumphed in the old Whig northern heartland, the Upper North. By 1858 there would be only three non-Republican Governors in the entire North, in Pennsylvania, Indiana and the infant state of Minnesota while by 1860 there would be only two (Pennsylvania and Indiana). The presidential election of 1860 would see this trend confirmed as Lincoln swept the entire North, with the exception of a portion of the electoral votes of New Jersey.

A comparable polarisation occurred in the South. In 1856 Buchanan carried every slave state apart from Maryland, which went to Fillmore. Yet it is important not to exaggerate this development. For these results perhaps masked the continuing strength of the Know Nothing (or American) Party in what was the other Whig heartland, the Upper South. Delaware, Maryland, and Kentucky all had Know Nothing Governors during at least some of the Buchanan years. Moreover across much of the Upper and Border South, and even in parts of the Lower South, ex-Whigs began after the collapse of the Know Nothings to call themselves an "Opposition" party and in 1860 they held twenty-three seats in the House of Representatives. Most of their strength was, once again, in the states that had previously had a strong Whig party. North Carolina, for example, remained highly competitive on the eve of the Civil War while in Tennessee the Opposition almost managed to unseat incumbent Democratic Governor Isham Harris in 1859 and took no fewer than seven of the state's ten congressional seats. In Kentucky too the Opposition made a strong showing in the gubernatorial election of 1859 and elected a number of Congressmen. More surprising, perhaps, was the success in Virginia, traditionally a banner Democratic state and still one whose politics attracted enormous interest throughout the nation. The Opposition in Virginia ran strongly in the 1859 congressional elections and took no less than forty-eight percent of the vote in that year's gubernatorial election. In Virginia as elsewhere the Opposition candidates espoused a strong, but still qualified unionism and in most of the Upper South campaigned on state as much as national issues.[218]

Nevertheless, the years in which Buchanan occupied the White House did witness the virtual completion of the realignment of the 1850s. By 1860 the Democrats held every Governorship in the South apart from one (that of Maryland), and the two Democratic presidential candidates in that year captured between them every southern state except Virginia, Kentucky and Tennessee. Although there were important divisions within each of the two major parties (especially the Democrats) and although each party had some support within the territory of the other (especially the Democrats), by the time Buchanan left office it was a pardonable exaggeration to say that a Republican North faced a Democratic South.

## II

The process by which the Republicans extended their control over the North in these years offers additional support for two hypotheses we have already encountered. First, it suggests once again that nativism played a relatively small part in the politics of the nation after the extraordinary events of 1854–1856. And second it confirms that the central Republican idea was the notion of slavery as a disorganising force.

After 1856 it was clear that the Republicans needed to broaden their appeal. In terms of the electoral college they needed to retain the states Frémont had carried and add to them Pennsylvania plus Illinois, Indiana or New Jersey. The lower North, traditionally an area with relatively close links to the South and traditionally an area where the Democrats had been highly competitive if not dominant, was the crucial battleground. Whilst the Republicans would, of course, welcome any further defections from the Democrats, they realised that the main new source of support would be from (in addition to new voters) those who had voted for Fillmore in 1856. This meant an appeal to former Know Nothings. The question was, however, whether it entailed any concessions to their nativist principles.

218. Daniel Crofts, *Reluctant Confederates: Upper South Unionists in the Secession Crisis* (Chapel Hill, 1989), pp. 52–54, 63; Link, *Roots of Secession*, pp. 144, 172–175; Allan Nevins, *The Emergence of Lincoln: Prologue to Civil War* (New York, 1950), pp. 58–68.; Bergeron, *Antebellum Politics in Tennessee*, pp. 131–134; Walter L. Buenger, *Secession and the Union in Texas* (Austin, TX, 1984), p. 69; Percy L. Rainwater, *Mississippi, Storm Center of Secession, 1856–1861* (Baton Rouge, 1938), p. 92; Anthony Carey, *Parties, Slavery and the Union in Antebellum Georgia* (Athens, GA, 1997), p. 216; Clarence C. Norton, *The Democratic Party in Ante-Bellum North Carolina, 1833–1861* (Chapel Hill, 1930), p. 244.

From its birth the Republican party had had important links with the Know Nothings. As we have seen, many in the East especially had moved from the Whig party to the Republicans via the Know Nothings. Some, though not all, had had genuine nativist sympathies, though they had not necessarily put nativism ahead of antislavery. Hence it would have been strange if the Republican party at any stage before the Civil War had lacked all traces of nativist principles.

These principles were perhaps most in evidence in Massachusetts, the state where the Know Nothings had probably been, for a time, strongest. Here there seemed to be a real opportunity to enact the major Know Nothing demand, an extension of the naturalisation period to a full twenty-one years. In fact, however, even after the Know Nothings had virtually swept the legislature in late 1854 they did not successfully press for this demand. Instead the period was to be fourteen years. Too many Republicans, however, found even five years too much and the Know Nothings, or former Know Nothings, by 1858 were having to settle for two years. The Republicans were, as a party, unwilling to tolerate any longer period, though they were prepared to support a literacy test for voting.[219] This was a genuine indication of the persistence of nativist principles within the Republican party, though it is important to note that a significant minority of Republicans (primarily the radicals) were strongly opposed to it. Moreover, the two-year constitutional amendment fell far short of original nativist demands, and the final vote on it produced only a small voter turnout.[220]

Elsewhere, however, even this concession was too much for Republicans. The Massachusetts two-year amendment drew a chorus of disapproval from large numbers of western Republicans, who viewed nativism as not merely unprincipled but also electorally damaging.[221] Nor was it adopted in any other state. Nevertheless in some other states, primarily in the East, nativists continued to display strength. Pennsylvania perhaps ranked second only to Massachusetts as a nativist stronghold. Here the Republican party was slow to achieve success. In 1857, following a relatively poor showing in the previous year's elections, Republicans coalesced with nativists to form the Union party. The following year a similar

---

219. Anbinder, *Nativism and Slavery*, pp. 247–253; Baum, *Civil War Party System*, p. 11.
220. It was even opposed by a former Know Nothing like Henry Wilson. Only just over a third of those who voted in the Gubernatorial election of the same year bothered to turn out. Only sixteen percent of the electorate voted. – Baum, *Civil War Party System*, p. 45.
221. These included Lincoln, Chase, and Trumbull together with important Republican newspapers like the *Chicago Tribune* and the *Ohio State Journal* – see Foner, *Free Soil, Free Labor, Free Men*, p. 251. See also Cook, *Baptism of Fire*, p. 113; Nevins, *Prologue to Civil War*, p. 241; Roy F. Basler (ed.), *The Collected Works of Abraham Lincoln*. 9 vols. (New Brunswick, 1953–1955), III, p. 392.

coalition took the field as the "People's Party" and in much of the state this was the official title as late as 1860. Pennsylvania, the largest state in the lower North, had traditionally had strong ties to the South and had traditionally been home to many southern sympathisers. The Know Nothings there had tended to combine genuine nativism with conservative Whig unionism (unlike in Massachusetts, for example, where they were far more uniformly antislavery). Consequently the various coalitions that challenged the Democrats in Pennsylvania both moderated the anti-Southernism and antislavery of the Republicans and enunciated some nativist principles.[222] In 1857, for example, the Union party state platform warned against enfranchising "any man who acknowledges a foreign supremacy which he cannot conscientiously and without mental reservations abjure and forever renounce, whether the supremacy be civil or spiritual." In that year the party ran David Wilmot for Governor and Wilmot wrote a letter in which he offered some criticisms of the Roman Catholic Church.[223]

Yet in terms of policies the Pennsylvania Republicans had to concede very little to their nativist allies. The former Know Nothings had to be content with minor successes such as the exclusion of aliens from the provisions of the Homestead measure of 1860 or the reaffirmation of the principle that would-be immigrants with a criminal record should not be allowed into the nation. The former Know Nothings were also given their share of offices following electoral victories. But these were modest gains, especially in a state where nativism had been strong. On the whole, as one historian puts it, Republicans "avoided open expressions of hostility to foreigners." Pennsylvania was regarded as the key battleground for 1860 and Republicans accordingly were prepared to emphasise measures like the tariff and were even prepared to moderate their antislavery policies. But although they needed the support of the nativists they were not prepared to adopt nativist principles to any significant degree.[224]

Much the same was true of New York. Here the main concession to nativism was a registry law. For some time in New York and elsewhere, there had been complaints about illegal voting, especially by immigrants and especially Irish Roman Catholic immigrants, and a registry law was intended to require the compilation of lists of legally eligible voters. A majority of New York Republicans, partly because of pressure from Know Nothings and former Know Nothings, proved willing to enact such a law, even though William Seward, the leading Republican in the state, was

---

222. Holt, *Forging a Majority*, p. 222.
223. Anbinder, *Nativism and Slavery*, pp. 261–264.
224. Holt, *Forging a Majority*, p. 288. Holt also notes that with more Germans and Irishmen among those emerging Republican leaders, they were much less clearly representative of established native born families than the Whigs had been – see p. 295.

opposed to it. The nativists were thought to be of critical importance in New York, even after 1856 (when Frémont had carried the state) because Republican control would be jeopardised if the Democrats ever managed to cease their customary infighting. Nevertheless, apart from the Registry law and a few offices, nativists got little from the Republicans and by 1860 had been swallowed up by them. And even the Registry law was an extremely mild measure. It fell far short of the old nativist demand for a twenty-one year naturalisation period and was in any case full of loopholes. By 1860 nativism counted for little more in the politics of the state than it had a decade earlier, before the Know Nothing upsurge.[225]

In most of the smaller states of the East, nativism achieved even less than in New York. In Connecticut, for example, the Republicans by 1859 had dropped even the mild nativist planks they had previously adopted. Meanwhile, in the West, where the Republicans had in any case organised earlier and with greater initial success, nativists had even less impact than in the East. Not only were there major foreign-born Republican leaders like Gustave Koerner in Illinois and Carl Schurz in Wisconsin but there were also large numbers of immigrant voters to whom the party felt it had to appeal. Although some Republicans continued to view the Roman Catholic Church with some hostility, it was, as we have seen, difficult to frame legislation that would discriminate against these more undesirable immigrants while allowing the more virtuous ones to escape. Thus Salmon P. Chase as Governor of Ohio opposed the attempt to extend the period between naturalisation and voting partly because he wanted the support of German Protestants. He and other Republicans successfully opposed a Registry law and in 1859 the Republican platform explicitly condemned the Massachusetts measure. The concessions that nativists won from Republians were extremely modest. They obtained a law requiring voters to have resided in the town in which they voted for twenty days and also a law requiring immigrants to produce naturalisation papers. These measures were little more than sops.[226]

The western state where nativists were strongest was probably Indiana and here, as in Pennsylvania, the Democrats were faced not by a Republican party but rather by a "People's Party." But even here, where immigration had been relatively light, the nativists were in sharp decline by 1856. In 1856 the party platform reaffirmed the need to retain the five-year naturalisation period and insisted that "the right of suffrage should accompany and not precede naturalization." Once again this was a minor

225. Anbinder, *Nativism and Slavery*, pp. 254–257.
226. Moreover, the requirement to produce naturalisation papers could be waived if the immigrants swore that they had lost them! Anbinder, *Nativism and Slavery*, pp. 237, 253–254, 258–259. See also Gienapp, *Origins of Republican Party*, p. 367; Holt, *Forging a Majority*, pp. 258–259.

concession to the nativists which, once again, fell well short of original Know Nothing demands. By 1860, however, even this had gone and the platform now contained a ringing endorsement of the equal rights of the immigrant. It was now "resolved That we are in favor of equal rights to all citizens, at home and abroad, without reference to the place of their nativity, and that we will oppose any attempt to change the present Naturalization laws." This was a blatant repudiation of the Massachusetts two-year amendment and of nativist principles generally.[227]

In other states of the northwest, where nativism was in any case weaker, similar resolutions were passed. This process culminated at the Republican national convention in Chicago in 1860 when the party officially disavowed nativism and nominated in Abraham Lincoln one who was as firmly opposed to nativism as one could be. The fourteenth plank of the platform again confirmed that the Republicans were a party that espoused the principle of equal rights for the immigrant and which opposed any real change in the naturalisation laws:

> The Republican party is opposed to any change in our naturalization law, or any state legislation by which the rights of citizens hitherto accorded to immigrants to foreign lands shall be abridged or impaired, and in favor of giving a full and efficient protection to the rights of all classes of citizens, whether native or naturalized, both at home and abroad.[228]

It was little wonder, therefore, that dedicated former Know Nothings were in general far from satisfied with the Republicans' handling of nativist issues. The election of 1856 had confirmed that they were the junior partners in the anti-Democratic coalitions that were emerging and in the next four years their influence shrank still further. The reason is not hard to find. The slavery question raised the most fundamental issues about the nation itself, its economic system, its democracy, even its ultimate purpose, and to all but a small minority of nativists these issues were more important than the naturalisation laws or the temporal power of the Pope. And contrary to the claims of the new political historians, anti-immigrant and anti-Catholic legislation did not in general mobilise the voters to a greater degree than the slavery issue. Thus when the Massachusetts two-year amendment was put to the people in 1859 only sixteen percent of them bothered to turn out (whereas almost three times

227. William G. Shade, *Banks or No Banks: The Money Issue in Western Politics 1832–1865* (Detroit, 1972), p. 81; William E. Henry (ed.), *State Platforms of the Two Dominant Political Parties in Indiana, 1850–1900* (Indianapolis, 1902), pp. 13, 21.
228. *The Tribune Almanac for the Years 1838 to 1868, inclusive, comprehending the Politician's Register and the Whig Almanac*, (New York, 1868), p. 31; Cook, *Baptism of Fire*, p. 57.

that number voted in the gubernatorial election of the same year).[229]
Similarly Congressmen in the late fifties frequently went armed to the
legislative chambers; they were guarding against assaults from their sectional enemies, not those with whom they disagreed over temperance or
nativism. In the entire history of the antebellum Republic there were, at
federal level, only two years in which ethnocultural issues could claim to
be at, or close to, the top of the political agenda. This pattern was only
slightly less evident within the states. In 1854 and 1855 nativism competed with the slavery question for dominance; by 1856 it was clearly
losing and by 1860 the battle was over. Nativism had clearly lost.[230]

## III

An examination of the attitudes of some of those who did move from
the Know Nothing to the Republican party lends further support to this
analysis. Rather than pretend that their new party was strongly nativist
in inspiration, they instead echoed the views of conservative Republicans and stressed its links with traditional Whiggery. Thus like conservative Republicans, these erstwhile Know Nothings venerated the memory of Henry Clay. Revealing their Whiggish antecedents, they joined in
1860 in the adulation of the great Kentuckian and claimed that Abraham
Lincoln was the Clay candidate. Members of the Know Nothing party
were, it was claimed, "men trained for the most part in the school of
Henry Clay, who learned from his lips those sentiments of national justice
and national brotherhood, which have inspired and ever will inspire, their
political actions." And for such men, supporting Lincoln was apparently
the natural course. "LINCOLN" a former Know Nothing announced,
"is the follower of CLAY." In fact "he sucked in the milk of his political
gospel from that most honored statesman." Accordingly, "we at least,
and you we believe, will rally to the support of a man who so nearly
represents the author of the American System." Indeed not only northerners, but southerners too, it was hoped, would rally to Lincoln once

229. Baum, *Civil War Party System*, p. 45.
230. Howard K. Beale (ed.), *The Diary of Edward Bates, 1859–1866* (Washington, DC,
1933), p. 129. Historians who stress ethnocultural factors sometimes employ a double standard, arguing that the merest mention of religious issues in political discourse
demonstrates a huge latent concern for these matters within the electorate. Yet since
Republicans statesmen and publicists devoted vastly more time and space to the slavery question, the evidence overall suggests the relative unimportance of ethnocultural
factors. It should also be noted that voter turnout figures do not support this case.
Ethnocultural issues were primarily state and local rather than federal issues. Yet in
general presidential elections drew the largest turnouts in the antebellum period. See
Huston, *Calculating the Value of the Union*, p. 261; Bergeron, *Antebellum Politics
in Tennessee*, p. 135; Formisano, *Birth of Mass Parties*, pp. 273–274.

his Clay credentials were properly recognised. George Babcock, another former Know Nothing, predicted that southerners would soon reconcile themselves to Lincoln. "And why" he asked, "should they not?" since "LINCOLN only echoes HENRY CLAY."[231]

The Republican desire to woo Fillmore voters meant that former Know Nothing speakers were much in demand in the late 1850s and in 1860. It would be wrong to suggest that they entirely ignored nativism. Thus Gustavus A. Scroggs, a leading New York nativist, claimed that the Republican party "has already inaugurated some of the reforms which were principles embraced in our political creed, and it has given its sanction to others which, if carried out, would go a great way towards accomplishing the aims of our political action." But Scroggs had to admit that he could not endorse the strongly antinativist plank of the Chicago platform and this was scarcely surprising since, as we have seen, it utterly repudiated the most fundamental principle of the Know Nothing movement.[232]

Scroggs in any case devoted only a small portion of his remarks to nativism. Other recent converts did not even do so much. All of them, including Scroggs, emphasised above all the sectional controversy. In the process they confirmed that for them, as for other Republicans, the key task was to deliver a rebuke to the slave interest, to prevent it continuing to exert a disorganising influence in the nation. Former Fillmore supporters had come to this conclusion more slowly and, in general, more reluctantly than mainstream Republicans but they had reached it nonetheless. Thus Scroggs himself acknowledged that "the agitation of the slavery question has increased and spread, until it now shakes the whole country from its centre to its remotest borders." "All other questions," he conceded, "of principle or governmental policy have shrunk into insignificance, and it alone has become the issue of a presidential campaign." How had this come about? The Know Nothing-Republicans had a clear, if not entirely accurate, view of the sectional conflict as it had developed in recent years. When Pierce had entered the White House in 1853, they noted, the slavery question had been quiet; the nation had had before it the prospect of "everlasting repose." But then had come the Kansas-Nebraska Act, the violence in Kansas, and the Dred Scott decision (which had cast aside, in a way that was deeply disturbing to neo-Whigs, the accumulated wisdom of the past). Now in 1860 there was the demand for a slave code in the territories. James Putnam reminded his audience that in 1856 the American party had "attempted to occupy a middle, conciliatory ground"

231. *Proceedings of the American Mass Meeting, And the Speeches of Hon. James O. Putnam, and Roswell Hart, Esq, Sept. 7, 1860* (Rochester, 1860), p. 3; *The Duty of Americans: Speech of Gen. G. A. Scroggs, and of Hon. Geo. B. Babcock, also of Hon James A. Putnam* (n.p., n.d.), pp. 8–9.
232. *Duty of Americans*, p. 5.

on the slavery question. But it had "all been in vain." Fillmore had been deserted by a significant number of southern "cowards" (here Putnam ignored northern defectors and "cowards") with the result that he had been left "high and dry on the beach in every Southern State, excepting gallant Maryland." There could be only one conclusion: "the business of redeeming the country from democratic license, and of suppressing slavery agitation, must devolve . . . on the northern opposition."[233]

Former Know Nothings not unnaturally dwelt on the experiences of their own party in the mid-1850s in order to demonstrate the futility of any strategy which did not combat southern aggression. The American party, Roswell Hart recalled, had been "a noble and patriotic organization." Its "great and cardinal principles" had been "to intensify an American sentiment, to purify the ballot box, to cultivate peace and fraternity between members of the National Confederacy who had become divided upon the unhappy dissensions of the slavery question." Know Nothings had been taught by "the experience of other parties" that "if we would hold together in knitted strength we must be especially solicitous to avoid the rocks on which they had shipwrecked, and to this end we purposely avoided the slavery question." But, Hart continued, southern Know Nothings had hurled among them the "firebrand" of Section Twelve which had confirmed the repeal of the Missouri Compromise and which prevented Congress from excluding slavery from any future territory. Here in microcosm was the problem: "the more we have labored to avoid all discussion of what we deemed this dangerous question to us as a party, the more determined have the South been to force from us some expression of opinion upon this very subject they were ever crying out to us not to agitate." "Thus it has been," Hart concluded, "from the origin of our party." Moreover, all parties would suffer this fate unless they were prepared to allow the South to be "dominant and supreme" in the nation."[234]

What Hart here ignored was the fact that for southern Know Nothings Section Twelve was itself an attempt to end agitation of the slavery question. But northerners simply could not accept what purported to be a resolution of the issue on these terms. And just as a resolution on southern terms inflamed northern opinion so northerners felt impelled to take the fateful step of supporting Lincoln and seeking a Republican resolution of the crisis regardless or unaware of the impact it would have on the South. In 1856 and in 1860, the party's enemies repeatedly emphasised the dangers of a Republican victory. But Know Nothings who joined the Republicans now ignored these warnings. They had by now reached the

233. *Duty of Americans*, pp. 5, 3. *Proceedings of the American Mass Meeting*, pp. 3–6.
234. *Proceedings of the American Mass Meeting*, pp. 9–10.

conclusion that the danger of inaction or of acquiescence in the wishes
of the South simply aggravated rather than resolved the nation's difficulties. Hence "we must choose between these striving forces. It is useless to
remain neutral." "We have been crying peace, peace," Scroggs lamented,
"but," he added in a phrase which signaled his adoption of the principal
Republican motif, "there is no peace."[235]

These former Know Nothings were agreed that it was essential to arrest
the progress of the slave interest. Their goal was not abolition but rather
the removal of the slavery question from politics. Ironically, however, this
strategy required an immediate confrontation with the South, so that no
further aggressions would be attempted. Scroggs argued that where it
existed, slavery should "remain undisturbed by any interference from the
free States" with "all the constitutional rights and immunities to which
it is legally and justly entitled ... faithfully enforced and preserved." But
"beyond this it cannot and will not be suffered to go." James Putnam was
similarly insistent. He noted that some conservative or Old Line Whigs
like Washington Hunt were claiming in 1860 that the Republicans had
achieved freedom for the territory of Kansas and thus had no further role
to play. To this he offered two rejoinders, each of which confirmed his and
his new party's view of slavery as a disorganising element in the Republic.
First he insisted that "we want some other force than civil war to settle the
institutions of every territory" and second, he warned that the next stage
in the southern proslavery offensive would be to declare slave property
inviolable in northern states too. This threat could not be ignored. Here
Putnam's views converged with those in the centre and on the radical wing
of the Republican party. Indeed he then echoed the opinion of William
Seward and confirmed that the conflict between slavery and freedom was
indeed "irrepressible."[236]

Nevertheless, these former Know Nothings remained on the conservative wing of the Republican party. They dissociated themselves from many
of the utterances of the radicals. Thus Putnam explained that although he
was supporting Lincoln, this was "not because I endorse every thing every
Republican orator has said." The radicals, he announced soothingly, were
not to be feared. Those (like Washington Hunt) who thought differently
were committing the error "of supposing that the irresponsible declama-
tion of the hustings is to be taken as the pole star of an Administration with
the weight of a government upon its shoulders." How could the nation
know that a Republican administration would indeed prove safe? The
answer would scarcely have reassured any southerners. The Republicans,

235. *Duty of Americans*, p. 3.
236. *Duty of Americans*, pp. 4, 14–15.

Putnam was confident, were not fools and an enlightened self-interest would prevent them from seeking to destroy southern society.[237]

Although these former Know Nothings were not without sympathy for the plight of African Americans, the welfare of the slave was of minor concern. Putnam stated explicitly that he did not believe that blacks were his "social equals" and he and those who thought like him scarcely even discussed the question of abolition, however gradual, in the South. Their priorities lay elsewhere. Where the radicals had a programme which they hoped would culminate in abolition, what the former Know Nothings wanted was to rid the federal government, and the territories, of the slavery question. Then the nation could attend to issues that were, or should be, of far greater importance, leaving slavery to continue in those states, and only those states, where it already existed. They believed that the demands of the South posed for the North a stark choice. Slavery had to be disposed of as a political question. There would be "no rest from the agitation with which we are now afflicted" unless one of two outcomes ensued. Either "the ascendancy of slavery" would be "permanently established" in the nation as a whole, or "its limits" would have to be "emphatically and definitely defined." The first outcome was clearly unacceptable; the second must therefore be expedited. Until this were achieved "questions of the greatest moment to our country's welfare" would not receive "any attention whatever, much less that attention which their importance demands." What were these issues? They were, of course, primarily those with which Whigs had traditionally been associated. Thus George Babcock, arguing that it was impossible for former Know Nothings in New York to support Stephen A. Douglas in 1860, explained that "in all matters of local or State policy, canals, railroads, the power of corporate monopolies and the numerous questions which affect your taxation at home, and the development of the resources of the Empire State, you are directly diametrically opposed to the democracy." Babcock then reminded his audience that "to you, practically, these questions are far more important than that of Slavery." Babcock here was referring to a single state but these Whiggish priorities were in evidence throughout the North, and they were equally relevant in federal politics too.[238]

The former Know Nothings were confident that the election of Lincoln would do much, perhaps everything necessary, to put the slavery question to rest. Historians know of course that the opposite occurred and that Lincoln's election instead marked a final and fatal escalation of the sectional controversy. It is ironic that a group who stressed above all the

237. *Proceedings of the American Mass Meeting*, p. 4; *Duty of Americans*, p. 12.
238. *Proceedings of the American Mass Meeting*, p. 4; *Duty of Americans*, pp. 4, 6.

need for enlightened statesmanship, cool judgment, and a prudential concern for the future should have been so catastrophically mistaken. One of them looked forward to a period "a month after his election, when Southern conservatives are in his cabinet, when Southern Whig statesmen in House and Senate support his policy [and] when Southern men are raised to high offices and are scattered all over the Slave States to defend and support the grand old Union of which he is the Representative man." As early as August 1860, fully two months before the election, this former Know Nothing argued that "the cry of disunion has already ceased at the South, and the people of that region are avowedly reconciling themselves to LINCOLN's election." "The election of Lincoln," Roswell Hart predicted, was essential because "the country needs repose on the subject of slavery, in its legislative halls."[239]

It is ironic too that the very means by which these northerners hoped to end the slavery agitation were precisely those which prompted southerners to leave the Union. These former Know Nothings believed that a northern majority, once mustered, would simply outvote the South and firmly, once and for all, put an end to her aggressions. They probably believed with James Putnam that once the Democratic party was defeated, the "reign of terror" in the South that prevented free and open discussion of the slavery question would cease and a real opposition in the southern states would emerge. But of course, what seemed to these northerners a healthy process of debate and discussion in the South was no less than the secessionist nightmare, the prospect of a ruinous division within southern society itself between slaveholders and the nonslaveholding majority. Thus these former Know Nothings, like other conservatives in the nation, for all their attempts to chart a middle, moderate course on the sectional question, were utterly unable to foresee the calamitous consequences of their own actions.[240]

## IV

Nevertheless the hope or fear that Lincoln and the Republicans might establish outposts within the South soon after his election was by no means entirely unfounded. The Opposition movement in the Upper South enjoyed, as we have seen, some success in the late 1850s. Some former Whigs in that region made no secret of the fact that they were opposed to the demands which southern militants were making in these years. Not only did they repudiate the movement for the reopening of the African slave trade, some of them made it clear that they did not like the

239. *Duty of Americans*, pp. 8–9; *Proceedings of the American Mass Meeting*, p. 4.
240. *Duty of Americans*, p. 14.

Lecompton constitution. John J. Crittenden, for example, made a speech opposing it which won accolades from the remnant of the American and the Whig parties in the South.

The result was a plan, or at least an aspiration, that the more moderate Republicans might be detached from their party and might unite with the southern Opposition in what would be in effect a reincarnated Whig party. In June 1857 a group of Whigs in New Orleans issued an address *To the People of Louisiana* in which they called for a revival of their old party. Meanwhile in Virginia John Minor Botts announced that he would ally with any group (including free blacks!) to overthrow the Democratic party and in the same state the Richmond *Whig* voiced the hope that "black Republicanism" might "soon become white Republicanism," whereupon it might form links with the opposition in Virginia. Even more remarkably, the *Whig*, which had long been one of the leading Whig newspapers in the entire South, in September 1859 pledged that the party in Virginia would "support Seward a thousand times sooner than any Democrat, Northern or Southern, in the land." And fittingly, Henry Clay's son, Thomas Clay raised the same possibility. "If the Black Republican party eschew sectional issues and have become national and conservative in their action," then "why," he asked, "should not all true Americans unite with it to cleanse the Augean stable at Washington and to purify the country from this baneful influence?"[241]

Utterances like these were often accompanied by ringing endorsements of the Union and denunciations of those southerners whose conduct seemed to be jeopardising it. Nevertheless in many cases, and especially in the Deep South, this was a highly conditional unionism, as the events after November 1860 would demonstrate. And in the Deep South countervailing pressure was being applied. Thus Alexander Stephens and Robert Toombs of Georgia who had scarcely acted with the Whigs since 1850 (and who had denounced the Know Nothings) joined the Democratic party before Buchanan's election; others followed their example both before and after the presidential contest. Judah P. Benjamin of Louisiana was among them and Henry Hilliard, perhaps the leading Whig in Alabama, announced that he would support the Buchanan administration on the grounds that "an undivided South" was a necessity. The

241. Richmond *Whig* quoted in William A. Link, *Roots of Secession: Slavery and Politics in Antebellum Virginia* (Chapel Hill, 2003), p. 172; Crofts, *Reluctant Confederates*, pp. 69, 75; Richmond *Whig* Sept. 30, 1859; Cole, *Whig Party in South*, pp. 332–334; Freehling, *The Reintegration of American History: Slavery and the Civil War* (New York, 1994), p. 211. Others, such as Henry Winter Davis of Maryland and the Opposition in North Carolina, made similar remarks about an alliance with the Republicans – see Cole, *Whig Party in South*, p. 327; Baker *Ambivalent Americans*, p. 152; De Roulhac Hamilton, *Party Politics in North Carolina, 1835–1860*, p. 192.

Democratic party must now be the party for "conservative men of all sections." Undoubtedly the alarming growth of the Republican party in the North was taking its toll upon southerners. The process of polarisation continued and even accelerated in each section in response to the polarisation that was taking place in the other.[242]

The movement for a national opposition foundered in these years for two reasons. First although some Republicans like Horace Greeley (whose influence was immense) were, on some occasions at least, favourable to the idea, the more common view was that the Republicans neither needed the Opposition for victory in 1860 nor could afford the surrender or dilution of principle that any fusion would require.[243] In other words the polarisation in the North damaged the project irretrievably. But secondly, the polarisation in the South was also damaging. These southerners were always vulnerable to the charge that they were disloyal to the South. After the Brown raid of 1859 this charge was even more potent. Although the Opposition continued in the South, and even, as we have seen, enjoyed considerable success, the alliance with the moderate Republicans failed to materialise. The Opposition in 1860 would ally not with the Republicans but instead with the small number of unreconstructed Whigs in the North and would fight the election as the Constitutional Union party. It would be the final curtain call for the Whig party.

## The Constitutional Union party

### I

The American presidential election of 1860 was perhaps the most momentous election in the history not merely of the United States but of the entire world. After its conclusion in November events moved with startling rapidity as first the states of the Deep South seceded, then the new Republican administration was inaugurated, then war broke out at Charleston and finally four more states left the Union.

As the election approached it was widely recognised that a crisis might be looming. The Republicans, although defeated in the presidential race four years earlier, had nevertheless run remarkably well and it was universally acknowledged that a relatively small swing in a relatively small number of states would be enough to send Lincoln into the White House. It was also feared, though less universally, that in such an eventuality, some of the southern states at least would take drastic action. In these

242. Cole, *Whig Party in South*, p. 327.
243. This was Lincoln's view – see Crofts, *Reluctant Confederates*, p. 69.

circumstances, it seemed, extraordinary efforts should be made in the name of sectional peace and to ensure the maintenance of the Union.

Such reasoning resulted in the creation in 1860 of the Constitutional Union party. The party nominated John Bell of Tennessee for the presidency and selected Edward Everett of Massachusetts as his running mate. Both were, of course, former Whigs and this was no coincidence. The Constitutional Union party was the closest thing to a resurrected Whig party that was imaginable in the final months of the antebellum Republic.[244]

There were some Democrats in the party but only one, Sam Houston of Texas, of any prominence. There were also some nativists like Jacob Broom of Pennsylvania, but he himself had previously been a Whig. In effect therefore this was the Whig party reincarnated. In the South at least, even its constituency was the old Whig heartland: the party was strongest in states like Maryland, North Carolina, Kentucky and Tennessee. In the North the party represented the more conservative, so called "national" Whigs who had not been willing to join the Republican party and who had, until his death in 1852, drawn inspiration from Daniel Webster.

The Constitutional Unionists did not disavow their heritage. They sometimes referred to themselves as Whigs in their own newspapers and their campaign sheet *The Union Guard* even sought to invoke the "spirit of 1840," thus recalling the Whig party's greatest electoral triumph. When John J. Crittenden of Kentucky delivered a speech on behalf of the party's candidates he announced himself a Whig from first to last while Gustavus Henry at the party's national convention declared that his ideal statesmen had always been Henry Clay and Daniel Webster.[245]

In 1856 the American party, as we have seen, also proclaimed itself the heir of Clay and Webster and was, by that time, a party principally concerned not with nativism but rather with unionism. The Constitutional Unionists were in this sense, therefore, also the lineal descendants of the Know Nothings. Yet nativism played little or no part in their appeal to the voters in 1860. Many of the former nativists had joined them but in

---

244. On the Constitutional Union party see John B Stabler, "A History of the Constitutional Union Party" (Unpublished Doctoral Dissertation, Columbia, 1954), though this work has little to say on the subject of ideology. See also Peter Knupfer, "Aging Statesmen and the Statesmanship of an Earlier Age: The Generational Roots of the Constitutional Union Party," in David W. Blight and Brooks D. Simpson (eds.), *Union and Emancipation: Essays on Politics and Race in the Civil War Era* (Kent, OH, 1997), pp. 57–78. This is a valuable essay, but I do not see the division within the party's ranks that Knupfer describes.

245. New York *Express* quoted in *Union Guard*, July 19, 1860, p. 28; *Union Guard*, Aug. 16, 1860, pp. 91, 95; *The Union, The Constitution, and the Laws, Speech of the Hon. John J. Crittenden, at Louisville, Ky ... Aug. 2, 1860* (Washington, DC, 1860), p. 7l; *Union Guard*, July 12, 1860, p. 6.

the North others, as we have seen, had continued to leave the party and enlist under the Republican banner. Although the example of Millard Fillmore's bid for the presidency in 1856 was scarcely an encouraging one, many in the new party began with extremely high hopes.[246]

## II

The crucial issue of the campaign was, of course, slavery and even though this was the issue which had done most to destroy both the Whigs and the Know Nothings, the Constitutional Unionists were compelled to engage with it. In fact as befitted conservative Whigs they gave little attention to the abstract question of slavery and rarely pronounced upon its morality. Least of all did they engage in the systematic comparisons between free and slave labour that were the stock-in-trade of both Republicans and proslavery enthusiasts. Instead they emphasised that, while there were legitimate differences between North and South, these need not and should not result in antagonism. According to Washington Hunt of New York such differences might be "inherent and unavoidable" but it did not follow that they should form the basis of party divisions. Indeed such dissimilarities placed a heavy burden of responsibility upon statesmen to ensure that they did not generate hostilities. In its *Address to the People of the United States* the party's national executive committee explained that "the fact that our Union is composed in part of slaveholding States, and in part of non-slaveholding States, imposes grave duties upon both sections." What were these duties? The committee spelled them out in terms that would have been entirely familiar to a conservative Whig a quarter century earlier. What was required were "duties of forbearance, concession and conciliation, respect for each other's convictions, tenderness in handling each other's sensitive points – in short, such rules of self-control and self-government as regulate in social life, and in the relations of business, the intercourse of gentlemen who may choose to differ widely on the gravest questions." Here was the traditional Whig emphasis upon self-control, prudence, moderation and self-restraint.[247]

Such qualities, it was held, were at an even higher premium when dealing with slavery than when other issues were under consideration, for

---

246. A very small number went in the opposite direction – from Republican to Constitutional Unionist. An example was Lew Campbell of Ohio but he took few with him – see Stabler, *History of the Constitutional Union Party*, pp. 542–543; Nashville *Patriot*, July 25, 1860 quoted in Dwight L. Dumond (ed.), *Southern Editorials on Secession* (New York, 1931), p. 148.
247. Washington Hunt quoted in *Union Guard*, July 19, 1860, p. 22; *Address of the National Executive Committee of the Constitutional Union Party to the People of the United States* (n.p., n.d.), p. 4.

there were "tremendous difficulties" surrounding the subject. Although an immense number of speeches had been delivered, how much progress had been made towards a resolution, or even a mitigation, of the problems? The National Executive committee noted quite rightly that northerners had no carefully elaborated policy for getting rid of slavery and instead spent their time denouncing it. Southerners meanwhile, also without a constructive policy, merely dismissed all practical suggestions as the ravings of abolitionism. This was the antithesis of the statesmanlike approach advocated by the conservative Whig.[248]

This did not mean, however, that the Constitutional Unionists themselves had a solution for the problems created by slavery. Rather they wished to contain them, as indeed they had been contained in previous decades. The leaders of the new party clearly felt it their duty to remind the electorate of some fundamental facts about the Union, facts which would encourage moderation and mutual respect between the sections, but facts which were being ignored in the fevered atmosphere of 1860. Above all they stressed, as Whigs had always done, the interdependence of North and South and, as they did so, confronted the central claim, made by leading Republicans, that there was an inevitable or, as William Seward had put it, "irrepressible" conflict between them. According to ex-Governor Charles S. Morehead of Kentucky there could be no possible basis for conflict between the sections since "the prosperity of one section is intimately blended with that of the other." Thus dissimilarities should produce not conflict but instead an enhanced interdependence. "Each branch of industry," Morehead observed, "harmonizes with, and, in a greater or less degree is dependent on some other." This was classic Whig doctrine, traditionally employed to stress the interdependence of the various interest or occupational groups within society as well as the two great sections. Similarly the *Union Guard* reminded its readers of the vast importance of the cotton industry to the prosperity of New England and then asked: "with these facts before them, how can the people of New England believe that there exists an 'irrepressible conflict' between free and slave labor?" The idea that the working men of New England had been disadvantaged by the existence of slavery in the South was, to the Constitutional Unionists, a palpable absurdity. "Where," the editor asked, having noted that wages were far higher in New England than in Europe, where there was no slave labour, "is the proof?"[249]

Alongside an appreciation of sectional interdependence, the Constitutional Unionists hoped to inculcate within the electorate a truer

248. *Address of National Executive Committee*, p. 5.
249. Morehead in *Union Guard*, Oct. 18, 1860, p. 238; *Union Guard*, Oct. 2, 1860, p. 202.

understanding of the issues involved in the current controversy. They affirmed, time and again, that the controversy over the extension of slavery, which had already divided the Democratic party and now threatened to divide the nation itself, was utterly futile and unnecessary. They adduced two reasons. First, the party's spokesmen repeatedly made it clear that the establishment of slavery in a territory would ultimately depend upon soil and climate. Where these were appropriate, slavery would go; where they were not, free labour would triumph. Hence there was simply no need for politicians to become involved.[250] Second, and even more important, the issue was by 1860 an "abstraction," devoid, it was said, of practical content or significance. According to the Constitutional Union party National Executive Committee "the whole question of slavery in the Territories, as now presented," was "an abstraction pure and simple, incapable of practical application, and prolific of serious mischief." It was, in the words of J. Thomas Stevenson of Massachusetts, "a senseless wrangle about a pure abstraction." At present, it was noted, there were no territories whose labour system remained to be determined, nor were there any plans to acquire additional territory. In these circumstances, John J. Crittenden concluded, it was folly to debate contentious issues that were unlikely ever to present themselves.[251]

Under these circumstances and given these beliefs, it was scarcely surprising that Constitutional Unionists did not wish to formulate a policy on the question of slavery in the territories. Nevertheless pressure in the South was intense and Bell in fact announced that in principle he upheld the principle of federal protection for slavery during the territorial stage, which was the orthodox position of the Breckinridge forces, but added the major qualification that it was inexpedient to assert the right at present, which was most certainly not the Breckinridge position. As we shall see, this attempt at even-handedness antagonised both extremes at least as often as it reconciled them.

Nor was it surprising that, rather than discuss future policy, the Constitutional Unionists preferred to voice their disapproval of the policies implemented in the past by their political enemies. Here the single event that bulked largest was, once again, the passage of the Kansas-Nebraska Act in 1854. For the Constitutional Unionists this measure was the negation of all their most cherished values and an utter repudiation of the style of statesmanship to which they were wedded. Stevenson, for example,

250. *Address of L. Madison Day, On the Union, The Constitution, and the Enforcement of the Laws ... New Orleans, Oct. 12, 1860* (New Orleans, 1862), p. 2; *Speech of J. Thomas Stevenson, of Boston, Delivered at Worcester, Sept. 12, 1860* (n.p., n.d.) p. 4; *Address of National Executive Committee*, p. 5.
251. *Address of National Executive Committee*, p. 6; *Speech of Stevenson*, p. 1; Crittenden, *Union, Constitution and Laws*, p. 14.

referred to "the wicked violation of the Missouri Compromise," while the Nashville *Patriot* denounced it as "unnecessary," "uncalled for," and "cruel." The reason was that "it displayed a faithlessness to pledges, a recklessness of the public peace and a disregard of the public weal, that is without parallel in the annals of the country."[252] The new party made much of John Bell's vote against the Act in 1854 and did not shrink from the claim that, if others had followed his example, there would have been no conflict over Kansas, no Republican party and no current threat to the safety and even the continued existence of the Republic.[253]

What had produced these calamitous errors? Here party spokesmen detected not merely individual mistakes but a more fundamental weakness in the nation's political system. In effect the Constitutional Unionists revived many of the old Whig fears that had been voiced during Andrew Jackson's presidency. In particular they insisted that government should be in the hands of a talented elite. Whereas Jackson had claimed that all men of even moderate abilities were qualified to hold office, Whigs had traditionally urged the voters to select instead members of an elite, whose powers and talents could then be used for the benefit of all. In 1860 the heirs of the Whigs now found that this elite was even more desperately needed. On behalf of the Constitutional Unionists, the *Union Guard* claimed credit for "the nomination, for the first time in sixteen years, of candidates for the Presidency and Vice-Presidency who were truly worthy of those lofty positions." Their candidates, Bell and Everett, would then resist the torrents of fanaticism that threatened to engulf the nation and would speedily resolve the current crisis.[254]

Constitutional Unionists did not, however, merely claim that the major parties happened to be led by men of insufficient stature. In addition they revived the old Whig charge that party itself had produced a degeneration in political leadership. Although accepting that political parties were necessary, Constitutional Unionists, like the Know Nothings earlier in the decade and the Whigs before them, held party zeal responsible for the nation's current afflictions. The *Union Guard* referred to "the mad fanatics and blind devotees to party, who have so heedlessly produced these results," while John J. Crittenden warned that "when we forget our country, and disobey our constitution, we listen to the summons of party." What was needed, according to Crittenden, was "a party for the country," one that would be "calm" and "patriotic" and which had "suitable

---

252. *Speech of Stevenson*, p. 2; Nashville *Patriot*, July 25, 1860, in Dumond (ed.), *Southern Editorials on Secession*, p. 146. See also Washington Hunt, in *Union Guard*, July 19, 1860, p. 22; Nashville *Republican Banner*, March 29, 1860, in Dumond (ed.), *Southern Editorials on Secession*, p. 63.
253. Crittenden, *Union, Constitution and Laws*, p. 19.
254. *Union Guard*, Sept. 6, 1860, p. 138.

and proper representatives at its head." Similarly, the North Carolina
*Whig* referred to "institutions wrenched from their legitimate spheres by
the violence of party faction," while J. Thomas Stevenson declared that
"government ought to be taken out of the hands of men, whose trade is
party politics."[255]

The Constitutional Unionists departed from contemporary practice in
having no real platform. Instead their party, they proclaimed, came "upon
a great and high principle," standing simply for "The Union, the Constitution and the Enforcement of the Laws." The lack of a real platform
was not, of course, the result of oversight. Instead it was the corollary
of the expanded role which the statesman, as opposed to the mere party
hack, was expected to play. Rather than be restricted by platforms, the
true leader should be left free to deliberate and reflect upon the major
issues of the day and act accordingly, untrammelled either by excessive
loyalty to parties, or by previously drawn up platforms. John J. Crittenden
announced his "natural aversion to platforms." "I hardly ever," he
declared, "read a platform in my life, and, when I did, tried to forget it as
soon as possible." "The Constitution," he affirmed, "is platform enough
for me." Other spokesmen for the Constitutional Unionists pointed out,
quite accurately, that before the era of Andrew Jackson, no party had a
platform in the contemporary sense of the term.[256]

Nor should the statesman be restricted by pledges. Although a candidate for the highest office, John Bell, it was emphasised, was "not in
the market to make bids for the Presidency: he is not upon the rack to
have pledges extorted." The rationale was the same: pledges would curtail the representative's freedom of movement, a freedom that was essential if the sometimes conflicting interests that were found in the political
arena were to be reconciled. Hence, according to Crittenden, Bell, and
Everett, untrammelled by platforms or pledges, stood ready to heal the
nation's self-inflicted wounds. "They come," Crittenden explained, "with
the Constitution in their hands. They come imploring their brethren to
forgive each other, to lay aside their hostilities, to cease these fierce broils
that are alienating section from section and men from men."[257]

The absence of pledges and platforms, together with the emphasis upon
the sterling qualities of their leaders, spoke to the Constitutional Unionists' concern for the values of republicanism rather than those of populistic

---

255. *Union Guard*, July 12, 1860, p. 10; Crittenden, *Union, Constitution and Laws*,
     pp. 12, 4. North Carolina *Whig*, Dec. 4, 1860; *Speech of Stevenson*, p. 1.
256. Crittenden, *Union, Constitution and Laws*, p. 14; *Address to the People of Mas-
     sachusetts, Adopted at the Union Convention, Held at Worcester, Sept. 12, 1860*
     (n.p., n.d.), p. 10. See also *To the People of the United States* (n.p., n.d.), p. 6.
257. *Union Guard*, Aug. 23, 1860, p. 105; Crittenden, *Union, Constitution and Laws*,
     p. 5.

democracy. Like the Whigs, and especially the conservative Whigs, before them they were inveighing against the populistic practices championed by Andrew Jackson. But whereas Jackson had acted in the name of an agrarian radicalism, the delinquent politicians of 1860 were motivated, or pretended to be motivated, by sectional animosities. The situations were nevertheless analogous: in each case mindless loyalty to party and unthinking passion were the illness, disinterested statesmanship on the part of an enlightened elite the cure.

In December 1860, immediately after the results of the election were known, John P. Kennedy of Maryland expressed a fear, common among leaders of the Constitutional Union party, that "passion will rule the hour." The party's national executive a few months earlier had offered a similar warning. "The great mass of law-abiding citizens," it claimed, "are looking on with amazement, and an ominous apprehension of mischief." "And yet," the readers were reminded, "there is no danger impending over the Republic which human passions have not created, and which human wisdom may not prevent." For the conservative Whigs and indeed the Federalists before them, democracy had always been susceptible to manipulation by the demagogue and the demagogue, in turn, had always spoken to the passions rather than to the reason of the electorate.[258]

Passionate appeals for loyalty to section were thus the disease afflicting the body politic. And if these were indeed the consequence of a mediocracy, they further ensured that none but the mediocre would wish to enter politics. The Constitutional Union party's National Executive explained the process: "The tendency of this sectional excitement" was "to repel wise and good statesmen from the sphere of politics, and thus to lower the tone of government." As a result "men endowed with statesman-like powers will not take part in an agitation which dwarfs the understanding while it inflames the passions." The result was political decline: "while we are rapidly increasing in wealth and all the indications of material civilization, and surely not declining in virtue and intelligence, the series of our public men marks a descending scale, and the standard of Congressional debate is constantly lowering."[259]

The solution was to abstain from unnecessary discussions of slavery and the sectional issues. But beyond that the solution was to cling to the classic safeguards of republicanism, the bulwarks that had traditionally been viewed as protection against an excessive populism. First, it was necessary to inculcate a deep respect for the majesty of the law. This meant an absolute obedience to the decisions of the Supreme Court, for example,

258.  Henry T. Tuckerman (ed.), *The Collective Works of John P. Kennedy*. 10 vols. (New York, 1871–1872), IV, p. 543; *To the People of the United States*, p. 4.
259.  *Address of National Executive Committee*, pp. 5–6.

however controversial they might be. More fundamentally, it meant "a sacred regard to law because it is law." This concern arose in part, but only in part, because the Personal Liberty laws of some northern states (passed in order to frustrate the Fugitive Slave Act) made "full allegiance to the United States, on the part of the individual, a crime." Respect for the law had always been viewed as a safeguard against anarchy, demagogy and radicalism, just as the radical, the anarchist and the demagogue prospered by promoting contempt for the law. Some Constitutional Unionists rehearsed the distinction, frequently made by conservative Whigs and Federalists before them, between liberty and license or anarchy. "The only difference between liberty and anarchy," according to one writer, was "the enforcement of *Law*."[260]

A second safeguard against the excesses of a populistic democracy lay in the accumulated wisdom of the past. As true conservative Whigs, Constitutional Unionists insisted that the past be viewed as a source of enlightenment for present and future. The old Jeffersonian and Jacksonian disdain for precedent and established practice had always struck Federalist and conservative Whigs as deeply alarming and in 1860 the party of their heirs sounded the same note. The Constitutional Unionist complained that the prescriptive force of the past and of tradition had been wantonly set aside or repudiated:

> the teaching of the fathers of the republic, the lights of history, the landmarks of constitutional power have been renounced, our old and revered traditions of policy spurned, and the welfare of the present and the hopes of the future been brought into jeopardy in the alternations of passionate challenge and defiance between the angry disputants."[261]

In the same way some Constitutional Unionists, again like conservative Whigs and Federalists before them, inveighed against the notions of "progress," invoked, it was claimed, in order to justify departures from past, time-honoured practice. This was the approach taken by the *Union Guard* in its very first issue:

> Every man of reflection, of whatever party, who will stop long enough to think, will admit that we are indebted more to false and mischievous ideas of progress for our present domestic troubles than to all other causes combined. They have given rise to new suggestions in relation to the theory of government, to new and experimental notions of policy which their advocates are seeking to introduce, to new modes of interpreting the laws, and to new, and till lately unheard

---

260. *Address of L. Madison Day*, p. 2; *Speech of Stevenson*, p. 5.
261. *To the People of the United States*, pp. 1–2.

of interpolations upon the Constitution. If we had kept more nearly to the lines of policy prescribed by our fathers, had more carefully heeded their admonitions and profited by their wisdom and example, it would have been far better for the country, because these evils would have been all escaped, and we should have gone on augmenting the prosperity which they sacrificed so much to establish, – developing, to the utmost extent, the immense resources with which Providence has so bountifully provided us."[262]

Here then was the set of problems.which the Constitutional Union party had been established to combat. An excessive sectionalism had triggered the formation of the new party, as former Whigs looked for a means by which harmony could be re-established and the Union preserved. But sectional asperity was itself seen as unnecessary, a product not of the differences between North and South, which were or should be, eminently containable, but rather of a more fundamental degeneration in American political practice and American political culture. The signs of that decline were an excessive partisanship, as the party spoilsman replaced the wise and sagacious statesmen, an appeal to the passions of the electorate and a failure to respect the hallowed wisdom of the past. The Constitutional Union party thus undertook to begin a transformation of the nation's political culture, the result of which would be peace, harmony and tranquillity.

## III

If there were any doubt about the Whiggish attitudes of the Constitutional Union party, its social philosophy and the policy objectives flowing from that philosophy would alone remove them. For just as Whigs from the 1830s had combined a political conservatism with a highly progressive attitude towards the nation's economy so the Constitutional Unionists in 1860 resurrected as much of the Whig economic programme as was viable. A national bank was still almost entirely absent from the political agenda in 1860. The tariff was another matter. The Constitutional Unionists made much of the problems Republicans had in formulating a single policy on the tariff (largely as a result of the presence of the former Democrats within their ranks) by proclaiming that they were the only true supporters of the protective principle. "Of all the candidates in the field," they boasted, "John Bell, of Tennessee, is the only one who is fully and without any compromise or equivocation committed to the *protection* of *American* industry." This appeal probably carried most weight in the states of New Jersey and Pennsylvania but Bell himself, though from neither of these

262. *Union Guard*, July 12, 1860, p. 10.

states, was able to claim that he had been in favour of the tariff for about twenty years. The *Union Guard* quoted at length from one of his recent speeches in which he told his audience what "the true policy of the country" ought to be:

> What is the true policy of this country? To encourage and protect, by all constitutional and just means, its internal trade and industry; to promote the division of labor and the diversity of industrial pursuits; to provide congenial and profitable employment, as far as practicable, for the whole population. Let all the arts of production and civilization be cherished by a discriminating patronage. Let the flame and smoke of the smelting furnace be seen rising from every hill and mountain side and from every valley where nature has stored her mineral wealth. Let beautiful villages spring up along the line of our railways, great and small, and dot over all the interiors; and, in or round all of them, let the stately factory appear, with its busy hum of looms and spindles, and hard by the great workshops be found in which that sort of machines are made that produce the wealth of New England.

With its invocation of small-scale rural capitalism this was indeed classic Whig doctrine. And the openly expressed admiration for the achievements of New England had been the hallmark of southern Whiggery since the party's inception.[263]

This demand for an active government which would foster and further diversify the various economic pursuits of its citizens had had an obvious appeal in both the North, which was the successful exemplar of the approach, and in the border South, where the North had long served as a model or inspiration. In the Deep South it had traditionally had less appeal, and in part for this reason the Whig party had traditionally been much weaker there. To advocate Whiggish economic policies in the Deep South (outside Louisiana perhaps where the sugar industry needed protection) was usually to voice criticisms of the existing economic structures in the region and to demand a fundamental change of course. This was the approach of the Vicksburg *Whig* which in 1860 asked and answered a highly pertinent question. "Why," the editor wanted to know "are we so far behind in the great march of improvement?" The answer was that it was "simply because we have *failed to act* in obedience to the dictates of sound policy. Simply because we have been criminally neglectful of our own pecuniary interests." Southerners should instead "encourage the mechanical arts." Referring to the South's "ignoble slumber," the editor urged his readers to "sedulously cultivate the sentiment, so true in itself,

---

263. *Union Guard*, July 19, 1860, p. 25; "Speech of John Bell in Philadelphia, April 27, 1859," quoted in *ibid.*, p. 14. See also *A Calm Appeal to the Friends of American Industry, Especially in the States of Pennsylvania and New Jersey* (n.p., n.d.), pp. 6–7.

that *labor is honorable and dignified.*" Only by such action could southerners end their excessive dependence upon the North.[264]

Yet in 1860 as in the 1850s such appeals made only a limited impression.
Except in the states of Pennsylvania and perhaps New Jersey the tariff
was not a major issue. In most of the North prosperity did not depend
on protection to domestic industry and in most of the Deep South the
tariff continued to be seen, as it had been seen since the time of Thomas
Jefferson and John Taylor of Caroline, as a device to transfer wealth
from agriculturists, now concentrated as never before in the South, to
industrialists, as always disproportionately located in the North. The neo-
Whiggery of the Constitutional Unionists was thus no more successful in
generating a mass appeal in 1860 than the Whig party itself had been in
the 1850s.


                                  IV

The task of the moderate in politics is to detach voters from more extreme
positions. Accordingly the task of the Constitutional Unionists in 1860
was to detach as many northerners as possible from the Republican party
(and even from the northern Democracy) and as many southerners as possible from the Breckinridge wing of the Democratic party. These might
then be allied to the natural Whiggish constituency of the new party to
create a winning coalition. But the very strength of the moderate position was also its weakness: the opportunity to recruit from both sides of
the political spectrum also meant that there was a real danger of being
squeezed from both sides, or, to change the image, of being caught in the
crossfire, denounced as insufficiently northern in the North and insufficiently southern in the South.

Such was the fate of the Constitutional Unionists. In the North Bell's
candidacy never really ignited and its lack of success bred further failure. Edward Bates was precisely the kind of conservative ex-Whig whom
the Constitutional Unionists had to recruit. But though he conceded that
Bell and Everett were "worthy and excellent men," Bates concluded that
they lacked popularity and therefore could do no good. Others were far
less complimentary. Everything depended not on the awareness that a crisis was at hand, which most observers acknowledged, but rather on the
explanation offered for it. As we have seen, the Constitutional Unionists attributed it to politicians, parties and the deteriorating political culture of the nation. Republicans attributed it instead to the encroachments of the Slave Power and the disorganising effect of slavery. Thus
Carl Schurz argued that the election of 1860 was a momentous struggle

264. Vicksburg *Whig*, Jan. 16, 1860 quoted in Dumond (ed.), *Southern Editorials on
    Secession*, pp. 15–16.

between liberty of speech and of the press on the one side, and a slave-holding tyranny on the other, between free homes for homesteaders, on the one side, and a monopolising sectional interest on the other. From this perspective the Constitutional Unionists' frequently expressed belief that the conflict could be ignored was foolhardy in the extreme. Were the voters being asked, Schurz wondered, to "ignore the fire that consumes the corner posts of your house?" Inaction would simply invite disaster.[265]

Massachusetts Senator Henry Wilson also rounded upon Bell and his supporters. The events of the 1850s seemed to Republicans to have demonstrated beyond all doubt that the slavery controversy could not be quelled except by a northern victory. Concessions, it seemed, simply invited more aggressions. Thus the concessions of 1850 had brought on the Kansas-Nebraska Act, which in turn had produced the strife in Kansas, the Dred Scott decision and the rest. Only by checking the aggression of the slaveholders, Wilson claimed, could harmony be restored. Yet who were the supporters of Bell in the North? Wilson's answer was polemical but highly accurate. "The class of men in the North now supporting John Bell," he observed, "were the first to falter on the Texas question, the first to surrender the Wilmot Proviso, the first to welcome and applaud the Compromise measures, the first to acquiesce in the Fugitive Slave act, and to execute it with alacrity." He concluded that "in all the contests of the last fifteen years, these men have come before they were called, and run before they were sent, to do the bidding of slave masters." Thus Bell's northern supporters were part of the problem, not the solution to it and to support them would be to intensify the nation's difficulties, not to resolve them. In the South, meanwhile, his supporters, according to Wilson, all too often favoured the extension of slavery, as when they voted to extend the Missouri Compromise line in the late 1840s, or when they supported the Dred Scott decision, or when they vied with Democrats in proclaiming their devotion to slavery and a slave code for the territories. According to Wilson, "the record of the supporters of John Bell in the South" was "with rare exceptions... a record of unfaltering fidelity to slavery, or fealty to the slave propagandists and perpetualists." In these circumstances a vote for Bell was a vote for the Slave Power.[266]

Bell was denounced to similar effect in the South. Richard Archer of Mississippi, like Wilson, referred to his attitude to the Missouri Compromise line. But where Wilson damned Bell for seeking to extend it,

265. *Diary of Bates*, p. 127; Frederic Bancroft (ed.), *Speeches, Correspondence, and Political Papers of Carl Schurz*. 6 vols. (New York, 1913), I, p. 137.
266. *The Position of John Bell And His Supporters: Speech of the Hon Henry Wilson...Sept. 18, 1860* (n.p., n.d.), pp. 6, 16–17.

Archer excoriated him as "the political Judas Iscariot" who in 1854 had said the Compromise was unconstitutional but who had nevertheless refused to vote against it simply because northerners were opposed to the repeal. Thus what to moderates might seem a statesmanlike attempt at even-handedness became in the eyes of extremists a craven and cowardly surrender to *force majeure*. Similarly, though Bell condoned a slave code for the territories, he nevertheless was attacked in the South for acknowledging that Congress could and in some eventualities should, abolish slavery in the District of Columbia. William Lowndes Yancey of Alabama seized upon this and denounced it as a precedent for more direct attacks upon slavery in the States. Once again a concession offered by moderates in the Constitutional Union party was easily presented by extremists as a dangerous capitulation and surrender of principle.[267]

Southerners denounced Bell on other grounds. As we have seen, the Constitutional Unionists maintained a studied silence on policies, especially those relating to the sectional controversy. William Yancey noted that, in refusing to offer pledges or to commit himself in advance, Bell in effect was announcing that "no candidate for the Presidency ought to let you know, if he is an Abolitionist or a Southern man." Moreover the Constitutional Union party platform, if the pronouncement in favour of "the Union, the Constitution, and the Enforcement of the Laws" could be termed a platform was, as John C. Breckinridge pointed out, utterly vacuous:

> I presume that there is scarcely a man in this assembly, perhaps no one North or South, who will admit that he is against the Union, the Constitution, and the enforcement of the laws, but yet they entertain the most diverse and opposite opinions as to the best mode of preserving the Union, of sustaining the Constitution and as the character of laws which ought to be passed. Mr Seward, of New York, Mr Burlingame of Massachusetts, Mr Giddings, of Ohio, and all those eminent gentlemen thoroughly identified with the ultra anti-slavery party of the United States, will tell you that they are for the Union; but it is their own sort of Union that they want. They say they are for the Constitution; but they construe the Constitution so as to take away all our rights. They tell you they are for the enforcement of the laws; but they are for laws which would take away our property. For the Union, the Constitution, and the laws, they shake hands with you on that, but you cannot agree on a single thing under heaven afterwards.

267. *Speech of Richard T. Archer, Esq., 10 Aug. . . . at Port Gibson, Mississippi* (Port Gibson, 1860), pp. 14–15; *Speech of Hon. William Yancey, of Alabama, Delivered at Memphis, Tennessee, Aug. 14, 1860* (Frankfort, KY, 1860), p. 18.

Breckinridge concluded, quite accurately, that the platform effectively declared nothing. As far as the Constitutional Unionists were concerned, the rationale was of course to avoid further escalation of the crisis. But to those who, like Breckinridge, Yancey and other southern militants, believed that the controversy had deeper roots, this was, once again, a highly dangerous approach.[268]

Battered therefore from both sides, the Constitutional Unionists experienced only disappointment in the election of 1860. Bell and Everett carried only the three states of Virginia, Kentucky, and Tennessee, the last two of which had previously been Whig strongholds. As far as the popular vote went, the results were no more impressive. The Constitutional Unionists attracted only one out of every eight voters who cast a ballot. The results showed that the attempted resurrection of the Whig party had failed; as a major force in American politics, the Whigs were still in their grave.[269]

## Secession and war, 1860–1861

### I

When Lincoln's victory was known Constitutional Unionists were deeply dismayed. Northerners feared the effect upon the South. Yet southern Constitutional Unionists, with few if any exceptions, along with many other former Whigs in the South, some of whom had recently defected to the Democracy, did not view the result as grounds for immediate secession. They had made this clear in advance of the polling[270] and in the fall and winter of 1860 –1861 they restated their position.[271] Many distinguished carefully between the radical Republicans, who did indeed, it

---

268. *Speech of Yancey*, p. 18; *Speech of Hon. J. C. Breckinridge, Delivered at Ashland, Kentucky, Sept. 5, 1860* (n.p., n.d.), p. 14.
269. Bell received 12.58 percent of the popular vote.
270. *Charlotte* (North Carolina) *Whig*, March 13, 1860; *Augusta Chronicle and Sentinel*. Feb. 13, 1860, Raleigh *Standard*, July 11, 1860, *Nashville Patriot*, July 25, 1860 in Dumond (ed.), *Southern Editorials on Secession*, pp. 35, 143, 148; John M. Botts, *Union or Disunion* (n.p., n.d.), p. 10; William Graham, "To the Knoxville Convention of the Constitutional Unionist Party," Sept. 22, 1860 in *Papers of Graham*, V, p. 176; Robert Tomlinson, "The Origins and Editorial Policy of the *Richmond Whig and Public Advertiser*, 1824–1865 (Unpublished Doctoral Dissertation, Michigan State University, 1971), p. 178.
271. *Charlotte* (North Carolina) *Whig*, Dec. 25, 1860; *Tuscaloosa Independent Monitor*, Nov. 6, 1860; *Louisville Journal*, Nov. 8, 1860; New Orleans *Picayune*, Nov. 4. 1860; Raleigh *Standard*, March 9, 1861; *Nashville Republican Banner*, March 14, 1861, in Dumond (ed.), *Southern Editorials on Secession*, pp. 219, 217, 478, 484; *Works of Kennedy*, IV, p. 583; "Alexander H. Stephens' Unionist Speech ... Nov. 14, [1860]," Benjamin H. Hill's Unionist Speech ... Nov. 15, [1860]," in William W. Freehling and Craig M. Simpson (eds.), *Secession Debated: Georgia's Showdown in 1860* (New York, 1992), pp. 51–79, 80–104.

was acknowledged, pose a threat to the South, and Lincoln, who was sometimes said to have the moderate, national outlook that befitted a Whig. Others argued that whilst the Republicans would control the executive, both the legislature and the judiciary would be in other hands and thus the new President would have little scope for hostile action against the South even if he desired to embark upon it. "Why, then," asked former Whig Alexander Stephens during Georgia's famous public debate over secession, "should we disrupt the ties of the Union when his hands are tied, – when he can do nothing against us?"[272]

Those opposing secession throughout the South, even those who had always been Democrats, offered such arguments. Similarly, some Constitutional Unionists revived the old Whig complaint that extremists on both sides, and not merely in the North, were responsible for the crisis. In much the same way, former Whigs like Alexander Stephens argued that the southern demand for a slave code in 1860 had been a major error. Stephens noted, quite uncontroversially, that it had split the Democratic party, and concluded, rather less uncontroversially, that without the split the Republicans could not have won.[273]

Stephens was one of many southerners who, in opposing immediate secession, argued that, if it ultimately proved unavoidable, it would be better for the South to have been seen to exhaust all other remedies first.[274] Yet this was not merely a cynical attempt to present secession in the best possible light. The anti-secessionists were convinced that compromise was eminently possible. This belief itself stemmed from a still more fundamental assumption: there was no necessary or inherent antagonism between slave and free labour systems. This was the classic southern Whig doctrine which had underpinned the southern Whig support for compromise in 1850.[275] Now, a decade later, and once again in sharp contrast to the stance of many who were urging disunion, those who opposed immediate secession struck the same note. Thus Benjamin Hill of Georgia claimed that just as greed had motivated antislavery in Britain and the North so the same motive had now impelled Britain to recognise her need for southern cotton and would soon produce the same effect on northerners.[276]

272. Botts, *Union or Disunion*, p. 22; *Louisville Journal*, Nov. 8, 1860, in Dumond (ed.), *Southern Editorials on Secession*, p. 219;"Stephens' Unionist Speech" in Freehling and Simpson (eds.), *Secession Debated*, p. 58.
273. *Louisville Journal*, Oct. 30, Nov. 8,1860, Jan. 26, 1861; Raleigh *Standard*, Feb. 5, 1861, in Dumond (ed.), *Southern Editorials on Secession*, pp. 195–198, 220, 422–423, 447. "Stephens' Unionist Speech" in Freehling and Simpson (eds.), *Secession Debated*, p. 58.
274. "Stephens' Unionist Speech," and "Hill's Unionist Speech," in Freehling and Simpson (eds.), *Secession Debated*, pp. 56, 102–104
275. See the first volume of this study, pp. 476–492.
276. "Hill's Unionist Speech," in Freehling and Simpson (eds.), *Secession Debated*, pp. 91–93.

Even more revealing was the lack of confidence displayed by many former Whigs in the prospects for an independent southern confederacy. Once again a more favourable view of the North underlay some of their pronouncements. The Nashville *Republican Banner*, for example, admitted that, however vital an interest to the South, slavery had "depended mainly for its existence upon the protection afforded it by the Constitution." Northern support within the Union, the paper held, had kept world antislavery sentiment at bay. Yet if, after disunion, the North became overtly hostile, "the doom of slavery" would be "irrevocably fixed." In neighbouring Kentucky, the Louisville *Journal* similarly asserted that a "northern majority, pleading the sacred obligation of the Constitution, has restrained and kept down the Abolition fanaticism." The *Journal* predicted that if the states of the Deep South left the Union, all the border states would be swiftly "abolitionised."[277]

This gloom was far more intense in the Upper South, the traditional southern Whig heartland, than in the cotton states. In North Carolina, for example, the Raleigh *Standard* feared that if the states of the Deep South were left in peace to form a separate confederacy, they would reopen the African slave trade and preside over a precipitate and catastrophic reduction in the value of all slaves. And if there were to be war, then with no market for slave produce, the same calamitous consequences would follow. Moreover, in war the slaves would become "restless and turbulent." The *Standard* was Democratic in affiliation. Similarly William Graham, perhaps the leading Whig and Constitutional Unionist in the state, warned that if war resulted in defeat, abolition would follow. But even if victory were secured, fugitive slaves would no longer be recoverable from the border areas. Hence abolition would triumph first in Virginia and then, by the same process, in North Carolina.[278]

This relative lack of confidence in the slave system coloured some southerners' responses to the prospect of war with the North. As we have seen, those who advocated immediate secession were on the whole confident that the North would be unable to subjugate the South militarily. Most indeed believed that any war would be swift and painless, resulting in a southern victory or at least a northern refusal to continue the fight. Some of the former Constitutional Unionists were not so sure, however. In some cases they actually scoffed at the South's military capacity. John Minor Botts, for example, argued that in war his own state of Virginia "could not furnish clothes for her men." Botts claimed that "it has taken all our

277. Nashville *Republican Banner*, Jan. 26, 1861, Louisville *Journal*, Jan. 26, 1861 in Dumond (ed.), *Southern Editorials on Secession*, pp. 425, 422–423. Crofts, *Reluctant Confederates*, p. 110.

278. Raleigh *Standard*, Dec 1, 1860, Feb. 5, 1861 in Dumond (ed.), *Southern Editorials on Secession*, pp. 284–245, 446; *Papers of Graham*, V, p. 219.

money to hang John Brown and his confederates." Southern Whigs had argued for many years that the North was simply more advanced than the South in economic terms; those who continued to believe it were necessarily wary about the prospects for an independent South, either in peace or war.[279]

Botts' attitude was, however, rare even among Constitutional Unionists and even in the Upper South. For all practical purposes Botts was an unconditional Unionist but, outside of areas like western Virginia, western North Carolina, northern Arkansas, and eastern Tennessee, this stance was not common in any of the eleven states that would ultimately secede. Others who had been Whigs and/or Constitutional Unionists expressed a variety of different responses to the emerging crisis. As a result whilst it was easy to identify those who opposed immediate secession, it was far more difficult, as the crisis unfolded, to determine what their preferred policy was. This problem was compounded by the dynamics of the secession crisis itself, which produced responses in the North and then counter-responses in the South the effect of which was to impel some individuals or groups to shift their ground, modify their demands, or harden their attitudes. Nevertheless, with these qualifications in mind, it is possible to see certain patterns in the responses of southern Whigs and neo-Whigs.

In the Deep South most of those who were described as Unionists or who made what have been termed Unionist speeches espoused a highly conditional unionism. Indeed they might just as appropriately be termed conditional secessionists. Moreover the conditions they attached, whilst put forward with, in most cases, perfect sincerity, were not such as a recently victorious Republican party was likely to accept. Thus Alexander H. Stephens, destined to become Vice-President of the new Southern Confederacy, in opposing secession when Lincoln's victory was first announced, nevertheless made it clear that he did not think that the South should simply acquiesce in the outcome, and especially not if the new President were to act in accordance with the platform on which he had been elected. Like many "Unionists" in the Deep South, Stephens expected the Republicans, in the very moment of victory, to offer new concessions to the southern states, in return for little more than their continued allegiance to the Union.

According to Stephens the election had produced a "fearful result" and far from meekly accepting it, he vowed that "if the policy of Mr. Lincoln and his Republican associates shall be carried out, or attempted to be carried out, no man in Georgia will be more willing or ready than myself to defend our rights, interest, and honor at every hazard and to the last extremity." As his listeners knew, this was shorthand for secession. In case

279. Botts, *Union or Disunion*, p. 15.

there could be any doubt Stephens announced that he would never "submit to any Black Republican aggression upon our Constitutional rights" and that the ultimatum for the Republicans would be either equality for Georgia or her withdrawal from the Union. More specifically Stephens declared that congressional exclusion of the South from the territories (the Chicago platform) should result in secession and that any attempt on the part of the federal government to repeal or weaken the Fugitive Slave Act should elicit the same response. These conditions were not new and had indeed been part of the famous "Georgia Platform" of 1850. What was new, of course, was an election victory by a party committed to one of the policies the Georgia platform sought to proscribe. But Stephens, in common with other Georgia Unionists, went further and added that if northern states refused to repeal their Personal Liberty Laws (designed to obstruct the Fugitive Slave Act) then he "should be willing, as a last resort, to sever the ties of our union with them." In other words, Stephens and those who thought like him expected the Republican triumph of 1860 to produce a shift in national policy – in favour of the South.[280]

The contest in Georgia therefore, although historians have not always recognised the fact, was more complex than it appeared. Although the immediate secessionists won by only a narrow margin, many of the so-called Unionists were in reality secessionists, whether they knew it or not, since they advocated an ultimatum to the Republicans that was certain to be rejected. Louisiana was another Deep South state where the anti-secessionists were thought to be in a position of strength and, with Georgia, the Deep South state where the Whigs had been strongest. But here again Unionist sentiment was deeply divided and many opponents of immediate secession were Unionists of the Stephens hue. Thus the New Orleans *Bee* espoused many of the anti-secessionist sentiments we have already encountered. In early 1860 the newspaper detected welcome signs of moderation in the North and, as if in return, the editor acknowledged that Kansas had been from the first unsuited to slavery. Like Stephens in Georgia the *Bee* believed that the demand for a slave code had been both unnecessary and unwise and like Stephens too the editor counselled caution when the Republican victory was announced. But once again, this moderate, conciliatory response belied the reality. Again there was to be an ultimatum. Either the North must give "ample guarantees of security and immunity for the future" or Louisiana would secede. By November 20, the *Bee* felt able to announce that it knew "pretty well what are the

---

280. "Stephens' Unionist Speech," in Freehling and Simpson (eds.), *Secession Debated*, pp. 54, 69, 58–59, 77. As Freehling and Simpson emphasise, similar demands were made by Benjamin Hill and Herschel Johnson – see pp. 98, 112.

views of at least a majority of the people of the Cotton States." They were "very generally in favor of secession, either immediate or eventual." Some, the editor continued, were for secession immediately, while others favoured a last ditch effort "to induce the North to abandon its iniquitous policy, and acknowledge our rights." Three quarters of the people of Louisiana, he claimed, were in one of these two categories. Although the *Bee* was initially in the first category, by mid-December it had given up the search for compromise. Reporting on the overwhelming defeat in the Vermont legislature of a bill to repeal the state's Personal Liberty law, the editor concluded that the Union could not be kept together. The alternatives had been either disunion or a "new compact" with the North; now only disunion remained. Such was the fate of unionism throughout the Deep South. The so-called Unionist of the Deep South easily became a secessionist.[281]

In the Upper South, however, the pattern was very different. While the states of the Lower South seceded, as we have seen, with a remarkable degree of unanimity, in the Upper South after Lincoln's election, the balance of opinion was strongly against immediate secession. In Delaware, Maryland and Kentucky Unionist sentiment was so strong that secession could not even be placed on the political agenda; in the other states of the Middle and Upper South (Virginia, North Carolina, Tennessee, Arkansas and Missouri) the voters pronounced against it in unmistakeable terms. Where conventions did meet (Virginia, Arkansas Missouri), Unionist majorities quickly formed; in other states (North Carolina, Tennessee) popular referenda ruled even against their being called. Among these seven states, secessionist sentiment was probably strongest in Virginia and Arkansas but an indication of its relative weakness even here is to be found in the composition of the Virginia convention, in which only about one in five delegates favoured secession.

Moreover, as the secession winter wore on, the Unionists in these states continued to prosper. Across the South as a whole, it seemed in November and December that secessionists had the initiative but by February and March 1861 outside the seven seceding states of the Deep South a reaction had set in and the prospects of Unionists seemed brighter than before. Unionists in the Upper South, in common with large numbers of Republicans and other northerners, clung to the belief that a peaceable reunion was possible, indeed imminent. The cotton states, it was held,

---

281. New Orleans *Bee*, Feb. 9, March 5, Nov. 8, 19, 23, Dec. 14, 1860 in Dumond (ed.), *Southern Editorials on Secession*, pp. 30–31, 48–50, 222, 249, 263, 335. Stephens himself was plagued by doubts, themselves characteristic of highly conservative Whigs, about the virtue of the masses and their ability to sustain secession – see Phillips (ed.), "Correspondence of Toombs, Stephens, and Cobb," pp. 457–458, 487, 504–505.

would quickly return first to their senses and then to the fold, provided that the Lincoln administration did nothing to antagonise them.

These Unionists were often deeply resentful not merely of northern antislavery zealots but also of southern proslavery extremists. Prominent North Carolinians, for example, had for many decades been highly contemptuous of the South Carolina school of statesmanship and it was those in the Whig, Know Nothing, and Constitutional Union tradition who displayed this contempt most openly. In Tennessee meanwhile Unionist Robert Hatton denounced secessionists as "madmen, drunken madmen," while from the Democratic side, William Polk put a number of rhetorical questions to his fellow Tennesseans which revealed his contempt for South Carolina: "will you obey the edict of South Carolina? Are we to be dragged out of the Union without even the courtesy of a consultation? Will we submit the neck of our proud state to a yoke shaped in an hour of madness and folly by *political desperadoes?*"[282]

Although Polk, brother of the late president, himself had a strong Democratic pedigree, most of these Unionists in the Upper South had been staunch Whig partisans. Many of them too were, as befitted southern Whigs, keen to see other interests besides slavery flourish in their region. This concern was a further factor which often (though by no means always) separated them from those further south. As one North Carolinian put it, while "Slavery is the great ruling interest of the extreme Gulf States," the Upper South, by contrast, had *"great interests besides slavery, which cannot be lightly abandoned."*[283] In some parts of the Upper South, such as northwestern Virginia, the local economy was far more intimately connected with free states like Ohio and Pennsylvania than with the Deep South but even where this was not the case, the old Whig dream of a diversified southern economy, with a developing industrial sector and an expanding commercial infrastructure, continued to exert its appeal. As we have seen, this creed had been articulated by the Constitutional Unionists as recently as the summer and fall of 1860, and it helped convince many that secession would he highly injurious to the region's interests.

Moreover, the typical Unionist of the border area was a different breed from his Deep South counterpart. In the states of Maryland, Missouri, Delaware and Kentucky a strong unionism held sway (though not, except in Delaware, unchallenged). Although these southerners would not have

---

282. Robert Hatton to Sophie Hatton, Dec. 31, 1860, William H. Polk to "My Dear Sir" Jan. 29, 1861, quoted in Crofts, *Reluctant Confederates*, pp. 114, 112. See also Raleigh *Standard*, July 11, 1860, in Dumond (ed.), *Southern Editorials on Secession*, p. 142.
283. Bartholomew F. Moore to his daughter, Dec. 1860, quoted in Crofts, *Reluctant Confederates*, p. 106.

accepted the abolition of slavery, the dominant view was that an ultimatum to the North was not needed and that Lincoln should be allowed to
take up the reins of office. In the Middle South a more qualified unionism
prevailed, one that was ideologically as well as geographically midway
between that of the Cotton States and that of the Border. Here the predominant reaction was that while secession was as yet undesirable, the
right to secede (perhaps by virtue of a right of revolution) must be maintained, for if the new Republican administration sought to coerce the Deep
South or to attack slavery in the states where it existed, then recourse to
disunion might yet be necessary. Thus the Raleigh *Standard*, which, as we
have seen, harboured suspicions of the Deep South and exhibited some
confidence in the people of the North, nevertheless warned that the South
would never submit to a "loss of honor and Constitutional right."[284]
Although there would be no ultimatum given to the North, and although
it was hoped that the Republicans would not need to implement their territorial policy, many of these Unionists made it clear that they would not
accept it, if the attempt were made. Instead they looked for a compromise.

## II

As the secession crisis unfolded, it became apparent that southern Unionists were mere bit players in this spectacular national drama, consigned
to react to events rather than initiate them. Their role seemed as limited
as that played by the Whig party since the election of 1852. For a time,
however, it had looked as though events might develop differently. After
Lincoln's victory was announced perhaps the most distinguished living
Whig, John J. Crittenden, stepped forward. The celebrated Whig leaders, Henry Clay and Daniel Webster, had excelled in effecting the great
compromises between the sections at moments of crisis. Clay had done
so three times: in 1820 over Missouri, in 1832 over nullification, most
recently and only a little before his death, at the time of the Compromise
of 1850. Plainly the election of Lincoln had now plunged the nation into a
crisis of unprecedented depth. And it was fitting that of all the compromise
attempts that were made during the secession winter of 1860–1861 the
most formidable was authored by John J. Crittenden, heir of Henry Clay
and like Clay representing Kentucky in the United States Senate. It was
even more fitting, in the light of the experience of Whigs and neo-Whigs
in the 1850s, that the attempt should end in abject failure.

Crittenden was the Constitutional Unionist Party's major figure and
could almost certainly have had its presidential nomination in 1860 if

---

284.  Raleigh *Standard*, Dec. 1, 1860, see also March 9, 1861 in Dumond (ed.), *Southern
      Editorials on Secession*, pp. 286, 476.

he had desired it. He now advanced an elaborate set of proposals. As we have seen, they were rejected by the Republicans, essentially on the grounds that they required a surrender of the platform on which the recent election had been fought and won. A party which opposed the South as a disorganising force and slavery as an undemocratic interest could scarcely have been expected to acquiesce in a proposal that would involve capitulation to a minority and the subversion, as it seemed, of the electoral process. Virtually all southern Unionists, from Alexander Stephens to John Minor Botts, and many secessionists too, would have been satisfied with the Crittenden formula but it soon became apparent that it could not succeed.

This did not, however, mean that the Unionists were a spent force. On the contrary, outside the Deep South, their election victories continued even after the demise of the Crittenden proposals (and the other attempts at compromise). Nor did Lincoln's Inaugural, a masterpiece of imprecision, alarm them unduly. The problems came a little later.

Although some Unionists toyed with the idea of a differently constituted Union (perhaps without the Deep South, perhaps without the New England states, perhaps without either), their predominant view was that peaceable reunion could and should take place, provided that the new administration refrained from provocative action. But as we have seen,[285] Republicans were themselves under pressure to act and it seemed to the new President that to surrender Fort Sumter to the newly formed confederacy would be to confer legitimacy upon a rebel regime. For this reason (among others) Lincoln resolved to send supplies to the Fort. Feeling itself impelled to defend its own territory from a foreign power, the Confederacy thus took the fateful step of firing the first shot. Lincoln quickly responded with a Proclamation that called for 75,000 troops to be enlisted in a war whose purpose was to put down the southern Confederacy. At this point unionism in most of the border states was placed under the severest strain while in the Middle South it abruptly collapsed.

The effect of the Proclamation on the Unionists was devastating. Many were at first so astonished that they believed it a forgery or a hoax. When it was proved genuine, they expressed intense resentment of what they believed to be a Republican betrayal. Thus William Graham of North Carolina made a speech on April 27 just twelve days after the Proclamation in which he expressed many of the attitudes of the Unionist-turned-secessionist. He argued that if Lincoln had relinquished the federal forts and supported the Crittenden compromise, the seceding states would have returned. But, he continued, with unmistakable bitterness, "it was not enough for the President that the conservative people of these [other slave]

285. See pp. 303–329.

states had been willing to acquiesce in his election." In addition Lincoln demanded the impossible: southerners must use force against other southerners. Thus North Carolina faced a choice: either "to join with him in a war of conquest, for it is nothing else, against our brethren of the seceding States, or . . . resistance to and throwing off the obligations of the Federal Constitution." It was a cruel choice, one which southern Whigs had spent much of their careers trying to avoid. But "of the two, we do not hesitate to accept the latter." For "blood is thicker than water" and "however widely we have differed from, and freely criticised the course taken by those States [of the Deep South], they are much more closely united with us by the ties of kindred, affection, and a peculiar institution . . . than to any of the Northern States." This was the predominant Unionist reaction in the Middle South. Many in the Upper and Middle South had warned that they would not tolerate the use of force against the states of the Deep South and these southerners now urged secession. In the Middle South they held sway. Within a few days Virginia had effectively left the Union. Within a few weeks Arkansas, North Carolina and Tennessee had done the same. The slaveholding counties of each were, unsurprisingly, those keenest on secession and the nonslaveholding areas sometimes warned of aristocrats trampling upon the liberties of the people. North Carolina was divided along regional lines, Tennessee still more so while Arkansas very nearly followed Virginia in splitting into two. In each case intimidation of those still wishing to remain in the Union occurred but there is no reason to believe that it was decisive in bringing about secession. These states had announced in advance that they would not tolerate coercion against their brethren in the Deep South and they now made good their promise.[286]

In Maryland, Missouri and Kentucky unionism still prevailed, but there were strong secessionist minorities in each of these states. (In Delaware, the other slave state, secessionism was a negligible force.) As Lincoln knew, if the stated purpose of the war in April 1861 had been to abolish slavery all three states might well have joined the Confederacy. As it was, in Maryland secessionist feeling was strong in the southern counties and

---

286. William Graham. "Speech Upon the Political Situation April 27, 1861," in *Papers of Graham*, IV, p. 245. See also William R. Smith (ed.), *The History and the Debates of the Convention of the People of Alabama, Begun and Held in the City of Montgomery, on the Seventh Day of January, 1861* (Montgomery, 1861), p. 387; Lynda Lasswell Crist *et al.* (eds.), *The Papers of Jefferson Davis*.11 vols. (Baton Rouge, 1971), VI, p. 113; Charles Bolton, *Poor Whites of the Antebellum South: Tenants and Laborers in Central North Carolina and Northeast Mississippi* (Durham, NC, 1994), pp. 142–152, 180–183; Woods, *Rebellion and Realignment*, pp. 120–142, 151–155; Norton, *Democratic Party in Ante-Bellum North Carolina*, p. 211; Crofts, *Reluctant Secessionists*, pp. 156, 342–346. As far as Virginia was concerned, the decision to secede could not be confirmed before a popular referendum was held on May 23 but the popular verdict was never in doubt. By April 17 Virginia was in effect a member of the Confederacy.

in large parts of Baltimore while in Missouri the same areas which had produced the "border ruffians" who had come to prominence during the repeated crises over Kansas were, not surprisingly, those keenest on secession. Kentucky was still more evenly divided and the state was to provide a large number of soldiers for the Confederacy. But even here unionism triumphed, though not without an attempt, temporarily successful, on the part of many southern sympathisers to declare the state neutral.[287]

## III

Historians have, of course, sought to explain the divergent courses of action taken by the different subregions of the South during the secession crisis. Here the contrast between the responses of the Deep and the Upper South has bulked large. The obvious explanation focuses upon slavery and the key statistic relates to the proportion of slaves within each state. The evidence is unmistakable that the greater the proportion of slaves, the greater the enthusiasm for secession. Thus the seven states that seceded in the first wave all, with the exception of Texas, had more than forty-three percent of their populations enslaved. The four that seceded only after the Proclamation had between twenty-five percent and thirty-three percent enslaved. Those that did not secede at all had less than twenty percent (Kentucky nineteen percent, Maryland thirteen percent, Missouri ten percent, and Delaware less than two percent).

The proportion of the population enslaved is, of course, only a proxy for another more fundamental characteristic: the extent to which the slave-holding interest dominated. Or to put it in the terms of this study, the extent to which the slaveholding class exercised a hegemonic control. As we have seen, this control was achieved partly, and especially in the Deep South, by outlawing all opposition to, and even critical discussion of, slavery, but also partly by more subtle and complex processes. In the Deep South, for example, there was a widespread fear that thousands of emancipated former slaves would act in a way reminiscent of events in Haiti at the turn of the century. The obvious and overwhelming dependence of those states upon slave labour produced a similar effect. As a result, and without organising a conspiracy to achieve it, the slaveholders were able to benefit from a common perception of what was, and what was not, politically and socially feasible, a common taken-for-grantedness and in

---

287. More than seventy percent of white Missourians who fought in the war fought for the Union. For Maryland the figure was only slightly lower. Kentucky was more evenly divided with more than forty percent enlisting with the Confederacy – see James M. McPherson, *Battle Cry of Freedom: The American Civil War* (New York, 1988), p. 293.

the Deep South this meant the continued existence and virtual immunity from criticism of the slave system.

In the Middle South, and still more, the Upper South, these processes were much weaker and opposition to slavery and slaveholders was correspondingly stronger. Although a state like Virginia actually had, in absolute numbers, more slaves or slaveholders than any other, it was universally recognised that Virginia was a moderate slaveholding state and her refusal to secede in the first wave was entirely predictable. The reason was simply that the slaveholding interest lacked in Virginia the control that it possessed in South Carolina or Mississippi.

These observations would not, perhaps, need to be made were it not for the fact that an alternative or perhaps supplementary explanation for the contrasting behaviour of the different slave states has been offered. Thus it has been argued that it was not the different degrees of commitment to slavery that accounted for the divergent courses taken by the states that seceded in the first and second waves of secession but rather their experience of partisan politics in the 1850s. In effect the claim is that the four states that seceded after the Proclamation had been able to take a more relaxed view of Lincoln's election because they had recent experience of partisan conflict, whereas in the Deep South the dominance of the Democratic party was so great that faith in the political process had been correspondingly dissipated: "extremism had been weakest, and faith in the political process to protect Southern Rights had been strongest where two-party systems flourished and loyalty to political parties consequently was strong." Hence the eagerness of the states of the Deep South to secede and the comparative reluctance of the Middle South to follow suit. This interpretation has also been advanced in a separate study of North Carolina.[288]

Yet it suffers from insuperable weaknesses. In the first place it cannot explain the course of events in Arkansas where the Democratic party had an overwhelming dominance but where immediate secession did not occur. Second, it cannot explain a still more fundamental fact: the failure of the slaveholding states of Kentucky, Missouri, Maryland and Delaware to secede at all. For here partisan conflict in 1860 for example, was at about the same level as in the Middle South. If commitment to slavery was not the decisive factor then why did these states stay in the Union at all?

This is not to say, however, that there was no correlation between Democratic supremacy and secession. Secessionists were either in no party at all or in the Democratic party; relatively few were in the ranks of the Opposition or Constitutional Unionist parties. Hence where Democrats were

288. Holt, *Political Crisis*, pp. 219–259, esp. p. 230; Marc W. Kruman, *Parties and Politics in North Carolina, 1836–1865* (Baton Rouge, 1983), pp. 180–181.

very strong, support for secession also tended to be strong. Yet this was a tendency rather than an iron law and the example of Arkansas reminds us that the Democratic party could triumph for other reasons too.

The error here lies not in identifying the correlation but instead in explaining it. The causal relationship is the opposite of the one these scholars have identified. It was not the lack of partisan conflict that produced a commitment to extremist proslavery politics in the Deep South but rather the commitment to extremist proslavery politics that produced a lack of partisan conflict. Otherwise how can we explain the lack of partisanship in most if not all the states of the Deep South other than by reducing it to coincidence? These scholars fail to explain why most of the states with low partisanship were in the Deep South; rather than being scattered randomly across the entire South. This problem disappears once the causal process is reversed and the underlying role of slavery recognised.

We must also resist the temptation to adopt an additive approach and claim that both factors, commitment to slavery and the absence of partisan conflict, were present.[289] The "slavery" interpretation explains why there were three different courses of action taken in the three subregions: the states where the slaveholding interest was strongest seceded most enthusiastically in the first wave, those where it was weakest did not secede at all, those where it was of intermediate strength seceded (often with some reluctance) in the second wave. The "partisanship" explanation, however, obscures the differences between Middle and Upper South. The slavery interpretation alone has no difficulty with the case of Arkansas and it alone explains (without resort to coincidence) the absence of partisanship throughout the Deep South. By combining the two factors we explain less rather than more. Historians are rightly aware of the danger of advancing monocausal explanations but are less aware of the dangers of multiplying causal factors and in the process implicitly increasing to improbable levels the role of chance and coincidence.

IV

In the North Constitutional Unionists and Old Line Whigs were equally dismayed by Lincoln's election, although they had been expecting it for some months. Yet their role in the national drama, in sharp contrast to that played by Clay and Webster a decade earlier, was to be a minor one. They could not even maintain any unanimity of opinion once the states of the Deep South had seceded. The *Cincinnati Times*, for example, dismissed secession as the illegal act of "bands of armed men, acting under

---

289. The approach adopted in Daniel Crofts's otherwise invaluable *Reluctant Confederates*, pp. 130–132.

the direction of temporary political juntos which profess to represent the 'sovereign nations' of South Carolina, Florida, Georgia, Alabama and Louisiana." The newspaper advocated the use of "force" if necessary to recapture federal property and even denounced the Republicans for being insufficiently assertive. Later, when war broke out the editor condemned the neighbouring state of Kentucky for attempting to remain neutral and proclaimed that "we of Ohio ... are for the Union, first last and all the time, and ... are willing to sacrifice our last dollar, and the last drop of our blood to maintain it."[290]

But earlier in the crisis, other former Whigs and Constitutional Unionists had favoured a different approach. In New York state the Troy *Daily Whig* for example, urged that no war be made against the seceding states, partly on the grounds that such a response would alienate the border states and partly because it doubted whether such a war was winnable. In common with many other northerners (and border state residents) the editor hoped that within a comparatively short space of time the seceding states would return. Similarly the Boston *Daily Courier* warned of the calamitous consequences that a war would have upon the economy of Massachusetts.[291]

Yet these differences of opinion largely disappeared after the fighting had broken out at Sumter. In Jersey City, the *American Standard* on April 12, when it learned that the Republicans intended to send provisions to Sumter, dismissed the plan as "a mere decoy to draw the first fire from the people of the South." It condemned the administration for seeking to bring on war and predicted that the border states would join the Confederacy and the Union be lost. But after the South had fired the first shot, the same newspaper announced that throughout the North there was no sympathy for the South "in its attitude of rebellion and disunion." Whilst there might be many in the North who believed that "war need not have been provoked," they were, with only a trivial number of exceptions, "unflinching enemies to the doctrine of the right of secession."[292]

Similarly the most famous northern Constitutional Unionists statesmen rallied to the Union cause after the encounter at Fort Sumter. Millard Fillmore, for example, attended a great Union rally and declared that the South had started the war and that it was now the North's duty to defend the government. The Constitutional Union party vice-presidential

290. *Cincinnati Times*, Feb. 14, April 3, 26, 1861 in Howard C. Perkins (ed.), *Northern Editorials on Secession*. 2 vols. (Gloucester, MA, 1942), I, pp. 231–232, II, pp. 665, 877–879.
291. Troy *Daily Whig*, April 4, 1861, Boston *Daily Courier*, Dec. 18, 1860, in Perkins (ed.), *Northern Editorials on Secession*, II, pp. 669–670, 575–577.
292. Jersey City *American Standard*, April 12, May 29, 1861, in Perkins, *Northern Editorials on Secession*, II, pp. 707–708, 762–763.

candidate, Edward Everett, adopted an equally firm stance. Everett excoriated southerners, who had, he claimed, controlled the federal government since the presidency of Thomas Jefferson, for refusing to accept the result of the election of 1860, for enacting unconstitutional and wholly illegal Ordinances of Secession and for starting the war. "We contend," Everett proclaimed "for the great inheritance of constitutional freedom transmitted from out revolutionary fathers." Undoubtedly this was one of the principal goals of not merely the Old Line Whigs and Constitutional Unionists but northerners in general. But if the outbreak of war brought the Constitutional Unionists in the North into line with mainstream northern opinion, it also shattered their own national unity. Even as Everett was rallying to the Union cause, John Bell, his running mate just a few months earlier, was sadly preparing to follow his home state of Tennessee out of the American Union. So ended the Constitutional Unionist attempt to resolve the sectional controversy.[293]

## V

Like their Whig and neo-Whig forebears in the 1850s, the Constitutional Unionists in 1860 were unable to effect a lasting peace between North and South. In this as in almost other respect Whiggery failed in the 1850s. There were many reasons. One which we have not yet noted, however, has to do with the patterns of economic growth in the final years of the antebellum Republic. As we have seen, in each section moderates were constantly in danger of being outflanked by more extreme groups, militant Democrats in the South, Republicans in the North. Both northern Whigs of the Webster stripe and southern Whigs who had been followers of Henry Clay were again and again the victims of this process. The growth of proslavery sentiment in the South and of antislavery sentiment in the North was in part a political phenomenon in that each fed off the other; extremists in each section could boost their support by pointing to the growing influence of extremists in the other. But the process also had deeper roots, in the economic developments of the decade.

This was most obviously true in the case of the South where confidence in slavery, captured in the image of "King Cotton," increased enormously in the final decade or so of the antebellum Republic. Those looking to the North for inspiration, as southern Whigs had done since the inception of their party, were necessarily damaged as a result. The experience of these

---

293. Severance (ed.), *Fillmore Papers*, II, p. 63; Edward Everett, *Orations and Speeches on Various Occasions*. 4 vols. (Boston, 1868–1870), IV, p. 330; "Address by Edward Everett, New York July 4, 1861," in Frank Moore (ed.), *The Rebellion Record* (New York ,1861–1869) I, pp. 7, 37, 42.

years confirmed that Whig national policies were in no sense a prerequisite of southern economic success. The South, it was now apparent, could thrive without federal banks, federal tariffs, or federally planned internal improvements. And if southern states did need banks or railroads, then experience confirmed that they could be promoted by the states themselves, without recourse to the federal government, and without an association with northern Whigs.

An analogous, but more complex, process operated in the North. It found expression in the patterns of regional development there and in the shifting balance of economic power which those patterns created. There is no question that important changes were taking place in interregional trade in the 1840s and especially the 1850s. As many historians have observed, northeast and northwest were becoming more closely tied in both absolute and relative terms, whereas North and South, in relative terms, were becoming less so. Thus the canals that were built in these and the preceding decades were overwhelmingly concentrated in the North and they carried freight from west to east. The Erie Canal for example, siphoned off a huge amount of trade that had once gone via the Mississippi and Ohio rivers. In 1836 almost eight times as much of the Trans-Appalachian West's commodity production was carried on those rivers as on the Canal but by 1860 near parity had been achieved. The impact of the railroads was similar. Although the South had railroads of her own, the great trunk routes went from east to west, principally from Northeast to Northwest, and increased western output (where it did not remain in the West) went not, as historians once believed, to the South but overwhelmingly to the East. The South remained largely self-sufficient in foodstuffs but the Northeast was a food deficit area. Moreover when northeastern manufactured goods left the region, they too went not to the South but rather to the Northwest. According to one estimate only two percent went to southern cotton producers and those goods accounted for only one percent of gross national product. These interdependencies, broadly between an agricultural northwest and an industrial northeast, underpinned the demand for Homestead legislation which, as we have seen, was viewed both as a means of stimulating western demand for eastern manufactures and. at the same time, a way of guaranteeing cheap and plentiful food for the East.[294]

---

294. Jeremy Atack and Peter Passell (eds.), *A New Economic View of American History*, 2nd ed. (New York, 1994), p. 151; Albert Fishlow, "Antebellum Regional Trade Reconsidered," *American Economic Review*, LIV (1964), pp. 352–364; Colleen Callahan and William Hutchinson, "Antebellum Regional Trade in Agricultural Goods: Preliminary Results, *Journal of Economic History*, XL (1980), pp. 25–32; Douglas North, *The Economic Growth of the United States, 1790–1860* (New York, 1961); North, "Location Theory and Regional Economic Growth" *Journal of*

This intimate and dynamic relationship between agriculture and man-ufacturing in the North was also reflected in the character of northern industrialism. It has been argued that the vanguard sector in the north-ern industrial revolution was not, as perhaps in Britain, textiles, in which southern cotton played a huge role, but rather agricultural machinery, where the role of the South, in terms of both production and consumption, was virtually negligible. One need not accept this thesis in its entirety to acknowledge that the agricultural implements industry, which produced ploughs, reapers, mowers, threshing-machines and the like, was of enor-mous importance on the American path to industrialism. The sector was highly dynamic and it facilitated great productivity gains in western agri-culture. According to one estimate, the value of agricultural implements manufactured in the West quadrupled in the 1850s, whereas in the same decade the value of those produced in the South declined absolutely.[295]

The problem for historians, however, has been to find a connection between these developments and the sectional conflict. Some have implic-itly or explicitly concluded that there was none;[296] others, writing from a Beardian or Marxist perspective, have taken the opposite view and suggested that they made virtually inevitable an assault upon southern slavery, perhaps on the grounds that it was a major obstruction to future capitalist growth in the nation.[297] Both views are unsatisfactory. It strains credulity to believe that the greater integration of the northern economy was unrelated to the region's new political integration, made manifest in the emergence and rise to dominance of a purely northern Republi-can party. On the other hand, it needs to be demonstrated, rather than assumed, that there was a mechanism at work which ensured that all social practices or economic interests that were not entirely functional for capitalist production would be removed. The assault upon slavery is a much more complex phenomenon. Why could the North, even an eco-nomically integrated North, not tolerate a South with whose economy it was not in any case in competition?

*Political Economy*, LXII (1955), pp. 243–258; Lawrence A. Herbst, "Interregional Commodity Trade from the North to the South and American Economic Devel-opment in the Antebellum Period," *Journal of Economic History*, XXXV (1975), pp. 264–270.

295. Gavin Wright, *The Political Economy of the Cotton South: Households, Markets and Wealth in the Nineteenth Century* (New York, 1978), pp. 108–109; Nevins, *House Dividing*, pp. 165–166, 256; Charles Post, "The American Road to Capitalism," *New Left Review*, CXXXIII (1982), pp. 30–51.

296. Thus for Nevins there was presumably no connection, since he argued that the Civil War "was caused primarily by social, moral, and political, not economic forces. Indus-trialism did not weaken the Union, but strengthened its fabric" – see Nevins, *House Dividing*, p. 244. Many other accounts of the origins of the War simply ignore these economic processes.

297. Post, "American Road to Capitalism," p. 37; George Novack (ed.), *America's Revo-lutionary Heritage* (New York, 1976), p. 213.

The experience of the Whig party in these years, and especially the conservative Whigs, sheds considerable light upon this issue. The conservative Whigs, whether the "cotton" Whigs of Massachusetts, the Silver Grays of New York, or their allies in other states, were the groups who represented interests, both manufacturing and mercantile, that were most closely dependent on the South. Throughout the era of the sectional conflict, they were among the groups who expressed most sympathy with the South and were (along with some northern Democrats) most willing to compromise with slavery and slaveholders. But the relative decline in their economic power, which we have just noted, was reflected in the decline of their political fortunes and influence. This decline is unmistakeable. In the 1830s and 1840s, these mercantile and textile manufacturing interests were hugely important within the Whig party: in Massachusetts, for example, perhaps the most important Whig state in the entire Union, they were in a position of dominance or near dominance until at least the mid-1840s. Daniel Webster was their spokesman. But in the 1850s, these interests carried far less weight politically. If they joined it at all, they scarcely found the Republican party a congenial home, and remained, for the most part, a conservative minority within its ranks, unable to influence events, often with only a lukewarm commitment to its policies and frequently displaying an alarming, as it seemed to party regulars, willingness to compromise when the sectional conflict was most intense. The mercantile interests that were dependent on the South and the manufacturing interests that depended upon southern cotton were in relative decline within the northern economy and within northern politics too.

The result was to strengthen antislavery sentiment, not directly by creating a narrowly economic imperative to dismantle slavery in the South, but instead indirectly by removing an impediment to antislavery's growth in the North. Here was the process by which changes in interregional trade facilitated the triumph of antislavery. The growth of wage labour, as I have argued throughout this work, generated a series of ideological shifts in the North, as a result of which slavery increasingly seemed, on political, moral and economic grounds, profoundly unsatisfactory and alien, and its extension unacceptable. Contrary to the Beardian (and, sometimes, the Marxist) view, this process entailed far more than a simple assault launched, perhaps in the name of profit maximisation, by one interest group upon another, since it involved the relations of wage workers to their employers, the relations of slaves to their masters, and, as it were, the relations between the relations. This network of relationships and interests was a disruptive force, a centrifugal tendency within the Republic. But the economic ties between North and South had traditionally operated as a counter-tendency. Hence as those ties became less important relatively and the northern interests which depended upon them lost ground politically, a barrier to the further growth of antislavery in the North was removed. This process, coupled with the comparable strengthening of proslavery sentiment in the South, consequently did much to undermine the efforts of those in the Whig tradition to maintain harmony between the sections.

## Conclusion

### I

Some historians have argued that the realignment of the 1850s was primarily the product of ethnocultural rather than sectional (or economic) factors. It has also been claimed that these ethnocultural issues could exert a decisive influence because of the broad agreement upon "fundamentals," the core values of capitalism and democracy, that united Americans in these years. This interpretation, however, can be criticised on a number of counts. First, it is doubtful whether the so-called ethnocultural factors played the decisive role that has been claimed. The realignment of the 1850s actually began as early as 1850 or 1851 when the second party system collapsed in the states of the Deep South where proslavery sentiment was strongest: Alabama, Mississippi and Georgia.[298] Sectional factors were by a wide margin the most important, indeed virtually the only, cause. As we have seen, even in the years when nativist sentiment was strongest, from late 1854 to mid-1856, the Know Nothing appeal in the North in most states was a blend of nativism and antislavery. And, from 1856 onwards, nativism and temperance were in sharp decline. The key event in the realignment was the Kansas-Nebraska Act, not merely its passage but also the turmoil in Kansas which it quickly produced.

Moreover, it is mistaken to argue that ethnocultural factors flourished because of an agreement on the fundamentals of democracy and capitalism. The temperance crusade focussed upon the dangers posed by, in particular, the wage labourer's consumption of alcohol and drew attention to the gains in productivity and output, as well as the enhanced social stability, that would ensue if he could be persuaded, or, more likely, compelled by legislation, to abstain from drinking. To a considerable extent therefore, temperance and prohibition were in these years a product of the shift towards wage-labour capitalism rather than functions of a pre-existing consensus upon it. In the case of nativism, the demand for a lengthening of the naturalisation period involved a reiteration of the arguments that

---

298. Here I exclude South Carolina from consideration because in that state the second party system had never properly existed – precisely because of the potency of sectional sentiment.

had been made in previous eras and which were still being made in contemporary Europe against the lower orders. The Irish Roman Catholic immigrant, upon whom attention centred, was castigated in the 1850s for his unfitness for the suffrage. Nativism was in this sense a product not of a consensus on democracy but rather of doubts about it, specifically doubts about the ability of a democratic polity to withstand the political influence of the group which (apart from African Americans, who, even in the North, could rarely vote in any case), seemed to have the smallest stake in society. Nativism thus continued the anti-democratic impulse that had been apparent in previous eras. It represented an animus that had once been directed against the lower orders in the United States but which had now been displaced or transferred onto one of the most conspicuously alien and disadvantaged groups in American society. Neither nativism nor temperance played the leading role in the destruction of the second party system but it was when they converged with class issues, and with traditional concerns about the suitability of the lower orders for inclusion in a democratic polity that they acquired their potency.

## II

Those Whigs who mourned the loss of Clay and Webster in 1852 and who did not in the 1850s defect either to the Republican party in the North or the Democracy in the South were unable to exert a decisive influence on the politics of the decade. After the upheaval of 1854–1855 those who retained their identity as Old-Line Whigs, or who formed the Opposition parties of the late 1850s in the South, or who created the Constitutional Unionist party of 1860 were unable, despite their best efforts, to arrest the process of sectional polarisation that would culminate in the secession of the South in 1860–1861 and the rapid slide into war. For these Whig or Whiggish groups there was, apart from the occasional victory at state level, little cause for satisfaction in these years. Meanwhile those neo-Whigs who agitated for temperance or for nativism enjoyed more success in the early or mid-1850s but once again their influence was limited. Thus the more that Whigs and neo-Whigs were loyal to the traditions of their party and faithful to the legacy of Henry Clay and Daniel Webster, the less they were able to shape events after midcentury.

Ironically, given that the Whig party had always stood for economic development, it was the expansion in the economy that was at the root of their difficulties. In these years, economic success confirmed the commitment of each section to its labour system. In the North satisfaction with a free-labour economy was nourished by the rapid growth in the region as industry as well as agriculture expanded at a faster pace than ever before, the regional infrastructure acquired a new maturity and sophistication, and the importance of economic ties with the South diminished in relative importance. In the South meanwhile, the prosperity of the decade largely banished the fears that had been voiced about monoculture and tended to undermine the (Whiggish) rationale for diversification. The result was a strengthening of the northern conviction that slavery was inferior and a parallel strengthening of the southern conviction that it was indispensable. Thus economic growth placed strains upon the unity of any party which aspired to win elections both north and south of the Mason-Dixon Line.

Beyond this, economic growth proved particularly damaging to the Whigs. Expansion of the nation's land and the need to settle the areas between the newly acquired territory on the Pacific and the older states created the most intense problems for the party. The attempt to organise Kansas on terms that were extremely generous to the South (given the prior existence of the Missouri Compromise) made it impossible for most southern Whigs to do anything other than accept the gift being offered in the form of the Kansas-Nebraska Act, much to the chagrin of their northern colleagues. Had the settlement of Kansas then proceeded smoothly the damage to the party might have been containable but this of course was not to be. So the territorial expansion of the late 1840s and the pressure to integrate that territory in the 1850s placed enormous strains upon both parties but especially upon the Whigs.

The vast majority of Whigs had not sought this territorial expansion and many had even warned of the threat to sectional harmony that it would pose. But if land had never been part of the Whig agenda for growth, capital assuredly had. Yet the expansion that took place in the nation's fund of capital in the late 1840s and 1850s, rather than bringing political dividends to the party, resulted instead in a serious erosion of support for its principal policies. Banking ceased to be a controversial issue at Washington and in most of the states, after 1846 there was little pressure for a protective tariff. Internal improvements meanwhile, though retaining their popularity, were no longer so reliant upon government involvement. Hence the growth in the nation's supply of capital brought fiscal stability and commercial development, but not according to the Whig blueprint. The result was to diminish the need for the party's economic policies still further.

Finally the expansion in the nation's labour supply, in the form of rapidly increasing levels of immigration, also proved a liability rather than an asset to the Whigs. The party had traditionally worried that the supply of labour for the factories of the East was insufficient to meet demand: this had been one of the reasons for opposing the rapid settlement of the West (to be achieved via pre-emption and graduation laws). In the North, the increasing availability of labour and the quickening pace of industrial development meant that the nation's economy was developing along lines that the Whigs might have anticipated and desired. But again there was no political payoff. There was now no need for the party's traditional land policy (which was strikingly reversed by the Republicans). Meanwhile the arrival of large numbers of immigrants, often difficult, it seemed, to assimilate into American society, brought its own problems. Thus with reference to each of the three primary economic resources of land, labour, and capital, expansion created difficulties for the Whigs.

The party had traditionally espoused both economic dynamism and political conservatism. But Whig political philosophy also lost much of its appeal as a result of economic expansion. The fear of radicalism and of demagoguery had, since the time of Jackson, led many Whigs to dissociate themselves from the populistic democracy espoused by their opponents. But as Democratic political radicalism waned, so the need for Whig political conservatism also diminished. Both were, to a considerable extent, casualties of the increasing prosperity of the final antebellum years.

For these reasons, the plight of the Whig party in the 1850s, and those who, after its demise, continued to espouse its values, was an unhappy one. Many Whigs, former Whigs and neo-Whigs yearned for a return to the disinterested statesmanship embodied by their heroes, Henry Clay and Daniel Webster, on the assumption that such statesmanship, if it could only be identified and sustained, would solve the nation's problems. The assumption was almost certainly erroneous; it ignored the social, economic and political processes that were in train and which were probably beyond the control of any statesman, however distinguished and disinterested. This the latter-day Whigs could not accept or even understand. What they could and did understand was that their nation was in peril, In the years following the death of Clay and Webster it was their melancholy fate to experience, to issue warnings about, but be unable to prevent, what they feared was a rapid and accelerating descent into a vortex of violence, bloodshed, and slaughter.

# Conclusion: Explaining the Civil War (2)

## I

When they went to war, northerners and southerners alike expected the conflict to be of short duration and foresaw little economic disruption. Both predictions proved hopelessly wrong. For the Confederacy, even more than for northerners, war was a devastating experience. Every significant feature of the southern economy was touched by the four years of bitter conflict and southern leaders were driven by economic as well as military necessity to employ ever more drastic measures and ultimately even to propose the arming of their slave population, an idea which, at the commencement of hostilities, would have struck virtually every white Confederate as utter lunacy. For the Confederacy, the war years were ones of increasingly severe economic dislocation, and for the overwhelming majority of her citizens, of unwontedly severe hardship.[1]

As I have argued throughout this study, southerners had been responding, for many years, to a set of problems whose existence they could not clearly recognise, but whose effects they could not avoid. Secession was the most drastic and the most radical of all attempts to overcome the weaknesses of slavery. But for reasons we have already examined, northerners were not, in practice, willing to allow the southern states to go in peace, and so war quickly erupted. This placed the severest strain upon the southern economic and social systems and the weaknesses of slavery came back to haunt southerners and to wreak havoc upon the nation they were trying to establish.

---

1. On the Confederacy see for example E. Merton Coulter, *The Confederate States of America 1861–1865* (Baton Rouge, 1950); Emory M. Thomas, *The Confederate Nation, 1861–1865* (New York, 1979); and the excellent essay in William L. Barney, *Flawed Victory: A New Perspective on the Civil War* (Lanham, 1980), pp. 81–120, which is equally valuable on the North during the War. For a fuller treatment of some of the issues I discuss here, see John Ashworth, "Capitalism and the Civil War," in Susan Mary Grant and Brian Holden Reid (eds.), *The American Civil War: Explorations and Reconsiderations* (Harlow, England, 2000), pp. 289–304.

## II

In 1861, the North enjoyed an enormous superiority in manpower and resources. With an advantage of more than five to two in population, three to one in the value of real and personal property, four to one in bank capital, two to one in railroad mileage, and more than ten to one in the value of manufactured products, the Union forces began with the odds heavily in their favour. Their advantage began to tell in economic terms almost immediately, although it took longer for the effects to work through to the battlefield.[2]

The Confederate economy was plagued by problems from the outset, problems which were the symptoms of the region's structural weaknesses. Southern wealth had always depended disproportionately upon the exporting of staple crops like cotton, but this left the economy highly vulnerable to the embargo and blockade which the Union almost immediately imposed after the outbreak of hostilities. The result was to reduce the cotton trade by perhaps as much as ninety percent.[3] This had catastrophic effects upon the financing of the War. Since southerners on the outbreak of war repudiated at least $300,000,000 in debts to northern banks and merchants, the Confederacy, now without its cotton crop to underwrite its borrowing, had to fall back upon its own financial infrastructure which itself lagged far behind that of the North. The result was that the Confederacy was starved of credit and capital. This made imports more difficult to finance. Except in New Orleans, banks suspended specie payments for the duration of the conflict, a reflection in part of the relative immaturity of the southern banking system. Faced with declining revenues and mounting expenditure, the Confederate government had little choice but to issue paper money in the form of treasury notes, which eventually totalled more than a billion dollars. Inevitably the money depreciated with the declining economic and military fortunes of the Confederacy so that rapid inflation and hoarding of foodstuffs occurred on an ever greater scale. Indeed a vicious cycle was created as the Confederate government authorised army officers to seize foodstuffs and pay for them at confiscatory prices; the result was yet more hoarding and a still deeper food crisis.[4]

2. Richard N. Current, "God and the Strongest Battalions," in David Donald (ed.), *Why the North Won the Civil War*," pp. 15–32, esp p. 15.

3. Other factors were also present. As we shall see in this chapter, southerners contributed to their own demise by voluntarily reducing the supply of cotton. A further difficulty arose since 1860 had seen a bumper cotton crop and the British market was all but glutted.

4. For the topics covered in this and the next paragraph, see Eugene M. Lerner, "The Monetary and Fiscal Programs of the Confederate Government, 1861–1865," *Journal*

With military reversals came disruption of supplies. The railroad network, which had in any case lacked trunk lines from the outset, was starved of funds and materials for essential repairs and maintenance, partly because such materials could not be imported and partly because they were needed elsewhere for the war effort. Thus even when food and other supplies were available they could not be distributed. Although there was a small shift out of agriculture in the South, with the government itself taking over the operation of factories for the processing of, for example, salt and the production of guns and other armaments, the enormous profits available from successful blockade running probably diverted productive capital out of manufacturing. Most damaging of all, perhaps, was the shortage of manufacturing itself in the South. Although southerners achieved near miracles with such resources as they possessed, they could not compete in this area. In what was perhaps the first major industrial military conflict, the southern economy simply could not be converted into an efficient war machine.

These structural weaknesses, encompassing the financial sector, the transportation network, and the allocation of resources between agriculture and manufacturing, undermined the southern war effort. Even on the land, where the Confederacy's essentially agrarian economy might have been thought to be at its strongest, signs of weakness and disintegration became apparent well before the final surrender. Despite an attempt to shift resources from cotton to grain and meat, large swathes of southern territory were home to a population threatened by famine during the final months of the War. By now the fledgling nation was on the verge of economic breakdown and there was no alternative other than capitulation. Again a vicious cycle had been established. The Confederacy failed to match the Union in economic performance and this was both cause and consequence of military collapse.

Very different was the experience of the North. Here was an economy that could be geared to war in an era of emerging industrialism. This is not to say, however, that all groups prospered in these years. Ironically

of Political Economy, LXII (1954), pp. 506–522; Lerner, "Money, Wages, and Prices in the Confederacy," *Journal of Political Economy*, LXIII (1955), pp. 20–40 reprinted in Ralph Adreano (ed.), *The Economic Impact of The Civil War*. 2nd ed. (Cambridge, MA, 1967), pp. 31–60. An older work is John C. Schwab, *The Confederate States of America: A Financial and Industrial History of the South During the Civil War* (New York, 1901), which is not fully superseded by Richard C. Todd, *Confederate Finance* (Athens, GA, 1954). On the blockade and its effects, see William.M. Robinson, Jr., *The Confederate Privateers* ( New Haven, CT, 1928); James L. Sellers, "Economic Incidence of the Civil War in the South," *Mississippi Valley Historical Review* XIV (1927), pp. 179–191 is a valuable article, reprinted in Andreano (ed.), *Economic Impact of Civil War*, pp. 98–108.

perhaps given that the party of "free labor" was in power, real wages fell.[5] The need to finance the War together with the balance of payments deficit entailed by the loss of cotton exports generated inflation and placed considerable pressure on the financial system. To this extent, the northern experience paralleled that of the Confederacy. But the outcomes were strikingly different. Whereas in the South the supply of banking capital fell during the Civil War decade by more than seventy percent, the financial network in the North acquired a new maturity and sophistication. The National Banking Acts of 1863 and 1864 placed the banking system on a far more secure basis than ever before. Moreover, the fiscal crisis gave rise to a revision of the tariff which, although intended to raise revenue, in fact gave considerable protection to American industry. The average rates rose from nineteen percent to forty-seven percent by the conclusion of the War. Lincoln and his party also continued the liberalisation of land policy that had been underway in the final antebellum decades, with the passage of the Homestead Act of 1862. Although speculators made windfall gains, the Act did promote the establishment of family farms in the West. The federal government continued to offer land grants not only to railroad companies, as it had done before the War, but also to States that established agricultural colleges. Finally, the War saw the introduction of a federal income tax.[6]

This was a bold economic programme and, partly as a consequence, large sectors of the northern economy experienced significant growth rates in the War years. But in addition to the direct and intended effects of the federal government's programme were the unintended consequences of the War: spiralling inflation, a great shortage of cotton, and an army of over a million men to feed and clothe. These together inevitably gave a boost to some industries, such was the untapped productive potential of the northern economy. Thus the iron industry boomed as a result of inflation, wartime needs and the protection afforded by the tariff. Woollen manufacturing also surged ahead, as consumers sought to

5. Wages actually rose by perhaps fifty percent during the war but failed to keep pace with prices. In the first two years of the War, wages rose twenty percent but prices rose by fifty percent. The following year prices rose even faster and the result was the organization of unions and the outbreak of strikes in the winter of 1863–1864. By the end of the War prices were perhaps more than two-thirds higher than on the eve of conflict – see Jeremy Atack and Peter Passell (eds.), *A New Economic View of American History* 2nd ed. (New York, 1994), p. 497; Wesley C. Mitchell, *Gold, Prices, and Wages under the Greenback Standard* (Berkeley, 1908); pp. 4, 279. See also the essays by Stanley Engerman and Reuben A. Kessel and Armen A. Alchian, reprinted in Andreano (ed.), *Economic Impact of Civil War*; Clarence D. Long, *Wages and Earnings in the United States, 1860–1890* (Princeton, 1960).

6. Leonard P. Curry, *Blueprint for Modern America: Nonmilitary Legislation of the First Civil War Congress* (Nashville, 1968), pp. 244–252.

substitute wool for cotton. In agriculture, an additional factor was the poor run of European harvests, increasing the demand for American wheat. Despite the absence of many farmers, more was produced than ever before. The number of sheep reared doubled, and the trend towards mechanisation in agriculture, already visible in the 1850s, continued in the war years.[7]

The War was thus a time of considerable prosperity for many northerners. Stockholders in railroads and telegraph companies enjoyed high dividend yields and the merger of some companies created oligopolies or monopolies which, whilst small compared to the corporate mammoths of the late nineteenth century, were large enough to cause considerable disquiet among sections of the northern public. Moreover, new industries, destined to be of enormous importance in the future, like the oil industry, emerged during the War.[8] In dozens of cities streetcars made their first appearance, again anticipating the changes of the gilded age. Thus the War produced effects on the northern economy that contrasted sharply with its impact on the South. These had been foreseen by no one at the outset of the War; they were partly planned, partly unplanned. But they were nevertheless testimony to the superior productivity and developmental dynamism of the northern economy.[9]

## III

The contrasting experience of the two belligerents in the four years of war reminds us once again of the weaknesses of the slave mode of production. The war years exposed the shortcomings of the southern economy as never before. The comparative lack of manufacturing and the heavy reliance upon a single crop, the weak financial infrastructure, and the inferior transportation network together inflicted immense damage upon

7. Lance Davis, "Capital Immobilities and Finance Capitalism: A Study of Economic Evolution in the United States, 1820–1920," *Explorations in Economic History* I (1963), pp. 88–105; Bray Hammond, *Sovereignty and an Empty Purse: Banks and Politics in the Civil War* (Princeton, 1970); Paul Studenski and Herman Krooss, *A Financial History of the United States* (New York, 1952); Wesley C. Mitchell, *A History of the Greenbacks* (Chicago, 1903), reprinted in Andreano (ed.), *Economic Impact of Civil War*, pp. 85–97; E. D. Fite, *Social and Industrial Conditions in the North during the Civil War* (New York, 1910); George W. Smith and Charles Judah (eds.), *Life in the North during the Civil War* (Albuquerque, New Mexico, 1966); Barney, *Flawed Victory*, pp. 158–194; J. Mathew Gallman, *The North Fights the Civil War: The Home Front* (Chicago, 1994), pp. 92–108.

8. Paul H. Giddens, *The Birth of the Oil Industry* (New York, 1938).

9. See Thomas Bender, *A Nation Among Nations: America's Place in World History* (New York, 2006) which effectively places some of the developments of the era in an international context.

the Confederate war effort and played a key role in bringing about Union victory.[10]

Historians, however, have only rarely linked the defeat of the Confederacy to the weaknesses of slavery. Although many scholars have looked at the reasons for Union victory, with very few exceptions their analyses have fallen into one of two categories. Some have focussed upon the disparities between the two sides in terms of manpower and material resources and have argued, quite tellingly, that this inequality, at least in the absence of any extraordinary occurrences, in effect doomed the South. Others have disputed this and have claimed instead and rather less tellingly that the reasons for northern victory must be found in the events of the war years themselves, in the ebb and flow of contingent events many of them military, in the errors and mistakes of politicians or generals, in the commitment of the troops on each side, or in the political structures and ideological traditions of the two sections. Common to both these approaches is a failure to appreciate that the Confederacy died for the same reason that it was born. The supreme irony of these years is that slavery gave birth to the bid for southern independence and slavery doomed it to almost certain failure.[11]

The second of these historiographical approaches is easily dealt with. In fact northern economic superiority was so pronounced that there were only three ways the Union might have lost. The first was if the struggle had become so costly, either in terms of resources expended or lives lost, as to be judged no longer worthwhile by northern opinion, or at least by key sections of it. The second was if the Confederacy had been aided by one or more foreign powers. The third was if the material advantages were negated by probably not one but a whole series of northern blunders. In fact the struggle did become extremely costly to the northern people, infinitely more costly than even the most pessimistic northern commentators had predicted in 1861. Yet the commitment to the Union was never really in doubt, even in the darkest hours. Nor was there ever much

---

10. See Raimondo Luraghi, *The Rise and Fall of the Plantation South* (New York, 1978), pp. 83, 110.

11. For a fuller discussion of the historiography of Union victory and Confederate defeat see the Appendix in this volume. For an analysis that in part resembles the one given here, see Roger L. Ransom, *Conflict and Compromise: The Political Economy of Slavery, Emancipation and the American Civil War* (New York, 1989). But the historian with whom I most agree is William W. Freehling. See Freehling, *The South vs. The South: How Anti-Confederate Southerners Shaped the Course of the Civil War* (New York, 2001). With a single exception – see note 25, I shall not consider my differences with Freehling here since they are the subject of a separate essay – see John Ashworth, "William W. Freehling and the Politics of the Old South," *American Nineteenth Century History* V (2004), pp. 1–29. See also Freehling's reply (pp. 30–33), though I should perhaps add that I have never subscribed to some of the views attributed to me here.

Conclusion

likelihood of foreign intervention. The Confederacy was in a double bind in that if military success required foreign intervention, foreign intervention (and even foreign recognition) depended on military success. From this vice there was no escape. And although northern leaders, military and civilian, (like their southern counterparts) did make major mistakes, these were never sufficient to offset the structural advantages their side enjoyed. Leadership in war is clearly enormously important but the success of northern military leaders, especially Ulysses S. Grant and William T. Sherman, lay precisely in bringing northern economic superiority to bear upon the struggle. And perhaps the greatest achievement of the Lincoln administration was (after a number of false starts) to find and select in Grant and Sherman the generals who could do this.

Northern superiority was in states and territory, in population, and in industry and cities. The vital issue, ignored by almost all historians who have sought the reasons for the defeat of the Confederacy, concerns the role of slavery in so constraining southern development as to produce this enormous northern superiority even before the first shot had been fired.[12] As far as states and territory are concerned, slavery had clearly shown itself unable to compete. When the nation was formed it existed in all thirteen of the new states. But it failed to sustain itself except in the South. Only where large-scale agriculture was possible, in highly favourable climatic conditions and where there was massive overseas demand for the staple crops produced, did the institution thrive and expand. Thus it proved unable to compete across much of the West even where white opinion was utterly indifferent to the welfare of the African American population. The inhabitants of first the upper then the lower North confirmed their commitment to free labor and in the Border South slavery was clearly weakening in the decades before war broke out. The Confederate failure to secure the loyalties of the four slaveholding states of Delaware, Maryland, Kentucky and Missouri offered the clearest possible evidence of slavery's relative weakness there and within the nation as a whole. Why was slavery rejected in most of the nation? In some parts of the North and the West, antislavery had moral and political underpinnings but, as we have seen, the economic shortcomings of the institution were decisive.

The South's failure to maintain slavery territorially was one of two reasons for its failure to keep pace demographically. Less territory implied, other things being equal, fewer people. But the other factor was still more important: the northern population was boosted by immigration. The populations north and south of the Mason-Dixon Line increased by

12. This is even a problem in Armstead Robinson, *Bitter Fruits of Bondage: The Demise of Slavery and the Collapse of the Confederacy, 1861–1865* (Charlottesville, VA, 2005), which stresses the role of slavery and slave resistance *during* but not prior to the war.

natural reproduction at approximately the same rate but immigrants went overwhelmingly to the North. This was in no sense attributable to the natural endowment of the region. It was simply that a free-labor economy offered the immigrant far greater opportunities. Moreover, as we have seen,[13] many southerners simply did not want immigrants. They made no secret of their twin fears: either the immigrants might bring antislavery opinions with them or they might, by their very economic successes, establish enclaves of free labor within the South whose mere existence would challenge the hegemony of the planters. So southerners were compelled to watch helplessly as the northern population outstripped their own.[14]

Finally there can be no doubt that slavery retarded both industrialisation and urbanisation in the South. Even Robert W. Fogel and Stanley L. Engerman, the most dogged defenders of the economic performance of slaves and slavery, concede that slavery slowed the development of industry in the Old South and the figures on urbanisation are equally unequivocal in confirming the southern lag, however it might be explained. Indeed even a cursory glance at a map of the Old South confirms that in general the more entrenched slavery was in a region, the less industry and the fewer cities were to be found there.[15]

The reasons for the South's failure to industrialise or urbanise remain highly controversial. I have argued in the first volume of this study, however, that they have to do with the essential characteristics of the slave mode of production. The relationship between slave and master was inevitably a conflict-ridden one, if only because the slaves did not wish to remain slaves and were highly, indeed painfully, conscious of the process by which the products of their labor were expropriated. As many southerners openly acknowledged, it was more difficult to control slaves in an urban or industrial environment. Finally the relationship between masters and nonslaveholding whites in the South was always critical for on the acquiescence of the latter depended the continued dominance of the.former. The use of slaves in cities and in industry placed considerable strains upon this relationship (and, as we have noted, was partly responsible for the absence of immigrants in the South). So for these (and other) reasons, the slaveholders in general preferred to keep their slaves in

13. See the first volume of this study, pp. 272, 280, 499–500, 504–505.
14. Here the example of Missouri in the final antebellum years is instructive. Many Missourians became alarmed at their state's inability to compete for population with free labor states like Illinois. The result was an attempt, even before war broke out, to rid the state of slavery. The attempt was unsuccessful but it both anticipated the course of many Missourians during the War and illustrated the relationship between slavery, population growth and territorial expansion.
15. Robert W. Fogel and Stanley L. Engerman, *Time on the Cross, The Economics of American Negro Slavery.* 2 vols. (London, 1974), I 257. See also the works reviewed in the first volume of this study, pp. 499–509.

agriculture and southern society continued to bestow its highest honours on those whose wealth was derived from slaves employed on the land. For this the regime would pay the ultimate price between 1861 and 1865.[16]

Thus slavery had inflicted incalculable damage upon the Confederate warmaking potential even before the first shot had been fired. As we have seen, some historians have stressed the importance of the northern superiority in numbers and resources. But overspecialisation has led them to treat this superiority as a given; they have not related it to the inherent characteristics of slave, as opposed to free, labor.[17] The simple fact is that the smaller population of the South and the smaller absolute size of the slave economy were themselves the most dramatic illustrations of the weaknesses, ultimately to prove fatal, of slavery in the United States.[18]

During the War the Confederacy continued to pay a high price for slavery. As we have seen, the economic imbalances and vulnerabilities for which it was in large measure responsible took a heavy toll. But there were other effects. The divisions engendered within southern society, were extremely severe, probably more severe than those at the North. In the South, there was much resentment of the War on the part of the non-slaveholders, some of whom complained bitterly that it was "a rich man's war and a poor man's fight." It is possible (though not certain) that this resentment was more intense and more damaging to the war effort than the equivalent resentment among lower-class northerners, which erupted most dramatically during the notorious New York city draft riots of 1863. More important, however, were the actions of the Confederacy's slaves. In the first place, this large population was, until the very end of the War, excluded from combat, thus further enhancing the northern advantage in population. Moreover, the slaves in their hundreds of thousands fled the plantations of the South, often (though by no means always) when the Union armies arrived in their locality. This, it should be noted, had no parallel in the North, whose wage laborers evinced no desire to take refuge in the arms of oncoming southern slaveholders. Similarly, Confederate

16. See Volume one of this study, pp. 80–121.
17. It may be worth noting that those who have compared slavery with free labor have usually ignored the confrontation of 1861–1865 and ignored the fact that by then slavery had failed in most of the nation. This vital fact is obscured by the per capita comparisons of income and wealth on which they have normally relied. As Raimondo Luraghi put it, the economic historian who ignores the performance of the South in the Civil War is akin to the person who goes to the zoo and misses the elephant – because it is too big. See Luraghi, *Rise and Fall*, p. 83.
18. To see this effect more clearly, let us imagine that slavery, because of its inability to compete with free labor, had shrunk in the United States to a single plantation in a single State of the Union. So long as the profits obtained by that one slaveholder were greater than the average rate of return in the rest of the nation, this would "prove" the economic superiority of slave labor. Yet this is the methodology employed by Fogel and Engerman (amongst others).

troops in the final months of the War began to desert in unprecedented numbers, partly because of the fears they had of their slaves back home. Again this had no parallel in the North.[19]

Material weakness, inadequate manpower, internal divisions – these were some of the fruits that slavery brought to the Confederacy. The peculiar institution had other effects. Some historians have claimed that the Confederates ought to have resorted to a guerrilla war and that such a strategy might have brought victory. But this was never a realistic option for a number of reasons chief among them the dangers that such a strategy would have brought to slavery. A temporary surrender of territory was simply unthinkable if it allowed large numbers of slaves to flee or in other ways to subvert the authority of their masters.

Even this does not exhaust the list of weaknesses slavery brought to the Confederates. For a variety of reasons, the slaveholders of the South utterly failed to understand the system they had created. Believing that the northern social order would ultimately be overwhelmed by its subordinate class of wage-earners, they were convinced that slavery by contrast was so finely attuned to the biological capabilities of blacks (or to the lack of them) that it would instead display a unique strength and stability. The discontented wage-worker might rise up and destroy the social order; the slave, provided he was properly supervised and controlled, would never even wish to do so. For this reason the Confederates grossly overestimated their chances of victory in the War.[20] "It may be safely estimated," a writer in *De Bow's Review* claimed, "that a population of twelve millions, one third of whom are slaves, are equal in time of war to a population of twenty millions without slaves."[21]

In this way slavery induced a quite unfounded optimism among its defenders. As we have seen, Confederates believed that the free-labor system that existed in Britain would be simply unable to withstand the removal of "King Cotton" and that British statesmen would consequently be impelled to recognise and come to the aid of, the new regime. Of course this proved a catastrophic error and it caused the South to misplay the cotton card during the War. Historians have tended to see this as nothing more than an error, or a series of errors. But it was indeed far more. It was yet another structurally generated misperception, on this occasion a direct consequence of southern confidence, indeed overconfidence, in slavery and of the slaveholders' failure to understand the conflict which was endemic in, and which ultimately undermined, their own social order. Thus among the many weaknesses that slavery generated in the South, not

19. See Robinson, *Bitter Fruits of Bondage*, for an excellent treatment of the wartime conflicts within the South between slaveholders and nonslaveholding whites and between slaveholders and slaves.
20. It should be added that others, British observers for example, made this mistake too.
21. *De Bow's Review*, XXXI (1861), p. 36.

the least significant was the conviction that slavery was uniquely free from weaknesses.

To claim primacy for slavery as a cause of Confederate defeat is not to reject or even necessarily to question some of the other factors that historians have identified.[22] Rather slavery was, above all, *a cause of a cause*, or even *a cause of a set of causes*, an underlying factor, creating a decisive imbalance in resources and manpower, precluding some military options, encouraging sabotage, disruption or flight on the part of slaves in the South, impelling African Americans, North and South, to make disproportionate military sacrifices. It operated, that is to say, at a deeper level than the factors upon which historians have usually concentrated.


# IV

Although Union victory was brought about primarily by the weaknesses of slavery, the victory was neither quick nor painless. The protracted nature of the struggle impelled Abraham Lincoln to exploit the enemy's vulner-ability by means of an attack upon the southern labor system itself. The Emancipation Proclamation, issued after the Union victory at Antietam in September of 1862, was in part a military strike against the enemy. To a lesser extent, it was a reflection of the concern held by some Republicans, including Lincoln himself, for the welfare of the African Americans held in bondage. Above all, however, it was a recognition that the struggle upon which the North had now embarked was so profound, the sacrifices made by ordinary northerners already so vast, that to restore slavery when the War was won, would be a palpable absurdity. As we have seen, from the inception of their party the Republicans' core belief had been that slavery was a dangerously disorganising force within the nation. Nothing could have more dramatically confirmed and deepened this belief than the onset of a bloody Civil War, a war for which slavery was so clearly responsible. Slavery had now brought about a Civil War, the ultimate form of national disorganisation and for this reason it had to be ended. "Those enemies," Lincoln announced, "must understand that they cannot experiment for ten years trying to destroy the government, and if they fail still come back into the Union unhurt." The Emancipation Proclamation, in conjunction with northern military triumph, would destroy their capacity for evil for ever.[23]

Although the Civil War and the emancipation of the slaves effected a revolutionary change in the nation's political and economic systems, it simultaneously brought to a climax many of the developments that had

---

22. See the Appendix to this volume for a review of some of these interpretations.
23. Roy F. Basler (ed.), *The Collected Works of Abraham Lincoln.* 9 vols. (New Brunswick, 1953–1955), V, pp. 350–351.

been in evidence in previous decades. Emancipation itself flowed from what had been the core belief of the Republican party, the conviction that slavery disorganised the nation. At the same time, as we have seen, Confederate defeat grew out of the weaknesses of slavery, to which the leaders of the South remained catastrophically oblivious, as they had been since the earliest years of the sectional controversy. In party political terms, the War completed the overthrow of Democratic hegemony. The party which had controlled the antebellum Republic until almost the very last and which had so often functioned in the interests of the slaveholders of the South had been in sharp decline in the dominant part of the nation since the mid-1850s. The Democracy had traditionally offered much covert support for slaveholders and for slavery by disabling antislavery sentiment and by promoting values behind which many northerners, including significant numbers who had no sympathy for slavery, could rally with enthusiasm. But the changes in northern society broke up the coalition between the planters of the South and the "plain republicans of the North" and drove the latter increasingly into the hands of a new Republican party, one whose appeal rested not upon slavery but rather upon antislavery with all its economic, political and moral underpinnings. In the war years northern Democrats, even when they were enthusiastic defenders of the Union, reacted angrily to the Emancipation Proclamation. Many of them continued to display sympathy for southerners and for slavery. But once again events showed how irrelevant they had become. It was a reflection of the extent to which the Democrats had lost the political initiative that Emancipation went ahead regardless of their opposition.

V

The most obvious consequence of the collapse of the Confederacy was, of course, the abolition of slavery throughout the United States. The war that effected that collapse was a unique event in the history of the nation and of the world and this is true not merely in the banal sense – what sequence of events is ever identical in all respects to another? – but in a more profound way too. In no other nation, with the possible exception of Haiti, was slavery destroyed in such a cataclysm of violence. Yet this should not blind us to the fact that the ending of slavery in the American South was part of a broader movement transcending national boundaries by which unfree labor systems were dismantled across the long nineteenth century. Slavery, rarely criticised before the final quarter of the eighteenth century, and serfdom, with an equally long and undistinguished pedigree, were supplanted by free-labour systems across much of the developed or developing world. In the first decades of the nineteenth century, slavery was abolished in the northern states of the Union, in Haiti, in Argentina,

Columbia, Chile and Central America (including Mexico). In the 1830s, 1840s and 1850s Bolivia, Uruguay, Ecuador, Peru and Venezuela followed suit. By the time of the Civil War, slavery had also been abolished in all British, French and Danish colonies, while in the 1860s the Czar of Russia presided over the emancipation of the serfs. Over the nineteenth century as a whole, slavery was destroyed across the Americas in most countries prior to the U.S. Civil War, in Cuba, Puerto Rico and in Brazil after it. So the freeing of the slaves, the most dramatic effect of the American Civil War, was part of a broader international movement that should be understood in its wider chronological and geographical context.

Those who have studied slavery in recent decades are now well-aware of this international dimension and many of them have incorporated a comparative perspective into their work. But this internationalism has not really extended to the study of the Civil War itself. Although historians have been willing, indeed eager, to compare the military conflict with other wars (usually in order to emphasise the possibility of Confederate victory), they have not considered an alternative possibility: that Confederate defeat was itself a function of the weaknesses of slavery, weaknesses that transcended national boundaries. To put it slightly differently, they have not considered the possibility that some of the same processes or factors that doomed unfree labor systems elsewhere on the globe resulted in the collapse, on the battlefield, of the South's slaveholding Republic and the ultimate triumph of the Union armies. It is in this sense that they have failed to situate the ending of American slavery in its geographical and historical context. The fundamental, inescapable fact is that throughout much of the developed and even semideveloped world unfree labor systems were being dismantled partly because they were thought to obstruct or impede economic growth and development.[24] Here is a priceless clue to Confederate defeat and Union victory. It is one that historians of the Civil War have almost entirely ignored.[25]

In other words, attributing the outcome of the Civil War to slavery and its weaknesses allows us to locate this decisive event – and what event has been more decisive in the American past? – within a broader international

---

24. An extended discussion of this issue is beyond the scope of the present work. I should state, however, that I do not wish to claim that a single formula can be offered which will explain the dismantling of unfree labor systems throughout the world in these years. Rather the claim is that there were economic factors which transcended national boundaries.

25. Even Freehling, who has indeed stressed the role of slavery, almost obliterates his own insights here by claiming that it was not slavery *per se* but rather its specifically American variant that was responsible for Confederate weakness. This again detaches Confederate defeat from its international and chronological context – see Freehling, *South versus the South*, pp. 201–206 and Ashworth, "William W. Freehling and the Politics of the Old South," pp. 19–20.

context. It opens up the possibility that the reasons for the dismantling of unfree labor systems across many advanced or developing countries stemmed from a common root. It allows us to recognise that in the United States from that root, the structural weaknesses of unfree labor systems, came not merely opposition to slavery in the American South but also the superiority in resources and manpower and the strategic advantages visible in the war that brought ultimate ruin to American slaveholders.

It remains true, of course, that in the United States the ending of unfree labor could be secured only by a blood-letting that had no equivalent in the rest of the world. This reminds us that slavery in the South, though unable to compete with the free-labor system of the North, either before the War or during it, was nevertheless immeasurably stronger than any other system of unfree labor observed in the modern world. This relative strength was in part political, since it enabled the slaveholders to control a large slice of the United States and to shape to an extraordinary degree the destinies of at least eleven of the states of the antebellum Republic. It was also economic in that for all its weaknesses the slave system of the South was nevertheless able to mount for four years an extraordinary struggle against one of the world's most dynamic economies. Indeed the Civil War reflects a perverse reality about slavery in the South: it was strong enough to make at least plausible the conviction that it could survive a protracted war with the North and it was strong enough to withstand four long years of debilitating warfare and unparalleled slaughter. Yet it was not, as the history of the prewar decades suggested and as the war years confirmed, strong enough to combat the free-labor system of the North. This is the comparative perspective in which southern slavery should be seen.

## VI

Southern weakness should thus be measured against the demanding standards of the North. It was not enough that the southern banking system or the southern railroad network, for example, compared favourably with those in most other nations. The point of comparison before the War had been with the North and it was failure by these standards that had produced the southern militants' concerns and the southern militants' strategies in the 1850s. In the same way it was the comparison, now a deadly rivalry, with the North in four years of war that would prove decisive.

Thus the location of southern slavery within an enormously successful national economy had contradictory effects. For many decades, northern and southern economies advanced together, with each benefiting from the success of the other. The tragedy of southern slavery, from the standpoint of the slaveholders, was that, while it derived immense advantages from its location within one of the world's most dynamic economies, its success would ultimately be measured by reference to the performance of the most dynamic region in that economy: the free-labor North.

For the southern economy the consequences of the War with the North were catastrophic. Whilst it would be wrong to conclude that all southerners were economically injured by the War, given the windfall gains available to blockade runners and successful speculators for example, there can be little doubt about its overall macroeconomic impact. It is no exaggeration to say that southern agriculture, by far the most important sector in the southern economy, was pauperised by 1865. The value of southern real estate fell by half while the value of farms, farm products and livestock in the older states of the Confederacy (that is, all except Arkansas, Texas and Florida) did not regain the levels of 1860 until 1900, by which time the value of farms in the North had doubled. In the decade of the Civil War, southern per capita output fell by thirty-nine percent.[26]

The combination of the War and the ending of slavery, together with a probable slowdown in the world demand for cotton, jointly produced these effects. The abolition of slavery was itself an act of confiscation of revolutionary proportions with catastrophic effects upon aggregate southern wealth. It is likely that the loss of perhaps three billion dollars worth of slave property represented about thirty percent of total southern wealth.

These effects were not of limited duration. On the contrary, southern agriculture and the southern economy as a whole sank into a position of weakness relative to the nation as a whole from which they would not recover until well after the Second World War. Despite the shift out of agriculture during the Civil War, the South's share of the nation's manufacturing output which had been a mere 7.2 percent in 1860 fell to 4.7 percent in 1870 and would not regain even the modest antebellum level until the end of the century. Indeed a central feature of the Confederate wartime economy, its fatal shortage of credit and capital, persisted as a characteristic and a chronic problem in the postbellum South.[27]

As we have seen, northerners and especially Republicans had hoped to remake the southern economy and southern society in the image of the North. In this they failed. Not only was commodity output in the South severely damaged but southern industrialisation, lagging far behind

26. Engerman, "Economic Impact," in Andreano (ed.), *Economic Impact of Civil War*, p. 180; Atack and Passell, *New Economic View*, pp. 373–374; Eugene Lerner, "Southern Output and Agricultural Income, 1860–1880," *Agricultural History* XXX (1959), pp. 117–125, reprinted in Andreano (ed.), *Economic Impact of Civil War*, pp. 109–122.
27. Atack and Passell, *New Economic View*, pp. 373–374, 378; Gavin Wright, *Old South, New South: Revolutions in the Southern Economy* (New York, 1986); Stephen Decanio, "Productivity and Income Distribution in the Postbellum South," *Journal of Economic History* XXXIV (1974), pp. 422–446.

the North in 1860, slipped still further behind. Moreover, the ending of southern slavery did not produce wage-labor in the region so much as a bewildering array of labor systems, including sharecropping, tenant farming, the crop-lien system and other contractual agreements, generally designed to give as little true freedom to the freedmen and to perpetuate racial inequality throughout the region. Thus the South emerged from the Civil War as a backward economic region, characterised by low wages, low productivity, underdevelopment and a chronic shortage of productive capital. By the mid-1870s, if not earlier, it was apparent that this part of the Republican project for the South lay in ruins.[28]

## VII

As we have seen, the northern economy performed very differently during the War and some historians have gone so far as to claim a special place for the War in the history of American capitalism. Thus Charles and Mary Beard and their followers argued that the Civil War played a key role in the transformation of the American economy which took place in the final decades of the nineteenth century and which made the United States by 1900 the world's leading capitalist power.[29]

These claims, however, are very much open to question.[30] For the Beards industrialisation was the key indicator of capitalist development. But the data require careful analysis. It is true that agriculture did decline in importance in the national economy in the 1860s but this was as a result of the collapse of southern agriculture, not of any absolute, or even relative, decline in the North. Indeed in the 1860s agriculture in the North expanded more rapidly in terms of total output than other sectors. In manufacturing, experience varied from industry to industry. Although

28. On economic conditions in the postbellum South, see, in addition to works already cited, three by Roger Ransom and Richard Sutch: "Debt Peonage in the Cotton South after the Civil War," *Journal of Economic History* XXXII (1972), pp. 641–667; "The Impact of the Civil War and of Emancipation on Southern Agriculture," *Explorations in Economic History* XII (1975), 1–28; *One Kind of Freedom: The Economic Consequences of Emancipation* (Cambridge, UK, 1977).

29. Charles and Mary Beard, *The Rise of American Civilization*. 2 vols. (New York, 1927), esp. II, pp. 54, 105, 166. See also Louis Hacker, *The Triumph of American Capitalism* (New York, 1940), esp. p. 339. This thesis stimulated a historiographical debate in which two of the major contributions were Thomas Cochran, "Did the Civil War Retard Industrialization?" *Mississippi Valley Historical Review* XLVIII (1961), pp. 197–210 and Stanley Engerman, "The Economic Impact of the Civil War," *Explorations in Economic History* III (1966), 176–199.

30. Some historians have accused the Beards of projecting the experiences of World War I, where the United States boomed, into the nineteenth century. See Beards, *Rise of American Civilization* II, pp. 53–54; Thomas Cochran, "Did the Civil War Retard Industrialization?" in Andreano (ed.), *The Economic Impact of the Civil War*, pp. 167–179.

Conclusion

the woollen industry expanded, cotton manufacturing not surprisingly fell back sharply. In some industries prices and profits rose, while production fell. Should this be viewed as a success for capitalists or a failure for capitalism? In any event the index of manufacturing productivity was almost static for the war years.[31]

Moreover, it is important to place the experience of the 1860s in historical perspective. Here it seems that there is little reason to see the war decade as a watershed. Annual growth in commodity output in the two decades before the war was higher than in the two decades after 1870. When value added in manufacturing is considered, no obvious conclusion emerges. The rate of growth was 7.8 percent for the years 1840–1860 but six percent for the final three decades of the century. On the other hand, the *per capita* rate was somewhat higher in the latter period, though this may have merely represented a catching up after the war decade. As far as the North's absolute growth performance is concerned, between 1840 and 1860 per capita income rose at an average annual rate of 1.3 percent; for the next two decades the figure was 1.75 percent and for the last two of the century 1.9 percent. Thus although there was an increase in the rate of growth after the war, it appears to have been part of a longer process. The data do not therefore give obvious support to the claim that the war has a privileged status in the history of American capitalism.[32]

As we have seen there were some important developments in the northern economy in the war years. The change in the nation's banking system and the raising of the tariff walls were of considerable importance but each decade in the late nineteenth century saw developments that were probably of similar significance. Once again there is no obvious reason to single out the war experience or the war decade as critical to the success or the development of American capitalism.[33]

VIII

With these consequences of the war in mind, it is appropriate to return to the question of origins. In 1860 and 1861, the states of the Deep South concluded that there could be no safety for them, and by this they meant essentially no safety for slavery, in the Union. Given the nature of northern opposition to slavery, and the heights it had reached by 1860, this was

31. Atack and Passell, *New Economic View*, pp. 363–364, 373.
32. Atack and Passell, *New Economic View*, pp. 363–374; Engerman, "Economic Impact," in Andreano (ed.), *Economic Impact of Civil War*, p. 192.
33. Engerman, "Economic Impact," in Andreano (ed.), *Economic Impact of Civil War*, 190–191; Roger L. Ransom, *Conflict and Compromise: The Political Economy of Slavery, Emancipation and the American Civil War* (New York, 1989), pp. 255–268.

an entirely rational response. Indeed, for those who believed that slavery could and should be perpetuated, there was no rational alternative.

As we have seen, when slaveholders left the Union they did so on a wave of optimism, and in the belief that slavery would provide an enviably stable foundation for their society and their nation. Nevertheless, what they did not know was that their actions were then, as they had been throughout the sectional controversy, heavily, indeed decisively, influenced by the slaves' resistance, both actual and potential, to their enslavement. This resistance gave rise to the many weaknesses of the regime, weaknesses that were manifest in the slaveholders' relationship not merely to northerners, but also to their own nonslaveholding white population, their free blacks and their slaves. Secession was the final, drastic attempt, to overcome the weaknesses of slavery. It failed – essentially because of those very same weaknesses.

In seeking to make the Union safe for slavery, southerners took a whole series of actions in the 1850s and earlier which fuelled northern resentment. The accusation that the South and even the nation itself were being controlled by a Slave Power was one of the most potent rallying cries of northern antislavery campaigners. But this should not blind us to the fact that antislavery had deep and growing roots in northern society and in the northern economy. As the North came to terms with the development of wage labor, it was driven to spell out the qualities and the advantages which the wage labourer enjoyed. These qualities and these advantages had the effect of making slavery in the South seem increasingly unacceptable, for political, economic and moral reasons. The crusade launched against the South and against southern slavery by the Republican party from the mid-1850s was the product of this deepening resentment of slavery and slaveholding, the conviction that slavery was at war with human nature and thus would, unless checked, inevitably and repeatedly disturb and disorganise any community in which it was located.

The Republican indictment of slavery was a potent mix of moral, economic and political criticisms. Which were primary? Although moral considerations played a considerable part, they were less in evidence than the other criticisms. Most important were the economic factors, not because they were more often cited than the political, but because the political case against slavery was, as we have seen, in large part derivative of the moral and economic critiques.

In the 1850s, the American political system was increasingly unable to contain the centrifugal pressures operating upon it. The need to conciliate an increasingly militant South took a heavy toll upon the Democratic party in the North and the polarisation of opinion on the slavery question undermined every effort to maintain a national party of Whigs or neo-Whigs, in whatever guise they might present themselves. Factors other than slavery played a part in the realignment of the 1850s but it was essentially the product of the growing sectionalisation of American politics.

In the course of the 1850s and the secession crisis, statesmen on both sides made many errors. There were many misperceptions, rather as the Civil War revisionists argued. But this is not to say that the war could have been avoided if superior statesmen had been at the helm. The question of inevitability is one which can never be finally resolved, of course, but it is surely apparent that those who claim the war was avoidable have an uphill task before them. It is easy to show that politicians made errors, and that these errors had momentous consequences. But as we have seen, they were all too often integral parts of entire world views, components of ideologies which themselves bore the imprint of fundamental economic interests. To convict the statesmen of errors, therefore, is not to demonstrate that error-free alternatives were actually possible.

Some historians have argued that North and South by 1860 consti-tuted nothing less than two distinct civilisations.[34] If the claim here is that in matters of high and popular culture the two sections were utterly dissimilar then it must surely be rejected.[35] What North and South had in 1860 were two different labor systems which generated values, essen-tially in the realm of political economy, that themselves clashed. In his interpretation of the war, Charles Beard perhaps glimpsed this incompat-ibility between the economic systems, but he mislocated its nature and its source. The struggle was not between agrarianism and industrial cap-italism, though it was certainly no coincidence that southern society was unable to industrialise. As many scholars have observed, there was no rea-son an industrialising North could not coexist with an agricultural South on the basis of a mutually advantageous and highly profitable interdepen-dence. Instead the struggle was between labor systems and the crucial need was to accommodate the subordinate classes in each section. As of 1860, this need was being met in that in neither section was there a danger of revolt from below. But the accommodation in the North with wage labor was made only by generating values that made southern slavery appear increasingly incongruous and increasingly unacceptable. If the war was indeed the result of an "irrepressible conflict," it is here that the roots of that conflict are to be found.

---

34. See, for example, Eugene Genovese, *In Red and Black: Marxian Explorations in Southern and Afro-American History* (London, 1971), pp. 315–353.
35. Thus David Potter has suggested that "there was probably more cultural homogeneity in American society on the eve of secession that there had been when the Union was formed, or than there would be a century later" – David M. Potter, *The Impending Crisis, 1848–1861* (New York, 1976), p. 472.

## IX

It is appropriate to refer to the Civil War as a "bourgeois revolution." Slavery was criticised, condemned, and finally destroyed in the United States essentially because by the norms of northern society it was increasingly unacceptable. These were the norms of a free-labor northern society, one characterised by "bourgeois social relations," as they are often termed, with wage labor at their core.

This is not to say, however, that the northern economy, in order to secure its future growth, in some sense required the dismantling of the southern labor system. It has been argued (essentially by those working within the Marxist tradition) that slavery was an impediment to northern capitalism and thus had to be removed. As far as straightforward economic (as opposed to ideological) criteria are concerned, this is an erroneous view. It is abundantly clear that northern capitalism had not come to a grinding halt in 1860, immobilised by the existence of southern slavery. The experience of the 1850s, the very decade when the North was progressing most rapidly, is the strongest possible evidence to the contrary. The northern economy of 1860 in no sense faced crisis or stagnation. With a huge area of land still to be settled, including most of California, a growing population, and a favourable international and regional environment, it did not need the South Atlantic states to expand into, still less the territory or states of the Southwest. The Civil War was not the product of a northern economy that was, or was soon to be, in crisis. Rather it was the product of a triumphant and booming northern economy, one which would almost certainly have continued to boom even if southern slavery had continued and one whose values were increasingly identified with the nation as a whole.[36]

We must also guard against an implicit functionalism, in which economic and social changes are assumed to be optimal for the dominant social order. As we have noted, the postbellum South was scarcely ideal for the development of capitalism in the South or in the nation as a whole. In other words, from the standpoint of American capitalism, after the war one set of suboptimal conditions in the South replaced another.[37]

After the war, however, the suboptimal conditions in the South no longer mattered in the same way. After the war northern values became the values of the nation as a whole. Although the attempts to remake the South in the image of the North failed, the result was in no sense to

---

36. Charles Post, "The American Road to Capitalism," *New Left Review* CXXXIII (1982), pp. 30–51, esp. p. 37. See also some of the essays in George Novack (ed.), *America's Revolutionary Heritage* (New York, 1976).
37. This is a tendency prominent within certain strains of Marxist writing and also within Beard's work.

discredit the North. Instead it was the South that remained discredited, increasingly viewed as a backwater, outside the national mainstream.

The Civil War thus marked a series of momentous transformations, not merely in the lives of the millions of newly freed African Americans, important though that was, but also in the politics, the economy and the political economy of the United States. The performance of the northern economy in the postbellum years confirmed that that economy could thrive without southern slavery. After the war although cotton production increased, neither cotton nor any other crop that had been produced by slave labor played more than a minor role in the economic growth of the nation. The shift in the balance of economic power, which had been so noticeable before the war, was confirmed after it.

Even more dramatic was the shift in political power. Before the war slaveholders had had a hold on the chief offices of the federal government that was, much as Republicans charged, entirely disproportionate to their numbers. Thus residents of the states that would form the Confederacy held the presidency for two-thirds of the years between 1789 and 1861, furnished almost the same proportion of Speakers of the House of Representatives and enjoyed a permanent majority on the Supreme Court. In the half-century after the war, no president, no Speaker, and only five out of twenty-five Supreme Court justices came from those states.[38]

Still more important were the ideological shifts. Historians have often recognised that the economic and political power that the southern ruling class had been able to wield within the nation was destroyed by the Civil War. They have less often recognised, however, that the ideology of the North now became identified with the nation itself, regardless of the situation in the South. Indeed the ideology of the victorious North, with its reconciliation of democracy and capitalism became the ideology of Americanism. The tenets of the Republican faith, social mobility, the dignity of labor, equal opportunity, underpinned by the acceptance of wage labour as a legitimate condition for the worthy citizen have become so integral a part of the nation's values that it is difficult to perceive that they were ever open to challenge. And yet before the era of the sectional conflict those who enthused about democracy had frequently entertained strong suspicions of wage-labour capitalism. Conversely those who welcomed wage-labour capitalism had frequently entertained strong suspicions of democracy. But the Republicans reconciled democracy and capitalism as never before and this powerful synthesis has been able to withstand virtually all challenges ever since. When Lincoln spoke at Gettysburg of "a new birth of freedom," he almost certainly said more than he knew.

---

38.  James McPherson, *Battle Cry of Freedom: The American Civil War* (London, 1988), pp. 859–860.

The unacknowledged foundation of antebellum American democracy, as exemplified in the tradition of Thomas Jefferson, John Taylor of Caroline and Andrew Jackson, had been slavery in the South, which had done so much to remove the opposition to popular government of the dominant class of the South and of the nation.[39] After the Civil War, this was no longer the case. American democracy now had a new foundation. Or, to alter the image: as a result of first, the growth and development of the northern economy, second, the ideological changes needed in part to contain the stresses and strains that resulted from that growth and development, and third, the continued resistance of the slaves themselves, American democracy had shed and consumed the skin in which it had been born.

There can, however, be no rigid separation between economy and ideology. The legitimation of northern capitalism that we have just outlined was not imposed conspiratorially by an elite determined to hoodwink the masses. In general that elite truly believed its own claims and genuinely invited the rest of the community to share its attitudes and outlook in the belief that they would prove beneficial to the nation as a whole. There was thus no capitalist conspiracy or plot. But immense benefits have accrued to the owners of capital in the United States as a result of the triumph of these values in the century and a half since they were enunciated. And this was no capitalist accident.

39.   This is a principal theme of the first volume of this study.

# Appendix: A review of some major works on the reasons for Confederate defeat[1]

David Donald (ed.), *Why the North Won the Civil War* (New York, 1960).

Richard E. Beringer, Herman Hattaway, Archer Jones, and William N. Still, Jr, *Why the South Lost the Civil War* (Athens, GA, 1986).

Gabor S. Boritt (ed.), *Why the Confederacy Lost* (New York, 1992).

James M. McPherson, *Battle Cry of Freedom: The American Civil War* (New York, 1988).

Gary W. Gallagher, *The Confederate War: How Popular Will, Nationalism, and Military Strategy Could Not Stave Off Defeat* (Cambridge, MA, 1997).

Most historical writing on the subject of Union victory and Confederate defeat in the Civil War has been characterised by certain unstated and indeed often unrecognised epistemological and even moral assumptions. Most scholars in the field have a tendency to stress agency rather than structure and, as a result, it might be suggested, to exaggerate the freedom of movement of individuals and even large groups (such as armies) whilst simultaneously neglecting or underestimating the structural constraints under which those individuals and groups operated. This has coloured many explanations of Confederate defeat. In a minority of cases, there has been a conspicuous failure to respect the integrity of the past by taking seriously moral codes that differ sharply from those of the twentieth or twenty-first centuries. Similarly, among some scholars there has been a clear preference for narrative over analysis and, though this may have brought some rewards, it must also be held partly responsible for some striking weaknesses in what is by now a very sizeable literature. This Appendix will not consider all the works or even all the major works on the subject of Confederate defeat or Union victory. It will, however, systematically assess some of the most important and most frequently cited among them.[2]

---

1. I shall not consider here the possibility that the Confederacy failed because its women did not sufficiently want it to succeed other than to observe that this interpretation clearly confuses symptoms (of impending defeat) and consequences (of defeats already sustained) with causes. See Drew M. Faust, "Altars of Sacrifice: Confederate Women and the Narratives of War," in Catherine Clinton and Nina Silber (eds.), *Divided Houses, Gender and the Civil War* (New York, 1992), pp. 171–199, especially p. 199.

2. The historian whose views are closest to mine is perhaps William W. Freehling. See, esp., his *The South versus the South: How Anti-Confederate Southerners Shaped the Course of the Civil War* (New York, 2001). I shall not, however, consider this work here because I have discussed Freehling's many books elsewhere – see John Ashworth, "William W. Freehling

## (1) Economic Factors

The modern debate over the reasons for Confederate defeat and Union victory was launched as a result of a slim volume published in 1960, which followed a conference held at Gettysburg College. The volume was entitled, *Why the North Won The Civil War*. It consisted of five essays each advancing a different explanation for northern victory.[3] The first, and without much doubt the most valuable, of these essays was by Richard N. Current and offered a neat and convenient summary of the economic interpretation. Current reminded his readers of the northern superiority in manpower and resources and succinctly summarised the key data. To this causal factor he unhesitatingly assigned primacy. "As usual," he concluded, "God was on the side of the heaviest battalions." Current did not entirely discount the possibility that other factors might have offset this northern advantage but he concluded that the Confederacy would have needed a miracle to win.[4]

Current did not, however, attempt to explain southern economic backwardness; this was instead taken as an established fact the explanation for which apparently had nothing to contribute to an understanding of the outcome of the war. It is striking that neither slavery nor the divisions within southern society featured in his analysis at all. Yet, as I have argued, slavery underlay the relative economic weakness of the Confederacy and Confederate defeat should be understood as part of the process by which unfree labor systems around the globe were dismantled – in large part because of their economic weaknesses.

How have historians responded to the claim that economic factors were paramount? In general, those who have challenged Current's argument, both his coauthors of 1960 and those who have written on the subject since, have tried to clear the way for their own competing interpretations by citing counter-examples taken usually from European or American history, where economically weaker nations have triumphed against stronger ones. The most frequently cited cases are the Dutch against Philip II's Spain, the American colonists against Great Britain and the North Vietnamese against the United States.

These examples, however, probably prove rather less than is sometimes claimed. To begin with, the American colonists and the North Vietnamese benefitted considerably from outside help offered by France and China, respectively. The Confederacy, by contrast, fought alone. More important perhaps, defeat for the larger country, even if it involved the loss of overseas or noncontiguous territory, was certainly a major blow to national prestige and, in some cases, the national economy too. It was not, however, anywhere near as catastrophic as the break-up of the nation itself. Yet this was precisely the prospect faced by Union forces in the 1860s. Throughout most of modern history the loss of colonies, or part of an

and the Politics of the Old South," *American Nineteenth Century History* V (2004), pp. 1–29. See also the author's reply (pp. 30–33). Nor shall I discuss the venerable state's rights interpretation of Frank L. Owsley, which has been almost entirely discredited in recent years. See Owsley. *State Rights in the Confederacy* (Chicago, 1925).

3. The essay by T. Harry Williams on military leadership has now been largely superseded by more recent works and will not be considered here.
4. David Donald (ed.), *Why the North Won the Civil War* (New York, 1960), p. 32.

empire, however painful, has proved far more palatable than the partition of the nation. This was particularly so in the nineteenth century when patriotic fervor reached hitherto unprecedented levels and especially in the United States, where an exuberant nationalism gripped northerners of both major parties. Finally, we should not forget that history records many examples of the stronger nation triumphing. The U.S. Civil War is often described as the first modern war and as a conflict which anticipated those of the twentieth century. But it resembled both World War I and World War II in a way that is sometimes forgotten. In all three conflicts the stronger battalions, as Current might have put it, eventually won. So the examples from the past may be less damaging to his thesis than is sometimes supposed.

### (2) Diplomacy

Also of considerable value in the 1960 volume was the contribution by Norman Graebner, who wrote "Northern Diplomacy and European Neutrality." But if Current's conclusions flowed directly from his evidence, then the value of Graebner's chapter lay rather in contradicting its author's explicit claim that diplomacy had played a vital role in determining the outcome of the war. The key question was foreign intervention. Of course, as virtually every historian (including Current) has recognised, intervention by one or more of the European powers on behalf of the Confederacy might well have been decisive. Such is the case with all wars: if a powerful ally can be recruited then the consequences can obviously be immense. But this begs the question: how likely was that intervention? And Graebner answered it quite convincingly: it was not at all likely. It was not, of course, impossible. Intervention on the part of Britain or France or Russia, or some combination of the three, required recognition of the nascent Confederate Republic, perhaps followed by, or following, an offer of mediation. The Union might, as Secretary of State William Seward had threatened, have declared war on a meddling European nation that actually recognised the Confederacy. Thus have nations sometimes been sucked into wars.

Yet, this was always an extremely improbable course of events. Russia was, of all the Great Powers, for her own reasons, the one most supportive of the Union. Not only would she not intervene alone but her steadfast refusal to give any encouragement to the Confederacy doomed any hopes of a concerted intervention or offer of mediation. Napoleon III was far more sympathetic but he made it clear that he would not intervene even diplomatically, let alone militarily, unless Great Britain joined him. Thus the attitude of the British government was crucial.

Unfortunately for the Confederacy the British premier, Lord Palmerston, mindful of the events of 1776–1783 and 1812–1815, neither had a desire to see British lives or resources wasted on yet another excursion to North America, nor wished to jeopardize British power in Canada. Although Lord John Russell, the Foreign Secretary, was more willing to offer to mediate, even he was prepared to pledge that the British would "take no part in the war unless attacked." Thus the Palmerston ministry did not recognise the Confederacy, and made no formal offer of mediation. It is far from certain that these steps would have resulted in military involvement but even they were never taken.

Ultimately European action or inaction was dictated not by sympathy for either of the belligerents in the Civil War but rather, as Graebner pointed out, by the European realist tradition of diplomacy, according to which national self-interest should determine foreign policy. The Confederacy in effect faced a cruel paradox: European states would never intervene until the Confederacy showed its military viability. But military viability required intervention. Thus military aid from the British and French, even had it occurred, would have been as much a symptom as a cause of Confederate military triumph.

Graebner concluded that the Union war effort "rested on the efficiency of its diplomatic as much as its military corps,"[5] but his own work actually refuted this contention. As he demonstrated, it would have taken a major diplomatic blunder, or set of blunders, on the part of the Union for a European power to intervene (in the absence of a Confederate victory). Similarly a military blunder, or set of blunders, might also have doomed the Union cause. But this does not demonstrate that diplomacy was as important in securing victory as the armed conflict. In what might be termed a "normal" (that is a blunder- or accident-free) situation the Union would win the war by virtue of its greater fighting power, not its diplomacy. In this way and despite himself, Graebner demonstrated not the significance, but rather the relative insignificance, of diplomacy. Those who have written on the subject since have fared no better.[6] What they have demonstrated is that foreign intervention, had it occurred, might have been decisive, not that its occurrence was at all likely.

## (3) "Died of Democracy"

David Donald, editor of the 1960 volume, found the key to Confederate defeat not in diplomacy or northern economic superiority but rather in the characteristics of the southern people at war. According to Donald, the Confederacy "died of democracy." The Confederate soldier was, he argued, simply too individualistic, too concerned to maintain his liberties. He would disobey orders he found unreasonable, he would insist upon electing his officers. Southern civilians meanwhile were equally dedicated to their liberties. They insisted on retaining the right of *habeas corpus* (less frequently suspended in the Confederacy than in the North) and their rights of free expression (so that while many newspapers were suppressed in the North none were in the Confederacy). Donald concluded that although lack of resources and manpower, weak leadership or defective strategy "were handicaps...none was fatal." "The real weakness of the Confederacy," he claimed, "was that the Southern people insisted upon retaining their democratic liberties in wartime"[7]

Few, if any, scholars have found this emphasis upon democracy convincing. In the first place, Confederate leaders like Jefferson Davis had at best a lukewarm

5. Donald (ed.), *Why the North Won*, p. 55.
6. See Howard Jones, *Union in Peril The Crisis over British Intervention in the Civil War* (Chapel Hill, 1992), p. 178. Like William W. Freehling I find that Jones's evidence does not support his overall interpretation.
7. Donald (ed.), *Why the North Won*, p. 90.

commitment to democratic values; they scorned political parties, for example, but this was not out of a commitment to popular rule but rather because, like John C. Calhoun, they believed parties gave too much scope to the populace and to the undisciplined majority. So what Donald was really describing was a death not so much from democracy as from libertarianism. This is perhaps only a minor quibble. More important, the Confederacy, as James McPherson, has observed, was far more vigorous in coercing its citizens than Donald allowed:

> As for the 'died of democracy" thesis, a good case can be made that, to the contrary, the Confederate government enforced the draft, suppressed dissent, and suspended civil liberties and democratic rights at least as thoroughly as did the Union government. The Confederacy enacted conscription a year before the Union, and raised a larger portion of its troops by drafting than did the North. And while Abraham Lincoln possessed more authority to suspend the writ of *habeas corpus* and used this power more often to arrest anti-war activists than did Jefferson Davis, the Confederate army suppressed Unionists with more ruthlessness, especially in east Tennessee and western North Carolina, than Union forces wielded against Copperheads in the North or Confederate sympathizers in the border states

Thus the Donald thesis simply lacks empirical support.[8]

### (4) Presidential leadership

Another contributor to the 1960 volume, David Potter, offered a significantly different explanation for Union victory. It was spelled out in the title of his chapter, "Jefferson Davis and the Political Factors in Confederate Defeat." Potter gave heavy emphasis to civilian leadership, especially that of the two presidents, and even went so far as to suggest that if they had exchanged places the Confederacy might have won. But he provided no means by which the relative importance of economic resources, for example, and civilian leadership could be assessed; he merely asserted that the latter was primary. In fact, like Graebner's, his chapter gave more support to Current that he appeared to realise. To begin with, he conceded that there were "innumerable measures – of manpower, of wealth, of railroad mileage, of industrial capacity – all of which point up the overwhelming advantage on the side of the Union." Then he added a further point in support of Current:

> One-sided as these statistical comparisons are, even they fail to reveal in full the economic handicaps of the South. No statistics can measure, for example, how much the Confederacy suffered from the fact that it had the kind of economy that is prostrated by war, in contrast to the Union which had the kind of economy that flourishes under wartime conditions.

8. Gabor S. Boritt (ed.), *Why the Confederacy Lost* (New York, 1992), pp. 24–25.

Then he moved from these points, which clearly furthered Current's case, to others that were intended to strengthen his own. But where the former were difficult to refute, the latter were equally difficult to sustain. In effect, he reduced problems that were societal in nature, deeply embedded in the most profound assumptions and values of the Old South, to mere individual errors. Thus he condemned Davis and other Confederate leaders who, he claimed, "embraced a fallacious belief – the King Cotton delusion – which caused them voluntarily to keep all of it [the cotton crop] at home." But whilst there can be no doubt that Davis and others misjudged the impact of a cotton embargo, to blame them for it simply misses the point. As we have seen, prior to the war the South had escaped the worst effects of the Panic of 1857 and this had further strengthened southerners' confidence in their social system. In his famous "King Cotton" speech a year later, James Henry Hammond of South Carolina had made explicit the assumptions that would subsequently govern Confederate policy. "What would happen if no cotton was furnished for three years," Hammond had asked. "England," he declared, "would topple headlong and carry the whole civilized world with her, save the South." This was the logic that underlay the cotton embargo. In fact the Confederate government did not officially sanction the cotton embargo and its implementation was due to public opinion. Cotton planters voluntarily destroyed their crops in the belief that they were striking a blow for Confederate independence. Thus the mistakes made over cotton, in any case more apparent with hindsight than at the time, grew out of southerners' most basic beliefs about the strength of their social system – with slavery as its foundation.[9]

Similarly it is all too easy to applaud Lincoln, leader of the victorious side, and castigate Davis, leader of the vanquished. Yet one of the most important tasks, perhaps the most important of all, that each president faced was the selection of generals. Here Davis did at least as well as Lincoln. Robert E. Lee is almost universally acknowledged, even by his critics, as the best the South had; he was given command of the Army of Northern Virginia in June 1862. Lincoln, however, took much longer before he found in Grant and Sherman generals who could win the war.[10] One can only wonder how historians would pillory Lincoln for having persevered so long with George McClellan, for example, if the Confederacy had won the war. But when it comes to establishing the relative importance of civilian leadership and resources (including manpower), contrary to Potter's claims, there can surely be no doubt: one can envisage a Union victory much more easily without Lincoln than without the Union's economic preponderance. This indeed is an objection that can be made to almost all the alternatives offered over many decades to Current's interpretation.

9. Donald (ed.), *Why the North Won*, pp. 91–95; *Selections from the Letters and Speeches of the Hon. James H. Hammond, of South Carolina* (New York, 1866), pp. 317–319. As Potter acknowledged, Davis's contemporary critics were actually more open to criticism than he. This again suggests we are dealing here with something more widespread, and deeper, than personal shortcomings.

10. Though he had, of course, attempted to give Lee command of the Union armies.

## (5) Confederate loss of will

In 1986 Richard E. Beringer, Herman Hattaway, Archer Jones, and William Still, Jr. published *Why the South Lost the Civil War*.[11] This volume thus appeared a quarter of a century after the Donald book and in the intervening years the United States had itself been at war in Vietnam. Although Beringer *et al.* did not devote any attention to this conflict, it had perhaps coloured their view of the Civil War. Perhaps they were conscious that the United States, despite its enormous advantage in resources and manpower, had lost. In any event, they focussed upon a factor that had surely been decisive in that struggle: the will to win. The United States had abandoned the Vietnam War because it lacked (or lost) the will to win; Beringer *et al.* advanced precisely the same explanation for Confederate defeat in the Civil War. "We contend," they wrote, "that lack of will constituted the decisive weakness in the Confederate arsenal." Like the United States in their own time perhaps, "the Confederacy succumbed to internal rather than external causes."[12]

Beringer *et al.* were convinced that, even in the second half of the war, "the South could still have won" had it not been for "the rapid diminution and ultimate death of morale, the will to win." In this sense, "the dynamics of giving up provide the key to why the South lost." Even when Lee surrendered at Appomattox, the Confederacy could still, they maintained, have continued the struggle, had the will been present. "No amount of argument," they insisted, "can obscure the fact that at the end the South still had large combat-ready armies and that these armies surrendered and went home." Thus even at that late stage "surrender was not the only choice open." As a result, for the authors "the key question" was: "why did not Confederates pursue another alternative? Why did they lack the will to make different decisions?"[13]

Much of the volume was concerned with supplying an answer to this question. Several factors were mentioned but at the heart of the argument was a claim about southern nationalism, or rather the lack of it. The Confederacy failed to generate a powerful enough sense of nationalism amongst its people. Here was the reason for Confederate lack of will: "an insufficient nationalism failed to survive the strains imposed by the lengthy hostilities." "The problem, in a nutshell," was that "the people of the South had no widely accepted mystical sense of distinct nationality."[14]

According to Beringer *et al.*, the Confederacy had only one source of this "mystical sense" of nationality and that was slavery. But slavery could not support Confederate nationalism for the simple reason that it too did not sufficiently command

11. Some of the authors' conclusions were, however, anticipated in a notable work by two of them. See Hattaway and Jones: *How the North Won: A Military History of the Civil War* (Urbana, IL, 1983). The lack-of-will thesis itself had also featured in some earlier works – see Charles R. Wesley, *The Collapse of the Confederacy* (Washington D.C., 1937); E. Merton Coulter, *The Confederate States of America, 1861–1865* (Baton Rouge, 1950).
12. Richard E. Beringer, Herman Hattaway, Archer Jones, and William N. Still, Jr., *Why the South Lost the Civil War* (Athens, GA, 1986), pp. 64, 439.
13. Beringer *et al.*, *Why the South Lost*, pp. 31, 20.
14. Beringer *et al.*, *Why the South Lost*, pp. 439, 66.

the loyalty of southerners. The authors then added their names to the lengthy list of historians who have signed up to the notion that southerners during and prior to the Civil War were consumed by guilt over slavery. "This probably widespread guilt," they concluded, "unconsciously compromised the initial determination and from the outset presaged the eventual defeat." Hence "the epitaph on the Confederacy's tombstone should read" not, as David Donald had earlier suggested, "Died of Democracy," but rather "'Died of Guilt and Failure of Will.'"[15]

There are many empirical problems with this thesis but the conceptual difficulties are still greater. Foremost among them is a problem that is associated with any explanation for military defeat that stresses lack (or loss) of will. This applies to any war, and not merely the Civil War. If a nation surrenders then it is, by definition, announcing that it lacks the will to continue the fight. Therefore any surrender, and thus almost any defeat, can, in this highly limited sense, be attributed to a "lack of will." An example may help here. When Japan surrendered in 1945 following the dropping of atomic bombs on her territory and citizens, she was announcing that, in a formal sense, she lacked the will to continue the fight. But does this mean that the Japanese lost the war because they had too weak a commitment to the values for which they were fighting? This is true only in the most literal and trivial sense. By any meaningful criteria the Japanese had a commitment to their country, their government and their society that has rarely if ever been exceeded in intensity in any belligerent nation in any armed conflict.

This does not mean, however, that lack of will is always and necessarily a vacuous concept. If Japan, to continue the analogy, had instead had only a lukewarm commitment to her values and interests then it would be entirely appropriate to explain her defeat by reference to a lack of will. In such circumstances, the phrase would be meaningful and not in any way misleading. In essence the problem with Beringer *et al.* is that they amply demonstrated the existence of a "lack of will" – but only in the literal and vacuous sense – and then drew conclusions that would be appropriate only if they had justified its use in the nontrivial and meaningful sense. In other words, there was an unrecognised slippage from one use of the term to the other.

In fact the Confederates did not lack will in the meaningful sense of the term. In 1997 Gary Gallagher published what was in part a book-length riposte to Beringer *et al.* entitled *The Confederate War*. The book was revealingly subtitled, *How Popular Will, Nationalism, and Military Strategy Could Not Stave Off Defeat* and in it Gallagher argued convincingly that the Confederates did not experience any significant degree of guilt over slavery, that their cause generated a strong sense of nationalism among civilians and soldiers alike and that the Confederates' commitment was so deep that they "sacrificed more than any other segment of white society in United States history." Thus Gallagher demonstrated that lack of will was not, in any meaningful sense, a cause of Confederate defeat.[16]

15. Beringer *et al.*, *Why the South Lost*, pp. 89, 34.
16. Gary W. Gallagher, *The Confederate War: How Popular Will, Nationalism, and Military Strategy Could Not Stave Off Defeat* (Cambridge, MA, 1997), p. 13. Gallagher also convicted Beringer *et al.* of some major logical inconsistencies. For example, he pointed

On the other hand, since final surrender by definition denotes lack of will to continue, every factor adduced by every historian who has attempted to explain the outcome of the war can be seen as contributing to a "lack of will" in this trivial sense of the term. But to cite lack of will in this trivial sense is merely to displace the question. What caused the lack of will? Sometimes Beringer *et al.* actually emphasised economic factors, even though elsewhere they denied that these were of major importance.[17] A similar confusion arose over desertion, which was recognised as a major cause of Confederate defeat. "Grant's brilliant campaign," they remarked, "did not... end the war" because "the Confederacy had lost long before, when its armies had melted away during the fall and winter." But what caused desertion? This was explained by reference to "the needs of destitute families at home." Economic suffering thus produced Confederate desertion and Confederate desertion apparently produced Confederate defeat.[18]

There are other problems with the thesis advanced by Beringer *et al.*[19] The key point however, is the conceptual one. The authors seem to have concluded that since all factors fed into a "lack of will," this must be the key cause. Hence their

out (p. 28) that "after discussing internal weaknesses in the Confederacy for more than 400 pages," they had then observed that "'Confederates fought harder than Americans ever fought, or needed to fight, facing far more formidable opposition than Americans ever confronted, and without allies.'" Clearly this raised questions about "lack of will."

17. For a denial of the role of economic factors, see Beringer *et al.*, *Why the South Lost*, p. 9. On p. 20, however, they argued that a "disintegrating economy" and a "deteriorating military situation" effectively "destroyed morale" and "created lack of will." Since the second is plainly no more than a symptom of impending defeat it cannot be adduced as a major cause: one cannot explain military defeat by a "deteriorating military situation." Thus Beringer *et al.*, whether they knew it or not, were giving primacy to the economic factors.

18. Beringer *et al.*, *Why the South Lost*, p. 333. They also cited (p. 327), as a cause of desertion, "the soldier's presumption of the inevitable outcome of the war," which tended "to persuade him that there was no more point in risking his life for a lost cause." But this was a circularity of argument: one cannot cite military defeats (the cause of this presumption) as the explanation of military defeat. Beringer *et al.* also sought (pp. 9, 424) to minimise the role of economic factors by arguing that no Confederate army lost a battle because of the lack of arms, munitions or other essential supplies." But this is an impossibly narrow understanding of the economy. In terms of "essential supplies" for an army, what can be more essential than men? Moreover, desertion became critical largely because of the South's original and overall lack of population, which made it almost impossible to replace the deserting troops.

19. For example, they seemed to believe that for a weakness to be "economic" – it must lie in the sphere of production and not distribution, even though Current (and others) always, and rightly, made much of the deficiencies of the Confederate railroad network. Elsewhere they declared that shortages of "raw materials" of which the Confederacy had, they recognised, an inadequate supply, "proved... as critical as manpower," having apparently forgotten that elsewhere they had argued that the Confederacy lost because of lack of manpower. Even more alarmingly, they argued that the North could survive a loss of will that might prove fatal to the Confederacy: "the battles took place on someone else's territory, and *the country [i.e. the North] had sufficiently abundant resources of manpower and treasure to leave ample margin for waste and error or to compensate for a lack of enthusiasm or flagging will* [emphasis added]. Many families could live relatively normal lives, disturbed only by an empty chair at the table and sometimes distressing newspaper headlines." In other words, morale was a significant factor only because of economic inferiority! – Beringer *et al.*, *Why the South Lost*, pp. 12, 25–26.

remark: "economic liabilities played an important role in Confederate fortunes *but primarily through the debilitating effect on the public will of the pervasive smell of defeat* [emphasis added]."[20] But here they were, without knowing it, using "lack of will" in its empty, trivial sense. The authors were correct in assuming that causal factors, in order to be effective, had to contribute to a "lack of will." But, not seeing that the term was devoid of meaning in this context, they drew exactly the wrong conclusion and ended by giving primacy to a factor that was in reality largely devoid of explanatory power. Thus Beringer *et al.*, despite claims to the contrary, were unable to dispose of, and indeed on occasion actually reinforced, Current's thesis.

It is important, however, to discuss their understanding of slavery and its impact on the War. Far more convincing than their claims about slavery-induced guilt was their analysis of the effect slavery had on determining Confederate strategy throughout, and especially at the end of, the War. The possibility of a guerrilla war had not received much attention from Donald and his colleagues in 1960 but by 1987 with many examples, including, one assumes, that of Vietnam, before them, Beringer *et al.* gave it much fuller consideration. They then explained that slavery had ruled this possibility out:

> But even if they [the Confederates] had wished to continue, slavery would have inhibited the usual war waged by small units and guerrillas against invading armies. Indeed, many slaves already had become sympathizers and recruits for the Union. The same bitter experience of Santo Domingo might have come to the South, just as southerners always had feared.

Then, lest there should be any misunderstanding, they hammered the point home:

> In any guerrilla resistance the black population in the Confederacy would constitute a resource for an enormously powerful indigenous counterinsurgency force. The turmoil introduced into the countryside would have made slavery more precarious, not less, and would have provided slaves with even more opportunity to subvert the Confederate war effort, perhaps by sabotage and espionage, but more likely by escape and enlistment in the Union army.

Slavery, the cause of secession and four years of military conflict, would thus have limited the extent and persistence of the Confederacy's resistance even had it wished to carry on beyond the defeat of the principal armies.

---

20. Beringer *et al.*, *Why the South Lost*, p. 13. Always their emphasis returned to "lack of will." Thus "a declining economy, added to other woes, caused southerners to recalculate the costs of war and to reconsider alternative decisions, with an effect on morale obvious to all" (p. 13). Again: "although economic factors affected the outcome of the war, they did so primarily in an indirect manner" (p. 13). Finally, they described the impact of Sherman's march through Georgia and the Carolinas: "vulnerability, suffering, and the apprehension that those conditions would continue indefinitely discouraged all southerners, not merely the population exposed to Sherman's raids" (p. 350).

Thus, although the overall thesis of their book gave no role to slavery other than as a source of moral wavering (and therefore as a factor promoting "lack of will"), here as elsewhere their reasoning was quite compatible with, and indeed pointed towards, a very different conclusion: slavery, not lack of will, played a key role in ensuring Confederate defeat by ruling out the only alternative to surrender.[21]

Nor was this of minor significance. As we have seen, the "lack of will" thesis entailed a claim that there were other options open to the Confederates when they surrendered; only the lack of a sufficient desire for victory prompted them to give up. This is perhaps the weakest point in the entire interpretive schema put forward by Beringer *et al.* Yet it needed to be the strongest. For "lack of will" to acquire real explanatory power and to rise above its status as a truism, it was essential for the authors to show that there was indeed a realistic alternative to surrender and that it would have been taken had the will been present. But the only alternative that Beringer *et al.* could cite was guerrilla warfare, which, as they themselves convincingly argued, would have fatally undermined, and would have been fatally undermined by, slavery. (This argument did not sit well with their emphasis upon slavery-induced guilt since Confederates might, one would have thought, have been less concerned to protect an institution that induced guilt among them and that was in any case a source of weakness.)

These conundrums are not easily resolved – as long as one is committed to the "lack of will" thesis. But the problems disappear if instead one maintains the following propositions: first that southerners fought to maintain slavery; second that slavery did not induce guilt (to any significant degree); third that there were no alternatives available at the end of the war other than the guerrilla war; fourth that the existence of slavery (amongst other factors) ruled that one out; and fifth that lack of will was not, therefore, in any meaningful sense, the reason for Confederate surrender and defeat.[22]

### (6) Generals, military strategy

In the early 1990s, history, or at least historiography, repeated itself. In 1991, another group of historians assembled at Gettysburg College, just as their predecessors had done a generation earlier, to discuss the outcome of the Civil War. In 1992, came the final product of their labors. Once again there were five contributions. The book appeared in 1992 under the title *Why the Confederacy Lost*.

In his introduction to the work, the editor, Gabor S. Boritt (who did not himself contribute a chapter) offered some general remarks about it. "We focus," he announced, "on military matters" and noted that this differentiated his colleagues from their predecessors who had instead "looked at various facets of the war such as economics, politics and so on." In this sense, the authors, he acknowledged, "do not so much replace as supplement the earlier book." But the focus on military matters was in no sense accidental. It probably owed much to the contributors'

---

21. Beringer *et al.*, *Why the South Lost*, pp. 436–439.
22. In what was one of his few areas of agreement with Beringer *et al.*, Gallagher too maintained that a guerrilla war was not a feasible option for the Confederacy – Gallagher, *The Confederate War*, p. 141.

overall view of history and the historical process, for all the scholars, according to Boritt, believed that "in the Civil War either side might have won." The result was an emphasis upon contingency. This was particularly evident in the views of James McPherson but Boritt stressed that "we all agree with McPherson on the contingent nature of history." Thus, the volume purported to be concerned with military issues and purported to illustrate the importance of contingency, rather than (one would presume) structure. But as we shall see, appearances were deceptive and, despite the considerable value of the book, the authors in fact demonstrated, as far as the outcome of the Civil War was concerned, neither the pre-eminence of military factors nor, in any meaningful sense, the contingent nature of the historical process.[23]

It will be appropriate to begin with the contribution of Gary Gallagher whose views we have already in part considered. Gallagher's purpose undoubtedly conformed to Boritt's overall characterisation of the volume since his very title stressed military factors, in this case the role of military leaders: "'Upon their Success Hang Momentous Interests': Generals." The underlying assumption of the chapter was that "generals made a very great difference in determining the outcome of the war." The obvious question was thus "which generals?" and here Gallagher was, once again, unequivocal. Without in any way criticising those who chose to study the lesser figures, he emphasised the big three, on whom historians have traditionally focused:

> if the campaigns of Grant, Lee and Sherman are removed from the equation, performances at the top levels of command on each side translate into largely negative influences on the respective populations. They convey no sense of building momentum toward eventual victory. In fact, it is difficult to imagine a scenario within which any other Union or Confederate general could either formulate or implement a decisive strategy.

Thus an emphasis upon the role of generals in fact amounted to an emphasis upon the acts and decisions of the triumvirate.[24]

Yet Gallagher did not claim that Confederate defeat was the product of defective Confederate strategy or defective Confederate generalship. On the contrary, he came riding to the rescue of Confederate General Robert E. Lee. Lee has been criticised by some historians for displaying an excessive degree of aggression: a more defensive strategy, his critics have claimed, would have prolonged the war and thus increased the likelihood of the Union abandoning the struggle. But Gallagher (in his book as well as his contribution to the Boritt volume) pointed out that this strategy also foundered on "southern military traditions" and southern "civilian expectations." "Morale," he observed, "required the type of victories Lee supplied from the Seven Days through Chancellorsville, and without which the Confederacy almost certainly would have collapsed sooner." Moreover, a more

---

23. Boritt (ed.), *Why the Confederacy Lost*, pp. 13–14.
24. Boritt (ed.), *Why the Confederacy Lost*, pp. 85, 88. Gallagher acknowledged that Winfield Scott might also be a contender for inclusion in this select list.

defensive strategy, if adopted by the Confederacy as a whole, would again have involved surrendering territory. It would therefore, Gallagher also observed, have conflicted with "the overwhelming imperative of maintaining white control in a slave-based society" and thus was necessarily rejected. "Too many critics of Lee's offensive movements," he concluded, "neglect to place them within the context of what the Confederate people would tolerate."[25]

This was an extremely important and valid point but it was not easily reconciled with the stress on the role of generals. For the recognition that generals were, to some degree, the prisoners of public opinion led towards an examination of social structure and ideology and away from the claim that generals themselves "made a very great difference" or, come to that, that contingency ruled. Gallagher devoted about half his chapter to Lee. At first sight this was fully justified since Lee's reputation is now probably more hotly contested than that of the two foremost Union commanders. But another problem confronted his analysis. The more he defended Lee and the more effective the defense – and Gallagher offered an extremely compelling defense – the more he demonstrated the irrelevance of generalship to the actual outcome of the war. "Far from hastening the demise of the Confederacy," he concluded, "Lee's generalship provided hope that probably carried the South beyond the point at which its citizens would otherwise have abandoned their quest for nationhood." Thus Gallagher's discussion of Lee in effect achieved precisely the opposite of the intended effect. It showed the unimportance of generalship to the outcome of the war. This difficulty went entirely unacknowledged by the author. Yet he was perhaps vaguely aware of it. "The generalships of Grant, Lee, and Sherman demand special attention," he wrote in his concluding sentence, "because to a significant extent those three officers determined not only which side would win *but also how long the contest would last* [emphasis added]." The problem was, of course, that here he had introduced a very different question, a perfectly valid one, and one whose answer might well require a full discussion of Lee's generalship. But the reasons the war lasted so long are not the same as the reasons for Confederate defeat.[26]

In a sense, therefore, Gallagher might have been better advised to spend more of his chapter discussing Sherman, who received two pages out of twenty-seven and Grant, who received three. But perhaps not, for again there were problems. One of Sherman's achievements, he explained, was to bring enormous pressure on Confederate civilians, with a consequent devastating impact upon civilian morale. "No officer," Gallagher suggested, "understood better the immense psychological damage large-scale raids could inflict on civilians (and by extension on their relatives and neighbors in the southern armies)." Gallagher clearly regarded this as a significant factor in Confederate defeat and the argument is difficult to challenge. But we are prompted to ask: why did the Confederacy not do the same in northern territory? Presumably it was not an error or oversight that prevented it, otherwise

25. Gallagher, *The Confederate War*, pp. 126–127, 10; Boritt (ed.), *Why the Confederacy Lost*, p. 25. Gallagher observed that every siege – when the Confederates did take the defensive role – ended in Union victory – *The Confederate War*, p. 134
26. Boritt (ed.), *Why the Confederacy Lost*, pp. 107–108.

Lee would once more be in the firing line. There can be only one answer: the Confederacy lacked the resources – in both manpower and materiel.[27]

So with Grant's contribution. His achievement was to bring superior northern resources to bear. "The North," according to Gallagher, "always enjoyed a substantial edge in manpower and almost every manufacturing category, but none of Grant's predecessors proved equal to the task of harnessing and directing that latent strength." But Grant was different and his "ability to do so stands as one of his greatest achievements."[28]

Thus the achievement of Grant and Sherman was essentially to fight a war in which the North's superiority in resources and manpower would be decisive. Yet such an emphasis – as evidenced in the work of Gallagher and others – is quite consistent with the argument of Current who, as we have seen, never claimed that the Union's superiority would automatically produce victory, no matter who led her troops. If a general succeeds in bringing superior resources to bear, should he or the resources receive the credit? Many historians of the Civil War, and especially military historians, seem to believe the former but this elevation of personal agency over structure is, at best, problematic. Although other capable generals might well have been found, there was simply no substitute for the Union's superiority in resources and manpower.

Gallagher himself seemed on occasion to recognise this. "The final failure," he wrote in *The Confederate Nation*, "lay not so much with Confederate strategy as with the men available to Davis to carry it out." By "final" he apparently meant not last chronologically but instead "ultimate" in a causal sense. And when he referred to "men" he meant not their quality but their quantity. As he later remarked, "persevering despite great adversity," the Confederates "surrendered only when their pool of manpower had been ravaged." Once again this is an interpretation that does not easily square with the emphasis upon generals and contingency. Gallagher had actually shown that generals did not in fact alter this decisive structural imbalance and that contingent factors did not in fact prevent that imbalance from determining the outcome of the war. What he had demonstrated was not that generals actually made a large difference but rather that they might have made a large difference (a proposition that no one has ever denied), but actually did not – a very different contention.[29]

Another of the contributors to the Boritt volume was Archer Jones, who, it will be recalled, was one of the authors of the 1987 book, *Why the South Lost the Civil War*. His contribution to the Boritt volume was a valuable discussion, essentially in narrative form, of strategy and of the links between strategy and politics. Indeed the chapter can be used as a good summary of the major military events of the War. Perhaps it was not intended to demonstrate the role of contingency because the

27. Boritt (ed.), *Why the Confederacy Lost*, pp. 92–94, 89–92.
28. Boritt (ed.), *Why the Confederacy Lost*, p. 91.
29. Gallagher, *The Confederate War*, pp. 153, 172. Gallagher also claimed that the Confederacy nearly won the war on several occasions, and this claim is crucial to his entire argument. Indeed it is difficult to see how the emphasis upon contingency, upon which all contributors to the volume were apparently agreed, can be sustained without this claim. As we shall see, however, it is a highly questionable claim.

author scarcely addressed this question. But it was presumably intended to explain Confederate defeat – otherwise why include it in the volume? Here, however, the achievement was entirely a negative one in that Jones demonstrated that strategy was not a significant factor. "In that neither belligerent outshone the other in its strategy," he concluded, "military strategy had a neutral effect in the war." One would have to look elsewhere for the explanation.[30]

## (7) Soldierly commitment

Reid Mitchell, another contributor to the same volume, did indeed look elsewhere and the title of his chapter, "The Perseverance of the Soldiers" announced where he had found it. Or perhaps it would be more accurate to say that it announced where he thought he had found it. For once again appearances were deceptive. Mitchell went some way to endorsing Current's interpretation and agreed that in the Civil War "the heaviest battalions" as usual won. But he added a further point: "the perseverance of the soldiers" or, more generally, the resolution of the Union forces and its leaders, had been indispensable. "Without that resolution," he declared, "the heaviest battalions could not have been brought into play." Thus, he stated flatly, "that resolution was the cause of Union victory and Confederate defeat in 1865."[31]

Here Mitchell seemed to imply that this factor was at least as important as the ones Current had emphasised. But there was some ambiguity. Elsewhere he argued that Union superiority in numbers and resources made victory "probable," though not "inevitable." Did the "perseverance of the soldiers" complement the Union's superiority in numbers and resources and thus convert a probability into a certainty? If so Mitchell's supplement to the Current thesis would certainly have been of great importance.[32]

Unfortunately Mitchell was unable to make good his claims for soldierly perseverance. The problem did not lie, however, in demonstrating that the Union soldiers did indeed "persevere." On the contrary he easily established the appropriateness of this term. Pointing out that the commitment of hundreds of thousands of northerners was not, in any sense, "foreordained," he reminded his readers of the importance of antislavery to a minority of them and of the Union to virtually all of them. But he also insisted that soldiers were not merely loyal to the Union. They were also, or soon became, loyal to their fellow soldiers. "Small unit cohesion," loyalty to others in the same mess, company or regiment was "even stronger" than loyalty to the Union. This was a factor that historians must not overlook.[33]

Yet it was also one that could scarcely help explain the outcome of the war, unless it could be shown not to have existed or not to have existed in the same degree, within the Confederacy. After all one can scarcely explain a victory by reference to factors that are present in equal measure on each side. Mitchell conceded

30. Boritt (ed.), *Why the Confederacy Lost*, p. 76.
31. Boritt (ed.), *Why the Confederacy Lost*, p. 131.
32. Boritt (ed.), *Why the Confederacy Lost*, p. 112.
33. Boritt (ed.), *Why the Confederacy Lost*, p. 113, 120–121.

that "the experience of fighting together should have created the same small-unit loyalties in the Confederate army." "And," he added, "it did create the same loyalties." In so doing he surrendered what was intended to be the main point of his contribution to the volume.[34]

Yet although it did not fulfill its stated purpose, Mitchell's chapter successfully made a different and much more important point. Running through his pages was a concern with slavery. First, he too confirmed that slavery prevented the Confederacy from adopting a guerrilla war. Second he demonstrated that it limited the Confederate war effort (Confederate "perseverance"?) by creating fears among the troops of what was happening back home as a result of slave flight or "insubordination." Here was a factor that assuredly could supplement Current's thesis because "slavery meant that the Confederacy went to war with its population divided." According to Mitchell, "far more so than in any other American war, the soldier in the field could not count on the unified support of the civilians back home." Thus, despite his explicit claims, Mitchell's argument actually made a case not for "the perseverance of the soldiers" but rather for the incorporation of slavery into a causal schema that could explain Confederate defeat in the Civil War.[35]

### (8) The role of African Americans

This emphasis upon slavery was, in a sense, continued in the volume by Joseph Glatthaar. Glatthaar's subject, however, was not so much slavery but rather "the African-American Role in Union Victory." In effect, he drew up a list of the achievements of African Americans during the war and assessed their overall role in bringing about Confederate defeat. He observed that some 180,000 served in the Union army overall with perhaps 100,000 serving at the end of the war. He argued that these troops, by helping tip the balance of power in favour of the Union, were "quite possibly" essential to victory, and he reminded his readers that this had indeed been the view of Abraham Lincoln. Moreover, African Americans furthered the Union war effort in other, less direct ways. Slaves who sabotaged work in the South, who were unruly or who challenged their masters or, what was then equally likely, their masters' wives, either damaged the Confederate economy or increased the pressure on Confederate soldiers to desert. Above all perhaps, African Americans themselves deserted the farms and plantations of the South, with perhaps as many as 500,000 or even 700,000 finding refuge with the Union armies. By the last months of the War, the cumulative effect was to unravel southern society and to cripple the southern war effort. In a sense, this crucial contribution was acknowledged when the Confederates, shortly before the end of the War, decided to arm and free some of their slaves. As Major General Patrick Cleburne, the principal advocate of the scheme, pointed out, "the fear of their slaves" was "continually haunting" southern whites with the result that "from silence and apprehension many of these soon learn to wish the war stopped on any terms."[36]

34.  Boritt (ed.), *Why the Confederacy Lost*, p. 122.
35.  Boritt (ed.), *Why the Confederacy Lost*, p. 125.
36.  Boritt (ed.), *Why the Confederacy Lost*, pp. 159–160.

Glatthaar's case was well made in that the African American contribution has until comparatively recently been neglected in the historiography of Union victory. In a sense, his argument was, however, very much compatible with the references to slavery as a cause of Confederate defeat which we have seen occasionally poking out of the historical literature. The only minor quibble that might be offered here is to the effect that, by casting his interpretation in racial terms, he emphasised not slavery but rather African Americans. Yet, as we have seen, in the larger scheme of things, it is slavery which deserves greater prominence.

### (9) Contingency

It remains to consider the contribution of James McPherson to the Boritt volume. McPherson is probably, and rightly, regarded as the leading scholar of the American Civil War. Amongst a long and imposing list of publications his 1988 Pulitzer Prize winning volume *Battle Cry of Freedom* stands out. Since McPherson specifically addressed the reasons for Confederate defeat in both works, it will be convenient to treat them together.[37]

In both works, McPherson discussed the interpretations that scholars had previously advanced. He pointed out many of the weaknesses in the various schools of thought. Indeed there is no better short introduction to the subject than the chapter in the Boritt volume entitled "American Victory, American Defeat." What of the Current thesis? Here he made an important acknowledgement. His conclusion was that "northern superiority in manpower and resources was a *necessary* but not a *sufficient* condition of victory."[38]

What then was McPherson's own view? At the heart of it was a denial of inevitability. "There was nothing inevitable," he wrote, "about northern victory in the Civil War." This was the key issue. Common to too many of the schools of thought, he complained, was the assumption that the outcome of the war was somehow preordained. But this gave too little room for the random play of events, individuals and forces. Instead the historian should emphasise "contingency." "It is this element of contingency," McPherson concluded, "that is missing from generalizations about the cause of Confederate defeat."[39]

To substantiate this claim he made specific reference to four "turning points" during the war. Two came in 1862, the first with McClellan's failure in June to capture Richmond (which ensured the war would go on), the second with Antietam (which boosted northern morale and Republican political fortunes, produced the Emancipation Proclamation and doomed Confederate hopes of European intervention). Another came in 1863 with Union triumphs at Vicksburg and Gettysburg (which also rescued northern morale). Finally, in 1864, the capture of Atlanta in conjunction with Sheridan's exploits in the Shenandoah again led to a resurgence

37. James M. McPherson, *Battle Cry of Freedom: The American Civil War* (New York, 1988). The following discussion of McPherson's work in no sense does full justice to it. *Battle Cry of Freedom*, for example, is narrative history at its best.
38. Boritt (ed.), *Why the Confederacy Lost*, p. 23. Thus, McPherson rejected the "lack of will" thesis by emphasising the sacrifices made for the Confederate cause and neatly demonstrated the difference between lack of will (not initially present in the South) and loss of will (essentially reducible to the underlying factors that were bringing defeat).
39. Boritt (ed.), *Why the Confederacy Lost*, p. 40.

of northern morale, ensured Lincoln's triumph in the presidential election, and put the Union firmly on the road to ultimate victory. McPherson ended his chapter by reasserting the importance of contingency.

> To understand why the South lost, in the end, we must turn from large generalizations that imply inevitability and study instead the contingency that hung over each military campaign, each battle, each election, each decision during the war. When we comprehend what happened in these events, how it happened, why it happened, and what its consequences were, then we will be on our way toward answering the question: Why did the Confederacy lose the War?

In *Battle Cry of Freedom* he explained that "this phenomenon of contingency" could "best be presented in a narrative format." Hence it was "a format this book has tried to provide."[40]

How is this argument to be assessed? It is, of course, true to say that superior resources and manpower did not, of themselves, make Union victory inevitable. After all if the Union had thrown away its advantages by appointing none but blundering generals or electing none but imbecilic leaders then victory might not have come. But, as we have seen, this was acknowledged from the start by Richard N. Current. And it is difficult to see how it could not be acknowledged. An impersonal factor that helps bring on victory is likely to make itself felt through human agency and the need for that agency creates the possibility that errors, misjudgment, or simple misfortune might intrude. In other words, the idea that any set of factors made victory utterly inevitable is problematic. We are dealing with probabilities, not certainties.

The *Oxford Dictionary* defines "contingent" as "happening by chance." So if contingency played, as McPherson claimed, a key role in Union victory then this is another way of saying that luck was, overall, on the side of the Union. Curiously, McPherson and others who take this view seem reluctant to state their argument in quite these terms. Nevertheless, the question becomes: were the Union forces, overall, lucky?

This has never been demonstrated. And *Battle Cry of Freedom* yields no such argument. Indeed might one not as easily argue that the Union won despite bad luck? Could it not be said that the Union was unlucky in her generals, for example, until the elevation of Grant and Sherman? More fundamentally, how are the different slices of good and bad luck to be weighed? This would seem a much more difficult task than McPherson allows.

Moreover, the emphasis on "contingency" poses an even greater problem. It would at first sight appear difficult to find a more anti-determinist approach. Yet appearances are deceptive. Let us consider a hypothetical possibility. Let us imagine that one side in a war because of its superiority in numbers and resources, and because slavery undermined the enemy's war effort, would, with merely

---

40. Boritt (ed.), *Why the Confederacy Lost*, pp. 41–42; McPherson, *Battle Cry of Freedom*, p. 858.

average luck, and no advantage or disadvantage in the quality of its leadership, civilian or military, inevitably win. How would this victory be secured? If even the weaker side could itself deploy hundreds of thousands of men, then a single encounter, involving only a portion of each side's available troops, would probably not be decisive. Instead a protracted conflict would probably ensue. There is no reason to assume that the weaker side would fail to gain some victories, and indeed some important ones, before the superior strength of the stronger won through. And this would probably happen in a way that would be, for the historian, so untidy as to suggest "contingency" was at play. There would also be "turning points." And some scholars would then be able to conclude that "contingency" had determined the outcome.

In other words, McPherson's position risks a determinism of its own. How is he to avoid a conclusion that *all* protracted struggles are decided by "contingency," that advantages in manpower and resources can *never* (in the absence of a single knock-out blow) be by a wide margin the most important cause of victory, precisely as Current claimed for the Civil War? Can we really claim, a priori, that all major conflicts are, to a crucial extent, determined by the throw of the dice? And if not, what distinguishes those that are from those that are not? A careful reading of *Battle Cry of Freedom* yields no answers to these questions.

The essential task for those who espouse "contingency" is to demonstrate that the weaker side almost won. This was the argument of several, perhaps all, the contributors to the Boritt volume, including McPherson himself. It was in this context that he drew attention to the four turning points. Yet these four turning points were really only three since that of June 1862, rather than promoting Union victory, actually benefited the Confederacy and thus prolonged the war. It therefore helps explain why the war lasted so long but not why the Union won it. What of the other turning points?

We have already considered the other turning point of 1862 and found that the prospects for European intervention, the only action that might then have been decisive, were in fact extremely remote. This leaves the turning points of 1863 and 1864. Of all Civil War campaigns, Vicksburg was surely one whose outcome was least explicable in terms of good fortune. The Confederates lacked the resources and manpower to compete in both the eastern and western theaters and also lacked the resources, including shipping, to challenge the Union effectively in the river war. And it might be worth noting that, according to McPherson, the surrender of Vicksburg was dictated by "inexorable circumstances."[41] The explanation for the Union victory at Gettysburg, on the other hand, is more complex but a strong case might be made for attributing it to Confederate strategy, for which Lee was primarily responsible but which, as we have seen, was grounded in some of the most fundamental attitudes of the Confederacy. Certainly there is no consensus among historians that it was attributable primarily to luck.[42]

The final turning point is the one on which the advocates of contingency normally rely. It is claimed that without the triumphs of 1864 at Atlanta and (perhaps)

---

41. McPherson, *Battle Cry of Freedom*, p. 635.
42. Nor is this the conclusion implied in McPherson's discussion – *Battle Cry of Freedom*, pp. 653–663.

in the Shenandoah, Lincoln might have lost the presidency to George McClellan who would, on assuming office, have stopped the war and then either successfully persuaded the Confederates to rejoin the Union or, failing in this effort, would have found himself unable to restart it. Thus it is not claimed that the victory at Atlanta was itself attributable to good luck (an extremely difficult proposition to maintain) but rather that its timing was not merely crucial but also highly fortuitous.

But as William W. Freehling has demonstrated, this scenario is highly improbable. First, there is no reason to believe that if stopped the war could not have been restarted. Second, McClellan was adamant on the need to restore the Union and even the Peace Democrats (outnumbered by the War Democrats in any case) would not contemplate a permanent separation. Third, McClellan finally, after some wavering, came out against even a temporary armistice. Fourth, the Confederacy would not have re-entered the Union even if a Democratic president had made concessions on slavery, so that war would then have recommenced. Fifth, over and above all these considerations, even a defeated Lincoln would have had until March 1865 to win the war. The President in fact made it clear that, if defeated, in those months he would fight with undiminished resolve. And by inauguration day the war would have been almost won.[43]

Perhaps the problem with McPherson's interpretation lay in a conceptual confusion about contingency. Those who have argued for northern superiority in resources and manpower have not claimed that this should necessarily have resulted, or that it did in fact result, in a smooth passage towards northern victory. In the absence of an early and sudden knockout blow (which itself would have required something more than an overall superiority in resources and manpower to achieve), the tide of the war would almost inevitably be subject to ebbs and flows. McPherson's stress on "contingency" in effect spoke to these vicissitudes. But this does not mean that, overall, luck was with the Union and McPherson, perhaps because of his commitment to a narrative form, mounted no sustained argument to that effect. What he showed was that contingent events operated within certain structural constraints, rather than that, in explaining Union victory and Confederate defeat, contingency itself defeated or even supplemented structural factors.

Whatever its merits, therefore, *Why The Confederacy Lost* must be judged at best only a partial success in addressing the central issue. And this criticism can be extended to the other works surveyed here. The Current thesis has stood up probably best. Those scholars who have accepted that northern superiority in numbers and resources was a necessary but insufficient condition – and no one has successfully challenged it – are in fact merely endorsing Current's own claims. But the attempts to adduce additional factors, and especially additional factors of equal weight, have been, on the whole, unsuccessful. They usually turn out, on closer examination, to be claims that such factors might have been crucial but in fact were not. Thus diplomacy might have been decisive – but only if an improbable series of blunders had been committed. Generals can make a great

---

43. Freehling, *South versus the South*, 186–188.

difference – but actually they did not. Civilian leadership can sometimes tip the balance – but it has not been shown that it did so in this war. "Contingency" sometimes rules in war but it has yet to be demonstrated that the Union enjoyed overall especially good fortune.

The one factor that emerges as a strong candidate for inclusion in a list of causes is one which has crept in, so to speak, almost unnoticed. This factor is slavery and it is one that none of the authors discussed has actually chosen to highlight or to dignify by heralding in the title of even a single chapter. But, contrary to what these scholars imply, slavery does not in fact sit alongside the Current thesis. Instead it underlies and indeed subsumes the Current thesis. Here, however, we encounter the problems posed by overspecialisation. As we have seen, those who have emphasised the Union's advantage in manpower and resources, including Current himself, have treated this superiority as a given. With their gaze fixed upon the war years themselves these scholars have taken northern superiority as an established fact. Of course to examine its roots they would need to journey far from the battlefield, far from the events of the War and into the darker recesses of economic history. This is forbidding territory indeed, especially since the question of southern economic performance and the impact of slavery upon it, is still unresolved. Yet just as the debates between economic historians over slavery help make the outcome of the Civil War more intelligible, the War, by illuminating the weaknesses of the peculiar institution sheds light upon the economics of slavery. In other words, overspecialisation has damaged the interpretations of scholars in both fields.[44]

## (10) Conclusion

It only remains to delineate the role of class within this causal framework. Historians have rarely emphasised class as a cause of Confederate defeat except when pointing to the class divisions implied in the slogan "a rich man's war and a poor man's fight." Yet, ironically, this is perhaps its least important manifestation and one must go beyond an approach which reduces class to divisions between rich and poor.

Unfortunately this is one of the two most common treatments of class in American historical writing. The other is the equation of class with class-consciousness. For the purpose of understanding the outcome of the Civil War, it is equally inadequate. The key effects of class relationships may or may not involve class-consciousness – that is itself a genuinely contingent question.

44. A few scholars over the years have emphasised the role of slavery. Thus Armstead Robinson in *Bitter Fruits of Bondage: The Demise of Slavery and the Collapse of the Confederacy, 1861–1865* (Charlottesville, VA, 2005) has stressed its damaging impact in the war years themselves – but without seeing the effect it had on the southern economy before the first shot was fired. Raimondo Luraghi has advanced a view closer to mine but without any emphasis upon slave resistance – Luraghi, *The Rise and Fall of the Plantation South* (New York, 1978). See also earlier works such as Wesley, *Collapse of the Confederacy*; W. E. B. Du Bois, *Black Reconstruction in America* (New York, 1935); Bell Irvin Wiley, *Plain People of the Confederacy* (Baton Rouge, 1949); Wiley, *Southern Negroes, 1861–1865* (New Haven, 1938).

Instead class should be understood as a richer, more subtle concept. Its effects are sometimes visible, but usually in a highly mediated form, in a society's trajectory of development for example (the inhibition of economic development in the South), in its choice of military strategy (the impossibility of a guerrilla war), in the loyalty or disloyalty of its people (the flight and the disruption caused by the slaves). Class creates not only conflict but also the potential for conflict.[45] Class precludes certain kinds of economic development, even as it makes others more probable. It sometimes generates class-consciousness and divisions between economic interest groups, but, equally often, it creates, in a far more subtle way, fault lines in a society whose impact must be traced with great care and sensitivity. This is not least because the outcome of great struggles can sometimes depend upon them.

45.  In this context, it may be worth repeating Gallagher's reference to "the risk of disrupting their [the Confederates'] social and economic control over 3.5 million enslaved black people." Needless to say, such evidence never feeds into a general assessment of the importance of class – because of the flawed understanding of the term.

# Index

Mississippi, 74, 160; and proslavery sentiment, 30; and secession, 150; banking in, 109; economy of, 50; mentioned, 52; politics in, 79, 92, 480, 481, 489, 490; slavery in, 102, 120, 617

*Mississippian*, and Compromise of 1850, 27, 30, 36; and Kansas-Nebraska Act, 548; and northern Democrats, 62; and northern opinion, 33; and slavery, 49, 120; and state's economy, 51; fear of northerners, 87; mentioned, 28; on Kansas, 47; on Kansas-Nebraska Act, 56, 57

Missouri, 48, 54, 58, 85, 142, 174, 322, 416, 418, 425, 546; abolition in, 408; admission of, 23, 245, 399; and events in Kansas, 69; antislavery in, 67, 137, 143; antislavery in, 88; politics in, 57–61, 64, 70, 96, 132, 252, 328, 461, 480, 573, 611, 612, 615, 616, 617, 634; slaveholders in, 71; slavery in, 57, 62, 63, 64, 68, 70, 72, 75–76, 86, 103, 105, 107, 169, 170, 230, 616

Missouri Compromise, 21, 174, 212, 420, 560; and Henry Clay, 546; Stephen A. Douglas on, 420; extension of, 317, 318, 322; provisions of, 46, 58, 418; repeal of, 47, 54, 59, 61, 67, 168, 173, 174, 183, 184, 249, 425, 469, 546, 597

Missouri crisis, 204

Mobile *Daily Advertiser*, 489

Monroe Doctrine, 386, 392

Montgomery *Advertiser*, 94, 160

Montgomery *Mail*, 141

Moore, Andrew B., 150

Moore, Oscar F., 571

Morehead, Charles S., 595

Morrill, Lott, 197, 201

Morris, Thomas, 245

Napton, William B., 70, 74

Nashville Conventions of 1850, 29, 32, 49, 85, 488

Nashville *Patriot*, 143, 597

Nashville *Republican Banner*, 608

National Banking Acts, 631

*National Democratic Review*, 347, 355, 356, 360, 361, 370, 377, 387, 389, 391, 395, 401, 426

*National Intelligencer*, 552

nativism, *see* Know Nothings, nativists

nativists (*see also* Know Nothings), 208, 521, 527, 534, 537, 542, 558, 562, 565, 567

Nebraska, 60, 344, 415, 416; territory of, 46

New Hampshire; economy of, 201; labor in, 295; politics in, 131, 200, 441, 558, 562; religious test in, 520

New Hampshire *Patriot*, 433

New Jersey; politics in, 112, 131, 443, 464, 558, 601

New Mexico; slavery in, 119, 120, 179; territory of, 24, 35, 45, 55, 317, 318, 320, 421, 422, 427

New Orleans *Bee*, 547, 610

New Orleans *Delta*, 137

New Orleans *Picayune*, 78

New York state; economy of, 291; politics in, 127, 131, 180–83, 194, 208, 213, 234, 275, 324, 360, 443, 454, 507, 519, 551, 558–59, 562, , 582–83, 619, 623, 636; temperance in, 372–73, 498, 514

New York *Courier and Enquirer*, 213, 234, 324

New York *Evening Post*, 193, 196, 200, 309

*New York Times*, 222, 230, 274, 326; and Whig party, 494; in war, 329; on secession, 306

New York *Tribune*, 234, 237, 291, 397; and secession, 323; and temperance, 511; and Whig party, 494; on secession, 306, 310, 311, 314, 315; on war, 329

Nicholson, A.O.P., 155

Niles, John M., 188

North Carolina; abolition in, 608; antislavery in, 88, 129; mentioned, 26, 53, 142, 484; politics in, 34, 52, 90, 98, 489, 554, 579, 593, 608, 609, 611, 612, 615, 617; slavery in, 107

northern Democrats, *see* Democrats

northern Whigs (*see also* Whigs) 205, 206, 207, 208, 231, 249, 472, 473, 486, 487, 491, 492; and Kansas-Nebrasak Act, 546, 551; and nativism, 537

Northwest Ordinance, 178, 222, 408, 421

O'Sullivan, John L., 370, 385

Ohio, 201, 249, 415, 561, 567; banking in, 109; economy of, 106; politics in, 131, 440, 558

*Ohio State Journal*, 325

Old Line Whigs, 485, 588, 618, 620

Olds, Edwon B., 351, 360, 404

Oliver, Mordecai, 569

Order of Star Spangled Banner, 519

Order of United Americans, 507, 519, 529, 536, 541

Oregon; acquisition of, 398

Orr, James L., 53, 114, 160, 360

Ostend Manifesto, 385, 395–98

## DATE DUE

| L687 | | | |
|------|--|--|--|
|      |  |  |  |
|      |  |  |  |
|      |  |  |  |
|      |  |  |  |
|      |  |  |  |
|      |  |  |  |
|      |  |  |  |
|      |  |  |  |
|      |  |  |  |
|      |  |  |  |
|      |  |  |  |
|      |  |  |  |
|      |  |  |  |
|      |  |  |  |
|      |  |  |  |
|      |  |  |  |
|      |  |  |  |